Managerial Finance

Managerial Finance

Second Edition

J. Fred Weston
Eugene F. Brigham
University of California, Los Angeles

HOLT, RINEHART and WINSTON

New York • *Chicago* • *San Francisco* • *Toronto* • *London*

Preface

The field of finance is undergoing significant change. The emphasis on acquisition of funds has been extended to a consideration of the effective use of funds. Descriptions of instruments and institutions have been incorporated into an analytical framework for measuring the effects of actions on the value of the enterprise.

Since 1962, when the first edition of this book appeared, significant developments in financial analysis and in the economic environment have occurred. We have tried to incorporate this new material into the text, and have substantially revised those chapters dealing with the tax environment, financial ratio analysis, and especially capital budgeting and the cost of capital. Also, four years of experience in our use of the book, as well as reports from other users, have revealed a number of errors and unclear sections. Particular effort has been devoted to clarifications to make the book easier to read and understand.

The emphasis of this book continues to be on decision making in the area of managerial finance. The central contribution of a school of business is the study of the management of business enterprise. Therefore the stress here is on managerial aspects of finance. The central decisions of research, engineering, production, and marketing are influenced by financial considerations. Hence the emphasis is on finance in relation to the other management functions. Good financial decisions must relate to the other areas of management decisions in the firm and to the changing external environment.

The balanced treatment of acquisition and effective utilization of funds is facilitated through the framework of financial planning and control materials. Extended treatment of analytical concepts for evaluating financial decisions is presented. Another emphasis is the orientation of financial decisions to help the firm achieve successful interaction with its external environment and to make an appropriate contribution to the operation of the economy.

Reflecting these objectives, the book begins with the nature of the economic, legal, and tax environment in which the firm operates. The tools of financial analysis and control are next set out, because they are essential for managerial decision making in finance. Following is a section on financial planning, including forecasting, budgets, profit planning, and planning the financial structure. The trade-off between accepting exposure to risk and opportunities for income is highlighted in the analysis of principles for formulating the financial structure. With this framework, guidelines for decisions in using alternative forms and sources of financing are developed. Finally, the financial strategies for stimulating and supporting the growth of the firm are developed.

The text seeks to emphasize principles and tools for analysis and decision making. Space limitations prevented full inclusion of illustrative materials and actual examples. As illustrative material becomes out of date quickly, we have found it more useful for classroom presentations to take examples from recent experiences or from developments reported currently in business newspapers, other periodicals, annual reports, and prospectuses. One of the functions of the instructor is to guide the student to critical testing of the theories against current practices, leading to improvement in both theory and practice.

Much of the specific content of the book is the result of our experience in presenting the material in executive development programs over a number of years, as well as in undergraduate courses. Consultation with business executives on financial problems and policies has helped identify what is most significant both to the responsibilities of financial managers and to practical decision making. The same topics are at the center of recent developments in the theory of business finance. Consequently, the book attempts to incorporate leading contributions to the literature of business finance. Some topics may be found difficult at places—but so are the issues faced by financial managers. Business managers must now be prepared to handle complex problems with advanced tools of analysis and techniques of effective decision making.

We acknowledge that the level of the material is quite uneven. Certain parts are simply descriptions of the institutional features of the financial environment, and as such are not difficult for the student to understand. Other parts—notably the material on capital budgeting and the cost of capital—are by nature rather abstract, and as such are difficult for those not used to thinking about abstract concepts. In some of the more complex sections, we have simply outlined procedures in the main body of the text, then justified the procedures in the chapter appendixes, recommended to the more able or mature student.

We have not sought to avoid consideration of the many unresolved areas of business financial theory and practice. The book could have been simplified in many places by avoiding the difficult issues, but we preferred to provide a basic framework and then to indicate the tentative nature of the state of knowledge on a number of important points. The reading references at the end of each chapter provide guides to further analysis of the evolving concepts of business finance. It is hoped that our presentation, along with the additional references, will stimulate the reader to further inquiry; whether he follows an academic or a business career.

The end-of-chapter questions and especially the problems have been extended and revised. In our opinion, practice with numerical problems is essential to an understanding of the basic principles. Cases are especially useful in this connection, but instructors in introductory courses frequently find it impossible to explore complex cases in the required depth and still have time to cover the necessary background material. Our own approach has been to use problems, or "essence cases," from which all extraneous material has been removed, thus permitting the essential principles to be illustrated in a minimum amount of time.

The problems seek to illustrate the concepts in the chapters which they follow. Because the computations can be made quickly, it is hoped that time will be taken to reflect on the generalizations illustrated by the problems and to fix in mind a method of attack for dealing with similar issues subsequently encountered.

The book is designed to serve as an introductory textbook, although it is also useful as a text for case courses and advanced finance courses.

For an introductory first course, the chapter appendixes and Parts VII and VIII may be omitted. The second course would consider the additional materials in the appendixes and the more advanced or specialized materials in Chapters 26 through 31. Some instructors will prefer to cover the entire subject matter in one semester.

We are grateful to the users of the first edition who have given us the benefit of their reactions and suggestions. The comments by Professor William F. Sharpe, University of Washington; Professor William J. Frazer, Jr., University of Florida; Professor Nathan L. Silverstein, Indiana University; and Professor Robert McKenzie, New York University, on a draft of the first edition were also useful in the revision. We are also grateful to Messrs. Walter R. Oreamuno, Jorge M. Gonzalez, and Raymond P. Kurshan for the opportunity to test the concepts in the environment of dynamic growth provided by the experience of Management Assistance, Inc.

We would like to express our appreciation to Messrs. Edward Altman, Robert Aubey, and Craig Johnson, who aided in the task of bringing the statistical tables up to date, in checking the numerical examples in the text, and in designing and checking the questions and problems. For typing the manuscript and for reproducing a number of ditto drafts of chapter revisions for testing in classroom use, we are grateful to Misses Pauline Grossman, Elaine Karalus, Rea Glazer, and Bertha Gutstein.

To Ing. León Avalos Vez, we express thanks for the continued opportunity to test the ideas in a different institutional setting through the programs of the Instituo de Administration Cienifica de las Empresas in Mexico. We are indebted to the Literary Executor of the late Sir Ronald A. Fisher, F.R.S., Cambridge, and to Dr. Frank Yates, F.R.S., Rothamsted, also to Messrs. Oliver & Boyd, Ltd., Edinburgh, for permission to reprint Table VI (Table 8A-1 in our text) from their book, "Statistical Tables for Biological, Agricultural and Medical Research." Dun & Bradstreet, Inc., kindly provided permission to reproduce a number of their materials as acknowledged in the text. Finally, we are indebted to various other persons and organizations for the use of their materials, also acknowledged in the text.

It is a source of great stimulation to participate in the exciting developments of the theory of the "new business finance." It is our hope that the present materials will contribute to the transmission and evaluating of those theories and to progress in the exercise of the new powers and responsibilities of financial executives.

University of California, Los Angeles
April 1966

J. FRED WESTON
EUGENE F. BRIGHAM

Contents

Part I

Financial Management and Its Environment

Chapter 1

The Finance Function

Traditionally, the finance function has been defined as obtaining the *funds needed* by the business enterprise for conducting its operations. In a broader sense, it has been described as dealing with the *fund flows* in the firm, a concept which encompasses the responsibility of having sufficient funds for carrying out the firm's goals. This is executed, for example, (1) by having funds for meeting maturing bills and for financing growth and new activities, (2) by combining different types and sources of funds at the lowest cost and under the best terms, and (3) by participating in the achievement of the efficient utilization of funds.

The newer emphasis in finance stresses *analysis* for achieving the most *effective utilization* of funds. In this broader framework, financial executives are concerned with the analysis related to all decisions that will affect the value of the firm. They also have responsibility for the design and operation of a system of information flows or accounts for efficient allocation of resources. Because financial executives participate in over-all management planning and control, they play an important role in decisions made by divisions or departments by evaluating such proposed decisions from the standpoint of over-all optimization for the firm as a whole. Finally, in formulating plans and in performing analysis of the results of operation, they acquire an understanding of the nature and quality of the firm's operations. This may lead to participation by financial executives in the important policy decisions of the firm, because of their knowledge of the vital information flows in the operations of the firm.

The range of responsibilities of financial management is suggested in Figure 1–1. The first column outlines the environmental factors that influence financial decisions, the economic, legal, and financial environment that defines the range of opportunities and choices confronting the financial executive. The second outlines the types of decision and policy areas

A. ENVIRONMENTAL FACTORS	B. FINANCIAL DECISION AND POLICY AREAS	C. MANAGEMENT FUNCTIONS
Economic Environment	How fast will our firm grow?	Analysis of decisions affecting value of the firm
	Industry, age, size, and growth rate of our firm determine amount of assets required to produce our products.	Planning
Legal and tax environment	What form of enterprise shall we use?	
Financial environment	Shall we lease or own plant and equipment? Shall we purchase parts or make them?	Design of system of accounts for effective resource allocation
Sources of Financing A. Commercial Banks B. Investment Banks C. Life Insurance Companies D. Finance Companies E. Equity Markets F. Other Business Firms G. Investment Development Companies H. Community Development Companies I. Friends and Relatives	Management of assets Capital budgeting Liquidity policies Cash flow patterns Policies for solvency How shall our assets be financed? Retained earnings	Budgeting Controlling
Cyclical and trend changes in cost and availability of funds	Common stock Debt Convertibles and warrants How shall we plan for growth? Diversification Mergers Financial reorganizations Timing of Financing Seasonal Cyclical Life cycle of firm and industry	Formulation of financial policies

Fig. 1–1. Areas of Responsibility of Financial Management

of financial management. The third shows general management functions in which financial managers participate and which are interrelated with the specific finance functions. Developments in the economy have greatly influenced the nature of the relation between performance of the specific finance functions and participation in general management functions.

EMERGING ROLE OF THE FINANCIAL MANAGER

Recent developments have introduced important changes in the environment in which the financial manager operates. These trends may be briefly summarized as follows:

1. Rise of large-scale business units, which makes the tasks formerly handled by the president too large for any one person
2. Increased product and market diversification by firms
3. Growth of spending on research and development, which has accelerated the tempo of change in the economy
4. Increased emphasis on growth in the economy and its major segments
5. Accelerated progress in transportation and communication, which has brought the countries of the world closer together
6. Narrowing profit margins, which reflect heightened competition

These changes have resulted in new ways of managing, which have had important impacts for the financial manager. First, large-scale operations require decentralization and divisional responsibility for profit. Methods must be developed for segregating the contributions of smaller groups of activities and evaluating these contributions. Second, the emphasis on growth and diversification requires both ability to finance expansion and considerable adaptability on the part of the firm. Third, increased competition and narrowing profit margins heighten the need for techniques to make operations more efficient.

These developments and their impact have produced what has been referred to as a management revolution.[1] Whether these changes deserve the term "revolution" or whether they simply reflect continuing changes that might be referred to as an "evolution," they have significantly broadened the responsibilities of financial management. The basic changes that have taken place in the environment have been associated with the development of powerful new techniques and new ways of managing. One such change is the revolution of information-processing techniques.

[1] T. F. Bradshaw, "The Place and Status of the Financial Executive Today," in *Financial Executive's Job*, Financial Management Series, No. 99 (New York: American Management Association, 1952), pp. 16–17.

This is the application of the computer for acquiring, storing, organizing, and retrieving all kinds of business information. The data are used to monitor the behavior of cash, receivables, inventories, and physical facilities. Another example is the accelerated development of techniques applicable to management generally, but particularly to the kinds of problems for which the financial manager is responsible. These are the techniques of operations research—linear programming, game theory, and simulation. All are essentially mathematical techniques dealing with complex relations among business data.

Related to the development of operations research is significant progress in management planning and control techniques. These involve (1) establishing of over-all profit goals, (2) establishing of departmental and divisional goals which, taken together, achieve the over-all profit goal, (3) measuring of progress and results against standards, and (4) action through adjustments to keep the company moving toward its goals.

The increased need for planning and control staffs to carry out the enterprise profit goal has made the financial manager a key executive. These developments have broadened his responsibilities and have determined the basic pattern of this book into the following broad areas:

1. Financial Analysis and Control
2. Financial Planning
3. Short-Term and Intermediate-Term Financing
4. Long-Term Financing
5. Capital Market Institutions
6. Financial Strategies for Growth

Emphasis is given to planning, analysis, and control, and also to the tasks of raising funds for the firm. In addition, consideration is given to the interactions with the broader environment in which the firm operates.

The remainder of this chapter covers the orientation of managerial finance, shows how financial management fits into the broader management framework, shows the relation of managerial finance to related disciplines, and gives illustrations of the crucial impact of finance during the life histories of individual firms. Succeeding chapters in Part I consider the selection of the legal form of the organization of a business enterprise and the impact of taxes on business decisions. This material seeks to provide the background necessary for the presentation of principles and procedures of financial analysis and control set forth in Part II.

ORIENTATION OF MANAGERIAL FINANCE

Scope of Financial Management

Traditionally, the literature of business finance has emphasized either management of working capital or acquisition of funds. The acquisition of funds, or episodic financing, typically commits the firm for long periods and involves sizable amounts of money. Errors here can be exceedingly costly. However, as the interval between episodes is long, the acquisition of funds takes only a small fraction of the financial manager's time.

A high proportion of the financial manager's time is concerned with management of working capital. For this reason some persons have suggested that finance books concentrate on this aspect of his duties. But a new and at least equally important emphasis is required: the place of the financial manager in the general management framework and the increased role of the financial manager in the vital activities of planning and control. However, the increased importance of new areas does not make traditional decision-making areas of less importance.[2] This book therefore attempts to give full emphasis to the three major approaches to the financial manager's functions: (1) financial planning and control, (2) management of working capital, and (3) individual financing episodes.

The Insider versus the Outsider View

Should the study of finance take the insider's or the outsider's point of view? Phrased in another way, should a finance book emphasize the administrative or the managerial point of view, or should it be aimed at the person who is interested in business finance as a customer, a stockholder, or a voter? These two points of view are not incompatible. Although this book emphasizes the professional manager's job, neither point of view can be effectively developed without consideration of the other.

The financial manager, whose preoccupation is the internal administration of the firm, must still take into account the reaction of outsiders to his operations. The claims and pressures of outsiders must also be adjusted to the responsibilities and problems of internal financial administration. Hence it seems essential to base financial decisions on a consideration of both points of view. Nevertheless, the managerial point of view deserves primary emphasis, because it is the financial manager who is responsible for the financial affairs of the enterprise.

Small-Firm versus Large-Firm Financing

Similarly, the issue of the large firm versus the small firm as the appropriate focus of attention of finance courses is a false one. Principles of business finance are just as applicable to the small firm as to the large. The basic ideas are fundamentally the same, even though there will be different factual environments in their application.

Similarly, the distinction between corporate finance and other forms of business financing is an artificial division. As the materials in Chapter 3 on the tax environment indicate, the boundaries between corporate and

---

2 The point is summarized well by Marshall D. Ketchum, "Looking Around: Financial Management," *Harvard Business Review*, 34 (January–February 1956), pp. 131–132.

noncorporate forms are becoming increasingly blurred, particularly for small firms. Further, important large-scale businesses are carried on in the form of business trusts.[3]

This book seeks to focus on generalizations that are applicable across a broad range of financing activities. It emphasizes effective use and adaptation to the firm's external environment and the role of the financial manager as a part of the general management process. A further foundation for this latter aspect is now developed.

MANAGEMENT FRAMEWORK

The last ten years have witnessed a blossoming of a literature on management theory and policy, which are the core of business school doctrine. These developments are too important to be ignored by any individual area of business studies. The contributions are particularly important for financial management. As a consequence of these developments, the financial manager's status has been elevated into a vital part of management. It is necessary to provide at least a summary statement of the nature of management activities in which the financial manager potentially performs a key role.

The process of managing is decision making—that is, choosing between alternatives. The job of the financial *manager* is to accomplish his tasks, both episodic and day-to-day financing, through people. Thus there are two aspects of management: (1) the general management activity— working with people and (2) the specific functions or activities—what gets done. The general and the specific functions of management as they relate to finance are outlined below.

Functions of Management

Lists of the functions of general management differ among different authorities; nevertheless, the following enumeration has gained wide acceptance:[4]

Organizing
Staffing
Directing
Planning
Controlling

Organizing is the identification and determination of activities which need to be undertaken in order to achieve enterprise objectives. Organi-

---

[3] An example is the American Optical Company, one of the leaders in its industry. It is organized as a Massachusetts trust, a form of organization described in Chapter 2.

[4] This section has benefited from Harold Koontz and Cyril O'Donnell, *Principles of Management* (New York: McGraw-Hill, 1959), pp. 1–59.

zation represents the grouping of activities into departments for the specialization of managerial activities and functions. Specialization in turn requires the definition of managerial authority and of responsibility relations for carrying out the activities to achieve the objectives.

Staffing involves the selection among candidates for positions, the training of subordinates, and the appraisal of activities. Job requirements must be defined, and inducements must be offered to elicit effective performance.

Directing requires the guidance and supervision of subordinates and their lines of communication.

Planning is the formulation of enterprise goals or objectives, the selection between alternative courses of action, and the initiation of policies and programs to achieve objectives.

Controlling is seeing that things get done and improving performance. It requires setting standards, measuring performance against enterprise objectives and standards, evaluating performance, and acting promptly to take corrective actions. Policies, programs, and procedures are modified in order to improve performance.

These general functions of management may now be contrasted with specific areas of management decisions. Four activities usually appear on most statements of the basic operations of a business: production, personnel, finance, and marketing. Finance is always included in such a list because financial activities are crucial for the well-being of a firm and play a strategic role in the performance of all general functions of management.

With this background on the nature of both general and specific activities of management, the role of financial management may now be set out.

Finance and General Functions of Management

The financial manager performs important activities in connection with each of the general functions of management. With respect to *organizing*, an important guideline is to group activities in such a way that areas of responsibility and accountability are defined. In the large-scale organization this procedure usually implies some degree of decentralization. The profit center (for example, a division) is a technique of decentralizing activities for developing strategic control points. Financial data are developed and analyzed for use in evaluating the performance of a related group of operations.

The determination of the nature and extent of *staffing*, or manpower requirements, is aided by the financial budget program. The ability of an enterprise to attract and to retain high-quality talent is greatly affected by its financial capabilities.

Direction is based to a considerable degree on instruments of financial reporting, such as budgets, balance sheets, and income statements. The information contained in these communication devices enables the manager to guide his subordinates.

Planning involves heavy reliance on financial tools and analysis. Forecasts and budgets are key instruments for financial planning.

Control requires use of the techniques of financial analysis and the development of financial ratios and standards. Financial reports must be supplemented, of course, by direct observation and a broad understanding of enterprise processes.

In summary, informed and enlightened use of financial information is necessary for coordinating the enterprise activities and for achieving harmony between individual motives and enterprise goals.

This completes a brief description of the nature of general management and the key role of finance in it. Description of financial management as an area of decision making is the subject matter of the remainder of this book. Now it will be possible to see the relation of financial decisions to the broader aspects of managing a business enterprise.

Place of Finance in the Organization

The financial manager in the firm often carries the title of treasurer. Sometimes he is called vice-president in charge of finance, controller, treasurer-controller, or secretary-treasurer. Whatever his title, the financial manager is usually close to the top of the organizational structure of the firm. Typically, he is a member of the first level of the corporate staff in a large organization.

Characteristically, financial planning is conducted by top-level management. Consequently, the chief financial manager is often a vice-president; or sometimes the president himself will carry the responsibilities of the financial manager. In large firms, major financial decisions are often made by a finance committee. For example, finance committees are used in General Motors, United States Steel, and American Telephone and Telegraph. In smaller firms the owner-manager himself typically conducts the financial operations, although he may delegate many other management functions.

One reason for the high place in the authority ladder occupied by financial managers is the key importance of the planning, analysis, and control operations for which they are responsible. Often a "financial control" staff reports directly to the president or operates as an analytical staff for vice-presidents in charge of production, marketing, engineering, and other operations.

Another reason why financial authority is rarely decentralized or delegated to subordinates is that many financial decisions are crucial for the survival of the firm. Decisions which have major financial implications, such as taking on a new product or discarding an old one, adding a plant or changing locations, floating a bond or stock issue, entering into sale and leaseback arrangements (or either) are all major episodes in the life of a corporation.

Also, significant economies can be achieved through centralizing financial operations. A large corporation requiring $50 million can float a bond issue at a much lower interest cost per dollar than the rate at which a small firm can borrow $1,000. A small firm borrowing $1,000 will probably pay from 6 to 8 percent up to 14 to 18 percent. The large corporation is likely to be able to borrow at a rate ranging from $2\frac{1}{2}$ to $5\frac{1}{2}$ percent. It would be misleading, however, to imply that the advantages of centralization lie only in interest savings. The terms of the financial contract are also likely to be improved—a matter that may be of greater importance to the borrower than the interest rate. Contract terms refer to the extent to which borrowers can buy additional fixed assets, declare dividends, incur debt, and so forth.

Although the responsibility for carrying out major financial decisions is likely to be centered in the hands of a high-level official, a large number of day-to-day operations are conducted by the treasurer's office. These tasks are likely to be carried out by subordinates in lower level jobs. They include handling cash receipts and disbursements, borrowing from commercial banks on a regular and continuing basis, and formulating cash budgets.

MANAGERIAL FINANCE AND RELATED DISCIPLINES

Paradoxically, although some aspects of the finance function are conducted at the highest levels of the organization, a person aspiring to become a financial manager in a large company is likely to start as a trainee in a job with a heavy accounting flavor. Therefore, questions about the relation of finance to other studies naturally arise.

Accounting and Finance

Some persons find it difficult to distinguish between accounting and finance. They observe that in both subjects the same terminology and financial records are often used. Hence it appears to them that accounting and finance are the same thing. But accounting is primarily data gathering; finance is data analysis for use in decision making. Though accounting has become increasingly useful in recent years in providing the information necessary for good management decisions, financial executives are responsible for analysis, planning, and control.

Quantitative Methods and the Behavioral Sciences

Financial management deals with data and with people. The responsibilities for data analysis provide opportunities for application of the new and powerful tools of linear programming, game theory, and simulation referred to previously. Many of the concepts set out in this book may be utilized most effectively in business operations in conjunction with these new techniques. As the financial area can make much use of these skills, the student of finance is well advised to acquire them.

Operating a business involves the interaction of physical assets, data, and people. The behavioral sciences are therefore also an essential part of the financial manager's training. Business involves authority relations between individuals and groups—political science. It also draws on sociology, which is the study of the behavior of people in groups. Of great importance, of course, is psychology, which deals with the mind, personality, and emotional make-up of both managers and managed.

Familiarity with these diverse areas of knowledge is required for sound financial decisions. But perhaps of most direct significance for financial policies is the *economic* environment, whose nature and impact need to be sketched at least briefly at this point.

Economics and Finance

Economics may be defined as a study of the efficient use of scarce resources or of the best means to fulfill socially defined ends or goals. The kinds of decisions made by firms in marketing, production, finance, and personnel are properly the subject matters of economics, and business finance is therefore an aspect of the economic theory of the firm. The characteristics of the economic environment are of vital significance for financial policies in ways now briefly indicated.

Separation of savings and investment. The United States is a money economy. Savings and investment are performed by different persons. People save through institutions such as savings banks, commercial banks, savings and loan associations, life insurance companies, and pension funds. These institutions are called "financial intermediaries." Businesses obtain funds from the intermediaries to make investments in land, buildings, equipment, and inventories. Financial intermediaries today own approximately two thirds (by value) of the securities of a firm, contrasted with less than one quarter (by value) of the securities at the turn of the century.[5]

Financing today is much more impersonal than it was earlier. Pre-

[5] Raymond W. Goldsmith, *The Share of Financial Intermediaries in National Wealth and National Assets, 1900–1949*. Occasional Paper No. 42 (New York: National Bureau of Economic Research, 1954), p. 4, Table A.

viously, wealth and income were not as equally distributed as they are today. People invested their funds directly in their own businesses or in local enterprises about which they had direct knowledge. Either they knew the persons running the firms or they were familiar with the operations. But today many people save through financial intermediaries, which in turn buy the securities of the firms. Finance, therefore, is fundamentally a process for allocating economic resources among different users. The ability to obtain funds is the ability to obtain command over the real resources of the economy. This suggests another basic characteristic of the economic environment.

Price and profit system. Prices and profits allocate resources in the United States. Allocation is made, not by administrative boards, but by relative prices and by income shares. Profit maximization, subject to risk-limiting strategies, is the framework for studying the operations of the firm. Most economics texts treat profit maximization, its variations and its substitute goals, in a formal way, with demand and supply curves to describe how the price system performs its functions. This book illustrates the concepts of profit maximization and other business strategies in terms of specific kinds of financial decisions.

A money economy, where savings and investment are performed by different groups of persons guided by prices and profits, has other characteristics which carry implications for financial managers.

Fluctuations and economic instability. Fluctuations in the general level of business are a major cause of changes in the level of an individual firm's sales. Such changes result in changes in the firm's financing requirements. Differences in the degree of fluctuations influence the extent to which a financial manager may take on the risk of fixed-interest or fixed-rental obligations. Economic fluctuations result in many diverse forms of financing contracts.

Growth. The economy of the United States has grown and will probably continue to grow from 3 to 5 percent a year. To maintain its place in the economy, an industry must grow at least as fast as this. To hold its share of its industry market, a firm must also grow. Sales growth implies a continued growth in the firm's plant and equipment, inventories, receivables, and other assets. The financial manager's job is to obtain the funds to finance the expansion of the firm's ownership of these means of production and sale.

Price movements. In addition to the fluctuations in business and in the growth of the economy as a whole, there are fluctuations in price levels. Financial planning is necessary if a firm is to benefit from price level changes. The financial structure of the firm should reflect expectations about future price level changes.

Interest rates and stock market prices. Fluctuations in interest rates and stock prices represent fluctuations in the cost of funds and the relative attractiveness of different forms and sources of financing. Interest rate levels are also an index of availability of loanable funds. These factors are used by the financial manager in analyzing the alternative forms of financing and in timing entry into the money markets.

Competition and technological change. Competition among firms, existing products, and newly created products pervades the economy. Technological changes present opportunities and threats to a firm. Adequate finances are required for the firm to make the adjustments necessary for survival and growth in the ever-changing economy, and it is the financial manager who must bear the responsibility for the availability of necessary funds.

Understanding the nature of the external environment, its impact on the firm, the role of the firm in the operation of the economy—are all crucial and vital aspects of the decision process. The aim of the present book is to provide a meaningful body of concepts to guide the use of a broad variety of tools for financial decisions that advance the progress of the firm and the society of which it is a part.[6]

CRUCIAL ROLE OF FINANCING DECISIONS

The role of finance in the conduct of the firm has been expressed most aptly in the following statement: "A firm's success and even survival, its ability and willingness to maintain production and to invest in fixed or working capital are to a very considerable extent determined by its financial policies, both past and present."[7] This statement can be amply documented by examples of the lives of many firms. Let us consider a few.

General Motors was established in 1908 by W. C. Durant as a consolidation of a few companies in the automobile industry. When the working-capital crisis of 1920–1921 developed, General Motors received financing aid from the Morgans and the du Ponts, and Durant lost his control of the company.

In contrast is the experience of Henry Ford. The Ford Motor Company needed some $75 million to meet its working-capital needs. A group of Wall Street bankers formed a committee and offered to help Ford out

---

[6] Cf. "It is important to recognize the fact that business also operates in a world of ideas. What business can or cannot do, as well as the way in which it must operate, is determined in part by the predominating concepts or theories in the society within which it exists. These may be religious, social, economic, or political and may be expressed in such forms as ethical standards, social values, and the objectives and methods of government."—H. M. Larson, *Guide to Business History* (Cambridge, Mass.: Harvard University Press, 1948), p. 5.

[7] Irwin Friend, "What Business Can Do to Prevent Recessions," in *Problems in Antirecession Policy* (New York: Committee for Economic Development, 1954), p. 6.

of his difficulty in return for a portion of the control of the Ford Motor Company. Ford declined their proposal.

But Ford had to raise $75 million. How did he do it? First, he shipped his auto inventories to his dealers, with a telegram requesting cash. This forced them to borrow individually. He raised $25 million in this manner. Second, he allowed accounts and bills payable for raw materials to accumulate. Third, he reduced overhead in the factory and in the office. Fourth, by vigorous collection methods he collected some outstanding accounts receivables, foreign accounts, and by-product accounts. Fifth, he sold some $8 million of liberty bonds on hand. By all these methods he was able to meet his working-capital needs and maintain complete control over his company.

A more recent illustration involves a consumer finance company. In 1946 the company sold promissory notes of $400,000 to an insurance company. Later the firm needed additional funds, but was unable to arrange with the holders of the original notes for an additional loan. The loan agreement had been so drawn that it was virtually necessary to call the entire issue and place a new one of $1 million with another institutional investor. Because calling the original issue involved a substantial penalty, the company made it a point to see that the new loan agreement provided that additional funds could be secured from either the same lender or other lenders without the consent of the present holders and without paying penalties if any of the existing notes were to be retired. This illustration points up some of the pitfalls of absence of planning in setting up loan agreements.

These examples illustrate a more general principle. It has been said with great truth that financing is the critical management function in that it provides the means of remedying weak management in other areas. If production or marketing efforts, for example, have deteriorated, adequate financial means may be used to rehabilitate and restore the weak departments to renewed effectiveness. On the other hand, money alone is no substitute for strength in the other operating areas of the firm. Finance is thus an interdependent part of the total fabric of the firm.

SUMMARY

The financial manager plays a key role in the guidance of the firm. He has a central responsibility in analysis, planning, and control which guide the firm's resources into the most profitable lines and hold a tight rein on costs.

The importance of the financial manager is recognized by his place at the top levels in the organization structure of the firm. Financial decisions are crucial for the well-being of a firm, because they determine the ability of the company to obtain plant and equipment when needed, to carry the requisite amount of inventories and receivables, to avoid burdensome fixed charges when sales and profits fall, and to prevent loss of effective control of the company.

SELECTED REFERENCES

American Management Association, *New Responsibilities in Corporate Finance*, AMA Management Report Number 71 (New York; American Management Association, 1962).

Curtis, Edward T., *Company Organization of the Finance Function*. AMA Research Study 55 (New York; American Management Association, 1962).

Donaldson, Gordon, "Financial Goals: Management vs. Stockholders," *Harvard Business Review*, 41 (May-June 1963), pp. 116–129.

Marting, Elizabeth and Robert E. Finley (eds.), *The Financial Manager's Job* (New York; American Management Association, 1964).

Weston, J. Fred, "The Finance Function," *Journal of Finance*, 9 (September 1954), pp. 265–282.

———— (ed.), *Financial Management in the 1960s: New Challenges and Responsibilities* (New York: Holt, Rinehart and Winston, Inc., 1966), selection "The New Power of the Financial Executive."

———— (ed.), *Readings in Finance from* Fortune (New York: Holt, Rinehart and Winston, Inc., 1958), selections 1, 3, 14, 15, and 16.

QUESTIONS

1–1 What are some similarities between business management and the management of the U. S. Department of Defense? some differences?

1–2 What has been the impact of the development of financial intermediaries on business finance?

1–3 Suppose you are called upon to take over as chief executive officer (usually the president) of a large firm that is struggling to avoid bankruptcy. Your first task is to reorganize the business. Prepare an organization chart showing the place of the financial manager within the managerial hierarchy.

1–4 Give illustrations of the financial implications of (1) production, (2) marketing, and (3) personnel decisions. In terms of the organization chart of question 3, do these illustrations suggest cross communications between the financial officer and the production, sales, and personnel officers?

1–5 Are financial decisions likely to be more crucial for a failing business or for a successful, growing business? Would you as chief executive officer be more concerned about your financial manager in the failing firm or in the thriving firm?

1–6 What are the most important activities of the financial manager in terms of their importance to the firm's future and the amount of the financial manager's time they take up? Are these relationships likely to the same for (1) large versus small firms, (2) stable versus growing firms, and (3) strong versus weak firms?

PROBLEMS

1–1 An appliance manufacturer has been selling directly to distributors on a net 15-day credit basis. His sales have been $1,080,000 per year and his average collection period is 20 days. He has 7 percent of sales in inventory. His balance sheet is as follows:

BALANCE SHEET

Cash	$ 15,000	Accounts payable	$ 75,000
Receivables, net	60,000	Other current liabilities . .	25,000
Inventories	75,000	Total current	100,000
Total current	150,000	Common stock	100,000
Net property	100,000	Earned surplus	50,000
Total assets	$250,000	Total claims on assets	$250,000

Because of excess production capacity and an attempt to increase the profit margin, the manufacturer begins to sell directly to retailers, in addition to selling to distributors. Standard terms on these sales are net 30.

1. How much additional financing will be required by the new sales if the additional sales amount to $540,000 and the average collection period is 40 days?
2. If this is the only change, how will the new balance sheet appear?
3. What aspect of finance does this problem illustrate?

(Use the convention of 360 days in a year.)

1–2 An office equipment retailer plans to add a new type of desk to his existing line. He expects annual sales of $540,000 from the new line. Net profit after salaries and taxes each year is 2.2 percent of sales. The owner takes no salary. The average payables for the new line will be 7 percent of sales.[8] However, the store will need 7 per cent of sales in its inventory at all times, and the average collection period will be 30 days.

BALANCE SHEET

Accounts receivable . .	———	Accounts payable	———
Inventory	———	Retained earnings	———
		Subtotal	———
		Additional financing (needed to balance) . . .	———
Total assets	———	Total claims on assets . .	———

Fill in the skeleton balance sheet above as of the end of the first year. Discuss the critical factors in the problem and the lesson to be learned from it.

---

[8] Payables would, of course, equal the payment period on purchases multiplied by average purchases per day. But if the ratio of materials costs to sales is constant, accounts payable can also be expressed as some multiple or percentage (in this problem, 7 percent) times sales.

Chapter 2

Promotion and Choice of Form of Organization

How do businesses come into being? What role does finance perform in this process? The formation of a new firm is called "promotion." Promotion is the act of bringing together the product ideas, the people, the plant, the machinery, and the other means of production into a coordinated organization necessary for creating a new operating activity.

PROMOTION

The practical identification of promotion and promotional opportunities is not clear cut. The concept of promotion is somewhat elastic, with the term being used in different ways by different people. However, some illustrations of promotional activities will indicate the range of activities to which the concept has been applied. A new commodity or service is developed. This results in the establishment of a new firm or of a new division or activity in an existing firm. Or a new process is developed which will reduce costs in an operation or activity already in existence. This development also leads to the establishment of a new firm or a modification of the operations of an existing firm.

The opportunity to establish a new competitor in an established field may also result in the formation of a new firm. Promoters may develop these and related opportunities by purchasing existing firms, by creating new divisions in existing firms, by creating new firms, or by merging firms already in operation. All the types of activity thus far described have been or could be called *promotion*. Basically, what is involved is changing the product or market activity of an existing firm or creating a new activity or enterprise.

Establishing a New Firm

To establish a new product or activity involves the full range of factors that determine the performance of any firm already in operation. It requires consideration of all the factors that determine the success of any business operation. These include the market potentials in the industry; the quality of management; the soundness of scientific, engineering, production, marketing, and financial policies in the firm; and the firm's competitive position.

A full evaluation of promotion, therefore, requires bringing together all the fields of knowledge covered in a business school curriculum. Obviously, it is not possible to attempt to repeat all such relevant material in this brief discussion of promotion. However, the nature of the factors reviewed in connection with providing financing for a new venture is suggested in Table 2-1, which indicates the kind of information required from applicants for venture capital financing. The table covers aspects of corporate structure, executive management and work force, nature of the industry and the business, financial statistics, and financing sought.

The task of the promoter is to convince others that the proposed venture can be successful. He must explain how the production process is feasible. He must establish his case that a market can be developed and that this is the time to exploit the market. He must indicate what the size of the potential market is and what share of that market his venture can obtain. He must have a clear understanding of the marketing strategy required.

If the promoter presents a sound and persuasive case, he can raise the funds needed to finance the operation. Funds for a new firm can come from a variety of sources, such as friends, local capitalists, financial enterprises, or the general public. If the promoter is seeking to establish or expand a division in an existing firm, he must be able to persuade top management that his project is worthy of an additional allocation of corporate funds to the proposed activity.

Investigation.   What techniques can the promoter use to establish his case? Essentially, he is forecasting an excess of revenue over costs. Revenues are estimated by the canvassing (or market survey) method. The *canvassing method* involves making sample surveys of the market and of the amount of the expected income. Essentially it is a market research analysis of the potential demand for the kind of product that the new firm contemplates producing.

TABLE 2–1

INFORMATION REQUIRED FROM APPLICANT FOR VENTURE CAPITAL FINANCING[1]

A. Corporate Structure
　　1. Name, where incorporated, date
　　2. Predecessor companies
　　3. Subsidiaries of subject
　　4. Securities and obligations outstanding
　　5. Names, ownership, and relation to firm of principal stockholders
　　6. Chronology of equity security sales

B. Executive Management and Work Force
　　1. Organization schematic with brief explanation
　　2. Background of all executive officers
　　3. Statistical table of employees and officers for past three years and for next three years
　　4. Data on payroll expense in relation to volume of sales, past and future

C. Business
　　1. Brief narrative history
　　2. Description of present product line
　　3. Total market for each product
　　4. Share of market, past and future
　　5. Identification of competitors in each line
　　6. Comparison of size with competitors
　　7. Evaluation of competitive position of products by price, performance, costs, and other factors
　　8. Description of uses of products
　　9. Description of marketing strategy
　　10. Analysis of ten main customers for each product line
　　11. Explanation of pricing policies
　　12. Description of product—market plans for next five years

D. Financial Statistics
　　1. Financial data for past five years
　　2. Financial plans for next three years
　　3. Cash flow analysis
　　4. Break-even profit point in time and volume
　　5. Explanation of any special financial methods

E. Financing Sought
　　1. Amount and form
　　2. Uses of funds
　　3. Effects of financing on *pro forma* balance sheets
　　4. Data on incremental earning power to be generated by application of financing
　　5. Cash flow and profit and loss forecasts, including bases for the forecasts
　　6. If further financing will be required in future, management's estimate of amount and timing

---

[1] This outline has been summarized and adapted from a more detailed checklist developed and used by Mr. David M. Goodman, a management consultant who has advised in the establishment of new firms and corporate divisions, with the sponsorship of venture capital groups, investment bankers, and corporations seeking growth and diversification.

Costs can be estimated by the *statistical method*, which is a cost accounting analysis of the probable cost of manufacturing the product. Often the cost analysis can be performed by obtaining data for a going concern in a similar line of business.

If there is no previous history for the product, engineering studies may be used in determining costs. The studies aid the estimates of costs by indicating the extent of technical complexities and of production problems. Forecasts can then be developed from the production costs of items of a similar nature.

The combination of the statistical and canvassing methods is called the *comparison method*. On the basis of a market and research analysis and a statistical analysis of costs, comparisons are made with the experience of other firms already established in a similar line of business.

The purpose of these investigations, whichever type is followed, is to forecast prospective revenues or sales and prospective costs, and from these two, to prepare an estimate of prospective profits and cash flows. Sound forecasting allows for the costs of developing the product designs, of planning the products in all their details, and of solving the chemical, physical, or engineering problems involved in getting into practical production. The marketing problem is to estimate what kind of products the consumer desires, how many will be sold, and at what prices.

Financial requirements in a new firm. The establishment of a new firm involves significant financial requirements. In the first place, some initial expenses will be involved. (1) Promotion and organization expenses will be required. (2) The firm will have to acquire the fixed assets—land, plant, and equipment—needed to produce the item. (3) The firm will need sufficient funds to pay salaries, to buy materials, to cover losses during the initial period of operations, and to carry receivables.

It is essential that organizers of the new firm clearly understand what they expect their financial requirements to be.[2] So that their initial cash needs may be provided appropriately, they should develop a cash budget for the first year or two of operation that predicts possible losses and other financial drains.[3]

The following composite of a number of newspaper advertisements represents a characteristic situation and suggests several financial pitfalls to be avoided during a promotion:

Business capital wanted—it's an old story. I built a plant. By the time it was completed, the product developed and the bugs eliminated, the cash reserve for sales effort was consumed. I am sitting here with a plant and a technical staff and an opportunity to build a fortune despite income taxes. It is an expensive and time-consuming effort to get established, but the reward is ample. We don't have

2 See Chapter 8 for procedures.
3 See Chapter 9 for procedures.

a sales force and that is why I need an additional $50,000. If you are influential in steel mills, steel foundries, or large industrial plants, so much the better. Please do not answer unless you are willing to spend money on a sales program, willing to accept a normal business risk, and patient enough to sweat out a growth situation. Prompt action is necessary.

This situation occurs over and over again. A person who is technically competent may have an idea for a new product; or he may be an exceptionally good salesman who wants to establish a retail store. Typically, he will accumulate his savings, he will probably mortgage his house, he may sell some of the family valuables, and he will borrow as much as he can from friends and relatives. Having amassed these funds, the promoter will rent or buy land, erect an attractive building, and install shiny new equipment. His funds are sunk in the form of fixed assets.

When the promoter is ready to begin operations, he is confronted with additional expenses. He needs cash to meet his payroll, to hire a sales force, to obtain product acceptance, and to obtain materials and supplies to get into production. He has exhausted his local sources of funds, so he must now go to the financial intermediaries. Since he has no record of profitable operation, he finds that banks or insurance companies, because of their financial standards, may not provide him with financing.

Overinvestment in fixed assets is, of course, only one way in which a promoter can get into financial difficulties. But the example illustrates some fundamentals of finance. *First,* sound financial planning is essential. A clear conception of how much financing will be required is necessary. This may appear to be a somewhat obvious prescription, but it is one that is frequently overlooked. *Second,* the development of a new product or a new firm always involves considerable risk taking. Consumer acceptance of the product and the volume of sales that is going to be achieved are always uncertain, whether or not a market research analysis has been made. Actual production is likely to vary from the forecast.

Consequently, a minimum amount of money should be sunk into brick and mortar at first. The land and factory and machinery should be rented if possible. If the machinery cannot be rented, secondhand machinery should be purchased. Expenses of marketing may be minimized by selling through already established channels in which the present product may be an added line. For example, a new type of vise or electric saw may be effectively marketed by wholesale hardware jobbers. The contract with the jobbers should be limited, so that the firm may develop its own sales outlets when it has attained sufficient volume. In short, a minimum of capital should be put into the initial operation in order to maintain operating flexibility to enable adjustments during a phase of rapid growth.

Third, despite all efforts to conserve costs, the owner of a new business may need more money from outside sources. If he has a clear conception of the production and marketing problems, if he can set out in detail a blueprint of expected project costs and income, if he is aware of alternative methods for selling the product, and if he can show budgets indicating his financial requirements, his prospects for obtaining funds will be substantially increased. In subsequent pages this book emphasizes techniques of financial management that enhance the prospects of businesses, both small and large, for obtaining funds.

Purchasing an Existing Firm

An alternative to establishing a new firm, from the standpoint of an individual businessman, involves purchasing a business that has been offered for sale. The classified section of newspapers often contains advertisements indicating the availability of going businesses for sale, such as restaurants, dry-cleaning establishments, small groceries, or ready-to-wear shops.

The prospective purchaser must consider at least two important factors. *First,* he should consider making the purchase only if he has had adequate experience in the particular line of business. *Second,* he should raise the question of why the business is for sale. The seller will obviously give reasons other than poor business, for example: "Grocery store available at tremendous sacrifice. Owner must sell because of ill health."

It is useful to check reasons for the offer to sell by securing additional information from other sources. Competitors frequently volunteer frank opinions on matters of this nature. Local bank officers often know what is happening to a particular firm, and even though they may not be able to talk frankly, they can sometimes imply much by what they say. In addition, members of a trade association in the line of business in which the seller is engaged will have useful information.

The creditors of the firm are another source of information. Does the firm pay its bills? Has it been slow or prompt? Has it taken discounts? If more information is needed, the Dun & Bradstreet or other mercantile agency reports give general background and financial information. The local credit managers' association also provides considerable information.

It is important, of course, for the enterpreneur to look at the financial records of the firm being offered for sale. Inadequate records are an indication of poor management or that information is being withheld. In either event, it is important to request an opportunity to review the proprietor's recent income tax returns.

In summary, when contemplating the purchase of an established concern, the prospective buyer should check the explanations of the seller against information obtained from other sources. Furthermore, factual

records, particularly income tax reports and financial statements, allow
the buyer to make an independent valuation of the worth of the firm.[4]

CHOOSING THE FORM OF BUSINESS ORGANIZATION

After deciding to start a business, a promoter is faced with the decision
of selecting the legal form of organization under which to operate. The
various forms are listed in Table 2-2. The importance of the various
types of partnerships are not shown, nor are statistics on joint companies,
business trusts, and cooperatives, all of which are included under the
figures for corporations. However, it is estimated that general partnerships account for well over 95 percent of all partnerships, and that regular
corporations (as opposed to joint stock companies, trusts, and cooperatives) make up 99 percent of the number and dollar amounts shown under
the heading Number of Firms for corporations.

It is obvious from the table that proprietorships are dominant in
terms of number of firms, whereas corporations produce the bulk of the
revenues. The significant features of each of the eight major forms are
presented in Table 2-3 (on page 35); a framework for choosing among
them is discussed at the close of the chapter.

Individual Proprietorship

The individual proprietorship is a business owned by one person.
The sole proprietor receives all the net income of the business, and is
responsible for all debts and losses that may be incurred. Some 9 million
of the 11 million enterprises in the United States are individual proprietorships. Proprietorships with fewer than four employees constitute
60 percent of all business concerns. Thus the proprietorship form is
widely used among the numerous small firms in the American economy.
These small proprietorships are concentrated in retail trade, such as food
stores, and in the services, such as barber shops and beauty parlors.

The proprietorship form possesses key advantages for small operations. It is easily and inexpensively formed. For example, to open a grocery
store it is necessary only to buy or rent a store, to buy or rent fixtures,
to obtain merchandise (often on credit), to obtain city licenses at nominal
fees—and the business is under way. No formal charter for operations is
required. The proprietorship is subject to few government regulations.
It pays no corporate income taxes, but the proprietor is required to file a
statement of income, because all profits of the sole proprietorship are
subject to federal *personal* income taxes, whether they are reinvested in
the business or are withdrawn.

---

[4] For formal procedures for establishing values, see Chapter 12.

Against the advantages of the ease of formation and freedom from government controls, the proprietorship has important limitations. Most significant is its inability to obtain large sums of capital. Chapter 8 demonstrates how, as a firm grows, its financing needs will often exceed

TABLE 2-2

MAJOR TYPES OF BUSINESS ORGANIZATIONS, 1961

Type of Organization	Number of Firms		Sales	
	Number	% of Total	Millions of Dollars	% of Total
Sole Proprietorships	9,242,000	81%	$ 170,981	16%
Partnerships:	939,000	8	73,413	7
General				
Limited				
Limited Association				
Joint Stock Companies*				
Business Trusts*				
Cooperatives*				
Corporations	1,190,000	11	823,943	77
	11,371,000	100%	$1,068,337	100%

Source: U.S. Bureau of the Census, *Statistical Abstract of the United States: 1964*, Eighty-fifth edition (Washington, D.C., 1964), p. 489.
* Figures for firms of this type are included under Corporations.

the amount of funds which is available from plowed-back earnings. Furthermore, potential lenders often require that additional ownership funds be invested in the business beyond the amounts available from retained earnings. Thus the proprietorship will often encounter financial barriers to growth. At such a point the proprietor is faced with the acceptance of retarded growth or a change to a form of organization which facilitates raising larger amounts of funds.

Another major disadvantage of the proprietorship is that creditors may look to both the assets of the business and the personal assets of the proprietor to satisfy their claims. That is, the proprietor has unlimited personal liability for the debts of the business. If the business incurs losses, the proprietor must be responsible for all debts incurred.

Finally, the proprietorship is bound up with the life and decisions of the individual who has created it. He may decide to terminate the business at will; the business ceases with his death. A limitation on salability of the business is that the success of the business may be tied directly to the owner's ability or personality. The difficulty of ownership transfer, coupled with impermanence of the proprietorship form of business organization, adds to the problem of obtaining needed funds.

Partnership

When two or more persons associate to conduct a business enterprise, a partnership is said to exist. A partnership may operate under different degrees of formality of agreement: an oral or informal understanding, a written partnership agreement, or formal articles of agreement filed with the proper state agency.

Like the proprietorship, the partnership has the advantage of ease and economy of formation, as well as freedom from special governmental regulation. Business income must be reported to the tax authorities, because the profits of the partnership are taxed as personal income in proportion to the claims of the partners, whether distributed to them or not.

One of the advantages of the partnership over the proprietorship is that it makes possible a pooling of resources. The partners may contribute different skills to the enterprise, in addition to pooling their funds. However, there are practical limits to the number of co-owners of a firm who can join in the enterprise without multiplying the possibilities of conflict. This fact also limits the capital-raising powers of the partnership.

Other drawbacks of the partnership form of organization are similar to those of the proprietorship: unlimited liability, difficulties of transferring ownership, and impermanence. Partners risk their personal assets as well as their investment in the business. Further, under partnership law the partners are jointly and severally liable for the debts of the business. If any partner is unable to meet the claims on him resulting from the partnership's liquidation, the remaining partners must take over the unsatisfied claims, drawing on their personal assets if necessary.

Most partnership agreements provide that a partner may not sell his share in the business to another person unless all other partners agree to accept the new partner. If a new partner comes into the business, the old partnership ceases to exist and a new one is created. The withdrawal or death of one of the partners also dissolves the partnership. Sometimes dissolution may be forced by one of the partners because of disagreements. In order to prevent disputes under such circumstances, the articles of partnership agreement should include provisions for terms of dissolution, including the method for valuing assets of the partnership. To avoid financial pressure for dissolution on the death of one of the partners, it is a common practice for each partner to carry life insurance, naming the remaining partners as his beneficiaries. The proceeds of such a policy may be used to buy out the investment of the deceased partner.

Limited Partnership

Limited partnership differs from a general partnership in that the liability of some partners is limited to the amounts they have actually invested in the business. This arrangement increases the ability of the firm to obtain outside funds. However, the agreement of a limited partnership must be formally registered with a designated state agency. Public notice is required to protect potential creditors of the firm who would otherwise be unaware of the limited extent of the obligation of some of the partners.

A limited partnership must include at least one general partner who is fully liable for partnership obligations. Furthermore, limited partners may not actively participate in the firm's over-all management. Because the notice of limited partnership is filed in one state pursuant to its laws, the organization is usually treated as a general partnership by other states.

Limited Partnership Association

A limited partnership association takes an additional step beyond the ordinary partnership form. It provides for the sale of shares of the partnership without thereby causing it to dissolve. However, the new purchasers must still be approved by the existing partners.

Joint Stock Company

The joint stock company takes still another step. Shares are freely transferable without the necessity for approval by existing shareholders. Although the liability of each owner is limited to obligations incurred while he is an owner of the company, each owner is jointly and severally liable for the debts of the organization. This provision handicaps the joint stock company in raising loan funds and is therefore used only to a small extent in the United States.

The Business Trust

A business trust is an arrangement in which the legal ownership of property is held by one party for the benefit of someone else. There are five essential parts to a trust:

1. *Creator.* The maker of the trust is the creator or trustor.
2. *Trustee.* The trustee manages the property for someone else.
3. *Beneficiary.* The person for whose benefit the property is managed is the beneficiary.
4. *Property.* Since a trust is a property arrangement, there cannot be a trust without property.
5. *Trust agreement.* A document containing a declaration of the purpose of the trust is necessary to guide the trustee.

Kinds of trusts. The business trust came into wide use in the 1880s for the purpose of conducting business operations when it was difficult to obtain corporate charters from state legislatures. The trust could be formed without cumbersome legislative procedures. Also, before 1889, corporations were not permitted to hold the shares of other corporations. The business trust was used to pool the ownership shares of a number of companies in the same industry. For example, the Rockefeller oil group induced stockholders in a number of oil companies to place their voting shares with a small group of trustees in exchange for trust certificates. This trust enabled the Rockefeller group to control the industry. The trust device was copied to such a degree that "trust" became synonymous with "monopoly," and the Sherman Act of 1890 is referred to as the "antitrust act." At the time the attack on trusts began, state incorporation laws began to permit corporations to hold stock in other corporations. The method of combining corporations then shifted from trusts to holding companies and mergers.

Today trusts perform many useful and socially beneficial functions, and they exist in almost as many forms as one can imagine. They are used primarily by persons in connection with bequests at death (testamentary trusts) and to conserve property for beneficiaries while the creator is still alive (living trusts). However, trusts continue to have a variety of business uses, although they are less important than they were before the turn of the century.

A business trust is different from a voting trust. A voting trust has only the power to vote the shares that have been deposited with it. A business trust, in contrast, engages in active management of property. The voting trust, usually of few years' duration, is designed to provide continuity of management decisions in a firm for a limited period. The voting trust is different from the business trust of the 1880s in that the voting trust involves only the common stock of one firm, whereas the business trust was used to vote the shares of a number of firms in the same industry.

Nature of the business trust. A business trust is formed by a trust agreement, which takes the place of a corporate charter. The trust may issue both bonds and shares, and the beneficiaries are often referred to as stockholders.

An illustrative abbreviated balance sheet for a typical trust is shown below.

GREAT NORTHERN IRON ORE PROPERTIES
BALANCE SHEET
December 31, 1964

Current assets	$ 7,031,000
Long-term assets	5,397,000
Total assets	$12,428,000
Current liabilities	$ 1,390,000
Capital stock and surplus*	11,038,000
Total	$12,428,000

* Includes 1,500,000 shares of common stock (no par) represented by 1,500,000 certificates of beneficial interest.

The board of trustees takes the place of the board of directors. But the board of trustees continues through the life of the trust and cannot be changed by either the creator or the beneficiary. The board itself fills vacancies. The beneficiaries of a trust are not liable for its affairs; neither may they participate in its management. Thus the business trust encourages separation of control and financial responsibility. Some states require that every document used by a trust give notice to third parties that beneficiaries are not liable. Where such notice is required, the procedure involved is time-consuming and operates as a deterrent to the use of the business trust.

The trustee manages the property and affairs of the trust. The trustee is liable only for the exercise of the judgment of a prudent man. Third parties must look to the funds of the trust for satisfaction of claims.

Duration.   The life of a business trust is limited to the designated life or lives of the creators, plus 21 years. The life of a business trust, therefore, is relatively limited in comparison to that of a business corporation.

Taxation and regulation.   At present, trusts are most generally taxed as corporations by the federal government. In addition, the legal status of a trust that conducts extensive business operations has not been fully clarified in state law. This fact likewise operates as a deterrent to the use of business trusts.

Appraisal of use.   The uses of business trusts are limited to the following situations:[5]

1. The business trust is used to conduct the business of real estate in some jurisdictions where corporations cannot legally own real estate. Some states do not permit corporations to hold real property unless it is essential to their business.

2. The business trust may be used in some special legal situations. For example, in Massachusetts a public utility corporation may not be owned by a "foreign" holding company corporation. "Foreign" in this sense refers to a firm chartered in a state other than Massachusetts. In such situations a business or Massachusetts trust is likely to be formed to operate in the place of a holding company.

3. The business trust may be used in temporary circumstances which make it desirable to place trustees in control of a business for a short period.

Cooperatives

A cooperative is an enterprise established and owned by its members to provide them with services at cost. Consumer cooperatives represent

---

[5] Examples of prominent businesses carried on under a declaration of trust are the Texas Pacific Land Trust, Great Northern Iron Ore Properties, American Optical Company, Eastern Gas and Fuel Associates, and the New England Gas and Electric Association.

some ten million families in the United States. Producer and marketing cooperatives are strong in a number of agricultural products. Manufacturing cooperatives are found to a limited degree in petroleum, farm machinery, electrical appliances, publishing, and telephones. Cooperative wholesalers are significant in the grocery and drug lines. Financial cooperatives are important in insurance, credit unions, and savings and loan associations.

The main rules governing cooperatives are these:

1. Each member has only one vote; there is no voting by proxy.
2. Share capital is paid a moderate, fixed return.
3. The surplus of the association is to be returned to members after reserves have been provided for.
4. Surplus is distributed on the basis of patronage for consumers cooperatives and either as price reductions or a fixed sum per member for cooperative wholesalers.

Cooperatives represent an effective financing device in some circumstances. By drawing on the deposits of a large number of members, cooperatives may raise substantial amounts of funds. Furthermore, cooperatives provide an opportunity for conserving funds, because in many instances they are completely or substantially exempt from income taxes. The special tax status of cooperatives results from the theory that the cooperative is a nonprofit enterprise, its dividends purporting to represent a discount in price rather than profits. Whether the tax advantage of cooperatives will continue to be an important source of funds is questionable, since the basis for their special tax status has become increasingly controversial. However, the importance of cooperatives in many lines of business suggests that their nature and role be more fully studied in the future.

The Corporate Form

The dominant position of the corporation in the private sector of the economy has been mentioned. While 77 percent of the total national income originates in corporate activities, 92 percent of manufacturing income is generated in corporate operations. Consequently, the corporate form deserves extensive treatment.

Fundamental characteristics. By legal definition a corporation is a person created by the state. This definition of the corporation is simple in itself. However, the chartering of corporations has resulted in some very complex consequences. These are set forth most colorfully in a commentary on the analogue which treats the corporation as a person.

The analogue, upon which an intricate legal code was built, turned out not to be the happiest of choices. The person is a human sort of biological organism, full of the weaknesses to which flesh and blood are heir, and blessed with the capacity to shuffle off the mortal coil. The corporation had no heart to be wrung, no body to be thrown in jail, no soul in mortal peril of being cast into hell. The person corporate draws its legal life from a sheet of paper. At its very birth it is deemed to have reached years of discretion. If in origin "domestic," it starts life as a mature being; if an emigré, it has to submit to no probationary period before taking out its second papers. It is endowed with a host of biological traits to which no son of Adam could ever aspire. Like the amoeba, it can in a twinkling resolve itself into two corporations; like the queen bee's mate it can, living only for one brief moment, exhaust its life in a single creative act; like the phoenix, it can cease to be yet resurrect itself from its own ashes. . . . Such is, at least by random sample, a little of what the common law let itself in for by calling the *corpus* a person.[6]

Growing out of the legal status of the corporation as a person are several characteristics.

Separate existence.   The corporation is a legal entity distinct from the individual stockholders or the individual managers of the firm.

Immortality.   The corporation has continuous life. It goes on despite the death of individual managers or stockholders.

Limited liability.   The liability of stockholders is limited to the amount of funds they have invested in the corporation. This rule facilitates the raising of funds and makes it easier to finance large-scale organizations. However, the limited liability feature shifts a considerable amount of risk to the creditors of the corporation. If the corporation fails, the creditors of the corporation have no redress against the stockholders. The only cushion provided is the amount of money the stockholders themselves have placed in the company and whatever earnings have been retained in the operation of the business.

In practice, the limited liability of stockholders for borrowed funds in the small corporation can be a fiction. A good credit manager requires that personal guarantees be made by the principal owners and managers of the small corporation. In addition, if the principal owners and managers do not have sufficient financial responsibility, guarantees from financially responsible relatives and friends will also be required.

Ready transferability of shares.   Shares may be freely sold by the owners of the corporation, and highly organized markets for conducting the sales and transferability of ownership have been developed. Voting in the corporation may be carried out through the use of proxies. A proxy is the transfer of the voting right by the owner of a share of stock to some other designated person or persons. Typically, the proxy is of limited duration.

Centralization of management.   In the large corporation a separation of ownership and control exists. Management typically owns fewer than 2 percent of the total shares of a large company. It is sometimes said

---

6 Walton H. Hamilton, "The Economic Man Affects a National Role," *American Economic Review, Proceedings*, 36 (May 1946), p. 737.

that a corporation facilitates more effective organization of responsibility and functions in a business. This may be true, but in any large organization responsibilities are delegated and departmentalized. The corporation, as such, is not unique in this regard.

Wide range of activities. Corporations have the power to carry on many diverse activities. The corporate purpose used to be narrowly defined by charter. Present-day corporate charters, however, are generally quite broad in scope. For example, the corporate purpose might read something like this: "This corporation shall have the power to manufacture steel and to do *any other things* necessary to carry out this activity."

Aspects of formation. Corporations formerly were created by special acts of state legislatures. Because of discriminatory treatment, the procedure was considered undemocratic and was discarded. States then passed charter regulations, which are applied without prejudice to all applicants. Under the present procedure, a certificate of incorporation is first drawn up. This certificate of incorporation carries the following information:

Name of proposed corporation
Purposes
Amount of capital stock
Number of directors
Names and addresses of directors
Duration, and so on

The certificate is notarized and sent to the secretary of the state in which the business seeks incorporation. The secretary of state examines the certificate. If it is satisfactory, he files the certificate. He notifies the applicant and sends a copy to the clerk of the county in which the corporation will have its principal office. The corporation is now in existence.

As a practical matter, attorneys and specialized companies will, in a very short time, perform all the steps required for incorporation. A fee is charged for the service. Some companies which specialize in incorporating procedures have offices located in Delaware, Nevada, and other states where incorporation is advantageous. They can perform the service in 24 hours or in even less time.

The charter. The corporate charter technically consists of (1) a certificate of incorporation and, by reference, (2) the general corporation laws of the state. Thus the corporation is bound by the general corporation laws of the state as they may be modified or particularized in its certificate of incorporation.

Bylaws. Once the corporation is established, it adopts bylaws. The rules governing the matters of internal management of the company cover a number of items:

Regulations for the issuance and transfer of stock
Stockholders' meetings

Directors' meetings
Election and qualifications of directors
Care and management of property and finance

Choosing the state of incorporation.   One of the interesting aspects of incorporating is selection of the state of incorporation. The question has been raised from time to time, "Why do corporations leave home?" The basic variables are (1) extent of the liabilities placed on stockholders, directors, and officers, (2) requirements concerning methods of paying for stock, and (3) amounts of taxes and fees required.

An analysis of the third factor, taxes and fees, indicates that this is probably not the major factor in a corporation's decision to domicile in a state other than that of its major activity, nor does it explain the concentration of corporation chartering in the state of Delaware.

The difference in costs of organization for a large corporation is not great enough to induce it to domicile in Delaware, as opposed to other states. In addition, because a foreign (out-of-state) corporation pays an income tax on the amount of business conducted in each state, no advantage is offered by incorporation in a state with a low corporate income tax rate. The major factors attracting a firm to incorporate in a state are nontax considerations.

The reasons for incorporation in Delaware publicized by companies advertising incorporation services include the following:

1. The charter is broad.
2. There are no requirements regarding residence of incorporators or directors.
3. Meetings of incorporators, stockholders, and directors may be held outside the state.
4. There is no limitation on the holding of shares of stock of other corporations.
5. There is no income tax on corporations.
6. There is no inheritance tax on nonresidents.
7. Nonresidents are not taxed on their holdings of stock in Delaware corporations.
8. Stock may be issued for labor done, money paid, and personal and real property or leases, and the judgment of directors governs the values.
9. Organization fees and annual taxes are low and are based on authorized capital.
10. Stated capital and paid-in surplus may be set up at times of issuance of shares.
11. A great variety of corporate structures is permitted.

Particularly significant is item 8, which gives promoters or incorporators discretion in evaluating their services in connection with the establishment of the firm. They may receive a substantial amount of stock in a company for the work performed in getting the company into operation. Other states do not allow the promoters as much flexibility on this point.

COMPARISON OF ALTERNATIVE FORMS

The foregoing material has described the essential elements of leading forms of business organization. Which form should the promoter choose?

The answer must depend upon the characteristics of the particular situation. No aspect of the problem should be omitted from consideration. The following list is adequate to cover most situations:

1. Ability to raise funds
   a) Personal liability of the owners for business debts—limited or unlimited
   b) Transferability and divisibility of ownership units, and *delectus personae* (that is, the right to choose associates)
2. Taxation
3. Expense and difficulty of formation
4. Ease of maintaining control
   a) Possibility of absentee control
   b) Relative percentage of ownership required for control
5. Other factors
   a) Ease of assignment of management functions
   b) Degree of government regulation

Table 2–3 is a comparative analysis of the forms of business organization. The chart has been set up verbally and numerically in describing the characteristics of the different forms of organization. Words are used to indicate in a general way the characteristics of each of the alternative forms. Numbers are used to provide some method for summarizing the general characteristics of each of the alternative forms of organization. As the key to the ratings indicates, the numbers are chosen in an arbitrary fashion to correspond to the five gradations of quality ratings. The chart makes a general comparison of the various forms.

The form used in Table 2–3 can be used in analyzing the facts in a particular case. The ratings on taxation will vary with the income position of the owners. The ease of assignment of management functions will vary also with the personalities of the principals. For example, the partnership is particularly vulnerable to disagreements. The increased formality of the corporate form defines organization responsibilities more clearly.

Because of its advantages for raising large sums of money through limited liability of owners and ease of transferring ownership, the corporate form is characteristic of large-scale enterprise. The predominance of the proprietorship and partnership forms in retail trade and service establishments reflect their ease and low expense of formation and greater flexibility.

TABLE 2-3

COMPARISON OF ALTERNATIVE FORMS OF BUSINESS ORGANIZATION

	Proprietorship	Partnership	Limited Partnership	Joint Stock Co.	Mass. Trust	Corporation
1. Ability to raise funds						
a) Liability of owners for business debts	Poor 2	Fair 4	Excel. 6	Poor 2	Excel. 7	Outs. 9
b) Transferability	Poor 2	Poor 0	Fair 3	Outs. 10	Excel. 6	Outs. 10
2. Taxation	Ave. 5	Ave. 5	Ave. 5	Ave. 5	Ave. 5	Ave. 5
3. Expense and difficulty of starting	Outs. 10	Outs. 8	Fair 3	Fair 3	Fair 3	Fair 4
4. Control	Poor 1	Poor 3	Excel. 7	Ave. 5	Outs. 8	Outs. 10
5. Other						
a) Ease of assigning management functions	Poor 1	Fair 3	Fair 4	Excel. 6	Ave. 5	Outs. 9
b) Government regulation	Outs. 9	Outs. 8	Ave. 5	Fair 4	Ave. 5	Fair 3
Total rating	30	31	33	35	39	50

Key:

Outstanding = Outs. = 8–10
Excellent = Excel. = 6–7
Average = Ave. = 5
Fair = 3–4
Poor = 0–2

SUMMARY

The promoter performs the economic function of establishing new business enterprises. He sees the opportunity for a new product or a new market to be exploited. He responds to the opportunity by the establishment of a new firm, the purchase and expansion of an existing firm, or the addition of a division to an existing firm.

Before a new firm is established, the first step is to make a market survey of the expected volume of sales and the nature of competition in the particular line of business. The second step is to analyze prospective selling prices and costs. These investigations will yield an estimate of sales, costs, and profits.

The ordinary financing problems of a firm are intensified in a new firm. Not only must it finance the requisite assets, but it must cover promotion and organization expenses as well as initial operating losses for a period. For these reasons and because the company's revenues are uncertain, it is important that the new, untried firm minimize its financing requirements. This work can be accomplished in several ways. The firm can rent rather than buy some of its land, building, and equipment needs. If it must buy equipment, it should seek to hold initial costs to a minimum by distributing the product through existing marketing organizations on a temporary basis until the firm is sufficiently well established to bear the costs of developing its own marketing organization.

A major decision in the process of forming a new firm is the choice of the form of organization. The alternative forms of financing were compared in a summary rating based on five criteria: (1) ability to raise funds, (2) amount of taxation, (3) expense and difficulty of starting the business, (4) ease with which management is able to function, and (5) degree of government regulation.

The choice of form of business organization depends on size of the operation, amount of funds needed, considerations of control of the firm, and severity of taxation. Generalization is not possible. Most large-volume and large-scale operations are conducted under the corporate form. Most small-scale operations are individual proprietorships or partnerships. In choosing among the various forms of business organizations, taxation is an important factor. The following chapter, The Tax Environment, deals with the importance of the tax factor in choosing among alternative forms of organization and in making other financial decisions.

SELECTED REFERENCES

Churchill, B. C., "The Business Population by Legal Form of Organization," *Survey of Current Business*, 31 (June 1951), pp. 9–23.
————, "Size Characteristics of Business Population," *Survey of Current Business*, 34 (May 1954), pp. 15–24.
Larcom, R. C., *The Delaware Corporation* (Baltimore: Johns Hopkins, 1937).
Milroy, Robert R., "The Small Business Corporation—Proceed with Caution," *Business Horizons,* Vol. 3, No. 2 (Summer 1960), 97–109.
Weston, J. Fred (ed.), *Financial Management in the 1960s: New Challenges and Responsibilities* (New York: Holt, Rinehart and Winston, Inc., 1966), selection "The Egghead Millionaires. "
———— (ed.), *Readings in Finance from* Fortune (New York: Holt, Rinehart and Winston, Inc., 1958), selections 1–7 and 14–16.

QUESTIONS

2-1 A friend of yours has just discovered a new product and plans to start a business to produce it. One of his goals is to maintain absolute control, but his own capital is limited. What are some ways he can reduce the amount of his initial outlay while still obtaining an efficiently large plant?

2-2 What are some sources of information on the past performance of a firm you are thinking of buying?

2-3 What are the major factors one should consider in choosing among different forms of business organizations?

2-4 What is the major difference between a sole proprietorship and a partnership?

2-5 What are the major advantages and disadvantages of corporations versus unincorporated forms of business?

2-6 In what sense is a corporation a person?

2-7 Would it be practical for U. S. Steel to be organized as a partnership?

2-8 In a large firm such as U. S. Steel many important decisions are made daily. In making a decision, the decision maker has some goal in mind.

1. Do you believe that the goal behind all decisions made in U. S. Steel is the maximization of the company's profits?
2. Explain how each of the following can help to bring the answer to question 1 more closely to an absolute "yes."
    a) Executive compensation schemes
    b) Employee stock option plans
    c) Profit-sharing plans

2-9 What is a closed corporation? Why is it formed? Give two or three examples.

2-10 What is a voting trust? Why is it used?

2-11 "Typically, officers and directors hold only a small percentage of the stock of large corporations but control the proxy machinery and voting." To what extent is this statement true? What is its significance?

2-12 If you were starting a business, under what circumstances would you incorporate in the state in which you live? Would you incorporate in Delaware? Why or why not?

PROBLEMS

2-1 J. L. Mason is a married man of 42, with two children. Practically all Mason's business experience has been in the production and selling of small and medium-size electric motors for industrial and commercial use.

Mason proposes to form a company to manufacture and sell electric motors. He possesses $40,000 capital. He has estimated that there is a ready market for electric motors that incorporate his new design, and forecasts total sales of $24,000 per month during the first two years of operation. He has secured an option on a vacant factory building in a Chicago suburb, which can be purchased and suitably remodeled at an estimated cost of $55,000. Equipment and machinery are estimated to cost $60,000.

All sales will be made on terms of one-third cash and the balance in sixteen equal monthly payments. The electric motors will have an average selling price of $40 per unit and an average total cost (including depreciation of $10,000 per year) of $32 per unit. Trade creditors will finance his initial inventory. Accounts payable at the end of one year will be $70,000; at the end of 18 months, $80,000. He will need 30 days' sales in inventory.

1. Knowing only the preceding facts and making any reasonable assumptions necessary, draw up a statement of the essential capital requirements for the proposed company as of the first day of business; at the end of one year; at the end of 18 months. What do you conclude from the statement developed? (Use the cash basis and do not consider income taxes.)
2. Indicate the additional facts and lines of investigation you would develop if you were one of the group of capitalists being approached to finance the company.

2-2 Recommend the form of business organization for the following, giving your reasons.

1. James Avery operates a small convenience auto repair shop in a residential neighborhood. His four children are all grown up. Avery is 52 years old; he completed only grade school. He has moderate savings and owns his house. He nets about $7,000 income per year.
2. Joan Baker is 38, is single, and operates a medium-priced-line women's dress shop in a local shopping area. She is a high school graduate with some artistic interests and background, which she feels contribute to her taste in selecting dresses. The store nets her about $8,000 per year.
3. Frank Root and Paul Henderson have been employed as application engineers in a large electronics company. They have an idea for producing a new type of precision measuring instrument. They estimate that $60,000 will be required to put the operation through the first six months. Each owns his house and has cash and securities amounting to some $80,000 each. They plan to limit their salaries to $10,000 until the enterprise proves successful.
4. Robert Jorgenson and John Clark have been junior members of two well-known management consulting firms. They plan to form their own firm; Jorgenson is a specialist in finance and Clark is strong in general management.

Chapter 3

The Tax Environment[1]

Numerous business policies including inventory policy, wage negotiations, sales and credit policies, asset purchases, and especially financing decisions are affected crucially by tax factors.[2] Choice of form of business organization, use of debt versus common stocks in financing, decisions about the timing of purchases of inventory and fixed assets, whether to lease or to buy, merger policies, and liquidation decisions—all these areas are influenced by tax factors. For these reasons a brief summary of the elements of the tax structure related to financial decision making are presented in this chapter.

OVERVIEW OF TAX AND EXPENDITURE PATTERNS

The overriding importance of governments—federal, state, and local —and the trend toward their increasing importance are shown by the figures in Table 3–1. In 1950, total tax revenues amounted to $57.3 billions, or 20.1 percent of the $285 billion gross national product that year. By 1963 taxes had climbed to $149.3 billion, which was 25.6 percent of 1963 GNP. State and local government taxes and expenditures rose somewhat more rapidly than those of the federal government, the former amounting to 42.1 percent of the total in 1963 versus 36.5 percent in 1950.

---

1 This chapter has benefited from the assistance of Mr. R. Wendell Buttrey, tax attorney and lecturer on taxation at the University of California, Los Angeles.
2 For many illustrations, see W. J. Vatter, *Management Planning For Corporate Taxes* (New York: Controllership Foundation, Inc., 1951).

TABLE 3–1

LEVEL OF TAXES AND SPENDING IN RELATION TO GROSS NATIONAL PRODUCT, 1950 and 1963

(dollars in billions)

	1950		1963	
	Tax Revenue	Percent of Total	Tax Revenue	Percent of Total
Federal Revenues	$ 36.4	63.5%	$ 86.4	57.9%
State and local government revenues	20.9	36.5	62.9	42.1
Total	$ 57.3	100.0%	$149.3	100.0%
Gross national product	$285		$584	
Government revenues as a percent of GNP	20.1%		25.6%	

Source: *Economic Report of the President* (Washington, D.C.: U.S. Government Printing Office, 1965), pp. 189, 260, 265.

Table 3–2 shows the principal sources of federal income for the years 1950 and 1963. Individual and corporate income taxes provided the bulk of the revenues in each of the years, with the percentage contributed by personal taxes rising over the period, because personal incomes rose more rapidly than corporate profits. The importance of excise taxes

TABLE 3–2

FEDERAL REVENUE BY SOURCES, 1950 and 1963

(dollars in billions)

	1950		1963	
	Amount	Percent	Amount	Percent
Individual income taxes	$18.1	48.8%	$47.6	55.1%
Corporate income taxes	10.9	29.4	21.6	25.0
Excise taxes	7.6	20.5	9.9	11.5
Estate and gift taxes	n.a.	n.a.	2.2	2.5
Customs.	0.4	1.0	1.2	1.4
Miscellaneous receipts	0.1	0.3	3.9	4.5
	$37.1	100.0%	$86.4	100.0%

Source: *Statistical Abstract of the United States*, 1953, p. 343; 1964, p. 392 (Washington, D.C.: U.S. Government Printing Office).

dropped markedly, and another sharp decline in this source of revenue will show up in future years as a result of the elimination of about half the remaining excise taxes by the Internal Revenue Act of 1965. Although the total of federal (and state) gift and estate taxes is not large, their impact on individuals and on individual businesses can be massive, so attention must be given to these taxes.

The main sources of state and local government revenue, shown in Table 3–3, are licenses and other fees, property taxes, and sales taxes. Income taxes, both personal and corporate, are of minor importance, but transfers from the federal government amounted to over 11 percent of

TABLE 3–3

STATE AND LOCAL GOVERNMENT REVENUES BY SOURCES, 1950 and 1962

(dollars in billions)

	1950		1962	
	Amount	Percent	Amount	Percent
Property taxes	$ 7.3	28.5%	$19.1	27.4%
Sales and gross receipts taxes	5.2	20.4	13.5	19.4
Individual income taxes	0.8	3.1	3.0	4.3
Corporation net income taxes	0.6	2.3	1.3	1.9
Revenues from the federal government	2.5	9.8	7.9	11.4
Licenses, fees, and other revenues	9.2	35.9	24.8	35.6
Totals	$25.6	100.0%	$69.6	100.0%

Source: Statistical Abstract of the United States, 1964 (Washington, D.C.: U.S. Government Printing Office), p. 422.

state and local revenues in 1962. The stability of income from the various sources is also worthy of note; while there were significant shifts in the importance of the different sources of federal revenues, such shifts have not occurred at the state and local levels.

CORPORATE INCOME TAXES
Rate Structure

The corporate income tax is 22 percent on income up to $25,000. For income in excess of $25,000, a surtax of 26 percent is applied, making a 48 percent total tax rate on corporate income over $25,000.

CORPORATE INCOME TAX RATES
(in percents)

Amount of Income	Normal Tax	Surtax	Total Tax Rate
First $25,000	22	0	22
More than $25,000	22	26	48

On income above $25,000 it makes no difference whether the corporation earns $50,000 or $50 million; the marginal tax rate is still 48 percent. If a firm's income were, for example, $100,000, the tax would be as follows: the 22 percent tax rate would apply to $25,000 and the 48 percent rate would apply to the remaining $75,000, resulting in a total tax of $41,500.

$$
\begin{array}{ll}
22\% \times 25,000 & \$\ 5,500 \\
48\% \times 75,000 & 36,000 \\
\hline
\text{Total} & \$41,500 \\
\end{array}
$$

Table 3–4 shows that the average corporate income tax is moderately

TABLE 3–4
MARGINAL AND AVERAGE TAX RATES OF THE CORPORATION INCOME TAX
(in percentages)

Corporate Income (in dollars)	Marginal Tax Rate	Average Tax Rate*
0–25,000	22%	22.00%
25,001–26,000	48	23.00
26,001–32,000	48	27.69
32,001–38,000	48	30.89
38,001–44,000	48	33.23
44,001–50,000	48	35.00
50,001–60,000	48	37.17
60,001–70,000	48	38.71
70,001–80,000	48	39.88
80,001–90,000	48	40.78
90,001–100,000	48	41.50
100,001–150,000	48	43.67
150,001–200,000	48	44.75
200,001–500,000	48	46.70
500,001–1,000,000	48	47.35
1,000,001–5,000,000	48	47.87
5,000,001–10,000,000	48	47.94
10,000,001–100,000,000	48	47.99
100,000,001–500,000,000	48	48.00

* Applied to the upper limit of each class interval.

progressive up to $1 million, when it becomes virtually 48 percent. These data are compared to the personal income tax rates in a subsequent section.

This relatively simple tax structure has wide implications for business planning. Because the tax rate on corporate income in excess of $25,000 is more than double the normal rate, some moderate-sized companies, which can practicably be broken down into smaller units, are motivated to form multiple corporations, thereby holding their tax rate at 22 percent.

For both the corporate and the personal income taxes, interest payments are deductible in determining the amount of income subject to taxation. Since dividends paid on the owners' investment are not deductible as an expense, some inducement is thereby provided for the use of debt as a source of financing. Moreover, profits used to retire debt do not create taxable income in the hands of shareholders, as would be true if they were distributed as dividends.

Depreciation is also a deductible business expense for the corporate income tax and for determining the business income of a proprietorship or a partnership. The accelerated depreciation methods, discussed in detail in the Appendix to Chapter 10, reduce the income tax in the earlier years of the life of an asset and thereby achieve a postponement of taxes. Postponing a payment of any kind is, of course, equivalent to receiving an interest-free loan.

Corporate Capital Gains and Losses[3]

Capital assets are defined as those used by a firm but not bought and sold in the ordinary course of its business. For example, a machine tool would be a capital asset to a manufacturing company that used the tool, but it would not be a capital asset to a dealer in machine tools or to the tool manufacturer. Gains and losses on capital assets are defined as *capital gains,* and under certain circumstances they receive special tax treatment.

The sale of capital assets held for six months or less gives rise to *short-term* capital gains or losses, while the disposal of property held for more than six months gives rise to *long-term* gains and losses. Net short-term gains (gains minus losses) are taxed at regular corporate income tax rates. For long-term assets, to the extent that a gain does not represent the recapture of depreciation, the tax is limited to 25 percent. For example, if a corporation holds the common stock of another firm as an investment for more than six months and then sells it at a profit, the gain is subject to a maximum tax of 25 percent.

On the other hand, suppose a firm buys a machine tool for $1,000, then sells it three years later for $800 after having taken $488 depreciation. The machine's book value is $512 at the time of sale ($1,000 — $488), so an accounting profit of $288 is reported ($800 — 512). But since the depreciation taken exceeds the profit, the amount of profit is reported as

---

[3] Corporate capital gains and losses (as well as most other tax matters) are subject to many technical provisions. This section and the others dealing with tax matters include only the most general provisions. For special cases the student is referred to *Federal Tax Course* (Englewood Cliffs, N.J.: Prentice-Hall, 1965), *passim.*

ordinary income (the amount of depreciation taken). Had the sale been for $1,800, thereby producing an accounting profit of $1,288, $488 would have been taxed as ordinary income, while $800 would have been a capital gain taxable at a maximum rate of 25 percent.

A net capital loss is not deductible from ordinary income. For example, if a corporation has an ordinary income of $100,000 and a net capital loss of $25,000 in 1967, it still pays a tax on the ordinary income at the normal rate of 22 percent on the $25,000 and 48 percent on the $75,000, a total tax of $41,500. But the net capital loss may be carried over for five years and used to offset any capital gains. If this corporation in 1968 has a net capital gain of $75,000, its *taxable net gain* in that year would be $50,000.

Another important rule is that 85 percent of dividends received by one corporation from another is exempt from taxation.[4] For example, if corporation N owns stock in corporation X and receives $100,000 in dividends from corporation X, it would have to pay taxes on only $15,000 of the $100,000. In addition, if it held the stock in corporation X for more than six months and sold the stock at a $300,000 profit, it would pay only a 25 percent tax, or $75,000, on that profit. Thus the present form of the tax law provides strong financial incentives for intercorporate investments.

Payment of Tax in Installments

Before 1952, corporations paid their tax obligations in quarterly installments in the year *following* the year in which the income was earned. For example, if a corporation earned $100,000 in 1949 and the tax payable on this was $50,000, the corporation would pay $12,500 in each of four quarterly installments on March 15, June 15, September 15, and December 15, 1950. Under the so-called Mills plan beginning in 1952, corporations were moved toward a pay-as-you-go basis. By 1960 the larger corporations were paying 25 percent of their tax liability on each September 15 and December 15 of the income year (on an estimated basis), and 25 percent of the tax liability on each March 15 and June 15 of the year following that in which the liability was incurred. New provisions of the Internal Revenue Act of 1964 speed up collection even more, and by 1970 large corporations will be paying 25 percent of their estimated tax bill on the 15th of April, June, September, and December of the *current* year.

As will be seen in a subsequent chapter, the amount of taxes owed to the government constitutes an interest-free source of funds. As the move-

---

[4] If the corporation receiving the dividends owns 80 percent or more of the dividend-paying firm, then the dividends are wholly deductible.

ment toward pay-as-you-go corporate taxes progresses, new sources of financing must be found, so planning for the speed-up in tax collections is important to American business.

Net Operating Carry-Back and Carry-Forward

For the years ending after December 31, 1958, any ordinary operating loss can be carried back three years and carried forward five years. The purpose of this provision is to avoid penalizing corporations whose income fluctuates widely. For example, if a corporation that earned $200,000 in 1966 suffered a $100,000 loss in 1969, it could carry the loss either backward or forward. It could recalculate the 1966 tax by deducting the $100,000 loss against the $200,000 income, so that taxable income in 1966 would be reduced to $100,000. The corporation should recompute its 1966 income tax and file for a refund.

The right to carry losses forward and backward made some corporations attractive buys. For example, Atlas Corporation and Howard Hughes bought RKO Pictures because of a $30 million tax-loss credit. A corporation may acquire another firm that has had a tax loss, operate it as a subsidiary, and then present consolidated returns for tax purposes. Newspapers frequently contain advertisements such as "Tax-Loss Corporation for Sale," "Attractive Tax Loss Available." The corporation may be a doubly attractive buy if the purchaser is able to operate the business effectively and turn it into a profitable corporation at the same time that he benefits from the tax-loss carry-forward or carry-back.

The tax law of 1954 placed certain restrictions on this privilege. (1) If more than 50 percent of the stock changes hands within two years after the purchase and (2) if the old business is essentially abandoned, no loss carry-over is provided. The objective of the limitation is to prevent a firm from merging for the sole purpose of taking advantage of the tax law. If it merges for this purpose and files consolidated returns, the loss privilege may be disallowed. Moreover, deductions are denied where an acquisition appears to have been motivated largely by the prospects of such deductions.[5]

Improper Accumulation

A special surtax on improperly accumulated income is provided for by Section 531 of the Internal Revenue Code (formerly Section 102). Section 531 provides that earnings accumulated by a corporation are subject to penalty rates if the purpose of the accumulation is to enable the stock owners to avoid the personal income tax. Of income not paid

---

[5] Sylvan Tobolowsky, "Tax Consequences of Corporate Organization and Distributions," *Journal of Taxation*, 12 (January 1960), pp. 8–15.

out in dividends, $100,000 is deducted as an amount *prima facie* retainable for the reasonable needs of the business. This again is a benefit for small corporations. But there is a penalty rate on all amounts over $100,000 shown to be unnecessary to meet the reasonable needs of the business. The penalty rate on the first $100,000 of improperly accumulated taxable income is 27.5 percent and 38.5 percent on all amounts over 100,000.

The 1954 law provided that the burden of proof of improper accumulation falls on the United States Treasury, if the taxpayer files a statement supporting his accumulation. In other words, if the taxpayer presents a statement explaining why he is retaining the earnings, it is up to the Treasury to prove that his statement is not justified. Before 1954, the burden of proof was on the taxpayer to convince the Treasury and the courts that retention was justified.

Retained earnings are used to pay off debt, to finance growth, and to provide the corporation with a cushion against possible cash drains caused by losses. How much a firm should properly accumulate for uncertain contingencies is a matter of judgment. Fear of the penalty taxes that may be imposed under Section 531 may cause a firm to pay out a higher rate of dividends than it would otherwise do.[6]

Sometimes Section 531 may influence financial policies other than dividend policy. A clear illustration is provided by the purchase of the Toni Company (home permanents) by the Gillette Safety Razor Company.[7] The sale was made early in 1948 when Toni's sales volume had begun to level off. Since earnings retention might be difficult to justify, the owners of Toni, the Harris brothers, were faced with the alternative of paying penalty rates for improper accumulation of earnings or of paying out the income as dividends. The income was $4 million per year, and, with an average personal income tax of 75 percent, only $1 million per year would have been left after taxes. By the sale of Toni for $13 million, the brothers realized a $12 million capital gain; after paying the 25 percent capital gains tax of $3 million, the Harris brothers realized $10 million after taxes. Thus Gillette paid the equivalent of three and one-third years' after-corporate-tax earnings for Toni. The Harris brothers received ten years' after-personal-income-tax net income for Toni. The tax factor made the transaction advantageous to both parties.

The broad aspects of the federal corporate income tax have now

---

[6] See materials in James K. Hall, *The Taxation of Corporate Surplus Accumulations* (Washington, D.C.: U.S. Government Printing Office, 1952), especially Appendix 3.

[7] See J. K. Butters, J. Lintner, and W. L. Cary, *Effects of Taxation, Corporate Mergers* (Boston: Harvard Business School, 1951), pp. 96–111. The lucid presentation by these authors has been drawn on for the general background, but the data have been approximated to make the illustration simple. The principle involved is not affected by the modifications of the facts.

been covered. For many business decisions, the federal income tax on individuals is equally important, so the main outlines of this part of the tax system must be discussed. First, however, it is necessary to indicate when corporations may elect to be taxed as individuals, and vice versa.

Election of Legal Form for Tax Purposes

The law makes provisions for certain qualifying sole proprietorships and partnerships to elect to be taxed as corporations while continuing to do business as proprietorships or partnerships. The principal qualifications include the following:

1. The business must be owned by not more than fifty individuals.
2. Capital assets must be a material income-producing factor.
3. No proprietor, or partner with more than a 10 percent interest in the business, can have more than a 10 percent interest in another such unincorporated business electing to be taxed as a corporation.

Similarly, certain incorporated businesses may elect to be taxed as proprietorships or partnerships. The main regulations governing permission to make this election include:

1. The firm must be a domestic corporation and must not be affiliated with a group eligible to file consolidated tax returns. (Ordinarily 80 percent ownership of a subsidiary is required for filing consolidated returns.)
2. The firm must not have more than ten stockholders, all of whom must be individuals.

This possibility of operating a business in one form but being taxed as another type of concern is highly important; it allows qualified firms to have the best of both worlds. In the next section the individual tax structure is examined and compared with the corporate tax structure, thus providing a basis for making an intelligent choice as to which form of organization a firm should elect for tax purposes.

PERSONAL INCOME TAX

Of some 4.6 million firms in the United States, approximately four million are organized as individual proprietorships or as partnerships. The income of businesses organized as individual proprietorships or partnerships is taxed as personal income to the owners or partners unless they have elected to have the firm taxed as a corporation. The net income of a proprietorship or a partnership is reported to provide a basis for determining the individual's income tax liability. Thus, as a business tax, the individual income tax may be as important as the corporate income tax.

Gross Income and Deductions

The general form of the personal income tax is as follows:

Gross income (wages, salaries, rent, and other income)
Deduct: Expenses incurred as necessary business expenses
Equals: Adjusted gross income
Less: Itemized personal deductions
   1. Contributions (limited to 20 percent of the adjusted gross income, with minor exceptions)
   2. Interest paid
   3. Medical and dental expenses
      a) Medical and drug expenses less 1 percent of adjusted gross income
      b) Excess drug expenses (from a) plus medical and dental expenses, all less 3 percent of adjusted gross income
   4. Taxes
   5. Child-care expenses
   6. Casualty losses and thefts (first $100 loss not deductible)
   7. Miscellaneous deductions
   (In lieu of itemization of deductions, the taxpayer may take the standard deduction of 10 percent of adjusted gross income up to a deduction of $1,000)
Less: Exemption of $600 each for wife, children, and other dependents
Equals: Taxable income

Individual Income Tax Structure

The tax rates applicable to taxable income are set forth in Tables 3–5 and 3–6. Table 3–5 shows the rates for single returns; Table 3–6 is for joint returns. Since joint returns are permitted whether or not one spouse earns the entire income, this privilege has the effect of lowering applicable tax rates.

For some decisions, the taxpayer will compare the top bracket (marginal) tax rates. If a taxpayer has income from other sources and is contemplating an additional venture, he will be concerned with the tax rate applicable to the additional income. In comparing the relative advantages of the corporate versus noncorporate form of business organization, he is likely to compare the top-bracket personal rates (the individual income tax rates to which his income will be subject) with the marginal corporate income tax rates.

When the taxpayer's income will be mainly from the enterprise he contemplates forming, he is more likely to compare the average rates of taxation. The marginal tax rates can be compared directly by reference to the tables provided in tax-information forms. In order to obtain the average tax rates, additional computations are required. The relation between the average tax rates of the corporate income tax and the individual income tax is shown in Figure 3–1. For single returns, the individual rate rises above the corporate rate at about $10,000. For joint returns, the individual tax rises above the corporate at $54,000, at which figure the amount of taxes on individual income is $19,320, while the corporate taxes would be $19,420. From this point on, the individual tax rate rises to 70 percent, while the corporate rate rises more slowly toward 48 percent.

Thus, for a firm with net income of $1 million, there is no question but that the corporate form of business will be used. This fact explains why most of our largest businesses utilize the corporate form of organi-

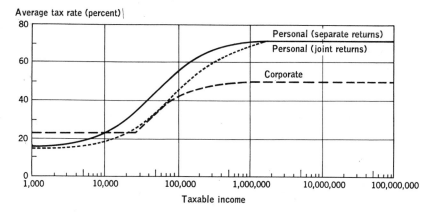

Fig. 3-1. Comparison between Average Rates of
Personal Income Tax and Corporation Income Tax

zation, especially since the corporation is also most effective for raising large sums of capital. At incomes in the region of the $54,000 dividing line, whether the corporate or noncorporate form will be most advantageous depends upon the facts of the case. If the corporation finds it necessary to pay out a substantial part of its earnings in dividends, the noncorporate form is likely to be advantageous, because the "double taxation" is avoided. On the other hand, the corporate form is satisfactory if it is possible to set up a number of corporations to keep the tax rate at 22 percent. In addition, the Revenue Act of 1964 made the corporate form somewhat more attractive by making an individual's income from investments in corporations partially tax-free. It provided for a dividends-received exclusion from income of $100. The $100 exclusion is available for each spouse.

Capital Gains and Losses

As with corporations, the distinction between short-term and long-term gains and losses is the six-month holding period. Net short-term gains are taxed at regular rates, while the tax on long-term gains may

TABLE 3–5

MARGINAL AND AVERAGE TAX RATES OF THE INDIVIDUAL INCOME TAX

1965 Rates

(Single taxpayers or separate returns)

Taxable Income	Tax Calculation			Average Tax Rate	
	Base Amount +	Marginal Tax Rate =	Tax*	Individual	Corporate
$0–$500	$0	14%	$70	14.0%	22.0%
500–1,000	70	15	145	14.5	22.0
1,000–1,500	145	16	225	15.0	22.0
1,500–2,000	225	17	310	15.5	22.0
2,000–4,000	310	19	690	17.3	22.0
4,000–6,000	690	22	1,130	18.8	22.0
6,000–8,000	1,130	25	1,630	20.4	22.0
8,000–10,000	1,630	28	2,190	21.8	22.0
10,000–12,000	2,190	32	2,830	23.5	22.0
12,000–14,000	2,830	36	3,550	25.3	22.0
14,000–16,000	3,550	39	4,330	27.0	22.0
16,000–18,000	4,330	42	5,170	28.7	22.0
18,000–20,000	5,170	45	6,070	30.3	22.0
20,000–22,000	6,070	48	7,030	31.9	22.0
22,000–26,000	7,030	50	9,030	34.7	23.0
26,000–32,000	9,030	53	12,210	38.1	27.7
32,000–38,000	12,210	55	15,510	40.8	30.9
38,000–44,000	15,510	58	18,990	43.1	33.2
44,000–50,000	18,990	60	22,590	45.2	35.0
50,000–60,000	22,590	62	28,790	48.0	37.2

Taxable Income	Tax Calculation				Average Tax Rate	
	Base Amount	+ Marginal Tax Rate	=	Tax*	Individual	Corporate
60,000–70,000	28,790	64		35,190	50.3	38.7
70,000–80,000	35,190	66		41,790	52.2	39.9
80,000–90,000	41,790	68		48,590	54.0	40.8
90,000–100,000	48,590	69		55,490	55.5	41.5
100,000–150,000	55,490	70		90,490	60.3	43.7
150,000–200,000	90,490	70		125,490	62.7	44.8
200,000–500,000	125,490	70		335,490	67.1	46.7
500,000–1,000,000	335,490	70		685,490	68.5	47.4
1,000,000–5,000,000	685,490	70		3,485,490	69.7	47.9
5,000,000–100,000,000	3,485,490	70		69,985,490	70.0	48.0

* Based on upper limit of each class interval.

TABLE 3-6
MARGINAL AND AVERAGE TAX RATES OF THE PERSONAL INCOME TAX

1965 Rates
(Joint returns)

Taxable Income	Tax Calculation			Average Tax Rate	
	Base Amount	+ Marginal Tax Rate	= Tax*	Individual	Corporate
$0–$1,000	$0	14%	$140	14.0%	22.0%
1,000–2,000	140	15	290	14.5	22.0
2,000–3,000	290	16	450	15.0	22.0
3,000–4,000	450	17	620	15.5	22.0
4,000–8,000	620	19	1,380	17.4	22.0
8,000–12,000	1,380	22	2,260	18.8	22.0
12,000–16,000	2,260	25	3,260	20.4	22.0
16,000–20,000	3,260	28	4,380	21.9	22.0
20,000–24,000	4,380	32	5,660	23.6	22.0
24,000–28,000	5,660	36	7,100	25.4	24.8
28,000–32,000	7,100	39	8,660	27.1	27.7
32,000–36,000	8,660	42	10,340	28.7	29.9
36,000–40,000	10,340	45	12,140	30.4	31.8
40,000–44,000	12,140	48	14,060	32.0	33.2
44,000–52,000	14,060	50	18,060	34.7	35.5
52,000–64,000	18,060	53	24,420	38.2	37.8
64,000–76,000	24,420	55	31,020	40.8	39.4
76,000–88,000	31,020	58	37,980	43.2	40.6
88,000–100,000	37,980	60	45,180	45.2	41.5

Tax Calculation

Taxable Income	Base Amount	+ Marginal Tax Rate	= Tax*	Average Tax Rate Individual	Average Tax Rate Corporate
100,000–120,000	45,180	62	57,580	48.0	42.6
120,000–140,000	57,580	64	70,380	50.3	43.4
140,000–160,000	70,380	66	83,580	52.2	43.9
160,000–180,000	83,580	68	97,180	54.0	44.4
180,000–200,000	97,180	69	110,980	55.5	44.8
200,000–300,000	110,980	70	189,980	60.3	45.8
300,000–400,000	180,980	70	250,980	62.7	46.4
400,000–1,000,000	250,980	70	670,980	67.1	47.4
1,000,000–10,000,000	670,980	70	6,970,980	69.7	47.9
10,000,000–100,000,000	6,970,980	70	69,920,980	70.0	48.0

* Based on upper limit of each class interval.

be computed in either of two ways. First, net long-term gains may be taxed at a flat rate of 25 percent. Alternatively, one may elect to pay the ordinary tax rate on *one half* the amount of the net long-term gains. The taxpayer should compute his tax under each of these methods, then select the one that gives him a lower tax bill. For joint returns the 25 percent option is beneficial only if the taxable income exceeds $44,000.

If capital losses exceed capital gains, the net loss may be deducted up to a maximum of $1,000. In other words, one may deduct against ordinary income only $1,000 of his net capital losses in any one year. If the net capital loss is in excess of $1,000, any amount above $1,000 may be carried forward until it is exhausted. Capital losses may not be carried back.

Moreover, the Revenue Act of 1958 provides that individuals who invest in the stock of small firms and suffer a loss on that stock may, for tax purposes, treat such a loss as an ordinary loss rather than a capital loss, up to $25,000 per year ($50,000 on a joint return). A corporation is treated as a small business corporation, and the loss on its stock can be treated as an ordinary loss, if the amount of the common stock does not exceed $500,000 per corporation and if the total net worth—common stock plus retained earnings—does not exceed $1 million. This provision also encourages the formation of and investment in small corporations.

Although the foregoing tax factors make it difficult to generalize on whether the corporate or noncorporate form is more advantageous from a tax standpoint, the essential variables for making an analysis are provided. In general, the advantage now seems to be on the side of the corporation, particularly since a firm may obtain the many benefits of its corporate status and yet elect to be taxed as a proprietorship or a partnership.

STATE AND LOCAL TAXATION

Besides the federal tax burden, the financial manager faces a complex of state and local taxes.

The main sources of state and local government revenues are property taxes, corporate income taxes, personal income taxes, licenses and fees, and sales taxes. Since sales taxes involve few major implications for business financial policy, they will not be discussed here.

State and local income taxes, both corporate and personal, are handled in relation to their federal counterparts. Property taxes, even though they are the major source of revenue for states and localities, are discussed only briefly because of their minor influence on business decisions.

State Corporate Income Taxes

State corporate income taxes have averaged about a 6 percent rate on taxable income. The state tax is deductible as an expense for the federal corporate income tax. If the corporation pays an average federal tax rate of 50 percent, the federal government is, in effect, absorbing one half the state income tax. Thus the effective rate of state corporate income taxes would be about 3 percent. Because of their low rate, state corporate income taxes would not have much significance for business financial policy were it not for the influence they have had in the past with regard to the selection of the state of incorporation. Formerly, corporations were taxable only in their state of incorporation.

On February 24, 1959, the Supreme Court of the United States ruled that states may tax the income of out-of-state companies, as well as local companies, on their local sales, even if the company merely sent salesmen into the state. However, the Interstate Income Law, effective September 14, 1959, essentially restored the situation that had existed prior to the 1959 Supreme Court decision. Only if a corporation has a warehouse or other indications of full business activity in the state is its income from the resulting sales in the state taxable by that state.

The present state corporate income taxes are not likely to have a bearing on selection of the state for incorporation, because the formulas for apportioning an interstate corporation's local state tax liability are not affected by the domicile of the corporation. The most generally used formula, known as the Massachusetts formula, is based on three factors:

1. The ratio of the company's sales in the state to its total sales
2. The ratio of the company's payroll in the state to its total employment expense
3. The ratio of the company's property holdings in the state to its total property holdings

The three ratios are averaged and applied to the company's total profits to determine the profits subject to the state's corporate income tax. The apportionment formulas vary from state to state; it is thus possible for a company to be taxed on more than 100 percent of its net income.

State Personal Income Taxes

The state personal income tax rates average about 3 to 7 percent. Capital gains are taxed at about one half these rates. State income taxes are deductible as an expense in determining the federal individual income tax liability. A person in a 65 percent federal tax bracket pays only 35 percent of the state individual income tax. Thus state personal income taxes are not likely to have great impact on business financial decisions.

State and Local Property Taxes

Property taxes are the main source of state and local revenues. Taxes on land and buildings are paid by the user either directly or in rentals. In most states property taxes are also levied on inventories. Inventories can be reduced at the assessment date in two ways: (1) scrapping programs can be carried out, and (2) taxpayers can avoid receiving large deliveries before the assessment date. States and localities also levy taxes on intangibles, such as bank balances, but at rates lower than on tangible property. A company with out-of-state branches can determine assessment dates at branch locations and reduce the bank accounts prior to local assessment dates.

The property taxes noted above have relatively little effect on financial decisions. Of greater significance are the estate and gift taxes levied by the states jointly with the federal government. This subject, requiring more detailed treatment, is developed in the next section.

ESTATE AND GIFT TAXES

Though estate and gift taxes do not raise substantial amounts of revenue in the aggregate, they can have a serious impact on individual firms if they have not been planned for properly. The matter has been put effectively as follows:

> Just as the successful operation of a business depends upon the owner's alertness and his ability to analyze complex situations, so the proper disposition of a business interest at death depends upon an accurate appraisal of numerous factors. If time and thought are not given to this question and if a carefully devised program is not adopted, the value of such an interest may suffer severe shrinkage after the owner's death, and a substantial portion of the fruits of a lifetime may wither and fade away.[8]

Estate taxes may be of major significance for several reasons. First, the impact of the estate tax can be great, because the marginal rates run as high as 77 percent. A taxable estate of $5 million pays approximately one half that amount in taxes. Problems of raising liquid funds to pay such taxes may be serious.

Second, the determination of the value of a closely held company may be subject to wide differences in judgment.[9] When a firm's stock has not been publicly traded, the value placed on the stock by the Internal Revenue Service for estate tax purposes may be greater than the value placed on the stock by the taxpayer. "The fear that property may be

---

[8] "Protecting the Value of a Business Interest," *Trusts and Estates* (Los Angeles: United California Bank, Trust Department, May 1957), p. 1.

[9] A table showing the difference between taxpayer valuations and Internal Revenue Service valuations is set forth in Butters, Lintner, and Cary, *op. cit.*, p. 87.

overvalued, besides striking the owner as arbitrary and unfair, greatly complicates his plans for providing funds adequate for the payment of his estate taxes and the other cash needs of his estate and heirs."[10] If a larger company with publicly quoted stock offers to buy the closely held company, with a partial payment in the form of stock, the attractiveness of the offer is increased by the desire to avoid valuation uncertainties of the estate tax.

Third, liquidity problems may arise. An example will make the third point clear.

A is a widower with a gross estate of $200,000. At his death, his debts, funeral expenses, and other costs of settling his estate are $15,000. Based on these facts, his gross federal estate tax is $28,200. The cash required to settle his estate will be $15,000 plus $28,200, giving a total of $43,200—more than one fifth of his total estate.[11]

Liquidity problems have been mitigated somewhat by the Revenue Act of 1958, which provides that taxes on an estate consisting largely of an interest in a closely held business may be paid in ten annual installments, subject to an interest rate of 4 percent.

Fourth, a decision must be made about the alternative methods for disposing of a sole proprietorship, a partnership interest, or the stock of a closely held corporation after the owner's death.

Before describing methods of preserving an estate in the face of the taxes mentioned above, a brief summary of the estate and gift tax provisions will be set forth.

There has been much dispute over the question of whether the federal government or the states should have authority to levy death taxes. A compromise was reached by the federal law of 1926, which provided that taxpayers could receive a credit against their federal estate tax for estate or inheritance taxes paid to the states.[12] By 1964 the state tax credits, however, were only about 10 percent of the federal estate tax, so in making provision for state death taxes the primary objective is to hold the state taxes to a level below the federal tax credit.[13]

The details of the state death and gift taxes vary, but are roughly parallel to the federal provisions. Consequently, the presentation is limited to a survey of the federal provisions.

Table 3–7 shows the elements of the federal estate tax computation.

---

10 *Ibid.,* p. 86.

11 "The Importance of Liquidity," *Taxes and Estates* (Los Angeles: United California Bank, Trust Department), August 1959, p. 2.

12 Some states term their death taxes "inheritance" taxes, whereas others call them "estate" taxes.

13 Currently, all states except Nevada levy a tax on the transfer of decedents' property, and about one fourth the states levy gift taxes. (Gifts are made during the lifetime of the donor in order to reduce his estate and thus lower the taxes on his estate.)

From the *gross estate* a group of miscellaneous deductions is first made. This gives the *adjusted gross estate*. If appropriate, the *marital deduction* of 50 percent of the *adjusted gross estate* can then be applied. This deduction is allowed for bequests to the decedent's spouse. A *specific exemp-*

TABLE 3-7

OUTLINE OF THE COMPUTATION OF ESTATE TAXES

Start with gross estate, including:

Value of personal and real property		$1,000,000
Life insurance		200,000
Total gross estate		$1,200,000

Four major types of deductions

1. Miscellaneous deductions

a) Funeral and last-illness expenses	$ 5,000	
b) Debts	70,000	
c) Administrative expenses	25,000	
d) Charitable gifts	100,000	
Total		200,000
Remainder is *adjusted gross estate*		$1,000,000

2. *Less:* Marital deduction (one half the adjusted gross estate) . . .   500,000

$ 500,000

3. *Less:* Exemption of $60,000   60,000

Equals: Net taxable estate . . . . $ 440,000

Federal estate tax on $440,000:

$65,700 on $250,000	$ 65,700	
32% of $190,000	60,800	
Total		126,500

4. *Less:* State inheritance tax (maximum)   10,000

Balance: Federal estate tax . . . . $ 116,500

tion of $60,000 is also deducted. The federal estate tax is applied to the remainder, the *net taxable estate*. The rates of the federal estate tax are shown in Table 3-8.

Conservation of Estates

With the preceding background, we may now turn to methods for conserving estates and business interests associated with estates.

Charitable bequests are deductible in arriving at the adjusted gross estate. By donating to worthwhile charities, the donor may avoid the high-bracket estate tax rates.

Gifts provide a method for reducing income and estate taxes, because gift taxes paid by the decedent may be deducted from the gross estate.

TABLE 3–8

FEDERAL ESTATE TAX

Net Taxable Estate (in dollars)	Tax (in dollars)	Plus Percentage (%)	Of Amount More Than (in dollars)
0–5,000	0	3	0
5,000–10,000	150	7	5,000
10,000–20,000	500	11	10,000
20,000–30,000	1,600	14	20,000
30,000–40,000	3,000	18	30,000
40,000–50,000	4,800	22	40,000
50,000–60,000	7,000	25	50,000
60,000–100,000	9,500	28	60,000
100,000–250,000	20,700	30	100,000
250,000–500,000	65,700	32	250,000
500,000–750,000	145,700	35	500,000
750,000–1,000,000	233,200	37	750,000
1,000,000–1,250,000	325,700	39	1,000,000
1,250,000–1,500,000	423,200	42	1,250,000
1,500,000–2,000,000	528,000	45	1,500,000
2,000,000–2,500,000	753,200	49	2,000,000
2,500,000–3,000,000	998,200	53	2,500,000
3,000,000–3,500,000	1,263,200	56	3,000,000
3,500,000–4,000,000	1,543,200	59	3,500,000
4,000,000–5,000,000	1,838,200	63	4,000,000
5,000,000–6,000,000	2,468,200	67	5,000,000
6,000,000–7,000,000	3,138,200	70	6,000,000
7,000,000–8,000,000	3,838,200	73	7,000,000
8,000,000–10,000,000	4,568,200	76	8,000,000
10,000,000–Balance	6,088,200	77	10,000,000

Source: U.S. Treasury Department.

Gifts reduce taxes, because gift tax rates are only three fourths as high as the estate tax rates and are on a graduated scale. Moreover, gift tax rates are applied after four deductions. The deductions that may be made by the taxpayer from his cumulative total of gifts are:

1. An exemption of $30,000 each for husband and wife
2. An annual exclusion of $3,000 each for husband and wife
3. All charitable gifts
4. A marital deduction of one half of any gift made by one spouse to the other

Moreover, even if gifts are subject to taxes, they divide the estate into one portion subject to the estate tax and another portion subject to the gift tax. Since the tax rates rise with the size of the estate or the gift, dividing the amount to be taxed reduces the applicable tax rate.

Trusts are a most important method of conserving an estate.[14] Also, trusts may operate without further probate costs or estate taxes through two or three generations of the trust's beneficiaries. One of the important kinds of trusts in this connection is that in which a living trust provides for its continuation after the death of the creator of the trust, and further provides that property be added to the principal of the trust by the grantor's will. Attorneys refer to this as "pouring over from the estate to the trust."[15] Furthermore, trusts may provide for transfers during the life of the grantor and for remainder interests to different people— another method involving only one property transfer subject to taxes.

The value of a business interest may be protected in a number of ways. For example, *business life insurance* performs an important function. Where used, it should be purchased by each participant on the lives of the other members of a closely held firm. If the firm buys the insurance, the amount to be raised by the remaining members, if they wish to buy the share of the deceased member, is larger than otherwise. If each person carries insurance on his own life in favor of the others, his own estate taxes are increased. A short-term trust may also be created for the purchase of the insurance for the benefit of selected members of the company.[16]

Tax avoidance certainly should not be the main consideration in estate planning. When it is, more important aims of the estate may be lost, and in the process even the tax advantages may be eliminated. The subject is so complex that the purpose of the abbreviated presentation in this chapter is to indicate the nature of the possibilities and the necessity of relying on experts for sound decisions.

SUMMARY

This chapter has attempted to provide some basic background for an understanding of tax factors bearing on financial decisions.

The corporate income tax rate structure is simple: 22 percent on the first $25,000 income; 48 percent on taxable corporate income over $25,000. Depreciation and interest on debt are deductible expenses for tax purposes. Operating losses may be carried back three years and forward five years.

Personal income tax rates affect some four million businesses organized as proprietorships or partnerships. The personal income tax rate structure is highly progressive, starting at 14 percent for taxable income in the lower brackets, reaching 50 percent on taxable income between $44,000 and $52,000 for joint returns, and rising to 70 percent on taxable income over $200,000.

---

[14] The general nature of trusts was described in Chapter 2 in connection with the explanation of business trusts.

[15] For an explanation and illustrations, see "Pour-Over to a Trust," *Taxes and Estates* (Los Angeles: United California Bank, Trust Department, November 1959).

[16] For a clear illustration of the use of a trust to provide for the continuation of a business, see "The Short-Term Trust," *ibid.* (November 1956), pp. 3–4.

Long-term capital gains are taxed at a maximum rate of 25 percent. This rate gives an advantage to income taken in the form of capital gains, such as investments in the common stocks of companies with good prospects for growth in sales and earnings. The tax amendments of 1958 offer several tax advantages to investors in small firms.

Estate and gift tax rates may result in substantial taxes, because both are steeply progressive, although the gift tax is less progressive than the estate tax. The estate tax allows a marital deduction up to 50 percent of the adjusted gross estate and a specific exemption of $60,000. Gifts made to charitable, educational, and other tax-exempt institutions are not subject to the gift or the estate tax. Gift taxes may be used to achieve substantial reductions in estate taxes.

In addition to minimizing taxes and maintaining the smooth course of the enterprise, the financial manager must take into account tax aspects of selecting the state of incorporation, choosing the legal form under which the firm will operate, establishing a dividend policy, and other matters. These are only a few of the situations in which the tax factors are important. Others are discussed in subsequent chapters.

The foregoing material on the United States tax system has not been designed to make tax experts of readers. It provides a few essentials for recognizing tax aspects of business financial problems and for developing an awareness of the kinds of situations that should be taken to tax specialists for further guidance.

SELECTED REFERENCES

Butters, J. K., J. Lintner, and W. L. Cary, *Effects of Taxation, Corporate Mergers* (Boston: Harvard Business School, 1951).

Miller, D. C., "Corporation Taxation and Methods of Corporation Financing," *American Economic Review* (December 1952), pp. 839–854.

Prentice-Hall Federal Taxes, 1965, 6 volumes (Englewood Cliffs, N. J.: Prentice-Hall, Inc.).

Seidman, J. S., "A Comparison of Tax Advantages of a Corporation versus Partnership or Sole Proprietorship," *Journal of Accountancy*, 90 (August 1950), pp. 104–112.

Smith, D. T., *Effects of Taxation: Corporate Financial Policy* (Boston: Harvard Business School, 1952).

Somers, H. M., "Estate Taxes and Business Mergers: The Effect of Estate Taxes on Business Structure and Practices in the United States," *Journal of Finance*, 13 (May 1958), pp. 201–210.

Standard Federal Tax Reporter, 7 volumes (Chicago: Commerce Clearing, 1965).

Statistics of Income (Washington, D. C.: U. S. Treasury Department, Internal Revenue Service, yearly). These volumes provide data for both individual returns and corporation income tax returns; they also include specimen returns and instructions for the years covered by the volumes.

QUESTIONS

3–1 Compare the marginal and the average tax rates of corporations with taxable incomes of $5,000, $50,000, $500,000, $5,000,000, and $50,000,000. Would it be possible to make such a comparison for sole proprietorships or for partnerships?

3–2 Which is the more relevant tax rate, the marginal or the average, in determining the form of organization for a new firm? Have recent changes in the tax laws made the form of organization more or less important than formerly?

3–3 How does the treatment of interest expense compare with the treatment of common stock dividends for tax purposes (1) from the standpoint of a firm paying the interest or the dividends? (2) from the standpoint of an individual recipient? (3) from that of a corporate recipient?

3–4 Compare the treatment of capital gains and losses with ordinary gains and losses in income tax returns.

3–5 What are the present corporate carry-back and carry-forward tax provisions, and what is their purpose?

3–6 What is the purpose of Section 531 of the Internal Revenue Code, dealing with the tax on improper accumulation of corporate surplus?

3–7 Does the corporate tax rate structure give small firms the incentive to operate as multiple corporations?

3–8 Why is personal income tax information important for a study of business finance?

3–9 How do the tax rates for capital gains and losses affect an individual's investment policies and opportunities for financing small business?

3–10 Which tax has the steeper rate of progression, the estate tax or the gift tax? What are the effects of this difference likely to be?

PROBLEMS

3–1 A corporation has an income of $100,000 after all expenses, including interest. Its profit margin on sales taxes is 5 percent.
1. What would be the amount of corporate income taxes?
2. Suppose that the operations of the company are such that it could justify setting up five separate corporations. (For example, a real estate company operating in five separate sections of a city or a state might have a corporation for each area served.) What is the tax paid by each of the five corporations, and the total tax paid by all five? (Assume that each of the five corporations had net profits of $25,000.)
3. A holding company whose stock is widely held receives the total after-tax income of the five corporations. What is the total amount of tax paid by the five corporations as a group?
4. The tax saving under 2 is equivalent to how much in additional sales?
5. The tax savings under 3 is equivalent to how much in additional sales?

3–2 A corporation has a net income of $43,350 before interest charges, which amount to $3,350.
1. What amount of corporate income tax would the corporation pay?
2. What is the marginal tax rate?

3–3 Warren T. Lasser is a married man with one child. His adjusted gross income for 1965 is $12,000, which includes $1,250 of corporate dividends received by his wife. He takes the standard deduction. What is his personal income tax liability for 1965? Assume he files a joint return.

3–4 The taxable income of the Austin Corporation, formed in 1961, is as follows (losses are in parentheses):

1962	$(300,000)
1963	150,000
1964	200,000
1965	300,000
1966	(150,000)

Corporate tax rate for these years are as follows:

1962 and 1963—first 25,000, 30%; excess, 52%

1964—first 25,000, 22%; excess, 50%

1965 and 1966—first 25,000, 22%; excess, 48%

What is the corporate tax liability during each of the five years?

3-5   The Western corporation has the following statement of income for 1965:

Gross taxable income	$150,000
Tax payable	60,000
Net income after taxes	$ 90,000

PSR Manufacturing Corporation had a $75,000 loss for 1965. Western feels that its managerial talent can turn PSR Manufacturing into a profitable operation. If the two companies merged prior to January 1, 1966, what would be the merged corporation's income for 1965 after the refund? What is the difference in tax liability for Western before and after the merger?

3-6   Alvin Manufacturing earned $150,000 after taxes on sales of $3 million. In 1963 it acquired working control of Markson Products, Inc., for $125,000 and disposed of the stock in 1965 for $350,000. (Alvin controlled less than 80 percent of Markson.) In addition, dividends paid by Markson to Alvin during 1965 amounted to $15,000.

1. What is Alvin's tax bill on the capital gain and dividends?
2. By how much does Alvin's income (including capital gains) after taxes increase?
3. By how much would Alvin's sales have had to increase to produce the equivalent additional income after taxes?
4. What would have been the benefit to Alvin if Markson had been able to declare a further dividend of $50,000 in 1965 and if Alvin had sold the stock, purchased in 1963, for $300,000?

Part II

Financial Analysis and Control

Chapter 4

Financial Analysis

The discussion of the environment of financial management in Part I has considered the nature and implications of the economy and the legal framework, particularly the tax structure. Within this environment the task of the financial manager is to determine the present position of his firm and to plan its future needs. Financial analysis, through the calculation of strategic relations, indicates the strengths and weaknesses of the business. Starting from the existing situation of the firm, the financial manager can proceed to plan future financial requirements by means of the forecasting and budgeting procedures described in succeeding chapters. This study of financial analysis also provides a review of elementary accounting and indicates the nature of the firm's operations. An understanding of these matters is required if the financial manager is to meet the requirements of general management, of investors, of the taxing authorities, and of the public.

The selection of financial ratios is discussed first in the chapter; then the applications of ratio analysis; and finally the analysis of sources and uses of funds.

SELECTION OF FINANCIAL RATIOS

In financial analysis, ratios are generally classified into four fundamental types:

1. *Liquidity ratios,* which are designed to measure the ability of the firm to meet its maturing short-term obligations

2. *Leverage ratios,* which measure the contributions of owners as compared with the financing provided by the firm's creditors
3. *Activity ratios,* which measure how effectively the firm is employing its resources
4. *Profitability ratios,* which measure management's over-all effectiveness as shown by the returns generated on sales and investment

Depending on the purpose of the analysis, one or another of these types is emphasized. For example, short-term creditors are especially interested in borrowers' liquidity positions. Since short-term loans mature in the near future and are large relative to the profits generated during the term of the loan, the debt must be repaid out of cash obtained from liquidating assets, not out of profits. Hence, profitability is less important than current assets. In contrast, long-term equity investors place far more emphasis on earning power and operating efficiency than on reported assets. They know that unprofitable operations will soon erode asset values, and that past and present earnings influence the estimates of future earnings, which form the basis of stock prices. Long-term creditors take an intermediate position, looking to the liquidity position to determine the firm's ability to meet current debt-servicing requirements, but to profits for ultimate repayment of the debt. In addition, this group of creditors is especially interested in the leverage ratios, because if leverage is high, even a small decline in the value of the firm may cause losses to holders of long-term debt.

In addition to these logical reasons for emphasizing different ratios from one situation to another, data availability sometimes influences the nature of the analysis. A creditor investigating a company before deciding on a loan application, for example, may be able to obtain information that would not be available to a potential stockholder. The financial manager, of course, has access to internal operating information not generally available to the outsider. Thus he is able not only to calculate and appraise those ratios of interest to long- and short-term creditors and stockholders and thus anticipate their reactions to attempts at raising new capital, but also to conduct a rather extensive evaluation of operating performance.

Each of the categories of ratios given above contains a large number of potential relationships, and the ones selected on any given occasion will depend on the nature of the analysis. The following list of ratios is a compromise between an exhaustive set designed to cover all situations and a limited list suitable only for a particular case. The discussion of each ratio covers six aspects: (1) the formula for the ratio; (2) a numerical example; (3) reference levels, consisting of a generally accepted rule of thumb or an industry average ratio, for evaluating a company's performance; (4) an evaluation of the performance of the company as shown by each ratio; (5) an explanation of details involved in calculating the ratio;

and (6) an indication of the information the ratio can provide the financial manager.

Illustrative Balance Sheet and Income Statement

Ratio analysis is most meaningful if specific balance sheet and income statement data are used to illustrate the nature, calculation, and significance of each ratio, and for this purpose a set of illustrative data is given in Tables 4–1 and 4–2. The forms of the balance sheet and in-

TABLE 4–1

COMPOSITE COMPANY
ILLUSTRATIVE BALANCE SHEET
December 31, 1966

Assets			*Claims on Assets*		
Cash		$ 5,000	Accounts payable		$ 6,000
Marketable securities . . .		15,000	Notes payable, 8%		10,000
Receivables, net		20,000	Accruals		1,000
Inventories		30,000	Provision for federal income		
Total current assets . . .		$ 70,000	taxes		13,000
Gross plant and			*Total current liabilities* . .		$ 30,000
equipment . . $180,000			First mortgage		
Less reserve for de-			bonds, 5%*		$50,000
preciation . . 50,000			Debentures, 6%		20,000
Net plant and equipment		130,000	Preferred		
			stock, 7% . . .	10,000	
			Common stock . .	50,000	
			Retained earn-		
			ings	40,000	
			Total net worth . . .		$100,000
Total assets		$200,000	*Total claims on assets* . . .		$200,000

* The annual sinking fund requirement is $2,000.

come statement presented here are not necessarily the best ones for all circumstances; indeed, no single form for financial statements meets all needs best. The formats used to present the illustrative data do, however, provide a terminology and breakdown that makes it possible to conduct the kind of analysis most significant from a financial manager's standpoint. In this regard, attention is called to the segregation of general and administrative expenses, rent, and depreciation.

Liquidity Ratios

Liquidity analysis is designed to measure a firm's ability to meet its maturing obligations. The Composite Company must satisfy $30,000 of current liabilities within the coming year. What is the likelihood that it

TABLE 4–2

COMPOSITE COMPANY
ILLUSTRATIVE INCOME STATEMENT
For Year Ended December 31, 1966

Net sales			$300,000
Cost of goods sold			258,000
Gross profit			$ 42,000
Less: Operating expenses:			
Selling		$2,200	
General and administrative		4,000	
Rent on office		2,800	9,000
Gross operating profit			$ 33,000
Depreciation			10,000
Net operating profit			$ 23,000
Add: Other income			
Royalties			1,500
Gross income			$ 24,500
Less: Other expense:			
Interest on notes payable		$ 800	
Interest on first mortgage		2,500	
Interest on debentures		1,200	4,500
Net income before income tax			$ 20,000
(tax at 40 percent*)			8,000
Net income after income tax			$ 12,000

* For most of the illustrations in the text a 50 percent corporate tax rate is used. A 40 percent rate is used here to avoid confusion between tax and after-tax elements.

can do this without undue stress? A full liquidity analysis requires the use of budgets, particularly the cash budget, which makes a forecast of funds flows in future periods. But liquidity ratios, by relating to current obligations the amount of cash and assets likely to be converted to cash in the near future, provide an easy-to-use measure of liquidity.

1. Current ratio. The current ratio is computed by dividing current liabilities into current assets. Current assets normally include cash, marketable securities, accounts receivable, and inventories, while current liabilities consist of accounts payable, short-term notes payable, current maturities of long-term debt, accrued income taxes, and other accrued expenses (principally wages). The current ratio is the generally accepted measure of short-term solvency, as it indicates the extent to which the claims of short-term creditors are covered by assets that are expected to be converted to cash in a period roughly corresponding to the maturity of the claims.

In Table 4–3, it is shown that the Composite Company has a current ratio of 2.3 to 1 versus the industry average of 2.5 to 1, indicating a satisfactory current condition. Since current assets are near-maturing, it is highly probable that they could be liquidated at close to book value. With a current ratio of 2.3, Composite Company could liquidate current assets at only 42.9 percent of book value and still pay off current creditors in full.

2. Quick ratio. The quick ratio is calculated by deducting inventories from current assets and dividing the remainder by current liabilities. Since inventories are typically the least liquid of a firm's current assets and the asset on which losses are most likely to occur in the event of liquidation, this measure of ability to pay off short-term obligations without relying on the sale of inventories is important.

Compared with the industry average of 1 to 1, the Composite Company's 1.3 to 1 quick ratio is good. The financial manager—and the firm's creditors—know that if the marketable securities of the firm can be sold at par, and if it can collect accounts receivable, it can pay off current liabilities without the necessity of selling any inventory.

3. Inventory to working capital. This ratio of inventory to working capital is calculated by dividing working capital—defined as current assets minus current liabilities[1]—into the inventory figure. Since the ratio shows the proportion of net current assets tied up in inventory, it can be used to indicate the potential loss to the company that would result from a decline in inventory values. Because a low ratio is best, the Composite Company's position of 75 percent compares favorably with the reference level of 87 percent.

Leverage Ratios

Leverage ratios, which measure the contributions of owners as compared with the financing provided by the firm's creditors, have a number of implications. First, creditors look to the equity, or owner-supplied funds, to provide a margin of safety. If owners have provided only a small proportion of total financing, the risks of the enterprise are borne mainly by the creditors. Second, by raising funds through debt, the owners gain the benefits of maintaining control of the firm with a limited investment. Third, if the firm earns more on the borrowed funds than it pays in interest, the return to the owners is magnified. For example, if assets earn 6 percent and debt costs but 4 percent, there is a 2 percent differential which accrues to the stockholders. Leverage cuts both ways, however; if the return on assets falls to 3 percent, the differential between that figure and the cost of debt must be made up from equity's share of

---

1 Sometimes businessmen and economists identify working capital with current assets and for that reason prefer the term "net working capital" or "net current assets." The definition used here is the one most commonly encountered in accounting and finance.

TABLE 4–3
COMPOSITE COMPANY
SUMMARY OF FINANCIAL RATIO ANALYSIS*

Name of Ratio	Formula for Calculation	Calculation	Industry Average	Evaluation
I. Liquidity				
1. Current	$\dfrac{\text{current assets}}{\text{current liab.}}$	$\dfrac{\$ 70,000}{\$ 30,000} = 2.3 \text{ times}$	2.5 times	Satisfactory
2. Quick, or acid test	$\dfrac{(\text{current assets} - \text{inventory})}{\text{current liabilities}}$	$\dfrac{\$ 40,000}{\$ 30,000} = 1.3 \text{ times}$	1 time	Good
3. Inventory to working capital	$\dfrac{\text{inventory}}{\text{current assets less current liabilities}}$	$\dfrac{\$ 30,000}{\$ 40,000} = 75\%$	87%	Satisfactory
II. Leverage				
4. Debt to total assets	$\dfrac{\text{total debt}}{\text{total assets}}$	$\dfrac{\$100,000}{\$200,000} = 50\%$	50%	Satisfactory
5. Times interest earned	$\dfrac{\text{profit before taxes plus interest charges}}{\text{interest charges}}$	$\dfrac{\$ 24,500}{\$ 4,500} = 5.4 \text{ times}$	8 times	Fair
6. Fixed charge coverage	$\dfrac{\text{net profit before fixed charges}}{\text{interest} + \text{rent} + \text{sinking fund} + \text{taxes related to sinking fund}}$	$\dfrac{\$ 27,300}{\$ 10,633} = 2.6 \text{ times}$	4 times	Fair
7. Current liabilities to net worth	$\dfrac{\text{current liabilities}}{\text{net worth}}$	$\dfrac{\$ 30,000}{\$100,000} = 30\%$	35%	Good
8. Fixed assets to net worth	$\dfrac{\text{fixed assets}}{\text{net worth}}$	$\dfrac{\$130,000}{\$100,000} = 130\%$	65%	Poor

Name of Ratio	Formula for Calculation	Calculation	Industry Average	Evaluation
III. Activity				
9. Cash velocity	$$\frac{\text{sales}}{\text{cash and equivalents}}$$	$$\frac{\$300,000}{\$\ 20,000} = 15 \text{ times}$$	10 times	Good
10. Inventory turnover	$$\frac{\text{sales}}{\text{inventory}}$$	$$\frac{\$300,000}{\$\ 30,000} = 10 \text{ times}$$	9 times	Satisfactory
11. Fixed assets turnover	$$\frac{\text{sales}}{\text{fixed assets}}$$	$$\frac{\$300,000}{\$130,000} = 2.3 \text{ times}$$	5 times	Poor
12. Average collection period	$$\frac{\text{receivables}}{\text{sales per day}}$$	$$\frac{\$\ 20,000}{\dfrac{\$300,000}{360}} = 24 \text{ days}$$	20 days	Satisfactory
13. Total assets turnover	$$\frac{\text{sales}}{\text{total assets}}$$	$$\frac{\$300,000}{\$200,000} = 1.5 \text{ times}$$	2 times	Low
IV. Profitability				
14. Gross operating margin	$$\frac{\text{gross operating profit}}{\text{sales}}$$	$$\frac{\$\ 33,000}{\$300,000} = 11\%$$	11%	Satisfactory
15. Net operating margin	$$\frac{\text{net operating profit}}{\text{sales}}$$	$$\frac{\$\ 23,000}{\$300,000} = 7.7\%$$	10%	Fair
16. Sales margin	$$\frac{\text{net profit after taxes}}{\text{sales}}$$	$$\frac{\$\ 12,000}{\$300,000} = 4\%$$	5%	Low
17. Productivity of assets	$$\frac{\text{gross income less taxes}}{\text{total assets}}$$	$$\frac{\$\ 16,500}{\$200,000} = 8.25\%$$	10%	Low
18. Return on net worth	$$\frac{\text{net profit after taxes}}{\text{net worth}}$$	$$\frac{\$\ 12,000}{\$100,000} = 12.0\%$$	15%	Somewhat low

* Additional illustrative ratios are given in Appendix B at the end of the book.

total profits. In the first instance, where assets earn more than the cost of debt, leverage is said to be favorable; in the second it is unfavorable.

In practice, leverage is approached in two ways. One approach involves looking at balance sheet ratios and determining the extent to which borrowed funds have been used to finance the firm. The other approach measures the risks of debt by income statement ratios designed to determine how well fixed charges are covered by operating profits. These sets of ratios are complementary, and most analysts examine both types of leverage ratios.

4. Debt to total assets. The debt ratio measures the firm's obligations to creditors in relation to all the funds that have been provided. Debt includes current liabilities and bonds, whether in the form of mortgages, notes, or debentures. Creditors prefer moderate debt ratios, since the lower the ratio, the greater the cushion against creditors' losses in the event of liquidation. For industrial corporations, creditors generally require owners to have as large an investment as the creditors themselves; therefore a frequent rule of thumb is a maximum debt ratio of 50 percent. Composite Company's ratio is 50 percent, the maximum, so it is not in a good position to do further debt financing without first raising some new equity capital.

In contrast to the creditors' preference for a low debt ratio, the owners may seek to use high leverage either to magnify earnings or because raising new equity will mean giving up some degree of control. But if the debt ratio is too high, there is a danger of encouraging irresponsibility on the part of the owners. The stake of the owners can become so small that speculative activity, if successful, will yield a substantial return to the owners. If the speculation is unsuccessful, only a moderate loss is incurred, because the owners' investment is small.

5. Times interest earned. The times-interest-earned ratio is determined by dividing earnings before interest and taxes by the interest charges. The before-tax profit figure is used in the numerator; because income taxes are computed after deducting interest expense, the ability to pay interest is not affected by income taxes. The times-interest-earned ratio measures the extent to which earnings could decline without a resultant financial embarrassment to the firm because of inability to meet annual interest costs. Failure to meet this obligation will bring legal action by the creditors, possibly resulting in bankruptcy.

The Composite Company's interest charges consist of three payments totaling $4,500 (see Table 4–2). The firm's gross income available to service these charges is $24,500 ($20,000 + $4,500), so the interest is covered 5.4 times. Since the industry average is 8 times, the company is covering its interest charges by a minimum margin of safety and deserves only a fair rating. This ratio reinforces the previous conclusion that the financial manager would likely have trouble raising additional funds from debt sources.

6. Fixed-charge coverage. The number of times fixed charges are covered is determined by dividing profit before fixed charges by the total fixed charges—interest, lease payments, sinking fund requirements, and the tax related to sinking fund payments.[2] This more inclusive ratio provides an important supplement to the times-interest-earned figure, as it recognizes that financial problems may arise from the nonpayment of lease obligations or sinking fund charges as well as from the failure to meet interest payments.

The Composite Company's fixed charges are covered 2.6 times, as opposed to an industry average of 4 times. Again, this indicates that the firm is somewhat weaker than creditors would prefer and further points up the difficulties the financial manager is likely to encounter should he attempt additional borrowing.

7. Current liabilities to net worth. The ratio of current liabilities to net worth measures the amount of funds supplied by owners against the amount raised by current debt. If the owners have not put enough funds into the firm, suppliers of long-term funds are likely to be un-willing to expose themselves to the risks and the firm will be forced to resort to short-term, stopgap financing to a greater extent. Hence the ratio of current liabilities to net worth will be large. As a consequence, the firm would be slow in paying its bills. The reference level for this ratio is 35 percent. The Composite Company's ratio of 30 percent is good.

8. Fixed assets to net worth. The ratio of fixed assets to net worth shows the extent to which ownership funds are sunk in assets with rela-tively low turnover. The yardstick for this measure is 65 percent for industrial firms. For the Composite Company, fixed assets are 130 percent of net worth. Judged by the reference level, this company has too large

---

[2] A sinking fund, discussed in detail in Chapter 19, is a required annual payment designed to amortize a bond issue. Sinking fund payments are not deductable for income tax purposes, so they must be paid with after-tax profits. This means, in effect, that the firm must earn sufficient profits before taxes to enable it to pay its tax bill and still have enough left over to meet the sinking fund requirement. For this reason the tax requirement must be included in the denominator of the fixed charge coverage ratio.

Since it is in the 40 percent tax bracket, the company must have a before-tax income of $3,333 to enable it to pay the tax and still have $2,000 left after taxes. The general equation for finding the tax-related figure is:

$$\text{taxes related to sinking fund} = \frac{\text{sinking fund payment}}{1.0 - \text{tax rate}} - \text{sinking fund}$$

$$= \frac{\$2,000}{1.0 - 0.4} - \$2,000 = \frac{\$2,000}{0.6} - \$2,000 = \$3,333 - \$2,000$$

$$= \$1,333$$

a commitment in fixed assets relative to ownership funds. The company's financial situation would be considered unsatisfactory in this regard, and the financial manager will more than likely find it necessary to finance future capital expenditures by selling common stock.

Activity Ratios

Activity ratios measure how effectively the firm is employing the resources at its command. One activity ratio analyzes the use of the total resources of the firm. This is the sales-to-total-asset ratio, a central measure in the du Pont system of financial control, which is discussed in some detail in the following chapter. But, in addition, the efficient use of the components of total assets should also be analyzed.

9. Cash velocity. Cash velocity is measured as cash and cash equivalents (short-term negotiable securities) divided into yearly sales, and indicates the number of times cash has been turned over during the year. In the typical business, cash is held for transactions, and a high cash velocity suggests that cash is being used effectively.[3] Against the industry average of 10, the Composite Company's cash velocity of 15 is entirely satisfactory.

10. Inventory turnover. Inventory turnover is calculated as **sales** divided by inventory. The Composite Company's inventory turnover of 10 times compares favorably with the industry average of 9 times.

Two problems arise in calculating and analyzing the inventory turnover ratio. First, sales are at market prices, and for the sake of comparability, inventories should also be at market values. If inventories are carried at cost, as they frequently are, then it would be more appropriate to use cost of goods sold in place of sales in the numerator of the formula. Established compilers of financial ratio statistics, such as Dun & Bradstreet, use the ratio of sales to inventories carried at cost. As financial ratios are used most frequently in comparative analysis and as the ratios are calculated in a consistent manner, inventory turnover calculated in this way is satisfactory.

The second problem lies in the fact that sales occur over the entire year, while the inventory figure is for one point in time. This makes it better to use an average figure, computed by adding the beginning and ending inventories and dividing by two. In the illustration for the Composite Company, data are provided for only one year, so it is not possible to calculate this average. If it is determined that the firm's business is highly seasonal, or if there has been a strong upward or downward sales trend during the year, it becomes essential to make this relatively simple adjustment.

---

[3] However, if the liquidity ratios are weak, a high cash velocity may simply be another indication of the liquidity problem faced by the firm.

11. Fixed assets turnover. The ratio of sales to fixed assets measures the turnover of capital assets. Composite's turnover of 2.3 times compares poorly with the industry average of 5 times, indicating that the firm is not using its fixed assets to as high a percentage of capacity as are the other firms in the industry. The financial manager should bear this fact in mind when the firm's production officers request funds for new capital investment.

12. Average collection period. The average collection period, which is an alternative ratio for measuring the accounts receivable turnover, is computed as follows: First, the annual sales are divided by 360 to get the average daily sales.[4] Second, daily sales are divided into accounts receivable to find the number of days' sales tied up in receivables. This is defined as the average collection period, for it represents the length of time, on the average, that the firm must wait after making a sale before receiving cash.

The calculations for the Composite Company show an average collection period of 24 days, which can best be evaluated by comparing it with the terms on which the firm sells its goods. For example, if this firm sells on a net 30-day basis, the 24-day collection period is excellent. Even if the firm sells on a net 20-day basis, the performance may still be satisfactory, because some spilling over in payment performance is customary. However, if the ratio's trend over the past few years has been rising and if the credit policy has not changed, this situation indicates that steps should be taken to expedite payments on accounts receivable.

One other financial tool should be mentioned in connection with accounts receivable analysis—the aging schedule, which breaks down accounts receivable according to how long they have been outstanding. This schedule for the Composite Company might look like the following:

Age of Account	Percent of Total Value of Accounts Receivable
0–10 days	50%
11–30 days	20
31–45 days	15
46–60 days	3
over 60 days	12
	100%

The 24-day collection period looked good by comparison with the 30-day terms, but the aging schedule shows that the firm is having serious

---

[4] Two points should be noted here. First, for convenience the financial community generally uses 360 rather than 365 as the number of days in the year for purposes such as the present one. Second, if cash sales are a significant percentage of the total, it is preferable to use *credit sales* when computing the average collection period.

collection problems with some of its accounts. Thirty percent are overdue, many for over a month. Many others pay quite promptly, bringing the average down to only 24 days, but the aging schedule shows this to be somewhat misleading.

13. Total assets turnover. Total assets turnover is computed by dividing yearly sales by total assets. As is true of fixed assets turnover, a high ratio indicates overtrading on assets; a low ratio indicates excessive investments. The Composite Company turnover of 1.5 times is low relative to the yardstick of 2 times. The financial manager has another indication of idle capacity.

Profitability Ratios

Profitability is the net result of a large number of policies and decisions of the business firm. Several measures of profitability are used, because any one measure may be greatly influenced by the peculiarities of the industry or accounting conventions as applied in particular circumstances. Both operating profits and net margins are measured to distinguish between results of operating and financial policies (see Table 4–3).

14. Gross operating margin. The gross operating margin—gross operating profit divided by sales—indicates the degree to which unit selling prices may decline without resulting in a loss on operations. For the Composite Company the ratio is 11 percent, the same as that of the average firm in the industry.

15. Net operating margin. The net operating margin is net operating profit divided by sales, and indicates the degree to which unit selling prices may decline without resulting in losses on an accrual basis rather than a cash basis. The figure is computed before nonoperating costs in order to facilitate comparisons among different firms with varying leverage—hence varying interest charges—and other nonoperating differences. Composite Company has a ratio of $23,000 divided by $300,000, or 7.7 percent, which is only fair by comparison with other firms in the industry.

16. Sales margin. This ratio relates profit to sales, and the next two ratios discussed compare profits to total assets and to net worth. Profits may be measured either before or after taxes, depending on the problem at hand. If comparisons are to be made among firms with varying tax rates, or if a trend analysis is to be made for a firm whose tax rates have changed over time, the before-tax figure may be best.

On an after-tax basis, the Composite Company has a profit margin of 4 percent ($12,000 net profit divided by $300,000 sales). This is somewhat lower than the industry average, indicating that the firm's sales prices are relatively low or that its costs are relatively high. It should also be noted that with a 4 percent margin, unit sales prices can decline by that percent before the firm suffers an over-all loss. In general, narrow profit margins indicate that a small percentage drop in prices will lead to losses, while large profit margins provide protection against losses due to falling prices.

17. Productivity of assets. This ratio, calculated by dividing the sum of net profits after taxes plus interest expenses (or gross income less taxes) by total assets, is designed to measure the rate of return on the firm's total resources. The numerator indicates the dollar returns to those who have invested funds in the firm, while the funds themselves are shown in the denominator. As Composite Company's rate of return is only 8.25 percent versus an industry-wide figure of 10 percent, Composite is on the low side.

18. Return on net worth. The ratio of net profit after taxes to net worth measures the productivity of the resources the owners of the firm have committed to the operation of the business. It is the kind of information the owners are desirous of having for determining whether their historical investments have performed better in this outlet than in others. The calculation for Composite Company is $12,000 to $100,000; the rate of return is therefore 12 percent. Compared with an average return of 15 percent in the industry, this is somewhat low.

USE OF FINANCIAL RATIOS

Thus far in the chapter we have looked at a rather long list of ratios and have seen, using illustrative data, what each of the ratios is designed to measure. Sometimes it will be unnecessary to go beyond a few calculations to determine that a firm is in very good or very bad shape, but often the analysis is equivalent to a detective-story investigation—what one ratio will not indicate, another may. Also, a relation vaguely suggested by one ratio may be corroborated by another. For these reasons, it is often useful to calculate a number of different ratios.

In numerous situations, however, a few ratios will tell the story. For example, a credit manager who has a large number of invoices flowing across his desk each day may limit himself to three ratios as evidence of whether the prospective buyer of his goods will pay promptly. (1) He will use the current ratio to determine how burdened the prospective buyer is with current liabilities. (2) He will use the debt ratio to determine how much of the prospective buyer's own funds are invested in the business. If the funds of the prospective buyer are low, he is probably short of working capital and is likely to fall behind in his payments. (3) He will use one of the profitability ratios to indicate whether or not the firm has favorable prospects.

If the profit margin is high enough, it may justify the risk of dealing with a slow-paying customer. If the profit margin is low relative to other firms in the industry, if the current ratio is low, and if the debt ratio is high, a credit manager probably will not approve a sale involving an extension of credit.

Of necessity, the credit manager is more than a calculator and reader of financial ratios. Qualitative factors may override quantitative analysis. Oil companies, for instance, in selling to truckers often find that the financial ratios are adverse and, if they based their decisions solely on financial ratios, they would not make sales. Or, to take another example, profits may have been low for a period, but if the customer understands why profits have been low and can remove the cause of the difficulty, a credit man may be willing to approve a sale to him. The credit man's decision will also be influenced by his own firm's profit margin. If the selling firm is making a large profit on sales, then it is in a better position to take credit risks than if margins are low. Ultimately, the credit manager must judge a customer with regard to his character and management ability, and intelligent credit decisions must be based on careful consideration of conditions in the selling as well as the buying firm.

EVALUATION OF THE COMPOSITE COMPANY

Although the qualitative considerations of financial analysis are necessary for a complete evaluation, the ratios calculated for the Composite Company may be brought together here in summary form to suggest their over-all implications. The fixed-assets-to-net-worth ratio of 130 percent exceeds the reference level of 65 percent. Also, the fixed assets turnover is too low, the result being a low profit margin on sales. Both ratios indicate excessive investment in fixed assets, which partially explains the high debt ratio and the low total assets turnover (1.5 times).

It should be noted that in acquiring the fixed assets the firm has incurred excessive fixed charges. This overcommitment is reflected in the low coverage of fixed charges of 2.6 times. Excessive fixed charges also partially explain the low net operating and sales margins. The gross margin is satisfactory; therefore the decline in the net profit margins is caused by excessive nonfactory overhead and fixed charges.

Apparently the company has built for the future. If it is able to increase sales, it may be able to benefit from the fixed assets it has acquired. However, if sales increase to the point at which they catch up with the fixed assets investment, working-capital needs will increase. As a consequence, the firm will face new financing requirements, and the high debt ratio will probably make it necessary to meet these requirements with equity capital.

The summary has been developed in a general manner rather than from one point of view. However, the management of the Composite Company should consider the steps which need to be taken in order to remedy the overcommitment in fixed assets. On the other hand, an outsider—a lender or an investor—is concerned with the actions of management if ratio analysis indicates a weakening of the firm's position.

COMPARATIVE RATIO ANALYSIS

From time to time in the above discussion, mention has been made of the value of comparative analysis in the use of ratios. For the most informative use of ratios and other measures, the experience of a firm is compared with that of other firms in its industry. If the firm's ratio is different from that of the industry, the cause of the deviation should be investigated.

Financial ratios of the individual firm may be compared either with those of selected firms in the industry or with averages for the industry, which are available from several sources.

Dun & Bradstreet. Probably the most widely known and used of the industry average ratios are those compiled by Dun & Bradstreet, Inc. "Dun & Brad" provides fourteen ratios calculated for a large number of industries. Sample ratios and explanations are shown in Table 4–4. The complete data give the fourteen important ratios, with the interquartile range[5] for 125 lines of business activity based on arrays of financial statements. The 125 types of business activity consist of 71 manufacturing and construction divisions, 30 wholesaling, and 24 retailing. Each of the business enterprises covered has a tangible net worth that, with few exceptions, exceeds $35,000.

Robert Morris Associates. Another group of useful ratios can be found in the annual *Statement Studies* compiled and published by the Robert Morris Associates (RMA), which is the national association of bank loan officers. These represent averages based on financial statements that banks have received in connection with loans made. Eleven ratios are computed for 156 lines of business. The firms represented in the sample tend to be the larger and financially stronger firms; the averages contained in the RMA studies therefore provide a relatively high-quality basis for comparison.

Quarterly financial report for manufacturing corporations. The

---

[5] The median and quartile ratios can be illustrated by an example. The median ratio of current assets to current debt of manufacturers of airplane parts and accessories, as shown in Table 4–4, is 2.01. To obtain this figure the ratios of current assets to current debt for each of the 55 concerns were arranged in a graduated series, with the largest ratio at the top and the smallest at the bottom. The median ratio of 2.01 was the ratio halfway between the top and the bottom. The ratio of 3.08, representing the upper quartile, was one quarter of the way down the series from the top (or halfway between the top and the median). The ratio of 1.52, representing the lower quartile, was one quarter of the way up from the bottom (or halfway between the median and the bottom).

TABLE 4-4 DUN & BRADSTREET RATIOS FOR SELECTED INDUSTRIES, 1963

Line of Business (and number of concerns reporting)	Current assets to current debt, (times)	Net profits on net sales, (per cent)	Net profits on tangible net worth, (per cent)	Net profits on net working capital, (per cent)	Net sales to tangible net worth, (times)	Net sales to net working capital, (times)	Collection period, (days)	Net sales to inventory, (times)	Fixed assets to tangible net worth, (per cent)	Current debt to tangible net worth, (per cent)	Total debt to tangible net worth, (per cent)	Inventory to net working capital, (per cent)	Current debt to inventory, (per cent)	Funded debts to net working capital, (per cent)
3722-23-29* Airplane Parts and Accessories (55)	3.08	4.48	17.29	29.23	5.39	7.58	26	11.1	27.7	34.0	56.5	53.8	76.9	24.7
	2.01	2.64	8.10	14.58	3.88	5.15	43	7.1	49.9	54.9	112.4	74.9	122.0	45.5
	1.52	1.26	3.46	5.83	2.47	3.98	66	5.3	75.6	105.7	142.9	133.5	215.2	83.0
3714 Automobile Parts & Accessories (89)	3.91	6.08	20.33	28.09	4.05	6.53	31	9.3	22.5	23.4	45.3	46.8	57.0	5.0
	2.97	3.63	11.15	16.68	2.96	4.41	42	6.6	32.4	36.3	69.5	71.7	85.5	23.9
	2.20	2.16	5.94	9.61	2.33	3.43	51	4.7	45.0	57.8	91.7	96.7	114.4	42.9
2515 Bedsprings & Mattresses (52)	5.63	2.02	8.38	10.39	5.29	8.45	24	10.2	16.3	15.1	38.5	49.2	39.0	9.9
	3.23	1.09	3.09	4.35	2.85	5.14	41	6.9	26.1	24.5	53.3	68.0	75.7	24.8
	1.97	0.30	0.77	1.41	2.22	3.10	49	5.8	47.6	68.9	107.7	88.2	113.0	60.2
2082 Breweries (36)	4.26	4.77	10.85	32.59	2.73	9.27	10	22.4	42.8	11.5	20.4	30.2	81.0	7.6
	3.02	3.12	6.34	17.52	2.24	6.62	17	14.1	56.2	15.9	28.4	43.1	123.7	35.0
	2.09	0.82	2.18	6.54	1.85	4.29	21	12.2	77.2	26.9	47.4	68.9	192.4	96.1
287 Chemicals, Agricultural (30)	4.22	3.20	11.43	27.13	4.92	13.92	26	14.8	24.0	17.1	73.6	37.1	63.4	34.6
	2.63	2.39	5.90	12.20	2.90	6.56	49	7.1	51.6	39.8	99.5	64.3	100.8	73.6
	1.36	0.47	1.95	2.27	1.66	2.23	97	5.4	87.5	89.6	204.2	117.0	239.5	198.5
281 Chemicals, Industrial (62)	4.12	7.37	12.26	34.78	3.08	7.36	37	8.9	41.8	18.3	40.7	46.3	55.1	40.8
	2.91	4.61	9.03	21.98	1.78	3.95	48	5.9	72.4	26.1	67.0	66.1	93.1	89.4
	1.82	2.67	5.79	8.02	1.32	2.80	62	4.5	99.4	60.3	108.5	95.0	145.2	135.5
1511 Contractors, Bldg. Constr. (164)	2.22	2.98	20.11	41.54	12.19	22.44	†	†	11.6	54.9	103.9	†	†	14.9
	1.53	1.48	11.50	18.76	7.52	12.60	†	†	26.3	107.6	143.8	†	†	44.9
	1.22	0.85	5.66	8.38	4.37	6.55	†	†	49.8	147.6	262.0	†	†	93.9

† Building trades contractors have no inventories in the credit sense of the term. As a general rule, they have no customary selling terms, such contracts being a special job for which individual terms are arranged.

Source: *Key Business Ratios in 125 lines,* 1963 (New York: Dun & Bradstreet, Inc., 1964).

Federal Trade Commission and the Securities and Exchange Commission jointly publish quarterly data on manufacturing companies. Both balance sheet and income statement data are developed from a systematic sample of corporations. The reports are published within perhaps six months after the financial data have been made available by the companies. They include an analysis by industry groups and by asset size, as well as financial statements in ratio form (or common-size analysis). The FTC-SEC reports are a rich source of information and are frequently used for comparative purposes.

Accounting Corporation of America. This firm provides an accounting service for small and medium-sized firms. Twice a year the Accounting Corporation of America publishes a *Barometer of Small Business,* based on reports from some 6,700 business firms grouped by fifty-one lines of business. As the name suggests, coverage is limited mainly to smaller firms; thus the *Barometer* provides a useful basis for comparison when smaller or newer firms are under analysis.

Individual firms. Credit departments of individual firms compile financial ratios and averages on (1) their customers in order to judge their ability to meet obligations and (2) their suppliers in order to evaluate their financial ability to fulfill contracts. The First National Bank of Chicago, for instance, compiles semiannual reports on the financial data for finance companies. The National Cash Register Company gathers data for a larger number of business lines.

Trade associations and public accountants. Financial ratios for many industries are compiled by trade associations and constitute an important source to be checked by a financial manager seeking comparative data. In addition, accounting firms specializing in certain lines (for example, textiles or canning) will compile averages of financial ratios for the confidential use of their clients. These averages are usually the best obtainable. In addition to balance sheet data, they provide detailed information on operating expenses, which makes possible an informed analysis of the efficiency of the firm.

Trend Analysis

Financial ratios may be put to effective use by observing the behavior of the ratios over time. Table 4–5 presents three selected ratios over a ten-year period for the Composite Company and another firm in its industry, Competitor X; Figure 4–1 presents the firms' ratios in graphic form. To aid in the comparisons industry averages are also shown for each of the ratios.

First, we note that the industry averages fluctuate somewhat, but they exhibit no noticeable trends. From this we infer that any trends in the companies' ratios are due to their own internal conditions, not to environmental influences affecting all firms. Second, the divergent trends of Composite Company and Competitor X are clear. Composite's liquidity position as measured by its current ratio has improved markedly over the ten-year period, while Competitor X has gone steadily downhill. Although Composite Company's current ratio is below the industry average, a

TABLE 4–5
THREE SELECTED RATIOS

	Composite Company									
	1957	1958	1959	1960	1961	1962	1963	1964	1965	1966
Current										
Company (times)	1.1	1.2	1.2	1.3	1.4	1.6	1.8	2.1	2.1	2.3
Industry (times)	2.5	2.6	2.5	2.6	2.4	2.6	2.7	2.4	2.3	2.5
Debt										
Company (percent)	65	62	63	58	60	57	57	55	55	50
Industry (percent)	52	50	51	50	49	50	51	51	49	50
Return on net worth										
Company (percent)	8	8	9	10	9	10	11	13	12	13
Industry (percent)	10	10	10	11	11	11	11	12	11	12
	Competitor X									
	1957	1958	1959	1960	1961	1962	1963	1964	1965	1966
Current										
Company (times)	2.8	2.8	2.7	2.8	2.6	2.4	2.4	2.2	1.8	1.2
Industry (times)	2.5	2.6	2.5	2.6	2.4	2.6	2.7	2.4	2.3	2.5
Debt										
Company (percent)	38	39	38	40	45	47	55	60	62	68
Industry (percent)	52	50	51	50	49	50	51	51	49	50
Return on net worth										
Company (percent)	12	9	8	7	4	(2)	(2)	(1)	2	(1)
Industry (percent)	10	9	10	11	11	11	11	12	11	12

credit analyst would not mark the firm down badly on this count, in view of the favorable trend. On the other hand, Competitor X would not have scored well even if its ratio had been above the industry average; with its unfavorable trend an analyst would question how long it would be before serious liquidity problems developed.

The debt ratios and returns on net worth show a similar picture—the profits of Composite Company are increasing, and it is using retained earnings to retire debt. Competitor X, meantime, has been suffering losses, and this condition has eroded its already weak working-capital and debt positions.

In the examples presented in Table 4–5 and Figure 4–1, only selected ratios are used. However, trend analysis can be performed for as many ratios as the financial manager judges useful for the problem at hand. By presenting a picture of operations over an extended period, trend and comparative analyses become a valuable tool for the financial manager. The trend of the ratios indicates where the company has been and the direction in which it is tending to go; the comparative analysis shows

TABLE 4–6

COMPOSITE COMPANY
BALANCE SHEET
December 31, 1966

Assets	Amount	Percent
Cash	$ 5,000	2.5
Marketable securities	15,000	7.5
Receivables	20,000	10.0
Inventories	30,000	15.0
Total current assets	$ 70,000	35.0
Net plant and equipment	130,000	65.0
Total assets	$200,000	100.0
Claims on assets		
Accounts payable	$ 6,000	3.0
Notes payable	10,000	5.0
Accruals	1,000	0.5
Provision for federal income tax	13,000	6.5
Total current liabilities	$ 30,000	15.0
First mortgage bonds	50,000	25.0
Debenture	20,000	10.0
Preferred stock	10,000	5.0
Common stock	50,000	25.0
Retained earnings	40,000	20.0
Total claims on assets	$200,000	100.0

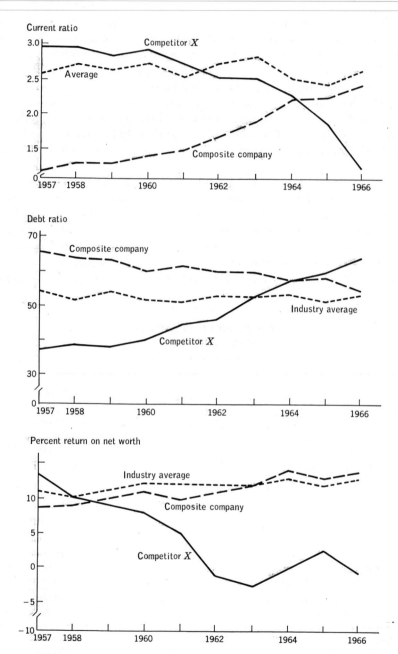

Fig. 4-1.   Trends in Three Selected Ratios

whether the firm has simply been riding an industry-wide trend or if its relative position has improved or deteriorated.

Common-Size Analysis

Another useful kind of financial evaluation is common-size analysis, which is made by expressing all items on the balance sheet as percentages of total assets and all items on the income statement as percentages of net sales. The nature of common-size analysis is illustrated by Tables 4–6 and 4–7.

TABLE 4–7

COMPOSITE COMPANY
INCOME STATEMENT
For Year Ended, December 31, 1966

			Amount	*Percent*
Net sales			$300,000	100.0
Cost of goods sold			$258,000	86.0
Gross profit			$ 42,000	14.0
Less: Operating expenses				
Selling	$2,200	0.7		
General and administrative . . .	4,000	1.3		
Rent on office	2,800	0.9	9,000	3.0
Gross Operating profit			$ 33,000	11.0
Depreciation			10,000	3.3
Net operating profit			$ 23,000	7.7
Add: Other income				
Royalties			$ 1,500	0.5
Gross income			$ 24,500	8.2
Less: Interest on notes payable	$ 800	0.3		
Interest on first mortgage	2,500	0.8		
Interest on debentures	1,200	0.4	4,500	1.5
Net income before income tax			$ 20,000	6.7
(tax at 40 percent)			8,000	2.7
Net income after income tax			$ 12,000	4.0

Common-size analysis is useful in that it makes firms directly comparable (from some standpoints) by standardizing all components of the financial statements. Caution should be exercised in making comparisons among firms of different sizes or ages, as these factors cause variation in normal relations. But with this reservation, firms that have somewhat different total assets or total sales may be compared directly by the use of the common-size analysis.

Summary of Financial Ratio Analysis

Financial ratio analysis enables the financial manager to gauge the progress of his firm and to judge how it appears to others, especially stockholders and creditors. The number and kinds of ratios he uses depend upon the nature of the industry and the size and age of the firm. The ratios discussed in this chapter are summarized with norms for large manufacturing firms, where such ratios are available, in Table 4–8. For

TABLE 4–8

SUMMARY OF FINANCIAL RATIOS AND REFERENCE GUIDES FOR LARGE MANUFACTURING FIRMS

Name of Ratio	*Reference Guide*
I. Liquidity	
1. Current ratio	2/1
2. Quick ratio	1/1
3. Inventory to working capital . .	varies
II. Leverage	
4. Debt to total assets	50 percent
5. Times interest earned	8 times
6. Fixed charge coverage	4 times
7. Current liabilities to net worth	35 percent
8. Fixed assets to net worth	65 percent
III. Activity	
9. Cash velocity	varies
10. Inventory turnover	8 times
11. Fixed assets turnover	varies
12. Average collection period . . .	30 days, compare with credit terms
13. Total assets turnover	2 times for large manufacturing 4 to 6 times for small firms
IV. Profitability	
14. Gross operating margin	varies
15. Net operating margin	varies
16. Sales margin	4 to 6 percent
17. Productivity of assets	10 to 12 percent
18. Return on net worth	13 to 15 percent

most types of analyses the financial manager need not utilize all the ratios indicated above. Usually only a selected few are necessary, but the financial manager will surely want to make trend comparisons, comparisons with other firms, or both.

The crucial idea is the realization that for many types of decisions financial ratios are only a beginning. They give the financial manager just a fraction of the information he needs for making a decision. Ultimately, the financial manager's success rests on his judgment of men and on future events.

SOURCES· AND APPLICATIONS OF FUNDS

The sources and applications (or uses) of funds statement is another useful tool in the financial manager's analytical kit. The basic purpose of this statement is to indicate, on a historical basis, where cash came from and where it was used. The statement is a counterpart to the cash budget (discussed in Chapter 13), since both are on a cash basis. The cash budget, however, is a projection into the future, whereas the statement of sources and applications of funds is historical. The latter deals with past data; the former deals with future projections.

From the standpoint of the financial manager, cash flow statements can be used in two ways. The first two questions a loan officer will ask are, "Why does the firm need the money?" and "What did the firm do with the money it had?" The first question can best be answered by the cash budget; the second question is answered by the sources and applications statement. The information it provides may indicate that the firm is making progress or that problems are arising. It will reveal the sources of funds and the principal uses to which they have been put.

Rough-and-Ready Sources and Applications Analysis

Rigorous development of a statement of sources and applications of funds is a time-consuming project. However, sufficient information is often obtained from an approximate analysis without the necessity of making elaborate adjustments. Where a detailed sources and applications statement is required, the financial manager will usually have it prepared for him by his accounting staff. For recurring decisions the financial manager may find it sufficient to make a rough analysis for himself in order to appraise the trend of developments in his company or for evaluating the performance of other companies.

To construct the financial manager's sources and uses statement it is initially necessary to tabulate the changes in balance sheet items from one year to the next. Each change in the balance sheet may be classified as either a source or a use (application) of funds, according to the following pattern:

> *Use of funds:* Increase in asset item; decrease in liability item.
> *Source of funds:* Decrease in asset item; increase in liability item.

Confusion sometimes arises on these points in connection with cash. Clearly, if inventories or fixed assets increase, funds have been used to obtain them. If cash is increased, this is also a use of funds; for example, drawer cash for use in conducting transactions in a department store. If cash in excess of current transactions needs has been accumulated and is then expended to purchase inventories, the transaction represents two flows of funds. Cash is drawn down—this is a source of funds; inventories are increased—this is a use of funds.

An illustration of the financial manager's rough-and-ready analysis of sources and uses of funds is embodied in Tables 4–9 and 4–10. Composite

TABLE 4–9

COMPOSITE COMPANY
CONSOLIDATED BALANCE SHEETS AND SOURCES
AND USES OF FUNDS
(in thousands of dollars)

	12/31/65	12/31/66	Sources	Uses
Cash	$ 10	$ 5	$ 5	
Marketable securities	25	15	10	
Net receivables	15	20		$ 5
Inventories	25	30		5
	75	70		
Gross fixed assets	150	180		30
Less: allowance for depreciation	40	50	10	
Net fixed assets	110	130		
Total assets	$185	$200		
Accounts payable	$ 10	$ 6		4
Notes payable	15	10		5
Other current liabilities	10	14	4	
Long-term debt	60	70	10	
Preferred stock	10	10	—	—
Common stock	50	50	—	—
Retained earnings	30	40	10	—
Total claims on assets	$185	$200	$49	$49

Company obtained funds by drawing down cash balances, by selling marketable securities, by increasing other current liabilities, by incurring long-term debt, and by retaining earnings. Total funds from these sources were $39,000. An additional $10,000 arose from the increase in the reserve for depreciation. Depreciation expense itself does not produce cash, but it is a noncash outlay. Since it was deducted from revenues to arrive at the retained earnings figure, it must be added back as a source of funds in cash flow analysis.

The total sources of funds, then, is $49,000. This amount was used to finance an increase in accounts receivable, to purchase inventories and fixed assets, and to reduce notes payable.

If Composite Company had net income of $12,000 in 1966 and paid out $2,000 in dividends, the retained earnings of $10,000 completely reconciles the surplus account. In some situations, however, there would be

TABLE 4–10

COMPOSITE COMPANY
STATEMENT OF SOURCES AND USES OF FUNDS, 1966
(in thousands of dollars)

Uses

Gross fixed assets expansion	$30
Inventory investment	5
Increase in receivables	5
Reduction in notes payable	5
Reduction in accounts payable	4
Total use of funds	$49

Sources

Increase in long-term debt	$10
Increase in retained earnings	10
Noncash depreciation outlay	10
Sale of marketable securities	10
Reduction in cash holdings	5
Increase in other liabilities	4
Total source of funds	$49

noncash transactions, such as debiting the reserve for insurance out of surplus. If such transactions are small in amount, they can be ignored by the financial manager in making a rough-and-ready statement of sources and uses of funds.

What does this rough-and-ready statement of sources and uses of funds tell the financial manager? It tells him that the firm's sales were growing, that plant size had to be expanded, and that therefore $30,000 of fixed assets were acquired. Inventories and net receivables also increased as sales increased. The firm needed funds to meet working-capital and fixed assets demands.

Previously, the firm had been financing its growth through bank credit (notes payable). In the present period of growth, management decided to obtain some of its financing from permanent sources (long-term debt). It obtained enough long-term debt not only to finance some of the asset growth but also to pay back some of its bank credit and reduce accounts payable. In addition to the long-term debt, funds were acquired from retained earnings and from depreciation charges of $10,000. Moreover, the firm had been accumulating marketable securities in anticipation of this expansion program, and these were sold to pay for new buildings and equipment. Finally, cash had been accumulated in excess of the firm's needs and was also worked down.

This example illustrates how the financial manager's rough-and-ready approach to sources and uses can give him a fairly complete picture of recent operations. Such an approach is not bogged down in details. Because refined adjustments usually amount to less than 4 to 5 percent of the total amounts involved, the financial manager can omit them and still obtain a good perspective on the flow of funds in his company or departments. The accountant still is required to make a formal sources and applications analysis. However, the financial manager's rough approach enables him to obtain the broad outlines of the firm's position quickly.

SUMMARY

An introduction to ratio analysis and the rough-and-ready statement of sources and applications of funds has been presented to show how the financial manager may chart the history of the firm and evaluate its present financial position. Thorough analysis also allows the manager to anticipate reactions of investors and creditors who use these techniques in evaluating the company.

Ratios are used in three basic ways: (1) comparative analysis with industry averages, (2) trend analysis, and (3) common-size analysis. Skilled use of ratio analysis provides valuable insights into the operations of the firm; unskilled use can lead to erroneous decision making. Ratios should therefore be used to point the way for further investigation.

The rough-and-ready statement of sources and applications of funds describes the cash flows through the firm. For most financial management purposes the rough-and-ready statement is sufficiently accurate.

Up to this point analytical techniques have been aimed at determining the present financial situation of the firm. Subsequent chapters will consider the determination of future needs and methods of meeting financial requirements.

SELECTED REFERENCES

Davidson, Sidney, George H. Sorter, and Hemu Kalle, "Measuring the Defensive Position of a Firm," *Financial Analysts Journal*, 20 (January-February 1964), pp. 23–29.

Foulke, Roy A., *Practical Financial Statement Analysis* (New York: McGraw-Hill, Inc., 1961).

Gold, Bela, and Ralph M. Kraus, "Integrating Physical with Financial Measures for Managerial Controls," *Academy of Management Journal*, 7 (June 1964), pp. 109–127.

Greeleaf, Robert W., *Corporate Financial Statements* (Indianapolis: Orchard House Press, 1964).

McCloud, B. G., Jr., "Pitfalls in Statement Analysis," *Bulletin of the Robert Morris Associates*, 39 (January 1957), pp. 143–148.

Sanzo, R., *Ratio Analysis for Small Business*, Small Business Management Series, No. 20 (Washington, D. C.: U. S. Government Printing Office, 1957).

QUESTIONS

4-1 "A uniform system of accounts, including identical forms for balance sheets and income statements, would be a most reasonable requirement for the SEC to impose on all publicly owned firms." Discuss.

4-2 There are four groups of financial ratios: (1) liquidity, (2) leverage, (3) activity, and (4) profitability. In addition, financial analysis is conducted by four types of analysts: (1) management, (2) equity investors, (3) long-term creditors, and (4) short-term creditors.

1. Explain the nature of each of the major types of ratios.
2. Explain the emphasis of each of the major types of analysts.
3. Could the same basic approach to financial analysis be taken by each group of analysts?

4–3 What are the uses and limitations of a composite or industry average as a standard or norm for comparison with the financial ratios of the individual firm?

4–4 Why can norms with relatively well-defined limits be stated in advance for some financial ratios but not for others?

4–5 What does common-size analysis accomplish?

4–6 Should most financial ratio calculations be supplemented by a trend analysis?

4–7 What are the similarities and differences between a sources and uses analysis and a cash budget?

4–8 How does a rough-and-ready sources and uses analysis differ from one ordinarily described in accounting texts?

4–9 In what sense is an increase in the cash item a use of cash?

4–10 Is depreciation a source of funds?

4–11 Is an increase in surplus a source of funds?

PROBLEMS

4–1 The consolidated balance sheets for the Moore Corporation at the beginning and end of 1966 are shown below.

MOORE CORPORATION
BALANCE SHEET
Beginning and End 1966
(in millions of dollars)

	Jan. 2 1966	Dec. 31 1966	Increase or (Decrease)	Source or Use
Cash	$ 20	$ 10		
Marketable securities	15	0		
Net receivables	30	40		
Inventories	70	100		
Total current assets	$135	$150		
Gross fixed assets	100	140		
Less: Reserves for depreciation	35	55		
Net fixed assets	65	85		
Total assets	$200	$235		
Accounts payable	$ 20	$ 25		
Notes payable	20	5		
Other current liabilities	10	15		
Long-term debt	10	30		
Common stock	50	50		
Retained earnings	90	110		
Total claims on assets	$200	$235		

The company brought $40 million of assets. The charge for current depreciation was $20 million. Earnings after taxes were $40 million, and the company paid out $20 million in dividends.

1. Fill in the amount of increase or decrease in the appropriate column.
2. Prepare a statement of sources and uses of funds.
3. State briefly a summary of your findings.

4–2 The following data were taken from the financial statements of the Medfone Corporation for the calendar year 1966. The norms given below are from Dun & Bradstreet financial ratios for the metal stamping industry.

Fill in the ratios for Medfone, then indicate, by comparison with the industry norms, what kinds of errors in management policies are reflected in these financial statements?

THE MEDFONE CORPORATION
BALANCE SHEET
December 31, 1966

Cash	$ 20,000	Accounts payable	$ 15,000
Receivables	25,000	Notes payable (5%) . . .	20,000
Inventory	75,000	Other current liab. . . .	10,000
Total current assets . . .	120,000	Total current liab. . .	45,000
Net property	55,000	Long-term debt (6%) . .	20,000
		Net worth	110,000
		Total claims on	
Total assets	$175,000	assets	$175,000

THE MEDFONE CORPORATION
INCOME STATEMENT
For Year Ended December 31, 1966

Sales		$250,000
Cost of goods sold		
Materials	$95,000	
Labor	60,000	
Heat, light, and power	9,000	
Indirect labor	15,000	
Depreciation (10%)	5,500	184,500
Gross profit		$ 65,500
Selling expenses	$25,000	
General and administrative expenses	20,500	45,500
Operating profit		20,000
Less: Interest expense		1,200
Net profit before taxes		18,800
Less: Federal income taxes		9,400
Net profit		$ 9,400

FINANCIAL RATIOS

Ratio		Medfone	Norm
$\dfrac{\text{current assets}}{\text{current liabilities}}$	. . . .	——	2.5 times
$\dfrac{\text{inventories}}{\text{net working capital}}$	. . . .	——	62.0%
average collection period	. . . .	——	33 days
$\dfrac{\text{sales}}{\text{inventories}}$	. . . .	——	9.9 times
$\dfrac{\text{sales}}{\text{net worth}}$	. . . .	——	3.0 times
$\dfrac{\text{sales}}{\text{total assets}}$	. . . .	——	1.3* times
$\dfrac{\text{current debt}}{\text{net worth}}$	. . . .	——	32.1%
$\dfrac{\text{total debt}}{\text{net worth}}$	. . . .	——	65.0%
$\dfrac{\text{fixed assets}}{\text{net worth}}$	. . . .	——	43.5%
$\dfrac{\text{net profit}}{\text{sales}}$	. . . .	——	3.3%
$\dfrac{\text{net profit}}{\text{total assets}}$	. . . .	——	3.8%
$\dfrac{\text{net profit}}{\text{net worth}}$	. . . .	——	10.7%

* Assumed.

4–3 The following data were taken from the financial statements of Snowfield Appliance Company for the years 1964, 1965, and 1966. The norms of the financial ratios given below for the household appliance industry are from Dun & Bradstreet.

What management problems are reflected in these financial data for each of the three years? Fill in the ratios on page 98.

THE SNOWFIELD APPLIANCE COMPANY
COMPARATIVE BALANCE SHEETS
For Years 1964–1966

Assets	*1964*	*1965*	*1966*
Cash	$ 5,000	$ 4,000	$10,000
Receivables, net	25,000	15,000	15,000
Inventories	22,000	34,000	25,000
Total current assets	$52,000	$53,000	$50,000
Net property	25,000	25,000	26,000
Other assets	2,000	2,000	2,000
Total assets	$79,000	$80,000	$78,000

Liabilities and Capital			
Accounts payable	$10,000	$12,000	$12,000
Notes payable (5%)	7,000	7,000	7,000
Other current liabilities	3,000	1,000	2,000
Total current liabilities	$20,000	$20,000	$21,000
Long-term debts (6%)	15,000	15,000	15,000
Net worth	44,000	45,000	42,000
Total claims on assets	$79,000	$80,000	$78,000

THE SNOWFIELD APPLIANCE COMPANY
COMPARATIVE INCOME STATEMENTS
For Years Ended 1964-1966

	1964		1965		1966	
Sales		$120,000		$110,000		$130,000
Material	$45,000		$39,000		$47,000	
Labor	40,500		37,000		43,000	
Heat, light, and power .	9,000		9,000		9,000	
Depreciation (10%) .	1,500	96,000	1,500	86,500	1,500	100,500
Gross profit		24,000		23,500		29,500
Selling expenses . .	10,000		10,000		10,000	
Gen. and admin. exp. .	9,500	19,500	9,250	19,250	8,750	18,750
Operating profit . . .		4,500		4,250		10,750
Less: Interest exp. .		1,250		1,250		1,250
Net profit before taxes .		3,250		3,000		9,500
Federal income taxes .		1,625		1,500		4,750
Net income		$ 1,625		$ 1,500		$ 4,750

	Ratio	1964 Company Ratio	1964 Average Ratio	1965 Company Ratio	1965 Average Ratio	1966 Company Ratio	1966 Average Ratio
1.	$\dfrac{\text{Current assets}}{\text{Current liabilities}}$	——	2.5	——	2.6	——	2.7
2.	$\dfrac{\text{Inventory}}{\text{Net working capital}}$	——	81.1	——	84.0	——	87.0
3.	$\dfrac{\text{Sales}}{\text{Inventory (at book)}}$	——	4.6	——	4.8	——	5.0
4.	Collection period (days)	——	53.0	——	51	——	48.0
5.	$\dfrac{\text{Fixed assets}}{\text{Net worth}}$	——	32.2	——	33.1	——	35.0
6.	$\dfrac{\text{Current debt}}{\text{Net worth}}$	——	46.8	——	48.0	——	50.3
7.	$\dfrac{\text{Total debt}}{\text{Net worth}}$	——	50.1	——	49.5	——	52.0
8.	$\dfrac{\text{Current debt}}{\text{Inventory}}$	——	75.8	——	77.3	——	81.8
9.	$\dfrac{\text{Sales}}{\text{Net worth}}$	——	2.5	——	2.8	——	3.0
10.	$\dfrac{\text{Net profit}}{\text{Sales}}$	——	3.4	——	3.5	——	3.7
11.	$\dfrac{\text{Net profit}}{\text{Net worth}}$	——	10.0	——	10.2	——	10.5
12.	$\dfrac{\text{Net profit}}{\text{Total assets}}$	——	4.3	——	4.9	——	5.7

Chapter 5

Financial Control

The preceding chapter described the tools for finding out what is going on in a company. The financial results mirror the effectiveness of management performance. The present chapter begins the discussion of the analysis of "what to do about it." Financial control deals with methods of improving operations of the enterprise. Effective financial control will lead to improved results as measured by the analytical yardsticks and ratios that have been set forth.

NATURE OF CONTROL

Control consists of three activities: (1) measuring performance against objectives; (2) evaluating performance by comparing the results of operations with pre-established standards; and (3) modifying policies, programs, and procedures of the enterprise with the purpose of improving performance. The nature of the control process is diagramed in Figure 5–1 and explained in the following discussion. Although some important aspects of control activities are nonfinancial, finance has a significant role to play in achieving the control goals of the enterprise.

The major purposes of the use of controls are:

1. To project desired results accurately
2. To identify and forecast major trends
3. To determine needs for changes
4. To detect operating problems in time to take corrective action before they become critical
5. To provide continuous guides for improving performance

99

The control process involves four important aspects.

First, control criteria must be formulated. As in variable budgeting, a cause-and-effect relation must be established as a basis for determining what variables influence other variables. In this way the logic of control relations may be understood.

Second, on the basis of the logical relations, standards may then be determined. These are the norms by which performance can be judged.

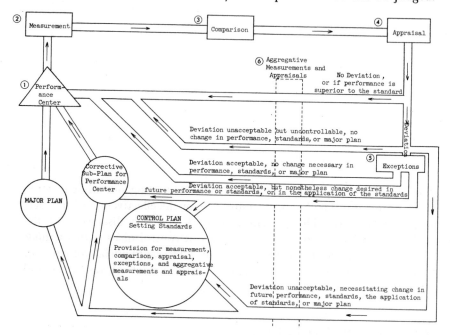

Fig. 5-1. Model of the Control Process

Third, actual performance is then compared with the pre-established norms. The comparison enables evaluation of performance.

Fourth, on the basis of the review and evaluation of actual results against the norms, remedial or *corrective action* may be required. Better performance may follow.

This general discussion may be put in more concrete terms by the use of illustrative material.

DU PONT SYSTEM OF FINANCIAL CONTROL

The du Pont system of financial control has achieved wide recognition in American industry, and properly so. Its essential technique is to begin with an analysis of the relation of investment in operating assets and the income statement pattern, all funneled into a final figure representing the rate of return on investment.[1]

The nature of the du Pont system, simplified somewhat, is set forth in Figure 5–2. The figure is divided into two main lines of relation. The upper group represents total current assets, plus fixed investment in the form of property, plant, and equipment. Sales divided by total investment

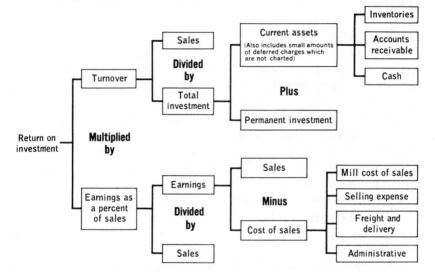

Fig. 5-2. The du Pont System of Financial Control
Source: How the du Pont Organization Appraises Its Performance,
AMA Financial Management Series, No. 94, Courtesy of T. C. Davis.

equals the total investment turnover, which is the final figure in the upper half of the chart.

The lower group begins at the far right with an analysis of the income statement. Sales minus cost of sales gives earnings, and earnings divided by sales gives the profit margin on sales, as the final figure in the lower level of relations. Turnover is then multiplied by earnings to sales to give return on investment. This can be shown in the following formula of relations.

$$\frac{\text{Sales}}{\text{Investment}} \times \frac{\text{Profit-return}}{\text{Sales}} = \frac{\text{Profit-return}}{\text{Investment}}$$

Thus the final figure provided by the du Pont approach is the return

[1] The best current description of the du Pont system is contained in T. C. Davis, *How the du Pont Organization Appraises Its Performance,* Financial Management Series, No. 94 (New York: American Management Association, 1950), and *Executive Committee Control Charts, prepared by Treasurer's Department;* E. I. du Pont de Nemours and Company, AMA Management Bulletin, No. 6 (New York: American Management Association, 1960).

on investment. The great value of the return-on-investment standard of control is that the duPont chart provides a framework for working back from the return on investment to check at each critical control point in the operation of the firm. In the hands of competent users of the duPont chart, the breakdown is carried to even further detail of critical points for checking controls than is indicated by the simplified chart in Figure 5–2.

Profit Centers

The du Pont system of financial control has two other areas that receive an important form of expression. The first is to apply the analysis by operating division, department, or product. This procedure has been viewed by some analysts as looking at performance in terms of *profit centers*. In the analysis by profit centers, portions of the total company's working capital, plus investment, are assigned to each of the profit centers or units of responsibility. Each of these departments or products must stand on its own feet. In deciding how or where to allocate additional capital funds—or the incentive bonuses to be paid to individual managers—the company compares department, division, or product performance.

When the analysis is by department, division, product, or some other profit-center basis, the important question is how the elements of investment and expense are allocated to these units. Some illustrative methods may be indicated. Cash can be allocated on the basis of an assumption of a uniform transaction velocity of cash in the company. In other words, cash could be related to the transfer price at which products or materials are valued as they leave a profit center.

Receivables would be a function of the terms of sale. For example, if average sales are $2,000 per day and terms are net 30, receivables would equal approximately $60,000. In actual practice, if terms of sale are net 30, actual collection would run from 35 to 40 days, with the result that receivables would run $70,000 to $80,000. Since intrafirm departments do not generate outside receivables, receivables could be allocated to departments on the basis of their contribution to product, what is usually referred to as value added to product, or some element of intrafirm transfer pricing.

Inventories can be taken on the basis of actual amounts in each area, with finished goods inventories allocated in the same way as receivables. Permanent investment could be allocated on the basis of factory space occupied by the activity.

So far as allocation of costs is concerned, direct material, direct labor, and other variable factory costs involve no problem. If there are departmental or product overhead rates, overhead would be assigned in this fashion. If these breakdown rates should not apply, the presumption is that over-all company rates are applicable by department or product.

Charting System

The second major contribution of the du Pont system lies in the expression of the large number of variables contained in its charting system. The procedure involves plotting on a simple time-trend chart a large number of the items whose behavior is to be analyzed. On the chart, time is on the horizontal axis, and the behavior of the item of investment, liabilities, net worth, or expense is on the vertical axis.

The du Pont chart may be used to pull out of the analysis crucial factors that analyze the operations of the firm in terms of three key factors: (1) money, (2) operations, and (3) people, in the form of customers and personnel. An illustrative basis for analysis is set out in Table 5–1.

TABLE 5–1

IMPORTANT SUMMARY CONTROLS
FINANCIAL CONTROL
Year to Date for _____ Weeks Ending _____, 196____

	Ratio	Actual to Date	Current Budget	Year Ago
A. *Money*				
1. Current assets to current liabilities	times			
2. Receivables to current assets	%			
3. Fixed assets to tangible net worth	%			
4. Total sales: working capital	times			
5. Net return on invested capital	%			
B. *Operations*—Net annual rate				
1. Gross margin to sales	%			
2. Operating expense to total sales	%			
3. Expense per unit	$			
4. Facilities cost, percentage of sales	%			
5. Net return on sales	%			
C. *People*				
I. *Customers*				
1. Transactions per month	No.			
2. Average sale per transaction	$			
3. Expense per transaction	$			
4. Payroll cost per transaction	$			
II. *Personnel* Avg. No.				
1. Sales per man-hour	$			
2. Average payroll per man-hour	$			
3. Payroll per unit	$			
4. Payroll, percentage of sales	%			

The kinds of relation suggested by this analysis can be portrayed in graphic form. Some of the different kinds of relations and the distinct methods of control implied by them are set out in the following series of charts.

Figure 5–3 presents the behavior of costs through time. The rapid increase or decline of costs calls attention to unusual behavior and results

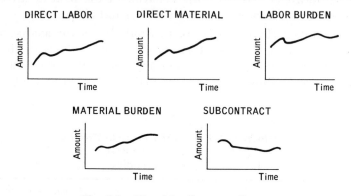

Fig. 5-3.   Monthly Contract Costs

in a study and analysis of why the costs have departed from usual patterns. Thus a simple time trend is useful, both as a record and for analytical purposes, in observing the behavior of trends.

Figure 5–4 shows another kind of analysis, the composition of costs expressed in percentage terms. If one type of cost is increasing in percentage more than others are, study to determine the reason may be indicated.

The best approach to costs is to look at them analytically. To do so, the cost must be related to the factors that determine what the level shall be. For example, in Figure 5–5, when general and administrative costs are related to sales, the graph suggests that sales will have an influence on general and administrative costs. When the two are shown together, any changes in general and administrative costs can be evaluated.

Figure 5–6a presents travel expense per month. In general, it is useful to have a record of the level of costs. It is more useful, however, if these costs can be related to some volume of operations figure that indicates the justification for whatever changes in the level of costs are taking place.

In the next presentation, two kinds of costs are shown. Figure 5–6b and c present telephone expense and wire-communication expense. Often the presentation of two kinds of expense in this way will tell a logical story. When telephone expense increases relative to volume of operations, wire-communications expense would be expected to increase at the same time, because it is also related to volume. However, if telephone expense increases while wire-communication expense falls, the indication is that

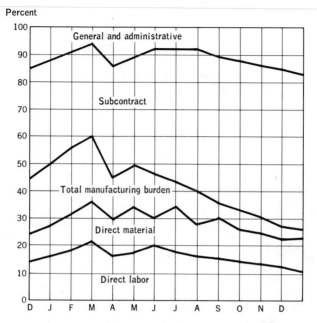

Fig. 5-4. Total Monthly Costs (in Percentages) by Elements

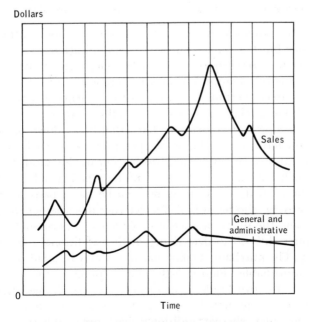

Fig. 5-5. General and Administrative Expense

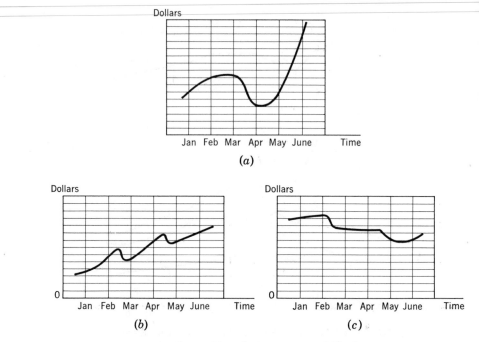

Fig. 5-6a.   Travel Expense per Month
Travel expense should be related to some volume of the operation figure.
Fig. 5-6b and c.   (b) Telephone Expense and (c) Wire-Communication Expense
These expenses should be related to some measure of volume.

employees are taking the easy way of using the telephone, rather than the less expensive but less convenient wire communication.

Another way to set up controls is to develop figures that seem reasonable as a standard. Figure 5–7 presents allowable direct overtime and allowable indirect overtime based on past experience. Current hours are then recorded and related to the standards thus developed.

Figure 5–8 presents a series of charts that break down payroll-section work load in terms of the kinds of operations performed and the total level of operations. In reviewing information of this kind, the financial controller will have a basis for determining whether a large number of employee hours will be required. Because he has a basis for estimating the work load, he also has a basis for determining whether the volume of operations and the items handled justify increased personnel.

It is often difficult to determine whether additional office machinery is necessary. The purchase of office machinery may be a fad, and purchases may be unjustifiable. Figure 5–9a and b presents the percentage of capacity used for two kinds of machines. The percentages that the key punch and sorter are actually in use gives a basis for indicating to the financial controller whether additional machines of this type are needed.

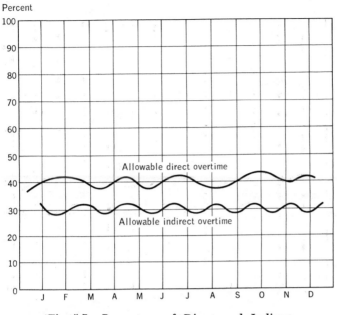

Fig. 5-7. Percentage of Direct and Indirect
Overtime Hours to Total Direct Labor Hours
Control based on experience and judgment.

Figure 5–10 charts monthly working capital, which is a measure of
the pile-up in inventories, receivables, and cash in comparison with the
pile-up in payables. This is another instance where a simple presentation
of the behavior of the item over time gives the basis for evaluating performance.

It is important to caution that sales volume alone is not always a
sufficient explanatory variable for all kinds of balance sheet items or expenses. For example, travel expense may not be a function only of sales
developed in a particular territory. It may also depend upon the size of
territory that a salesman must cover. It will reflect whether the customers
in the territory are large or small, and thus also reflect the amount of time
per customer that must be spent by the salesman. In addition, the number
of customers in the territory will influence the amount of sales expense
associated with activity in that area.

In analyzing elements of cost control and expense items, a simple
statistical relation is often not adequate. Even a time-trend analysis may
be misleading. There may be an excessive number of calls per account.
Salesmen may call too frequently on the account, or may spend an excessive amount of time per call. In short, a salesman's quality of selling
may be too high, and he may thus unproductively overapply resources in
certain directions. Statistical techniques are no substitutes for firsthand

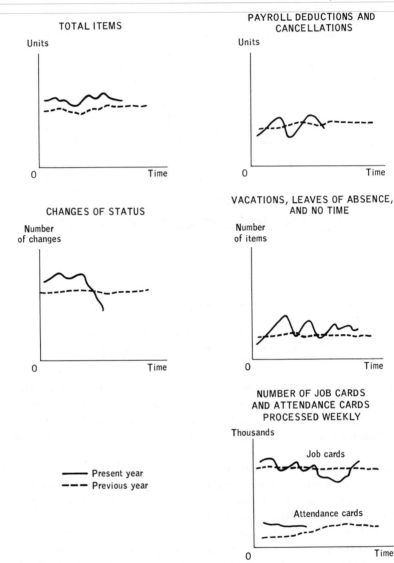

Fig. 5-8. Payroll Section Work Load

direct understanding of the activity, which will provide a basis for the exercise of informed judgments by those responsible for financial controls.

MAKING FINANCIAL CONTROL WORK

It should be emphasized that financial controls are tools of management and not substitutes for management. Like any tools, they have uses and limitations. Their effective use is assured if management carries out the

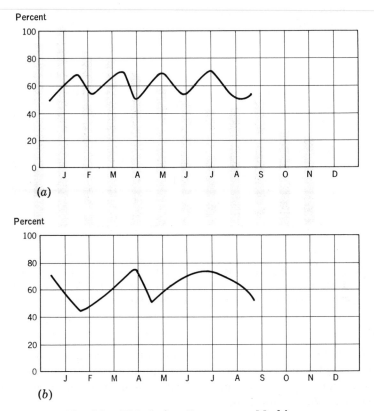

Fig. 5-9. Tabulating Department Machine
Usage—(a) 024 Key Punch; (b) 082 Sorter
*Data on percent utilization provide a basis for deter-
mining whether additional machines will be needed.*

requirements of a system of financial control that emphasizes the following
factors.

Coverage

Does management maintain the controls necessary to accomplish
the objectives set out by the firm in its planning activities? Top management should periodically appraise and question every control, every
record, and every report, to eliminate those which do not contribute
information clearly required.

Accountability

Management controls and reports must be related to objectives and
to standards at various levels of authority—for the organization as a whole
and for each department for which a single executive is finally held
accountable.

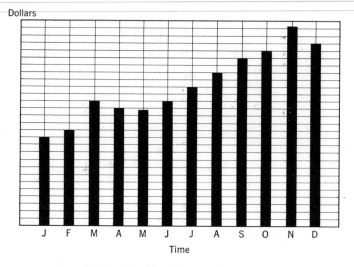

Fig. 5-10. Monthly Net Working Capital
*A measure of pile-up in inventories and receivables compared
with pile-up in payables (current assets minus current liabilities).*

Economy

Controls must be economical. They must be simple in design, easy
to use, easy to understand, and easy to administer and to maintain. They
must be few so that the time and expense involved in preparing and
using them will be minimal.

Participation

An important means of making plans and controls work is making
certain that those who are expected to carry out, to administer, and to
live with them take part in their preparation. Wide organizational participation is advisable for developing acceptance of plans. In a like manner,
budget making, an instrument of planning and control, will succeed if
there is wide participation in the development of the budgets. The most
valuable by-products of budgeting are the information, education, and
understanding that grow out of budget discussions. Communication is
enhanced whenever people are called in to help set budget goals and to
develop standards.

Cycling and Review of Projections

An important factor in the success of the control process is provision
for review and adjustment of initial projections. Some firms make a
budget for a 12-month period. During each month in the budget period,
the actual figures are compared with those that were forecast, and an over-

or under-budget percentage factor is computed. Departures from budget (or forecast) require explanation and correction.

Another device is the use of a cycling process. For example, from 15 to 20 days before the start of each quarter, a projection is made for the following four quarters, by month for the proximate quarter and by quarter for the last three quarters of the year. Thus each quarter is forecast four times during the cycling process. A comparison of actual with budget is made and reviewed each month. Variances will call for explanations and corrections.

Figure 5–11 indicates how the cycling process operates. Selling expense is the subject of the forecast. Selling expense is expressed as a per-

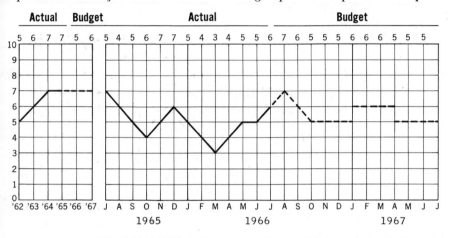

Fig. 5-11. Selling Expense as a Percent of Sales*
*Current standard is 5 percent of sales.
Data of budget projection, June 10, 1966. The proximate quarter is forecast by months; the following three quarters are forecast by quarters.

cent of sales, to provide a standard for control of selling expenses. The current standard is specified as 9 percent. Data for six years on an annual basis are provided. The figure by months represents 12 months of actual performance, a quarter forecast by months, and a forecast for three quarters by quarter.

The date of the forecast is given as June 10, 1966. The forecast is made for four quarters, encompassing the third and fourth quarters of 1966 and the first two quarters of 1967. The forecast is by month for the third quarter of 1966 and by quarter for the following three quarters.

Three months later, approximately September 10, 1966, another forecast would be made for one quarter on a monthly basis and for three additional quarters on a quarterly basis. The forecast is repeated on December 10, 1966, and on March 10, 1967.

Thus any given quarter is forecast four times. The first three times the forecast is on a quarterly basis. The fourth time the forecast is on a monthly basis. Thus, four broken lines would appear on the chart for each quarter, representing the four forecasts that would be made. If the broken-line marks are retained after the actual solid-line data are entered, an excellent historical record of a sequence of forecasts is provided. Thus after actual performance is entered, a comparison between the trend of the forecasts and the actual is provided.

The entire process provides an excellent vehicle for testing the ability of the operating managers to demonstrate an understanding of the factors affecting the operations of their departments. The evaluation of the managers is not based on the accuracy of the forecast. What is more important is the manager's ability to explain the factors affecting his operations and his ability to improve performance related to the potentials of the economic and competitive environment in which his division operates.

Appraisal of Performance

Appraisal of performance requires a comparison with standards. For direct tasks of the kind found on the assembly line and in other production areas, it is usually feasible to develop standards.

As one attempts to appraise the performance of larger units, however, difficulties are often encountered. For example, accounting department performance could be judged in terms of the trend in its cost in relation to the volume of activity carried on by the firm, or in its relation to the firm's total volume of business compared with the costs of accounting departments in other firms. There is danger here, of course, that the degree of responsibility carried on by the accounting departments in the firms compared may not be the same.

Appraisal of performance may require the use of substitute or proxy standards. For example, often it is not meaningful to make comparisons among firms on the basis of profit rates in relation to investment, because accounting procedures are not comparable. Proxy measures may therefore be employed, for example, trends in the firm's share of the industry market, or the behavior of the market price of the firm's common stock if it is a publicly owned corporation.

For complex kinds of activity, however, judgment must be exercised in making an appraisal of performance. The difficulty with judgments is that there may not be an objective basis for making comparisons between points of time or between different firms.

Correction of Deficiencies

It is important that there be a follow-through between an appraisal of performance, the observation of departures from standards, and the study and analysis of the reasons for these departures. Study conferences and discussions of reasons for deviations from standards can be a valuable source of increasing understanding of the process or the area of activity. Thus, just as there is great value in the process of setting up standards and budget goals, there is likewise great value in discussing the *results* of performance in relation to budgets. It is to be hoped, of course, that such discussions will be productive and not merely a process of placing blame and criticism.

NONBUDGETARY CONTROL DEVICES

The previous discussion of budgets emphasized how useful they are in setting up projections that may be used as standards for comparing actual performance. Many important things may be accomplished through the use of nonbudgetary devices, many of which are distinct from budgeting as such.

Special Reports and Analyses

Although regular reports and analyses can provide much information, special analyses will often provide information not otherwise easily developed. Through these special studies, opportunities for cost improvement or more effective utilization of capital may be discovered, which may not be observable from statistical charts.

Internal Audit

Internal auditing traditionally deals with accounting methods, procedures, and systematic behavior. But, in addition, internal auditing has been developed into management audits to appraise the policies, procedures, use of authority, quality of management, effectiveness of methods, and other phases of operations. Though analysis of integrity of accounts and of corporate assets is a valuable function, internal auditing can, in addition, be broadened into internal management audits for control in this way.

Personal Observation

Statistical and mechanical methods of control are valuable. They summarize information quickly and bring it to the attention of the reader dramatically. However, the manager who relies on these devices alone has cut himself off from vital information. Effective planning and control must get to the level of face-to-face contacts and discussions with people before the manager can obtain a full understanding of what is going on in the organization. This is an especially important injunction for financial managers, who, by training and traditions, are accustomed to the use of formal, impersonal control instruments.

SUMMARY

By way of summary, it is clear that the financial manager plays a very important role in carrying out the control function in the firm. His work is concerned to a major degree with planning, setting standards, preparing reports on performance, appraising performance, and participating in decisions for improving performance.

In an important sense, everything the financial manager does is tied to financial control. This fact is reflected in the organization of the materials that will be discussed in the following chapter. Their significance for control is so great that the nature of the relation is set out to provide guidelines to the following chapters. Effective management of assets (Chapter 6) controls the amount of resources required for operations.

The financial planning activities (Part III) are crucial for setting targets and providing reference points. Financial planning is expressed through profit planning, forecasting financial requirements, valuations, and budgeting for facilities and manpower.

Sound choices of financing forms and of sources also contribute to the effectiveness of business operations (Parts IV and V). In these decisions, financial management is interrelated with other activities of the enterprise. Sound sales forecasting and effective marketing policies are essential for sound financial forecasting and choice of appropriate kinds of financing. Effective engineering and production operations are required to produce a healthy business. Inadequate finances may reflect unsound management, not lack of adequate financing sources. Poor management cannot be remedied by repeated doses of money. However, unsound financial policies may hamper engineering, production, and marketing operations to the point where the performance of the firm will suffer.

The great responsibility of the financial manager is his contribution to effective timing of executive decisions (Part VIII). The finacial manager operates in an environment in which the timing of the purchase of money is critical. The costs of money may change by as much as 100 percent within 12 to 18 months. More important, the terms and conditions under which funds may be obtained may vary greatly with changes in the economic and financial environment. Thus an understanding of the general economic environment, including trends in capital market conditions, has become of crucial significance for the financial manager. Because good financial management places heavy emphasis on systematic planning, the financial manager may contribute importantly to effective planning in other strategic decision areas of the firm.

With progress in the ability to forecast, many aspects of cash management, which may have been handled on a rule-of-thumb basis during the pre-World War II period, are now amenable to the application of analytical tools of forecasting. Thus financial administration has come to be of importance parallel to, and indeed intertwined with, participation in major investment or financing decisions confronting the firm. At every level, therefore, financial management performs a vital role in carrying out a firm's program of planning and control for profit.

The present chapter is called "Financial Control" because it introduces the subject. It provides a foundation for understanding how the subsequent topics contribute to the control task of improving the performance of the firm.

SELECTED REFERENCES

Arisman, G. M., *Company Planning and Production Control* (Paris, France: Organization for European Economic Cooperation, 1958).

Chane, G. W., "Closer Planning through Forecasting Techniques," *N.A.C.A. Bulletin*, 38 (May 1957), pp. 1106–1113.

Financial Controls and Break-Even Points, Financial Management Series, No. 91 (New York: American Management Association, 1941).

Frank, G. W., "Let's Develop Return-on-Investment Consciousness," *N.A.C.A. Bulletin*, 38 (October 1956), pp. 200–207.

Graham, Ben S., "Techniques for Lightening the Lord of Paper Work—Work Simplification and Integrated Systems," *N.A.A. Bulletin*, 41 (September 1959), pp. 3–10.

Henning, Dale A., *Non-Financial Controls in Smaller Enterprises* (Seattle, Wash.: University of Washington, College of Business Administration, 1964).

Jasinski, F. J., "Use and Misuse of Efficiency Controls," *Harvard Business Review*, 34 (July-August 1956), pp. 105–112.

Kempster, J. H., "Economic Yardsticks in Management Reports," *N.A.A. Bulletin*, 40 (September 1958), pp. 5–16.

Koontz, H., "Management Control: A Suggested Formulation of Principles," *California Management Review*, 1 (Winter 1959), pp. 47–55.

Malcolm, D. G., and A. J. Rowe, "An Approach to Computer-Based Management Control System," *California Management Review*, 3 (Spring 1961), pp. 4–15.

A Program of Financial Planning and Controls, Financial Management Series, No. 103 (New York: American Management Association, 1953).

Strong, William L., "Decentralized Operations—Control Program," *Controller*, 26 (January 1958), pp. 11–40.

QUESTIONS

5–1 "The higher the rate of return on investment, the better the firm's management." Is this statement true for all firms? Explain. If you disagree with the statement, give examples of businesses in which it might not be true.

5–2 What factors would you attempt to change if you wanted to increase a firm's rate of return on (1) investment or (2) net worth?

5–3 Profit margins and turnover rates vary from industry to industry. What characteristics of different industries account for these variations? Give some contrasting examples to illustrate your answer.

5–4 What are the characteristics of a successful control system? Briefly explain the most important ingredient for a control system.

5–5 Why is it particularly important for a rapidly growing young firm to concern itself with systems of control?

5–6 A simplified control system for evaluating a newly created department might consist of the following aspects: (1) selecting control criteria, (2) establishing cost and sales standards, (3) establishing procedures for evaluating actual performance, and (4) prescribing procedures for remedial actions. What are some factors that should be considered at each step?

PROBLEMS

5-1   For one set of the pairs of companies listed below, chart the following financial ratios over the past seven years:

a) Current
b) Total debt to net worth
c) Sales to total assets
d) Average collection period
e) Sales to inventory turnover
f) Profit after fixed charges and taxes to sales
g) Profit after fixed charges and taxes to net worth

> General Motors and Chrysler
> Boeing and Douglas Aircraft
> Sperry, Rand and International Business Machines
> Standard Oil of New Jersey and Standard Oil of California
> General Electric and Westinghouse

(Data may be obtained from company reports or from an investment manual such as Moody's Industrials or Standard & Poor's Industrials.)

1. Compare the trends in the return on net worth for the two companies in the pair of companies you are analyzing.
2. Indicate the reasons for any difference in trends in rate of return on net worth suggested by your time-trend analysis.

5-2   Fill in the following outline of the du Pont pattern of analysis for one set of the pairs of companies in problem 5-1.

Sales to operating investment _____%	Cash to sales, percentage _____
	Average collection period, days _____
	Inventory turnover, times _____
Return on investment _____%	Net fixed asset turnover, times _____
	Total operating assets $_____
	Operating expenses to sales, percentage _____
Profit to sales _____%	Net income before fixed charges and taxes to total assets, percentage _____
	Net income after fixed charges and taxes $_____

(Data may be obtained from company annual reports or from an investment manual such as Moody's Industrials or Standard & Poor's Industrials.)

1. Using data for the most recent year available, compare the return on investment for the two companies.
2. Indicate the reasons for the difference in observed rates of return suggested by the du Pont analysis.

Chapter 6

Management of Assets

The discussion in the preceding two chapters focused primarily on aspects of financial analysis and financial control. Another important aspect of financial control is management of investment in assets, which is now considered both in detail and from the standpoint of the basic theory involved.

This material represents a link between *control,* which we have emphasized up to this point, and *planning,* which is the major emphasis of the chapters that follow. Planning is the formulation of enterprise goals and the selection between alternative policies and actions to achieve the goals. Control is the comparison between goals and performance, and criteria and policies for modifying behavior to improve performance. Though the subjects are related, the distinctive emphasis of each is shown by the following relations:

Components of Control:
    Standards
    Reference ranges
    Norms
    Bases for evaluation
    Corrective actions

Components of Planning:
    Cause-and-effect relations
    What leads to what
    Behavior relations
    Equations
    Correlation relations

Standards or reference ranges, once developed, provide a basis for exercising control. These are in a sense norms or bases for comparing results against the reference standards. The process of planning involves an understanding of cause-and-effect relations so that a basis for projections into the future can be established. Management of assets will provide foundations for developing both standards and cause-and-effect relations. In this way it provides the link between financial control and financial planning.

The four main categories of assets to be covered in this chapter are (1) cash, (2) receivables, (3) inventories, and (4) fixed assets. Investments in other companies, another category frequently found on the asset side, are covered in Chapters 26 and 27.

Managing assets of all kinds is basically an inventory-type problem. It applies to cash, receivables, and fixed assets, as well as to inventories as such. First, a basic stock must be on hand to balance the inflows and outflows of the items, with the size of the stock depending upon the patterns of flows—whether regular or irregular. Second, because the unexpected may always occur, it is necessary to have safety stocks on hand. They represent the little extra to avoid the costs of not having enough to meet current needs. Third, additional amounts may be required to meet future growth needs. These are anticipation stocks. Related to anticipation stocks is the recognition that there are optimum purchase sizes—economical ordering quantities. In borrowing money or in buying raw materials for production or plants and equipment, it is cheaper to buy more than one at a time or just enough to meet immediate needs. This general rule should be kept in mind in connection with the following presentation on managing investment in cash, receivables, inventories, and fixed assets.

The primary responsibility for managing some items falls on the financial manager. Particularly in matters of management of cash and receivables, his may be the major responsibility. The financial manager will doubtless be involved importantly in fixed assets management, because the amounts involved are so large and their management so vital for the continued well-being of the firm. Inventory management will be more directly the responsibility of the production department, but the financial manager must be familiar with the procedures for inventory management and with the standards for evaluating their effectiveness.

Finally, modern developments in operations research are likely to prove useful in connection with determining asset acquisition policy. Operations research has made and is making impressive strides in inventory model building, and since all assets are in a sense inventories, these new techniques are likely to provide an efficient means of handling acquisition problems. Because the procedures are highly technical, the services are best performed by specialists. Our presentation seeks to indicate the nature of the problems on which assistance may be received, and to develop standards so that the financial manager may judge whether the complicated procedures are producing good results.

CONTROLLING INVESTMENT IN CASH

The starting point in the conservation of investment in assets is effective control of cash and cash equivalent. Cash equivalent includes marketable securities, characteristically held for liquidity purposes. "Cash" primarily signifies, of course, balances held with commercial banks, largely in the form of demand deposits. Approximately 85 to 90 percent of all transactions in the United States are accomplished through the use of "cash" in the form of demand deposits.

The cash holdings by firms throughout a wide range of manufacturing industries vary from about 3 to 5 percent of sales and about 6 to 10 percent of total assets. Among industries generally, including utilities and trade, a wider variation in the ratios of cash to sales and total assets is observed.

Economic theory has now established that businesses or individuals have three primary motives for holding cash: (1) the transaction motive, (2) the precautionary motive, and (3) the speculative motive. These theoretical terms may be clothed with certain concrete aspects in terms of business operations.

The transactions motive for holding cash is to carry out the purchases and sales of the firm. The management of cash is so important in finance that Chapter 13 is devoted entirely to the analysis of the flow of cash into inventories at various stages and of payments for labor, rent, and other items necessary in a production process. The expenses are ultimately embodied into finished inventories. These inventories are sold, and usually result in receivables. At some later date the receivables are collected and once again become cash.

These flows indicate the kinds of needs involved in the transactions use of cash. In some lines of business, such as the utilities, where billings can be cycled throughout the month, cash flows can be scheduled and synchronized closely with the need for the outflow of cash. Hence the cash-to-revenues or cash-to-total-assets ratios for utility firms would be expected to be relatively low. By contrast, in retail trade, a large number of transactions may actually be conducted by physical currency. As a consequence, retail trade requires a higher ratio of cash to sales and cash to total assets.

The seasonality of a business may give rise to a need for cash for the purchase of inventories. For example, raw materials may be available only during a harvest season and may be perishable, as in the food-canning business. Or sales may be seasonal, as are department store sales around the Christmas and Easter holidays, or various phases of sports seasons, giving rise to an increase in needs for cash.

Studies of the ratios of cash to sales and cash to total assets indicate also that the ratios are likely to be somewhat higher among the profitable firms. This fact shows that holding cash is a matter of ability as well as necessity.

The two other traditional motives for holding "cash" are actually satisfied in large part by holdings of near-money assets—short-term government securities and the like. The precautionary motive relates primarily to the predictability of cash inflows and outflows. If the predictability is high, less cash will need to be held against an emergency or other contingency. Another factor that will strongly influence the precautionary motive for holding cash is the ability to obtain additional cash on short notice when circumstances necessitate. Borrowing flexibility is primarily a matter of the strength of the firm's relations with banking institutions and other sources of potential augmentation of its cash holdings.

The speculative motive for holding cash is to be ready for profit-making opportunities that may arise. By and large, accumulations of cash for speculative purposes are not widely found. Holding cash is more a function of the behavior of individual investors. However, the cash and marketable securities account may rise to rather sizable levels as a temporary basis for accumulating the means of financing. The dramatic example of this is the rise in cash and marketable securities of Montgomery Ward in 1958 to $149 million, representing 22 percent of total assets. At a somewhat different level it is interesting to note that to finance its very rapid growth, the International Business Machines Corporation has carried cash and marketable securities as high as 23 percent of its assets in recent years.

To this point the general nature of cash flows has been discussed. With an understanding of the anatomy of cash flows, the financial manager seeks to improve the inflow-outflow pattern of cash. He seeks to improve the inflow rate (1) by better synchronization of flows, (2) by reduction of float, and (3) by prevention of pilferage.

Synchronization of Cash Flows

As an example of synchronization, cash flows may be improved by more frequent requisitioning of funds by divisional offices from the central office. A concrete illustration makes the point clearly.

Some Gulf Oil Corporation divisional field offices, for instance, used to requisition funds once or twice a week; now the treasurer's office insists on daily requisitions, thus keeping some cash on tap as much as four days longer. John Shaw, assistant treasurer, told an American Management Association seminar last year that, on the basis of ten offices, each requiring $500,000 a week, these staggered requisitions free the equivalent of $10 million for one day each week. At 3 per cent interest, this earns better than $42,000 a year.[1]

In addition, effective forecasting can reduce the investment in cash. The cash flow forecasting at Universal Commercial Investment Trust Credit Corporation exemplifies this truth.[2] An assistant treasurer forecasts planned purchases of automobiles by the dealers. The assistant treasurer estimates daily the number of cars shipped to the 10,000 dealers who finance their purchases through Universal CIT. He then estimates how much money should be deposited in Detroit banks that day to pay automobile manufacturers. On one day he estimated a required deposit of $6.4 million; the actual bill for the day was $6.397 million, a difference of one tenth of 1 percent.

Though such close forecasting cannot be achieved by every type of firm, the system enables Universal CIT to economize on the amount of money it must borrow, and thereby to avoid interest expense.

Reduction of Float

Another important method of economizing on the volume of cash required is by reduction of "float." Float refers to funds in transit between cities. Checks received from customers in distant cities are subject to two types of delays: the time required for the check to travel in the mail, and the time required for clearing through the banking system. To reduce these two types of float, a "lock-box plan" can be used. If our firm makes sales in large amounts at far distances, we can establish a lock box in a city in the customer's area. We can arrange to have a bank in the city pick up the checks daily, deposit them, and remit by wire to our bank or banks of deposit. The only lag remaining may be the practice of the distant bank of making certain that the customer has funds in his account before notifying our bank of the availability of the funds.

If our distant customers are scattered, we can establish the lock box in our local city to be picked up by our bank. The bank begins the clearing process, notifying us that the check has been received. In this way the clearing process starts before our firm processes the check.

By these methods float may be reduced by one to five days. Examples of freeing funds in the amount of $1.5 million or more by these methods have been cited by firms.

---

[1] *Business Week* (July 12, 1958).
[2] *Finance* (May 15, 1954), pp. 56–58.

Avoidance of Losses

Control of cash leakages through theft is best worked out in cooperation with the development of effective accounting systems. The fundamental principle here is that both inflows and outflows of cash should be broken into a number of steps. Each step should be in the charge of a different person. In addition, these jobs should be subject to relatively frequent rotation. Such procedures establish conditions under which collusion, even between a large number of people, would be almost impossible because of the checks and cross checks of record keeping that are provided.

Investment of Funds

A firm may have cash to invest for a number of reasons. One is seasonal or cyclical fluctuations in business. As sales expand, inventories and receivables build up. As sales fall off, inventories and receivables, if sound, decrease and become cash. Thus, during a seasonal or cyclical expansion, the firm will need to finance an increase in inventories and receivables. Some firms may borrow as their seasonal or cyclical needs for financing expand. Others, particularly firms in the capital goods industries in which the amplitude of fluctuations is violent, attempt to accumulate cash or near-cash during a downturn to be ready to finance an upturn in business volume.

Firms may also accumulate resources to protect against a number of contingencies. Where uninsurable product warranties are made by firms, they must be ready to meet claims that may arise. Firms in highly competitive industries must have resources to carry them through substantial shifts in the market structure. A firm in an industry in which new markets are developing, for example, foreign markets becoming of increased importance, will find it necessary to have resources to make the change.

Thus a firm may have cash funds to invest for a few weeks, a few months, a few years, or indefinitely because of uncertain contingencies. Investment alternatives are available to meet the needs of the firm. Taking both yield and risk considerations into account, the alternatives are shown at the top of the following page.

The forecast period in which the funds will exceed the needs will determine the maturity pattern of the investments that will be selected by the financial manager. The numerous alternatives can be selected and balanced in such a way that he obtains the maturities and risks appropriate to the financial situation of his firm. From commercial bankers, investment bankers, and brokers, the financial manager can obtain detailed information on each of the forms of investments listed below. Since their characteristics change with shifts in money market conditions, it would be misleading to attempt to give detailed descriptions of these investment outlets. Their characteristics are a matter on which the financial manager must keep up to date. He should follow the principle of making

	*Approximate Maturities**
U. S. Treasury bills	91 to 182 days
U. S. Treasury certificates	9 to 12 months
U. S. Treasury notes	1 to 5 years
Prime commercial paper	Varies up to 270 days
Negotiable certificates of deposit†	
Savings certificates at commercial banks	6 months
Savings accounts at commercial banks	
Savings accounts at savings and loan associations	
Bonds and stocks of other corporations	
Bonds and stocks of the firm in question‡	

* The maturities are those at issue date. For outstanding securities, maturities varying almost by day or week are available.
† See Roy L. Reierson, "A New Money Market Instrument" (New York: Bankers Trust Company, March 24, 1961).
‡ See L. A. Guthart, "More Companies Are Buying Back Their Stock," *Harvard Business Review*, March 1965.

investment selections that offer maturities, yields, and risks appropriate to his firm.

Because some funds are to be held for extended periods, they may be invested with the objective of a higher return than that available from government securities. Such investments may be made in the shares of other companies. "Mostly, however, these are investments pure and simple, not for the sake of control. They were purchased to put the buyer's surplus cash to work hard, producing a larger return than it could, say, in the government bond market."[3]

A long list of the investments is contained in the *Forbes* article. Several patterns are discernible. The percentage of ownership is characteristically small; thus the dominant motive cannot be said to be control. Often the investments are made in firms in related industries. This practice is followed partly because the nature and outlook for such industries are better understood and partly because such investments may yield additional information useful for purchasing or sales activities. For example, suppliers to larger firms may often hold shares in the larger firms for the contacts that will be provided by shareholders' information and meetings. Clearly, control cannot be exercised by the smaller firm. However, the smaller firm may for this reason obtain market information that might otherwise be more difficult to obtain.

MANAGEMENT OF INVESTMENT IN RECEIVABLES

In the present chapter, trade credit refers to accounts *receivable* and is discussed from the standpoint of the use of credit to support and

3 "Part-Time Portfolios," *Forbes* (May 15, 1961), pp. 16–17.

expand sales and from that of the resulting investment required by the firm. In Chapter 14, trade credit refers to accounts *payable* and is discussed from the standpoint of its potentials and limitations as a source of funds.

The ratio of receivables to sales runs in the range from 8 to 12 percent, representing an average collection period of approximately one month. The ratio of receivables to total assets centers from about 16 to 20 percent. However, wide variations are experienced in these ranges, particularly when consideration of nonmanufacturing industries is included.

The major determinants of the level of receivables are (1) volume of credit sales, (2) seasonality of sales, (3) rules for credit limits, (4) terms of sales and credit policies of individual firms, and (5) collection policies. Variations in the ratios of receivables to sales (or the average collection periods) observed in different firms reflect the differential impact of the factors listed.

Variations in terms of sale reflect the customs of the line of business. A very important influence, however, is the perishability of the product. For example, very low ratios are observed in the following industries: bakery products, milk products, meat products, and textiles. On the other hand, relatively high ratios of receivables to sales are observed in the construction, industrial machinery, agricultural machinery, office equipment, and printing and publishing industries.

In addition, higher ratios of receivables to sales are observed among larger firms. Larger firms are able to obtain funds at lower cost and tend to be wholesalers of credit obtained from financial institutions and reloaned to smaller firms. An analysis of the ratio of receivables to sales or total assets on the basis of differential profitability of firms indicates that profitability, as such, has no great influence on the extent to which a firm will be holding receivables.

Credit Policy

The starting point in formulating a credit policy is the characteristic credit terms of the industry. A firm must meet the terms provided by other firms in the industry. However, when the customer is a poor credit risk, the terms will be altered in a downward direction to protect the firm extending trade credit. A central task in formulating credit policy is an evaluation of the credit worthiness of the potential customer.

To evaluate the credit risk, the credit manager considers the C's of credit: *character, capacity, capital, collateral, conditions.* "Character" refers to the probability that the customer will honor his obligations. This factor is of considerable importance because every credit transaction implies a *promise* to pay. There is thus a moral hazard of whether the promise will be fulfilled.

"Capacity" is judgment of the ability of the customer. This is gauged by the past record of the business, supplemented by observation of the customer's plant or store and business methods. "Capital" is measured by the general financial position of the firm, which is indicated by a financial-ratio analysis, with special emphasis on the tangible net worth of the enterprise. "Collateral" is represented by assets which the customer may offer as a pledge for security of the credit that is extended to him. Finally, "conditions" refers to the impact of general economic trends on the firm or special developments in certain areas of the economy that may affect the customer's ability to meet his obligations.

The C's of credit represent the factors by which the credit risk is judged. How information on these items is obtained is now considered. Information will be obtained from the firm's previous experience with the customer, supplemented by a well-developed system of information-gathering groups. In this presentation two major sources of external information will be described.

The first is the work of the credit associations. By periodic meetings of local groups and by direct communication, information on experience with creditors is exchanged. More formally, credit interchange is provided. Credit interchange is a system developed by the National Association of Credit Management for assembling and distributing information on the ledger experience of creditors. The interchange reports show the paying record of the debtor, industries from which he is buying, and the trading areas in which his purchases are being made.[4]

The second is the work of the credit-reporting agencies. Dun & Bradstreet is the well-known general reporting agency. Agencies that specialize in coverage of a limited number of industries also provide information. Representative of these are the National Credit Office and the Lyon Furniture Mercantile Agency. Some of the services of Dun & Bradstreet are briefly described to indicate the nature of the information obtainable.

The Dun & Bradstreet Reference Book is published six times a year and covers the entire United States and Canada. Regional and state editions are also published. The Reference Book contains listings of firms and their credit ratings by town location, town population, and names of local banks. The credit ratings shown in Table 6–1 indicate both estimated financial strength and a composite credit appraisal. A credit appraisal of "high" indicates that financial affairs appear healthy and meet a number of important tests with reference to the C's of credit.

---

4 For additional information, see *Credit Management Handbook*, Second Edition (Homewood, Ill.: Irwin, 1965), a publication of the National Association of Credit Management.

TABLE 6-1

KEY TO RATINGS

ESTIMATED FINANCIAL STRENGTH			COMPOSITE CREDIT APPRAISAL			
			HIGH	GOOD	FAIR	LIMITED
AA	Over	$1,000,000	A1	1	1½	2
A+	Over	750,000	A1	1	1½	2
A	500,000 to	750,000	A1	1	1½	2
B+	300,000 to	500,000	1	1½	2	2½
B	200,000 to	300,000	1	1½	2	2½
C+	125,000 to	200,000	1	1½	2	2½
C	75,000 to	125,000	1½	2	2½	3
D+	50,000 to	75,000	1½	2	2½	3
D	35,000 to	50,000	1½	2	2½	3
E	20,000 to	35,000	2	2½	3	3½
F	10,000 to	20,000	2½	3	3½	4
G	5,000 to	10,000	3	3½	4	4½
H	3,000 to	5,000	3	3½	4	4½.
J	2,000 to	3,000	3	3½	4	4½
K	1,000 to	2,000	3	3½	4	4½
L	Up to	1,000	3½	4	4½	5

CLASSIFICATION AS TO BOTH ESTIMATED FINANCIAL STRENGTH AND CREDIT APPRAISAL

FINANCIAL STRENGTH BRACKET			EXPLANATION
1	$125,000 to	$1,000,000 and Over	When only the numeral (1, 2, 3, or 4) appears, it is an indication that the estimated financial strength, while not definitely classified, is presumed to be within the range of the ($) figures in the corresponding bracket and that a condition is believed to exist which warrants credit in keeping with that assumption.
2	20,000 to	125,000	
3	2,000 to	20,000	
4	Up to	2,000	

NOT CLASSIFIED OR ABSENCE OF RATING

The absence of a rating, expressed by the dash (—), or by two hyphens (- -), is not to be construed as unfavorable but signifies circumstances difficult to classify within condensed rating symbols and should suggest to the subscriber the advisability of obtaining additional information.

SEE REFERENCE BOOK FOR EXPLANATION OF ABSENCE OF A LISTING AND ADDITIONAL SYMBOLS USED IN REFERENCE BOOK

When the rating of a firm is less than high, the financial manager may wish to obtain more specific information, which can be obtained from credit reports sold by Dun & Bradstreet. The credit reports follow the forms indicated in Table 6–2. They provide a synopsis of the main information about the customer: his credit rating and history, discussion of the business operations and their location, financial information, and payment experience. The payment experience indicates whether the customer takes discounts, whether he pays promptly, and by how many days he delays payment if he does not pay promptly.

The above information can be translated into risk classes, grouped according to the probability of risk associated with sales to a customer. The combination of rating and supplementary information might lead to the following groupings of loss experience:

Group Number	Loss Ratio, in Percentages
1	none
2	0–½
3	½–1
4	1–2
5	2–5
6	5–10
7	10–20
8	over 20

TABLE 6-2

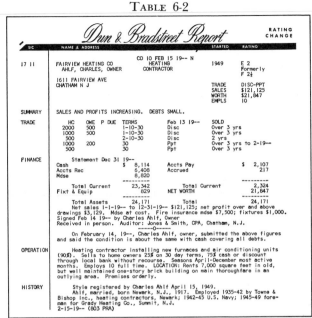

If the selling firm has a margin over the sum of direct operating costs and of all delivery and selling costs of 20 percent, and is producing at less than full capacity, it may adopt the following credit policies. It may sell on customary credit terms to groups 1 to 5, sell to groups 6 and 7 under more stringent credit terms, such as cash on delivery, and require advance payments from group 8 customers. So long as the bad debt loss ratios are less than 20 percent, the additional sales are contributing something to overhead.

Credit limits, which may be related to risk classes, are management procedures that set a maximum on the total amount of credit which may be extended to a firm without a review of the customer's general credit position. They may be based on experience with the customer and related to a calculation of his appropriate needs for credit. Credit limits may be set at some fraction of working capital or net worth. For example, a customer with current assets of $80,000 and current liabilities of $50,000 has working capital of $30,000. If the supplying firm applies the rule of one fifth of working capital, the buyer's credit limit is $6,000. On the other hand, the limit may be relative to the net worth of the buyer. For example, if a customer has $50,000 net worth and the credit limit is one fifth of net worth, the credit department will allow an outstanding balance of $10,000.[5]

In reviewing the granting of credit, the financial manager should not

---

5 A credit limit of one fifth of net worth is based on the following logic. Credit should not exceed the owner's stake. Assuming that the customer has four other major suppliers, the seller should not extend credit of more than one fifth of the total credit.

be guided by bad debt loss ratios alone. These must also be related to the potential contribution that additional sales have made to overhead costs. Accounts receivable represent an investment. The return on this investment can be calculated by taking the contribution to additional net earnings and determining the return from the investment in receivables, as in any capital budgeting problem, described in the following chapter.

Two remaining aspects of the management of investment in receivables should be noted.

Collection.   Though bad debts and overdue collections may be justified for their contribution to additional sales and profits, controls must be established. One useful control device is the "aging schedule." This is a tabulation of receivables outstanding by the length of time they are outstanding. A summary tabulation provides a succinct picture of collection effectiveness.

Outstanding	Amount	Percentage
Fewer than 30 days	$1,300,000	65
30 to 59 days	400,000	20
60 to 89 days	200,000	10
90 days or more	100,000	5
Total	$2,000,000	100

The aging schedule is a valuable supplement to ratios of receivables to sales or to the average collection period. The aging schedule calculated periodically will reveal any tendency of slowing collections. It will be a danger signal of the possibility of deterioration in the accounts and unusual bad debt losses. Aging schedules may be required by loan officers from prospective borrowers as a regular procedure.

Credit insurance.   Credit insurance exists, as do other forms of insurance, to protect the firm against catastrophe hazards. When a large percentage of a firm's sales is made to a small number of accounts, credit insurance should be seriously considered. Though there are many forms of coverage, the essential elements are

1. *Primary loss:* The average bad debt loss ratio for the industry that will not be covered by insurance
2. *Coinsurance:* Portion of loss that must be carried by the insured
3. *Coverage:* Maximum insurance for each customer of the insured, related to the account's credit rating (admissible losses)

An example will illustrate the application of these concepts.

Customer	Coverage	Loss	Admissible Losses
Jones Paper Co.	$10,000	$12,000	$10,000
Smith Paper Co.	15,000	5,000	5,000
Brown Paper Co.	30,000	20,000	20,000

Assume that the coinsurance is 10 percent. The primary loss is 1 percent of covered sales, and the policyholder's sales volume for the year on insured accounts is $200,000.

The amount collectible from the insurance company can be calculated as follows:

Total admissible credit losses on insured accounts	$35,000
Coinsurance (10% of credit loss on insured accounts)	3,500
Net covered loss after deduction of coinsurance	31,500
Amount of primary loss (1% of $200,000)	2,000
Net recoverable loss from insurance company	$29,500

Credit insurance, like other forms of insurance, provides an economic function in protecting firms from unusual credit hazards. The primary determinant of whether such insurance should be carried is the existence of catastrophe hazards.[6]

Summary. A firm can economize on the amount of funds tied up in receivables by following a number of policies. One is to have the financial manager guide the credit manager and have him work closely and effectively with the sales manager. In addition, well-thought-out pre-established credit limits will minimize the investment in receivables without adverse effects on the volume of sales. Finally, alert collection methods, together with good credit-granting policies, will hold down bad-debt-loss ratios, as well as minimize the amount of funds tied up in accounts receivable.

The central decision in the evaluation of receivables management involves balancing bad debt losses against sales losses. If credit policies are extremely stringent, bad debt losses may be held to virtually zero. However, to refuse to sell to marginal customers means reduced sales. Reduced sales result in lowered profits. A proper evaluation requires balancing the contributions to net profits from increased sales against the potential increases in bad debt loss ratios resulting from accepting orders from customers of doubtful credit worthiness.

INVENTORY CONTROL

Manufacturing firms generally have three kinds of inventories: *raw materials, work in process,* and *finished goods.* The levels of raw material inventories are influenced by levels of anticipated production, seasonality

6 For excellent examples of situations in which credit insurance was effectively used, see the section "Case Histories of Credit Insurance in Use," *Credit Management Handbook,* Second Edition (Homewood, Ill.: Irwin, 1965).

of production, reliability of sources of supply, and efficiency of scheduling purchases and production operations.

Work in process inventory is strongly influenced by the length of the production period, which is the time between placing raw material in production and completing the finished product. Inventory turnover can be increased by decreasing the production period. One means of accomplishing this end is perfecting engineering techniques to speed up the manufacturing process. Another means of reducing work in process is to buy items rather than to make them. Standards formulated by the financial manager may lead to substantial improvements in the levels of work in process inventory.

The level of finished goods inventories is a matter of coordination of production and sales. The financial manager can stimulate sales by changing credit terms or by allowing credit to marginal risks. Whether the goods remain on the books as inventories or as receivables, the financial manager has to finance them. Many times firms find it desirable to make the sale and thus take one step nearer to realizing cash. The potential profits can outweigh the additional collection risk.

Determinants of Size of Inventories

Although wide variations occur, a concentration of inventory to sales ratios may be observed in the 12 to 20 percent range, and a corresponding concentration of inventory to total asset ratios in the 16 to 30 percent range.

The major determinants of investment in inventory are the following: (1) length and technical nature of the production processes, (2) durability versus perishability or style factor in the end product. Inventories in the tobacco industry are high because of the long curing process. Likewise, in the machinery-manufacturing industries, inventories are large because of the long work in process period. On the other hand, inventory ratios are low in coal mining and in oil and gas production; no raw materials are used and the goods in process are small in relation to sales. Because of the seasonality of the raw material, inventories are large in the canning and the carpet industries.

With respect to the durability and style factors, large inventories are found in the hardware and the precious-metals industries, because durability is great and the style factor is small. Inventory ratios are low in baking because of the perishability of the final product. Inventories are low in printing because the items are manufactured to order and require negligible finished inventories.

A potential for tremendous improvement in inventory control is offered by the use of computers and operations analysis. Though the techniques are far too diverse and complicated for treatment in this text, the financial manager should be prepared to make use of the contributions of specialists who have developed effective procedures for minimizing the investment in inventory.[7]

Inventory Decision Models

As an illustration of the systematic approach to inventory control, the use of a basic EOQ (economical ordering quantity) procedure may be illustrated.[8] The level of inventories is determined by reliability of sources of supply, degree of integration of the firm, perishability of the item, and other factors which depend upon the nature of the product. Within these limits, however, the manager can reduce inventory commitments. Analytical work in recent years has shown that the optimum size of investment in inventory can be controlled by determining the economical ordering quantity (EOQ). Ordering quantity serves as an indicator of the investment in inventory in the following manner. If it is assumed that (1) the ordering quantity is 100 units, (2) the firm's inventory is virtually zero by the time the new order arrives, and (3) inventory is withdrawn at a regular rate, the amount of inventory on the average will be

$$\frac{100 + 0}{2} = 50$$

Thus the average size of inventory may be approximated by the order quantity divided by 2. A widely used formula for the determination of EOQ is

$$EOQ = \sqrt{\frac{2 \times R \times O}{P \times I}} = \sqrt{\frac{2 \times 100 \times 10}{1 \times 0.2}} = 100$$

where

EOQ = economical order quantity
R = sales for the period in units = 100

---

[7] Illustrative of the techniques at the practical level is the following:

Raytheon's new system works like this: Tabulator cards are inserted in each package of five electronic tubes leaving Raytheon's warehouse. As the merchandise is sold, the distributor collects the cards and files his replacement order without doing paperwork. He simply sends in the cards which are identified by an account number, the type of merchandise, and the price of the units he orders.

Western Union Telegraph Co. equipment accepts the punched cards and transmits information on them to the warehouse, where it is duplicated on other punched cards. A typical order of 5,000 tubes of varying types can be received in about 17 minutes, Raytheon says. It can be assembled in about 90 minutes and delivered to Boston's Logan Airport in an additional 45 minutes. "Orders from 3,000 miles away can be delivered within 24 hours, a saving of 13 days in some cases.—Roger B. Rowand, "Tactics Vary As Firms Try to Cut Warehouse Costs, Speed Service," *Wall Street Journal* (May 26, 1961), pp. 1, 11.

[8] For elaborations of the technique, see R. B. Fetter and W. C. Dalleck, *Decision Models for Inventory Management* (Homewood, Ill.: Irwin, 1961).

P	= price paid per unit	= \$1
O	= purchasing cost per order	= \$10
I	= inventory carrying charge as a percentage of the inventory value	
		$= 20\% = 0.2$

$$A \quad = \text{average inventory} = \frac{EOQ}{2} = 50$$

Had sales been estimated at 200 units, the *EOQ* would have been 144 and the average inventory 72. Notice that a doubling of sales leads to less than a doubling of inventories.

The formula may be utilized to determine the EOQ and the average inventory, under a series of assumptions with regard to values of the variables, as is shown in Table 6–3. The results of the calculations are graphed in Figure 6–1. The graph shows sales and the corresponding

TABLE 6–3

RELATION BETWEEN SALES AND INVENTORY LEVELS RESULTING FROM USE OF ECONOMICAL ORDER QUANTITY

	Situation Number								
I		II		III		IV		V	
$P = \$1$		$P = \$1$		$P = \$1$		$P = \$1$		$P = \$1$	
$I = 20\%$		$I = 20\%$		$I = 10\%$		$I = 5\%$		$I = 30\%$	
$O = \$10$		$O = \$5$		$O = \$10$		$O = \$10$		$O = \$20$	
S	A	S	A	S	A	S	A	S	A
1,000	158	1,000	112	1,000	224	1,000	316	1,000	183
2,000	224	2,000	158	2,000	316	2,000	447	2,000	258
3,000	274	3,000	194	3,000	387	3,000	548	3,000	316
4,000	316	4,000	224	4,000	447	4,000	632	4,000	365
5,000	354	5,000	250	5,000	500	5,000	707	5,000	408
6,000	387	6,000	274	6,000	548	6,000	774	6,000	447

S = Level of sales in units.
A = Level of inventories in units.

average level of inventories as a series of lines somewhat curved over. The height and the slope of each line are different; they depend upon the values of such critical factors as purchasing costs and inventory carrying costs. But the significant fact from the standpoint of the financial manager is that a stable and dependable relation exists between sales and inventories when the strategic variables influencing inventory policy are known. The financial manager can work with the production department in determining the EOQ. From the EOQ he can develop financial standards for inventory levels.

The use of economical order quantity models not only contributes to

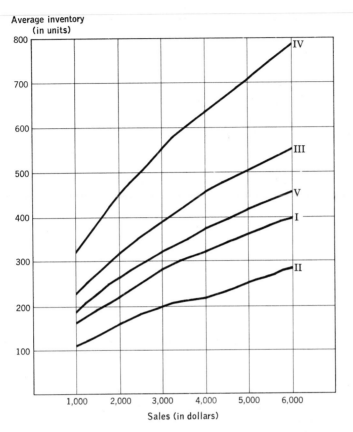

Average inventory
(in units)

Sales (in dollars)

(*See Table 6-3 for data*)

Fig. 6-1. Relation between Inventory and Sales Based
on the Formula for the Economical Order Point

sound inventory management but also provides a basis for projecting requirements for investment in inventories.[9] In other words, sound asset management results in stable relations, which facilitate forecasts of financing requirements.

INVESTMENT IN CAPITAL ASSETS

The purchase of fixed assets is of particular significance to a firm, because the amounts involved are relatively large and represent commitments for a relatively long period, as long as 20 to 30 years. The amount

---

[9] The newer operations research techniques for inventory control that have been investigated by the authors also result in stable relations between the level of sales and the size of inventories.

of investment in fixed assets as measured by the ratio of net fixed assets to sales runs as high as 80 to 85 percent of the total assets of public utilities, and as low as 10 percent or less of the assets of firms in wholesale trade. The general range for net fixed assets to sales for manufacturing firms is 15 to 40 percent, and ratios of net fixed assets to total assets are found in the 30 to 50 percent range.

Investments in fixed assets tend to be very high in the producer-goods industries, such as industrial machinery and machine tools, and in producer-materials industries, such as iron and steel, petroleum, and chemicals. The ratios of fixed assets to total assets are considerably lower in the clothing, apparel, meat, and tobacco industries.

A firm may economize on the use of fixed assets by buying second-hand rather than new assets. This procedure, however, often involves buying obsolete items that require more maintenance or which do not provide as high an output per dollar of investment as those provided by more modern equipment. Sometimes a firm can economize on an investment in fixed assets by renting rather than owning. As will be shown in Chapter 16, however, leasing uses up a portion of the financing ability of a firm; it cannot therefore be regarded as complete avoidance of investment.

In evaluating the control of investment in all the items discussed, as in our presentation of the materials of financial analysis, a financial manager will rely heavily on the use of the following. (1) *Industry norms:* Comparisons with achievements of the industry on the average or with close competitors will provide a guide to the effectiveness of investment in assets by an individual business firm. (2) *Historical norms:* A time-trend analysis of investment items, especially if related to the causal factors that produce the investment, will provide a basis for evaluation of management effectiveness in investing in individual asset items.

Overriding both the preceding tests, which are necessarily comparative or relative, are the formal methods of capital budgeting. Whether the investment is in current assets or in fixed assets, the fundamental principles must be the same. Commitment of funds in assets must produce sufficient profits to justify tying up funds in these items. An understanding of how these techniques can be used requires an understanding of capital budgeting, which is a profitability analysis of the effectiveness of investment decisions by business firms. Capital budgeting is the subject of the following chapter.

SUMMARY

Financial managers are primarily interested in minimizing asset investment in order to increase profits for a given level of sales. Elements of policy for conservation of asset investment are basic decisions that must be made by the firm.

Identifying and eliminating the least profitable markets will increase gross margins. Such action eliminates the need for funds in the one area and releases them for use in more profitable operations. Furthermore, effective management requires policies related to the nature of the asset itself.

SELECTED REFERENCES

Andrews, Victor L., "Captive Finance Companies," *Harvard Business Review* (July-August, 1964), pp. 80–92.

Bierman, Harold, Jr., and Alan K. McAdams, *Management Decisions for Cash and Marketable Securities* (Ithaca, N. Y.: Cornell University Press, 1963).

Carroll, R. P., and F. E. Schneider, "Developing Order Points and Quantities for Inventory Control," *N.A.A. Bulletin*, 42 (December 1960).

Dun & Bradstreet, *How to Control Accounts Receivable for Greater Profits* (New York: Dun & Bradstreet, 1959).

Magee, John F., "Guides to Inventory Policy," *Harvard Business Review*, 34 (January-June 1956).

Oline, Robert H., "Rapid Reference Charts for Economical Production Order Quantities," *N.A.A. Bulletin*, 42 (December 1960), pp. 75–78.

Robbins, Sidney M., "Getting More Mileage Out of Cash," *N.A.A. Bulletin*, 42 (September 1960), pp. 65–74.

Snyder, Arthur, "Principles of Inventory Management," *Financial Executive*, 32 (April 1964), pp. 13–21.

Whitin, T. M., "Inventory Control in Theory and Practice," *Quarterly Journal of Economics*, 46 (November 1952), pp. 502–521.

QUESTIONS

6–1 Better methods of communications are making it less necessary for firms to hold large cash balances. Why?

6–2 The highly developed financial system of the United States, with its myriad of different near-cash assets, has greatly reduced cash balance requirements by reducing the need for transactions balances. Discuss.

6–3 Assuming its volume of business remained constant, would you expect a firm to have higher cash balances (demand deposits) during a "tight-money" or an "easy-money" period? Does this situation have any ramifications for federal monetary policy?

6–4 If a firm sells on terms of net 30 and its accounts are on the average 30 days overdue, what will its investment in receivables be if its credit sales approximate $720,000?

6–5 "It is difficult to judge the performance of many of our employees, but not that of the credit manager. If he's performing perfectly, credit losses are zero, and the higher our losses (as a percent of sales), the worse his performance." Evaluate the statement.

6–6 Explain how a firm may reduce its investment in inventory by having suppliers hold raw materials inventories and customers hold finished goods inventories. What are the limitations of such a policy?

6–7 What factors are likely to reduce the holdings of inventory in relation to sales in the future? What factors will tend to increase the ratio? What is your judgment of the net effect?

6–8 What are the probable effects of the following on inventory holdings?

1) Manufacture of a part formerly purchased from an outside supplier.
2) Greater use of air freight.
3) Increase, from 7 to 17, in the number of styles produced.
4) Your firm receives large price reductions from a manufacturer of bathing suits if they are purchased in December and January.

PROBLEMS

6–1   The Hill Production Company sells 150,000 oil-pipe connector units at $25 per unit. The costs of production are as follows:

Selling price		$25
Cost of goods sold per unit:		
Direct material	$8	
Direct labor	7	
Factory overhead	5	20
Gross margin		$5
General and administrative expenses	$1	
Selling expense	1	2
Net profit per unit		$3

The firm is operating with one shift. It can sell an additional 150,000 units and go to a second shift at the $25 price with a probable credit loss of 10 percent on additional sales and additional collection costs of $50,000. With the additional sales, factory overhead will rise by $250,000 and general and administrative expenses by $50,000, because of the increased collection costs.

1. Based on the data given, should the additional credit sales be made?
2. What other factors would be taken into account for such a decision?

6–2   The Wayne Machinery Company has sales of $40 million per year in good years and $25 million in poor years. Its fixed assets are $12 million; receivables and inventories are 40 percent of sales. Total assets are $30 million; the difference between total assets and operating assets is cash available for investment.

   The firm must have liquidity because of substantial risks under product warranties. In addition, the firm must be ready to meet extended terms provided by foreign competitors.

1. How much cash does the firm have to invest in good years? in poor years?
2. Suggest three kinds of investments to be used by this firm.

6–3   The following relations for inventory purchase and storage costs have been established by analysis for the Irwin Manufacturing Corporation.

1) Orders must be placed in multiples of 100 units.
2) Requirements for the year are 50,000 units (use 50 weeks in a year for calculations).
3) Price per unit, $3.
4) Inventory carrying charge, 10 percent of average inventory.
5) Purchasing cost per order, $18.75.
6) Desired safety stock is 3,000 units.
7) Two weeks are required for delivery.

1. What is the economical order size?

2. What is the optimal number of orders to be placed?

3. At what inventory level should a reorder be made?

6-4 A firm has sales of $2.5 million. The primary loss is 0.008 percent of sales. The coinsurance clause is 20 percent. The insurance coverage on each account in the following classes of accounts is as follows:

D & B Rating	Coverage Limit per Account
C 1½	$40,000
D 1½	30,000
E 2	15,000

Losses are incurred on one account in each class as follows:

D & B Rating	Amount of Loss
C 1½	$25,000
D 1½	25,000
E 2	25,000

What amount can be collected from the insurance company on the losses incurred?

Chapter 7

Capital Budgeting

Capital budgeting involves the whole process of planning expenditures whose returns are expected to extend beyond one year. The choice of one year is arbitrary, of course, but it is a convenient cutoff time for distinguishing between types of expenditures. Obvious examples of capital outlays are expenditures for land, buildings, and equipment. Also, an advertising or promotion program or a program of research and development expenditures is likely to have an impact beyond one year and hence comes within the classification of a capital budgeting expenditure.[1]

It is not the purpose of this definition to set out artificial boundaries or criteria for particular kinds of outlays. The basis for the distinction is a practical one. When outlays are made and the results continue over an extended period, several implications of considerable importance for the firm follow.

SIGNIFICANCE OF CAPITAL BUDGETING

A number of factors combine to make capital budgeting one of the most important areas of strategic decision making with which financial management is involved. First and foremost, the fact that the results continue over an extended period means that the decision maker has lost

---

[1] Though this discussion is focused on capital budgeting related to expenditures on fixed assets, the theory and techniques are equally applicable to all kinds of asset investments by business. Hence, while the authors follow traditional practices of relating capital budgeting to investment in fixed assets, it should be remembered that the techniques discussed are widely applicable.

some of his flexibility. He has made a commitment into the future. For example, the purchase of an asset with an economic life of ten years requires a long period of waiting before the final results of the action can be known. The decision maker has committed funds for this period, and he is now a hostage of future events.

Asset expansion is fundamentally related to expected future sales. A decision to buy or to construct a fixed asset that is going to last five years involves an implicit five-year sales forecast. Indeed, the economic life of an asset purchased represents an implicit forecast for the duration of the economic life of the asset. Hence failure to forecast accurately will result in overinvestment or underinvestment in fixed assets.

An erroneous forecast of asset needs can result in serious consequences for a firm. If the firm has invested too much in assets, it will be incurring unnecessarily heavy expenses. If it has not spent enough on fixed assets, two serious consequences may arise. First, its equipment may not be sufficiently modern to enable it to produce competitively. Second, if it has inadequate capacity, it may lose a portion of its share of the market to rival firms. To regain lost customers characteristically requires heavy selling expenses or price reductions, or both.

Another problem is to phase properly the availability of capital assets. For example, the executive vice-president of a decorative-tile company recently gave the authors an illustration of the importance of capital budgeting. His firm tried to operate near capacity most of the time. For about four years there had been intermittent spurts in the demand for their product, and when these spurts occurred the firm had to turn away orders. After a sharp increase in demand, the firm would add capacity by renting an additional building, then purchasing and installing the appropriate equipment. But it would take six to eight months to have the additional capacity ready. At about this point the company would find that there was no demand for its increased output—other firms had already expanded their operations and had taken an increased share of the market, with the result that demand for this firm had leveled off. If the firm had properly forecast demand and had planned its increase in capacity six months or one year in advance, it would have been able to maintain its market—indeed, to obtain a larger share of the market.

Good capital budgeting will also improve the timing of asset acquisitions and the quality of assets purchased. This situation follows from the nature of capital goods and of their producers. Capital goods are not ordered by firms until they see that sales are going to press on capacity. Such occasions occur simultaneously for many firms. When the heavy orders come in, the producers of capital goods find that they go from a situation of idle capacity to one where they cannot meet all the orders that have been placed. Consequently, large backlogs of orders pile up.

Since the production of capital goods involves a relatively long work in process period, a year or more of waiting may be involved before the additional capital goods are available. This factor has obvious implications for purchasing agents and plant managers.

Another reason for the importance of capital budgeting is that asset expansion typically involves substantial expenditures. When a firm is going to spend a considerable amount of money, it must make the proper plans—large amounts of funds are not available automatically. A firm contemplating a major capital expenditure program may need to arrange its financing several years in advance in order to have the funds required for the expansion.

Finally, it has been said with a great deal of truth that many firms fail not because they have too much capital equipment, but because they have too little. While the conservative approach of having a small amount of capital equipment may be appropriate at times, such an approach may also be fatal if a firm's competitors install modern, automated equipment that permits them to produce a better product and sell it at a lower price.

Evidence suggests that American business has erred on the side of having replacement criteria which are too stringent, with the result that replacement is too slow. A 1958 survey made by the McGraw-Hill Department of Economics estimated that a $95 billion equipment modernization program was needed by American business.[2] In another survey the *American Machinist* found that, in 1958, 60 percent of machine tools were ten years old or older, and 23 percent were 20 years old or older.[3] Though these data did not prove that the machine tools were obsolete, they do suggest that replacement may not be as prompt as the vigorous growth of the economy requires.

AN OVER-ALL VIEW OF CAPITAL BUDGETING

Capital budgeting is, in essence, simply an application of the classic economic theory of the firm; namely, a firm should operate at the point where its marginal revenue is just equal to its marginal cost. When this rule is applied to the capital budgeting decision, marginal revenue is taken to be the percentage rate of return on investments, while marginal cost is the firm's cost of capital.

A greatly simplified version of the concept is depicted in Figure 7–1. Here the horizontal axis measures the dollars of investment during a year, while the vertical axis shows both the percentage cost of capital and the

---

2 *Electronics*, October 24, 1958, p. 65.
3 November 17, 1958.

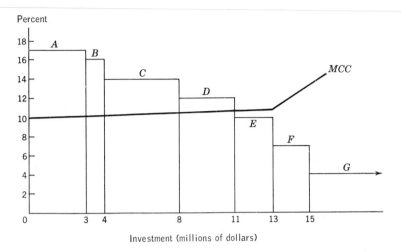

Fig. 7-1.   Illustrative Capital Budgeting Decision Process

rate of return on projects. The projects are themselves denoted by the boxes—project A, for example, calls for an outlay of $3 million and promises a 17 percent rate of return; project B requires $1 million and yields about 16 percent; and so on. The last investment, project G, simply involves buying 4 percent government bonds, which may be purchased in unlimited quantities.

The curve *MCC* designates the marginal cost of capital, or the cost of each additional dollar acquired for purposes of making capital expenditures. As it is drawn in this hypothetical illustration, the cost of capital is constant at 10 percent until the firm has raised about $13 million, after which it turns up. To maximize profits, the firm should accept projects A through D, obtaining and investing $11 million, and should reject E, F, and G.

At the applied level, the process is considerably more complex than this simple example would suggest. Projects do not just appear; a continuing stream of good investment opportunities results from hard thinking, careful planning, and often, large outlays for research and development. In addition, some very difficult measurement problems are involved; the sales and costs associated with particular projects must be estimated, frequently for many years into the future. Last, some difficult conceptual problems arise over the method of calculating rates of return and the cost of capital.

Businessmen are required to take action, however, even in the face of the kinds of problems described, and this requirement has led to the development of certain procedures that assist in making optimal investment decisions. One of these procedures, forecasting, is discussed in the following chapter, while the important subject of the cost of capital is deferred to Chapter 12. The essentials of the other elements of capital budgeting are taken up in the remainder of this chapter.

Investment Proposals

Aside from the actual generation of ideas, the first step in the capital budgeting process is to assemble in a coherent manner the proposed new investments, together with the data necessary to appraise them. Though practices vary from firm to firm, proposals dealing with asset acquisitions are frequently grouped according to the following categories:

1. Replacements
2. Expansion: additional capacity in existing product lines
3. Expansion: new product lines
4. Other

These groupings are somewhat arbitrary, and it is frequently difficult to decide the appropriate category for a particular investment. In spite of such difficulties, the scheme is used quite widely and, as shall be seen, with good reason.

Ordinarily, replacement decisions are the simplest to make. Assets wear out and become obsolete, and they must be replaced if production is to continue. The firm has a very good idea of the cost savings to be obtained by replacing an old asset, and it knows the consequences of non-replacement. All in all, the outcomes of most replacement decisions can be predicted with a high degree of confidence.

An example of the second investment classification is a proposal for adding more machines of the type already in use or the opening of another branch in a city-wide chain of food stores. Expansion investments are frequently incorporated in replacement decisions. To illustrate, an old, inefficient machine may be replaced by one both larger and more efficient.

A degree of uncertainty—sometimes extremely high—is clearly involved in expansion, but the firm at least has the advantage of having built up production and sales experience with similar machines or stores. When it considers an investment of the third kind, expansion into new product lines, little if any experience data are available on which to base decisions. To illustrate, when General Motors decided to develop the diesel engine for commercial application, it had very little idea of either the development costs or the specific applications to which the engine could be put. Under such circumstances, any estimates must at best be treated as very crude approximations.

The "other" category is a catchall and includes intangibles, for example, a proposal to boost employee morale by installing a music system.

Major strategic decisions such as plans for overseas expansion or merger acquisitions might also be included here, but more frequently they are treated separately from the regular capital budget.

Administrative Details

The remaining aspects of capital budgeting involve administrative matters. Approvals are typically required at higher levels within the organization as we move away from replacement decisions and as the sums involved increase. One of the most important functions of boards of directors is to approve the major outlays in a capital budgeting program. Such decisions are crucial for the future well-being of the firm.

The planning horizon for capital budgeting programs varies with the nature of the industry. When sales can be forecast with a high degree of reliability for ten to 20 years, the planning period is likely to be correspondingly long. Also, when the product-technology developments in the industry require an eight-to-ten-year cycle to develop a new major product, as in certain segments of the aircraft or the electronics industries, a correspondingly long planning period will be necessary.

After a capital budget has been adopted, payments must be scheduled. Characteristically, the finance department is responsible for scheduling payments and for acquiring funds to meet payment-schedule requirements. In addition, the finance department will be primarily responsible for cooperating with other members of operating divisions to compile systematic records on the uses of funds and the uses of equipment purchased in capital budgeting programs. Effective capital budgeting programs require such information as the basis for periodic review and the evaluation of capital expenditures.

The foregoing represents a brief overview of the administrative aspects of capital budgeting; the analytical problems involved are considered next.

CHOOSING BETWEEN ALTERNATIVE PROPOSALS

In most firms there are more proposals for projects than the firm is able or willing to finance. Some proposals are good, others are poor; and methods must be developed for distinguishing between them. Essentially, the end product is a ranking of the proposals and a cutoff point for determining how far down the ranked list to go.

In part, proposals are eliminated because they are *mutually exclusive*. Mutually exclusive proposals are alternative methods of doing the same job. If one piece of equipment is chosen to do the job, the others will not be required. Thus, if there is a need to improve the process control system in a chemical plant, the job may be done by additional instruments, by new types of instruments, or by the application of computers. The selection of one method of doing the job makes it unnecessary to use the others. They are mutually exclusive items.

Independent items are pieces of capital equipment that are being considered for different kinds of projects, or tasks that need to be accomplished. For example, in addition to the items mentioned, a chemical firm may need equipment to package and to measure the end items. The work would call for a packaging machine, and the purchase of equipment for this end item would be independent of the equipment purchased for process control.

To distinguish among the many items that compete for the allocation of the firm's capital funds, a ranking procedure must be developed. This procedure involves, first, calculating the estimated benefits from the use of equipment; and secondly, translating the estimated benefits into a measure of the advantage of the purchase of the equipment. Thus an estimate of benefits is required, and a conversion of the benefits into a ranking measure must be developed.

Most discussions of measuring benefits are relatively brief, but it is important to emphasize that in the entire capital budgeting procedure, probably nothing is of greater importance than a reliable estimate of the cost savings or revenue increases that will be achieved from the prospective outlay of capital funds. But these estimates are likely to be more closely related to the facts of particular situations than they are subject to generalizations.

The nature of the task of calculating savings from a proposed investment is indicated by a brief consideration of the items that may affect benefits, for example, changes in quality and quantity of direct labor, in amount and cost of scrap and rework time, and in maintenance expenses, down time, safety, flexibility, and so on. So many variables are involved that it is obviously impossible to make neat generalizations. Yet each capital equipment expenditure must be examined in detail for possible additional costs and additional savings. The inability to generalize, however, should not minimize the crucial importance of the savings analysis required.

All the subsequent elaborate procedures for ranking projects are no better than the data input. Above all, the data formulation requires good judgment in expressing the amount of the benefits. This is not a routine clerical task to be performed on a mechanical basis. It requires continuous monitoring and evaluation of estimates by individuals competent to make such evaluations: engineers, economists, cost analysts, and other qualified persons.

After the benefits estimates have been made, they are utilized for ranking alternative investment proposals. How this grading is accomplished is the next topic.

RANKING INVESTMENT PROPOSALS

Among the many methods for ranking investment proposals, four are relatively widely used. The name and a brief description of each are set forth below. Future returns are, in all cases, defined as the net proceeds before depreciation but after taxes that result from a project. In other words, returns are synonymous with cash flows from investments.

Financial Analysis and Control

1. Payback method: Number of years required to return the original investment
2. Average-rate-of-return method

$$\frac{\text{sum of earnings (after depreciation)}}{\text{number of years}} \div \text{average investment}$$

3. Internal rate method: Interest rate which equates the present value of future returns to the investment outlay
4. Net present value method: Present value of future returns discounted at the appropriate cost of capital minus the present value of the investment outlay

The nature and characteristics of each method will be illustrated and explained. To make the explanation more meaningful, the same data are used to illustrate each method. Assume that two projects are being considered by a firm. Each requires an investment of $1,000. The firm's cost of capital is taken to be 10 percent.[4] The net returns from investments A and B are as follows:

NET CASH FLOWS

Year	A	B
1	$500	$100
2	400	200
3	300	300
4	100	400
5		500
6		600

Payback Period

The payback period method represents the number of years required to return the original investment by net returns before depreciation but after taxes. It is two and one-third years for project A and four years for

---

[4] A discussion of how the cost of capital is calculated is presented in Chapter 12.

project B. If the firm were employing a three-year payback period, project A would be accepted but project B would be rejected.

Though the payback period is very easy to calculate, it can lead to the wrong decisions. As the illustration demonstrates, it ignores income beyond the payback period. If the project is one maturing in later years, the use of the payback period can lead to the selection of less desirable investments. Projects with longer payback periods are characteristically those involved in long-range planning—developing a new product or tapping a new market. These are just the strategic decisions which determine a firm's fundamental position, but they also involve investments which do not yield their highest returns for a number of years. This means that the payback method may be biased against the very investments that are most important to a firm's long-run success.

In spite of its shortcomings, the payback method has been widely used by American industry. A survey made by the Machinery and Allied Products Institute indicated that 60 percent of the surveyed firms use the payback period. On equipment with a service life of ten years or more, 28 percent of those using the method set a three-year payback and 34 percent set a five-year payback. Only 16 percent use a payoff period of more than five years. Thus the relatively belated initiation of effective long-range planning by American firms is probably related to the widespread use of the payback period in analyzing alternative investments. Since its emphasis is on the very short run, the payback method simply does not require inquiry into the far-distant future.

Recognition of the longer period over which an investment is likely to yield savings points up another weakness in the use of the payback method for ranking investment proposals—its failure to take into account the interest factor. This factor can be quite important at high rates of interest, but the matter is best deferred until after the interest factor is considered in more detail.

The use of the payback period is sometimes defended on the ground that returns beyond three or four years are fraught with such great uncertainty that it is best to disregard them altogether in a planning decision. However, this is clearly an unsound procedure. Some of the investments with highest returns are those which may not come to fruition for eight, nine, or ten years. The new product cycle in industries involving advanced technologies may not have a payoff for eight or nine years. Furthermore, even though returns that occur after three or four or five years are most uncertain, it is important to make a judgment about the likelihood of their occurring. To ignore them is to assign a zero probability to these distant receipts. This can hardly produce the best results.

A final defense of the payback method is that a firm which is short of cash must necessarily give great emphasis to a quick return of its funds so that they may be put to use in other places or in meeting other needs. It can only be said that this does not relieve the payback method of its many shortcomings, and that there are better methods for handling the cash-shortage situation.

Average Rate of Return

Another fundamentally unsound approach to ranking investment opportunities is called the average-rate-of-return method. Actually, there are quite a number of different procedures for calculating average rates of return. One procedure requires the following steps: (1) add all the after-tax-and-depreciation returns, then divide the sum by the project's economic life to obtain an average earnings figure; (2) divide average earnings by the average investment over the period to get the average rate of return. An example of the calculation for the illustrative data is given in Table 7–1.

TABLE 7–1

CALCULATION OF AVERAGE RETURN ON INVESTMENT

A			B		
Earnings after Taxes	Depre- ciation	Earnings after Depreciation*	Earnings after Taxes	Depre- ciation	Earnings after Depreciation*
$500	$250	$250	$100	$167	$ (67)
400	250	150	200	167	33
300	250	50	300	167	133
100	250	(150)	400	167	233
		300	500	167	333
			600	167	433
					$1,098

$$\frac{\dfrac{\$300}{4}}{\dfrac{\$1000}{2}} = \frac{\$75}{\$500} = 15\%$$

$$\frac{\dfrac{\$1098}{6}}{\dfrac{\$1000}{2}} = \frac{\$183}{\$500} = 37\%$$

* Figures in parentheses indicate losses. A consideration of the tax implications of losses is deferred until later in the chapter.

Assuming the firm uses straight line depreciation, the annual depreciation charge is $250 for project A ($1,000/4 years) and $167 for project B ($1,000/6 years). With this depreciation method and assuming a zero salvage value, the average investment in each project is $500, the initial cost divided by 2. Had a salvage value been involved, average investment would have been computed as the initial investment plus the ending book value divided by 2. Project A is seen to have an average rate of return equal to 15 percent versus one of 37 percent for project B.

The average return method of ranking investment proposals is superior to the payback method in that it does take into account benefits over the entire economic life of the project. However, it still carries one of the fundamental weaknesses of the payback period; namely, it disregards the time value of money. A dollar received at the end of the fifth or sixth year is given just as much weight as one received during the first year, but we know (from Appendix 7A if not from earlier courses) that this should not be. With this weakness, rankings obtained by the average-rate-of-return method are highly suspect.

Internal Rate of Return

As the flaws in the payback and the average-rate-of-return methods were recognized, people began to search for methods of evaluating projects that would recognize that a dollar received immediately is preferable to a dollar received at some future date. The internal-rate-of-return method was the first widely used method in which this recognition was accomplished. The internal rate of return itself is defined as "the interest rate that equates the present value of the expected future receipts to the present value of the investment outlay."[5]

The internal rate of return must be found by trial and error. First, compute the present value of the cash flows from an investment, using an arbitrarily selected interest rate. Then compare the present value so obtained with the investment's cost. If the present value is higher than the cost figure, try a higher interest rate and go through the procedure again. Conversely, if the present value is lower than the cost, lower the interest rate and repeat the process. Continue until the present value of the flows from the investment are approximately equal to its cost. *The interest rate that brings about this equality is defined as the internal rate of return.*[6]

This calculation process is illustrated in Table 7–2 for projects A and B. First, the 4 percent interest factors are obtained from Table 7–3. These factors are then multiplied by the cash flows for the corresponding years, and the present values of the annual cash flows are placed in the appro-

---

[5] Anyone who has not recently been exposed to the arithmetic of compound interest should go over the first section of Appendix 7A before completing the remainder of the chapter.

[6] In order to reduce the number of trials required to find the internal rate of return, it is important to minimize the error at each iteration. One reasonable approach is to make as good a first approximation as possible (probably taking the average rate of return as a starting point), then "straddling" the internal rate of return by making fairly large changes in the interest rate early in the iterative process. In practice, if many projects are to be evaluated or if long periods are involved, one would not work out the calculations by hand but would use a computer.

priate columns. For example, the IF (interest factor) 0.96 is multiplied by $500, and the product, $480, is placed in the first row of column A.

The present values of the yearly cash flows are then summed to get the investment's total present value. Subtracting the cost of the project from this figure gives the net present value. As the net present values of both investments are positive at the 4 percent rate, increase the rate to 10 percent and try again. Once again the net present values are positive, so the rate is stepped up to 15 percent. At this point the net present value of investment A is approximately zero, which indicates that its internal rate of return is approximately 15 percent. Continuing, B is found to have an internal rate of return of approximately 20 percent.

Assuming the firm uses a cost of capital of 10 percent and the two projects are independent, both will be accepted. If they are mutually exclusive, B ranks higher and thus will be accepted, while A will be rejected.

Net Present Value Method

Another discounted cash flow technique for analyzing investment opportunities is called the net present value method, or sometimes simply the present value method. To implement this approach, simply find the present value of the expected net cash flow of an investment, discounted at the cost of capital, and subtract from it the initial cost outlay of the project.[7] If the net present value is positive, the project should be accepted; if negative, it should be rejected. If the two projects are mutually exclusive, the one with the higher net present value should be chosen over the other.

If the assumption of a 10 percent cost of capital is continued, the net present values of our illustrative projects A and B have already been found. The second set of calculations in Table 7–2—that for a 10 percent interest factor—shows investment A to have a net present value of $80, B to have one of $400. On this basis, both would be accepted if they are independent, but B would rank ahead of A (and thus be the one accepted) if they are mutually exclusive.

Both discounted cash flow methods—the internal rate of return and net present value—meet the objections to the payback and the average rate of return methods. They consider all the revenues from a project, and they take account of the time value of money. Under ordinary circumstances, the two approaches will give identical investment decisions; there are, however, differences between them. For the theoretical reasons

---

[7] If costs are spread over several years, this fact must be taken into account. Suppose, for example, that a firm bought land in 1965, erected a buiding in 1966, installed equipment in 1967, and started production in 1968. One could treat 1965 as the base year, comparing the present value (as of 1965) of the costs to the present value of the benefit stream.

Table 7-2
PRESENT VALUE CALCULATIONS

Investment = $1,000

Year	A	B
1	500	100
2	400	200
3	300	300
4	100	400
5		500
6		600

	4 Percent			10 Percent			15 Percent		
		Present Value			*Present Value*			*Present Value*	
	*IF**	*A*	*B*	*IF**	*A*	*B*	*IF**	*A*	*B*
1.	0.96	480	96	0.91	455	91	0.87	435	87
2.	0.92	368	184	0.83	332	166	0.76	304	152
3.	0.89	267	267	0.75	225	225	0.66	198	198
4.	0.86	86	344	0.68	68	272	0.57	57	228
5.	0.82		410	0.62		310	0.50		250
6.	0.79		474	0.56		336	0.43		258
Present value		1,201	1,775		1,080	1,400		994	1,173
Net present value		201	775		80	400		(6)	173

	20 Percent			24 Percent			32 Percent		
		Present Value			Present Value			Present Value	
	IF*	A	B	IF*	A	B	IF*	A	B
1.	0.83	415	83	0.81	405	81	0.76	380	76
2.	0.69	276	138	0.65	260	130	0.57	228	114
3.	0.58	174	174	0.52	156	156	0.43	129	129
4.	0.48	48	192	0.42	42	168	0.33	33	132
5.	0.40		200	0.34		170	0.25		125
6.	0.33		198	0.28		168	0.19		114
Present value		913	985		863	873		770	690
Net present value		(87)	(15)		(137)	(127)		(230)	(310)

* IF stands for interest factor.

TABLE 7–3
PRESENT VALUE OF $1

Year	1%	2%	3%	4%	5%	6%	7%	8%	9%	10%	12%	14%	15%	16%	18%	20%	24%	28%	32%	36%	40%	50%	60%	70%	80%	90%
1	.99	.98	.97	.96	.95	.94	.93	.93	.92	.91	.89	.88	.87	.86	.85	.83	.81	.78	.76	.74	.71	.67	.62	.59	.56	.53
2	.98	.96	.94	.92	.91	.89	.87	.86	.84	.83	.80	.77	.76	.74	.72	.69	.65	.61	.57	.54	.51	.44	.39	.35	.31	.28
3	.97	.94	.92	.89	.86	.84	.82	.79	.77	.75	.71	.68	.66	.64	.61	.58	.52	.48	.43	.40	.36	.30	.24	.20	.17	.15
4	.96	.92	.89	.86	.82	.79	.76	.74	.71	.68	.64	.59	.57	.55	.52	.48	.42	.37	.33	.29	.26	.20	.15	.12	.10	.08
5	.95	.91	.86	.82	.78	.75	.71	.68	.65	.62	.57	.52	.50	.48	.44	.40	.34	.29	.25	.21	.19	.13	.10	.07	.05	.04
6	.94	.89	.84	.79	.75	.70	.67	.63	.60	.56	.51	.46	.43	.41	.37	.33	.28	.23	.19	.16	.13	.09	.06	.04	.03	.02
7	.93	.87	.81	.76	.71	.67	.62	.58	.55	.51	.45	.40	.38	.35	.31	.28	.22	.18	.14	.12	.09	.06	.04	.02	.02	.01
8	.92	.85	.79	.73	.68	.63	.58	.54	.50	.47	.40	.35	.33	.31	.27	.23	.18	.14	.11	.09	.07	.04	.02	.01	.01	.01
9	.91	.84	.77	.70	.64	.59	.54	.50	.46	.42	.36	.31	.28	.26	.23	.19	.14	.11	.08	.06	.05	.03	.01	.01	.01	
10	.91	.82	.74	.68	.61	.56	.51	.46	.42	.39	.32	.27	.25	.23	.19	.16	.12	.08	.06	.05	.03	.02	.01	.01	.01	
11	.90	.80	.72	.65	.58	.53	.48	.43	.39	.35	.29	.24	.22	.20	.16	.13	.09	.07	.05	.03	.02	.01	.01			
12	.89	.79	.70	.62	.56	.50	.44	.40	.36	.32	.26	.21	.19	.17	.14	.11	.08	.05	.04	.03	.02	.01				
13	.88	.77	.68	.60	.53	.47	.42	.37	.33	.29	.23	.18	.16	.15	.12	.09	.06	.04	.03	.02	.01	.01				
14	.87	.76	.66	.58	.51	.44	.39	.34	.30	.26	.20	.16	.14	.13	.10	.08	.05	.03	.02	.01	.01					
15	.86	.74	.64	.56	.48	.42	.36	.32	.28	.24	.18	.14	.12	.11	.08	.06	.04	.02	.02	.01	.01					
20	.82	.67	.55	.46	.38	.31	.26	.21	.18	.15	.10	.07	.07	.05	.04	.03	.01	.01								
25	.78	.61	.48	.38	.30	.23	.18	.15	.12	.09	.06	.04	.03	.02	.02	.01										
30	.74	.55	.41	.31	.23	.17	.13	.10	.08	.06	.03	.02	.02	.01	.01											
35	.71	.50	.36	.25	.18	.13	.09	.07	.05	.04	.02	.01	.01	.01												
40	.67	.45	.31	.21	.14	.10	.07	.05	.03	.02	.01	.01														
45	.64	.41	.26	.17	.11	.07	.05	.03	.02	.01	.01															
50	.61	.37	.23	.14	.09	.05	.03	.02	.01	.01																

discussed in Appendix 7A, the authors recommend the net present value approach when capital is not rationed, and the internal rate of return approach when it is.

DETERMINING CASH FLOWS

Thus far the problem of measuring cash flows—the benefits used in the present value calculations above—has not been dealt with directly. In particular, the impact of taxes and depreciation has not been considered. These matters will now be discussed and a few simple examples given.

Simplified Model for Determining Cash Flows

One way of considering the cash flows attributable to a particular investment is to think of them in terms of comparative income statements such as those shown in Table 7–4. The upper part of the table is general, the lower part uses figures taken from the example below.

TABLE 7–4

COMPARATIVE INCOME STATEMENT FRAMEWORK FOR
CONSIDERING CASH FLOWS

	Without New Investment	With New Investment	Difference
Sales	S_1	S_2	$S_2 - S_1$
Operating costs	$- C_1$	$- C_2$	$- (C_2 - C_1)$
Depreciation	$- D_1$	$- D_2$	$-(D_2 - D_1)$
Taxable Income	Y_1	Y_2	$Y_2 - Y_1$
Income Taxes	$- T_1$	$- T_2$	$- (T_2 - T_1)$
Profit after taxes	P_1	P_2	$P_2 - P_1$
Cash flow $(P + D)$	CF_1	CF_2	$CF_2 - CF_1$
Sales	$10,000	$11,000	$1,000
Operating costs	7,000	5,000	2,000
Depreciation	500	1,000	−500
Taxable income	$ 2,500	$ 5,000	$2,500
Income taxes	1,250	2,500	1,250
Profit after taxes	$ 1,250	$ 2,500	$1,250
Cash flow $(P + D)$	$ 1,750	$ 3,500	$1,750

If the firm does not make the new investment, then its income statement will be as shown in the first column of the table. But if it does make a particular investment, then certain changes will occur. Sales will increase if the investment is undertaken to raise capacity. Costs may rise with sales, or if the investment is made simply to replace an inefficient machine with an efficient one, costs will fall. Depreciation generally rises after a new investment has been made, as do taxes and profits. The resultant of all these changes is a change in the firm's cash flows, and the difference between cash flows of the first and second columns, $CF_2 - CF_1$, is the figure representing the net annual benefits from the investment.

This conceptual framework may be thought of as applying to the whole firm, to divisions within it, or even to individual assets. Also, the analysis is thought of as extending over time—that is, the firm can project into the future the effects of a new investment. The following example illustrates how a new investment affects a firm's cash flows and how the investment is evaluated.

The Widget Division of the Culver Company, a profitable, diversified manufacturing firm, purchased a machine seven years ago at a cost of $7,500. The machine had an expected life of 15 years at time of purchase, is being depreciated on a straight line basis, and has a book value of $4,000 at present. The division manager reports that he can buy a new machine for $10,000 (including installation) which, over its ten-year life, will expand sales from $10,000 to $11,000. Further, it will reduce labor and raw materials usage sufficiently to cut operating costs from $7,000 to $5,000. The old machine has no salvage value. Taxes are at a 50 percent rate and are paid quarterly, and the firm's cost of capital is 10 percent. Should Culver buy the new machine?

The decision calls for three steps: (1) estimate the actual cash outlay attributable to the new investment, (2) determine the present value of the incremental cash flows, and (3) see if the net present value is positive.

1. *Estimated cash outlay.* Culver must make a $10,000 payment to the manufacturer of the machine, but its next quarterly income tax bill will be reduced by $2,000. The tax reduction occurs because the old machine, which is carried at $4,000, will be written off immediately if the new one is purchased.[8] The result is that the purchase of the new machine involves a net cash outlay of $8,000; this is its cost for capital budgeting purposes.

2. *Present value of benefits.* The first column in the lower section of Table 7–4 shows the Widget Division's estimated income statement as it would be without the new machine. The second column shows the statement on the assumption that the investment is made, and the third

---

[8] It is also useful to point out at this time that, for most firms, the outlay cost of new investments in machinery and equipment is reduced by the amount of the investment tax credit. In other words, if the asset has a cost of $1,000 and a depreciable life of at least eight years, the outlay cost will be reduced by a 7 percent tax credit, or by $70. This obviously raises the net present value over what it would otherwise be, and thus stimulates investment. It is for this reason, of course, that Congress created the investment tax credit.

TABLE 7-5
PRESENT VALUE OF AN ANNUITY OF $1

Year	1%	2%	3%	4%	5%	6%	7%	8%	9%	10%	12%	14%	15%	16%	18%	20%	24%	28%	32%	36%
1	0.99	0.98	0.97	0.96	0.95	0.94	0.93	0.93	0.92	0.91	0.89	0.88	0.87	0.86	0.85	0.83	0.81	0.78	0.76	0.74
2	1.97	1.94	1.91	1.89	1.86	1.83	1.81	1.78	1.76	1.74	1.69	1.65	1.63	1.61	1.57	1.53	1.46	1.39	1.33	1.28
3	2.94	2.88	2.83	2.78	2.72	2.67	2.62	2.58	2.53	2.49	2.40	2.32	2.28	2.25	2.17	2.11	1.98	1.87	1.77	1.67
4	3.90	3.81	3.72	3.63	3.55	3.47	3.39	3.31	3.24	3.17	3.04	2.91	2.86	2.80	2.69	2.59	2.40	2.24	2.10	1.97
5	4.85	4.71	4.58	4.45	4.33	4.21	4.10	3.99	3.89	3.79	3.60	3.43	3.35	3.27	3.13	2.99	2.75	2.53	2.35	2.18
6	5.80	5.60	5.42	5.24	5.08	4.92	4.77	4.62	4.49	4.36	4.11	3.89	3.78	3.68	3.50	3.33	3.02	2.76	2.53	2.34
7	6.73	6.47	6.23	6.00	5.79	5.58	5.39	5.21	5.03	4.87	4.56	4.29	4.16	4.04	3.81	3.60	3.24	2.94	2.68	2.46
8	7.65	7.33	7.02	6.73	6.46	6.21	5.97	5.75	5.53	5.33	4.97	4.64	4.49	4.34	4.08	3.84	3.42	3.08	2.79	2.54
9	8.57	8.16	7.79	7.44	7.11	6.80	6.52	6.25	5.98	5.76	5.33	4.95	4.47	4.61	4.30	4.03	3.57	3.18	2.87	2.60
10	9.47	8.98	8.53	8.11	7.72	7.36	7.02	6.71	6.42	6.15	5.65	5.22	5.02	4.83	4.49	4.19	3.68	3.27	2.93	2.65
11	10.37	9.79	9.25	8.76	8.31	7.89	7.50	7.14	6.81	6.50	5.99	5.45	5.23	5.03	4.66	4.33	3.78	3.34	2.98	2.68
12	11.26	10.58	9.95	9.39	8.86	8.38	7.94	7.54	7.16	6.81	6.19	5.66	5.42	5.20	4.79	4.44	3.85	3.39	3.01	2.71
13	12.13	11.35	10.63	9.99	9.39	8.85	8.36	7.90	7.49	7.10	6.42	5.84	5.58	5.34	4.91	4.53	3.91	3.43	3.04	2.73
14	13.00	12.11	11.30	10.56	9.90	9.30	8.75	8.24	7.79	7.37	6.63	6.00	5.72	5.47	5.01	4.61	3.96	3.46	3.06	2.74
15	13.86	12.85	11.94	11.12	10.38	9.71	9.11	8.56	8.06	7.61	6.81	6.14	5.85	5.58	5.09	4.68	4.00	3.48	3.08	2.75
20	18.05	16.35	14.88	13.59	12.46	11.47	10.59	9.82	9.13	8.51	7.47	6.62	6.26	5.93	5.35	4.87	4.11	3.55	3.11	2.77
25	22.02	19.52	17.41	15.62	14.09	12.78	11.65	10.67	9.82	9.08	7.84	6.87	6.46	6.10	5.47	4.95	4.15	3.56	3.12	2.78
30	25.81	22.40	19.60	17.29	15.37	13.76	12.41	11.26	10.27	9.43	8.06	7.00	6.57	6.18	5.52	4.98	4.16	3.57	3.12	2.78
35	29.41	25.00	21.49	18.67	16.37	14.50	12.95	11.65	10.57	9.64	8.18	7.07	6.62	6.22	5.54	4.99	4.16	3.57	3.12	2.78
40	32.83	27.36	23.11	19.79	17.16	15.05	13.33	11.92	10.76	9.78	8.24	7.10	6.64	6.23	5.55	5.00	4.17	3.57	3.12	2.78
45	36.09	29.49	24.52	20.72	17.77	15.46	13.61	12.11	10.88	9.86	8.28	7.12	6.65	6.24	5.55	5.00	4.17	3.57		
50	39.20	31.42	25.73	21.48	18.26	15.76	13.80	12.23	10.96	9.91	8.30	7.13	6.66	6.25	5.55	5.00	4.17			

column gives the difference between the first two. (It is assumed that these figures are applicable for each of the next ten years; if this is not the case, then cash flow estimates must be made for each year.) The figure at the bottom of the third column gives the incremental cash flow produced by the new machine; this is the benefit stream to be discounted at the cost of capital.

The interest factor for a ten-year, 10 percent annuity is found to be 6.15 from Table 7–5. This factor, multiplied by the $1,750 incremental cash flows, shows the investment to have a present value of $10,762.

3. *Net present value.* Subtracting the $8,000 cost figure from the $10,762 gives the investment a net present value of $2,762. Since the net present value is positive, the new machine should be purchased.[9]

Replacement Assumption

In the preceding example it is assumed that the old machine is re-placed in the eighth year, the end of its economic life, and the replace-ment results in a continuation of the $500 depreciation deduction (the "tax shield"). It could also be assumed that the depreciation tax shield on the old machine stops at the end of the eighth year. The solution under this assumption is set out in Table 7–6. The pattern of the table is suggested as an orderly framework for keeping track of all the factors affecting the decision. The net present value becomes $2,967. The re-conciliation of the two results is shown below.

Tax saving of $250 for 10 years × present value factor of 6.15	$1,538
Tax saving of $250 for 8 years × present value factor of 5.33	1,333
Difference	$ 205
Net present value of investment, assuming no replacement	$2,967
Net present value of investment, assuming replacement	2,762
Difference	$ 205

Thus the difference in the net present values is attributable entirely to the assumptions made regarding the nature and the timing of replace-ment.

Accelerated Depreciation

In the solution provided in Table 7–6 it is assumed that straight line depreciation was used, thus enabling us to derive uniform cash flows

---

[9] Alternatively, the internal rate of return on the project could have been computed, and found to be 18 percent. Since this is substantially in excess of the 10 percent cost of capital, the internal rate of return method also indicates that the investment should be undertaken.

TABLE 7–6

PATTERN FOR REPLACEMENT DECISION

	Amount before Tax	Amount after Tax	Year Event Occurs	Present Value Factor at 10%	Present Value
Outflows					
Investment in new equipment	10,000	10,000	—	1.00	$10,000
Salvage value of old*	—	—	—	1.00	—
Tax loss on sale	(4,000)	(2,000)	—	1.00	(2,000)
Total outflows (present value of costs)					$ 8,000
Inflows					
Benefits†	3,000	1,500	1–10	6.15	9,225
Depreciation on new (annual)	1,000	500	1–10	6.15	3,075
Depreciation on old (annual)	(500)	(250)	1–8	5.33	(1,333)
Salvage value on new*	—	—	—	—	—
Total inflows (present value of benefits)					$10,967

Present value of inflows less present value of outflows = $2,967

Present value of inflows divided by present value of outflows = 1.37 times

* Salvage value is not an issue in this example. However, the table is structured to show how salvage values would be handled in cases where they are applicable.
† $1,000 sales increase + $2,000 cost saving = $3,000 benefit.

over the life of the investment. Realistically, however, firms usually employ accelerated depreciation methods; when such is the case, it is necessary to modify the procedures outlined thus far. In terms of the framework given in Table 7–4, accelerated depreciation makes it necessary to recompute the differential cash flow for each year during the life of the investment. In terms of the approach given in Table 7–6, the depreciation figures are modified simply by applying another present value factor.

Table 7–7 contains present value factors for accelerated depreciation; the table is constructed as follows.

1. Assume that an asset with a $1 cost, a five-year depreciable life, and zero salvage value is to be depreciated by the sum-of-years'-digits method (see Appendix to Chapter 10 for an explanation of the method).
2. Assume that the firm's cost of capital is 10 percent, and discount the depreciation tax savings at this rate; this produces the present value of the depreciation flows.
3. Calculations:

Year	Depreciation Fraction Applied to Asset Cost	Amount of Depreciation	10% Discount Factor	Sum-of-Years'-Digits Depreciation Factor
1	5/15	$0.33333	0.909	$0.303
2	4/15	0.26667	0.826	0.220
3	3/15	0.20000	0.751	0.150
4	2/15	0.13333	0.683	0.091
5	1/15	0.06667	0.621	0.042
Totals	1.00	$1.00000		$0.806

4. Thus, the present value of the depreciation from a $1 investment, discounted at 10 percent, when sum of years' digits and a five-year life are used, is $0.806. The factor 0.806 can be found in Table 7–7. All the other factors in the table were constructed in a similar manner.

To modify the results given in Table 7–6 to allow for accelerated depreciation, it is necessary to change only that section of the table headed "Depreciation on new (annual)." In place of the annual depreciation, use the total depreciation and apply a factor taken from Table 7–7. In Table 7–8, where the modification is made, assume that the new investment is depreciated by the double declining balance method over a ten-year period; hence the factor 0.685 is applied to the after-tax depreciation figure of $5,000, obtaining a present value of $3,425 for the depreciation tax shelter.

No modification is necessary for the old machine's depreciation—its tax shelter is still a straight line annuity; hence the present value of the shield is still found to be $1,333. Had it been desired to modify the example still further—to have the old machine being depreciated by an accelerated method—the procedure would have been handled exactly the same as for the new machine. Naturally, the present value of the old machine's tax shield would be larger if the deductions came sooner because of accelerated depreciation.

Note that the modifications incorporated in Table 7–8 make the new machine an even more advantageous investment. The reason for this, of

TABLE 7-7

TABLES FOR PRESENT VALUE OF DEPRECIATION FOR SUM-OF-YEARS'-DIGITS AND DOUBLE-DECLINING-BALANCE METHODS

Period	*Sum of Years' Digits*						
	6%	*8%*	*10%*	*12%*	*14%*	*15%*	*16%*
1	—	—	—	—	—	—	—
2	—	—	—	—	—	—	—
3	0.908	0.881	0.855	0.831	0.808	0.796	0.786
4	0.891	0.860	0.830	0.802	0.776	0.763	0.751
5	0.875	0.839	0.806	0.775	0.746	0.732	0.719
6	0.859	0.820	0.783	0.749	0.718	0.703	0.689
7	0.844	0.801	0.761	0.725	0.692	0.676	0.661
8	0.829	0.782	0.740	0.702	0.667	0.650	0.635
9	0.814	0.765	0.720	0.680	0.643	0.626	0.610
10	0.800	0.748	0.701	0.659	0.621	0.604	0.587
11	0.786	0.731	0.683	0.639	0.600	0.582	0.565
12	0.773	0.715	0.665	0.620	0.581	0.562	0.545
13	0.760	0.700	0.648	0.602	0.562	0.543	0.526
14	0.747	0.685	0.632	0.585	0.544	0.525	0.508
15	0.734	0.671	0.616	0.569	0.527	0.508	0.491
16	0.722	0.657	0.601	0.553	0.511	0.492	0.475
17	0.711	0.644	0.587	0.538	0.496	0.477	0.460
18	0.699	0.631	0.573	0.524	0.482	0.463	0.445
19	0.688	0.618	0.560	0.510	0.468	0.449	0.432
20	0.677	0.606	0.547	0.497	0.455	0.436	0.419

Period	*Double Declining Balance*						
	6%	*8%*	*10%*	*12%*	*14%*	*15%*	*16%*
1	—	—	—	—	—	—	—
2	—	—	—	—	—	—	—
3	0.920	0.896	0.873	0.851	0.831	0.821	0.811
4	0.898	0.868	0.840	0.814	0.789	0.777	0.766
5	0.878	0.843	0.811	0.781	0.753	0.739	0.727
6	0.858	0.819	0.783	0.749	0.718	0.704	0.689
7	0.840	0.796	0.756	0.720	0.687	0.671	0.656
8	0.821	0.774	0.731	0.692	0.657	0.641	0.625
9	0.804	0.753	0.708	0.667	0.630	0.614	0.597
10	0.787	0.733	0.685	0.643	0.605	0.588	0.571
11	0.771	0.714	0.664	0.620	0.582	0.564	0.547
12	0.755	0.696	0.644	0.599	0.559	0.541	0.524
13	0.740	0.678	0.625	0.579	0.539	0.521	0.504
14	0.725	0.661	0.607	0.560	0.520	0.501	0.484
15	0.711	0.645	0.590	0.542	0.502	0.483	0.466
16	0.697	0.630	0.573	0.526	0.485	0.466	0.450
17	0.684	0.615	0.558	0.510	0.469	0.451	0.434
18	0.671	0.601	0.543	0.495	0.454	0.436	0.419
19	0.659	0.587	0.529	0.480	0.440	0.422	0.405
20	0.647	0.574	0.515	0.467	0.427	0.409	0.392

TABLE 7–8

PATTERN FOR REPLACEMENT DECISION

	Amount before Tax	Amount after Tax	Year Event Occurs	Present Value Factor at 10%	Present Value
Outflows					
Investment in new equipment	10,000	10,000	—	1.00	$10,000
Salvage value of old*	—	—	0	1.00	—
Tax loss on sale	(4,000)	(2,000)	0	1.00	(2,000)
Total outflows (present value of costs)					$ 8,000
Inflows					
Benefits	3,000	1,500	1–10	6.15	$ 9,225
Depreciation on new (total)	10,000	5,000	1–10	0.685	3,425
Depreciation on old (annual)	(500)	(250)	1–8	5.33	(1,333)
Salvage value on new*	—	—	—	—	—
Total inflows (present value of benefits)					$11,317
Present value of inflows less present value of outflows			= 3,317		
Present value of inflows divided by present value of outflows = 1.41 times					

* Salvage value is not an issue in this example. However, the table is structured to show how salvage values would be handled in cases where they are applicable.

course, is that with accelerated depreciation the cash flows accrue faster. If the comparison was made by the method outlined in Table 7–4, computing a different cash flow for each year, this would have been seen quite clearly.

Other alternative assumptions could have been made regarding the action taken by the firm at the end of the eighth year, the depreciation method used, and so on. The procedures described are sufficiently flexible to be shaped to fit any situation that might be devised.

The final point to be emphasized in this section is that the numbers used in the above calculations are estimates and that the decisions indicated by the computations are no better than the estimates and assumptions on which they are based. Savings estimates are subject to great variation, especially over a five-to-ten-year period. Estimates of salvage values for the old and the new machines are also subject to error, and the possibility that better machines may come along faster than expected and thus affect the obsolescence rates must be considered. The business manager will attempt to incorporate all these factors into the formal analysis, but it will not always be possible for him to do so. This very fact makes it essential that the actual decision *not* be made mechanically, solely on the basis of a set of processed numbers, but be tempered with subjective business judgment.

THE COMPOSITION PROBLEM

A general fallacy is to consider that what is true of the individual parts will be true of the whole. This problem also arises in connection with capital budgeting. Though individual projects appear to promise a relatively attractive yield, when they are taken together difficulties might be involved in achieving all the favorable projects simultaneously. One problem is that other firms in the same industry may be engaging in similar capital expenditure programs to increase their capacity or, by cost reductions, in an attempt to obtain a larger share of the product market. For a given growth rate in the industry, it is obviously impossible for every firm to obtain increases in sales that would fully utilize all the capital expenditure projects being undertaken.

Another problem is that while individual projects promise favorable yields, to undertake a large number of projects simultaneously might involve a very high rate of expansion by the individual firm. Such substantial additional personnel requirements and organizational problems may be involved that over-all rates of return will be diminished. Top management, at some point in the capital budgeting process, must therefore make a decision regarding the total volume of favorable projects that may be successfully undertaken without causing a significant reduction in the prospective returns from individual projects.

CAPITAL RATIONING

Ordinarily, companies operate as illustrated in Figure 7–1; that is, they take on investments to the point where the marginal returns from investment are just equal to the marginal cost of capital. For firms operating in this way the decision process is as described above—they make those investments having positive net present values, reject those whose net present values are negative, and choose between mutually exclusive investments on the basis of the higher net present value.

However, a firm will occasionally set an absolute limit on the size of its capital budget during any one year. In part, this policy can be justified by the composition problem discussed above, but sometimes it simply reflects an unwillingness to engage in external financing. Some managements, recalling the plight of firms with substantial amounts of debt in the 1930s, may simply refuse to use debt. Other managements, which have no objection to selling debt, may not want to sell equity capital for fear of losing some measure of voting control. Still others may refuse to use any form of outside financing, considering safety and control to be more important than additional profits. These are all cases of capital rationing, and here the investment decision is somewhat different.[10] For reasons discussed in Appendix 7A, the authors recommend that investments be ranked by the internal rate of return whenever capital rationing is imposed. The firm should start at the top of its list of projects, taking investments of successively lower rank until the available funds have been exhausted. However, no investment with an internal rate of return less than the cost of capital should be undertaken.

A firm might, for example, have the investment opportunities shown in Table 7–9 and only $6 million available for investment. In this situa-

TABLE 7–9

THE PROSPECTIVE-PROJECTS SCHEDULE

Nature of Proposal	Amounts of Funds Required	Cumulative Total	Internal Rate of Return
1. Purchase of leased space	$2,000,000	$ 2,000,000	23%
2. Mechanization of accounting system . .	1,200,000	3,200,000	19
3. Modernization of office building . . .	1,500,000	4,700,000	17
4. Addition of power facilities	900,000	5,600,000	16
5. Purchase of affiliate	3,600,000	9,200,000	13
6. Purchase of loading docks	300,000	9,500,000	12
7. Purchase of tank trucks	500,000	10,000,000	11
			10% cutoff
8. Installation of conveyer system	200,000	10,200,000	9
9. Construction of new plant	2,300,000	12,500,000	8
10. Purchase of executive aircraft	200,000	12,700,000	7

[10] It is not correct to interpret as capital rationing a situation where the firm is willing to sell additional securities at the going market price but finds that it cannot because the market will simply not absorb more of its issues. Rather, such a situation indicates that the cost of the capital curve is rising. If more acceptable investments are indicated than can be financed, then the cost of capital being used is too low and should be raised. This matter will be discussed further in Chapter 12.

tion, the firm would probably accept projects 1 through 4 and project 6.[11] Under no circumstances should it accept projects 8, 9, or 10, as they all earn less than the cost of capital.

SUMMARY

Capital budgeting is of the greatest significance because it involves commitments for large outlays whose benefits (or drawbacks) extend well into the future. Decisions in these areas will therefore have a major impact on the future well-being of the firm. The chapter focused on how such decisions might be made more effective and might contribute to the health and growth of a firm. The material emphasized the development of systematic procedures and rules for preparing a list of investment proposals, for evaluating them, and for selecting a cutoff point.

The chapter emphasized that one of the most crucial phases of the process of evaluating capital budget proposals is obtaining a dependable estimate of the savings or increases in revenues that will be obtained from undertaking the project. It cannot be overemphasized that the firm must allocate competent and experienced personnel for making these judgments.

If estimates of benefits and of investment outlays required are available, alternative methods may be used for ranking investment proposals. The chapter concluded that among the alternative methods the net present value approach is generally the most defensible. However, in those instances where the firm is subject to capital rationing, it may be better to employ the internal rate of return criterion rather than the net present value.

SELECTED REFERENCES

Baldwin, R. H., "How to Assess Investment Proposals," *Harvard Business Review*, 37 (May–June 1959), pp. 98–104.

Bennion, E. G., "Capital Budgeting and Game Theory," *Harvard Business Review*, 34 (November–December 1956), pp. 115–123.

Bierman, Harold, Jr., *Topics in Cost Accounting and Decisions* (New York: McGraw-Hill, Inc., 1963), Chs. 8 and 9.

Dean, Joel, *Capital Budgeting* (New York: Columbia University Press, 1951).

———, "Four Ways to Write Off Capital Investment: Management Should Have a Wider Tax Choice," *Journal of Business*, 29, No. 2 (April 1956), pp. 79–89.

———, "Measuring the Productivity of Capital," *Harvard Business Review*, 32 (January–February 1954), pp. 120–130.

———, "The Present Cost of Investing in the Company's Future," *Planning Ahead for Profit* (New York: American Management Association, 1958), pp. 87–103.

Edson, Harvey O., "Setting a Standard for Your Company's Return on Investment," *Controller*, 26 (September 1958), pp. 411–415.

Gordon, Myron J., and Eli Shapiro, "Capital Equipment Analysis: The Required

---

[11] Linear programming techniques have been worked out to provide optimal decisions when capital constraints are present. To our knowledge, however, such procedures have not been employed by any businesses, and it is unlikely that they will. The type of firm that is sufficiently sophisticated to understand, let alone use, such techniques is not likely to subject itself to capital rationing.

Rate of Profit," *Management Science*, 3 (October 1956), pp. 102–110.

Grayson, C. Jackson, Jr., "Introduction of Uncertainty into Capital Budgeting Decisions," *N.A.A. Bulletin*, 43 (January 1962), pp. 79–80.

Griswold, John A., "More for Your Capital Dollar—Finding the Realistic Rate of Return" (Hanover, N. H.: Amos Tuck School of Business Administration, 1957).

Schwab, Frank, Jr., "Capital Expenditure Evaluation," *Controller*, 26 (August 1958), pp. 359–365, 393.

Solomon, Ezra, "The Arithmetic of Capital-budgeting Decisions," *Journal of Business*, 29 (April 1956), pp. 124–129.

————, *The Management of Corporate Capital* (New York: Free Press, 1959).

Terborgh, George, *Business Investment Policy* (Washington, D. C.: Machinery and Allied Products Institute, 1958).

————, "Some Comments on the Dean-Smith Article on the Mapi Formula," *Journal of Business*, 29 (April 1956), pp. 138–140.

QUESTIONS

7-1   What reasons can you suggest why companies often continue to use obsolete equipment instead of installing new replacements? How does the use of this obsolete equipment affect the company and the economy?

7-2   Are there conditions under which a firm might be better off if it chooses a machine with a rapid payback rather than one with the largest rate of return?

7-3   Company X uses the payback method in evaluating investment proposals and is considering new equipment whose additional earnings will be $150 per year. The equipment costs $500 and its expected life is ten years (straight line depreciation). The company uses a three-year payback as its criterion. Should the equipment be purchased under the above assumptions?

7-4   What are the most critical problems that arise in calculating a rate of return for a prospective investment?

7-5   For firms with no capital rationing restriction, what should be the simple criterion for accepting or rejecting a project?

7-6   What other factors in addition to rate of return analysis should be considered in determining capital expenditures?

7-7   Would it be beneficial to a firm to review its past capital expenditures and capital budgeting procedures? Why?

7-8   Fiscal policy is a tool used by the government to stimulate the economy. Explain, using the analytical devices developed in this chapter, how each of the following might be expected to stimulate the economy by stimulating investment.

1. The investment tax credit (see footnote 8, page 154 for a description of the credit)
2. A speed-up of tax-allowable depreciation (for example, the accelerated methods permitted in 1954 or the guideline revisions of 1962)
3. An easing of interest rates
4. Passage of the War on Poverty Program

PROBLEMS

7-1   The Jordan Company is using a machine whose original cost was $10,000; it is three years old and has a salvage value of $2,000. The asset is being depreciated over a ten-year life toward a zero salvage value. Depreciation is on a straight line basis.

Management is contemplating a purchase of a replacement whose cost is $10,000 and whose salvage value would be $2,000; the expected savings with the new machine will be $3,000 per year. Depreciation is on a straight line basis over a ten-year life and the cost of capital is 10 percent.

1. Should the firm replace the asset?
2. What factors in addition to the quantitative factors listed above are likely to require consideration in a practical situation?

Set up your solution in such a way that the total initial transaction is illustrated under the *outflows* heading. Assume a 50 percent tax rate.

7–2 For the following groups of companies, compare the incremental and average returns on total assets for the period 1959–1964. The incremental return is defined as the change in profits for the five-year period (profits 1964 − profits 1959) divided by the change in total assets (assets 1964 − assets 1959). The average return is the average of the six individual yearly returns.

Auto Manufacturers	*Oil Companies*
General Motors	Standard Oil, N.J.
Ford	Standard Oil, Calif.
Chrysler	Tidewater Oil

Comment on the significance of your findings, if the relevant cost of capital for these firms was 10 percent.

7–3 The Denver Company is considering the purchase of a machine tool to replace an obsolete one. The machine being used for the operation has a tax book value of zero; it is in good working order and will last, physically, for at least an additional ten years. However, the proposed machine will perform the operation so much more efficiently that Denver Company engineers estimate that labor, material, and other direct costs of the operation will be reduced $3,000 a year if the proposed machine is installed. The proposed machine costs $12,000, delivered and installed. Its economic life is estimated to be ten years, with zero salvage value. The company expects to earn 14 percent on its investment after taxes. The tax rate is 50 percent.

1. Should Denver buy the new machine?
2. Assume that the tax book value of the old machine had been $4,000, that the annual depreciation charge would have been $400, and that it had no sale value. How do these assumptions affect your answer?
3. Change part 2 to also give effect to the sale of the old machine for $2,000.
4. Change part 2 to assume that the annual savings would be $4,000. (The old machine is *not* sold for $2,000.)
5. If the relevant cost of capital were 5 percent, how would your answers to parts 1 through 4 be affected? What is the significance of this?
6. What other factors are likely to affect investment decisions of this type?

7–4 Each of two projects involves an investment of $1,000. After tax, savings from S are $660 for two years; from L $265 for six years.

1. Rank the projects if the firm's cost of capital is 6 percent, 10 percent, 20 percent.
2. Graph your results.
3. What is the significance of your results?

7–5   Each of two projects requires an investment of $1,000. The firm's cost of capital is 10 per cent. The pattern of income returns after taxes is as follows:

Year	A	B
1	$400	$100
2	400	200
3	200	200
4	100	200
5		300
6		400

1. Rank the investments by the following methods:
   a) Three-year payback
   b) Average return on average investment
   c) Internal rate of return (discounted return)
   d) Present worth at cost of capital
2. Calculate the present value of each project at the following cost of capital: 0%, 4%, 6%, 10%, 15%. (Present value equals present worth less investment cost.)
3. Graph the results of part 2 with cost of capital on the horizontal axis and (a) present value on the vertical axis and (b) present worth on the vertical axis.
4. What is the practical significance of your findings in 1, 2, and 3?

The Interest Factor
in Financial Decisions

Most financing decisions involve commitments over extended periods. Bonds mature in 5, 20, 50, or 100 years. Buildings and equipment have lives of 2, 5, 20, or even 50 years. Whether the commitment is in real assets, such as buildings and equipment, or in financial obligations, such as notes or bonds, the interest factor will have a crucial effect on the soundness of the decisions. Compound interest has an amazing force. At 6 percent, money doubles in 12 years;[1] at 8 percent, it doubles in 9 years; at 16 percent, in 4½ years.

For most financial decisions the interest factor is of vital importance. Should the firm engage in a refunding operation? Or suppose a firm decides to obtain funds through a bond issue. Several offers are made, some with high interest rates requiring sale of the issue at a premium; others with low interest rates and sale of the issue at a discount. How shall the financial manager choose between the different offers? Many requests come from production managers for new and better equipment. Which should be accepted and which rejected? Equipment is offered under leasing arrangements. Is it better to lease or to buy? In all these applications the correct decision will hinge upon the effects of compound interest.

BASIC INTEREST RELATIONS

Many people are afraid of the subject of compound interest, hence they simply avoid it. It is certainly true that many successful businessmen—even some bankers—know essentially nothing of the subject. However, as

---

1 "The rule of 72" is employed here. This is a quick way of observing the effect of compound interest. Divide 72 by the interest rate to determine how long it takes the initial amount to be doubled. Or, given the number of years required to double the initial amount, divide this number into 72 to obtain the interest rate. For example, if it takes 12 years for a firm's total assets to double, its total assets are growing at a rate of 6 percent a year.

technology advances, as more and more engineers become involved in general management, and as modern business administration programs turn out more and more highly qualified graduates, this "success in spite of himself" pattern will become more and more difficult to find. Furthermore, a fear of interest rates is quite unfounded—the subject matter is simply not that difficult. Practically all problems involving compound interest can be handled quite satisfactorily with only three basic formulas.

Compound sums. A person deposits $1,000 in a savings and loan association that pays 4 percent interest compounded annually. How much will he have at the end of one year? To treat the matter systematically, let us define the following terms:

P = principal, or beginning amount

i = interest rate

I = dollar amount of interest earned during a period

S = ending amount, or the sum of $P + I$

S may now be calculated as:

$$S = P + I$$
$$= P + Pi$$
$$= P(1 + i) \tag{7A-1}$$

This last equation shows that the ending amount is equal to the beginning amount times the factor $(1 + i)$. For the example, P is $1,000. Now suppose the person leaves the $1,000 on deposit for five years; to what amount will it have grown at the end of that period? Equation (7A-1) can be used to construct Table 7A-1, which indicates the answer.

TABLE 7A-1

COMPOUND INTEREST CALCULATIONS

Year	Beginning Amount (P)	times	(1 + i) =	Ending Amount (S)
1	$1,000		1.04 =	$1,040
2	1,040		1.04 =	1,082
3	1,082		1.04 =	1,125
4	1,125		1.04 =	1,170
5	1,170		1.04 =	1,217

Note that S_2, the balance at the end of the second year, is found as:

$$S_2 = P_2(1 + i) = P_1(1 + i)(1 + i) = P_1(1 + i)^2$$

Similarly, S_3, the balance after three years, is found as:

$$S_3 = P_3(1 + i) = P_1(1 + i)^3$$

In general, S_n, the compound amount at the end of any year n, is found as:

$$S_n = P(1 + i)^n \qquad (7A\text{-}2)$$

This is the fundamental equation of compound interest, and it can readily be seen that equation (7A–1) is simply a special case of equation (7A–2) where $n = 1$.

While it is necessary to understand the derivation of equation (7A–1) in order to understand much of the technical material in the remainder of this appendix (as well as the material on the cost of capital), the concept can be applied in a mechanical sense quite readily. Tables have been constructed for values of $(1 + i)^n$ for wide ranges of i and n.

Letting *IF* (interest factor) $= (1 + i)^n$, equation (7A–2) may be written as $S = P(IF)$. It is necessary only to go to an appropriate interest table to find the proper interest factor. A set of illustrative interest tables is provided in the Appendix in the back of the book. The correct interest factor for the above illustration is found in Table A–1 of that appendix. Go down the Year column to 5 and across to the appropriate value in the 4% column to find the interest factor—1.217.

Present values. Suppose you were offered the alternative of either $1,217 at the end of five years or X dollars today. There is no question but that the $1,217 will be paid in full (perhaps the payer is the U. S. Government), and having no current need for the money, you would deposit it in a savings association paying a 4 percent dividend. (Four percent is defined to be your "opportunity cost.") How small must X be to induce you to accept the promise of $1,217 five years hence?

Referring to Table 7A–1, it is seen that the initial amount of $1,000 growing at 4 percent a year yields $1,217 at the end of five years. Hence, barring any personal quirks such as liking the idea of being able to withdraw the funds from the savings and loan association if your plans should change, you should be indifferent in your choice between $1,000 today and $1,217 at the end of five years.

Finding present values (or discounting, as it is commonly called), is simply the reverse of compounding, and equation (7A–2) can quite readily be transformed into a present value formula. Transposing, and dropping the subscripts:

$$P = \frac{S}{(1 + i)^n} = S \left[\frac{1}{(1 + i)^n} \right] \qquad (7A\text{-}3)$$

Tables have been constructed for the term in brackets for various values of i and n; Table A–2 in the Appendix is an example. For the illustrative case being considered, look down the 4% column to the fifth row. The figure shown there, .822, is the interest factor used to determine the present value of $1,217 payable in five years, discounted at 4 percent.

$$\$1,217 \times 0.822 = \$1,000$$

Compound sum of an annuity. An annuity is defined as a series of payments of a fixed amount for a specified number of years. For example, a promise to pay $1,000 a year for five years is a five-year annuity. If one were to receive such an annuity and were to deposit each annual payment in a savings account paying 4 percent interest, how much would he have at the end of five years? The answer is shown graphically in Figure 7A–1. The first payment is made at the end of year 1; the second at the end of year 2; and so on.[2] The last payment is not compounded at all; the next to last is compounded for one year; the second from last for two years; and so on back to the first, which is compounded for $N - 1$ years.

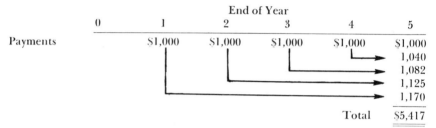

Figure 7A–1. Graphic Illustration of an Annuity: Compound Sum

When the compound amounts of each of the payments are added, their total is the sum of the annuity. For the example, this total is $5,417.

Expressed algebraically, with S_a defined as the compound sum, R as the periodic receipts, and n as the length of the annuity, the formula for S_a is

$$S_a = R_1(1+i)^{n-1} + R_2(1+i)^{n-2} + \ldots + R_{n-1}(1+i)^1 + R_n$$
$$= R[(1+i)^{n-1} + (1+i)^{n-2} + \ldots + (1+i)^1 + 1] \qquad (7A\text{–}4)$$

The expression in brackets has been given values for various combinations of n and i; a set of these annuity interest factors is given in Table A–3 in the Appendix. To find the answer to the five-year $1,000 annuity problem, simply turn to Table A–3; look down the *4%* column to the row for

---

[2] Had the payments been made at the beginning of the period, each receipt would simply have been shifted back one year. The annuity would have been called an *annuity due*; the one in the present discussion, where payments are made at the end of each period, is called a *deferred annuity*.

the fifth year; and multiply the factor 5.416 by $1,000. The answer differs only by a rounding error from the $5,417 derived by the long method.

$$S_a = R \times IF$$
$$= \$1,000 \times 5.416 = \$5,416 \qquad (7A-5)$$

Annual payments to accumulate a future sum. Suppose it was desired to know what amount must be set aside, on deposit at 5 percent, for each of the next five years in order to have $10,000 available to pay off a debt due at the end of the fifth year. Transposing equation (7A–5) we get

$$R = \frac{S_a}{IF} \qquad (7A-6)$$

Looking up the interest factor for five years at 5 percent in Table A–3, then dividing this figure into $10,000, we get

$$R = \frac{\$10,000}{5.526} = \$1,810$$

Thus, if the sum of $1,810 were deposited each year in an account paying 5 percent interest, at the end of five years the account will have accumulated $10,000.

Present value of an annuity. Suppose you were offered the following alternatives: a five-year annuity of $1,000 a year or a lump-sum payment today. You have no need for the money during the next five years, so if you accept the annuity you would simply deposit the receipts in a savings account paying 4 percent interest. Ignoring flexibility and any risk differentials that might exist, how large must the lump-sum payment be to make it equivalent to the annuity? Again, a graphic illustration will help explain the problem.

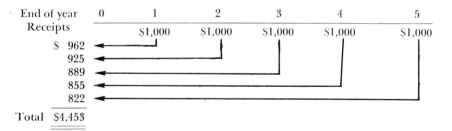

End of year	0	1	2	3	4	5
Receipts		$1,000	$1,000	$1,000	$1,000	$1,000
$ 962						
925						
889						
855						
822						
Total $4,453						

Figure 7A–2. Graphic Illustration of an Annuity: Present Value

The present value of the first receipt is $R/(1 + i)$, the second is $R/(1 + i)^2$, and so on. Defining the present value of an annuity of n years as A_n, we may write the following equation:

$$A_n = \frac{R_1}{(1 + i)} + \frac{R_2}{(1 + i)^2} + \ldots + \frac{R_n}{(1 + i)^n}$$

$$= R\left[\frac{1}{(1 + i)} + \frac{1}{(1 + i)^2} + \ldots + \frac{1}{(1 + i)^n}\right] \qquad (7A\text{--}7)$$

Again, tables have been worked out for the interest factor, the term in the brackets; Table A–4 is illustrative. From this table the *IF* for a five-year, 4 percent annuity is found to be 4.452. Multiplying this factor by the $1,000 annual receipt gives $4,452, the present value of the annuity. This figure differs from the long-method answer shown in Figure 7A–2 by a rounding error.

$$\begin{aligned} A_n &= R \times IF \\ &= \$1{,}000 \times 4.452 \\ &= \$4{,}452 \end{aligned} \qquad (7A\text{--}8)$$

Annual receipts from an annuity. Suppose you receive from an aunt an inheritance of $7,000, which is on deposit in a savings account yielding 4 percent and which is all you have for support while working on your degree. You expect to be in school for four years in addition to the present year. How much of the money can you withdraw at the beginning of each of the next four years to leave exactly zero at the end of the fourth year? Transposing in equation (7A-8) and finding the 4 percent 4-year factor in Table A-4, we get:

$$R = \frac{A_n}{IF}$$

$$= \frac{\$7{,}000}{3.630} = \$1{,}928 \qquad (7A\text{--}9)$$

Thus, starting one year from now, you may withdraw $1,928 at the beginning of each year for four years.

Present Value of an Uneven Series of Receipts

Suppose you were offered your choice of a lump-sum payment of $500 now or a series of payments consisting of $300 after one year, $100 after two years, and $200 after three years. Your opportunity cost is 4 percent. Which offer would you choose? Using the interest factors found in Table A–2, the present value is found to be $558.90, so you would choose the series of payments.

$$\text{P.V.}^* = \frac{R_1}{(1+i)} + \frac{R_2}{(1+i)^2} + \frac{R_3}{(1+i)^3}$$

$$= R_1 \left[\frac{1}{(1+i)} \right] + R_2 \left[\frac{1}{(1+i)^2} \right] + R_3 \left[\frac{1}{(1+i)^3} \right]$$

$$= R_1(IF) + R_2(IF) + R_3(IF)$$

$$= \$300\,(.962) + \$100\,(.925) + \$200\,(.889)$$

$$= \$558.90$$

* Present value.

Had the series been somewhat different—say $300 the first year, then thirty annual payments of $100 each—we would find the present value as follows.

1) P.V. of $300 due in one year: $300 (0.962) $ 288.60
2) P.V. of 30-year annuity with $100 receipts:
   a) P.V. at beginning of next year: $100 (17.292)
      = $1,729.20
   b) P.V. of $1,729.20: $1,729.20 (0.962) $1,663.49
3) P.V. of total series $1,952.09

In such an example, we would clearly want to make use of the annuity formula, but note that the value of the annuity must itself be discounted, as it does not begin until the second year.

SOME FINANCING DECISIONS INVOLVING INTEREST

Terms of a Bond Issue

A corporation needs $1 million cash. Investment banking houses have made the following offers:

1) 6 percent 20-year bonds at 110 percent of par (par = $1,000)
2) 5 percent 20-year bonds at 100 percent of par
3) 4 percent 20-year bonds at 90 percent of par

Which offer should the company accept on cost considerations alone?

First, the company must choose which interest rate to use in making the calculations. Since the bonds carrying the 5 percent interest rate sell at par, 5 percent appears to be the prevailing market rate. The solution requires the computation of (1) the present value of the principal to be repaid at the end of 20 years and (2) the present value of the interest payments (annuity) for 20 years.

The principal amount for repayment will be different, depending on whether the bonds are sold at a premium or a discount.

Calculation of Amount of Bonds to Be Sold

1) 6% bonds at 110: $\dfrac{\$1,000,000}{1.10} = \$\ \ 909,091$

2) 5% bonds at 100: $\dfrac{\$1,000,000}{1.00} = \$1,000,000$

3) 4% bonds at 90: $\dfrac{\$1,000,000}{0.90} = \$1,111,111$

Annual Interest Payment on Bonds Sold

1) 6% bonds: $0.06 \times \$\ \ 909,091 = \$54,545$
2) 5% bonds: $0.05 \times \$1,000,000 = \$50,000$
3) 4% bonds: $0.04 \times \$1,111,111 = \$44,444$

Calculation of Present Value of Sum of Principal and Interest

1) 6% bonds: Principal of $909,091 at 5%: $909,091 × 0.377* . .   342,727
    Interest of $54,545 at 5%: $54,545 × 12.462   679,740
        Total $1,022,467

2) 5% bonds: Principal of $1,000,000 at 5%: $1,000,000 × 0.377*   377,000
    Interest of $50,000 at 5%: $50,000 × 12.462   623,100
        Total $1,000,100

3) 4% bonds: Principal of $1,111,111 at 5%: $1,111,111 × 0.377*   418,889
    Interest of $44,444 at 5%: $44,444 × 12.462   553,861
        Total   . . . . $ 972,750

* IF for 5%, 20 years.

The 4 percent bonds will involve the least expense under the assumptions of this example. The sum of the present value of the outlay is the lowest of the three. Because the same amount of funds is received from each of the offers, the offer with the lowest present value of costs is the cheapest.

Refunding of a Bond Issue

The Culver City Company has outstanding a $60 million 20-year bond issue, carrying a $6\frac{1}{2}$ percent interest rate. The bond indenture carries a call provision making it possible for the company to retire the bonds by calling them in at a 6 percent premium. Investment bankers have assured the company that it could sell an additional $60 to $70 million worth of 20-year bonds at an interest rate of 5 percent. The company would net 96 percent of par value. Should the company refund the $60 million worth of bonds?

Step 1: How much will it cost the company to redeem the bonds?

$$\$60,000,000 \times 1.06 = \$63,600,000$$

Step 2: How much money will the company have to raise in order to redeem the outstanding bonds? The investment bankers said they could sell the bonds at 5 percent if they were sold at a discount of 96. If the new bonds are sold at a discount of 96, the company would find it necessary to sell bonds with a face value of $66.25 million.

$$\frac{\$63,600,000}{0.96} = \$66,250,000$$

Step 3: Analyze the interest cost of the two plans. Originally, $60 million at 6½ percent represented an interest cost per year of $3.9 million. The company will now pay 5 percent on $66,250,000, or $3,312,500.

Interest on 6.5% bonds	$3,900,000
Interest on 5% bonds	3,312,500
Savings per year	$ 587,500

The savings will be $587,500 a year, but the company has one other factor to take into consideration. Before the refunding, it would have had to pay off $60 million at maturity. With the refunding operation, it has an additional $6.25 million to pay off at the end of the 20-year period.

The company will deduct from the annual savings of $587,500 an amount which, paid out or set aside each year would accumulate to $6.25 million at the end of 20 years. By Formula 7A-6 the sum equals the annual rent times the interest factor; with n equal to 20 years and an interest rate of 5 percent, we find the interest factor to be 33.07 (from Table A-3).

$$\frac{\$6,250,000}{33.07} = \$188,993$$

We divide the 33.07 into $6.25 million, obtaining approximately $189,000. The $189,000 is deducted from the annual savings of $587,500, so the annual net savings for the company will be about $400,000 a year. The refunding operation appears to be a profitable one.

An alternative but equivalent approach to this problem is to find the present values of each of the issues—the present value of the interest payments for 20 years, plus that of the principal to be repaid at maturity. These calculations are shown below.

Costs of Old Issue:	*Amount*	*Discount Factor**	*Present Value*
Annual interest payments	$ 3,900,000	12.462	$48,601,800
Principal amount	60,000,000	0.377	22,620,000
Present value of costs			$71,221,800

Costs of New Issue:

Annual interest payments	$ 3,312,500	12.462	$41,280,375
Principal amount	66,250,000	0.377	24,976,250
Present value of costs			$66,256,625
Present value of costs of old issue			$71,221,800
Present value of costs of new issue			66,256,625
Present value of net savings			$ 4,965,175

* The discount factor used is 5 percent.

Since the present value of the costs of the new issue is less (by about $5 million) than those of the old issue, the company should refund the bonds.

COMPARISON BETWEEN INTERNAL RATE OF RETURN AND NET PRESENT VALUE METHODS

In Chapter 7 the internal rate of return was defined as the value of r that equates the two sides of the following equation:

$$\text{Initial outlay} = R_1\left[\frac{1}{(1+r)}\right] + R_2\left[\frac{1}{(1+r)^2}\right] + \ldots + R_n\left[\frac{1}{(1+r)^n}\right]$$

The value of r is found by trial and error.

The other theoretically correct ranking technique, the net present value method, found the difference between the present value of the annual receipts, discounted at the cost of capital (i), and the initial outlay.

$$\text{Net present value} = R_1\left[\frac{1}{(1+i)}\right] + R_2\left[\frac{1}{(1+i)^2}\right]$$
$$+ \ldots + R_n\left[\frac{1}{(1+i)^n}\right] - \text{cost}$$

Referring to Table 7A–1, it will be recalled that the entire concept of present value as it has been developed hinges on the assumption of reinvestment. In the example used in Table 7A–1, we started with $1,000, added the interest received during the first year, reinvested the sum at the same 4 percent, and so on. Exactly the same concept is involved in the capital budgeting equations. The internal rate of return calculation assumes that the cash flows from the projects—the R's—can be reinvested in other projects that will yield the same internal rate of return. The net present value calculation, by contrast, implicitly assumes that cash flows are reinvested at the cost of capital.

Which is the better assumption? In general, if the firm is not subject to artificial capital restraints (capital rationing), the net present value method is more nearly correct. The reason for this is that, conceptually, a firm will invest to the point where its marginal rate of return on new investment (the internal rate of return on the last acceptable project) is just equal to its cost of capital. As cash flows come in, they simply replace other sources of investment capital; hence they save the firm the cost of the replaced capital. From this it is concluded that the rate of return at which cash flows are invested is equal to the marginal cost of capital. Therefore, the assumption of the net present value method—that funds are reinvested at the cost of capital—is the correct one.

It has been argued that some firms are subject to capital rationing, meaning that they can spend no more than a fixed sum regardless of the amount of profitable investment opportunities open to them. This situation is illustrated in Figure 7A-3. A capital rationing edict might set the

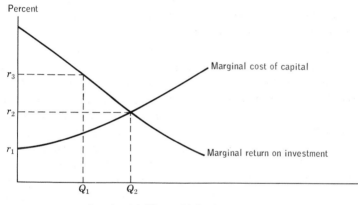

Fig. 7A-3. Hypothetical Investment and Cost of Capital Schedules

maximum that could be spent on capital assets at Q_1, while, without capital rationing, investment would be taken on to Q_2. At a level of investment Q_1, the cost of capital is r_1—well below r_3, the minimum rate of return earned on new investment. Under such circumstances it might well be that cash flows can be invested at the internal rate of return, and it certainly appears that assuming reinvestment at the cost of capital involves an understatement. This lends appeal to the internal rate of return method. Without capital rationing, on the other hand, the minimum return earned is just equal to the marginal cost of capital, r_2. Under this condition, the present value assumption is the better one.

Would a firm actually submit itself to a self-imposed capital rationing and thus pass up profitable investment opportunities? In the case of large, publicly owned firms that are sophisticated enough to be employing these capital budgeting techniques, the answer is that probably they would not. But it might be perfectly rational for a small, closely owned firm simply to refuse to expand faster than it can be financed internally. It may well be that the owner-manager is more interested in control than in maximizing profits. This topic will be discussed in greater detail later.

ALTERNATIVE APPROACHES TO NET PRESENT VALUE METHOD

In Chapter 7, the net present value of an investment was defined as the present value of its receipts minus the initial outlay. When ranking mutually exclusive investments, the investment with the higher net present value was assigned the higher rank. There is, however, an alternative approach that calls for dividing the net present value of a project by its cost, thus getting the net present value per dollar of outlay and ranking on the basis of this ratio. This procedure has the effect of standardizing for size of investment.

Such an adjustment would have no bearing on the rankings of the hypothetical projects A and B in Chapter 7—the net present values are both divided by the same cost figure; hence the relationship of the ratios is exactly the same as that of their net present values. But in many instances it might make a difference. Suppose, for example, that we are comparing project A—which calls for an investment of $1 million in a conveyor belt system for handling goods in a storage warehouse—with project B, which calls for an expenditure of $300,000 to do the same thing by employing a fleet of fork trucks. The conveyor belt system has lower operating costs, so its cash flows are larger; the net present values are found to be $200,000 for A and $100,000 for B. Using this as the criterion, we would select project A. However, if we compute the ratios of net present value to cost, we find A's to be 20 percent, B's to be 33.3 percent. Using the ratios for ranking, we would select project B, because it produces higher net returns per dollar invested.

Given this conflict, which project should be accepted? Alternatively stated, is it better to use the net present value approach on an absolute basis or on a relative basis? Barring capital rationing, the authors recommend the absolute values for the following reason. First, the differential between the initial outlays of the two projects ($700,000) can be looked upon as an investment itself, project C. This differential investment produces a net present value equal to the differential between the net present values of the first two projects, or $100,000. Since the hypothetical project has a positive present value, it should be accepted. The result is to accept project A.

	A	−	B	=	C
Cost	$1,000,000		$300,000		$700,000
Net present value	200,000		100,000		100,000

Put another way, project A can be split into two components, one costing $300,000 and having a net present value of $100,000, the other costing $700,000 and having a net present value of $100,000. Since each of the two components has a positive present value, both should be accepted. But if project B is accepted, in effect the second component of project A is being rejected. Hence the conclusion that, since the ratio method selects project B while the absolute value method selects project A, the absolute value method is the better one.

Under certain circumstances, the ratio method obviously gives the better answer. If one project cost $1 million and had a net present value of $100,000, while another cost $100,000 and had a net present value of $99,000, the latter would certainly be selected. The benefits are almost as great but the amount of funds invested, hence the risk, is much smaller. However, such an example is not very realistic. Mutually exclusive investments represent alternative ways of doing essentially the same thing, and it is unlikely that they will involve such substantial cost differentials. But if they did, this would simply be one more among many examples demonstrating that no mechanical rule can be substituted for judgment.

QUESTIONS

7A–1 What types of financial decisions are importantly contingent upon the interest factor concept?

7A–2 At a growth rate of 8 percent, how long does it take a sum to double?

7A–3 Which is worth more at 5 percent: $1,000 today or $1,400 after seven years?

7A–4 What is one main difference between the internal rate of return concept and the present value concept? Restrict your answer to reinvestment considerations.

7A–5 Compound interest relations are important for decisions other than financial ones. Why are they important to marketing managers?

PROBLEMS

7A–1 The Harris Company has $100,000 long-term bonds outstanding. The debt has an additional ten years to maturity and bears an interest rate of 8 percent. The firm now has the opportunity to refinance the debt with ten-year bonds at a rate of 6 percent. The firm's cost of capital is 6 percent. The bond redemption premium on the old bond would be $5,000; issue costs on the new would be $6,000. If tax effects are ignored, should the firm refund the bonds?

7A–2 On December 30, Philip P. Potter buys a building for $20,000, payable 10 percent down and the balance in twenty-five equal annual installments that are to include interest at 6 percent on a compound annual basis. What are the equal installments?

7A–3 1. What amount would be paid for a $1,000 ten-year 5 percent coupon bond, interest paid semiannually, sold to yield 6 percent?

2. What would be paid if the bond were sold to yield 4 percent?

3. What would be paid if the coupon were 6 percent and the bond were sold to yield 10 percent?

7A–4 The Westwood Company wishes to establish a sinking fund to retire a $200,000 mortgage on December 31, 1975. The company plans to put a fixed amount into the fund each year. The first payment will be made on December 31, 1966. The company anticipates that the fund will earn 5 percent per year. What annual contributions must be made to accumulate the $200,000 as of December 31, 1975?

7A–5 You are considering two investment opportunities, A and B. A is expected to pay $100 per year for the first ten years, $200 a year for the next 20 years, and nothing thereafter. B is expected to pay $200 per year for eight years, nothing thereafter. You find that alternative investments of similar risk yield 8 percent and 3 percent for A and B respectively.

1. Find the present value of each investment. Show calculations.

2. Which is the more risky investment? Why?

3. Assume that your rich uncle will give you your choice of investments without cost to you, and that: (a) you must hold the investment for its entire life (cannot sell it) or (b) you are free to sell it at its going market price. Which investment would you prefer under each of the two conditions?

Make or Buy Decisions

Another important decision may be approached through the methodology described in Chapter 7—the decision to make or to buy component parts. A component should be purchased if it can be obtained at a price lower than the production costs involved if it were produced by the user firm. Typically, making the part requires an investment in specialized machinery that can be used effectively only if volume is sufficiently high. Thus, the reason firms buy parts from vendors is that the supplier firms may, by selling components to several users, generate a volume that will enable them to sell the product at a price below that at which the buyer could produce it. The nature of the analysis may be illustrated by the following example.

The Hansen Electronics Company's demand for a component is expected to be between 10,000 and 15,000 units per year during the next ten years. A manufacturing firm has offered to supply Hansen with this part at a price of $3 per unit. The company can manufacture the part in its own plant for $1 per unit if it purchases a special machine. The machine costs $80,000, and has an economic life of ten years, with no terminal salvage value. Hansen's cost of capital is 10 percent. Assuming double declining balance depreciation and a 50 percent income tax rate, should the company make or purchase this part?

The solution follows the pattern set out in Table 7–6, and is given in Table 7B–1. The inflows (savings) depend upon the volume the Hansen Company is able to achieve. At 5,000 units, it is much cheaper to buy the items from the outside. At 10,000 units, it is cheaper to buy the machine and gain the benefits of large volume and low unit costs. The break-even volume occurs at 8,534 units. The firm would doubtless require some margin of safety over the break-even point, as more risk is involved in making the $80,000 investment for the machine than buying the units as needed. However, if the company is confident of the forecast that its volume requirements will in fact exceed 10,000 units per year, then the choice of purchasing the equipment and making the component is indicated.[1]

---

[1] Another consideration is the assurance of a continued supply of quality components. Firms are often willing to sacrifice some cost advantages in order to produce a part themselves and thus be sure of getting parts of a sufficiently high quality when they are needed.

Net present value

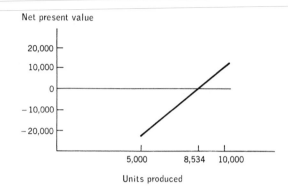

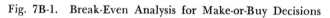

Units produced

Fig. 7B-1.   Break-Even Analysis for Make-or-Buy Decisions

TABLE 7B–1

SOLUTION TO THE HANSEN ELECTRONICS PROBLEM

Outflows	Amount before Tax	Amount after Tax	Year Event Occurs	Present Value Factor at 10%	Present Value
Investment in new equipment	80,000	80,000	0	1.00	$80,000
Inflows					
Depreciation	80,000	40,000	1–10	.69	27,600
P.V. of outflows after depreciation					$52,400
Savings					
1) 5,000X2	10,000	5,000	1–10	6.14	30,700
2) 8,534X2	16,650	8,534	1–10	6.14	52,399
3) 10,000X2	20,000	10,000	1–10	6.14	61,400

Net P.V. of investment:		P.V.-savings	P.V.-costs	Net P.V.
	5,000 units	$30,700	52,400	(21,700)
	8,534 units	52,399	52,400	0
	10,000 units	61,400	52,400	9,000

Part III

Financial Planning

Chapter 8

Financial Forecasting

The preceding chapter, dealing with capital budgeting, set forth procedures for determining the desired amount of a firm's equipment financing in a given period and provided a method for ranking individual investment proposals. Thus, by summing up the acceptable investments, management can obtain an accurate measure of total capital expenditures. Capital budgeting does not, however, necessarily reflect what the firm's over-all need for funds will be. Sales may increase (up to the limit of capacity) independently of new capital investment, and as sales increase so does the need for funds to carry higher levels of inventories, accounts receivable, and so forth. Further, capital budget plans or facilities planning in total must be viewed in the framework of over-all sales forecasting and financial planning.

Such long-range planning is vitally important. As will be seen in subsequent chapters, additional long-term debt and especially equity funds are raised infrequently and in large amounts. Further, the cost (per dollar raised) of selling such securities decreases as the size of the issue increases, thus reducing the tendency to raise outside capital at frequent intervals. Because of these considerations, it is important that the firm have a working estimate of its total needs for funds for the next few years. It is therefore useful at this point to examine methods of forecasting the firm's over-all needs for funds.

A distinction should be made between the material covered in the present chapter and that of the following chapter dealing with budgeting. The term "forecasting" deals essentially with the impact of the external environment on the firm's sales and in turn on its total resource needs.

185

Budgeting, however, begins with the forecast of external factors as basic premises. With these forecasts as a foundation, budgeting involves the effective allocation of the firm's resources among different products and projects.

The discussion in this chapter is thus focused on determining the amount of resources that will have to be financed. The following chapter centers on the allocation of a firm's resources among the alternative internal uses.

The most important causal variable in determining financing requirements is a firm's projected dollar volume of sales. Hence a good sales forecast is an essential foundation for forecasting financial requirements. The two principal methods of forecasting financial requirements are described in the following sections. Both use sales as the starting point for the forecast; the first method uses a ratio relation between sales and asset components; the second, a regression relation.

PERCENT OF SALES METHOD

The simplest approach to forecasting financial requirements expresses the firm's needs in terms of the percentage of annual sales invested in an individual balance sheet item. For example, a firm may require 2 percent of sales in cash, 17 percent in receivables, 20 percent in inventories, and 30 percent in fixed assets. On the liability side, accounts payable may represent 10 percent of sales, and accruals 5 percent. If the firm's net worth is $200,000 and sales are $500,000 per year, the above information is enough to tell us that the firm will need to raise $70,000 in new funds. The results of these calculations are shown on the balance sheet for the Moore Company:

MOORE COMPANY
BALANCE SHEET
December 31, 1966

Cash	$ 10,000	Accounts payable	$ 50,000
Receivables	85,000	Accruals	25,000
Inventories	100,000	Net worth	200,000
Fixed assets	150,000	Additional funds needed	70,000
Total	$345,000	Total	$345,000

This brief example illustrates the relationships between sales and the balance sheet items and a necessary tie-in between forecasting sales and financial requirements. The percent-of-sales method is a relatively simple procedure. The difficult problem is to establish valid relations.

One way of developing the relationships between sales and the individual balance sheet items is based on a consideration of basic business practices. For example, suppose the Moore Company sells on credit terms of 60 days net. The firm could therefore expect to have about two months' sales in receivables at any one time. Barring seasonality, this is two twelfths of annual sales, or about 17 percent. If credit sales are $500,000 per year, then 17 percent of this figure, or $85,000, will be tied up in receivables. If credit sales should rise to $700,000, accounts receivable may be expected to increase to $119,000. This demonstrates how the level of sales influences the size of individual asset components.

This procedure is illustrated in Table 8–1 for the Radio Corporation of America for the years 1963 and 1964. In the first column, the balance sheet items and selected income statement items for 1963 are shown. In the second column, those asset components which should be closely related to sales are expressed as a percentage of sales. The third column multiplies the percentages contained in the second column by 1964 sales, and adds in the remaining balance sheet figures (not directly tied to sales) to produce a *pro forma* balance sheet.[1]

Reinvested earnings are calculated as follows: The percentage of profits after tax to sales is calculated; an estimate of profits after taxes is thus obtained. The company's dividend-payout percentage is applied to profits after tax. This amount, *pro forma* dividends, is deducted from profits after tax to obtain reinvested earnings for the year. The amount of the retained earnings is added to reinvested earnings of the previous year to obtain reinvested earnings for the forecast year.

The total of retained earnings for 1964 was $45 million. These data illustrate that the importance of retained earnings as a source of financing is inversely related to the rate of growth of the firm. This is shown by generalizing how the percentage-of-sales method directly establishes the amount of financing requirements. For any increase in sales for a given year, the increase in financing requirements for RCA may be indicated:

Percentage-of-sales increase in asset requirements as a consequence of increase in sales		*Percentage-of-sales increase in financing provided from internal sources*	
Cash	4	Accounts payable	13
Receivables	15	Federal income tax and	
Inventories	10	other current liabilities	4
Fixed assets	15	Total (before retained	
Total	44	earnings)	17

[1] Since the increase in assets due to the increase in revenues was small, random fluctuations in assets would have a larger influence on the change in assets than would be the case when a 4 to 5 percent increase took place because of the increase in revenues.

TABLE 8-1

PERCENTAGE OF SALES METHOD OF FORECASTING FINANCING REQUIREMENTS
RADIO CORPORATION OF AMERICA, 1963-1964
(in millions of dollars)

	(1) 1963	(2) Percentage of Sales	(3) 1964 Pro Forma	(4) Actual	(5) Pro Forma Less Actual	(6) (5) ÷ (4) Percent Error
Sales	$1,779		$1,800	$1,797		
Cash	79	4.4	79	65	14	21.5
Marketable securities	250		234	234		
Receivables	268	15.1	272	263	9	3.4
Inventories	186	10.4	187	201	(14)	(7.0)
Prepayments	34		34	34		
Total current	$ 817		$ 806	$ 797		
Investments	39		37	37		
Net property	269	15.1	272	294	(22)	(7.5)
Miscellaneous	4		4	4		
Total assets	$1,129		$1,119	$1,132	(13)	(1.1)
Accounts payable	$ 228	12.8	$ 230	$ 235	(5)	(2.1)
Federal income tax	70	3.9	70	59	11	18.6
Other current liabilities	9	0.5	9	14	(5)	(35.7)
Total current	$ 307		$ 309	$ 308		
Long-term debt	255		255	255		
Other liabilities	36		45	45		
Preferred stock*	15		3	3		
Net worth*	516	2.2*	556	521*	(35)	(6.7)*
Total claims	$1,129		$1,168	$1,132		

Financing Needed (or ???)

Memorandum Information	1963	Percentage of Sales	1964 Actual
Profits after tax	66		82
Percent of sales	3.7	3.7	4.6
Dividends paid	26		37
Payout percentage	39.4		45.1
Reinvested earnings	40	2.2	45
Percent of sales	2.2		2.5

* The *increase* in retained earnings is 2.2 percent of 1964 sales and is added to the 1963 net worth to obtain 1964 net worth. RCA's 1964 net worth was affected by transactions in RCA preferred and common stock. If these changes had not taken place, the reinvested earnings of RCA during 1964 would have increased by the amount of retained earnings of $45 million for 1964.

The difference between the automatic increase in financing requirements and the automatic increase in financing sources is 27 percentage
points. Thus, for any given amount of increase in sales, for example, $100
million, RCA's net additional financing requirement before the increase
in retained earnings will be $27 million. In the present illustration, RCA's
sales increased by $21 million on a *pro forma* basis. The additional funds
needed beyond the funds provided from the "automatic" increase in the
current liability items is 27 percent of the $21 million, which is $5 million.
But retained earnings alone were $45 million, so that over $40 million was
available for increasing the investment in marketable securities or reducing debt and preferred stock obligations.

The important role of retained earnings is emphasized by the above
example. The relations may now be generalized. Retained earnings can
be expressed as a percent of *total* sales. The increased net financing requirements are expressed as a percent of the *increase* in sales. The amount
of additional external financing required can then be determined directly.
To illustrate for an increase in sales of $60 million for a company with
sales of $600 million:

	Percent	Amount (millions)
Increase in sales	10%	$60
Net financing requirements	25% of 10% (or 2.5% of total sales)	15
Retained earnings	2% of total sales*	13.2
Additional outside financing required	3% of increase in sales, or 0.5% of total sales	1.8

* The new total sales of $660 million.

Thus, when RCA experienced a 2 percent sales increase (from a $1.8
billion base) in a given year, the funds provided would be determined as
follows:

	Percent	Amount (millions)
Increase in sales	2%	$36
Net financing requirements	27% of 2%, or 0.54% of total sales, or 27% of increase in sales	$10
Retained earnings	2.5% of total sales of $1,836 million	$46
Additional outside financing required (available)	(1.96%) of total sales	($36)

The increase in sales is 2 percent. Net financing requirements are 27 percent of the 2 percent, which is 0.54 percent of total sales. Retained earnings are 2.5 percent of total sales. Thus net additional external financing requirements are 1.96 percent of total sales of $1,836 million, or a total of $37 million.

This illustration should reinforce the generalization about the relation between the rate of growth of sales and the amount of external financing requirements. The higher the rate of growth of sales for a given net financing requirements pattern, the greater the size of additional external financing requirements. Small increases in sales are likely to result in funds availability if profit margins are maintained. It will be interesting to apply these relations to the RCA data for 1965, the first year in which the massive impact of the expansion in color television was felt. At the time of this writing the final sales figures were not available, but estimates placed 1965 sales at $2 billion, 11 percent above those of 1964.

The authors wish to caution the reader that they do not intend to convey the impression that the use of percentage of sales as a method of forecasting financial requirements is simple and mechanical. To explain the ideas requires simple illustrations. The authors' experience in applying the technique in practice suggests the importance of understanding the underlying local technology and logic of the relation between sales and the asset investment requirements that will be experienced by the firm. In addition, a substantial amount of experience and judgment will be required to apply the technique in actual practice.

The percentage-of-sales method is most appropriately used for forecasting month-to-month or other short-term changes in financing needs. It is less useful for longer term forecasting for reasons that are best described in connection with the analysis of the regression method of financial forecasting.

SCATTER DIAGRAM, OR REGRESSION, METHOD

An alternative method used to forecast financial requirements is the scatter diagram, or regression, method. A scatter diagram is a graphic portrayal of joint relations. Statistical sophistication is not necessary, but practice is required to use scatter diagrams properly.

Table 8-2 and Figure 8-1 illustrate the use of the regression method and also demonstrate its superiority over the percentage-of-sales method. As in all financial forecasting, the sales forecast is the starting point. The financial manager is given the sales forecast, or he may participate in formulating it. Suppose that the financial manager has data through 1965 and is seeking to make a forecast of inventories for 1970, as indicated in

TABLE 8-2

RELATIONS BETWEEN INVENTORY AND SALES

Year	Sales	Inventory	Inventory as a Percentage of Sales
1960	$ 50,000	$22,000	44
1961	100,000	24,000	24
1962	150,000	26,000	17
1963	200,000	28,000	14
1964	250,000	30,000	12
1965	300,000	32,000	11
1970	500,000	40,000	8

Table 8-2. If the regression method is used, a line is drawn through the points for 1960 through 1965, as shown in Figure 8-1. The line that fits the scatter of points in this example is a straight line. It is called the line of best fit, or regression line.[2] Of course, all points will seldom fall exactly on the regression line. The line itself may be curved as well as linear.[3]

If the percentage-of-sales method had been used, some difficulties immediately arise. Table 8-2 gives percentages of sales for 1960 through 1965. What relation should be used? the 44 percent for 1960? the 11 percent for 1965? some average of the relations? If the relation for 1965 had been used, a forecast of $55,000 for inventories in 1970 would have been made. This forecast represents a large error.

The regression method is thus seen to be superior for forecasting financial requirements, particularly for longer term forecasts. When a firm is likely to have a base stock of inventory or fixed assets, the ratio of the item to sales declines as sales increase. In such cases the ratio, or percentage, method will result in large errors.[4]

---

[2] The word "regression" has a fascinating origin. In 1885-1886 Sir Francis Galton, in a paper entitled "Regression towards Mediocrity in Hereditary Stature," observed that sons did not grow progressively taller than their fathers because tall sons came predominantly from fathers of medium height through random mutations in heredity. But the sons of these tall sons followed the predominant strain of medium height in their inherited characteristics. Galton observed the data on heights on a graph and called attention to the "regression" of the heights of sons toward the heights of fathers.

Regression line simply means the average relation between the two variables being correlated—in our example, the average relation between sales and inventories.

[3] In these illustrations inventories are used as the item to be forecast. Much theory suggests that inventories increase as a square root of sales. This characteristic would tend to turn slightly downward the line of regression between inventories and sales. Also, improvement in inventory control techniques would curve the line of relation downward. However, the increased diversity of types, models, and styles tends to increase inventories. Applications by the authors' students of the regression method to hundreds of companies indicates that the linear straight line relations typically represent the line of best fit or at worst involve only small error. If the line were truly curved over, a curved line could be fit to the data and used for forecasting purposes.

[4] The widespread use of the percentage method makes for lax control. It should be

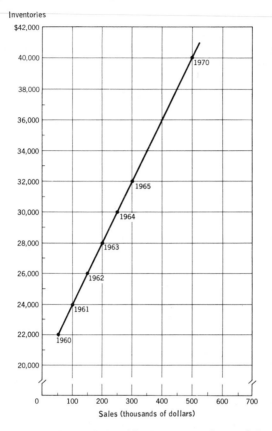

Fig. 8–1. Illustrative Relationship between Sales and Inventory

In Table 8–3 the data for the Standard Oil Company of California are used to demonstrate the scatter diagram method for a complete financial forecast. In Figure 8–2, only selected variables are plotted. Chart *a* shows the relation between gross national product (hereafter called GNP) and the Standard Oil Company sales. A forecast of GNP, a good measure of the general level of business activity, is used to project company sales in chart *a* of Figure 8–2. Charts *b, c,* and *d* relate Standard Oil Company sales to net accounts receivable, inventories, and net fixed assets.

The procedure for carrying out a scatter diagram analysis is outlined below.

1. Forecast or project the sales of the firm by GNP, industry sales, or other logical business indicators.

---

easy to improve on a $55,000 inventory level and still be inefficient, because the correct target amount is closer to $44,000. A clear example of the use of correlation relations rather than ratios to set controls for travel expenses is set out in W. A. Wallis and H. V. Roberts, *Statistics* (New York: Free Press, 1956), pp. 549-555.

TABLE 8-3

GROSS NATIONAL PRODUCT AND STANDARD OIL COMPANY OF CALIFORNIA DATA
(in millions of dollars)

Year	GNP (billions of dollars)	Sales	Cash, marketable securities	Inventories	Receivables	Total current assets	Net fixed assets	Misc. assets	Accounts payable	Provision for income tax
1958	444.5	$1,559	$193	$243	$250	$686	$1,629	$136	$164	$54
1959	482.7	1,565	189	238	253	675	1,759	143	165	48
1960	502.6	1,663	217	219	318	754	1,864	164	226	53
1961	518.7	2,046	219	252	347	820	2,105	191	286	56
1962	556.2	2,150	202	240	399	871	2,274	208	333	50
1963	583.9	2,203	204	267	446	917	2,397	230	344	50
1964	622.6	2,285	172	279	519	971	2,589	236	347	60

Year	Other current liab.	Long-term debt	Common stock and capital surplus	Retained earnings and surplus reserves	Total assets and claims on assets	Net income to common	Cash dividends to common	Payout percentage	Retained earnings
1958	$259	$179	$ 797	$1,215	$2,451	$258	$126	$49%	$132
1959	259	175	797	1,347	2,578	254	126	50	128
1960	324	173	797	1,487	2,782	266	126	47	140
1961	394	172	962	1,569	3,117	286	126	44	160
1962	434	185	1,148	1,563	3,353	305	133	44	172
1963	451	183	1,148	1,741	3,545	314	139	44	175
1964	478	216	1,378	1,724	3,796	337	144	43	193

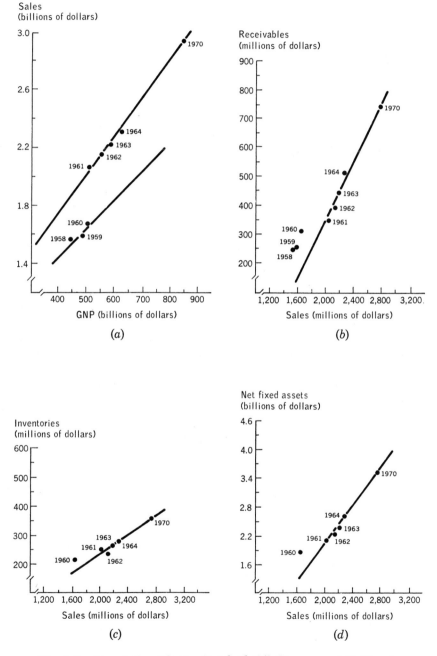

Fig. 8–2. Correlation Charts: Standard Oil Company of California

2. Plot the scatter diagrams for major asset, liability, and net worth categories related to sales.
3. Fit the regression line by free hand (inspection) or by numerical calculations.
4. Project the regression lines and determine the level of balance sheet category for the forecast value of sales. (Projections for the Standard Oil Company of California are summarized in Table 8–4.)
5. The difference between asset requirements and financing sources directly related to sales indicates financial requirements.

As is true of the ratio methods of forecasting financial requirements, the regression method can be used to forecast only the items of the balance sheet that are directly influenced by sales. Some items are directly tied to sales; others are not.

Balance sheet items directly tied to increase in sales		Balance sheet items not directly tied to increase in sales	
Assets	*Liabilities*	*Assets*	*Liabilities*
Cash	Accounts payable	Investments	Notes payable
Receivables	Provision for income		Long-term debt
Inventories	tax		Preferred stock
Fixed assets	Accruals		Common stock
	Retained earnings		

As the above listing indicates, most of the asset items—the balance sheet items to be financed—vary with the increase in sales. When sales increase, these items are likely to increase in some predictable fashion. On the right-hand side of the balance sheet, some items increase with incremental sales in a similar fashion. Retained earnings, as indicated in the discussion of the ratio method, increase with total sales, not just incremental sales.

In the example provided in Table 8–4, the company's sales are shown to increase by some $400 million over the six-year period. Total assets rise from $3,796 million to $5,213 million, an increase of $1,417 million. The increase in retained earnings and other selected current liability items provide part of the additional funds required. But additional financing of some $123 million will be needed.[5]

The difference between the financing required (increases in the asset items) and the financing provided (increases in certain liability and net worth items) is the additional financing required. This financing will come from four major sources: notes payable, long-term debt, preferred stock, and common stock.

These are the major alternative sources of financing. Forecasting

---

[5] The authors do not presume to have made the careful study required to establish that these are forecasts that would be used to guide company policy. The figures here presented for the Standard Oil Company of California are used only to illustrate a methodology.

TABLE 8–4

STANDARD OIL COMPANY OF CALIFORNIA
PRO FORMA BALANCE SHEETS
1964 Estimates Compared With 1964 Actual
(in millions of dollars)

	1964 Actual	1964 Estimated	1970 Estimated
GNP (in billions of dollars)	$ 622.6	$ 622.6	$ 850*
Company sales	2,285	2,285	2,780
Assets			
Cash and marketable securities	173	210	223
Receivables	519	480	750
Inventories	279	275	355
Total current assets	971	965	1,328
Miscellaneous assets	236	236	345
Net fixed assets	2,589	2,590	3,540
Total assets	$3,796	$3,791	$5,213
Liabilities			
Accounts payable	$ 348	$ 348	$ 455
Income tax	60	60	74†
Other current liabilities	70	57	63
Total current liabilities	478	465	592
Long-term debt	216	216	216
Total liabilities	694	681	808
Capital			
Common stock	1,378	1,378	1,378
Retained earnings	1,724	1,724	2,904
Total capital	3,102	3,102	4,282
Subtotal	3,796	3,783	5,090
Additional financing needed	0	8	123
Total	$3,796	$3,791	$5,213

* 5.5 percent growth rate.
† Assumed 20 percent of net income.

financial requirements thus leads to an estimate of financing needed. How the needed financing will be raised is the subject matter of Parts IV, V, and VI of this book.

COMPARISON OF FORECASTING TECHNIQUES

The scatter diagram method can be used for an individual firm, an industry, or the economy as a whole. Like the percentage of sales method, however, the scatter diagram is subject to a margin of error. For more dependable forecasting, additional analysis based on the characteristics of the line of business must be carried out.[6]

If a good sales forecast is made, the scatter diagram method can yield results such as those appearing in Table 8–5. The largest percentage

TABLE 8–5

STANDARD OIL COMPANY OF CALIFORNIA
PERCENTAGE ERROR IN 1964 ESTIMATES

	(1) Actual figures in millions of dollars	(2) Estimates in millions of dollars	(3) Percentage error $\frac{(2)-(1)}{(1)}$
Sales	$2,285	$2,285	—
Assets			
Cash	$ 173	$ 210	21
Receivables	519	480	(17)
Inventories	279	275	(1)
Total current assets	971	965	
Miscellaneous assets	236	236	—
Net fixed assets	2,589	2,590	—†
Total assets	$3,796	$3,791	—†
Liabilities			
Accounts payable	$ 348	$ 348	—
Income tax	60	60	—
Other current liabilities	70	57	(19)
Total current liabilities	478	465	(3)
Long term debt	216	216	—
Total liabilities	694	681	(2)
Capital			
Common stock	1,378	1,378	
Retained earnings	1,724	1,724*	—
Total capital	3,102	3,102	—
Subtotal	3,796	3,783	—†
Additional financing needed			
Total	$3,796	$3,791	—†

* Since special adjustments were made to this account, the forecast reflects these policy determinations.
† Negligible.

errors occur in the accounts that combine several categories and in receivables. The latter suggests further analysis of credit policies. More than one half the errors are below 5 percent. The accuracy depends upon

[6] Multiple regression techniques, for example, might help improve forecasts.

the stability of the relations, which in turn depends upon the nature of the business.

For short-term forecasts, such as month to month, either the ratio method or the correlation method, appropriately supplemented with judgment and knowledge of special developments in the company, may be employed. For longer term forecasts, it is best to use the regression method to avoid major errors that might result from systematic shifts in the ratios. Where the points on the scatter diagrams deviate widely from the regression lines (as they are likely to do as credit or inventory policies change), additional study and application of judgment are required for an accurate forecast.

The use of mechanical methods of financial forecasting described in this chapter are not expected to do the entire job of financial forecasting.

Justification for describing the methods in this book rests on three considerations. One, a review of the considerable literature describing how individual firms forecast their financial requirements indicates that companies generally employ either the ratio method or the correlation method, directly or indirectly. To forecast at all requires the use of some cause-and-effect relations; these are the basis for the use of the correlation method. Thus one justification is that the methods are implicitly widely used.

Two, the use of these methods avoids the twin errors frequently encountered in growing businesses. On the one hand, a firm that seeks to grow 20 percent a year may run into financial difficulties because of failure to plan for the requisite financing of the assets required to support such sales growth. Often a top executive will give a directive such as, "We will increase sales by 50 percent during the next three years, but we will hold the line on investment in inventories and fixed plant." A consideration of the logic of the forecasting methods recommended suggests that such a directive may be unrealistic and may place subordinates in impossible situations. On the other hand, growth in sales and profits may be accompanied by a sense of corporate affluence, which leads to profligate expenditures on equipment and to lax inventory and receivables control. The use of the forecasting methods just described provides standards for control.

Three, it is not presumed that the methods described provide a finished forecast. But, typically, they will put the financial manager "in the ball park." They set limited boundaries on what financing requirements are likely to be. If the financial manager starts with this foundation, he can take into account all the special circumstances and individual factors bearing on the particular situation of a business (and which, because of their unique and different patterns, cannot be expressed in general relations). This specific knowledge can be used to refine the financial forecast arrived at by the use of the methods described here.

SUMMARY

Because asset requirements are generated by sales activity, sales levels can be used as a basis for estimating financing requirements. The ratio method based on the percentage of sales is simple and is useful for forecasting changes in financial requirements over short periods. The regression method is more dependable for longer term forecasts.

Both methods, when used appropriately, are valuable for providing a perspective on financing trends in a firm. Both may be used to indicate a first approximation to financing requirements. With the foundation they provide, consideration of individual factors and special influences can be used to modify these mechanical forecasts and achieve a dependable guide to the future financing needs of the firm.

SELECTED REFERENCES

Binshadler, Edward W. "Financial Planning and Control—The Key to Efficient Management," *The Arthur Young Journal,* 6 (April, 1959), pp. 30–37.

Forecasting Financial Requirements, Financial Management Series, No. 103 (New York: American Management Association, 1947).

How H. J. Heinz Manages Its Financial Planning and Controls, Financial Management Series, No. 106 (New York: American Management Association, 1953).

Jerrett, Robert, Jr., "Total Financial Planning," *Financial Planning for Greater Profits.* Management Report Number 44. (New York: American Management Association, 1960) pp. 44–51.

"Minnesota Mining and Manufacturing Company Case," *N. A. C. A. Bulletin,* 38 (October 1956), pp. 307–340.

Peterson, H. G., "The Co-ordination of Company Financial Planning with External Economic Conditions," *N. A. C. A. Bulletin,* 27 (March 1946), pp. 575–587.

Planning for Growth: Three Company Programs, General Management Series, No. 185 (New York: American Management Association, 1957).

Villers, Raymond, *Research and Development: Planning and Control* (New York: Financial Executives Research Foundation, Inc., 1964).

QUESTIONS

8–1 What is the logical first step in forecasting financial requirements? Why?

8–2 For what reasons does a firm hold cash?

8–3 Compare the relative advantages of holding cash as opposed to investing in short-term marketable securities.

8–4 If a firm's average collection period is 25 days and its credit sales per day are $1,000, what is the theoretical amount for accounts receivable on the balance sheet?

8–5 What is the regression method for forecasting financial needs?

8–6 What should be the approximate point of intersection between the sales-asset regression line and the vertical axis for the following: inventory, accounts receivable, fixed assets. State your answer in terms of positive, zero, or negative. Can you think of any accounts that might have a negative intercept?

8–7 How does forecasting financial requirements in advance of needs help the financial manager perform his responsibilities more effectively?

PROBLEMS

8-1 The Granite Company expects to double its sales by the end of 1967 from the present level of $720,000 to $1,440,000 per year. The net profit after taxes is expected to be 5 percent of sales. Each balance sheet account will have the following percent of sales tied up in it:

1) Cash	2%
2) Receivables	6%
3) Inventory	12%
4) Fixed assets	5%
5) Accounts payable	5%

On December 31, 1966, the common stock account is $100,000 and the retained earnings are $44,000. No dividends are paid to holders of common stock.

1. Complete two balance sheets, one ending December 31, 1966, and the other December 31, 1967, using U. S. Government bonds to balance on the asset side or financing needed on the liability side.
2. What is the significance of your results?

8-2 The Grossman Supply Company is a warehouse and wholesale distributor of steel. It purchases steel in carload lots from more than twenty producing mills; the items include shapes, plates, sheets, wire products, bolts, windows, pipe, and tubing.

The company owns two warehouses of 10,000 square feet each and contemplates the erection of another warehouse of 15,000 square feet. The nature of the steel-supply business requires that the company maintain large inventories to take care of customer requirements in the event of mill strikes or other delays.

In examining the pattern of sales and balance sheets from 1960 through 1965, the company found a rather consistent relation between the following accounts as a percentage of sales.

Current assets	50%
Net fixed assets	20%
Accounts payable	5%
Other current liabilities, including accruals and provision for income taxes but not bank loans	5%
Net profit after taxes	2%

The company's sales for 1966 were $4 million, and its balance sheet on December 31, 1966, was as follows:

GROSSMAN SUPPLY COMPANY
BALANCE SHEET
December 31, 1966

Current assets . . .	$2,000,000	Accounts payable	$	200,000
Fixed assets	800,000	Notes payable		600,000
		Other current liabilities . .		200,000
		Total current liabilities . .		1,000,000
		Mortgage loan		200,000
		Common stock		500,000
		Earned surplus		1,100,000
	$2,800,000			$2,800,000

The company expects its sales to grow by $300,000 each year. If it does so, what will its financial requirements be at the end of the five-year period? Assume other accounts remain the same, that is, notes payable, etc.

1. Construct a *pro forma* balance sheet for the end of 1971, using "additional financing needed" as the balancing item.
2. What are the crucial assumptions made in your projection method?

8–3 The annual sales of the Townsend Company are $1 million. The percentages of sales in each balance sheet that carries sales are as follows:

Cash	4%
Receivables	12
Inventories	12
Net fixed assets	18
Accounts payable	10
Provision for income tax	4
Other current liabilities	5
Profit rate on sales	6

1. Complete the balance sheet below.

TOWNSEND COMPANY
BALANCE SHEET
December 31, 1966

Cash		Accounts payable	
Receivables		Notes payable	$ 80,000
Inventory		Provision for income tax . .	
Current assets . .		Other current liabilities . .	
Fixed assets		Current liabilities . . .	
		Common stock	100,000
		Retained earnings	90,000
Total assets . .		Total	

2. Now suppose that in one year sales increase by $200,000, to $1.2 million. What will be the new balance sheet (no dividends paid)?
3. For any given increase in sales in one year, what will be the additional external financing requirements, expressed as a percentage of sales?

Calculation of Correlation Relations

In the text, "freehand" methods of estimating the regression line were indicated. The regression line can also be calculated by numerical methods.

The procedure outlined below illustrates the calculation of the regression equation $(Y = a + bX)$, the standard error of estimate (S_y), the standard error of the regression coefficient (S_b), and the correlation coefficient (r). For practical situations, computer programs would be used. However, a better understanding will be obtained by the experience of going through the actual calculations with simple data for forecasting a firm's inventories.

Year	X	Y = inventories Y	X²	Y²	X = sales XY (X − X̄)		(X − X̄)²
1962	1	3.4	1	11.56	3.4	−4	16
1963	3	4.6	9	21.16	13.8	−2	4
1964	5	5.5	25	30.25	27.5	0	0
1965	7	6.6	49	43.56	46.2	2	4
1966	9	7.4	81	54.76	66.6	4	16

$\Sigma X = 25$ $\Sigma Y = 27.5$ $\Sigma X^2 = 165$ $\Sigma Y^2 = 161.29$ $\Sigma XY = 157.5$ 0 $\Sigma(X - \overline{X})^2 = 40$

$\overline{X} = 5$ $\overline{Y} = 5.5$

$$b = \frac{N\Sigma XY - \Sigma X\Sigma Y}{N\Sigma X^2 - (\Sigma X)^2} = \frac{5(157.5) - 25(27.5)}{5(165) - 625} = \frac{787.5 - 687.5}{200} = 0.5$$

$$a = \overline{Y} - b\overline{X} = 5.5 - 0.5(5) = 3$$

$$Y_c = 3 + 0.5X$$

$$S_Y = \sqrt{\frac{\Sigma(Y^2) - [a\Sigma(Y) + b\Sigma(XY)]}{N - 1}} = \sqrt{\frac{161.29 - [3(27.5) + 0.5(157.5)]}{4}}$$

$$= \sqrt{\frac{161.29 - (82.5 + 78.75)}{4}} = \frac{\sqrt{0.04}}{2} = 0.1$$

$$S_b = \frac{S_Y}{\sqrt{\Sigma(X - \bar{X})^2}} = \frac{0.1}{\sqrt{40}} = 0.016$$

$$
\begin{aligned}
r &= \frac{N\Sigma XY - \Sigma X\Sigma Y}{\sqrt{N\Sigma X^2 - (\Sigma X)^2}\ \sqrt{N\Sigma Y^2 - (\Sigma Y)^2}} \\[2mm]
&= \frac{5(157.5) - 25(27.5)}{\sqrt{5(165) - 625}\ \sqrt{5(161.29) - (27.5)^2}} \\[2mm]
&= \frac{787.5 - 687.5}{\sqrt{825 - 625}\ \sqrt{806.45 - 756.25}} = \frac{100}{\sqrt{200}\ \sqrt{50.2}} \\[2mm]
&= \frac{100}{\sqrt{10,040}} = \frac{100}{100.2} = 0.998
\end{aligned}
$$

The standard error of the regression coefficient (the slope of the line, the numerical value in front of the b in the regression equation) is S_b. Its numerical value is 0.016. The value of b, which is 0.5, is probably significant if it is greater than $2 \times S_b$ or $2 \times 0.016 = 0.032$. This is, of course, the case in the present example. The value of b also meets the more rigorous test of being greater than three times S_b (0.048).

The correlation can be tested for significance by use of Table 8A–1. Since two degrees of freedom are lost (one for the estimate of a and one for the estimate of b), we look in the D.F. column (degrees of freedom)

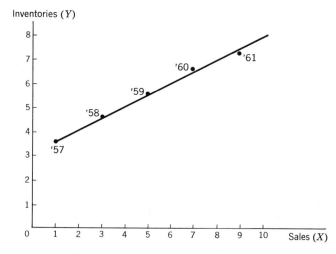

Fig. 8A–1. Scatter Diagram of Inventory to Sales, 1957–1961

TABLE 8A-1

CRITICAL VALUES OF THE CORRELATION COEFFICIENTS*
The entry in the table is the minimum value of the correlation coefficient r, which, for a given number of degrees of freedom, rejects the null hypothesis for the indicated probability level.

	Probability				Probability	
D.F.	0.05	0.01		D.F.	0.05	0.01
1	0.997	1.000		24	0.388	0.496
2	0.950	0.990		25	0.381	0.487
3	0.878	0.959		26	0.374	0.478
4	0.811	0.917		27	0.367	0.470
5	0.754	0.874		28	0.361	0.463
6	0.707	0.834		29	0.355	0.456
7	0.666	0.798		30	0.349	0.449
8	0.632	0.765		35	0.325	0.418
9	0.602	0.735		40	0.304	0.393
10	0.576	0.708		45	0.288	0.372
11	0.553	0.684		50	0.273	0.354
12	0.532	0.661		60	0.250	0.325
13	0.514	0.641		70	0.232	0.302
14	0.497	0.623		80	0.217	0.283
15	0.482	0.606		90	0.205	0.267
16	0.468	0.590		100	0.195	0.254
17	0.456	0.575		125	0.174	0.228
18	0.444	0.561		150	0.159	0.208
19	0.433	0.549		200	0.138	0.181
20	0.423	0.537		300	0.113	0.148
21	0.413	0.526		400	0.098	0.128
22	0.404	0.515		500	0.088	0.115
23	0.396	0.505		1,000	0.062	0.081

* Portions of this table were abridged from Table VI of Fisher and Yates, *Statistical Tables for Biological, Agricultural, and Medical Research,* published by Oliver & Boyd, Ltd., Edinburgh, by permission of the authors and publishers.

at the value 3. The minimum value of the correlation coefficient at the 5 percent probability level is 0.878, and at the 1 percent level it is 0.959. The observed correlation coefficient of 0.988 meets both tests.

If the firm's sales are forecast as 12 for 1967, the firm can be 95 percent confident that its inventories will lie within $Y = 3 + 0.5(12) \pm 2(0.1)$. We estimate that the inventories will lie within 8.8 and 9.2. The point estimate, without consideration of the range, would be 9.0. The forecasting error is potentially 0.2/9, or 2 percent. Knowledge of internal developments in the firm may enable the financial manager to arrive at a judgment estimate of inventories for 1967. Conceivably, this estimate might fall outside the range of 8.8 to 9.2.

PROBLEMS

8A–1 Forecast the firm's inventories for 1967 if the facts are as shown below and sales in 1967 are 10. Calculate the regression line, the correlation coefficient, the standard error of estimate, and the standard error of the regression coefficient.

Year	Inventories	Sales
1962	0.7	1
1963	2.1	3
1964	3.0	5
1965	4.1	7
1966	5.1	9

8A–2 Now change inventory values in 1962 to 0.5 and in 1966 to 5.3. Make the same calculations as in problem 1.

8A–3 Forecast the firm's inventories for 1967 if the facts are as follows and sales in 1967 are 12. Make the same calculations as in problem 1.

Year	Inventories	Sales
1962	0.5	1
1963	2.3	3
1964	3.2	5
1965	3.9	7
1966	5.1	9

8A–4 Forecast the firm's inventories for 1967 if the facts are as follows and sales in 1967 are 20. Make the same calculations as in problem 1.

Year	Inventories	Sales
1962	0.7	11
1963	2.1	13
1964	3.0	15
1965	4.1	17
1966	5.1	19

8A–5 What generalizations can you make about the behavior of forecasting lines (regression lines or equations) in relation to the pattern of the underlying data?

Chapter 9

Budgeting

The methods of financial forecasting described in the preceding chapter represent an over-all approach to estimating the financial requirements of an enterprise. These methods are valuable for providing a framework for viewing the financing needs of the firm in broad perspective. Further, they indicate the logical basis for establishing relations that can be used in formulating a budgetary system. Thus the preceding chapter represents an artist's preliminary sketch. This chapter completes the picture by describing a budget system.

In the discussion of financial forecasting, the center of focus was on the balance sheet. The asset side represented the items to be financed. The liability and net worth side indicated how the financing is to be accomplished. In budgeting, additional types of financial statements are considered—and in greater detail. The interrelations are shown among the cost accounting system, the production and materials schedules, the income statement, the balance sheet, and the cash budget. Because of the greater detail, it is possible to show lead-and-lag relations, which are the heart of financial planning.

NATURE OF BUDGETS

The budget system is both a "plan" and a "control."[1] On the one hand, it expresses in financial form a firm's plans for a period of time into the future. The relations required to establish a budget system are forecasting

---

[1] Andrew C. Stedry, *Budget Control and Cost Behavior* (Englewood Cliffs, N.J.: Prentice-Hall, 1960), p. 3.

relations. Based on these relations, the budget sets forth a careful and orderly plan for the firm. Preparing the budget requires the financial manager to look ahead. This advance planning leads to improved performance, since problems can be identified and studied before they suddenly emerge.

In addition, since budgeting steps depend upon a proper relation between one set of factors and another, "standards" must be established. Standards represent reference levels for comparing plans with performance. Establishing standards is, of course, one of the essential steps in a control process. In providing them, budgets thereby aid managers in performing the control function. This leads to the second major use of budgets—*as a control device which makes possible the successful delegation of authority to subordinates without loss of control.*

Budgets are subject to abuse, but this characteristic is true of most important instruments. It is useful, however, to express some *caveats* in connection with budgeting. Budgets should not be used as a bargaining device to obtain excessive allocations of funds for a department, nor should they be used to obtain lower standards in order to improve the apparent performance of an operating unit. Budgets should be based on realistic expectations, and this requires effective communication between different operating levels of a firm. Extensive evidence indicates that budgets established with the wide participation of the subordinates whose actions are constrained by the budgets are more effective (that is, produce "better" results) than budgets promulgated in an authoritative procedure. Finally, a budget system should be flexible. It should allow for unusual circumstances. The budget system should recognize and adapt to significant changes in the fundamental operating conditions of the firm.

This discussion of the nature of budgets could proceed to great lengths. However, unless one has had some direct experience with budgets, such discussions will have little meaning. The nature and significance of budgets may best be conveyed by simulating some budgetary experience.[2] Just as "management games" telescope years of experience into a few hours, the use of a simplified but complete budget system will convey more understanding about how a budget system is established than will hundreds of pages of description. By utilizing a brief and simplified budget system, the underlying logic of the relations will also be high-lighted.

AN ILLUSTRATIVE BUDGET SYSTEM

A complete system includes (1) a production budget, (2) a materials purchases budget, (3) a budgeted income statement, (4) a budgeted balance

---

[2] More elaborate budget systems can also be constructed, programmed for "playing" them on the computer and used to test the consequences of alternative policies and decisions by management. Since the full consequences of alternative courses of action can be delineated in advance, decisions should be improved.

sheet, and (5) a capital expenditure budget. Since capital expenditures are related directly to problems of the firm's growth, they have been considered separately in Chapter 7.[3]

Tables 9–1 through 9–7 carry out a hypothetical budget system. In Tables 9–2 through 9–7 the lines are numbered consecutively from 1 to 54. This procedure has the advantage of making it easy to see the relations among the various budgets. Table 9–1 outlines the highly summarized cost accounting system. It is based on the standard costs of goods sold per unit. Standard costs include direct material, direct labor, and variable and fixed manufacturing expense. Standard costs are the costs of goods produced when the firm is operating at a high level of efficiency and when operations are near a level that may be regarded as "normal."[4]

TABLE 9–1

STANDARD COSTS BASED ON VOLUME OF 1,000 UNITS PER MONTH

	Per Unit
Direct material: 2 pieces—$1	$2
Direct labor: 1 hour—$2 per hour	2
Variable manufacturing expense: $1 per unit	1
Fixed manufacturing expense: $1,000 per month* . .	1
Cost of goods produced per unit	$6

* Includes $200 depreciation charges.

Production Budget

The illustrative production budget is based directly on the sales forecast and the estimated unit cost of production. It is assumed that the firm maintains its finished goods inventory at 50 percent of the following month's sales. In any month, the firm must produce the unit sales plus ending inventory less the beginning inventory level.

This example illustrates the financial consequences of a rise in sales from a $10,000-per-month level to a new plateau of $12,000. As production rises in response to increased sales, the (standard) cost of goods produced also rises. But the standard cost of goods produced increases faster than actual costs increase because the unit cost of $6 includes fixed

---

3 Outlays for capital equipment do, of course, affect the cash budget, the income statement, and the balance sheet. For consideration of the influence of capital expenditures on operating budgets, the reader is referred to A. Matz, O. J. Curry, and G. W. Frank, *Cost Accounting* (Cincinnati: South-Western, 1952), pp. 450–451.

4 The terminology in this chapter follows accounting usage, but anyone familiar with economics can readily translate it into economic terms. For instance, "$6 per unit at standard output" is "average total (production) cost"; "marginal production cost" is "$5 per unit"; and so on.

charges of $1 per unit. An increase of one unit of production actually raises total costs by only $5. The estimated cost per unit, however, increases by $6. Estimates of the cost of goods produced are made and then adjusted by the amount of under- or overabsorbed burden. Of course, the same result for calculating the adjusted cost of goods produced (Table 9–2, line 9) is obtained by multiplying $5 by the number of units produced to get total variable costs, and adding $1,000 in fixed costs to reach total adjusted cost of goods produced.

The per unit adjusted costs of goods produced ($5.91 for the first month) is required to calculate the ending inventory. The first-in, first-out method of inventory costing is employed. The calculation of the ending inventory value is required for the work sheet (Table 9–6) used in developing the budgeted balance sheet (Table 9–7).

TABLE 9–2

PRODUCTION BUDGET

Item	Monthly Average 1966	First Month	Second Month	Third Month	Source of Data
		Estimated 1967, First Quarter			
1. Sales at $10 per unit	$ 10,000	$ 10,000	$ 12,000	$ 12,000	Assumed
2. Unit sales . .	1,000	1,000	1,200	1,200	Line 1 divided by $10
3. Beginning inventory (units).	500	500	600	600	One half of current month's sales
4. Difference (units)	500	500	600	600	Line 2 minus line 3
5. Ending inventory (units) . .	500	600	600	600	One half of next month's sales
6. Production in units	1,000	1,100	1,200	1,200	Line 4 plus line 5
7. Estimated cost of goods produced . . .	$ 6,000	$ 6,600	$ 7,200	$ 7,200	Line 6 times $6
8. Burden absorption, under or (over)	0	(100)	(200)	(200)	Line 6 times $1 less $1,000 fixed mfg. expense
9. Adjusted cost of goods produced	$ 6,000	$ 6,500	$ 7,000	$ 7,000	Line 7 less line 8
9a. Adjusted cost per unit . . .	$ 6	$ 5.91	$ 5.83	$ 5.83	Line 9 divided by line 6
10. Value of ending inventory (finished goods)	$ 3,000	$ 3,545	$ 3,500	$ 3,500	Line 5 multiplied by line 9a (rounded)

Materials Purchases Budget

The level of operations indicated by the production budget in Table 9–2 is based on sales forecast and inventory requirements. The materials purchases budget (Table 9–3) contains estimates of materials purchases which will be needed to carry out these production plans. Raw materials purchases depend in turn upon materials actually used in production, material costs (Table 9–1), size of beginning inventories, and requirements for ending inventory.

The example in Table 9–3 does not take into account economical ordering quantities as discussed in Chapter 6. EOQ's are not integrated, primarily because they assume a uniform usage rate for raw materials, an assumption that is not met in the example. Also, the EOQ analysis assumes a constant minimum inventory, but the desired minimum inventory (Table 9–3, line 13) shifts with production levels. In a practical situation,

TABLE 9–3

MATERIALS PURCHASES BUDGET

	Monthly Average 1966	Estimated 1967, First Quarter			
Item		First Month	Second Month	Third Month	Source of Data
11. Production in units	1,000	1,100	1,200	1,200	Line 6
12. Material used (units)	2,000	2,200	2,400	2,400	Line 11 times 2
13. Raw materials, ending inventory	2,200	2,400	2,400	2,400	Raw material requirements next month
14. Total	4,200	4,600	4,800	4,800	Line 12 plus Line 13
15. Raw materials, beginning inventory . . .	2,000	2,200	2,400	2,400	Raw material requirements this month
16. Raw materials purchases . . $ 2,200		$ 2,400	$ 2,400	$ 2,400	(Line 14 less line 15) times $1

these assumptions might be approximated, and EOQ's can then be used to determine optimum purchase quantities. Or the more sophisticated operations research techniques may be used.

Cash Budget

The cash budget—to the financial officer perhaps the most interesting of these statements—is generated from information developed in the production and materials purchases budgets. In addition, estimates for other expense categories are required.[5] In the illustration, only cash receipts from operations are considered in order to emphasize the logic of the budget system. No account is taken of receipts or expenditures for capital items because of the emphasis in this illustration on budgeting consequences of short-term fluctuations in the sales volume of the firm, though for practical situations it is a simple matter to incorporate capital expenditures into the cash budget. However, the fact that capital expenditures are ignored does not diminish their impact on cash flows. Capital expenditures occur sporadically and in amounts that sometimes overwhelm operating transactions.

Period. The three-month period used in the cash budget, Table 9–4, is not necessarily the length of time for which a firm will predict cash flows. Although this period does coincide with the length of traditional 90-day bank loans, the firm is more likely to utilize a six-month or one-year period. Normally, a six-month forecast is prepared on a monthly basis. Briefly, the cash budget period will vary with the line of business, credit needs, the ability to forecast the firm's cash flows for the distant future, and requirements of suppliers of funds.

Illustrative cash budget. The cash flow for a given period is the difference between receipts and expenditures for that period. In Table 9–4, for the 1966 monthly averages, cash from operations ($1,200) is the difference between accounts receivable collected ($10,000) and total disbursements ($8,800). Note that collections from accounts receivable and accounts payable paid depend upon sales and purchases from the preceding months rather than on current sales.

The significant figure for the manager is cash available (or needed). Cash from operations during the first month, 1967, plus the initial cash balance at the beginning of the month, total $6,900. The financial manager has previously determined that only $5,000 is needed to handle this level of sales. Consequently, the firm will have surplus cash of $1,900 by the end of the month, and $3,100 by the end of the third month. In the *pro forma* balance sheet (Table 9–7), it is assumed that these cash surpluses are used to pay off notes payable.

Use. As mentioned earlier in the chapter, the financial manager uses the cash budget to anticipate fluctuations in the level of cash. Normally, a growing firm will be faced with continuous cash drains. The cash budget tells the manager the magnitude of the outflow. If necessary, he can plan to arrange for additional funds. The cash budget is the primary document presented to a lender to indicate the need for funds and the feasibility of repayment.

---

[5] These are assumed to be paid in the months the expenses are incurred, in order to reduce the volume of explanatory information.

TABLE 9–4

CASH BUDGET

Item	Monthly Average 1966	First Month	Second Month	Third Month	Source of Data, 1967
		1967			
Receipts					
17. Accounts receivable collected .	$ 10,000	$ 10,000	$ 10,000	$ 12,000	Sales of previous month
Disbursements					Raw materials
18. Accounts payable paid . . .	$ 2,000	$ 2,200	$ 2,400	$ 2,400	purchases of previous month
19. Direct labor . .	2,000	2,200	2,400	2,400	Line 6 times $2
20. Indirect labor .	700	700	700	700	Assumed
21. Variable manufacturing expenses . . .	1,000	1,100	1,200	1,200	Line 6 times $1
22. Insurance and taxes	100	100	100	100	Assumed
23. General and administrative expenses . . .	2,500	2,500	2,500	2,500	Assumed
24. Selling expense .	500	500	600	600	5% of line 1
25. Total disbursements	$ 8,800	$ 9,300	$ 9,900	$ 9,900	Sum of lines 18–24
26. Cash from operations . .	$ 1,200	$ 700	$ 100	$ 2,100	Line 17 less line 25
26a. Initial cash . .	5,000	6,200	6,900	7,000	Preceding month, line 26b
26b. Cumulative cash	6,200	6,900	7,000	9,100	Line 26 plus line 26a
27. Desired level of cash	5,000	5,000	6,000	6,000	50% of current month's sales; approx. 4.2% of annual sales
27a. Cash available (needed) cumulative . .	$ 1,200	$ 1,900	1,000	$ 3,100	Line 26b less line 27

In Table 9–4 the opposite situation is illustrated. The firm will have excess cash of at least $1,000 during each of the three months under consideration. The excess can be invested or it can be used to reduce outstanding liabilities. In this example the firm retires notes payable (Table 9–7, line 44). Such a small amount as $1,000 might be held as cash or a demand deposit, but the alert financial manager will not allow substantial amounts of cash to remain idle.

Budgeted Income Statement

After a cash budget has been developed, two additional financial statements can be formulated—the budgeted income statement, Table 9–5, and the budgeted balance sheet, Table 9–7. They are prepared on an accrual rather than a cash basis. For example, the income statement accounts for depreciation charges. Expenses recognized on an accrual basis are included in total expenses (Table 9–5, line 32); thus, calculated net income is lowered. The only accrual item assumed in this exhibit is depreciation, and this is assumed to be $200 monthly. Hence the before-tax profit figure in the third month in the budgeted income statement (line 33) differs from line 26 in the cash budget only by the amount of depreci-

TABLE 9–5
BUDGETED INCOME STATEMENT

Item	Monthly Average 1966	Estimated 1967, First Quarter			Source of Data
		First Month	Second Month	Third Month	
28. Sales	$ 10,000	$ 10,000	$ 12,000	$ 12,000	Line 1
29. Adjusted cost of sales	6,000	5,955	7,045	7,000	Line 54
30. Gross income .	$ 4,000	$ 4,045	$ 4,955	$ 5,000	Line 28 less line 29
31a. General and administrative expenses . . .	2,500	2,500	2,500	2,500	Assumed
31b. Selling . . .	500	500	600	600	5% of line 1
32. Total expenses .	$ 3,000	$ 3,000	$ 3,100	$ 3,100	Line 31a plus 31b
33. Net income before taxes . .	1,000	1,045	1,855	1,900	Line 30 less line 32
34. Federal taxes .	500	522	927	950	50% of line 33
35. Net income after taxes	$ 500	$ 522	$ 927	$ 950	line 33 less line 34

ation.[6] This illustration makes clear the effect of noncash expenses on the income statement.

The preparation of the budgeted income statement follows standard accounting procedures. The major calculation involved is adjusted cost of sales, explained in Table 9–6.

------

[6] This agreement holds only in a "steady state," that is, when inventories and receivables are not being raised or lowered. Prior to the third month this condition does not hold.

TABLE 9–6

WORK SHEET

Item	Monthly Average 1966	Adjusted Cost of Sales Estimated 1967, First Quarter			Source of Data
		First Month	Second Month	Third Month	
50. Adjusted cost of goods produced	$ 6,000	$ 6,500	$ 7,000	$ 7,000	Line 9
51. *Add:* Beginning inventory . . .	3,000	3,000	3,545	3,500	Line 10 lagged one month
52. Sum	$ 9,000	$ 9,500	$ 10,545	$ 10,500	
53. *Less:* Ending inventory . . .	3,000	3,545	3,500	3,500	Line 10
54. Adjusted cost of goods sold* . .	$ 6,000	$ 5,955	$ 7,045	$ 7,000	Line 52 less line 53

* Note difference from line 9, adjusted cost of goods produced.

The budgeted income statement shows the impact of future events on the firm's net income. Comparison of future income with that of past periods indicates the difficulties which will be encountered in maintaining or exceeding past performance. A forecast indicating low net income should cause management to increase sales efforts as well as make efforts to reduce costs. Thus anticipation and prevention of difficulties can be achieved by a sound budgeting system.

Budgeted Balance Sheet

Lenders are interested in the projected balance sheet to see what the future financial position of the firm will be. Balance sheet projections discussed in Chapter 8 were focused on year-to-year forecasts, and they assumed stable underlying relations. The budget technique deals with shorter term projections, but is based on the same fundamental kinds of stable relations between the volume of sales and the associated asset requirements. Either method can be used, and each can operate as a check on the other. The budgeted balance sheet presented in Table 9–7, however, is the result of a more detailed and analytical forecast of future operations. It is the logical culmination of the budget system and provides a complete reconciliation between the initial balance sheet, the cash budget, and the income statement.

The required information is readily available from past balance sheets or is contained in other elements of the budget system. For example, the initial balance of notes payable is $3,200. An increase in cash available (Table 9–4, line 27a is used to repay notes payable; a decrease is met by

TABLE 9–7

BUDGETED BALANCE SHEET

	Monthly Average 1966	Estimated 1967, First Quarter			
Item		First Month	Second Month	Third Month	Source of Data
Assets					
36. Cash	$ 5,000	$ 5,000	$ 6,000	$ 6,000	Line 27
37. Govt. securities .	0	0	0	0	Excess of line 27a over line 44
38. Net receivables	10,000	10,000	12,000	12,000	Sales of current month
39. Inventories					
Raw materials .	2,200	2,400	2,400	2,400	Line 13
Finished goods .	3,000	3,545	3,500	3,500	Line 10
40. Current assets .	$ 20,200	$ 20,945	$ 23,900	$ 23,900	Total lines 36 through 39
41. Net fixed assets	80,000	79,800	79,600	79,400	$80,000 less $200 per month depreciation
42. Total assets . .	$100,200	$100,745	$103,500	$103,300	Total lines 40 and 41
Liabilities					
43. Accounts payable . . .	$ 2,200	$ 2,400	$ 2,400	$ 2,400	Raw material purchases this month
44. Notes payable, $3,200	2,000	1,300	2,200	100	$3,200 less line 27a
45. Provisions for federal income tax	500	1,022	1,950	2,900	Cumulation of line 34
46. Long-term debt	25,000	25,000	25,000	25,000	Assumed
47. Common stock, $50,000 . . .	50,000	50,000	50,000	50,000	Assumed
48. Surplus, $20,000	$ 20,500	$ 21,023	$ 21,950	$ 22,900	Cumulation line 35 plus $20,000
49. Total claims .	$100,200	100,745	103,500	103,300	Sum of lines 43 through 48

additional borrowing from a commercial bank. Other new items, such as long-term debt and common stock (Table 9–7, lines 46 and 47), are taken from previous balance sheets.

The foregoing exhibits present a simplified yet complete budget system. It contains all the elements found in a voluminous and complex actual budget system of a firm. If a person understands the logic and flow of this relatively simple budget system, he can approach an actual budget with perspective, looking for the fundamental relations involved. He can then apply the patterns to actual budget systems of any degree of complexity.

VARIABLE OR FLEXIBLE BUDGETS

Budgets are planned allocations of a firm's resources based on forecasts for the future. But it is not always possible to know what volume of operations will actually be attained. For the establishing of budgets that provide meaningful standards in guiding operations and in judging performance, some flexibility is desirable.

One way of introducing flexibility into budgets is to recognize the need to vary some aspects of expenditures with the factors that determine the variation. Accordingly, the firm might have alternative budgets for different levels of operation—high, low, and medium. Management, of course, decides which budget is in effect at any given time.

Linear regression analysis can be used to provide budget flexibility. Suppose that a retail store has had the experience indicated by the historical data in Table 9–8. It is apparent from the data that the number

TABLE 9–8

HUBLER DEPARTMENT STORE

Month	Sales (in thousands of dollars)	Number of Employees
January	4	42
February	5	51
March	6	60
April	7	75
May	10	102
June	8	83
July	5	55
August	9	92

of employees the firm needs is dependent upon the dollar volume of sales which occurs during a month. This is seen more easily from a scatter diagram like that in Figure 9–1. The freehand regression line is sloped positively, because the number of employees will increase as the volume of sales increases.

The independent variable, dollar volume of sales, is called the control variable. Variations in the control variable cause changes in total expenses. The volume of sales can be forecast, and the number of employees can be read from the regression chart. The relations can be expressed in tabular form (Table 9–9). Given the forecast of the volume of operations,

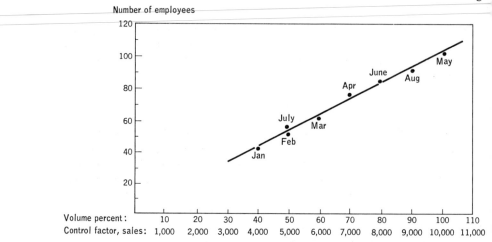

Fig. 9–1. Hubler Department Store Scatter Diagram and Regression Line

TABLE 9–9

HUBLER DEPARTMENT STORE: BUDGET ALLOWANCE

Volume (in percentages)	Employees	Weekly Payroll Estimate (average wage, $100)
60	62	$ 6,200
70	72	7,200
80	82	8,200
90	92	9,200
100	102	10,200
110	112	11,200

standards are provided for the expected number of employees and the weekly payroll.[7]

GENERAL CONSIDERATIONS

Problems Encountered in Budgeting

Four major problems are encountered in the use of budget systems. First, budgetary programs can grow to be so complete and so detailed that they become cumbersome, meaningless, and unduly expensive. Overbudgeting is dangerous.

Second, budgetary goals may come to supersede enterprise goals. But budgets are a tool, not an end in themselves. Enterprise goals by defi-

---

[7] Note that the regression analysis provides even more flexibility in budgeting than do the high, medium, and low levels mentioned earlier.

nition supersede subsidiary plans of which budgets are a part. Also, budgets are based on future expectations which may not be realized. There is no acceptable reason for neglecting to alter budgets as circumstances change. This reasoning is the core of the argument in favor of more flexible budgets.

Third, budgets tend to hide inefficiencies by continuing initial expenditures in succeeding periods without proper evaluation. Budgets growing from precedent usually contain undesirable expenditures. They should not be used as umbrellas under which slovenly, inefficient management can hide. Consequently, the budgetary process must contain provision for re-examination of standards and other bases of planning by which policies are translated into numerical terms.

Finally, some case study evidence suggests that the use of budgets as a pressure device defeats their basic objectives. Budgets, if used as an instrument of tyranny, cause resentment and frustrations, which in turn lead to inefficiency. In order to counteract this effect, it has been recommended that top management increase the participation of subordinates during the preparatory stages of the budgets.

Some Qualitative Aspects of Budgeting

Surprisingly, budgeting is still not employed by some firms, particularly small ones. In fact, budgeting is often inadequately used even by medium sized firms. One of the important functions of business management is to assess changes in the firm's environment and in its sales activities as they take place, and to check and recheck the assumptions of its financial plans which have also been expressed in its pricing, procurement, and labor policies. As these changes take place, the plans of the firm as represented by its budget system need to be altered.

Another aspect of budgeting is the choice of the appropriate planning period or unit of time. Conventionally, budgets are presented in terms of one year, six months, or one month. However, depending upon the natural production cycle of the particular line of business or industry in which the firm is situated, a one-week budget or a two-week budget, or even a daily budget, might be appropriate for some purposes. The important thing is not to be overinfluenced by the conventional calendar unit but to choose a budget period that will be most meaningful and informative for the individual firm.

SUMMARY

Budgeting is an integral step in the process of forecasting financial requirements. The illustrative budget system shows the logic underlying actual budget systems. The chain flows from the sales forecast through the production and materials purchase budgets to the cash budget. Information from these sources is required for the budgeted income statements and balance sheets.

The cash budget is a key tool for financial decisions. It indicates the amount and timing of requirements for additional financing. It is a necessary part of financial planning and is an indispensable instrument in arranging for borrowing from financial institutions.

The errors in budgeting can create hazards: (1) overbudgeting may occur; (2) budgetary goals may supersede enterprise goals; (3) budgets may not be readjusted periodically; (4) budgets may become pressure devices. Budgeting is a *tool* of financial management, not an end in itself.

SELECTED REFERENCES

Argyris, Chris, "Human Problems with Budgets," *Harvard Business Review,* 31 (January-February 1953), pp. 97–100.

Keller, I. W., "Budgeting for Small Business," *Journal of Accountancy,* 107 (January 1959), pp. 44–49.

Peirce, J. L., "The Budget Comes of Age," *Harvard Business Review,* 32 (May-June 1954), pp. 58–66.

Villers, Raymond, "The Managerial Approach to Budgeting," *The Controller,* 26 (October 1958), pp. 44–49.

Wasley, R. S., "Position Budgeting: Bulwark of Small Business," *N.A.C.A. Bulletin,* 38 (February 1957), pp. 783–791.

Werolin, A. W., "Setting Up a Flexible Budget," *N.A.A. Bulletin,* 45 (January 1964), pp. 21–30.

Willson, James D., "Dynamic Budgeting," *Dun's Review* 62 (June 1957), pp. 127–132.

QUESTIONS

9–1 Explain the difference between reporting on a cash basis as opposed to reporting on an accrual basis. In budgeting, what information would you desire to adjust from an accrual to a cash basis?

9–2 Can the individual consumer derive any benefit from financial planning concepts?

9–3 Do net profits after taxes indicate the increase in cash available? What is cash flow and why is it an important budgeting tool?

9–4 What are some of the problems involved in developing a budget system?

9–5 What items are common to a budgeted income statement and a budgeted balance sheet?

9–6 The control function in any business can be explained in three steps. What are these steps and do budgets relate to any or all of them?

9–7 What factors should be considered in establishing a planning period for budgets?

PROBLEMS

9–1 The Byproducts Corporation's Department B budgets its major expenses on a fixed and per man-hour basis. Salaries are fixed at $700 per month; operating material averages $2 per man-hour; maintenance has a fixed portion of $300 per month and varies at a rate of 40 cents per man-hour worked.

The budget is projected for each month on the basis of estimates of man-hours to be worked.

For one month, the department estimated that 22,000 man-hours would be worked. Actually, employees worked only 17,000 man-hours.

Actual expenditures were:

Salaries	$ 700
Operating material	38,000
Maintenance	8,000
Total	$46,700

1. Compare actual and budgeted results. Are they favorable or unfavorable?
2. Compare the actual with the budgeted expenses if the department had varied its budget to meet the actual number of man-hours the employees would work. Is the variance favorable or unfavorable?

9–2 The Aubey Corp. has a variable budget for product C, expressed by the following relation: total costs are $400 plus 25 cents per unit. For the past month's operation, volume is 840 units and the actual cost is $600. Normal equals 900 units.

Calculate and evaluate as favorable or unfavorable the following variances:

1. Accounting variance, which is actual versus absorbed costs
2. Volume variance, which is budgeted amount versus absorbed amount
3. Spending variance, which is the difference between budgeted amount and actual amount

9–3 The following is a complete budget system for six months, except for February and April, data for which are not filled in after the sales forecast figure. From the relations set out in the key in the last column, fill in the required data for the two months.

1. What is the role of the sales forecast in developing a company budget?
2. Why is inventory a lead item?
3. Why are receivables a lag item?
4. A budget is a form of projection. Why is it possible to make the projections employed in setting up a budget system?

ILLUSTRATIVE COMPLETE BUDGET SYSTEM

Item	January 1966 I	February 1966 II	March 1966 III	April 1966 IV	May 1966 V	June 1966 VI	Key
Production budget							
1. Sales forecast ($10 per unit)	$ 10,000	$ 10,000	$ 12,000	$ 12,000	$ 8,000	$ 8,000	(1) Assumed
2. Unit sales	1,000		1,200		800	800	(2) Line 1 ÷ $10
3. Beginning inventory	500		600		400	400	(3) 50% of current month's sales
4. Difference	500		600		400	400	(4) Line 2 − line (3)
5. Ending inventory	500		600		400	400	(5) 50% of following month's sales
6. Production in units	1,000		1,200		800	800	(6) Line 4 + line (5)
7. Cost of goods produced	$ 6,000		$ 7,200		$ 4,800	$ 4,800	(7) Line 6 × $6
8. Burden absorption—under (over)	0		(200)		200	200	(8) $1,000 − line (6) × $1
9. Adjusted cost of goods produced	$ 6,000		$ 7,000		$ 5,000	$ 5,000	(9) Line 7 + line (8)
10. Adjusted cost per unit of production	$ 6		$ 5.83		$ 6.25	$ 6.25	(10) Line 9 ÷ line (6)
11. Value of ending inventory	$ 3,000		$ 3,498		$ 2,500	$ 2,500	(11) Line 5 × line (10)
Materials purchases budget							
12. Production in units	$ 1,000		$ 1,200		$ 800	$ 800	(12) Line 6
13. Materials used	2,000		2,400		1,600	1,600	(13) Line 12 × (2)
14. Raw materials, ending inventory	2,200		2,000		1,600	1,600	(14) Following month's raw material needs
15. Total	4,200		4,400		3,200	3,200	(15) Line 13 + line (14)
16. Raw materials, beginning inventory	2,000		2,400		1,600	1,600	(16) Raw materials required this month
17. Raw materials purchases ($1 per unit)	$ 2,200		$ 2,000		$ 1,600	$ 1,600	(17) Line 15 − line (16)

Item	January 1966 I	February 1966 II	March 1966 III	April 1966 IV	May 1966 V	June 1966 VI	Key
Cash budget receipts							
18. Accounts receivable collected	$ 10,000		$ 10,000		$ 12,000	$ 8,000	(18) Sales of previous month
Disbursements							
19. Accounts payable paid	2,000		2,400		1,600	1,600	(19) Purchases of previous month
20. Direct labor	2,000		2,400		1,600	1,600	(20) Line 6 × $2
21. Indirect labor	700		700		700	700	(21) Assumed
22. Variable mfg. expense	1,000		1,200		800	800	(22) Line 6 × $1
23. Insurance & taxes	100		100		100	100	(23) Assumed
24. Gen'l. & admin. expense	2,500		2,500		2,500	2,500	(24) Assumed
25. Selling expense	500		600		400	400	(25) 5% of line 1
26. Total disbursements	$ 8,800		$ 9,900		$ 7,700	$ 7,700	(26) Sum of lines 19 thru (25)
27. Cash from operations	$ 1,200		$ 100		$ 4,300	$ 300	(27) Line 18 − line 26
28. Desired level of cash	$ 5,000		$ 5,000		$ 5,000	$ 5,000	(28) Assumed
Budgeted income statement							
29. Sales	$ 10,000		$ 12,000		$ 8,000	$ 8,000	(29) Line 1
30. Adjusted cost of sales							(30)
31. Adjusted cost of goods produced	6,000		7,000		5,000	5,000	(31) Line 9
32. Add beginning inventory	3,000		3,546		2,400	2,500	(32) Line 11 for previous month
33. Total	$ 9,000		$ 10,546		$ 7,400	$ 7,500	(33) Sum Line 31 + line 32
34. *Less:* Ending inventory	3,000		3,498		2,500	2,500	(34) Line (11)
35. Adjusted cost of sales	$ 6,000		$ 7,048		$ 4,900	$ 5,000	(35) Line (33) − Line (34)

(Table continued on following page.)

Item	1/'66, I	2/'66, II	3/'66, III	4/'66, IV	5/'66, V	6/'66, VI	Key
36. Gross income	$ 4,000		$ 4,952		$ 3,100	$ 3,000	(36) Line (29) − Line (35)
37. Gen'l & admin. expense	2,500		2,500		2,500	2,500	(37) Line (24)
38. Selling expense	500		600		400	400	(38) 5% of Line (1)
39. Total expense	$ 3,000		$ 3,100		$ 2,900	$ 2,900	(39) Line (37) + Line (38)
40. Net income before taxes	1,000		1,852		200	100	(40) Line (36) − Line (39)
41. Federal income taxes	500		926		100	50	(41) ½ Line (40)
42. Net income after taxes	$ 500		$ 926		$ 100	$ 50	(42) Line (40) − Line (41)
Budgeted balance sheet							
43. Cash	$ 5,000		$ 5,000		$ 5,000	$ 5,000	(43) Assumed
44. Government securities	1,200		2,000		9,400	9,700	(44) Cumulative sum of Line (27)
45. Net receivables	10,000		12,000		8,000	8,000	(45) Line (1)
46. Inventories							(46)
47. Raw materials	2,200		2,000		1,600	1,600	(47) Line (14)
48. Finished goods	3,000		3,498		2,500	2,500	(48) Line (11)
49. Current assets	$ 21,400		$ 24,498		$ 26,500	$ 26,800	(49) Sum of Lines (43) thru (48)
50. Net fixed assets	79,800		79,400		79,000	78,800	(50) $80,000 − $200 depreciation per month
51. Total assets	$101,200		$103,898		$105,500	$105,600	(51) Line (49) + Line (50)
52. Liabilities							(52)
53. Accounts payable	$ 2,200		$ 2,000		$ 1,600	$ 1,600	(53) Line (17)
54. Notes payable	3,000		3,000		3,000	3,000	(54) Assumed
55. Federal income taxes payable	500		1,949		2,950	3,000	(55) Line (41) cumulative
56. Long-term debt	25,000		25,000		25,000	25,000	(56) Assumed
57. Total liabilities	30,700		31,949		32,550	32,600	(57) Sum of Lines (53) thru (56)
Net worth							
58. Common stock	50,000		50,000		50,000	50,000	(58) Assumed
59. Earned surplus	20,500		21,949		22,950	23,000	(59) $20,000 + Line (42) cumulative
60. Total liabilities & net worth	$101,200	$102,446	$103,898	$105,300	$105,500	$105,600	(60) Sum of Lines (57, 58, 59)

Chapter *10*

Profit Measurement and Planning

Part II of this book has dealt with financial control; Part III deals with planning. Chapters 8 and 9 have focused on important aspects of financial planning: financial forecasting and budgeting. This chapter is the first of three discussing interrelations between control and planning, with an ultimate focus on planning for profit. This phase of the planning process introduces the many factors that influence future earnings and consequently values.

Four major aspects are involved in planning for profits:

1. Measurement and control of revenues and costs
2. Turnover
3. Operating leverage
4. Financial leverage

The first three aspects are discussed in this chapter; the fourth is analyzed in the following one. Then, in Chapter 12, the planning process is drawn together to consider both earnings and their capitalized values (market prices or wealth) and the interrelations between earnings and values.

MEASUREMENT OF INCOME

A number of accounting conventions and practices have an important impact on the measurement of income. Among the most important are (1) measuring costs of inventories, (2) measuring depreciation charges, and (3) treating other types of income and losses that occur from time to time.[1]

---

[1] The treatment here will be relatively brief and in summary. For detailed analysis, see the Appendix to this chapter.

It is now well recognized that the use of a first-in, first-out (fifo) method of inventory costing during a period of rising price levels will result in higher reported profit than will alternative methods of inventory costing. While prices are rising, the fifo method charges income with the first-in items, which carry lower prices. The items remaining in the inventory are the higher priced items. As a consequence, reported profits are higher, but amounts in the inventory account on the balance sheet will be larger. Thus, to maintain the same physical quantity of inventories will require more dollars. On these grounds, it has been argued that fifo overstates profits.

The use of the last-in, first-out (lifo) method of costing inventories will, of course, have the opposite effect, and since different companies even in the same industry do use different inventory valuation methods, it is important that consideration be given to possible profit differentials when making comparative financial analyses.

Similarly, the use of historical costs for charging off depreciation expense during a period of rising price levels is said to understate the true costs of using capital equipment during such periods. Without entering into long, involved, and extended arguments, we can simply recognize that measuring depreciation on the basis of historical costs of fixed assets results in smaller charges to income and higher reported profits. For purposes of comparative analysis, however, this is not a particularly important problem; practically all companies report depreciation on the basis of historical cost.[2]

Gains or losses on sale of assets, gains or losses from damage suits, and large royalties received or paid also have important effects on reported income. Some argue for excluding such "nonrecurring" items from the income statement so that current profit will not be affected (a charge would be made directly to the earned surplus account on the balance sheet). Others urge that it is "normal" for a succession of events with major effects on income to take place, that these are actually "recurring" events and should be reflected in current measures of net profit for the firm.

Without attempting to settle these long-continued controversies, it is important to recognize their potential effects on reported net income. What is being sought is a measure of income that will provide a basis for estimating profits into the future, because it is future earnings that determine values. In the subsequent discussion it will be understood that the measure of net income being used is the one that is meaningful and relevant for a dependable estimate of the future stream of net incomes,

---

[2] One aspect of depreciation does, however, pose something of a problem to the analyst—accounting for accelerated depreciation. See the chapter Appendix for a discussion of the problem.

and that when interfirm comparisons are made, we assume that reported profits have been adjusted for accounting variances.

COST CONTROL AND TURNOVER

Profit planning depends importantly upon (1) the extent to which costs are controlled and (2) the turnover of investment in assets of all kinds. The du Pont chart of control encompasses the many factors involved.

Figure 10–1 shows the du Pont chart depicting characteristic relations for a composite manufacturing firm in the United States. Profits and return on investment depend upon control of costs and of investment. If costs are too high, profit margins on sales fall. If investment is not controlled, the turnover (activity ratios) will decline.

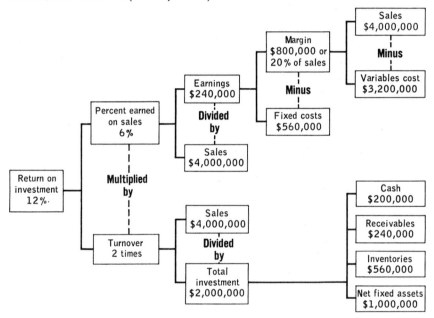

Fig. 10–1.   Return-on-Investment Analysis

Cost control requires detailed study of the operations of the individual firm, but no general formula can be given for how cost control can best be accomplished. To cut costs while paying necessary attention to quality and at the same time attempting to meet a profit target, management must employ a concerted, continued effort. The kind of continued analysis required is illustrated by the following excerpt.

Three men sit around a desk and ponder a small electric motor. Then the comments begin to flow.

"I don't think it needs two labels."

"Do we have to use this high-grade electrical steel?"
One of the men peers inside. "Why does it have to be painted in there?"
The motor is broken open and the innards studied.
"We could cut the amount of copper wire by winding the coils tighter."
"How about those nylon washers? Does it need so many or could we use something cheaper?"

And so it goes, until a dozen or so suggestions for cutting the cost of producing the motor have been tossed up.

The three men are Westinghouse Electric Corporation vice-presidents, giving an impromptu demonstration of how the company's new cost-reduction program works. The savings their offhand suggestions might bring may seem trifling—elimination of one label on the motor, for example, might cut costs a tiny fraction of a cent, while tighter winding of the coils might save a dime's worth of copper. But when similar suggestions are multiplied many times over and put into effect in a company the size of Westinghouse, they can mean savings of several million dollars a year.[3]

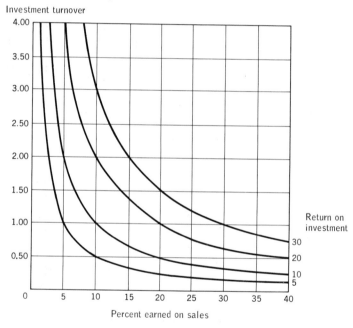

Fig. 10–2. Return on Investment Related to Profit Margin and Investment Turnover

Through efforts along the lines suggested by this example, effective cost control can be achieved, and cost control can widen the profit margin.

For a given profit margin on sales, the resulting return on investment is determined by turnover. The relationship is illustrated in Figure 10–2. This chart shows a number of equal return-on-investment lines in relation

---

[3] *Wall Street Journal*, January 3, 1957.

to turnover. The 20 percent line shows that with a turnover of 2, a profit margin of 10 percent on sales would be required to yield a 20 percent ROI.[4] However, to attain a 20 percent ROI when turnover is 4 requires only a 5 percent profit margin on sales.

Table 10–1 illustrates the way turnover and profit margins interact with each other to produce varying returns on assets, and also of the way financial leverage (discussed in detail in the following chapter) affects the return on net worth. Monsanto, with its very heavy fixed asset investment, is seen to have a relatively low turnover, while Safeway, a typical chain food store, has a very high sales-to-assets ratio. However, since it ends up with about the same rate of return on assets, Monsanto's profit margin on sales compensates for its low turnover. Both Safeway and Monsanto use financial leverage to increase their returns on net worth.

Profit planning focuses attention on the profit margin on sales and the turnover of investment. Thus far the analysis has been based on a given level of sales. Another important aspect of profit planning analyzes operating leverage in relation to different volumes of sales.

TABLE 10–1

TURNOVER, PROFIT MARGINS, AND RETURNS ON NET WORTH, 1963

	Sales to Total Assets	Profit to Sales	Profit to Total Assets	Debt to Total Assets	Profit to Net Worth*
All Manufacturing Firms . . .	2.05X	4.7%	9.6%	36%	15.0%
Monsanto Company (chemical producer)	0.89	8.5	7.5	43	13.2
Safeway Stores (food retailer)	5.22	1.7	8.8	38	14.2

* The figures in this column may be found as:

$$\text{profit to net worth} = \frac{\text{profit to total assets}}{1 - \text{debt to total assets}}$$

Sources: Moody's Investors Service, SEC-FTC Bulletins, Robert Morris Associates, and Annual Statement Studies.

BREAK-EVEN ANALYSIS

Break-even analysis is basically an analytical technique for studying the relation between the level of fixed and variable costs, and profits. If a firm's costs were all variable and none were fixed, the problem of break-

---

4 From time to time return on investment will be referred to as "ROI," the widespread practice.

even volume would never arise. But by having some fixed costs, the firm
will suffer losses up to a given volume. To indicate why these relations
obtain, some details of break-even analysis are now presented.

Break-even analysis is a formal profit-planning approach based on
established relations between costs and revenues. It is a device for determining the point at which sales will just cover total costs. If the firm is to

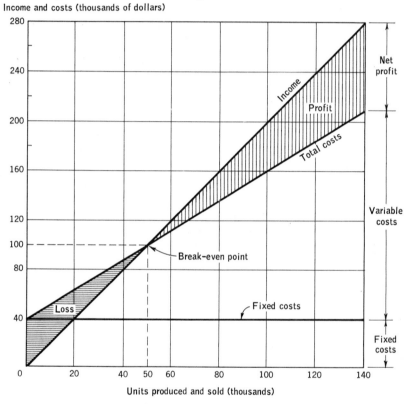

Fig. 10–3. Break-Even Chart

avoid losses, its sales must cover all costs—those which vary directly with
production and those which do not change as production levels change.
Costs that fall into each of these categories are outlined below.

Fixed Costs	*Semivariable Costs**	*Direct or Variable Costs*
Depreciation on plant and equipment	Salaries of research staff	Factory labor
Rentals	Salaries of executive staff	Materials
Interest charges on debt	General office expenses	

* In the break-even analysis to follow, semivariable costs are included with those that
are fully variable.

The nature of break-even analysis is depicted in Figure 10–3, the basic break-even chart. The chart is on a unit basis, with volume produced shown on the horizontal axis and costs and income measured on the vertical axis. Note that fixed costs of $40,000 create a horizontal line: that is, they are the same (fixed) regardless of the number of units produced. Variable costs, assumed to be $1.20 per unit, cause the total-cost line to rise as production increases; every time another unit is produced, costs rise by $1.20. Production is assumed to be sold at $2 per unit, so the total income is pictured as a straight line, which also must increase with production. The positive slope (or the rate of ascent) of the total-income line is steeper than that of the total-cost line. This must be true because the firm is gaining $2 of revenue for every $1.20 paid out for labor and materials, the variable costs.

Up to the break-even point, found at the intersection of the total-income and total-cost lines, the firm suffers losses. After that point the firm begins to make profits. Figure 10–3 indicates a break-even point at a sales and costs level of $100,000 and a production level of 50,000 units.

More exact calculations of the break-even point can be carried out by trial and error or algebraically. In section A of Table 10–2 profit-and-

TABLE 10–2

RELATIONS AMONG UNITS PRODUCED, TOTAL VARIABLE COSTS, FIXED COSTS, TOTAL COSTS, AND TOTAL INCOME

A. Trial-and-Error Calculations

Units Sold	Total Variable Costs	Fixed Costs	Total Costs	Total Income	Net Profit (Loss)
20,000	$ 24,000	$40,000	$ 64,000	$ 40,000	$(24,000)
40,000	48,000	40,000	88,000	80,000	(8,000)
50,000	60,000	40,000	100,000	100,000	—
60,000	72,000	40,000	112,000	120,000	8,000
80,000	96,000	40,000	136,000	160,000	24,000
100,000	120,000	40,000	160,000	200,000	40,000
120,000	144,000	40,000	184,000	240,000	56,000
140,000	168,000	40,000	208,000	280,000	72,000

B. Algebraic Solution to Break-Even Volume

1) The break-even quantity is defined as that volume of output at which revenue is just equal to total costs (fixed costs plus variable costs).

2) Let:

$$P = \text{sales price per unit}$$
$$Q = \text{quantity produced and sold}$$
$$F = \text{fixed costs}$$
$$V = \text{variable costs per unit}$$

3) Then:

$$P \cdot Q = F + V \cdot Q$$
$$P \cdot Q - V \cdot Q = F$$
$$Q(P - V) = F$$
$$Q = \frac{F}{P - V} \text{ at break-even } Q$$

4) Illustration:

$$Q = \frac{\$40,000}{\$2.00 - \$1.20}$$
$$= 50,000 \text{ units}$$

loss relations are shown for various levels of sales, while in section B the algebraic calculations are carried out.

Break-Even Point Based on Totals

Calculating break-even points on the basis of dollar sales rather than on units of output is especially useful (Table 10–3). The main advantage

TABLE 10–3

CALCULATION OF BREAK-EVEN POINT BASED ON TOTALS

$$\frac{\text{Break-even point}}{\text{(sales volume)}} = \frac{\text{total fixed costs}}{1 - \dfrac{\text{total variable costs}}{\text{total sales volume}}}$$

Procedure: Take any quantity and use the related data to determine the break-even point. For example, assume that 20,000 units are produced and use the data from Table 10–2.

$$\text{Break-even point} = \frac{\$40,000}{1 - \dfrac{\$24,000}{\$40,000}} = \frac{\$40,000}{0.4} = \$100,000$$

Rationale:

1) At the break-even point, sales (S) are equal to fixed cost (FC) plus variable cost (VC):

$$S = FC + VC \qquad (1)$$

2) Because both the sales price and the variable cost per unit are assumed to be constant in break-even analysis, the ratio VC/S is also constant and can be found from any annual income statement.

3) Since variable cost is a constant percentage of sales, equation (1) can be rewritten as:

$$S = FC + \frac{VC}{S}(S)$$

$$S\left(1 - \frac{VC}{S}\right) = FC$$

$$S = \frac{FC}{1 - \dfrac{VC}{S}} \text{ at break-even } S$$

of this method is that it enables one to determine a general break-even point for a firm that sells several related products at varying prices. Furthermore, the procedure requires a minimum of data. Only three values are needed: sales, fixed costs, and variable costs. Sales and total-cost data are readily available from annual reports of corporations and from investment manuals. Total costs can be determined by deducting net profits from sales. Total costs must then be segregated into fixed and variable components. The major fixed charges (rent, interest, depreciation, and general and administrative expenses) can be taken from the income statement. Finally, variable costs are calculated by deducting fixed costs from total costs.

Operating Leverage

Operating leverage is defined as the extent to which fixed costs are used in operations, and break-even analysis can be used to reflect the degree of operating leverage employed. The formal definition does not fully convey the meaning of leverage, but an example may help. If you were trying to lift the end of a large box in order to place a roller under it, you might insert an iron rod under the box with a sturdy object like a stone as the fulcrum to obtain leverage in lifting. With this lever system a relatively small amount of pressure can lift a very heavy box. To complete the analogy, the fixed cost element is the lever that allows a small change in sales to induce a relatively large change in profits.

The significance of the degree of operating leverage is further brought out by Figure 10–4. Three firms, A, B, and C, with differing degrees of leverage are contrasted. Firm A is considered to have a normal amount of fixed costs in its operations. It uses automated equipment, with which one operator can turn out a few or many units at the same labor cost, to about the same extent as the average firm in the industry. Firm B has lower fixed costs, but note the steeper rate of increase in variable costs of firm B over firm A. However, firm B will break even at a lower level of operations than firm A. At a production level of 40,000 units, firm A is losing $8,000, but firm B breaks even.

On the other hand, firm C has the highest fixed costs. It is quite highly automated, using expensive, high-speed machines that require very little labor per unit produced; with such an operation its variable costs rise slowly. Because of the high overhead resulting from charges associated with the expensive machinery, C's break-even point is higher than that for either A or B. Once firm C reaches its break-even point, however, its profits rise faster than those of the other firms.

High fixed costs and low variable costs provide the greatest percentage change in profits both upward and downward. The profit behavior follows from economic logic. High fixed costs arise from the employment

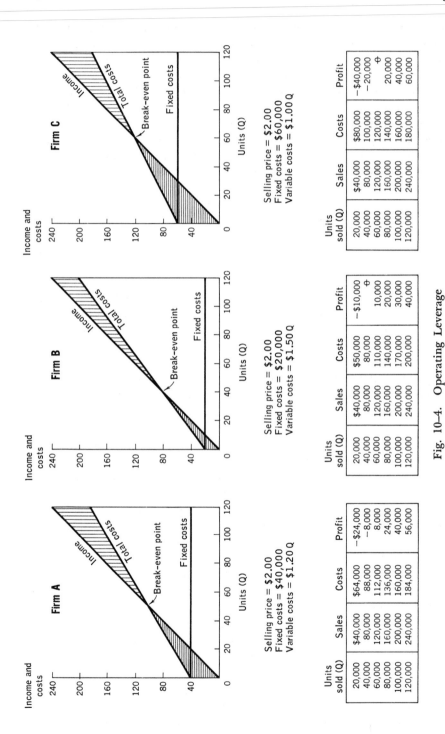

Fig. 10-4. Operating Leverage

Firm A

Selling price = $2.00
Fixed costs = $40,000
Variable costs = $1.20 Q

Units sold (Q)	Sales	Costs	Profit
20,000	$40,000	$64,000	-$24,000
40,000	80,000	88,000	-8,000
60,000	120,000	112,000	8,000
80,000	160,000	136,000	24,000
100,000	200,000	160,000	40,000
120,000	240,000	184,000	56,000

Firm B

Selling price = $2.00
Fixed costs = $20,000
Variable costs = $1.50 Q

Units sold (Q)	Sales	Costs	Profit
20,000	$40,000	$50,000	-$10,000
40,000	80,000	80,000	⌀
60,000	120,000	110,000	10,000
80,000	160,000	140,000	20,000
100,000	200,000	170,000	30,000
120,000	240,000	200,000	40,000

Firm C

Selling price = $2.00
Fixed costs = $60,000
Variable costs = $1.00 Q

Units sold (Q)	Sales	Costs	Profit
20,000	$40,000	$80,000	-$40,000
40,000	80,000	100,000	-20,000
60,000	120,000	120,000	⌀
80,000	160,000	140,000	20,000
100,000	200,000	160,000	40,000
120,000	240,000	180,000	60,000

of great amounts of capital, which permit the firm to operate with reduced labor and thereby smaller variable costs.

The relative importance of fixed costs is likely to reflect both the technology of the industry and the stability of sales. The nature of the business influences how much equipment will be reduced in the production
process. If sales are stable, the firm will use more specialized equipment.
If sales fluctuate greatly, the firm will seek more flexibility by using less
machinery relative to more purchased parts or labor.

Cash Break-Even Analysis

Another use of break-even analysis is to analyze the firm's situation
on a cash basis. Some of the firm's fixed costs are noncash outlays, and
for a period some of its revenues may be in receivables. The cash break-

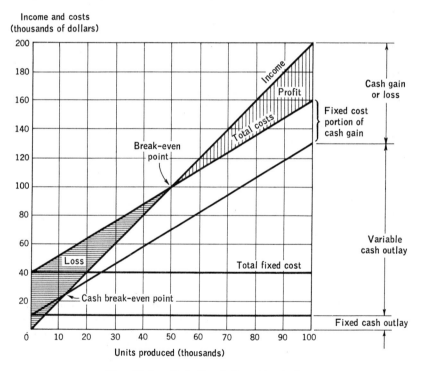

Fig. 10–5. Cash Break-Even Analysis

even chart for firm D, constructed on the assumption that $30,000 of the
fixed costs from the previous illustration are depreciation charges and
therefore a noncash outlay, is shown in Figure 10–5. Because fixed cash
outlays are only $10,000, the cash break-even point is at 12,500 units
rather than 50,000 units, which is the profit break-even point.

Cash break-even analysis does not fully represent cash flows—for this a cash budget is required. But the cash break-even analysis is useful, because it provides a picture of the flow of funds from operations. A firm could incur a level of fixed costs that would result in losses during periods of poor business but in large profits during upswings. If cash outlays are small, even during periods of losses the firm might still be operating above the cash break-even point. Thus the risks of insolvency, in the sense of inability to meet cash obligations, would be small. This allows a firm to reach out for higher profits through automation and operating leverage.

Limitations of Break-Even Analysis

Break-even analysis is useful in studying the relations among volume, prices, and cost structure, and is thus useful for making pricing, cost control, and financial decisions. It has limitations, however, as a guide to managerial actions.

Break-even analysis is especially weak in what it implies about the sales possibilities for the firm. Any given break-even chart is based on a constant selling price, so in order to study profit possibilities under different prices a whole series of charts is necessary, one chart for each price.

With regard to costs, break-even analysis is also deficient—the relations indicated by the chart do not obtain at all outputs. As sales increase, existing plant and equipment are worked to capacity, and both this situation and the use of additional workers and overtime pay causes variable costs to rise sharply. Additional equipment and plant will be required, thus increasing fixed costs. Finally, over a period the products sold by the firm will change in quality and quantity; such changes in product mix influence the level and slope of the cost function. In short, break-even analysis is useful as a first step in developing the basic data required for pricing and making financial decisions. More detailed analysis is required before final judgments can be made.

SUMMARY

Profit planning involves controlling costs and boosting turnover, and is facilitated by break-even analysis. Break-even procedures introduce the concept of operating leverage, which is the use of fixed assets (with their attendant fixed costs) in a firm's operations for the purpose of reducing variable costs and increasing total profits. There are significant weaknesses in break-even analysis, but they do not obliterate the usefulness of the technique. In the following chapter the basic break-even ideas are used to extend the concept of leverage to the financing characteristics of the firm.

SELECTED REFERENCES

Bachofer, John B., "Short- and Long-Term Forward Planning Based on Contribution Margin," *N.A.A. Bulletin*, 45 (March 1964), pp. 11–20.
Dean, J., "Cost Structures of Enterprises and Break-even Analysis," *American Economic Review*, 38 (May 1948), pp. 153–164.

Dearden, John, "Profit-Planning Accounting for Small Firms," *Harvard Business Review,* 41 (March-April 1963), pp. 66–76.

Gardner, F. V., "Break-even Point Control for Higher Profits," *Harvard Business Review,* 32 (September-October 1954), pp. 123–130.

Robbins, Sidney M., "Emphasizing the Marginal Factor in the Break-even Analysis," *N.A.A. Bulletin,* 42 (October 1961), pp. 53–60.

————, and E. Foster, Jr., "Profit Planning and the Finance Function," *Journal of Finance,* 12 (December 1957), pp. 451–467.

Soldofsky, R. M., "Accountant's vs. Economist's Concepts of Break-even Analysis," *N.A.A. Bulletin,* 41 (December 1959), pp. 5–18.

Vatter, William J., "Toward a Generalized Break-even Formula," *N.A.A. Bulletin,* 43 (December 1961), pp. 5–10.

QUESTIONS

10–1 One of the departments in a large merchandising store specializes in auto repairs. Which of the following expenses should be charged to this department? Which would be most likely to vary with the activity level in the department? Make any assumptions clear as you explain your conclusions.

1) Direct salaries
2) Automobile paint
3) Heat and electricity
4) Tools
5) Advertising

10–2 Can the statement be made that lower total costs are *always* beneficial to a company? Why?

10–3 Which relationship would you, as a financial manager, prefer: a profit margin of 10 percent with a capital turnover of 2 or a profit margin of 25 percent and a capital turnover of 1? Can you think of any firm with a relationship similar to the latter?

10–4 What benefits can be derived from break-even analysis?

10–5 What is operating leverage? Explain how profits or losses can be magnified in a firm with a great deal of operating leverage as opposed to a firm without this characteristic.

10–6 How would you determine how much of the selling price of a product is going toward covering fixed costs? How is this procedure related to marginal cost analysis?

10–7 What data are necessary to construct a break-even chart?

10–8 What is the general effect of each of the following changes on a firm's break-even point?

1. An increase in selling price with no change in units sold.

2. A change from leasing a machine for $5,000 to a purchase of the machine for $100,000. The useful life of this machine will be 20 years, with no salvage value. Assume straight line depreciation.

3. A reduction in variable labor costs.

10–9 What determines fixed asset and inventory requirements for a manufacturing firm?

10–10 Why do turnover ratios differ for firms in the same industry?

PROBLEMS

10-1 The Mikall Company indicates that the following statement is representative of its operations:

Net sales (1,250,000 units @$4)		$5,000,000
Less: Cost of goods sold:		
Materials	$1,000,000	
Labor	1,400,000	
Overhead	1,600,000	4,000,000
Gross profit		$1,000,000
Less: Operating expenses:		
Selling expenses	$ 350,000	
Administrative expenses	250,000	600,000
Profit		$ 400,000

Costs and expenses in the income statement are redistributed as follows:

	Total	Variable	Fixed
Materials	$1,000,000	$1,000,000	
Labor	1,400,000	1,400,000	
Factory overhead	1,600,000	400,000	$1,200,000
Selling expenses	350,000	150,000	200,000
Administrative expenses . . .	250,000	50,000	200,000
	$4,600,000	$3,000,000	$1,600,000

1. From the above information construct a break-even chart in its conventional form and designate areas and points of particular significance.
2. Indicate the special assumptions involved in break-even analysis as well as any limitations that may be found in such analysis.

10-2 For the Ajax Corporation the following relationships exist. Each unit of output is sold for $20. For output up to 20,000 units the fixed costs are $60,000. Variable costs are $8 per unit.

1. What is the firm's gain or loss at sales of 4,000 units? of 6,000 units?
2. What is the break-even point? Illustrate by a chart.
3. What occurs to the break-even point if the selling price rises to $24? What is the significance for financial management of the change? Illustrate by a chart.
4. What occurs to the break-even point if the selling price rises to $24 but variable costs rise to $12 a unit? Illustrate by a chart.

Income Determination

Funds generated from operations provide most of the long-term financing for many firms, and dividends and capital gains are related to profitable operations. Financial managers and investors rely primarily upon income statement data as a measure of profit. Consequently, accounting methods that distort income measurement will result in erroneous guides for decision-making purposes. Though there are many issues involved with income flows, three are of special interest to the financial manager and will now be discussed. They are (1) inventory accounting, (2) reserves,[1] and (3) depreciation accounting.[2]

INVENTORY ACCOUNTING

Inventory accounting has important financial implications. During and after World War II, the general price rise was so great that historical costs differed markedly from current replacement costs. In a period of rising price levels, the choice of inventory costing will have an important effect on reported profits, on balance sheet values, and on dividend policy. The issues can best be discussed through a specific illustration.

The Alverado Company purchased 100 units of material on December 5 at $5 per unit, 100 units on December 20 at $10 per unit, and during January an additional 900 units at $10 per unit. In January it sold 1,000 units at $20 per unit. All other costs per unit were $5 for this volume of operations. The income statement and balance sheet are shown below.

Income statements are prepared under three methods of inventory costing: first-in, first-out (fifo), last-in, first-out (lifo), and weighted average cost, or average cost, method. The raw material cost under fifo is the 100 units purchased at $5 plus 900 units purchased at $10, or a total of $9,500. Net income in this instance is $5,500. Under lifo the cost of the last 1,000

---

[1] An accounting reserve is not a cash fund but a measure of expired cost, an estimate of a contingency, or a restriction upon the distribution of earned surplus.
[2] It should be noted that most large firms keep at least two sets of records: one for stockholder reporting and one for tax accounting. The firm will thus use whatever accounting methods result in the lowest profits for purposes of tax computation, and figures that they "believe" for purposes of stockholder reporting.

units purchased at $10 is $10,000; net income is therefore $5,000. Under the average cost method, the computed cost of the number of units used is $9,546, and the net income $5,454.[3]

ALVERADO COMPANY
INCOME STATEMENTS
Month of January 1966

	Fifo	Lifo	Average Cost
Sales	$20,000	$20,000	$20,000
Cost of sales, excluding raw materials . . .	5,000	5,000	5,000
	$15,000	$15,000	$15,000
Raw material cost	9,500	10,000	9,546
Net profit	$ 5,500	$ 5,000	$ 5,454

Thus the fifo method, which applies historical cost of purchase to cost of goods sold, causes the highest amount of apparent income.

TABLE 10A–1

COMPUTATION OF AVERAGE COST OF INVENTORIES

	Received			Issued			On Hand		
	Number	Cost per Unit	Total Cost	Number	Cost per Unit	Value	Number of Units	Value	Computed Average Cost
12/5	100	$ 5	$ 500				100	$ 500	$5.00
12/10	100	10	1,000				200	1,500	7.50
12/20	900	10	9,000				1,100	10,500	9.54
January				1,000	9.54	9,546	100	954	9.54

The balance sheet effects of alternative methods of inventory costing are now considered. The beginning balance sheet for December 31 shows cash of $500, inventory of 100 units at $5 and 100 units at $10, common stock of $1,800, and retained earnings of $200. Under fifo, the inventory is the last 100 units purchased at $10, with a total value of $1,000, and net income for the period of $5,500. The addition of net income for January to initial retained earnings ($200) results in retained earnings $5,700. Under lifo, ending inventory is the first 100 units purchased at $5. Net income and retained earnings are correspondingly reduced by $500. The

---

[3] Computation of inventory value under the average cost method is carried out in Table 10A-1.

average cost method values inventory at $954, as indicated, and results in retained earnings of $5,654.

In each of the balance sheets, cash is shown at $6,500 on January 31. The amount of cash is the same under each method of inventory costing, because cash flows are not affected by accounting entries. The ending cash of $6,500 is shown by the cash budget for January.

ALVERADO COMPANY
CASH BUDGET
Month of January 1966

Cash receipts from sales		$20,000
Cash outlays for cost of sales	$5,000	
Cash outlays for raw materials	9,000	
Total cash disbursements		14,000
Cash inflow or (outflow)		6,000
Add initial cash		500
Balance sheet value of cash, 1/31		$ 6,500

ALVERADO COMPANY
BALANCE SHEET

Alverado Company, 12/31				*Fifo, 1/31*			
Cash . .	$ 500	Common stock . .	$1,800	Cash . .	$6,500	Common stock . .	$1,800
Inventory .	1,500	Retained earnings .	200	Inventory .	1,000	Retained earnings .	5,700
	$2,000		$2,000		$7,500		$7,500

Lifo, 1/31				*Average, 1/31*			
Cash . .	$6,500	Common stock . .	$1,800	Cash . .	$6,500	Common stock . .	$1,800
Inventory .	500	Retained earnings .	5,200	Inventory .	954	Retained earnings .	5,654
	$7,000		$7,000		$7,454		$7,454

The average cost method yields intermediate results. Consequently, the discussion will be confined to the contrast between fifo and lifo. Fifo, which represents a historical basis for costing, results in the highest reported current income and also the highest stated inventory on the balance sheet. Lifo, on the other hand, reports $500 less income and inventory value that fifo does.[4]

---

[4] The discussion shall not presume to conclude which method is more accurate. Ac-

The alternative methods of costing inventory have implications for the financial manager. The amount by which income is greater under fifo than under lifo does not reflect earnings available for dividends. Fifo therefore overstates the apparent degree of internal financing which is available from net income. The amount by which earnings are greater under fifo is exactly matched by the additional amount of funds required to be held in inventory. This equality is a partial explanation of the distortion in reported income relative to sales, total assets, and net worth during the immediate postwar period. As price indexes rose, incomes were in substantial measure inventory profits, and inventory values on balance sheets rose, as would be expected under the previous fifo illustration. Consequently, dividend payouts as a percentage of net income fell from the historical level of two thirds to approximately a 50 percent level.

These, then, are the implications of the various inventory-costing procedures. Accounting procedures affect reported incomes, dividend policy, and inventory accounts carried on the balance sheet.

RESERVES

Financial planning is affected by three main types of reserve accounts: (1) valuation reserves, (2) estimated liabilities, and (3) contingency reserves.[5]

Valuation reserves record the expiration of costs of fixed assets. As they are primarily associated with fixed assets, they are closely related to depreciation policy. The term "reserve" is also sometimes applied to *estimated liabilities*. "Estimated liabilities," or "liability reserve," is used most appropriately when the exact amount of the obligation or the parties to whom payment must be made cannot be definitely determined. If the obligation is determinable, it will be recorded as a liability rather than a reserve. Deferred revenues—income received but not earned—are often likewise called reserves. Because they are definite liabilities, however, they should be so labeled. Contingency reserves are earmarked surplus or retained earnings. A liability is a certainty; a contingency is not. The effect of each type of reserve on income and dividend policy, the debt-to-equity ratio, and the liquidity of the firm are of interest to the financial manager.

Liability Reserves

With regard to estimated liabilities, the financial question often arises whether a cash fund should be set aside to meet estimated current liabili-

---

counting standards require adherence to historical costs. Economic theory, however, would use current replacement costs to value inventory, but it would also call for taking unrealized inventory gains as profits. Adherence to accounting conventions may produce information which is either useless or misleading for sound management decisions.

5 The term "reserve" does not imply the existence of a cash fund.

ties, particularly federal income taxes, as they mature. It is argued that since the obligation comes due at a definite date, the firm should make provision to meet it by building up cash balances or buying liquid securities.

An equally valid argument could be made for providing funds to pay off a 60- or a 90-day bank loan, which may have about the same maturity as the estimated liability on federal income tax. Since the amount of the federal income tax liability is known, provision for meeting the obligation should be made through an appropriate cash analysis and cash-budgeting procedure. It is not necessary to set aside funds in order to meet this maturing obligation. It is necessary to have or to raise the funds at the time payment falls due. The income tax liability is just as much a source of funds as any other item on the right side of the balance sheet and should be treated as such.

Contingency Reserves

It is important to distinguish and understand contingency reserves, or earmarked surplus. When earnings are retained, they generally become a source of financing for receivables, inventories, or fixed assets. Earmarking specifically by means of contingency reserves commits earnings to internal use rather than to distribution. Sometimes surplus is also earmarked for repayment of debt, often as a result of a bond indenture provision, which restricts dividend payments and requires such earmarking to provide for bond retirement. This fund indicates that long-term debt will be paid off from retained earnings. Then the accounting entry may be made as follows:

Reserve for bond retirement $100,000
　　　Surplus $100,000

When the book value per share or the debt-equity ratio is calculated, contingency reserves or earmarked surplus should be included in equity as a part of surplus or retained earnings.

Depreciation

Magnitude. During the period 1953–1964, for all nonfinancial corporations, depreciation and amortization charges, which are allocations of costs among time periods, amounted to over $250 billion. The gross sources and uses of corporate funds in this period amounted to $575 billion. Thus depreciation funds represent about 43 percent of the total sources of funds—the largest single source of funds for financing the gross growth of business operations. As such they have considerable significance for financial management.

Tax effects. Tax depreciation allowance provides considerable leverage from the standpoint of capital formation. One dollar of depreciation is worth about two dollars of taxable income. A dollar reported as taxable business income is reduced by the applicable income taxes and by any consumption expenditures made by the owners from amounts distributed by the firm. Annual depreciation charges of the *manufacturing* sector of nonfinancial corporations are now close to $15 billion, or some 11 percent of their net property accounts. The ratio of depreciation to the gross and net property accounts (that is, depreciation to fixed assets) has been rising slowly (Table 10A–2, columns 5 and 6). This is a reflection of liberalized depreciation provisions in the federal income tax laws.

TABLE 10A–2

PROPERTY ACCOUNTS AND DEPRECIATION CHARGES ON ALL UNITED STATES MANUFACTURING CORPORATIONS
(in billions of dollars)

	1	2	3	4	5	6
Years Ended Dec. 31	*Gross Prop. Acct.**	*Accrued Deprec. Res.†*	*Net Prop. Acct.**	*Annual Deprec. Chges.†*	*Deprec. to Prop. Gross*	*Deprec. to Prop. Net*
1939	$ 41.6	$ 18.5	$ 23.1	$ 1.6	3.9%	7.1%
1940	42.7	19.1	23.6	1.7	4.1	7.3
1941	44.9	20.2	24.7	1.9	4.3	7.9
1942	49.1	22.5	26.6	2.3	4.8	8.8
1943	51.6	24.6	27.0	2.7	5.3	10.1
1944	52.0	26.1	25.9	3.0	5.7	11.5
1945	53.9	28.7	25.1	3.5	6.6	14.1
1946	59.2	29.7	29.4	2.4	4.1	8.3
1947	66.8	31.4	35.4	3.1	4.7	8.8
1948	74.0	32.8	41.2	3.9	5.2	9.4
1949	79.1	35.0	44.1	4.1	5.2	9.2
1950	83.3	36.9	46.4	4.4	5.3	9.6
1951	92.1	39.5	52.6	5.3	5.7	10.0
1952	100.6	42.8	57.7	6.0	6.0	10.4
1953	112.6	50.2	62.4	6.3	5.6	10.0
1954	121.3	54.9	66.4	6.8	5.6	10.2
1955	129.1	59.4	69.6	7.6	5.9	10.9
1956	145.1	65.9	79.2	8.6	5.9	10.8
1957	159.3	72.4	86.9	9.4	5.9	10.8
1958	169.1	79.0	90.1	9.8	5.8	10.9
1959	180.1	85.6	94.5	10.3	5.7	10.9
1960	193.9	93.4	100.5	10.9	5.6	10.8
1961	206.8	101.1	105.7	11.6	5.6	11.0
1962	220.9	110.1	110.8	12.8	5.8	11.6
1963	232.8	117.7	115.1	13.5	5.8	11.7
1964	251.7	126.6	125.1	14.4	5.7	11.5

* Includes land.
† Includes amortization charges on defense facilities, and depletion charges on natural resources of minerals, petroleum, etc.
Sources: United States Treasury, annual *Statistics of Income* for 1939–1952; FTC-SEC *Quarterly Financial Report*, 1953–1964.

Depreciation as a source of funds. Some do not view depreciation as a source of funds; others see depreciation as an important source of financing gross capital formation by business. In fact, there is really no conflict between these two points of view. Depreciation holds funds in the firm in the sense that it is a *noncash expense*. What then happens to this noncash expense depends upon the growth rate of the firm and upon its financial policy.[6]

The three balance sheets for the Diverto Manufacturing Company illustrate the significance of depreciation charges. It is assumed that five years have elapsed between the first and second balance sheets and that all balance sheet items are related to the level of sales. If the firm's sales are stable and have not increased over a five-year period, the amount of funds required in all the balance sheet items is unchanged. Fixed assets, however, are assumed to have depreciated over this five-year period. The $500 depreciation charges do not increase earned surplus, because they reduce recorded net income. Under the assumption that they would remain in cash, cash is shown to increase from $100 to $600 in balance sheet 2. Observe further that although cash has increased to $600, total assets are the same under balance sheet 2 as they are under balance sheet 1.

DIVERTO MANUFACTURING COMPANY
BALANCE SHEET 1
December 31, 1965

Assets			*Liabilities and Net Worth*	
Cash	$ 100		Current liabilities	$ 300
Accounts receivable	200		Long-term debt	300
Inventories	300		Net worth	500
Total current assets . . .	$ 600			
Fixed assets $500				
Less: Reserve for depreciation . . 0				
Net fixed assets	$ 500			
			Total liabilities and net	
Total assets	$1,100		worth	$1,100

In balance sheet 3, Diverto sales have doubled, and all balance sheet items, with the exception of net worth and net fixed assets, have also doubled. Gross fixed assets are assumed to have doubled. Since the original $500 of the gross fixed assets is fully depreciated, net fixed assets are $500. Net worth has not increased, because of the assumption that all earnings

---

[6] Depreciation, of course, does not initiate a flow of funds into the firm. Revenue realized from sales is the source of funds. Depreciation charges serve to keep a portion of revenue inside the firm.

Effect of depreciation on a firm with a stable level of operations:

DIVERTO MANUFACTURING COMPANY
BALANCE SHEET 2
December 31, 1970

Assets			*Liabilities and Net Worth*	
Cash		$ 600	Current liabilities	$ 300
Accounts receivable		200	Long-term debt	300
Inventories		300	Net Worth	500
Total current assets . .		$1,100		
Fixed assets	$500			
Less: Reserve for				
depreciation . .	500			
Net fixed assets		0		
			Total liabilities and net	
Total assets		$1,100	worth	$1,100

Effect of depreciation on a growing firm:

DIVERTO MANUFACTURING COMPANY
BALANCE SHEET 3
December 31, 1970

Assets			*Liabilities and Net Worth*	
Cash		$ 200	Current liabilities	$ 600
Accounts receivable		400	Long-term debt	600
Inventories		600	Net worth	500
Total current assets . .		$1,200		
Fixed assets	$1,000			
Less: Reserve for				
depreciation . .	500			
Net fixed assets		500		
			Total liabilities and net	
Total assets		$1,700	worth	$1,700

Assumptions:

(1) Sales and all working capital items are doubled.

(2) Depreciation charges of $500 are utilized to help finance the increased assets, $1,000 (gross), needed to carry on larger scale operations.

Uses of Funds		*Sources of Funds*	
Increase in cash	$ 100	Increase in current liabilities .	$ 300
Increase in receivables . . .	200	Increase in long-term debt . .	300
Increase in inventories . . .	300	Depreciation charges	500
Increase in gross fixed assets .	500		
	$1,100		$1,100

have been paid out in dividends. In this situation, depreciation charges of $500 do not appear as an increased amount of cash, because they have been utilized to help finance the increase in assets which were needed to carry on the larger scale of operation (see the analysis of sources and uses of funds).

Cash has increased by $100, receivables by $200, inventories by $300, and gross fixed assets by $500. The new assets were financed partially by increases in current liabilities and long-term debt. Depreciation charges provided the remaining $500 needed.

It is sometimes said that depreciation reserves were used to purchase an equal amount of additional fixed assets. But it is not possible for a going concern to state how the specific sources were allocated to specific uses. Because one source happens to equal a specific use does not prove that the specific source was used to finance the use.

The Diverto Manufacturing illustration also shows why confusion arises over depreciation as a source of funds. In this situation, $500 has been reserved through depreciation charges against net income. Depreciation charges, in this sense, are simply a vehicle for retaining revenues that are the source of funds.

The last balance sheet shows the effects of reduced sales for Diverto

Effect of depreciation on a firm with declining sales:

DIVERTO MANUFACTURING COMPANY
December 31, 1970

Assets			Liabilities and Net Worth		
Cash		$300	Current liabilities		$150
Accounts receivable		100	Long-term debt (paid off) . . .		0
Inventories		150	Net worth		400
Total current assets . . .		550			
Fixed assets	$500				
Less: Reserve for depreciation . . .	500				
Net fixed assets		0			
			Total liabilities and net worth		$550
Total assets		$550			

Sources			Uses		
Decreases in cash		$ 50	Loss (decrease in net worth) . .		$100
Decreases in receivables . . .		100	Decrease in current liabilities .		150
Decreases in inventories . . .		150	Decrease in long-term debt . .		300
Depreciation		500	Increase in cash		250
		$800			$800

Manufacturing Company. When sales decline 50 percent, the needs for assets are assumed to drop by the same amount. Thus the need for cash decreases to $50, and the need for accounts receivable and inventories drops to $100 and $150, respectively. Thus the net decrease in the need for current assets amounts to a total of $300. The need for current liabilities decreases from $300 to $150. In order to maintain the initial current ratio of 2 to 1, only $300 in current assets is required. The depreciation charges, however, retained funds in the firm that were not used to purchase assets. Consequently, cash balances were built up and the current ratio rose to 3.7 to 1.

Accelerated depreciation methods. These illustrations emphasize that depreciation is a powerful means of increasing the retention of a firm's revenues. For this reason the new methods of depreciation have significant effects.

The most familiar method of allocating the costs of a fixed asset over time (the depreciation charge) is the straight line method. It provides an equal depreciation charge for each year of the life of an asset. The depreciation charge for an asset with a five-year life would be 20 percent of the original cost of the asset for each of the five years. The sum-of-years'-digits method provides for absorption of a higher percentage of initial cost in the early years than in the succeeding years. The charge for the first year is calculated by summing the years of life of the asset and dividing the sum into the life of the asset. For the second year, the numerator is decreased by 1 and again divided by the sum of the years' digits. The double declining balance method simply doubles the straight line rate, but applies the percentage to the undepreciated portion of the original cost of the assets. (Each method is demonstrated in Table 10A–3.)

The new methods (sum of the years' digits and double declining balance) of depreciation increase the rate at which deductions are made in the early years. At the end of two years, under the sum-of-the-years'-digits method, $\frac{9}{15}$, or 60 percent of the asset has been depreciated, instead of 40 percent under the straight line method. Under the double declining balance method, by the end of the second year, depreciation amounts to 64 percent of the original value of the assets. About halfway through the estimated life of the asset, the rate under the sum-of-the-years'-digits method of depreciation becomes slightly higher than that under the double declining balance method.

The financial effects of the accelerated depreciation methods should be noted at this point.

First, since the amount of depreciation is increased during the early years, income taxes are concomitantly decreased. Second, the increased funds and the savings on taxes can be reinvested and thereby used to increase the firm's earning power for both the present and the future. Third,

TABLE 10A-3

COMPARISON OF ALTERNATIVE METHODS OF DEPRECIATION

Cost of Asset, $100; Life, 5 years

	Straight Line			Sum of Years' Digits				Double Declining Balance			
Year	Amt. of Deprec.	Per-centage of Total	Cum. Per-centage	Ratio	Amt.	Per-centage of Total	Cum. Per-centage	Ratio	Amt.	Per-centage of Total	Cum. Per-centage
1	$20	20	20	5/15	$33	33	33	2/5(100)	$40.0	40.0	40
2	20	20	40	4/15	27	27	60	2/5(60)	24.0	24.0	64
3	20	20	60	3/15	20	20	80	2/5(36)	14.4	14.4	78.4
4	20	20	80	2/15	13	13	93	2/5(21.6)	8.6	8.6	87.0
5	20	20	100	1/15	7	7	100	Remainder	13.0	13.0	100.0

since accelerated depreciation is higher than the depreciation that would obtain under the straight line method, profits for the year are lower than would otherwise be reported.

Though the accelerated depreciation methods provide for new patterns of writeoff, they are generally applied to historical costs, with no adjustment for the effects of inflation. It has been argued that during a period of rising price levels the use of historical costs as a base for depreciation is insufficient for the restoration of the real capital used up in production. It has been estimated that, as a consequence of inflation, the use of historical costs has understated true depreciation in recent years by about $6 billion a year.[7]

SUMMARY

An understanding of the effect of accounting methods on the measurement of income will enable the financial manager to avoid errors in analyzing cash flows. In particular, it will aid him in formulating dividend policy. The first-in, first-out method of inventory valuation (fifo) overstates net income relative to income calculated under last-in, first out (lifo) during a period of rising price levels. Fifo also results in larger values of inventories and retained earnings on the balance sheet.

Accounting for reserves likewise influences the measurement of income and consequently the measure of liquidity and the debt-to-equity ratio on the balance sheet. Depreciation allowances represent a source of funds in the sense that they are noncash expenses. Accelerated depreciation reduces taxes in the early years relative to later years and thereby holds a larger volume of funds in the business for reinvestment.

SELECTED REFERENCES

American Management Association, *Direct Costing*, Management Bulletin 54 (New York: American Management Association, 1964).

Bodenhorn, Diran, "An Economist Looks at Industrial Accounting and Depreciation," *Accounting Review*, 36 (October 1961), pp. 583–588.

Dobrovolsky, S. P., "Depreciation Policies and Investment Decisions," *American Economic Review*, 41 (December 1951), pp. 906–914.

Hobbs, James B., "Volume-Mix-Price/Cost Budget Variance Analysis: A Proper Approach," *Accounting Review*, 39 (October 1964), pp. 905–914.

Jaedicke, Robert K., and Alexander A. Robicheck, "Cost-Volume-Profit Analysis under Conditions of Uncertainty," *Accounting Review*, 39 (October 1964), pp. 917–926.

Jones, R. C., *Effects of Price Level Changes on Business Income, Capital and Taxes* (Columbus, Ohio: American Accounting Association, 1956).

Morrissey, L. E., *The Many Sides of Depreciation*, Tuck Bulletin 23 (Hanover, N. H.: Dartmouth College, February 1960), pp. 1–24.

Norr, David, "Accounting and Analysis," *Financial Analysts Journal*, 20 (May-June 1964), pp. 38–45.

Raun, Donald L., "The Limitations of Profit Graphs, Breakeven Analysis, and Budgets," *Accounting Review*, 39 (October 1964), pp. 927–946.

Spencer, Milton H., "Axiomatic Method and Accounting Science," *Accounting Review*, 22 (April 1963), pp. 310–316.

---

[7] "Underdepreciation from Inflation," *Capital Goods Review*, No. 29 (February 1957) (Washington, D.C.: Machinery and Allied Products Institute, 1957), p. 5.

QUESTIONS

10A–1 What economic trends in the United States have been the main cause of inventory valuation problems? Why would the problem be nonexistent if this occurrence were to stop?

10A–2 What arguments can you give for the use of fifo as an inventory valuation method?

10A–3 What effects would the use of the lifo, fifo, and average cost inventory valuation methods have on a corporation's profits during a period of inflation?

10A–4 There are many reasons why some form of accelerated or reducing charge depreciation method is advantageous. How many can you think of?

10A–5 In what year will the depreciation expense be equal for the sum-of-the-years'-digits method and the straight line method if a machine has a five-year life?

10A–6 In what ways can overstated profits due to understated depreciation caused by inflation be avoided?

PROBLEMS

10A–1 Westbrig Company has the following balance sheet:

WESTBRIG MANUFACTURING COMPANY
BALANCE SHEET
December 31, 1966

Cash	$ 800	Current liabilities . . .	$1,000
Other current assets	1,200		
Total current assets . . .	$2,000	Long-term debt . . .	800
Gross fixed assets	2,000	Total debt	$1,800
Less: Reserve	0		
Net fixed assets	2,000	Net worth	2,200
Total assets	$4,000	Total claims . . .	$4,000

The company's sales in 1966 amounted to $8,000. All earnings are paid out in dividends. Assets are depreciated on a straight line 20 percent rate.

1. Present the balance sheet at the end of 1971, assuming that sales remain at $8,000 per year, that asset requirements remain unchanged, and that the firm has not replaced any fixed assets or paid off debt.

2. Present the balance sheet at the end of 1971 under the same assumptions except that any cash in excess of $1,600 is used to pay off long-term debt and then current liabilities.

3. Present the balance sheet at the end of 1971, assuming that sales rise to $12,000, that other current asset requirements increase by 50 percent, that fixed assets are not replaced, that current liabilities have increased by 30 percent, and that the firm does not use additional external financing.

10A–2 The Edbob Company has an inventory turnover every three months. The company keeps on hand an inventory of 400 items at all times. The cost per item during each quarter in 1966 was: first quarter, $4; second, $6; third, $8; and fourth, $10. The inventory on hand December 31, 1965, was 400 items at $2 each.

1. In tabular form, show the quarterly dollar volume of a) beginning inventory, b) purchases, c) materials used, and d) ending inventory, if inventory cost is determined on the following basis: first-in- first-out, and last-in, first-out.
2. The firm had annual net sales of $12,000. Its only cost was that of materials used. By constructing a simple income statement, show the effect of each method of inventory costing on net income.
3. What will be the effect of each method in a period of declining prices?

Chapter 11

Capital Structure and Use of Financial Leverage

In the preceding chapter break-even analysis was used to show how operating leverage magnifies the earnings of a company in both upward and downward directions. We now turn to a related concept, financial leverage, and examine the way it can be used to increase the return on stockholders' investment.

BASIC DEFINITIONS

To avoid ambiguity in the use of key concepts, the meanings of frequently used expressions are given here. *Asset structure* refers to the left-hand side of the balance sheet—the firm's resources that must be financed. *Financial structure* refers to the right-hand side of the balance sheet—the financing of the resources acquired by the firm. *Capital structure* is the permanent financing of the firm, represented by long-term debt, preferred stock, and net worth. *Net worth* is the *common* stockholders' equity and includes common stock, capital surplus, earned surplus (retained earnings), and net worth reserves.[1]

---

[1] Note that preferred stock is excluded from net worth here, although it was included in net worth when leverage ratios were calculated in Chapter 4. This is not an inconsistency; rather, it reflects the fact that preferred stock is a hybrid security with some of the characteristics of common stock and some of the characteristics of bonds. When viewed from the point of view of the firm's creditors, preferred is very much like common. From the viewpoint of common stockholders, preferred shares are similar to debt. Consequently, preferred stock can be classified either as a part of net worth or as debt, depending on the purpose of the analysis. In Chapter 4, we looked at leverage from the creditors' point of view; now we are concerned with the position of the common stockholder. This seemingly ambiguous point is discussed in more detail in Chapter 18.

$$\text{Capital structure} = (\text{long-term debt} + \text{preferred stock} + \text{net worth})$$
$$= (\text{total assets} - \text{current liabilities})$$

Finally, our key concept for this chapter is *financial leverage,* or the *leverage factor,* defined as the ratio of total debt to total assets. For example, a firm having assets of $100 million and total debt of $50 million would have a leverage factor of 50 percent. Some writers use only long-term debt in the numerator of the ratio, but this is not a generally accurate measure of financial leverage. While long-term debt might be more or less appropriate in an industry such as electric utilities, where little short-term debt is employed, it would be clearly inappropriate in other industries, such as aerospace, where firms rely on current debt as an important source of financing. Further, the smaller firms in most industries tend to make extensive use of short-term liabilities. Therefore, to ignore current debt in measuring the risk incurred by using financial leverage would be to ignore the major (sometimes the only) form of debt employed.

Financial leverage is also referred to as "trading on the equity." By using debt (obligations having seniority over common stock), the firm is able to conduct operations with assets in excess of the stockholders' contributions (equity of the owners). Stockholders' equity provides the financial base on which the ability of the firm to incur debt is established. For this reason the ratio of total debt to either equity (net worth) or total assets is a measure of leverage or trading on the equity.

THEORY OF FINANCIAL LEVERAGE

Perhaps the best way to understand the proper use of financial leverage is to analyze its impact on profitability under varying conditions. Suppose there are three firms in a particular industry, and these firms are identical except for their financial policies. Firm A used no debt and consequently has a leverage factor of zero; firm B, financed half by debt and half by equity, has a leverage factor of 50 percent; firm C has a leverage factor of 75 percent. Their balance sheets are shown below.

FIRM A

	Total debt	$ 0
	Net worth	200
Total assets $200	Total claims	$200

FIRM B

	Total debt (6%)	$100
	Net worth	100
Total assets $200	Total claims	$200

FIRM C

		Total debt (6%)	$150
		Net worth	50
Total assets	$200	Total claims	$200

How do these different financial patterns affect stockholder returns? As can be seen from Table 11–1, the answer depends upon the state of

TABLE 11–1

STOCKHOLDER RETURNS UNDER VARIOUS LEVERAGE AND ECONOMIC CONDITIONS

	Economic Conditions				
	Very Bad	*Bad*	*Normal*	*Good*	*Very Good*
Rate of return on total assets before interest	2%	5%	8%	11%	14%
Dollar returns on total assets before interest	$4	$10	$ 1	$22	$28
Firm A. Leverage Factor 0%					
Earnings in dollars	$4	$10	$16	$22	$28
Less: Interest expense	0	0	0	0	0
Gross income	4	10	16	22	28
Taxes (50%)*	2	5	8	11	14
Available to common stock	2	5	8	11	14
Percent return on common stock . . .	1%	2.5%	4%	5.5%	7%
Firm B. Leverage Factor 50%					
Earnings in dollars	$4	$10	$16	$22	$28
Less: Interest expense	6	6	6	6	6
Gross income	(2)	4	10	16	22
Taxes (50%)*	(1)	2	5	8	11
Available to common stock	(1)	2	5	8	11
Percent return on common stock . . .	—1%	2%	5%	8%	11%
Firm C. Leverage Factor 75%					
Earnings in dollars	$4	$10	$16	$22	$28
Less: Interest expense	9	9	9	9	9
Gross income	(5)	1	7	13	19
Taxes (50%)*	(2.5)	.5	3.5	6.5	9.5
Available to common stock	(2.5)	.5	3.5	6.5	9.5
Percent return on common stock . . .	—5%	1%	7%	13%	19%

* The tax calculation assumes that losses are carried back and result in tax credits.

the industry's economy. When the economy is very depressed, sales and profit margins are low and the firms earn only 2 percent on assets. When conditions become better but are still bad, the return on assets is 5 percent. Under normal conditions the returns rise to 8 percent, while in a moderate boom the figure goes to 11 percent. Finally, under extremely favorable circumstances the companies have a 14 percent return on assets. These percentages, multiplied by the $200 of assets, give the earnings before interest and taxes for the three companies under the various states of the economy.

Note how the use of financial leverage magnifies the impact on the stockholders of changes in the rate of return on assets. When economic conditions go from normal to good, for example, returns on assets go up by 37.5 percent. Firm A uses no leverage, gets no magnification, and consequently experiences the same 37.5 percent jump in the rate of return to stockholders. Firm B, on the other hand, enjoys a 60 percent increase in stockholder returns as a result of the 37.5 percent rise in returns on assets. Firm C, which uses still more leverage, has an 86 percent increase. Just the reverse holds in economic downturns, of course: the 37.5 percent drop in returns on assets, when the economy goes from normal to bad, results in return-on-net-worth declines of 37.5 percent, 60 percent, and 86 percent for firms A, B, and C, respectively.

Using the same illustrative numbers, Figure 11–1 gives a graphic

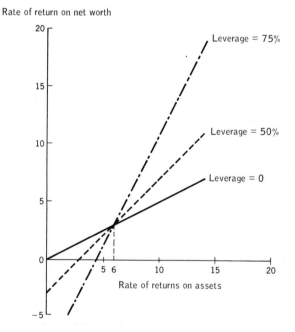

Fig. 11–1. Relationship between Rates of Return on Assets and Rates of Return on Net Worth under Different Leverage Conditions

presentation of the interaction between the rates of return on assets and net worth, given the three different leverage factors. The interesting point to note here is the intersection of the three lines at the point where assets are returning 6 percent, the interest cost of debt. When returns on assets are higher, leverage improves stockholder returns and is said to be *favorable;* when assets earn less than 6 percent, returns to stockholders are reduced and the leverage is defined as *unfavorable.* In general, whenever the return on assets exceeds the cost of debt, leverage is favorable, and the higher the leverage factor the higher the rate of return on common equity.

EFFECTS OF FINANCIAL LEVERAGE

To show that the results of alternative financial decisions are useful in judging the relative merits and demerits of various plans, a specific example is given. This example illustrates how future earnings prospects affect financing decisions.

The Universal Machine Company, whose latest balance sheet is shown in Table 11–2, manufactures equipment used by steel producers. As is typically

TABLE 11–2

UNIVERSAL MACHINE COMPANY
BALANCE SHEET
December 31, 1966

Assets		*Liabilities*	
Cash	$ 20,000	Accounts Payable	$120,000
Receivables (net)	110,000	Other current liabilities . .	80,000
Inventories	160,000	Total liabilities . . .	$200,000
Plant (net)	250,000	Common stock ($10 par) . .	500,000
Equipment (net)	280,000	Surplus	120,000
Total assets	$820,000	Total claims on assets .	$820,000

the case for the producers of durable capital assets, its sales fluctuate widely, far more widely than does the over-all economy. For example, during nine of the last 25 years, sales have been below the break-even point, so losses have been relatively frequent. In the last few years, however, machinery demand has been heavy and actually rising, and if Universal is to continue sharing in this expansion it will have to increase capacity. For this increase, $300,000 is required. James Forsite, the financial vice-president, learns that he can net $300,000 by selling $320,000 of bonds with a 5 percent coupon. Alternatively, he can raise the $300,000 by selling 35,000 shares of common stock.

During the past five years, Universal's sales have fluctuated between $50,000 and $400,000; at the latter volume the firm was operating at full capacity and had to turn down orders. With the additional plant expansion, sales capacity will increase to $600,000. Although net profits before taxes and interest will fluctuate with the degree of capacity utilization, to simplify calculations it is assumed that the profit margin is 20 percent of sales.

Although Forsite's recommendation will be given much weight, the final decision for the method of financing rests with the company's board of directors. Procedurally, the financial vice-president will analyze the situation, come to a conclusion, and then present his recommendation to the board. For his own benefit, as well as for presentation to the board, Forsite prepares the material shown in Table 11-3 and Figure 11-2.

In Table 11-3, Forsite computes earnings per share under each of the financial alternatives for levels of sales ranging from zero to $600,000; Figure 11-2 is simply a break-even chart constructed from the data in the table. With $200,000 in sales, it can be seen that the two methods of raising capital produce the same earnings per share. Below that level of sales, the earnings per share

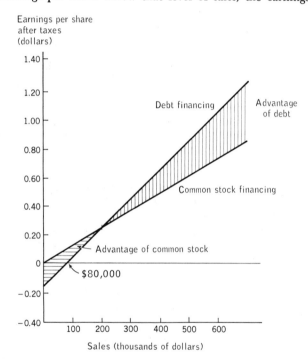

Fig. 11-2. Break-Even Chart for Financial Leverage:
Earnings per Share versus Sales

are higher under common stock financing than under bond financing. Above $200,000 the earnings per share on common stock are higher if bonds are used instead of common stock. This is shown by a break-even chart (Figure 11-2), which relates sales to earnings per share after taxes. The break-even point is at sales of $200,000.

If Forsite and the board *know for sure* that sales will never again fall below $200,000, their decision will be a simple one—bonds would be the logical choice. But they do not know this, and in fact they probably have good reason to expect future business cycles to drive sales down to and even below this

TABLE 11–3

UNIVERSAL MACHINE COMPANY

PROFIT CALCULATIONS AT VARIOUS SALES LEVELS

Financing by Bonds

Sales	$ 0	$ 50,000	$100,000	$200,000	$400,000	$600,000
Income before interest and taxes	0	$ 10,000	$ 20,000	$ 40,000	$ 80,000	$120,000
Interest (5% × $320,000)	16,000	16,000	16,000	16,000	16,000	16,000
Profit before taxes	$−16,000	$− 6,000	$ 4,000	$ 24,000	$ 64,000	$104,000
Less: Income taxes (50%)	(8,000)	(3,000)	2,000	12,000	32,000	52,000
Net profit after taxes	$− 8,000	$− 3,000	$ 2,000	$ 12,000	$ 32,000	$ 52,000
Earning per share on 50,000 shares of common	$− 0.16	$− 0.06	$ 0.04	$ 0.24	$ 0.64	$ 1.04

Financing by Common Stock

Sales	$ 0	$ 50,000	$100,000	$200,000	$400,000	$600,000
Net Income	0	$ 10,000	$ 20,000	$ 40,000	$ 80,000	$120,000
Less: Income taxes (50%)	0	5,000	10,000	20,000	40,000	60,000
Net profit after taxes	$ 0	$ 5,000	$ 10,000	$ 20,000	$ 40,000	$ 60,000
Earnings per share on 85,000 shares of common	$ 0	$ 0.06	$ 0.12	$ 0.24	$ 0.47	$ 0.70

level. They know, for example, that within the past five years sales were as low
as $50,000. If this level is reached again, the company will not be earning
enough to cover its interest charges. Such a situation, if it continued for several
years, could jeopardize the very existence of the firm. On the other hand, if
sales continue to expand, there will be pronounced benefits from using bonds,
and no officer or director would want to forgo these substantial advantages.

Forsite's recommendation and the individual decisions of each of the
directors will probably depend upon their own appraisals of the future. The
optimists will tend to favor bonds, while the pessimists will prefer to finance
with common stock. This example, which is typical of many real-world situations, suggests that the major disagreements over the choices of forms of financing are likely to reflect uncertainty about the future levels of the firm's sales.
Such uncertainty, in turn, reflects the characteristics of the firm's environment—
general business conditions, industry trends, and quality and aggressiveness of
management.

VARIATIONS IN FINANCIAL STRUCTURE

As might be expected, wide variations in the use of financial leverage
may be observed among individual firms, among groups of firms, and
among industries. Illustrative of these differences is the range of ratios of
total debt to total assets shown in Table 11–4 for certain broad groups of
industries. Service industries use the most leverage, reflecting the facts
that (1) services include certain financial institutions that typically have
high liabilities and (2) there are many smaller firms in the service industries (small firms as a group are heavy users of debt). Public utility
use of debt stems from a heavy fixed asset investment coupled with
extremely stable sales. Mining and manufacturing firms use relatively
little debt because of their exposure to fluctuating sales.

These broad industry groupings understate the differences in leverage
that are found when the data are disaggregated. Industry data represent
an averaging among the different firms, and the averages necessarily
fluctuate less than the individual companies. Whereas the range for the
averages in Table 11–4 is only from 63 to 36 percent debt to total assets,
statistics on the individual firms shown in Table 11–5 range from 81.6
percent for International Shoe to only 6.1 percent for Texas Gulf
Sulphur.[2]

Even within a given industry there are wide variations in the use of
financial leverage; this is illustrated for the electric utility industry in
Table 11–6. These variations reflect a number of different considerations,

---

[2] During 1964, Texas Gulf Sulphur announced the discovery of one of the largest
ore bodies ever found. These deposits, located in a relatively remote section of Canada,
were estimated to contain several *billions* of dollars worth of silver, lead, zinc, nickel,
and other valuable metals. The costs of developing the property—putting in access
roads, mills, and smelters, and sinking mine shafts—will require the company to
raise additional capital. Given its very conservative debt ratio, it would be safe to
bet that debt is employed.

including volatility of business in the companies' operating areas, extent to which they are using preferred stock, and managements' willingness to assume risk. Montana Power, for example, sells a large amount of electricity to copper producers, whose volume of business, hence demand for

TABLE 11-4

VARIATIONS IN FINANCIAL LEVERAGE IN INDUSTRY GROUPS, 1961-1962

Name of Industry	*Total Debt to Total Assets (in percentages)*
Service	63
Public utilities	58
Wholesale trade	53
Agriculture	49
Retail trade	48
Mining	38
Manufacturing	36

Source: United States Treasury Department, Internal Revenue Service, *Statistics of Income, U.S. Business Tax Returns, 1962*, (Washington, D.C.: U.S. Government Printing Office, 1964).

TABLE 11-5

DEBT-TO-TOTAL-ASSETS RATIOS
Selected Largest Firms in Product Line, 1960

International Shoe	81.6	Great A. & P. Tea	31.9
Boeing Aircraft	61.9	Standard Oil, N. J.	31.5
United Air Lines	61.4	General Motors	30.8
R.C.A.	59.4	Swift	29.8
Reynolds Tobacco	48.9	du Pont	26.5
Penn. R.R.	41.8	National Lead	26.4
A. T. & T.	41.6	Cincinnati Milling	22.5
Burlington Ind.	40.6	Hercules Powder	21.4
General Electric	39.5	Eastman Kodak	19.2
International Business Machines	39.2	Johns Manville	17.7
Continental Can	38.5	Lone Star Cement	17.5
Sears Roebuck	36.8	Singer	15.4
U.S. Steel	35.2	Coca Cola	13.9
Aluminum Co. of Amer.	33.4	Procter & Gamble	13.7
Harbison Walker	32.9	Armstrong Cork	13.5
General Foods	32.4	Goodyear	12.5
Time Inc.	32.4	Consolidation Coal	12.2
J. C. Penney	32.3	Ohio Oil	11.8
American Home Prods.	32.1	Weyerhauser Timber	6.8
American News	32.1	Texas Gulf Sulphur	6.1

Compiled from *The News Front Directory of 3,000 Leading U. S. Corporations* (New York: Year, Inc., 1960), pp. 14–74.

DEBT-TO-TOTAL-ASSETS RATIO
Selected Electric Utility Companies, 1962

Montana Power	37
Detroit Edison	41
Central Illinois Light & Power	54
Consolidated Edison	56
Tampa Electric	57
Missouri Public Service	63

Source: Moody's Public Utility Manual, 1963

power, is quite cyclical. This largely explains its low debt ratio. Missouri Public Service, by contrast, has a stable demand pattern, which takes much of the risk out of its relatively high leverage factor.

FACTORS INFLUENCING FINANCIAL STRUCTURE

Thus far the discussion has alluded to some of the factors that are generally considered when a firm establishes its financial structure. The more important of these capital structure determinants are now listed and briefly discussed.

Growth rate of future sales
Stability of future sales
Competitive structure of the industry
Asset structure of the industry
Control position of owners and management and attitudes toward risk
Lender attitudes toward firm and industry

Growth Rate of Sales

The future growth rate of sales is a measure of the extent to which the earnings per share of a firm are likely to be magnified by leverage. If sales and earnings grow at an 8-to-10 percent rate per year, for example, financing by debt with limited fixed charges should magnify the returns to owners of this stock.[3]

On the other hand, the common stock of a firm whose sales and earnings are growing at a favorable rate will command a high price, and thus it would appear that equity financing is inexpensive. The firm will weigh the benefits of trading on the equity against the opportunity of broadening its equity base for future financing alternatives. Such firms would be expected to have a moderate-to-high rate of debt financing. For example, at the end of 1960 International Business Machines had a debt

---

[3] Such a growth rate is typically associated with a high profit rate.

ratio of 37 percent. Litton Industries, another growth company, had a debt ratio of 60 percent.[4]

Sales Stability

Sales stability and debt ratios are directly related. With greater stability in sales and earnings, a firm can incur the fixed charges of debt with less risk than it can when its sales and earnings are declining; in the latter instance it will have difficulty in meeting its obligations. The stability of the utility industry, combined with relatively favorable growth prospects, has resulted in high leverage ratios in that industry.

Competitive Structure

Debt servicing ability is dependent upon the profitability as well as the volume of sales; hence the stability of profit margins is as important as the stability of sales. Most important in determining margins is the competitive environment within which a firm is operating: Are profit margins subject to erosion either from new firms entering the industry or from the expansion of other firms already in the business; or are the existing firms relatively secure from excessive competitive pressures? Profit margins in a growing industry are likely to narrow if the industry is one in which the number of firms is likely to multiply rapidly. For example, pleasure-boat manufacturing and neighborhood bowling alleys are likely to be subject to increased competition over time, because of the relative ease of establishing competitive businesses.[5] On the other hand, to duplicate the unique technical and distribution facilities of the International Business Machines Corporation is much more difficult, a fact suggesting that profit margins for this firm are less subject to erosion.

Asset Structure

Asset structure influences the sources of financing in several ways. Firms with heavy fixed assets, for example, utilities, use long-term mortgage debt to a greater degree. Firms with current assets predominant in their balance sheets, for example, those in wholesale and retail trade, rely

---

[4] There is, however, another consideration at work in the case of profitable, growing firms. The fact that they are profitable means that relatively large amounts of funds are being generated, and these are equity funds that can be used to finance further expansion. On this basis, one might expect to find *low* debt ratios among rapidly growing firms, and in fact such a situation was observed when a sample of 70 electric utility companies was examined. Others have reported similar findings; for example, Gordon Donaldson, *Corporate Debt Capacity*, (Boston: Harvard University, 1961). Nevertheless, in general it appears that growing firms are the ones that employ debt to the greatest extent.

[5] This sentence was taken *verbatim* from the first edition of the book, written in 1961. It is interesting to note that in the short span of five years the prediction has been borne out decisively.

on short-term debt financing to a greater degree. Asset structure is, however, relatively less important than are stability and growth of earnings as a measure of ability to carry long-term debt.

Management Attitudes

The aspects of management attitudes that most directly influence the choice of financing are (1) control of the enterprise and (2) attitudes toward risk. In large corporations whose stock is widely owned, additional sales of common stock will have little influence on the control of the company. Also, because management represents a stewardship for the owners, it is often less willing to take the risk of heavy fixed charges.[6]

Smaller firms, controlled by the owners, may prefer to avoid the issue of common stock in order to be assured of continued control. Because they generally have confidence in the prospects of their company and because they can see the large potential gains to themselves resulting from leverage, they are often willing to incur debt ratios.

Lender Attitudes

Regardless of managements' feelings about the proper leverage factor for their firms, there is no question but that lenders' attitudes are frequently an important—sometimes the most important—determinant of capital structures. Lender influence ranges in significance from zero for those firms whose managements are more conservative than the most risk-conscientious lenders, to *the* determining force in situations where management is supremely confident of the future and anxious to trade on the equity to the maximum extent possible. In between lie the majority of cases, where the corporation discusses its capital structure with lenders and gives some degree of weight to their advice. Illustrative of this position is the unnamed electric utility company whose financial vice-president stated that his policy is "to determine how much debt we can carry and still maintain an AA bond rating,[7] then use that amount less a small margin for safety."

---

[6] It would be inappropriate to delve too far into motivational theory in an introductory finance textbook, but it is interesting to note that the managers of many larger, publicly owned corporations have a relatively small ownership position and derive most of their income from salaries. Some writers assert that in such cases managements do not strive for profits, especially if this effort involves using leverage with its inherent risk. Presumably, these managers feel that the risks of leverage for them, the ones who actually decide to use debt or equity, outweigh the potential gains from successful leverage. If sales are low, there is a chance of failure and the loss of their jobs, while if sales and profits are high, it is the stockholders, not management, who receive the benefits. While there is undoubtedly some merit to this argument, it should be pointed out that companies are increasingly using profit-based compensation schemes—bonus systems and stock-option plans—to motivate management to seek profitability as well as stability.

[7] Bond ratings, which are discussed in detail in Chapter 19, are basically indices of the risk that lenders incur when buying particular bonds. A rating of AAA is the highest, denoting the lowest risk, and AA is just below it.

GUIDELINES FOR FINANCIAL STRUCTURES

On the basis of the foregoing considerations, broad guidelines or reference levels for the financial structures of wide industrial segments are presented in Table 11–7. In examining these figures, keep in mind all

TABLE 11–7

REFERENCE LEVELS FOR FINANCIAL STRUCTURES

	Percentage of Total Assets					
	Current Liabilities	Long-term Debt	Preferred Stock	Net Worth	Current Ratio	Coverage of Fixed Charges
Large, established firms						
Manufacturing	20–25%	6–10%	0–4%	65–70%	2×	7×
Utilities . . .	5–10	45–50	10–15	30–35	1	4
Trade	30–35	6–8	0–2	60–65	2.5	7
Small, rapidly growing profitable firms						
Manufacturing	40–45%	0–5%	0–10%	40–60%	1×	8×
Trade	50–60	0–5	0–5	30–40	1.5	10

that has been said about the importance of carefully appraising the individual situation and the dangers of relying on industry norms. The guidelines do, however, have a rational basis, and it would be wise to question the reasons behind any given company's decision to step outside the prescribed bounds.

Manufacturing Industries

Detailed studies of financial ratios among manufacturing firms reveal wide variations among industries and, to a lesser degree, among firms in the same industry. Within a given industry, firms tend to cluster about a certain financial structure, as the major factors influencing financial structure all tend to operate in the same direction.

Table 11–7 suggests that the percentage of the financial structure in current liabilities should be smallest for utilities, next for manufacturing, and highest for firms engaged in wholesale and retail trade. As a group, manufacturing firms tend to operate with relatively small percentages of long-term debt in their financial structures. They incur long-term debt during periods of rapid expansion and follow the policy of paying off debt as rapidly as permitted by earnings retention or flotation of new shares of common stock. Preferred stock is used mainly as a substitute for debt where firms seek to gain the benefits of trading on the equity but are unwilling to bear the risks of fixed charges.

The reference ranges suggested for manufacturing indicate that debt-to-total-assets ratios should approximate 33 percent, or that debt should be about one third of total assets.

Utility Industries

Current debt is a much smaller ratio of total assets for utilities than for any other industry. Cash is small because of the synchronization of inflows and outflows of cash. Receivables are small because terms of sales are on presentation of invoice, and service may be cut off if bills are not paid. By the nature of the business, inventories are small. Because of heavy fixed plant and stability of earnings, long-term debt is large. Preferred stock is used to a greater extent by utilities than by any other category of firms. The tax disadvantages of preferred stock is somewhat mitigated, because rates are determined on the basis of earning power after taxes.

For utilities, the ratio of preferred stock and debt to total assets runs about 60 to 65 percent. Greater clustering occurs in utility companies' debt ratios than in other industrial categories, even though here, as was seen from Table 11–6, variations can occur.

Wholesale and Retail Trade

Firms engaged in wholesale and retail trade utilize current debt to the highest degree, but their use of long-term debt and preferred stock is smallest. Net worth percentages are moderately smaller for wholesale and retail trade than for manufacturing firms, with the ratio of debt to total assets rising to between 36 and 43 percent.

Current Ratio

The levels of current ratios reflect the characteristic asset structures in the three categories of industrial activity. The traditional 2 to 1 rule-of-thumb ratio fits most categories in the industrial field, but because of relatively small amounts of current assets, the 1 to 1 ratio for utilities is appropriate. Since trade firms have heavier inventories and receivables, a ratio of 2.5 or 3 to 1 is desirable here.

Fixed-Charge Coverage

Coverage of fixed charges is one of the tests widely applied by investors. The coverage suggested here reflects characteristic recommendations found in works on investments and security analysis.[8] Because these

---

[8] See, for example, B. Graham, D. L. Dodd, and S. Cottle, *Security Analysis* (New York: McGraw-Hill, 1961), pp. 343–352.

are the coverages expected by investors, the determination of the appropriate levels must reflect investor preferences as well as financial structure considerations. The logic involved here is to protect creditors by having expected earnings adequately cover fixed charges. The earnings level to be used should reflect the best judgment of future earnings levels, taking into account past experience and prospective changes in the economic environment that may affect earnings in the industry and company under study, with allowance for unexpected declines.

The coverages suggested are based on earnings before deduction for income taxes. For operating companies, the logic here appears clear— interest is paid out of earnings before taxes, so taxes, as such, cannot impair the ability of the firm to meet its interest obligations.

Modification of Standards for Small Firms

In formulating broad reference guides for evaluating the financial structures of business firms, a number of factors in addition to the industry of the firm are important. Among these are the age, size, growth rate, and profitability of the firm. To reflect these factors and yet avoid unduly proliferating the categories, the second section of Table 11–7 indicates suitable modifications in the basic reference ranges for small, rapidly growing, profitable firms. A new, small firm starts from such a limited base that success, measured by profitability, is likely to be accompanied by rapid growth. Since they are likely to occur together, the influence of age, size, growth rate, and profitability may be conveniently grouped.

The small, successful firm is likely to employ leverage to a much greater degree then its older, larger counterpart. Current ratios will be lower, and the firm may actually be slow in meeting its bills. Because of this, the required coverage of fixed charges should be somewhat greater for protection to creditors. Debt-to-total-assets ratios may run as high as 60 percent for manufacturing firms and 70 to 75 percent for trade firms. As the firm grows and begins to present a record of success, its access to the equity markets is likely to improve. Then it will likely have a common stock flotation that will help bring its financial structure into better balance.

The guidelines presented to this point have been very broad. They have been developed for the purpose of providing basic reference guides that can be kept in mind when evaluating the financial structures of firms. Finer distinctions must be made, however, and the following section describes how financial structures can be developed to reflect the characteristics of individual industries.

USE OF FINANCIAL RATIO COMPOSITES IN DETERMINING THE FINANCIAL PLAN

Chapter 4 described how financial data tabulated by industries could be used to evaluate the financial ratios for individual firms in these industries. Such composite data, or averages, can also be used to provide a basis for formulating the financial plan of an individual firm. Financial structures so developed will conform to general industry practice. While simply conforming to the structure of other firms in a particular line of business is not necessarily desirable, such a standard can be a useful starting point, especially if the capital structure of a new enterprise is being planned.

Developing a *pro forma* balance sheet, based on the average of financial ratios of firms in a given line of business, is the first step. To use the method of financial-ratio composites to construct the *pro forma* financial plan, it is necessary to know only two things: (1) the industry of the hypothetical firm and (2) its estimated annual sales. To illustrate, it is assumed that the firm is an industrial-machinery manufacturer with estimated annual sales of $120,000.

The Dun & Bradstreet median financial-ratio composites for the industry for the most recent year are:

Sales to net worth	3 times
Current debt to net worth	40 percent
Total debt to net worth	60 percent
Current ratio	3 times
Net sales to inventory	4 times
Average collection period	42 days
Fixed assets to net worth	40 percent

On the basis of this information, the following *pro forma* balance sheet can be constructed:

Pro Forma Balance Sheet

Cash	$ 4,000		Current debt	$16,000
Accounts receivable	14,000		Long-term debt	8,000
Inventory	30,000		Net worth	40,000
Current assets		$48,000		
Fixed assets		16,000		
		$64,000		$64,000

Calculations:

1. Net worth = sales ÷ net worth turnover

$$\frac{\$120,000}{3} = \$40,000$$

2. Total debt = 60% of net worth
$$\$40,000 \times 60\% = \$24,000$$

3. Current debt = 40% of net worth
$$\$40,000 \times 40\% = \$16,000$$

4. Long-term debt = total debt − current debt
$$\$24,000 - \$16,000 = \$8,000$$

5. Total claims on assets = net worth + total debt
$$\$40,000 + \$24,000 = \$64,000$$

6. Current assets = current debt × current ratio
$$\$16,000 \times 3 = \$48,000$$

7. Inventory = sales ÷ inventory turnover
$$\frac{\$120,00}{4} = \$30,000$$

8. Accounts receivable = average collection period × sales per day
$$\frac{\$120,000}{360} \times \frac{42}{1} = \$14,000$$

9. Cash = current assets − (receivables + inventory)
$$\$48,000 - (\$14,000 + \$30,000) = \$4,000$$

10. Fixed assets = net worth × 40%
$$\$40,000 \times 40\% = \$16,000$$

11. Total assets = current assets + fixed assets
$$\$48,000 + \$16,000 = \$64,000$$

Pro forma balance sheets, based on financial ratio composites, may be developed for a firm if only its industry and size, measured by actual or expected sales, are known. Profitability and income statement relations can also be developed by reference to industry data, with the data being based on any of the wide variety of sources of financial ratio compilations described in Chapter 4. Alternatively, a financial manager may develop his own guidelines by constructing averages based on a selected number of firms most similar (in his judgment) to his own business—for example, those firms operating in his same geographic market area.

The use of financial ratio composites as a guideline to financial structures may be questioned on theoretical grounds. Because these composites are computed averages, some firms must be above the average and some below. But it is of interest to know on which side of the average an individual firm stands. Further, a strong practical consideration reinforces the value of such comparisons—bank lending officers and other credit and financial analysts place heavy reliance on such comparisons between individual firms and industry norms. Thus the financial structure of the firm will in practice be checked against industry data.

Of course, neither financial managers nor lenders need be held in a strait jacket by an industry average. The average is primarily a standard for reference, and many factors may cause an individual firm to depart from the industry pattern. For example, it has already been noted that age, size, growth rate, control position of owners, and management attitudes toward risk may exert a strong influence on the financial policies of a firm.

Financial structures suggested by industry practices represent only a starting point. Sound reasons may exist why an individual firm's financial structure will depart from the reference levels provided by industry data. But it is important that the financial manager understand the reasons for these differences and be able to explain them effectively to potential creditors. Sometimes the differences may represent elements of strength or the almost unavoidable growing pains of a rapidly developing company. However, departures from industry norms may also signal weaknesses, which should be corrected at the earliest opportunity.

SUMMARY

Financial leverage, which deals with the use of debt to boost rates of return on net worth over the returns available on assets, is the primary topic covered in this chapter. Whenever the return on assets exceeds the cost of debt, leverage is favorable and the return on equity is raised by using it. However, leverage is a two-edged sword, and if the returns on assets are less than the cost of debt, then leverage reduces the returns on equity. This reduction is greater the more leverage a firm employs. As a net result, leverage may be used to boost stockholder returns, but using it is at the risk of increasing losses if the firm's economic fortunes decline.

Financial structure, defined as the method of financing a firm's assets, represents another way of looking at the leverage question. In part, financial structures are determined by management. But firms are constrained by the amount of debt lenders are willing to advance, and this willingness is partially conditioned by the characteristics of the industry and by the financial structures of other firms in the industry. For this reason, the authors have analyzed the factors causing capital structures to differ among industries.

Thus far, the analysis has been more conversational than rigorous. In the following chapter, the concepts developed up to this point will be extended to the formal theory of the cost of capital and the theory of security valuation. The way investors appraise the relative desirability of increased returns versus higher risks will be seen to be a most important consideration, and one that, in general, invalidates the theory that firms should strive for maximum earnings per share regardless of the risks involved.

SELECTED REFERENCES

Donaldson, Gordon, *Corporate Debt Capacity* (Boston: Harvard University, 1961).

Foster, Louis O., *Corporate Debt and the Stockholder: The Effects of Borrowing on Rates of Return* (Hanover, N. H.: Amos Tuck School of Business Administration, Dartmouth College, 1956).

Hubbard, Philip M., Jr., "The Many Aspects of Dilution," *Financial Analysts Journal*, 19 (May-June, 1963), pp. 33–40.

Kuznets, Simon, *Capital in the American Economy—Its Formation and Financing* (Princeton, N. J., Princeton University Press, 1961).

Marris, Robin, *The Economic Theory of Managerial Capitalism* (New York: Free Press, 1964).

Meiselman, David, and Eli Shapiro, *The Measurement of Corporate Sources and Use of Funds* (New York: National Bureau of Economic Research, 1964).

Sauvain, H. C., "Has Business Borrowed Too Much?" *Business Horizons*, No. 1 (Winter 1958), pp. 48–55.

Schwartz, Eli, "Theory of the Capital Structure of the Firm," *Journal of Finance*, 14 (March 1959), pp. 18–39.

Weston, J. Fred (ed.), *Financial Management in the 1960s: New Challenges and Responsibilities* (New York: Holt, Rinehart and Winston, Inc. 1966), selections "The Optimistic World of Henry Kaiser," and "Is A. T. & T. Playing It Too Safe?"

———. *Readings in Finance from Fortune* (New York: Holt, Rinehart and Winston, Inc., 1958), selections 8 and 9.

QUESTIONS

11–1 How will each of the following be changed by the occurrences listed below: financial structure, capital structure, and net worth?

1. The firm has retained earnings of $100 for the year.
2. A preferred stock issue is refinanced with bonds.
3. Bonds are sold for cash.
4. The firm repurchases 10 percent of its outstanding common stock with excess cash.
5. An issue of convertible bonds is converted.

11–2 From an economic and social standpoint, is trading on the equity justifiable? Explain by listing some advantages and disadvantages.

11–3 Financial leverage and operating leverage are similar in one very important respect. What is this similarity and why is it important?

11–4 What are some reasons for variations of debt ratios among the firms in a given industry?

11–5 Why is the following statement true? "Other things the same, firms with relatively stable sales are able to incur relatively high debt ratios."

11–6 Why do public utility companies usually pursue a different financial policy from that of trade firms?

11–7 The use of financial ratios and industry averages in the financial planning and analysis of a firm should be approached with caution. Why?

11–8 Some economists believe that the swings in the business cycles have not been as wide in recent years as they were in the past. Assuming that they are correct in their analysis, what effect can this added stability have on the types of financing used by firms in the United States? Would your answer be true for all firms?

PROBLEMS

11–1 One useful test or guide for evaluating a firm's financial structure in relation to its industry is by comparison with financial ratio composites for its industry. A new firm or a firm contemplating entering a new industry may use such industry composites as a guide to what its financial position is likely to approximate after the initial settling-down period.

The following data represent the ratios for the furniture manufacturing industry for 1963:

Estimated annual sales	$400,000
Sales to net worth	4 times
Current debt to net worth	50%
Total debt to net worth	80%
Current ratio	2.2 times
Net sales to inventory	8 times
Average collection period	40 days
Fixed assets to net worth	70%

EXCELSIOR FURNITURE DESIGNS
PRO FORMA BALANCE SHEET
1963

Cash	$———	Current debt	$———
Accounts receivable	———	Long-term debt	———
Inventory	———	Total debt	———
Current assets	———	Net worth	———
Fixed assets	———	Total liabilities and	
Total Assets	$——	net worth	$——

1. Complete the above *pro forma* balance sheet. (Round to nearest 000.)
2. What does the use of the financial ratio composites accomplish?
3. What other factors will influence the financial structure of the firm?

11–2 In November 1965, Gusher Company raised $300 million additional funds to finance growth. In September 1966, Streamer Company raised $100 million to finance growth in sales.

From data given below, which firm is likely to have sold 4.5 percent debentures and which to have sold common stock?

GUSHER AND STREAMER OIL COMPANIES
BALANCE SHEETS
June 30, 1966
(in millions of dollars)

	Gusher	*Streamer*
Current assets	$3,000	$ 650
Investments	400	100
Net fixed assets	4,600	1,750
Total assets	$8,000	$2,500
Current liabilities	$1,400	$ 300
Long-term debt	1,600	200
Total debt	$3,000	$ 500

Common stock: Outstanding

Gusher (200 million shares)—$10 par	$2,000	
Streamer (40 million shares)—$25 par		$1,000
Earned surplus	3,000	1,000
Net worth	5,000	2,000
Total claims	$8,000	$2,500

Sales (in billions of dollars):

1962	5.4	1.7
1963	5.6	1.7
1964	5.8	1.8
1965	6.4	1.9
1966	7.1	2.0

Net income (in millions of dollars):

1962	540	136
1963	560	136
1964	580	144
1965	640	152
1966	700	152

GUSHER AND STREAMER OIL COMPANIES
INCOME STATEMENTS
For Period Ended June 30, 1966
(in millions of dollars)

	Gusher	*Streamer*
Sales	$7,100	$2,000
Total costs	6,128	1,820
Net income before taxes	972	180
Interest on debt (4.5%)	72	(4.0%) 8
	$ 900	$ 172
Federal income taxes	200	20
Net income after taxes	$ 700	$ 152
Sales to total assets	0.089	0.080
Earnings per share	$3.50	$3.80
Dividends per share	1.85	1.25
Price-earnings ratio	20×	15×
Market price	70	57

11–3 The Beaumont Company plans to expand assets by 50 percent. It is attempting to choose between a straight 6 percent debt issue and common stock. Its current balance sheet and income statement are shown below.

BEAUMONT COMPANY
BALANCE SHEET
December 31, 1966

Total assets	$200,000	Debt, 5%		$ 40,000
		Common stock, $10 par. . .		100,000
		Earned surplus		60,000
		Total claims		$200,000

INCOME STATEMENT
Year Ended December 31, 1966

Sales	$600,000
Total costs (excluding interest) . .	538,000
Net income before taxes	62,000
Debt interest	2,000
Income before taxes	60,000
Taxes @ 50%	30,000
	$ 30,000

Earnings per share: $\dfrac{30,000}{10,000} = \$3$

Market price: $12 \times 3 = \$36$

If Beaumont Company finances the $100,000 expansion with debt, the rate on the incremental debt will be 6 percent and the price-earnings ratio of the common stock will be 10 times. If the expansion is financed by equity, the new stock can be sold at $33 1/3, the rate on debt will be 5 percent and the price-earnings ratio of all the outstanding common stock will remain at 12 times earnings.

1. Assuming that net income before interest on debt and before taxes is 10 percent of sales, calculate earnings per share at sales assumptions of $0, $50,000, $200,000, $400,000, $600,000, $800,000, and $1,000,000, when financing is with common stock in contrast to debt.
2. Make a break-even chart for the earnings under 1.
3. Using the price-earnings ratio indicated calculate the market value per share of common stock for each sales level assumption for the debt versus the equity methods of financing.
4. Make a break-even chart of market value per share of the company for data found in number 3.
5. If the firm follows the policy of seeking to maximize the market price of its stock, which form of financing should be employed?
6. What other factors should be taken into account in choosing between the two forms of financing?

Chapter 12

Valuation and the Cost of Capital

In the discussion of the capital budgeting process in Chapter 7, the discount rate used in the present value calculations was seen to be of vital importance. Relatively small changes in this figure produced significant changes in computed net present values and frequently caused a complete reversal in the decision to accept or to reject a particular project. In the discussion of capital budgeting, it was simply *assumed* that the cost of capital—the discount rate used in the present value process—was known, and this rate was used in the calculations. Now, however, it is necessary to devote attention to the problem of deriving the cost of capital for individual firms.

Since the cost of capital to the firm is integrally connected with investors' returns on capital, the basic principles underlying valuation theory are first discussed. Then, building on valuation theory, the costs of the various types of capital that a firm may employ are discussed. Finally, the costs of the individual components of capital are averaged to produce the firm's over-all cost of capital, the fundamental quantity used in capital budgeting.

VALUATION

While it is impossible to ascribe any monetary returns to certain types of assets—works of art, for instance—the fundamental characteristic of business assets is that they give rise to income flows. Sometimes this flow is easy to see and measure—the interest return on a bond is an example. At other times the cash flows attributable to the asset must be estimated, as was done in Chapter 7 in the evaluation of projects. But regardless of the difficulties of measuring income flows, it is the likelihood that business assets will produce revenues that gives them value.

Liquidating versus Going-Concern Value

Several different definitions of "value" exist in the literature and are used in practice, with different ones being appropriate at different times. The first distinction that must be made is that between *liquidating value* and *going-concern value*. Liquidating value is defined as the amount that could be realized if an asset or a group of assets (the assets of an entire firm, for example) were to be sold for use by another. If the owner of a machine shop decided to retire, he might auction off his inventory and equipment, collect his accounts receivable, then sell his land and buildings to a grocery wholesaler for use as a warehouse. The total sum that he received would be the liquidating value of the assets. If his debts were subtracted from this amount, the difference would represent the liquidating value of his ownership in the business.

On the other hand, if the firm was sold as an operating business to a corporation or another individual, then the purchaser would have paid an amount equal to the going-concern value of the company. If the going-concern value exceeds the liquidating value, then the difference represents the value of the organization as distinct from the assets.

Book Value versus Market Value

Another distinction must be made between *book value,* or the accounting value at which an asset is carried, and its *market value,* the price at which it can be sold. If the asset in question is a firm, then it will actually have two market values—a liquidating value and a going-concern value. Only the higher is generally referred to as *the* market value.

Market Value versus Intrinsic Value

The distinction between *intrinsic values* and *market values* has been stated clearly yet succinctly by Graham, Dodd, and Cottle.

A general definition of intrinsic value would be "that value which is justified by the facts, e.g., assets, earnings, dividends, definite prospects, including the factor of management." The primary objective in using the adjective "intrinsic" is to emphasize the distinction between value and *current market price,* but not to invest this "value" with an aura of permanence. In truth, the computed intrinsic value is likely to change at least from year to year, as the various factors governing that value are modified. But in most cases intrinsic value changes less rapidly and drastically than market price, and the investor usually has an opportunity to profit from any wide discrepancy between the current price and the intrinsic value as determined at the same time.[1]

---

[1] Graham, Dodd, and Cottle, *Security Analysis.* (New York, McGraw-Hill, 1961), p. 28.

Although these authors develop this concept for security (that is, stocks and bonds) valuation, the idea is applicable to all business assets. What it involves, basically, is estimating the future revenues attributable to an asset, determining an appropriate capitalization rate, then finding the present value of the future income. This is, of course, exactly what was done in Chapter 7 when the present values of investment opportunities were found.

Capitalization of Income

This procedure for determining an asset's intrinsic value is known as the *capitalization of income method of valuation*. Example 1 illustrates the technique for a perpetuity.

Example 1. The future earnings from an asset have been estimated at $1,200 per year and are expected to continue indefinitely. The average rate of return on long-term assets of this kind is 6 percent. The value of the asset is therefore obtained by dividing 6 percent into $1,200.

$$\text{value} = \frac{\text{earnings}}{\text{capitalization rate}} = \frac{\$1,200}{0.06} = \$20,000^2$$

Although methods of valuing assets differ widely in details, they depend fundamentally upon the two basic factors set out above: the estimate of future earnings and the selection of an appropriate capitalization rate. The data in example 1, however, do not supply complete

---

2 For those students curious about the justification for this procedure, the following explanation is offered:

1) The value (V) of an asset is equal to the sum of its revenue in each future year (R_t), discounted at an appropriate capitalization rate (r):

$$V = \frac{R_1}{(1+r)^1} + \frac{R_2}{(1+r)^2} + \cdots + \frac{R_N}{(1+r)^N} = \sum_{t=1}^{N} \frac{R_t}{(1+r)^t} \tag{1}$$

2) If R is constant and the earnings are expected to continue forever, that is, $n = $ infinity, equation 1 may be rewritten as:

$$V = R \sum_{t=1}^{\infty} \frac{1}{(1+r)^t} \tag{2}$$

3) The summation component on the right-hand side of equation 2 is the sum of a geometric progression, summed to infinity, and algebra books prove that:

$$\sum_{t=1}^{\infty} \frac{1}{(1+r)^t} = \frac{1}{r} \tag{3}$$

4) Therefore:

$$V = R \cdot \frac{1}{r} = \frac{R}{r} \tag{4}$$

If the revenue stream is not constant, then the simplification procedure cannot be carried out. The problems involved in such cases are discussed in the Appendix to this chapter.

valuation information even for this simple illustration. The 6 percent capitalization rate was stated to be the *average* for assets of this kind. If for some reason this particular asset is thought to be more risky than the average, the earnings figure may be cut down by what is called variously a discount factor, a probability factor, or a margin-of-safety factor. Example 2 assumes a probability factor of 75 percent.

Example 2

a) Probability factor applied to the capitalization rate:

$$\frac{0.06}{0.75} = 0.08 = \text{adjusted capitalization rate}$$

$$\frac{\$1,200}{0.08} = \$15,000 \text{ asset valuation}$$

b) Probability factor applied to earnings:

$0.75 \times \$1,200 = \$900$ adjusted earnings per annum

$$\frac{\$900}{0.06} = \$15,000 \text{ asset valuation}$$

Note that the asset value is $15,000, whether the probability factor is applied to earnings or to the capitalization rate.

The technique can be applied equally well to a business situation:

Example 3. Howard Smith contemplates the purchase of a small metal-working firm. Expected sales of the company are $5 million per year. On the average, firms in this type of business earn about 6.5 percent after taxes on sales. Smith feels that in an area as risky as metalworking, his investment should earn a 25 percent return. What is the greatest amount he should pay for the metal-working firm?

Answer

$$\$5,000,000 \times 0.065 = \$325,000 = \text{indicated earnings}$$

$$\text{capitalization of indicated earnings} = \frac{\$325,000}{0.25} = \$1,300,000$$

Thus, if Smith is to earn a 25 percent return on his investment, he should pay no more than $1.3 million for the company. His first bid for the company would probably be $1 million or less. Smith would then bargain with the seller to reduce his initial asking price, which might be as high as $2 million, to bring the purchase price closer to what Smith can pay if he is to earn a 25 percent return on his investment.

Security Valuation

Securities—stocks and bonds—are simply special kinds of assets, and they are valued by essentially the same techniques.[3] How this works will be illustrated for bonds, preferred stocks, and common stocks.

---

[3] Some would argue that securities, especially common stocks, are valued by an essentially irrational process involving psychological factors, stockbroker recommenda-

Bonds. Compared with common stocks, bond values are easy to determine. So long as the bond is not expected to go into default, the expected returns are simply the annual interest payments plus the principal amount paid when the bond matures. Capitalization rates differ among bonds, depending primarily upon differences in risk of default; and appropriate rates are easily determined. The calculation procedures are illustrated by the following examples.

Example 4. A bond of the Ceramic Company pays perpetual interest of $50 per year. Bonds of equal quality are yielding 4 percent. What is the value of the bond?

$$\text{value} = \frac{\text{interest income}}{\text{capitalization rate}} = \frac{\$50}{0.04} = \$1,250$$

Values for the bond at various interest rates are given below.

Interest Rate	Capital Value[4]
0.02	$2,500.00
0.03	1,666.67
0.04	1,250.00
0.05	1,000.00
0.06	833.33
0.07	714.29

Example 5. Suppose these same bonds are not perpetuities but actually mature in three years. How will this alteration affect their value? The solution requires the long form of the present value equation:[5]

Year	Receipt	4 Percent Discount Factors	Present Value
1	$50	0.962	$ 48.10
2	$50	0.925	46.25
3	$50 + $1,000	0.889	933.45
		bond value	$1,027.80

---

tions, and other factors. Such essentially random phenomena do have a profound influence on short-run price movements; but nevertheless, the authors argue that the long-run value of a stock is determined by investors capitalizing expected future returns. As the more sophisticated institutional investors assume an increasingly important role in the stock market, this is becoming increasingly true.

[4] Bonds are generally traded in $1,000 denominations. (Some are sold in smaller denominations in certain instances, but these are exceptions to the rule.) Prices, however, are quoted in dollars and 32ds of a dollar. For example, United States Treasury bonds which mature in 1990 and carry an interest rate of $3\frac{1}{2}$ percent per year have been quoted at 93.24. This is $93.75 per $100 face value. Buying in $1,000 units means an outlay of $937.50 per unit.

[5] If the bond had a longer maturity, 20 years for example, we would certainly want to calculate its present value by finding the present value of a 20-year annuity and then adding to that the present value of the $1,000 principal amount received at maturity. Special bond tables have been devised to simplify the procedure further.

At the various rates of interest used in the preceding example, this three-year bond would have the following values:

Interest Rate	Capital Value
0.02	$1,086.15
0.03	1,056.45
0.04	1,027.80
0.05	1,000.00
0.06	973.65
0.07	947.20

Note how much less the bond value changes with given changes in interest rates when the term to maturity is only three years. At a going rate of interest equal to 5 percent, both the long- and short-term bonds are valued at $1,000. When rates fall to 2 percent, the long-term bond rises to $2,500, while the short-term security only goes to $1,086. A similar situation occurs when rates rise above 5 percent. *This differential responsiveness to changes in interest rates always holds true—the longer the maturity of a security, the greater its reaction to a given change in capitalization rates.*

Preferred stock. Most preferred stocks entitle their owners to regular, fixed dividend payments similar to bond interest. Although some preferred issues are retired, for the most part they are perpetuities whose values are found in exactly the same manner as was described for bonds in example 4.

Common Stock Valuation

While in theory the same principles apply to the valuation of common stocks as to bonds, preferred stocks, or other assets, two features make their analysis much more difficult. First is the degree of certainty with which receipts can be forecast. For bonds and preferred stocks, this forecast presents very little difficulty, as the interest payments or preferred dividends are known with relative certainty. But in the case of common stocks, the forecasting of future earnings, dividends, and stock prices is exceedingly difficult, to say the least. The second complicating feature is that, unlike interest and preferred dividends, common stock earnings and dividends are generally expected to grow, not remain constant. Hence standard annuity formulas cannot be applied, and more difficult conceptual schemes must be used. The detailed calculations are given in Appendix 12A.

Price-Earnings Ratios and Dividend Yields

Two simple calculations used in the valuation of common stock in relation to market prices are (1) the price-earnings ratio (P/E ratio) and (2) the dividend yield. The *price-earnings ratio,* equal to market price per share divided by earnings per share, represents the amount of money an investor is willing to pay for $1 of current earnings. *Dividend yield* is the percentage of market price that is currently being paid to the share-holders. Example 6 is based on the assumption that the Ceramic Company is paying out in dividends 40 percent of its earnings, or $2.

Example 6

$$\text{Price-earnings ratio} = \frac{\text{price per share}}{\text{earnings per share}} = \frac{\$100}{\$5} = 20 \text{ times earnings}$$

$$\text{Dividend yield} = \frac{\text{dividend per share}}{\text{market price}} = \frac{\$2}{\$100} = 2\%$$

At times it is desirable to calculate the reciprocal of the price-earnings ratio, or the earnings-to-price ratio. For Ceramic Company the ratio is 5 percent. In the past, the current earnings-to-price ratio was frequently used as the capitalization rate in the same sense that capitalization rates were used in bond and preferred stock analysis. *The authors cannot em-phasize too strongly, however, that this is not a proper procedure. The capitalization rate applied to the income from an asset is the rate of return that the investor must receive in order to be induced to invest in the asset. For common stocks, this is most emphatically not the current earnings-to-price ratio.*

Some estimates of common stock capitalization rates are given in Table 12–1, which is based on the figures developed in Appendix 12A. The table is most important, as it forms the basis for measuring the cost of equity when calculating a firm's cost of capital. This calculation is dis-cussed in the following section.

TABLE 12–1

ESTIMATED RATES OF RETURN ON COMMON STOCK

Risk Class of Firm	Stock Market Conditions		
	High	*Normal*	*Low*
Low risk	6½	7	9½
Average risk	7	8	12
High risk	8	12	20

COST OF INDIVIDUAL CAPITAL COMPONENTS

In the preceding section, the nature of the valuation process and the con-cept of expected rates of returns on investments were considered and dis-cussed. (These are also dealt with in Appendix 12A.) Now we turn to the cost of capital, in which extensive use will be made of these valuation concepts. First the costs of different kinds of capital—bonds, preferred stock, and common stock—are examined. Then the various capital components are combined to form a weighted, or over-all, cost of capital.

Debt Capital

If a firm borrows $100,000 for one year at 6 percent interest, its before-tax dollar cost is $6,000 and its before-tax percentage cost is 6 percent. *As a first approximation, the cost of debt is defined as the rate of return that must be earned on debt-financed investments in order to keep unchanged the earnings available to common shareholders.*[6] Hence the cost of debt turns out to be the interest rate on debt, for if the firm borrows and invests the borrowed funds to earn a before-tax return just equal to the interest rate, then the earnings available to common stock remain unchanged.

Example 7. The ABC Company has sales of $1 million, operating costs of $900,000, and no debt, and is taxed at the rate of 50 percent. Its income statement is shown in the Before column below. Now it borrows $100,000 at 6 percent and invests the funds in assets whose use causes sales to rise by $7,000 and operating costs to rise by $1,000 (hence, profits rise by $6,000 before interest). The new situation is shown in the After column.

	Income Statements	
	Before	*After*
Sales	$1,000,000	$1,007,000
Operating costs	900,000	901,000
Earnings before interest and taxes (EBIT)	$ 100,000	$ 106,000
Interest	1,000	7,000
Earnings before taxes (EBT)	$ 99,000	$ 99,000
Taxes	49,500	49,500
Earnings after taxes (EAT)	$ 49,500	$ 49,500

Earnings after taxes are unchanged, as the investment just earned its cost of capital.

Note, first, that the cost of debt is applicable to *new* debt, not to the interest on old, previously outstanding debt. The primary concern with the cost of capital is to use it in a decision-making process—the decision to obtain capital to make new investments; the fact that the firm borrowed at high or low rates in the past is quite irrelevant. The second point to note is that the definition is merely a *first approximation;* it will be modi-

---

[6] Note that this definition is a *first approximation;* it will be modified to take account of the deductibility of interest payments for income tax purposes. Also, note that the cost of debt is considered in isolation. The impact of the debt on the cost of equity, as well as on future increments of debt (in a sense, the true marginal cost of debt), will be treated when the weighted cost of capital is derived.

fied later to take account of the fact that interest payments are deductible for income tax purposes, so the federal government pays a portion of the cost of debt.

Preferred Stock

Preferred stock, described in detail in Chapter 18, is a hybrid between debt and common stock. Like debt, preferred stock carries a fixed commitment on the part of the corporation to make periodic payments, and in liquidation the claims of the preferred stockholders take precedence over those of the common stockholders. Unlike debt, however, a failure to make the preferred dividend payment does not result in bankruptcy. Preferred stock is thus somewhat more risky than common stock to the firm, but it is less risky than bonds. Just the reverse holds for investors. To the investor, preferred is less risky than common, but more risky than debt.

The definition of the cost of preferred stock is similar to that of the cost of debt—it is that rate of return which must be earned on preferred-stock-financed investments in order to keep unchanged the earnings available to common shareholders. This required rate of return turns out to be the preferred dividend (D_p) divided by the net price that the firm could realize from the sale of a new issue of preferred stock (P_n):

$$\text{cost of preferred stock} = \frac{D_p}{P_n}$$

For example, if a firm sells an issue of $100 par value preferred stock with a $6 dividend and nets $95 per share after underwriting commissions, then its cost of preferred stock is 6.3 percent ($6/$95).

Tax Adjustment

As they stand, the definitions of the cost of debt and preferred stock capital are incompatible, because of the differential treatment of interest payments and preferred dividends for tax purposes. Example 8 is an illustration (see next page).

As can be seen from the tabulations, if the funds are invested to yield 6 percent before taxes, earnings available to common stockholders are constant if debt is used, but they fall if the financing is with preferred stock. To maintain the $49,500 net earnings requires that funds generated from the sale of preferred stock be invested to yield 12 percent before taxes or 6 percent after taxes.

Cost of capital calculations may be made either on a before-tax or an after-tax basis. Ultimately, however, business decisions must consider after-tax effects. Therefore, just as was done in Chapter 7 in the discussion of the rates of return on investments, only the cost of capital after taxes

Example 8. The ABC Company learns that it can borrow $100,000 at 6 percent, or it can sell 1,000 shares of $6 preferred stock to net $100 per share. Its before-investment situation is given in the Before column below. At what rate of return must it invest the proceeds from the new financing to keep the earnings available to common shareholders from changing?

| | | | Invest in Assets Yielding: | |
| | | | 6% | 12% |
	Before	*Debt*	*Preferred*	*Preferred*
EBIT	$100,000	$106,000	$106,000	$112,000
I	1,000	7,000	1,000	1,000
EBT	99,000	99,000	105,000	111,000
T (50%)	49,500	49,500	52,500	55,500
Preferred dividends	0	0	6,000	6,000
Available for common dividends	$ 49,500	$ 49,500	$ 46,500	$ 49,500

will be dealt with. The cost of preferred stock is already on an after-tax basis as defined, but a simple adjustment is needed to arrive at the after-tax cost of debt. It is simply recognized that interest payments are tax deductible, meaning in effect that the government pays a share of the interest cost of profitable corporations, and the cost of debt capital is reduced as follows:

$$\text{after-tax cost} = (\text{before-tax cost}) \times (1.0 - \text{tax rate})$$

Example: before-tax cost = 6 percent, tax rate = 48 percent
$$\text{after-tax cost} = (0.06)(1 - 0.48) = (0.06)(0.52) = 3.12 \text{ percent}$$

Had the tax rate been 50 percent, as it is usually assumed for ease of calculations, the after-tax cost of debt would have been one half the interest rate.

Cost of Equity

The cost of equity capital is defined as the minimum rate of return that must be earned on equity-financed investments to keep unchanged the value of the existing common equity. In other words, if 7 percent is a corporation's cost of equity capital, then an equity-financed investment raises the price of the firm's stock if—and only if—the internal rate of return on the investment exceeds 7 percent. In the main body of the chapter, this required rate of return will be assumed for different risk class companies under different stock market conditions, as in Table 12–1. Although this is a gross simplification, it is appropriate for purposes of illustration.

Some of the many complexities involved in deriving accurate estimates of the cost of equity capital are discussed in Appendix 12B. It is useful to state here the main conclusions. First, if stockholders' before-tax required rate of return is equal to k, say 8 percent, then the cost of equity capital from depreciation and retained earnings is less than k. Under certain assumptions the cost of depreciation and retained earnings turns out to be:

$$k_d = k_r = (1 - T)k$$

where k_d = the cost of depreciation-generated funds; k_r = the cost of retention-generated funds; and T = the tax rate paid on capital gains. If a firm's stockholders pay a 30 percent marginal tax rate on normal income and a capital gains tax of one half that rate, and if $k = 8$ percent, then the cost of depreciation and retention-generated funds is:

$$k_d = k_r = (1 - 0.15)8 = (0.85)8 = 6.8 \text{ percent}$$

New outside equity obtained from the sale of stock (k_s) has a higher cost:

$$k_s = \frac{k}{(1 - F)}$$

where F = the percentage cost of floating new stock issues. If $k = 8$ percent and $F = 15$ percent, the cost of new outside equity is:

$$k_s = \frac{8}{(1 - 0.15)} = \frac{8}{(0.85)} = 9.4 \text{ percent.}$$

The costs of internally generated equity and new outside equity are averaged in proportion to their usage, and the resulting weighted average cost of equity is used in the calculation of the over-all average cost of capital. An example of the computation of a weighted average cost of equity is given in Appendix 12B; in the main body of the text it is simply assumed that all equity capital is from internal sources.

WEIGHTED AVERAGE COST OF CAPITAL

The marginal concept is often used erroneously in connection with the cost of capital. Suppose a particular firm's cost of debt is estimated to be 2½ percent (the interest rate on new debt issues is 5 percent), its cost of equity is found to be 8 percent, and the decision has been made to finance next year's projects by selling debt. The argument is frequently advanced that the cost of these projects is 2½ percent, because debt will be used to finance them.

This position contains a basic fallacy. To finance a particular set of projects with debt implies that the firm is also using up some of its potential for obtaining new low-cost debt. As expansion takes place in subsequent years, at some point the firm will find it necessary to use additional equity financing, or else the debt ratio will become too large. On this basis, the authors argue that the firm should be viewed as an on-going concern and that its cost of capital should be calculated as a weighted average of the various types of funds it uses: debt, preferred stock, and equity.

The Calculating Procedure

Before discussing the proper set of weights to employ in computing the weighted average, it is useful to look briefly at the calculating procedure. The method is demonstrated in example 10.

Example 10. The right-hand side of the Simple Company's balance sheet is shown in column 2 of the table below, and the dollars are converted to percentages of the total in column 3. Column 4 gives the after-tax costs of the different types of capital: debt, preferred stock, and equity; column 5 shows the product of column 3 and column 4. Summing column 5 gives the weighted average cost of the firm's capital—0.0605, or 6.05 percent.

SIMPLE COMPANY

(1) Capital Components	(2) Balance Sheet Figures	(3) Percent of Total	(4) Component Cost (after taxes)	(5) Column 3 times Column 4
Debt	$ 30,000,000	30%	2%	0.0060
Preferred stock . .	5,000,000	5	5	0.0025
Net worth	65,000,000	65	8	0.0520
Total	$100,000,000	100%		0.0605 or 6.05%

An alternative method that gives identical results is to multiply the dollar figures in column 2 by the component costs in column 4, sum the three products, and divide the sum by the total amount of capital. The authors prefer the method given in the table, as it proves to be somewhat more convenient in later applications.

The Weighting System

Although both financial theorists and corporate financial managers disagree about particular aspects of debt policy, there is general agreement that firms do have optimum capital structures.[7] "Optimum" is defined as the capital structure that minimizes the average cost of capital;

---

[7] This view was universally held among financial theorists until 1958, when Franco Modigliani and Merton Miller published a famous paper denying the existence of an optimal capital structure. ("The Cost of Capital, Corporation Finance, and the Theory of Investment," *American Economic Review*, June 1958.) Subsequently, these men recognized an error in their original work, and their corrected theory leads to an optimum. ("Corporate Income Taxes and the Cost of Capital: A Correction," *American Economic Review*, June 1963.)

the concept is illustrated by Figure 12–1. To avoid cluttering the graph unnecessarily, it is assumed that firms in these hypothetical industries have no preferred stock.

Shown in the figure is the cost of capital for firms in industry Z, which is moderately risky, and for those in industry A, which is relatively stable. Industry Z consists of diesel locomotive manufacturers and industry A of electric utilities. The highest line on the graph shows the relation-

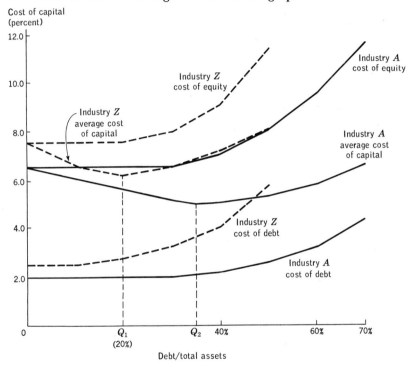

Fig. 12–1. Hypothetical Cost of Capital Schedules
for High-Risk and Low-Risk Industries

ship between the cost of equity and the debt ratio for firms in industry Z. With no debt, their cost of equity is $7\frac{1}{2}$ percent. It remains at this level until the debt ratio reaches 20 percent, at which point it begins to rise at an increasing rate because of the increasing risk attached to the assumption of more and more debt. The second curve from the bottom shows the relationship between the cost of debt capital and the debt ratio for the Z firms. This curve is depicted as starting at $2\frac{1}{2}$ percent after taxes, then rising as a larger and larger percentage of assets is financed with debt. The average cost of capital for firms in this industry starts at $7\frac{1}{2}$ percent, where all financing is with relatively expensive equity capital; falls for a while as more and more low-cost debt is averaged in with equity; then rises after debt has reached 20 percent of total capital. Beyond this point, the fact that both debt and equity are becoming more expensive offsets the fact that debt costs are lower than those on common equity.

While the same principles apply to firms in the less risky industry A, its cost functions are quite different from those of the more risky industry. In the first place, the over-all risk is lower and gives rise to lower debt and equity costs at every debt ratio. Further, its relative stability means that less risk is attached to any given percentage of debt, so its cost of both debt and equity and consequently its average cost of capital turn up further to the right than do those for firms in industry Z. The optimum debt ratio (Q_2) is at 35 percent as against only 20 percent for industry Z firms.

Determining the optimum capital structure of actual firms is partly a matter of analysis and partly a matter of judgment, and it is up to a firm's financial management to decide on the best capital structure for his company. Once this decision has been reached, the weighting system for the average cost of capital calculation is also determined.

Some interesting problems are involved when a firm decides to make a marked departure from its existing capital structure. For example, it may decide to go from a zero debt ratio to one of 30 percent, and it may estimate that several years will be required to reach the new position. During the transition period, when most new financing is by debt, what weighting scheme should be used when computing the cost of capital? It might be argued that the firm should go to the newly defined optimum as soon as the decision to change the capital structure is reached. Conversely, it might be argued that since the firm still has the old structure, the old weights should be used. Neither of these suggestions, however, produces the best results in terms of maximizing stockholders' wealth (the present value of future dividends). This result is accomplished by setting a cost of capital close to the debt cost early in the transition period, then having it rise year by year until it is just equal to the cost of capital computed on the optimal capital structure at the end of the transition period.[8]

Book or Market Weights?

It is clear that *current costs*, not historical costs, should be used for costing the individual capital components when calculating the weighted average cost of capital. If, for example, a firm finds that new debt will cost 5 percent, then the fact that it was able to borrow for 3 percent ten years ago, when most of its long-term debt was taken on, is quite irrele-

---

[8] The reason is that, by setting a low rate, the firm takes on new investments faster and thus gets to the new optimum faster. A rigorous proof requires some complicated mathematical analysis, and the (changing) average cost of capital, year by year during the adjustment period, will itself depend upon a number of factors, most importantly the firm's investment opportunity schedule.

vant. But what about the weights applied to these component costs? Should they be based on capital structure percentages taken at book value or at market value? Suppose the common stock of the Simple Company, which was described in example 10, sells at twice book value, while debt and preferred sell at book value. Then, different percentage capital structures are obtained, and consequently different average cost of capital figures are computed, depending on which weighting scheme is employed. This is illustrated below.

	(1) Capital Dollars	(2) Structure Percent	(3) Component Cost (after tax)	(4) Column 2 times Column 3
Book Value				
Debt	$ 30,000,000	30.0%	2%	0.0060
Preferred . . .	5,000,000	5.0	5	0.0025
Net Worth . . .	65,000,000	65.0	8	0.0520
	$100,000,000	100.0%		0.0605, or 6.05%
Market Value				
Debt	$ 30,000,000	18.2%	2%	0.0036
Preferred . . .	5,000,000	3.0	5	0.0015
Net Worth . . .	130,000,000	78.8	8	0.0630
	$165,000,000	100.0%		0.0681, or 6.81%

The second calculation, which weights the more expensive equity capital more heavily, gives the higher over-all cost of capital.

Note that, except in the unlikely event that book and market values are equal for each of the firm's securities, an expanding firm cannot maintain both sets of capital proportions. If new funds are raised in proportion to the market value percentages, then these proportions will be maintained, but the book value percentages will change.

Which set of weights, and consequently which of the two average cost of capital figures, is correct? Actually, either may be, depending upon whether management defines the optimum capital structure in terms of book or market value. Interviews and case studies suggest that book value is used most frequently.

CALCULATING COST OF CAPITAL FOR CONTINENTAL CAN COMPANY

The procedures discussed above are now applied to an actual company, the Continental Can Company, to illustrate the cost of capital calculation. Continental Can is a large firm, with assets of over $850 million and sales over $1 billion. Sales and earnings are relatively stable, as food and beverage companies make up the bulk of the firm's customers. Dividends have been paid since 1923, even during the depression of the 1930s. Based on an indicated dividend rate of $2 and a current price of $50 per share, the dividend yield is 4 percent. Over the past ten years, dividends have grown at a rate of about 4 percent, and all indications suggest that this same rate of growth will be maintained in the foreseeable future. From this it is assumed that the required rate of return on equity is 8 percent (4 percent plus 4 percent), which is in line with historical returns on low-to-average risk common stocks during "normal" market periods (see Table 12–1). Since internally generated funds provide sufficient equity, only the costs of internal equity, taken to be $0.85 \, k = 7$ percent, need be considered.

The average interest rate on Continental Can's outstanding long-term debt at the end of 1964 was 4.1 percent, but much of this debt was issued in earlier years when interest rates were generally lower than they are now (1966). Current market yields are about 4.7 percent, and approximately this cost will be associated with new debt issues. After a 48 percent income tax, the cost of debt is estimated to be 2.44 percent. The preferred stock is stated to be 3.75 percent preferred, but it was also issued when rates were low. Based on current market yields, the estimated cost of preferred stock is 4.8 percent.

The right-hand side of Continental Can's balance sheet is given in Table 12–2. A considerable portion of the firm's funds are "free" in the

TABLE 12–2

CONTINENTAL CAN COMPANY
RIGHT-HAND SIDE OF BALANCE SHEET
December 31, 1964
(millions of dollars)

			Long-Term Funds Only	
Payables and accruals	$107.1	12.6%		
Current portion of long-term debt	3.7	0.4		
Tax accruals	26.1	3.1		
Total current liabilities	$136.9	16.1%		
Reserve for deferred taxes	50.0	5.9		
Other reserves (primarily pension fund)	11.1	1.3		
Total reserves	61.1	7.2%		
Long-term debt	164.8	19.3	$164.8	25.2%
Preferred stock	11.3	1.3	11.3	1.7
Common equity	478.4	56.1	478.4	73.1
	$852.5	100.0%	$654.5	100.0%

sense that no interest is charged for them—accounts payable, accruals, and reserves are in this class. Some would argue that in the calculation of the over-all cost of capital, this "free" capital, plus short-term debt, should be included. Under certain circumstances this procedure is valid; usually, however, only permanent, long-term capital should be considered. The principal reason for ignoring short-term and "free" capital is a practical one: the cost of capital is used primarily in capital budgeting for long-term assets, which are generally financed with long-term, permanent funds.[9] Of the permanent capital structure, 25.2 percent is debt, 1.7 percent is preferred stock, and 73.1 percent is common equity.

If management believes that some other capital structure is optimal, then other weights would be used, but for purposes of illustration it is assumed that the existing structure is determined to be the optimum. On the basis of these weights and the previously determined costs of debt, equity, and preferred stock, the calculations shown in Table 12–3 indicate

TABLE 12–3

CONTINENTAL CAN COMPANY
CALCULATION OF COST OF CAPITAL

	(1) *Capital* *Proportions*	*(2)* *Component* *Costs*	*(3)* *Column 1* *times* *Column 2*
Debt	25.2%	2.44	0.0061
Preferred stock	1.7	4.80	0.0008
Common stock	73.1	7.00	0.0512
	100.0%		0.0581, or 5.8%

that Continental Can's average cost of capital is 5.8 percent. This after-tax rate of return, perhaps rounded to 6 percent to allow a margin for error, should be used as the discount factor in the capital budgeting process.

SUMMARY

The first part of this chapter, in which the question of valuation is considered, showed that there are a number of different concepts of value: (1) liquidating versus going-concern value, (2) book versus market value, and (3)

---

[9] In theory, it would be better to consider all sources of funds and cost them at their proper costs, zero or otherwise. In practice, it is somewhat tenuous to plan to finance the purchase of an asset out of a reserve for deferred taxes (or other such source) that will materialize only if the firm continues to expand at a sufficiently rapid rate to allow the tax deferment to continue. Given the fact that crude estimates are involved in the entire cost of capital procedure, it simply does not seem worthwhile to carry the calculation to the point of including accruals, deferred items, and short-term debt unless changes in these items can be forecast with some certainty and the items are relatively important.

market versus "intrinsic value." This last concept, the intrinsic value, is fundamentally dependent upon discounted cash flow concepts and procedures, and it involves estimating future cash flows and discounting them back to the present at an appropriate rate of interest. This rate of interest, defined as the "required rate of return," is a function of the investment's risk and the investor's opportunity costs.

As investors generally dislike risk, the required rate of return is higher on more risky securities. Bonds, as a class, are less risky than preferred stocks, and preferred stocks, in turn, are less risky than common stocks. As a result, the required rate of return is lowest for bonds, next for preferred stocks, and highest for common stocks. Within each of these security classes, there are variations among the issuing firms' risks; hence, required rates of return vary among firms.

Note also that risk is of two types: (1) a basic business risk having to do with the nature of the industry and the firm and (2) a financial risk dependent upon the extent to which financial leverage is employed. A firm that manufactures producers' durables—for example, railroad locomotives—is inherently more risky than an electric utility or chain of grocery stores. However, firms can and do alter their basic risks by using more or less financial (and also operating) leverage. As a result, a firm in a relatively stable industry may, because of excessive financial leverage, end up in a more risky position than one in an unstable industry.

The required rates of return, adjusted for selling costs when necessary, on each of its classes of securities constitute the cost of a firm's capital from that type of capital, assuming that the securities are sold in such a manner as to maintain a stable capital structure. (Of course, in practice firms sell debt at one time, equity at another, and oscillate about their target capital structures.) The over-all, or average, cost of capital is found by computing a weighted average of the costs of the separate components of the capital structure with the weights based on the capital structure proportions defined by management as optimal. This average cost of capital is the figure that should be used in capital budgeting: if the firm accepts only those investments yielding returns equal to or greater than its cost of capital, then stockholder wealth will be maximized.

While the procedures outlined in this chapter are widely accepted, this acceptance is by no means universal—there are areas of controversy over which both academicians and businessmen argue. Some of these are taken up in Appendix B to this chapter.

SELECTED REFERENCES

Barges, Alexander, *The Effect of Structure on the Cost of Capital* (Englewood Cliffs, N.J.: Prentice-Hall, Inc., 1963).

Beranek, William, *The Effect of Leverage on the Market Value of Common Stock* (Madison, Wisc.: University of Wisconsin, Bureau of Business Research and Service, 1965).

Boness, A. James, "A Pedagogic Note on the Cost of Capital," *The Journal of Finance,* 19 (March 1964), pp. 99–106.

Bosland, Chelcie C., "The Valuation of Public Utility Enterprises by the Securities and Exchange Commission," *Journal of Finance,* 16 (March 1961), pp. 52–64.

Brewer, D. E., and J. B. Michaelsen, "The Cost of Capital, Corporation Finance, and the Theory of Investment: Comment," *American Economic Review* (June 1965), pp. 516–524.

Duesenberry, James S., *Business Cycles and Economic Growth* (New York: McGraw-Hill, Inc., 1958).

Gordon, Myron, J., *The Investment, Financing and Valuation of the Corporation* (Homewood, Ill.: Richard D. Irwin, Inc., 1962).

———, "Security and Investment: Theory and Evidence," *Journal of Finance,* 19 (December 1964), pp. 607–618.

Herzog, John P., "Investor Experience in Corporate Securities: A New Technique for Measurement," *Journal of Finance,* 19 (March 1964), pp. 46–62.

Kuh, Edwin, *Capital Stock Growth: A Micro-Econometric Approach* (Amsterdam: North-Holland Co., 1963).

Lerner, Eugene M., and Willard T. Carleton, "The Integration of Capital Budgeting and Stock Valuation" *American Economic Review* (September 1964), pp. 683–702.

———, and ———, *A Theory of Financial Analysis* (New York University, Mimeograph, 1965).

Lintner, John, "Dividends, Earnings, Leverage, Stock Prices and the Supply of Capital to Corporations," *The Review of Economics and Statistics,* 44 (August 1962), pp. 243–269.

———, "Optimal Dividends and Corporate Growth under Uncertainty," *Quarterly Journal of Economics,* 78 (February 1964), pp. 49–95.

Malkiel, Burton G., "Equity Yields, Growth, and the Structure of Share Prices," *American Economic Review* (December 1963), pp. 467–494.

Meyer, John R., and Robert R. Glauber, *Investment Decisions, Economic Forecasting and Public Policy* (Boston: Harvard University, 1964).

Modigliani, F., and M. H. Miller, "The Cost of Capital, Corporation Finance, and the Theory of Investment," *American Economic Review,* 48 (June 1958), pp. 261–297. "Reply," *ibid.,* 49 (September 1958), pp. 655–669. "Taxes and the Cost of Capital: A Correction," *ibid.,* 53 (June 1963), pp. 433–443. "Reply," *ibid.,* 55 (June 1965), pp. 524–527.

Ortner, Robert, "The Concept of Yield on Common Stock," *Journal of Finance,* 19 (May 1964), pp. 186–198.

Sharpe, William F., "Capital Asset Prices: A Theory of Market Equilibrium," *Journal of Finance,* 19 (September 1964), pp. 425–442.

Soldofsky, Robert M., and James T. Murphy, *Growth Yields on Common Stock—Theory and Tables* (Iowa City, Iowa: State University of Iowa, 1963).

———, "The Return on Common Stock: Growth Yield or Current Yield" *Quarterly Review of Economics and Business,* 2 (May 1962), pp. 21–30.

Solomon, Ezra (ed.), *The Management of Corporate Capital* (New York: Free Press, 1959).

Weston, J. Fred, "A Test of Cost of Capital Propositions," *Southern Economic Journal,* 30 No. 2 (October 1963), pp. 105–112.

QUESTIONS

12-1 Most inheritance tax laws state that for estate tax purposes property shall be valued on the basis of "fair market value." Describe how an inheritance tax appraiser might use the valuation principles discussed in this chapter to establish the value: (1) of shares of a stock listed on the New York Stock

Exchange and (2) of shares representing 20 percent of a stock that is not publicly traded.

12-2 How does the level of interest rates influence stock and bond prices?

12-3 Suppose that, for each industry, the basic business risks to all firms in the industry are similar.

1. Would you expect all firms in each industry to have about the same cost of capital?
2. How would the industry averages differ?

12-4 Why are internally generated equity funds (depreciation and retained earnings) less expensive than equity raised by the selling of stock?

12-5 Prior to the 1930s the corporate income tax was not very important, as rates were fairly low. Also prior to the 1930s preferred stock was much more important than it has been since that period. Is there a relationship between the rise of corporate income taxes and the decline in importance of preferred stock?

12-6 Describe how each of the following would affect the cost of capital to corporations in general:

1. The federal government solves the problem of business cycles (that is, cyclical stabilty is increased).
2. The Federal Reserve Board takes action to lower interest rates.
3. The cost of floating new stock issues rises.
4. Depreciation charges are liberalized.

12-7 Describe some actions the government might take to stimulate investment by reducing the cost of capital.

PROBLEMS

12-1 (1)   The Bay State Company is earning $4 million a year. It has common stock of $10 par value, with three million shares authorized and one million shares outstanding. What are the company's earnings per share?

(2)   Common stocks of electronic companies such as Bay State are selling on a 5 percent earnings-yield basis. What would be the expected price of Bay State's stock? Why?

(3)   On what price-earnings ratio basis does Bay State common sell?

(4)   If Bay State common sold on an 8 percent earnings-yield basis, what would be its price? What is the price-earnings ratio now?

(5)   Bay State pays a dividend of $2 a year per share. If Bay State sells on a 5 percent earnings yield basis, what is the dividend yield basis on which it sells?

12-2 (1)   The bonds of the Carolina Corporation are perpetuities and bear a 5 percent coupon. Aaa bonds of this type yield 4 percent. What is the price at which Carolina's bonds will sell?

(2)   Interest rate levels rise to the point where such bonds now yield 6.25 percent. What will be the price of the Carolina bonds now?

(3)   Interest rate levels drop to 5 percent. At what price will the Carolina bonds sell?

(4)   How would your answers change if the bonds had a definite maturity date?

12-3 James Smith contemplates purchase of a small electronics firm. Expected sales of the company are $2 million per year. For this line of business, firms earn 5.5 percent on sales after taxes.

Smith feels that his money should earn a 20 percent return on investment in an area as risky as electronics. What is the largest amount he would pay for the electronics firm?

12–4 Because of ill health Robert McKenzie contemplates the sale of his hardware store. He shows the following balance sheet:

Assets		*Liabilities and Net Worth*	
Cash	$ 8,000	Notes payable—bank . . .	$ 3,500
Receivables, net	3,000	Accounts payable	5,000
Inventories	19,000	Accruals	1,500
Fixed property—less			
$10,000 res. for			
deprec.	20,000	Net worth	40,000
	$50,000		$50,000

Annual earnings (after interest and salaries) for the preceding three years have averaged $12,000.

McKenzie has set a price of $60,000, which includes all the assets of the business except cash; the buyer assumes all debts. The assets include the five-year rental option and the goodwill associated with the name of McKenzie Hardware.

The balance sheet is a fair and honest statement based on traditional accounting practices.

1. Is the price of $60,000 a reasonable one?
2. Explain your reasons for the answer to 1.
3. What other factors should be taken into account in arriving at a selling price?

12–5 The Slauson Company is a small machine-tool manufacturer. It has been successful and has grown. Slauson is going to sell an issue of common stock to the public for the first time. It faces the problem of setting an appropriate price on its common stock. The company feels that the proper procedure would be to select firms similar to Slauson with publicly traded common stock and to make relevant comparisons.

The company finds eight machine-tool manufacturers similar to it with respect to (1) product mix, (2) size, (3) asset composition, and (4) debt-equity proportions.

Of these Western and Olympic are most similar.

Relation	*Western*	*Olympic*	*Slauson totals*
Earnings per share, 1966	$ 3.00	$ 5.00	$ 800,000
Average, 1960–1966	2.00	4.00	600,000
Price per share, 1966	24.00	50.00	—
Dividends per share, 1966	1.50	2.50	400,000
Average, 1960–1966	1.20	2.50	300,000
Book value per share	20.00	50.00	6,000,000
Market-book	120%	100%	—

1. How would these relations be used in guiding Slauson in arriving at a market value for its stock?
2. What price would you recommend if Slauson sells 200,000 shares?

12–6 Next year the XYZ Company plans to expand assets (net expansion) by 50 percent. Its capital structure, shown below, is considered to be optimal.

Debt (3% coupon bonds)	$ 35,000,000
Preferred stock (4%)	15,000,000
Net worth	50,000,000
	$100,000,000

New bonds will have a 4 percent coupon rate and will be sold at par. Preferred will have a 5 percent rate and will also be sold at par. Common stock, currently selling at $50 per share, can be sold to net the company $45 per share. Stockholders' required rate of return is estimated to be 8 percent, the average marginal tax rate is 30 percent. It is estimated that internally generated funds will be $20 million, consisting of $15 million of depreciation and $5 million of retained earnings. The marginal corporate tax rate is 50 percent.

1. Assuming all asset expansion to be included in the capital budget, what is the dollar amount of the capital budget?
2. To maintain the present capital structure, how much of the capital budget must be financed by equity?
3. Show the breakdown of the equity funds by source; new outside equity, retained earnings, and depreciation.
4. Calculate the cost of each of the equity components.
5. Compute the weighted average cost of equity.
6. Compute an over-all average cost of capital for XYZ.
7. According to the information given, would the over-all average cost of capital have been higher or lower if the firm's rate of expansion had been lower? Why?

A Discussion of the Theory of Valuing Common Stocks

When the future receipts of an asset are expected to be constant and to continue indefinitely, its value is found as:

$$V = \frac{R}{r} \tag{12A-1}$$

where V = value, R = the constant annual return, and r = the capitalization rate.

Although this is an appropriate procedure for valuing many types of assets, the fact that it assumes constant receipts makes it inappropriate for evaluating most common stocks. Corporate earnings and dividends, on the average, have had a history of growth, with some firms growing more rapidly than others. To allow for such growth, a valuation scheme that considers growth is needed.

DIVIDENDS AND STOCK VALUES

Before the actual valuation techniques are discussed, it is necessary to pause briefly to consider the nature of the revenue stream that is being discounted. It will be shown that dividends, and only dividends, go into the calculation of the intrinsic value of common stocks held as investments.[1] This fact can be demonstrated as follows:

1) Suppose an average investor buys a stock, planning to hold it for one year. What is the value of the stock to him? It is the value of the dividend, discounted back one year, plus the discounted value of the price that he expects to receive on selling the stock. (Taxes are ignored, though it would be simple enough to adjust for them.)

$$P_o = \frac{D_1}{1+k} + \frac{P_1}{1+k} \tag{12A-2}$$

---

[1] If stock is held to enable its owner to control a corporation, then its value is not necessarily dependent upon expected dividends.

where:

P_o = price of the stock today
D_1 = dividend to be received at the end of the first year
P_1 = price of the stock at the end of the first year
k = appropriate capitalization rate

2) Some other "typical" investor will buy the share at the end of the year, paying P_1. If this investor also expects to hold the stock for only one year, he establishes the value as:

$$P_1 = \frac{D_2}{1+k} + \frac{P_2}{1+k} \qquad (12A\text{--}3)$$

3) P_2, the price at the end of the second year, and all future prices are determined in the same manner, so equation (12A–2) may be expressed as:

$$P_o = \frac{D_1}{(1+k)^1} + \frac{D_2}{(1+k)^2} + \frac{D_3}{(1+k)^3} + \ldots \qquad (12A\text{--}4)$$

If the initial stockholder plans to hold the stock for some period longer than a year, say two years, then equation (12A–2) would simply be written as follows:

$$P_o = \frac{D_1}{(1+k)^1} + \frac{D_2}{(1+k)^2} + \frac{P_2}{(1+k)^2} \qquad (12A\text{--}5)$$

and we would continue as before. In similar fashion, any time period may be accommodated. Thus, the present intrinsic value of a share of stock is dependent upon its future dividends.

But is this statement really true? What about a person who buys a stock, such as Litton Industries, that has never paid a cash dividend? Can it be said that dividends determine this stock's value? Again, the answer is yes, it can. Litton pays no dividend today, but, by retaining earnings, it is building up to its earning power base and will, some time in the future, be able to pay quite large dividends. In terms of equation (12A–4), the first few D_t values are zero, but at some point investors expect the firm to begin to pay dividends.

STOCK VALUES WITH ZERO GROWTH

Returning now to the valuation technique, suppose the rate of growth is measured by the rate at which dividends are expected to increase. If future growth is expected to be zero, the value of the stock is simply:

$$\text{price} = \frac{\text{dividends}}{\text{capitalization rate}}$$

$$P = \frac{D}{k} \qquad (12A\text{--}6)$$

"NORMAL" GROWTH

Year after year the earnings and dividends of most companies have been increasing. In general, this growth is expected to continue in the foreseeable future at about the same rate as GNP. On this basis, it is expected that an average, normal company will grow at a rate of from 3 to 5 percent a year. Thus, if such a company's most recent dividend is D_0, its dividend in any future year may be forecast as $D_t = D_0 (1 + g)^t$, where g = the expected rate of growth. For example, if the ABC Company's last dividend was $1 and a 3 percent growth rate is expected, the estimated dividend five years hence will be:

$$D_t = D_0 (1 + r)^t$$
$$= \$1.00 (1.03)^5$$
$$= \$1.00 (1.159)$$
$$= \$1.16$$

Using this method of estimating future dividends, equation (12A–4) may be rewritten as:

$$P_0 = \frac{D_1}{(1 + k)^1} + \frac{D_2}{(1 + k)^2} + \frac{D_3}{(1 + k)^3} + \cdots$$

$$= \frac{D_0(1 + g)^1}{(1 + k)^1} + \frac{D_0(1 + g)^2}{(1 + k)^2} + \frac{D_0(1 + g)^3}{(1 + k)^3} + \cdots$$

$$= \sum_{t=1}^{\infty} \frac{D_0(1 + g)^t}{(1 + k)^t} \qquad (12A\text{-}7)$$

It can be shown, by algebra, that equation (12A–7) may be rewritten as:[2]

$$P_0 = \frac{D_0}{k - g} \qquad (12A\text{-}8)$$

To illustrate, suppose company G is growing at a rate of 3 percent per year; the latest dividend is $1, and the risk on investments of this type calls for an 8 percent capitalization rate. The estimated value of the firm's stock is:

$$P_0 = \frac{\$1.00}{0.08 - 0.03} = \frac{\$1.00}{0.05} = \$20$$

If the stock is bought at this price, it provides a 5 percent initial dividend yield ($1/$20 = 5%), but the dividend rises at the rate of 3 percent per year. And as the dividend rises, the price of the stock rises pro-

---

[2] The proof is omitted here.

portionately, so the investor has a 3 percent capital gain per year. The 3 percent capital gain plus the 5 percent dividend yield totals to the 8 percent required rate of return.[3]

Note that equation (12A–8) is sufficiently general to encompass the no-growth case described above. If growth is zero, this is simply a special case and equation (12A–8) is exactly equal to equation (12A–6).

"SUPERNORMAL" GROWTH

As will be seen in Chapter 31, firms typically go through "life cycles," during part of which their growth is much faster than that of the economy as a whole. Automobile manufacturers in the 1920s and television makers in the 1950s are examples. Figure 12A–1 illustrates such supernormal growth and compares it with normal, zero growth, and declining situations.[4]

The illustrative supernormal growth firm is expected to grow at a 10 percent rate for ten years, then to have its growth rate fall to 3 percent, the norm expected for the economy. The value of a firm with such a growth pattern is determined by the following equation:

$$P_o = \sum_{t=1}^{N} \frac{D_o(1 + g_s)^t}{(1 + k)^t} + \sum_{t=N+1}^{\infty} \frac{D_N(1 + g_n)^t}{(1 + k)^t} \qquad (12A\text{--}9)$$

where g_s = the supernormal growth rate and g_n = the normal growth rate. The first summation is the present value of the dividends received during the early, rapid-growth period, while the second is the present value of the remainder of the expected dividends.

Working through an example will help make this clear. It was seen that the supernormal growth company pays a $1 dividend at present and is expected to grow by 10 percent a year for ten years and thereafter at 3 percent a year indefinitely. If stockholders' required rate of return is 8 percent on an investment with this degree of risk, what is the value of the stock? Based on the calculations in Table 12A–1, the value is found to

---

[3] This can also be seen by solving equation (12A–8) for k:

$$k = \frac{D_o}{P_o} + g$$

In this form, it is easy to see that for normal growth companies—those whose growth is expected to continue indefinitely—the required rate of return is equal to the current dividend yield plus the expected growth rate.

One technical point should at least be mentioned here. The logic underlying the analysis implicitly assumes that investors are indifferent to dividend yield or capital gains. Empirical work has not established if this is true or not.

[4] A declining company is simply one with a negative growth rate.

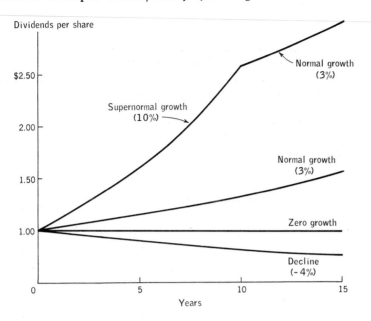

Fig. 12A–1.   Illustrative Dividend Growth Rate

be $35.12, the present value of the dividends during the first ten years plus the present value of the stock at the end of the tenth year.

If desired, equation (12A–9) could be expanded to include as many different growth periods as seem desirable. For example, it might be desired to evaluate a firm expected to grow at 15 percent for the next five years; at 10 percent for the following five years; then at 5 percent indefinitely. To handle this situation additional terms could simply be added to equation (12A–9). Given the roughness of the data on which these assumptions are based, however, there is no particular point in making such refinements for practical purposes.

COMPARING COMPANIES WITH DIFFERENT EXPECTED GROWTH RATES

It is useful to summarize this section of the Appendix by making certain comparisons of the four illustrative firms whose dividend trends are shown in Figure 12A–1. Using the valuation equations developed above, the conditions assumed in the preceding examples, and the additional assumption that each of the firms pays out 75 percent of its reported earnings (therefore earnings per share currently are $1.33 for each company), prices, dividend yields, and price-earnings ratios (hereafter written P/E) are shown in Table 12A–2.

Table 12A–1

METHOD OF CALCULATING THE VALUE OF A STOCK WITH SUPERNORMAL GROWTH

1) *Assumptions*
   a) Stockholder's capitalization rate (k) is 8 percent
   b) Growth rate is 10 percent for ten years, 3 percent thereafter
   c) The initial dividend is $1.

2) *Present value of dividends during rapid growth period*

Year	Dividend $1 (1.10)^t$	Discount Factor $\dfrac{1}{(1.08)^t}$	Present Value
1	1.100	0.926	$ 1.02
2	1.210	0.857	1.04
3	1.331	0.794	1.06
4	1.464	0.735	1.08
5	1.611	0.681	1.10
6	1.772	0.630	1.12
7	1.949	0.583	1.14
8	2.144	0.540	1.16
9	2.358	0.500	1.18
10	2.594	0.463	1.20
			$11.10

3) *Value of stock at end of year 10*

$$P_{10} = \frac{D_{10}}{k - g} = \frac{\$2.594}{0.05} = \$51.88$$

4) *Value today of price in year 10*

$$P_{10}\left(\frac{1}{1 + k}\right)^{10} = \$51.88(0.463) = \$24.02$$

5) *Value of stock today*

$$P_0 = \$11.10 + \$24.02 = \$35.12$$

Investors expect a return of 8 percent on each of the stocks. For the declining firm, this return consists of a relatively high current dividend yield combined with a capital loss amounting to 4 percent per year. For the no-growth firm, there is neither a capital gain nor a capital loss expectation, so the 8 percent return must be obtained entirely from the dividend yield. The normal growth firm provides a relatively low current dividend yield, but a 3 percent per year capital gain expectation. Finally, the supernormal growth firm has the lowest current yield but the highest capital gain expectation.

The relationships among the P/E ratios are also similar to what one

TABLE 12A-2
PRICES, DIVIDEND YIELDS, AND PRICE-EARNINGS RATIOS FOR 8 PERCENT RETURNS UNDER DIFFERENT GROWTH ASSUMPTIONS

		Price	Current Dividend Yield	P/E Ratio
Declining firm	$P_o = \dfrac{D}{k-g} = \dfrac{\$1}{0.08-(-0.04)} = \dfrac{\$1}{0.12}$	$ 8.33	12%	6.3
No-growth firm	$P_o = \dfrac{D}{k} = \dfrac{\$1}{0.08}$	$12.50	8%	9.4
Normal growth firm	$P_o = \dfrac{D}{k-g} = \dfrac{\$1}{0.08-0.03} = \dfrac{\$1}{.05}$	$20.00	5%	15.0
Supernormal growth firm	$P_o =$ (See Table 12A–1)	$35.12	3%	26.4

would intuitively expect—the higher the expected growth, the higher the P/E ratio.[5]

CHANGES IN REQUIRED RATE OF RETURN

Up to this point, 8 percent has been used as k, the rate of return stock-holders require on investments in common stocks as risky as the ones in the examples. If the risk is higher, investors will require a larger return; on less risky securities they will accept a lower expected return. For ex-ample, the 8 percent return considered thus far might be the one ap-plicable to the automobile-parts manufacturing industry, one with about average risk as compared with other industrial sectors. For the electric utility industry, with its more stable sales and more predictable prices, risks are lower, and a 6 percent expected return might be appropriate. Using 6 percent in the valuation formulas and assuming the same earn-ings, dividends, and expected growth rates, the stock prices, dividend yields, and P/E ratios are found as given in Table 12A–3. Here stock prices and P/E ratios are very much higher for the various growth rates than they were at the higher required rate of return, while the dividend yields are considerably lower. This is seen by a comparison of Tables 12A–2 and 12A–3.

TABLE 12A–3

PRICES, DIVIDEND YIELDS, AND PRICE-EARNINGS RATIOS FOR 6 PERCENT RETURNS UNDER DIFFERENT GROWTH ASSUMPTIONS

	Price	Current Dividend Yield	P/E Ratio
Declining firm ($g = -4\%$)	$10.00	10%	7.5
No-growth firm ($g = 0$)	$16.67	6%	12.5
Normal growth firm ($g = 3\%$)	$33.33	3%	25.1
Supernormal growth firm ($g = 10\%, 3\%$)	$67.49	1.5%	50.7

HISTORICAL RATES OF RETURN

Required rates of return differ among firms because of differences in the inherent risks of the firms, but they also differ for all stocks in differ-

---

[5] Although the fact has not been demonstrated, the longer the supernormal growth rate is expected to continue, the higher the current price, the lower the cur-rent dividend yield, and the higher the current P/E ratio.

ent periods. If the demand for funds is particularly heavy and at the same time the supply is restricted, the law of supply and demand requires that the price of funds—the interest rate on debt or the required rate of return on equity—be higher than when supply and demand conditions are reversed. In the late 1940s, for example, many corporations were expanding and seeking funds to finance this expansion, while many investors expected a serious postwar depression and consequently were not interested in purchasing stocks. The result was a very high required rate of return on equity issues and low stock prices and P/E ratios. As it became clear that the economy was booming and was not headed into a depression, investors began putting more money into the equity markets. At the same time, productive capacity began to catch up with demand, so corporate investment and the attendant demand for funds slowed down. The net result was a pronounced decline in required rates of return and a much higher level of stock prices and P/E ratios. On the average, P/E ratios of industrial stocks were about 7.5 in 1949, but by 1958 stocks were selling for 18 to 20 times earnings. At the recent peak, in 1961, the average industrial P/E ratio was just over 24.

A change in average P/E ratios may result from either of two causes —a change in the required rate of return or a change in growth expectations. For example, the 1949–1961 increase in P/E ratios may have been caused by a lowering of the required rate of return or by an increase in the expected rate of growth, or by some of each. In fact, both these factors were probably operating.

Various financial researchers have investigated stockholder returns over long periods and found them to average about 7½ percent. When returns are measured from a point in time when the stock market is low, returns are relatively high. Conversely, when the market is high in the base period, stockholder yields are relatively low. For example, the combined dividend-yield-plus-growth-yield on a group of average-risk common stocks purchased when the market is low, as in 1949, has in the past worked out to about 12 percent; the same group of stocks, bought in a high market, has in the past yielded about 7 percent.

Some rough averages of estimated stock yields on firms subject to different risks and with the purchases made under different market conditions are shown in Table 12A–4. To the extent that (1) the future approximates these estimates of past stock performance and (2) investors base expected future returns on those which have been realized in the past, the figures in the table should give some idea of stockholders' required rates of return under different market and risk conditions.[6]

---

[6] Cf. John P. Herzog, "Investor Experience in Corporate Securities," *Journal of Finance,* XIX (March 1964) pp. 46–62.

TABLE 12A-4

ESTIMATED RATES OF RETURN ON COMMON STOCKS (k values)

	Stock Market Condition		
	High	*Normal*	*Low*
Low risk	6½	7	9½
Average risk	7	8	12
High risk	8	12	20

Some Issues in the Dynamics of Cost of Capital

Even though the treatment of the cost of capital thus far may appear complicated, the material presented in the main body of the chapter and in Appendix A involved some gross simplification, particularly with regard to the cost of equity capital. In this Appendix it will be shown how some of the issues glossed over earlier can affect the cost of capital calculation. The purpose here is as much to raise questions as to answer them, and the material is more theoretical than practical. However, anyone engaged in financial management must understand all the implications underlying the practical, rule-of-thumb procedures that the financial manager will necessarily be forced to follow.

COST OF RETAINED EARNINGS[1]

Whenever a firm retains a portion of its net income rather than pay it out in dividends, there is an "opportunity cost" to the stockholders. If the firm in question has a required rate of return (k) equal to 8 percent, then presumably its shareholders could have invested the retained earnings in other firms of similar risk and received an 8 percent return. This 8 percent is, under certain assumptions, the opportunity cost of retained earnings. The two assumptions are (1) that the stockholder pays no income tax on dividends and (2) that he incurs no brokerage costs when reinvesting dividend receipts. To the extent that these assumptions are not met, the opportunity cost of retained earnings, hence the cost of capital from retained earnings, is lower than the cost of new common stock. Example 1B is an illustration.

Example 1B. The ABC Company has net earnings of $1 million, and all its stockholders are in the 30 percent marginal tax bracket. Management estimates that under present conditions stockholders' required rate of return is 8 percent.

---

[1] There is a question of whether investors prefer to receive their rewards from stock investments in the form of dividends or capital gains. The question is considered in some detail in Chapter 20, but here it is assumed that investors are indifferent as between dividends and capital gains.

If the earnings are paid out as dividends, the recipients will pay income taxes, then reinvest the proceeds in the stock of similar firms and obtain an 8 percent return. The brokerage costs to the stockholders will average 3 percent of the new investments. What rate of return must be earned internally to provide the stockholders with incremental earnings equal to what they would receive externally?

1) After-tax proceeds of dividend payment   = $1,000,000 — taxes
                                          = $1,000,000 — $300,000
                                          = $ 700,000
2) Net investment after brokerage costs   = $700,000 — brokerage
                                          = $700,000 — $21,000
                                          = $679,000
3) Earnings on new investment = ($679,000) (0.08) = $54,320
4) Internal rate of return (k_r) necessary to provide stockholders with incremental income of $54,320:

$$\$54,320 = (\$1,000,000)(k_r)$$
$$(k_r) = 5.432\%$$

5) Therefore, if the firm is able to earn 5.432 percent on retained earnings, the stockholders will be as well off as they would be if all earnings were paid out and then reinvested to yield 8 percent.
6) In general, the internal opportunity cost, or the required rate of return on retention-financed investments, is less than stockholders' required rate of return and may be calculated as follows:

$$k_r = k(1 - T)(1 - B)$$

Where k_r = the required return on retention-financed investments, k = stockholders' required rate of return, T = the stockholders' marginal tax rate, and B = the percentage brokerage cost. In the example being considered,

$$k_r = 0.08(0.7)(0.97) = 0.054, \text{ or } 5.4\%$$

This procedure actually involves an overstatement. The retained earnings will give rise to an increase in the price of the stock, and if the investor sells it he will be subject to a capital gains tax. The capital gains tax rate is lower than the rate applicable to dividends (generally), and, as it is deferred, it has a lower present value.

Two limiting cases can be applied. First, it can be assumed that the stockholder never sells the stock, passing it on to his heirs, who do the same, *ad infinitum*. In this case, the procedures in the example are correct. At the other limit, it can be assumed that the investor holds the stock for the minimum holding period (six months) to receive capital gains tax treatment, then sells the stock and pays a tax at one half his normal tax rate (or 25 percent, if this is lower). In this case, the value of T for the example should be 15 percent, and the resultant cost of retained earnings is computed to be:

$$k_r = 0.08(0.85)(0.97) = 0.066, \text{ or } 6.6\%$$

The correct figure probably lies somewhere between these two extremes, but there is no way of knowing exactly where. For conservatism the higher cost figure will generally be used in the remainder of the illustrations.

The example shows that, in general, the required rate of return on retention-financed investment (k_r) is less than the regular required rate of return (k) by the amount of brokerage costs on reinvested dividends receipts and by stockholders' marginal tax rates. But suppose there are many stockholders, and their marginal tax rates range from zero to 70 percent. Now what should be done? There simply is no one correct answer. One could use one half the average marginal tax rate of individual stockholders in general—it was 46 percent in 1965,[2] the 25 percent maximum capital gains tax, the tax rate of the controlling stockholder, or could try to estimate the average tax rate of all the firm's stockholders and use one half that number.

The authors suggest the latter figure, but admit that it, like the selection of the basic required rate of return, is highly arbitrary. For simplicity, in the examples it is assumed that the product of one half the marginal tax rate and brokerage cost is 15 percent, and the cost of retained earnings is defined as:

$$\text{cost of retained earnings} = .85 \text{ (required rate of return}$$
$$\text{on new common stock)}$$
$$k_r = 0.85k$$

COST OF DEPRECIATION-GENERATED FUNDS

The very first increment of equity funds used to finance any year's capital budget is depreciation-generated funds. In their statements of sources and uses of funds, corporations generally show depreciation charges to be one of the most important sources of funds, if not the most important. For capital budgeting purposes should depreciation be considered "free" capital; should it be ignored completely; or should a charge be assessed against it? The answer is that a charge should indeed be assessed against these funds, and that their cost is approximately equal to the cost of retained earnings (k_r).

The reasoning here parallels that dealing with the cost of retained

---

[2] The 46 percent was found by getting a weighted average of the marginal tax rates paid by individual dividend recipients. Tax rates for 1965 were used and applied to the distribution of dividends among taxpayers in 1962. The weights are based on the dollar amounts of dividends received by stockholders in each tax bracket, and the tax rates are those of married persons filing joint returns.

Since this figure applies to taxpayers only, a firm with many tax-exempt stockholders would probably want to adjust it downward.

earnings. If the firm so desired, it could distribute the depreciation-generated funds to its stockholders, who would then reinvest the proceeds in the stock of similar corporations and receive a return equal to the required rate of return.[3] Thus, if the firm cannot earn a return equal to stockholders' after-tax opportunity costs, the depreciation-generated funds should be paid out in the form of dividends. The authors conclude that, except in those unusual situations where the firm has no earned surplus, the cost of depreciation is equal to the cost of retained earnings.

COST OF NEW OUTSIDE EQUITY CAPITAL

The final source of equity capital is new outside equity raised by floating stock issues.[4] Here, as was discussed in the main body of the chapter, the cost of capital is simply the required rate of return adjusted for flotation costs:

$$k_s = \frac{k}{(1-F)}$$

where k_s = the cost of capital from new stock issues, k = the required rate of return, and F = the percentage cost of floating a new stock issue.

WEIGHTED AVERAGE COST OF EQUITY CAPITAL

Because equity funds are obtained from depreciation, retained earnings, and new flotations, and because these different sources involve different costs, it is necessary to calculate a weighted average cost of equity capital. This particular weighted average is the one that should be used in figuring the firm's over-all weighted average cost of capital. Example 2B illustrates the calculation of the weighted average cost of equity.

Example 2B. The directors of the Simple Company have decided that the firm's optimum capital structure calls for 30 percent debt, 5 percent preferred stock, and 65 percent common equity, all measured at book value. Current plans call for capital expenditures of $15 million. Earnings after preferred dividends and taxes are forecast at $7.5 million, but $4 million of this is committed to dividends on the common stock. Depreciation-generated funds will amount to $5 million. New debt will carry a 4 percent interest cost, hence its cost after a

---

[3] Assuming that the firm has no earned surplus, the dividend would constitute a return of capital. Recipients would not be taxed on the dividend but would simply be required to reduce the cost basis of their stock by the amount of the tax-free dividend. If the firm has earned surplus, then dividend payments made out of depreciation-generated funds are taxable. In this case, it is appropriate to treat the cost of depreciation-generated funds as being equal to that of retained earnings. Since the vast majority of firms do in fact have earned surplus, this latter treatment is generally the correct one.

[4] Or, as shall be seen in Chapter 22, by the conversion of convertible securities.

50 percent tax is 2 percent. Preferred stock has a cost of 5 percent; the required rate of return (k) is estimated to be 8 percent; retained earnings and depreciation are estimated to cost 85 percent of k; and flotation costs on new equity issues are 15 percent. What is the company's over-all cost of capital?

Estimate new funds needed

1. The first estimate of the capital budget is $15 million. (This figure includes an estimate of added working capital.) Since depreciation charges are forecast at $5 million, net investment will be $10 million (assets will increase by $10 million).
2. In order to maintain the capital structure, 65 percent of this $10 million, or $6.5 million, must be in the form of equity. Retained earnings will provide $3.5 million ($7.5 — $4.0); the other $3 million must be obtained from the sale of new equity.

Weighted average cost of equity

1. Thus, the total equity-supplied funds amounts to $11.5 million ($3.5 million retained earnings, $3.0 million new stock, and $5.0 million depreciation), and its average cost is computed as follows:
   (a) *Costs of equity components*

$$\text{new stock:} k_s = \frac{k}{(1-F)} = \frac{0.08}{(0.85)} = 0.094$$

Depreciation and retained earnings: $k_d = k_r = 0.85k = 0.068$

(b) *Weighted average cost of equity*

	Dollars (millions)	Percent $\times$	Component cost $=$	Product
New equity	$3.0	26.1%	0.094	0.025
Retained earnings	3.5	30.4	0.068	0.021
Depreciation	5.0	43.5	0.068	0.030
	$11.5	100.0%		0.076, or 7.6%

Over-all weighted average cost of capital

The optimal capital structure has been specified, and estimates have been obtained of the costs of debt, preferred stock, and equity. This is sufficient information to determine an over-all cost of capital figure.

	Percentage weights $\times$	Component cost $=$	Product
Debt	30%	0.020	0.006
Preferred	5	0.050	0.003
Equity	65	0.076	0.049
	100.0%		0.058, or 5.8%

Several points should be noted. First, it is seen that the cost of equity depends upon the amount of equity raised. Up to the amount of internally generated funds available, its cost is 6.8 percent; beyond that point, the average cost of equity rises as the firm is forced to go to the more expensive outside equity capital market. And, with the rising cost of equity, the over-all cost of capital is also an increasing function of the amount of funds raised.[5]

Figure 12B–1 will perhaps help to make this point clear. Using the values given in Example 2B, the cost of equity capital is constant at 6.8 percent up to $8.5 million, the amount of internally generated funds. Beyond this point, expensive outside equity capital must be averaged in with

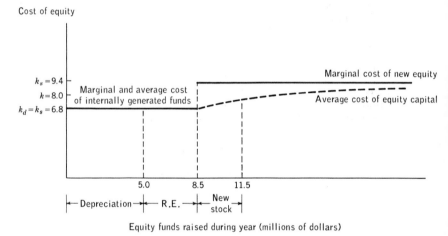

Fig. 12B–1. Hypothetical Relationship between Cost of Equity and Amount of Equity Funds Needed

the internal funds, and this produces a rising average cost of equity capital. The average cost of equity approaches k_s, the cost of outside equity funds, as more and more funds are raised. The main assumptions underlying this construction are (1) that the firm continues to employ the optimum mix of debt and equity capital (otherwise k—hence k_s, k_d, and k_r —will not remain constant), and (2) that k and k_s do not vary with the amount of funds raised. Depending upon how these assumptions are modified, the curves in Figure 12B–1 will themselves be modified. Empirical evidence suggests that k and k_s are probably increasing functions of the amount of new outside equity raised during any given period; hence the

---

[5] The increase in the cost of capital with the amount of funds raised is boosted still more by the fact that flotation costs rise if a *given-sized firm* tries to float more and more securities. For example, it might cost a firm with a net worth of $10 million 10 percent to sell $1 million of stock. But if it tried to sell $5 million of new stock, the underwriting costs might rise to 20 or 25 percent. This increase in cost is caused by the fact that the market must absorb more stock in the second case, and this involves more underwriting risk and more underwriting sales effort.

average cost of new equity probably rises faster than the figure would indicate.

The second point to note is that the cost of capital figure was described as a *first approximation*. The capital budget was estimated at $15 million, and this figure was used as the basis for the cost of capital calculation. If, given the first approximation cost of capital, only $10 million of the proposed investments are found to have positive net present values, then the cost of capital should be recomputed on the basis of this new budget. The process would then be repeated, and this would continue until the capital budget and the cost of capital were found to be consistent. This is simply another way of saying that the capital budget and the cost of capital must be simultaneously determined.

Theories of the Financial Structure

In contrast to the view contained in Chapters 11 and 12, Modigliani and Miller have set forth a different body of theory.[1] They have formulated two main propositions. The first proposition is Durand's NOI approach expressed in different language. Durand compared two theories of the valuation of the earnings of a corporation, describing one as the capitalization of net operating earnings (NOI approach) and the other as capitalization of net income (NI approach).

In the NOI approach the value of a corporation is determined by capitalizing the corporation's net operating income. The value of the company's stocks and bonds must conform to this total. In the NI approach the cost of debt is deducted from net operating income to give net income. The appropriate capitalization rate is applied to net income available to common stock to determine the value of the company's common stock. The market value of the common stock is then added to the market value of the company's bonds to determine the total value of the company.

Durand's net operating income approach and Modigliani and Miller's proposition I are logically equivalent. Both state that the net operating income of a firm, divided by the appropriate capitalization rate, gives the value of the enterprise to which the value of the bonds and stocks of the firm must conform.

The NOI approach can be expressed in the symbols of Modigliani and Miller.

$$V_j = (S_j + D_j) = \overline{X}_j / \rho_k \equiv (\text{NOI})_j / \rho_k \qquad \text{(Proposition I)}$$

Where:

$V_j =$ market value of all the firm's securities or market value of the firm

---

[1] Franco Modigliani and Merton H. Miller, "The Cost of Capital, Corporation Finance, and the "Theory of Investment," *American Economic Review*, June 1958, pp. 261–296. "Reply," September 1959, pp. 655 669. "Taxes and the Cost of Capital: A Correction," *Ibid.* (June 1963), pp. 433–443. "Reply," *Ibid.* (June 1965), pp. 524–527.

$S_j =$ market value of the firm's common shares

$D_j =$ market value of the debts of the firm

$\overline{X_j} =$ expected return on the assets owned by the firm, which equals its net operating income—NOI

$\rho_k =$ capitalization rate appropriate to the risk class of the firm

It appears that Modigliani and Miller also imply that the market value of the firm is equal to its book value. Their proposition II can be derived directly from the accounting identity that assets equal debt plus equity and from the expression for profit available to common stockholders.[2] Profit available to common stock is net operating income less interest paid on debt. This can be expressed in the Modigliani and Miller symbols:

$$\Pi = \rho_k(D_j + S_j) - rD_j$$

Where:

$S_j =$ market value of the firm's common shares

$D_j =$ market value of the firm's debts

$\Pi =$ net income available to common stock

$r =$ expected cost of debt

From the definition of profit available to common stock, the Modigliani and Miller proposition II is readily derived without the long and confusing analogies and economic arguments.

$$\Pi = \rho_k(D_i + S_j) - rD_j \text{ definition of profit}$$

$$\Pi = \rho_k S_j + \rho_k D_j - rD_j \text{ multiply by } \rho_k$$

$$\frac{\Pi}{S_j} = \rho_k + (\rho_k - r)\frac{D_j}{S_j} \text{ divide through by } S_j$$

$$i = \rho_k + (\rho_k - r)\frac{D_j}{S_j} \text{ define } i \text{ as } \frac{\Pi}{S_j} \qquad \text{(Proposition II)}$$

Thus it is clear that the Modigliani and Miller propositions are tautologies. It is not surprising, therefore, that their empirical tests are consistent with the propositions. However, a replication of their tests suggests that their empirical tests were deficient in not taking growth into account.[3] Initially, their tests for the electrical utility industry were replicated exactly. (The procedure followed is described in detail in the reference cited in footnote 3.)

---

2 This is set forth in Eugene M. Lerner and Willard T. Carleton, *A Theory of Financial Analysis* (Mimeograph, 1965), Ch. VI, pp. 2, 3.

3 J. F. Weston, "A Test of Cost of Capital Propositions," *Southern Economic Journal*, 30 (October 1963), pp. 105–112.

The initial results are set forth in Table 12C–1. (The symbols of Modigliani and Miller are generally followed.) The Modigliani-Miller findings for 1947–1948 are compared with those for 1959. The findings for the earnings-price ratio are almost identical in form. The intercept is somewhat lower, and the slope is somewhat smaller, which is consistent with the change in equity markets between the two periods of time. The correlation coefficient is somewhat smaller, but almost of equal significance in view of the fact that the sample size is approximately 30 percent larger than that of Modigliani and Miller.

TABLE 12C–1

COST OF CAPITAL CALCULATIONS, ELECTRIC UTILITIES, 1959

Year	M & M 1947–1948	Weston 1959
(A) Earnings to price ratio	$z = 6.6 + 0.017\,h$ $(\pm\,0.004)$ $r = 0.53$	$z = 4.91 + 0.014\,h$ $(\pm\,0.004)$ $r = 0.43$
(B) Cost of capital (investor viewpoint)	$x = 5.3 + 0.006\,d$ $(\pm\,0.008)$ $r = 0.12$ $n = 43$	$x = 4.27 + 0.027\,d$ $(\pm\,0.007)$ $r = 0.46$ $n = 55$
(C) Cost of capital (financial manager viewpoint)		$x = 5.07 - 0.010\,d$ $(\pm\,0.007)$ $r = -0.193$
(D) Cost of capital (risk measure of leverage)		$x = 5.25 - 0.017\,d*$ $(\pm\,0.008)$ $r = -0.283$

Where: $z =$ yield on common stock

$h =$ market value of senior securities divided by market value of common stocks

$x =$ cost of capital equals total earnings after taxes divided by market value of all securities

$d =$ market value of senior securities divided by market value of all securities

$d* =$ market value of debt divided by market value of all securities

The significant contrast occurs, however, when the cost of capital function is calculated. Three measures of the cost of capital are set forth. Equation B takes the investor viewpoint (as did Modigliani and Miller) in which the cost of debt is taken at its full value into the weighted cost of capital calculations. The second method, under part C of the table, takes the financial manager's viewpoint in which the cost of debt is on an after-tax basis.[4] A third concept of cost of capital takes the financial manager's viewpoint, but removes preferred stock from the numerator of the leverage measure. Only fixed charges on debt carry risks of insolvency. Dividends on preferred stock do not constitute a fixed

---

[4] The rationale for the distinction and the circumstances under which the investor viewpoint versus the financial manager viewpoint would be taken are set forth cogently in John F. Childs, *Long-Term Financing* (Englewood Cliffs, N. J.: Prentice-Hall, 1961), Ch. X, "Profit Goals—Cost of Capital," especially pages 340–344.

charge in this sense. It is logical therefore to measure leverage from the risk standpoint as the ratio of debt to the total market value of the company.[5]

When the investor viewpoint is taken, the cost of capital function has a positive slope. The regression coefficient is significant as well as is the correlation coefficient. This result differs fundamentally from Modigliani and Miller's findings. When the financial manager's viewpoint is taken, the cost of capital function has a negative slope, but is no longer significant. When the risk measure of leverage is used, the negative slope of the cost of capital function becomes significant at the 5 percent level.

INFLUENCE OF GROWTH ON THE COST OF CAPITAL

To this point the analysis . . . follow[s] . . . the original paper of Modigliani and Miller, including their empirical tests. Since the size of firms and the growth rate of their earnings are additional possible influences on the cost of capital, the study was broadened to include these additional variables. The investor viewpoint was used in these studies to permit direct comparison with the Modigliani-Miller data.

Table 12C–2 shows that the growth in earnings per share has a significant influence on the *cost of equity financing*. However, the partial regression coefficient for the influence of leverage on equity yields is no longer significant. The

TABLE 12C–2

MULTIPLE REGRESSION ANALYSIS OF COST OF CAPITAL, ELECTRIC UTILITIES, 1959

(A)	z	$= 6.75$	$-$	$0.0029h*$	$+$	$0.0A$	$-$	$0.1352E$
				(± 0.0059)	$+$	(± 0.0002)		(± 0.0454)
				$\beta = 0.0253$				$\beta = 0.4110$
	R	$= 0.4032$						
(B)	x	$= 5.91$	$-$	$0.0265d*$	$+$	$0.0A$	$-$	$0.822E$
				(± 0.0079)	$+$	(± 0.0001)		(± 0.0024)
				$\beta - 0.4333$				$\beta = 0.4702$
	R	$= 0.5268$						
(C)	d	$= 51.66$	$-$	$1.78E$			$r = -0.58$	
				(± 0.34)				
(D)	$d*$	$= 39.59$	$-$	$1.16E$			$r = -0.48$	
				(± 0.29)				

Where: $z =$ yield on common stock
$x =$ cost of capital equals total earnings after taxes divided by market value of all securities
$d =$ market value of senior securities divided by market value of all securities

[5] Of course, preferred stock (typically nonparticipating) enables a firm to trade on the equity. For an analysis of the effectiveness of trading on the equity, preferred stock would be included in senior obligations. In the present situation where risk aspects of leverage are being investigated, it is more appropriate to exclude preferred stock from senior obligations.

$h^* = d^* =$ market value of debt divided by market value of all securities
$A =$ total assets at book value
$E =$ compound growth rate in earnings per share per annum, 1949–1959
$\beta =$ beta coefficient which normalizes the regression coefficient to measure its relative influence on the dependent variable
$R =$ multiple correlation coefficient

influence of growth on the *total cost of capital* is also highly significant. But the sign of the leverage term is now negative, consistent with the declining segment of the cost of capital function predicted by traditional theory. Thus, when the influences on the cost of capital are partitioned through multiple regression analysis, the results are consistent with traditional theory. In view of the strong influence of growth on the cost of capital function, the relation between the cost of capital and leverage will depend on how growth is correlated with leverage. The regression equations in sections C and D of Table 12C–2 show that leverage is a negative function of growth.

Thus the apparent positive correlation between leverage and equity yields observed by Modigliani and Miller actually represents the negative correlation between current equity yields and growth. The partial regression relationships show that when the influence of growth is removed, leverage is not significantly correlated with current earnings-price ratios for the range of leverage employed.

The partial regression analysis of the weighted cost of capital yields similar results. When the influence of growth is isolated, leverage is found to be negatively correlated with the cost of capital. Traditional theory suggests that firms have an aversion to debt and are likely to be operating in the range of a declining cost of capital.[6] The apparent lack of influence of leverage on the *over-all cost of capital* observed by Modigliani and Miller is due to the negative correlation of leverage with earnings growth. When the net effects are measured, the cost of capital is found to be significantly negatively correlated with both leverage and growth. The reason why Modigliani and Miller found no correlation between the cost of capital and leverage is that leverage is correlated with other influences which change the gross relationship between cost of capital and leverage.[7]

The data showing the influence of growth on equity yields and the cost of capital function help explain the positive slope obtained for the cost of capital function for 1959 in Table 12C–1. The empirical data utilized by Modigliani and Miller were for the late 1940s, when equity prices were depressed and earnings-price ratios were high. Interest yields were low and inflexible, reflecting the support of the Government bond market by the Federal Reserve System. In contrast, this study for the year 1959 was in a period of buoyant equity prices, large premiums for prospective growth, and low current earnings to current price ratios. The current cost of equity money relative to the cost of debt money was low. . . .

The strands may now be brought together. These data show that leverage is negatively correlated with growth. Growth also lowers the (current) cost of

---

[6] N. H. Jacoby and J. F. Weston, "Financial Policies for Regularizing Business Investment," *Regularization of Business Investment* (Princeton, N. J.: Princeton University Press, 1954), pp. 386–387. See also Gordon Donaldson, *Corporate Debt Capacity* (Boston: Harvard University, 1961), passim.

[7] The beta coefficient for earnings growth in the regression for the yield on equity funds is much larger than the beta coefficient for leverage. In the regression for cost of capital, the two beta coefficients are approximately equal.

equity money. Hence both studies found that the cost of equity money is a positive function of leverage. The Modigliani-Miller data indicate a rising cost of equity function and a constant and lower cost of debt function. As leverage is increased, the cost of capital is pushed up by the rising cost of equity function, but is pulled down because the lower cost of debt is weighted more heavily. Modigliani and Miller's data for the late 1940s indicate that the pull of the opposing forces was about balanced so that the cost of capital function appeared not to have a significant slope.

In the data for 1959, the current cost of equity money was relatively low, because current prices reflected the future growth of earnings. Cost of debt was somewhat higher. Hence in equation B of Table 12C–1 where the cost of debt is taken into the measurements at its full level, the cost of capital function would rise with leverage. The rising cost of equity is offset only slightly because the cost of debt is relatively high. When the cost of debt is reduced by one half, the greater weighting of debt cost as leverage increases pulls down the cost of capital, as shown in equation C of Table 12C–1.

MEASUREMENT OF COST OF EQUITY FUNDS WITH GROWTH

In the studies utilized by Modigliani and Miller, the ratio of current earnings to the current market price of common stock is used as a measure of the cost of equity financing. This is invalid. As their own subsequent writing has demonstrated, the cost of equity financing must add to current yields a corrective for a growth factor in order to obtain a relevant measure of the cost of equity financing.[8] For example, in this study the average dividend yield on common stock for the year 1959 was 3.96 percent. The average compound rate of growth in either dividends or earnings per share over the eleven-year period, 1949–1959, was approximately 6 percent. The estimate of the electrical utility industry cost of equity money for 1959 is 9.96 percent, employing the Modigliani and Miller formula.[9] The current earnings-price ratio understates the cost of capital of a company with growing earnings.

These data suggest that the original Modigliani and Miller analysis is at best incomplete and probably invalid. Modigliani and Miller themselves have acknowledged that the original article was in error.[10] In their correction to the original article, Modigliani and Miller recognize the tax advantage of debt. Since they concluded that capital structure did not affect the cost of capital in their original article, the logical implication of the tax advantage of debt would suggest the maximum use of debt in capital structures.

But Modigliani and Miller argue that the reason the implications of their corrected model are not observed is that "other forms of financing, notably retained earnings, may in some circumstances be cheaper still

---

[8] Merton H. Miller and Franco Modigliani, "Dividend Policy, Growth, and the Valuation of Shares," *Journal of Business,* October 1961, pp. 411–32.
[9] *Ibid.,* p. 422.
[10] Franco Modigliani and Merton H. Miller, "Taxes and the Cost of Capital: A Correction," *American Economic Review,* 53 (June 1963), pp. 433–443.

when the tax status of investors under the personal income tax is taken into account."[11] But this statement would still imply that no outside equity financing would be employed. Obviously this is not the case in the real world.

Modigliani and Miller's answer to this confrontation is that lenders impose limits on the leverage ratios that may be employed.[12] This is simply an acknowledgment of the traditional business finance theory. As economists, Modigliani and Miller must recognize that "limitations" imposed by lenders has meaning only in terms of a cost of capital supply function. To recognize that lenders impose limits on debt ratios is to recognize a sharply rising cost of capital function as leverage increases. The authors conclude, therefore, that the cost of capital is affected by financial policy.

NET-MONETARY DEBTOR-CREDITOR THEORY[13]

The net-monetary debtor-creditor theory is in direct contradiction to the Modigliani-Miller propositions in that it asserts that the value of the common stock of a firm will be greatly influenced by its capital structure.

The Alchian-Kessel theory suggests that the relative cost of debt versus equity financing is influenced by expected price level movements. It makes the following assertions:

Net-monetary debtors gain during inflation.
Net-monetary creditors lose during inflation.
Net-monetary debtors lose during deflation.
Net-monetary creditors gain during deflation.

Balance sheet items are classified as monetary assets or liabilities (M), or real assets or liabilities (R), as set forth below.

Classification of Balance Sheet Items

(M)	Cash	(M)	Accounts payable
(M)	Marketable securities	(M)	Notes payable
(M)	Receivables	(M)	Provisions for income tax
		(M)	Accruals
(R)	Inventories	(M)	Bonds and long-term notes
(R)	Investments	(M)	Preferred stock
(R)	Fixed plant		
		(R)	Common stock
		(R)	Surplus

---

11 *Ibid.*, p. 442.
12 *Ibid.*
13 The theory and its empirical tests are set forth in R. A. Kessel, "Inflation-caused Wealth Redistribution: A Test of a Hypothesis," *American Economic Review*, 46 (March 1956), pp. 128–141. Other writings by Kessel and A. A. Alchian suggest use of the expression "the Alchian-Kessel theory."

A net-monetary debtor is one whose monetary liabilities exceed his monetary assets. A net-monetary creditor is one whose monetary assets exceed his monetary liabilities. A firm may have either high leverage or low leverage from a debt standpoint and be either a monetary debtor or a monetary creditor. The following balance sheets show the distinction between monetary-debtor status and the degree of trading on the equity.

1. HIGH-LEVERAGE MONETARY DEBTOR

(M)	Cash and receivables . .	$ 40	(M)	Accounts, notes, and bonds payable	$ 60
(R)	Inventories and fixed assets	60	(R)	Equity accounts	40
		$100			$100

2. LOW-LEVERAGE MONETARY DEBTOR

(M)	Cash and receivables . .	$ 10	(M)	Accounts, notes, and bonds payable	$ 20
(R)	Inventories and fixed assets	90	(R)	Equity accounts	80
		$100			$100

3. HIGH-LEVERAGE MONETARY CREDITOR

(M)	Cash and receivables . .	$ 80	(M)	Accounts, notes, and bonds payable	$ 60
(R)	Inventories and fixed assets	20	(R)	Equity accounts	40
		$100			$100

4. LOW-LEVERAGE MONETARY CREDITOR

(M)	Cash and receivables . .	$ 80	(M)	Accounts, notes, and bonds payable	$ 20
(R)	Inventories and fixed assets	20	(R)	Equity accounts	80
		$100			$100

In the first balance sheet, the firm has a heavy debt-to-equity ratio of 150 percent and is a net-monetary debtor, because monetary assets are 40 and monetary debts are 60. In the third balance sheet, the firm has the same debt-to-equity ratio, but becomes a net-monetary creditor, because the composition of assets shifted as shown. Similarly, in the other two balance sheets, a small amount of trading on the equity is associated with both types of debtor-creditor relations.

The influence of a firm's net-monetary position on equity values is shown by the following illustration. We start with a firm's balance sheet at a price level of 100.

BALANCE SHEET
Price Level, 100

Cash	$20	Accounts payable		$40
Fixed assets	40	Equity		20
Total	$60	Total		$60

The price level and all nonmonetary asset values are now assumed to double. Cash and payables, however, do not change in value, because they are fixed dollar claims. However, fixed assets would double in value. The value of equity is a residual. Since total assets are now 100 (20 cash and 80 fixed assets) and accounts payable are 40, equity must be 60. Equity tripled in value as the price level doubled, because the firm had been a net-monetary debtor of 200 percent, the ratio of monetary debts (accounts payable of 40) to monetary assets (cash of 20).

The Alchian-Kessel studies of the experience of companies during both inflationary and deflationary periods confirm that in fact the common stocks of net-monetary-debtor companies gained during inflation. Furthermore, the relative advantage of net-monetary-debtor companies during inflations was in proportion to the ratio of monetary debts to monetary assets. During deflations, net-monetary creditors gained in proportion to their net-monetary-creditor status.

The theory and empirical findings that support the "debtor-creditor" theory suggest that prospective price level changes may be another important variable influencing choice of financial structure. If financial managers correctly anticipate the direction of changes, and lenders erroneously expect smaller than actual price changes, the choice of an appropriate financial structure will increase the value of a firm's common stock. The cost of capital to the firm will thereby be affected by its net-monetary-debtor or -creditor position.

The crucial assumption of the net-monetary-debtor-creditor theory is that lenders on the average underestimate future price level changes. If lenders on the average overestimated the extent of future price changes, debtors would lose in inflation and creditors would gain. If expectations about future price level changes were correct, prices would reflect these judgments and neither gains nor losses would result from price level changes. Expected price level changes would have been correctly taken into account both by investor-lenders and by firms in their planning.[14]

---

[14] Professor Sorge has described how the net-monetary-debtor position may be used in international business finance as an inflation hedge. He recommends that a firm with monetary claims in the currency of a country with a record of inflation should hedge these claims. Among the methods of hedging he describes is that of incurring monetary obligations in the currency of the same country to offset in a debtor position the firm's position as a creditor in monetary claims of a depreciating currency.

(*Footnote continued on opposite page.*)

The difference in the conclusions of the two theories discussed in this Appendix rests upon different assumptions about the correctness of investor-lender expectations. The Modigliani-Miller propositions assume that their anticipations are correct. The Alchian-Kessel theory assumes that anticipations of lenders underestimate the degree of future price change.

See Barthold W. Sorge, *The Prevention of Financial Losses in Foreign Operations* (Ph.D. Dissertation, Graduate School of Business, University of California at Los Angeles, 1965), Chapter IX.

Part IV

Short-Term and Intermediate-Term Financing

IV

Short-Term and Intermediate-Term Financing

Chapter 13

The Cash Cycle

The preceding sections have laid the foundation for decisions about forms and sources of financing which are discussed in Parts IV and V. Financing choices depend upon many attributes of the firm which have been treated in the previous sections on financial control and planning.

Chapters 11 and 12 set out the factors that determine the broad outlines of the firm's financial structure. The next task is to consider the detailed breakdown of the liability and net worth side of the firm's balance sheet. A large number of different forms of short-term and long-term financing may be available to a firm. In addition, many sources of lending provide different kinds of financing under varying terms and conditions. How to make good decisions in choosing among these many alternatives is the subject matter of the following sections.

MEANING OF WORKING CAPITAL

Working capital may best be defined as current assets minus current liabilities. Gross working capital is total current assets, which are represented mainly by cash and government securities, accounts receivable, and inventories of raw materials, goods in process, and finished goods. Increases in the level of inventories and receivables throughout the production process use up cash. Hence there is a need for financing to carry the firm through its production cycles. This chapter discusses the nature of the cash cycle as an introduction to Chapter 14, "Major Sources of Short-Term Financing," and Chapter 15, "Forms of Secured Short-Term Financing."

The amount by which current assets exceed current liabilities is significant in financial management for two reasons. First, the amount of working capital represents the extent to which current assets are financed from long-term sources. If the current assets of a firm are $100,000 and its current liabilities $40,000, the remaining $60,000 has been financed from other than current sources. Although current assets are turned over within relatively short periods, they always represent some percentage of sales. In this sense, a portion of current assets must be owned by the firm permanently. Consequently, it is appropriate that a portion of current assets be financed from permanent sources.

Second, working capital represents a margin of safety for short-term creditors. Current assets are likely to yield a higher percentage of their book value on liquidation than do fixed assets. Fixed assets are likely to be more specialized in use and suffer larger declines from book values in a forced liquidation. Hence short-term creditors look to the current assets as a source of repayment of their claims. The excess of current assets over the total of short-term claims indicates the amount by which the value of current assets could drop from their book values and still cover the claims of short-term creditors without loss. To short-term creditors the working capital concept is therefore critical.

The growth in a firm's gross working capital (total current assets) may represent a financial problem for a firm. The point to be emphasized is that current assets need to be financed just as do fixed assets. That this is true may be shown by examining the flow of cash in the operations of a business firm.

CASH CYCLE

Effects on Balance Sheet

The budgets discussed in Chapter 9 laid the foundation for the present discussion by showing how financing follows changes in the level of sales. But the relations may be shown more directly by following through the balance sheet consequences of a series of transactions.

1. An initial investment of $50,000 cash is made in a dress-manufacturing business. Plant and equipment is bought with $30,000 of the cash. The resulting financial situation is shown by balance sheet 1.

2. The firm receives an order to manufacture 10,000 cotton dresses. The receipt of an order in itself has no effect on the balance sheet. However, in preparation for the manufacturing activity, the firm buys $20,000 worth of cotton cloth on terms of net 30 days. Without additional investment by the owners, total assets increase by $20,000.

3. Direct labor of $20,000 is applied to the material to be cut to the required pattern. Of the labor costs, $10,000 is paid in cash and $10,000

BALANCE SHEET 1

Assets		Liabilities	
Current Assets			
Cash	$20,000		
Fixed Assets		Capital stock	$50,000
Plant and equipment . .	30,000	Total liabilities and net	
Total assets	$50,000	worth	$50,000

is owed in the form of accrued wages. These transactions and the one above are reflected in balance sheet 2.

BALANCE SHEET 2

Assets		Liabilities	
Current Assets		Accounts payable .	$20,000
Cash	$10,000	Accrued wages pay-	
Inventories: Work-		able	10,000
in-process:			
Materials . .	20,000	Total	$30,000
Labor	20,000		
Total	$50,000	Capital stock	50,000
Fixed Assets			
Plant and equipment . .	30,000	Total liabilities and net	
Total assets	$80,000	worth	$80,000

Total assets have expanded to $80,000. Working capital is still unchanged, but the current ratio has declined to 1.67, and the debt ratio has risen to 37 percent. The financial position of the firm is weakening. If it sought to borrow at this point, it could not use the work in process inventories as collateral, because a lender could find little use for partially manufactured dresses.

4. In order to complete the dresses, additional labor costs of $20,000 are incurred and paid in cash. It is assumed that the firm desires to maintain a minimum cash balance of $5,000. Since the cash balance is $10,000, the firm must borrow $15,000 from its bank to meet the wage bill. The borrowing is reflected in the notes payable account in balance sheet 3. Total assets have risen to $95,000, with a finished goods inventory of $60,000. The current ratio has dropped to 1.4, and the debt ratio has now risen to 48 percent. These ratios represent a further weakening of the firm's financial position.

5. The firm ships the dresses on the basis of the original order, invoicing the purchaser for $100,000 on terms of net 30 days. Accrued wages and accounts payable have to be paid; the firm then has to borrow an additional $30,000 in order to maintain the minimum cash balance of

BALANCE SHEET 3

Assets			Liabilities		
Current Assets			Accounts payable .	$20,000	
Cash	$ 5,000		Notes payable . .	15,000	
Inventory: Fin.			Accrued wages pay-		
goods	60,000		able	10,000	
Total		$65,000	Total		$45,000
Fixed Assets			Capital stock		50,000
Plant and equipment . .	30,000		Total liabilities and net		
Total assets . . .		$95,000	worth		$95,000

$5,000. Note that in balance sheet 4 the borrowing is almost as large as the original capital placed in the enterprise by the owners. Also, finished goods inventory is replaced by receivables with the markup reflected as retained earnings.

Since the receivables are carried at selling price, the current assets in balance sheet 4 increase to $105,000. The current ratio rises to 2.3, and the debt ratio drops to 33 percent. Compared with the conditions reflected in balance sheet 3, most of the financial ratios have improved. However, the absolute amount of debt is large.

Whether the firm's financial position has really improved depends upon the credit worthiness of the purchaser of the dresses. If the purchaser is a good credit risk, the seller may be able to borrow further on the basis of the accounts receivable.

BALANCE SHEET 4

Assets			Liabilities		
Current Assets			Notes payable . .	$45,000	
Cash	$ 5,000		Total current liabilities .		$ 45,000
Accounts receiv-			Capital stock . . .	50,000	
able	100,000		Retained earnings .	40,000	
Total		$105,000	Total net worth . . .		90,000
Fixed Assets					
Plant and equipment . .	30,000		Total liabilities and net		
Total assets		$135,000	worth		$135,000

6. The firm receives payment for the accounts receivable, pays off the bank loan, and is now in the highly liquid position shown by balance sheet 5. If a new order for 10,000 dresses is received it has no effect on the balance sheet, but a cycle similar to the one described above would begin.

The idea of the cash cycle can now be generalized. An order that requires the purchase of raw materials is placed with the firm. The purchase in turn generates accounts payable. As labor is applied, work in

BALANCE SHEET 5

Assets		Liabilities	
Current Assets		Capital	$50,000
Cash	$60,000	Earned surplus	40,000
Fixed Assets			
Plant and equipment . .	30,000	Total liabilities and net	
Total assets	$90,000	worth	$90,000

process inventories build up. To the extent that wages are not fully paid at the time a balance sheet is drawn up, accrued wages will appear on the liability side of the balance sheet. As goods are completed, they move into finished goods inventories. The cash needed to pay for the labor to complete the goods may make it necessary for the firm to borrow.

Finished goods inventories are sold, usually on credit, which gives rise to accounts receivable. As the firm has not received cash, this point in the cycle represents the peak in financing requirements. If the firm did not borrow at the time finished goods inventories were at their maximum, it may do so as inventories are converted into receivables by credit sales. Income taxes, which were not considered in the example, can add to the problem. As accounts receivable become cash, short-term obligations can be paid off.

How Sales Require Financing: An Example

How the process described above results in the need for increased financing as the volume of sales rises can be illustrated by actual data for the Radio Corporation of America during 1949–1964 (Table 13–1). During the first ten years of this period sales rose by $800 million, which represents a 200 percent increase. Current assets increased by 220 percent, net plant and equipment by only 167 percent. The $800 million increase in sales gave rise to the need to finance a $230 million increase in current assets and a $125 million increase in net fixed assets. Thus current assets rose by about 30 percent of the increase in sales, and net fixed assets at somewhat over 15 percent of the increase in sales. Stated differently, for every $10 million increase in sales, RCA had to finance an additional $3 million in current assets and $1.5 million in net fixed assets.

During the decade covered by the RCA data, increased operating assets were financed about two thirds by debt and one third by shareholders' equity. Long-term debt increased by 525 percent; thus working capital increased from $90 million to $305 million.

The data for 1949–1958 may be compared with those for the subsequent six years, thus testing to see if the generalizations made from the early years hold for the latter period. Since a shorter period is involved and since the base amount of the figures is larger, the percentage figures

TABLE 13-1

RADIO CORPORATION OF AMERICA, 1949-1964
(dollars in millions)

	1949	1958	1964	Percentage of Increase 49–58	58–64
Sales	$400	$1,200	$1,800	200	50
Current assets	150	480	800	220	67
Net plant and equipment	75	200	300	167	50
Total	225	680	1,100	202	62
Current liabilities	60	175	310	192	77
Long-term debt	40	250	300	525	20
Shareholders' equity	140	300	525	114	75
Total	$240	$ 725	$1,135	202	57

Source: RCA Annual Report, 1958–1964. Totals do not balance because only the significant items were taken from the report.

are smaller. However, there is strong confirmation of the generalizations made with respect to the decade between 1948 and 1958. During the later period, 1958 through 1964, sales increased by 50 percent and total assets by 62 percent. Note again the close correspondence between the percentage increase in sales and the percentage increase in financing requirements. When sales increased by 50 percent, net plant and equipment also increased by precisely 50 percent. Current assets increased by 67 percent.

An interesting contrast is provided by the methods of financing growth. In the earlier period, current liabilities increased by about the same percentage as sales increased. However, in that earlier period long-term debt increased by over 500 percent, while net worth increased by somewhat over 100 percent. In the years 1958–1964, long-term debt increased by a much smaller percentage than did sales, and net worth increased by a much larger percentage.

These data, drawn from RCA's actual experience, illustrate the close relation between the changes in the level of sales and changes in financing requirements. This close relation obtains not only over long periods but during short-term fluctuations in sales as well.

Financing Patterns

The influence of sales on current asset levels was illustrated above. Over the course of several cycles the fluctuations in sales will be accompanied in most industries by a rising long-term trend. Figure 13–1 shows the consequences of such a pattern.[1] Total permanent assets increase stead-

---

[1] Seasonal influences are omitted for the sake of simplicity.

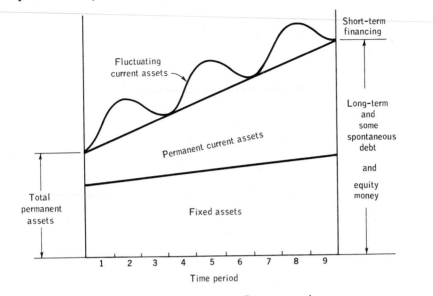

Fig 13–1. Fluctuating versus Permanent Assets

ily in the form of current and fixed assets. Increases of this nature should be financed by long-term debt, equity, and, of course, "spontaneous" increases in liabilities such as accrued taxes and wages, and by accounts receivable, which naturally accompany increasing sales. On the other hand, temporary increases in assets can be covered by short-term liabilities. The distinction between temporary and permanent asset levels may be difficult to make in practice. However, it is neither illusory nor unimportant. Short-term financing to finance long-term needs is dangerous. A profitable firm may become unable to meet its cash obligations if short-term borrowing has become tied up in permanent asset needs.

CASH BUDGET

Short-term (temporary) and long-term (permanent) financing needs can be distinguished by analyzing a cash budget. The nature of the cash budget was indicated in Chapter 9, but its importance demands that a more complete illustration be provided. Table 13–2 is a cash budget for Glendon Plastics Company for the period July 1 through December 31, based on assumed data. The form of the cash budget should be noted carefully. Receipts minus payments equals the cash gain or loss. This figure is added cumulatively to the initial cash. The minimum (or desired) level of cash is deducted from this cumulative figure to arrive at the "cash above minimum needs" or the "financing needs."

In the table, the Glendon Company is shown to have ample money

TABLE 13-2
GLENDON PLASTICS COMPANY
WORK SHEET AND CASH BUDGET

Work Sheet

	May	June	July	Aug.	Sept.	Oct.	Nov.	Dec.	Jan.
Sales	$10,000	$10,000	$20,000	$30,000	$40,000	$20,000	$20,000	$10,000	$10,000
Collections									
First month (20%)	$ 2,000	2,000	4,000	6,000	8,000	4,000	4,000	2,000	2,000
Second month (70%)		7,000	7,000	14,000	21,000	28,000	14,000	14,000	7,000
Third month (10%)			1,000	1,000	2,000	3,000	4,000	2,000	2,000
Total	$ 2,000	$ 9,000	$12,000	$21,000	$31,000	$35,000	$22,000	$18,000	$11,000
Purchases (70% next month's sales)	$ 7,000	$14,000	$21,000	$28,000	$14,000	$14,000	$ 7,000	$ 7,000	
Payments		7,000	14,000	21,000	28,000	14,000	14,000	7,000	7,000

Cash Budget

	May	June	July	Aug.	Sept.	Oct.	Nov.	Dec.	Jan.
Receipts									
Collections			$12,000	$21,000	$31,000	$35,000	$22,000	$18,000	$11,000
Payments									
Purchases			14,000	21,000	28,000	14,000	14,000	7,000	
Wages and salaries			1,500	2,000	2,500	1,500	1,500	1,000	
Rent			500	500	500	500	500	500	
Other expenses			200	300	400	200	200	100	
Total payments			$16,200	$23,800	$31,400	$16,200	$16,200	$ 8,600	
Net cash gain (loss)			(4,200)	(2,800)	(400)	18,800	5,800	9,400	
Initial cash			6,000	1,800	(1,000)	(1,400)	17,400	23,200	
Cumulative cash			1,800	(1,000)	(1,400)	17,400	23,200	32,600	
Desired level of cash			5,000	5,000	5,000	5,000	5,000	5,000	
Cash above minimum needs (or financing needs)			(3,200)	(6,000)	(6,400)	12,400	18,200	27,600	

in cash at the end of the six-month period. However, during the period it faced a cash shortage, which required borrowing. Short-term sources would be appropriate. On the other hand, if the cash budget had been developed for three to five years and if consistent cash deficits had appeared, the need for long-term financing would have been signaled. Cash surpluses, conversely, would raise the question of their efficient utilization by management. Thus the cash budget has been used to distinguish between temporary and permanent financing needs and to facilitate the efficient use of cash.

During a major depression or in a declining industry or firm, the needs for cash may decline. As sales fall, the need for permanent current assets and even fixed assets declines. The firm improves its cash position as inventories are worked off (if sold) and accounts receivable are repaid (if debtors are solvent).

Two additional observations with regard to financing patterns should be mentioned. First, physical volume is not the only influence on asset levels. Price changes cause higher (or lower) balances in accounts receivable and increases (or decreases) in inventories. Second, the existence of time lags is apparent. Asset levels and financing needs rise in anticipation of the actual increase in sales. But a sales decline does not provide an immediate reduction. Assets and financing decline only after the period needed to reduce inventories and accounts receivable.

PRODUCT LIFE CYCLE

An important aspect of cash management is the recognition of cash flows over the life cycle of individual products. A new product or new firm typically experiences an initial period of cash flow deficits which must be financed from external sources. A typical product life cycle cash flow is shown in Figure 13–2 and Table 13–3, and is described below.

Net cash flows are small and negative while the firm completes the necessary preliminary organization activities leading to engineering outlays and preparations for manufacturing activities. When manufacturing begins, inventories of raw materials, work in process, and finished goods are generated before sales are made. Sales result in receivables, so some additional time may elapse before a positive cash flow begins.

An illustrative pattern is indicated in Table 13–3. After two years, when the preliminary studies have been completed, $15,000 has been spent. Engineering and manufacturing activities begin in 1968, and actual production and sales are started in 1969. Net cash flows are still negative at the end of 1970, at which time negative cash flows of $305,000 have been accumulated. This represents a total amount that the organizers of the firm, or product managers responsible for new product activities, must recognize as a total investment outlay.

By 1971 positive cash flows begin. At first they are relatively small; then, with product acceptance, they become large. By 1973 positive cash inflows are substantial and cumulative cash flows on a nondiscounted basis become zero.

TABLE 13–3

GOODMAN MANUFACTURING CORPORATION
PRODUCT LIFE CYCLE CASH FLOW AND
RATE OF RETURN ANALYSIS

Year	Net Cash Flows	Cumulative Cash Flows	Present Value Factor at 20%	Present value of inflows or (outflows)	Present Value Factor at 32%	Present Value
			Present Values at 20%		*Present Values at 32%*	
1966	($5,000)	($5,000)	0.833	(4,165)	0.758	(3,790)
1967	(10,000)	(15,000)	0.694	(6,940)	0.574	(5,740)
Completion of preliminary studies						
1968	(50,000)	(65,000)	0.579	(28,950)	0.435	(21,750)
1969	(200,000)	(265,000)	0.482	(96,400)	0.329	(65,800)
1970	(40,000)	(305,000)	0.402	(16,080)	0.250	(10,000)
Positive cash flows begin						
1971	30,000	(275,000)	0.335	10,050	0.189	5,670
1972	50,000	(225,000)	0.279	13,950	0.143	7,150
1973	225,000	—	0.233	52,425	0.108	24,300
1974	250,000	250,000	0.194	48,500	0.082	20,500
1975	300,000	550,000	0.162	48,600	0.062	18,600
1976	350,000	900,000	0.135	47,250	0.047	16,450
1977	200,000	1,100,000	0.112	22,400	0.036	7,200
1978	200,000	1,300,000	0.083	16,600	0.027	5,400
1979	100,000	1,400,000	0.078	7,800	0.021	2,100
1980	50,000	1,450,000	0.065	3,250	0.016	800
Net present value				$118,290		$1,090

The remainder of Table 13–3 illustrates how the material of Chapters 7, 11, and 12 can be integrated with cash flow analysis. Present value factors are applied to the cash outflows, cash inflows, and cumulative present values of cash flows. A discount factor of 20 percent is applied, because any new product activity involves considerable estimating risks. It will be noted in the table that positive cash flows are not generated until some eight years after preliminary analysis of the product potential has begun. It is not implied that it always takes 8–10 years to begin to achieve positive cash flows. However, for the successful launching of many

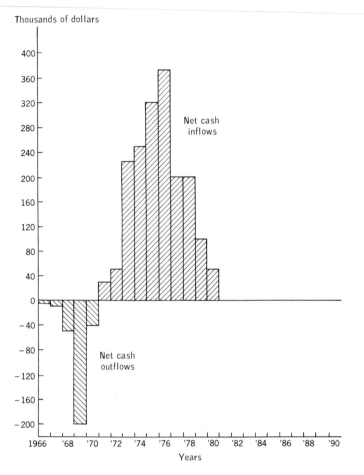

Fig. 13–2.   Cash Flows over the Product Life Cycle

new products, such a development period is not unusual. In an industry of fast-moving technology or in relatively simple industries such as wholesale or retail trade, the duration of the life cycle may be substantially compressed.

On the basis of the discounted cash flows, a "break-even" is not achieved until the tenth year (see Figure 13–3). From that point on, positive net cash flows from the project are achieved. The success of this product invites competition, so in the year of maximum profits, 1976, it begins to attract additional capacity into the industry. As a consequence, profit margins and total profits begin to decline. By the end of 1980, profits have declined to the point where serious consideration should be given to abandoning business activity in this particular product line.

It will be noted that over the 15-year product life cycle analyzed, in

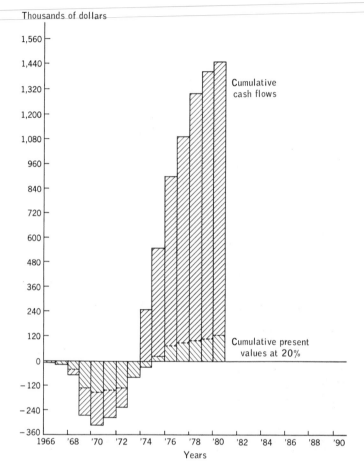

Fig. 13–3.   Cumulative Cash Flows over the Product Life Cycle.

which a 20 percent discount factor was applied, the cumulative net present value of the project is $118,290. Analysis indicates that this project would provide a substantial cumulative positive present value of returns. The internal rate of return of this product life-cycle is 32 percent.

The main thrust of this exposition, however, has been to illustrate the cash requirements of new project activities. The necessity for taking into consideration the heavy cash outlays required before beginning engineering and manufacturing activities is frequently overlooked. Also, there is often inadequate understanding of the cash requirements for financing raw material purchases and labor payrolls used to build up the initial work in process and finished goods inventories. In addition, an investment in receivables is required. The total amount of cash outflows in the period over which negative cash flows are incurred is frequently larger than a careful analysis would indicate. For new product activity, therefore, the typical short-term monthly cash budget analysis should certainly be augmented by a product life-cycle cash flow analysis.

CASH MANAGEMENT

Seasonality, Cycles, and Growth

Fluctuating seasonal sales confront producers and sellers of such products as beer, sporting goods, toys, farm machinery, fertilizers, autos, and wearing apparel. Also, some producers, such as canners and ore producers, are faced with seasonal buying periods for their raw materials. Superimposed on seasonal influences are changes in the cyclical level of business activity and secular influences which reflect long-run growth trends in the economy.

Since seasonal, cyclical, and secular factors are operating simultaneously, financial managements sometimes make serious mistakes in planning their financing needs. In some instances seasonal working-capital needs are not clearly recognized, and management has erred by having to sell profitable investments to meet temporary working-capital needs. The firm could have financed these temporary needs from short-term bank loans at moderate interest rates.

On the other hand, it is equally erroneous to assume that all fluctuating working-capital needs are seasonal, and not to recognize cyclical and secular influences. For example, a firm will approach a banker for a short-term loan when it really needs a long-term loan. The firm has a good sales outlook and adequate financial ratios. Yet the bank refuses to make the loan on the grounds that the financing needs of the firm are permanent. Since the bank's liabilities are primarily short term, it cannot make permanent commitments.

Advantages of Adequate Cash

The cash budget and balance sheet examples presented above assumed a minimum level of cash. It is a management decision problem to determine this desired minimum. Sound working-capital management requires maintenance of an ample amount of cash for several reasons. First, it is essential for the firm to have sufficient cash to take trade discounts. A firm that buys on terms 2 percent 10 days, net 30, can reduce costs by taking the discounts. Failure to take the discount means paying 2 percent of the amount of purchases for using the money an additional 20 days. This sum represents an annual interest rate of 36 percent (2 percent times 360 divided by 20). Most firms are able to borrow at a rate substantially lower than 36 percent per year.

Second, since the working-capital ratio is a key item in credit analysis, it is essential that the firm, in order to maintain its credit standing, meet the standards of the line of business in which it is engaged. A strong credit standing enables the firm to purchase goods from trade suppliers on favorable terms and to maintain its line of credit with banks and other sources of credit.

Third, ample cash is useful for taking advantage of favorable business opportunities that may come along from time to time. Finally, the firm should have sufficient liquidity to meet emergencies, such as strikes, fires, or marketing campaigns of competitors.

Disadvantages of Excessive Cash[2]

There are, of course, disadvantages in holding excessive cash. The firm ties up funds unnecessarily and bears an additional cost, which reduces the return on its total assets. Moreover, if the firm finances its temporary needs from permanent sources, it may have idle cash for long periods. Even if the firm utilizes excess funds by investing them in marketable securities, it is not likely to earn as high a rate of return from temporary investments as it pays for its permanent funds. The financial manager must also keep in mind that he will lose credit contacts if he acquires permanent funds and leaves the short-term market for an extended period. Borrowing potential is lost if abused or not used. The firm may be unable to develop new lines of credit as promptly as required when the need arises.

The crux of effective cash management, in brief, is in synchronizing the rate of inflow of cash receipts with the rate of outflow of cash disbursements. As pointed out previously, the cash budget is the planning or forecasting instrument with which to analyze this problem. The management of cash in a rational manner does not conflict with the goal of having the optimum amount of accounts receivable and inventories necessary to conduct the business effectively and efficiently.

SUMMARY

The financial manager is interested in the influence of the cash cycle and price level changes on financing requirements. He should be aware that financing needs follow sales with a lag as sales both rise and decline.

The cash budget is the basic tool in cash cycle analysis. It aids the financial manager in distinguishing between temporary and permanent financing requirements, as well as in determining their magnitude. Another influence on financing requirements is the minimum cash balance that the firm maintains. Cash should be adequate (1) to take trade discounts, (2) to maintain a good credit rating, (3) to take advantage of opportunities, and (4) to meet emergencies. Excessive cash, however, is costly and causes the loss of credit contacts. One of the tasks of the financial manager is to determine the optimum cash level.

---

2 See also previous discussion in Chapter 6.

SELECTED REFERENCES

Corcoran, Wayne A., "A Simplified Worksheet for the Funds and Cash-Flow Statements," *N.A.A. Bulletin* 46, Section 1 (September 1964), pp. 35–44.

Donohue, William A., and Erwin Kaufman, "Leveling Cash Flow Through a Mechanized Receivable System," *N.A.A. Bulletin* (September 1963), pp. 51–56.

Federal Reserve Bank of Philadelphia, *Business Review* (August, 1962).

Griswold, J. A., *Cash Flow Through a Business* (Hanover, N.H.: Amos Tuck School of Business Administration, Dartmouth College, 1955).

Mason, Perry, *Cash Flow Analysis and the Funds Statement* (New York: American Institute of Certified Public Accountants, 1961).

Toan, Arthur B., Jr., "The Impact of Corporate Policy on Cash Flow," *Financial Executive*, 31 (November 1963), pp. 13–15, 19.

Weston, J. Fred (ed.), *Readings in Finance From Fortune* (New York: Holt, Rinehart and Winston, Inc., 1958), selections 10 and 11.

QUESTIONS

13–1 Do you suppose the management of working capital would occupy more of the financial manager's time in a retailing concern or in an electric utility company? Why?

13–2 "The longer the cash cycle, the better off a firm; consequently, one of the financial manager's goals should be to lengthen the cycle as much as possible." Discuss the statement.

13–3 Explain how a downturn in the business cycle could either cause a cash shortage for a firm or have the opposite effect and generate excess cash.

13–4 Why do many "young" firms have difficulties obtaining working-capital loans from commercial banks? Do you suppose that a given young firm would have an easier time getting a working-capital loan than a loan to finance fixed assets?

13–5 What alternatives are available to a company when it finds it has excessive working capital in the form of cash?

13–6 Explain this statement: "Current assets to a considerable extent represent permanent assets."

13–7 If the United States lacked a highly developed banking system, making it difficult if not impossible for business to borrow to meet seasonal needs, what would be the effects on the cash balances maintained by business firms? What would be the effect on the general level of business and economic activity?

PROBLEMS

13–1 You are called upon to prepare a cash budget for Crystal Stores for the period July 1 through December 31. You are provided with the following data:

1) All sales are for credit. Payment for 10 percent of the sales is received during the month in which the sales are made, 60 percent in the month following, and 30 percent in the second month following.

2) Purchases during each month equal the requirements for the following month's sales. Payment for purchases is made in the month following the purchase.

3) Inventory equals $8,000 plus purchases for the following month.

4) The firm's minimum level of cash is $5,000. Initial cash is $6,000.
5) The firm buys no additional fixed assets during the period.
6) Accrued wages and salaries remain unchanged at the end of the period.
7) Borrowings are in the form of notes payable.
8) Other current liabilities remain unchanged at the end of the period.
9) The firm is a corporation that pays no dividends.
10) The gross profit margin on sales averages 25 percent.
11) Sales data and wages and salaries data are:

	Actual	
	Sales	*Wages and Salaries*
May	$20,000	$2,000
June	20,000	2,000

	Forecast	
	Sales	*Wages and Salaries*
July	30,000	2,500
Aug.	50,000	3,000
Sept.	50,000	3,000
Oct.	60,000	3,500
Nov.	30,000	3,000
Dec.	20,000	2,000
Jan.	20,000	2,000
Feb.	20,000	2,000

12) Rent is $500 per month, depreciation is $400 per month, and other cash expenses are 2 percent of sales.

Prepare a cash budget for the six-month period.

13-2 The following is the current balance sheet of the Merton Corporation.

MERTON CORPORATION
BALANCE SHEET
December 31, 1966

Assets		*Liabilities and Net Worth*	
Cash	$ 50,000	Accounts payable	$ 45,000
Accounts receivable . . .	240,000	Accruals	35,000
Inventories	180,000	Federal taxes payable . . .	40,000
Total current	$470,000	Total current	$120,000
Fixed assets, net	120,000	Net worth	470,000
Total assets	$590,000	Total claims on	
		assets	$590,000

The level of business activity is expected to rise 20 percent by the end of the six-month period January through June 1967. An expansion program requiring an additional investment of $60,000 in fixed assets is planned for this period. Assume that receivables, inventories, payables, and accruals increase by 20 percent. The estimated income statement for the six-month period is as follows:

MERTON CORPORATION
INCOME STATEMENT
For Six Months Ended June 30, 1967

Net sales		$900,000
Cost of goods sold	$620,000	
Other operating expenses	210,000	
Depreciation expense	30,000	
Total cost of sales		860,000
Net income before federal income taxes		$ 40,000
Federal income taxes		19,200
Net income after federal income taxes		$ 20,800

1. Prepare a cash budget covering the six-month period as one unit of time.
2. Construct an estimated balance sheet for the end of the six-month period.
3. Calculate the current ratio and total debt-to-net-worth ratio of the firm on June 30, 1967.
4. Assume that Merton raises $100,000 cash by selling long-term debt. What will be the effect on the two ratios obtained in 3?
5. What is the financial significance of the problem of rapidly expanding sales?

13–3 Indicate the effects of the transactions listed below on each of the following: (1) total current assets, (2) working capital, (3) current ratio, and (4) net profit. Use + to indicate an increase, − to indicate a decrease, and 0 to indicate no effect. State necessary assumptions and assume an initial current ratio of more than 1 to 1.

Transaction	Total Current Assets	Working Capital	Current Ratio	Effect on Net Profit
1. Cash is acquired through issuance of additional common stock.	_____	_____	_____	_____
2. Merchandise is sold for cash.	_____	_____	_____	_____
3. Federal income tax due for the previous year is paid.	_____	_____	_____	_____
4. A fixed asset is sold for less than book value.	_____	_____	_____	_____
5. A fixed asset is sold for more than book value.	_____	_____	_____	_____
6. Merchandise is sold on account.	_____	_____	_____	_____
7. Payment is made to trade creditors for previous purchases.	_____	_____	_____	_____
8. A cash dividend is declared and paid.	_____	_____	_____	_____

Transaction	Total Current Assets	Working Capital	Current Ratio	Effect on Net Profit
9. Cash is obtained through bank loans.	_____	_____	_____	_____
10. Notes receivable are discounted (interest bearing).	_____	_____	_____	_____
11. Previously issued stock rights are exercised by company stockholders.	_____	_____	_____	_____
12. A profitable firm increases its fixed asset depreciation allowance account.	_____	_____	_____	_____
13. Marketable securities are sold below cost.	_____	_____	_____	_____
14. Uncollectible accounts are written off against the allowance account.	_____	_____	_____	_____
15. Advances are made to employees.	_____	_____	_____	_____
16. Current operating expenses are paid.	_____	_____	_____	_____
17. Promissory notes are issued to trade creditors for prior purchases.	_____	_____	_____	_____
18. Ten-year notes are issued to fund accounts payable.	_____	_____	_____	_____
19. A wholly depreciated asset is retired.	_____	_____	_____	_____
20. A cash sinking fund for the retirement of bonds is created: a reserve for bond sinking fund is also created.	_____	_____	_____	_____
21. Bonds are retired by the use of the cash sinking fund.	_____	_____	_____	_____
22. Accounts receivable are collected.	_____	_____	_____	_____
23. A stock dividend is declared and paid.	_____	_____	_____	_____
24. Equipment is purchased with short-term notes.	_____	_____	_____	_____

Transaction	Total Current Assets	Working Capital	Current Ratio	Effect on Net Profit
25. The allowance for doubtful accounts is increased.	_____	_____	_____	_____
26. Merchandise is purchased on credit.	_____	_____	_____	_____
27. Controlling interest in another firm is acquired by the issuance of additional common stock.	_____	_____	_____	_____
28. Earnings are added to the reserve for bond sinking fund.	_____	_____	_____	_____
29. A subsidiary paid the firm a cash dividend from current earnings.	_____	_____	_____	_____
30. The estimated taxes payable has been increased.	_____	_____	_____	_____

Chapter 14

Major Sources of Short-Term Financing

Thus far the nature of the cash cycle and leading methods for projecting cash needs have been described. The three major sources of funds with short maturities are discussed in this chapter. Ranked in descending order by volume of credit supplied to business, the main sources of short-term financing are (1) trade credit between firms, (2) loans from commercial banks, and (3) commercial paper. To a lesser degree these institutions also supply funds for longer terms, but their primary importance in short-term financing justifies treatment at this point.

TRADE CREDIT

Trade credit is interfirm debt, which usually is recorded as accounts receivable by the seller and as accounts payable by the buyer. The receivables of nonfinancial corporations increased from $66 billion in 1953 to $160 billion by the end of 1963, or by 142 percent during the decade. Of the increase in the receivables of nonfinancial corporations, about 20 percent represents extensions to consumers. The other 80 percent is primarily to business firms.[1] Accounts payable, the largest single category of short-term credit, represents about 40 percent of total current liabilities of nonfinancial corporations. As smaller firms frequently have difficulty obtain-

---

[1] *Economic Report of the President,* 1965 (Washington, D.C., U.S. Government Printing Office, 1965), pp. 270–271.

ing financing from other sources, they rely relatively heavily on trade credit.

Trade credit is a "spontaneous" source of financing in that it arises from ordinary business transactions. For example, suppose a firm makes average purchases of $2,000 per day on terms net 30. On the average it will owe thirty times $2,000, or $60,000. If its sales, and consequently its purchases, double, then accounts payable will also double. The firm will have spontaneously generated an additional $60,000 of financing. Similarly, if the terms of credit are extended to 40 days, the firm will owe $80,000.[2] It is clear that the length of credit terms largely determines the extent to which trade credit may be used as a source of financing.[3]

Credit Terms

Any transaction agreement must include a statement of the date when the buyer is obligated to make payment. The terms of sale, or credit terms, formulate the payment obligation of the buyer. The four main factors that influence the length of credit terms are outlined below.

1. *Economic nature of product.* Commodities with high sales turnover are sold on relatively short credit terms. Groceries have a high turnover, but perishability also plays a role. The credit extended for fresh fruits and vegetables might run from five to ten days, whereas the credit extended on canned fruits and vegetables would more likely be 15 to 30 days. Terms for items that have a slow retail turnover, such as jewelry, may run six months or longer.

2. *Seller circumstances.* Financially weak sellers must require cash or exceptionally short credit terms. For example, farmers sell livestock to meat-packing companies on a cash basis. In some industries, variations in credit terms can be used as a sales promotion device. Although the use of credit as a selling device endangers sound credit management, the practice occurs. This is especially true when the seller's industry has excess capacity. Also, a large seller could use his position to impose relatively short credit terms. However, the reverse appears more often in practice; that is, financially strong sellers are suppliers of funds to smaller firms.

3. *Buyer circumstances.* In general, financially sound retailers who sell on credit may, in turn, receive slightly longer terms. Some classes of retailers regarded as selling in particularly risky areas (such as clothing) receive extended credit terms, but they are offered large discounts to encourage early payment.

4. *Cash discounts.* A cash discount is a reduction in price based on

---

[2] It will be noted that these relations also provide a basis for financial forecasting.
[3] Small, growing firms may be slow in paying their accounts. Arrears of one month in paying its bills would add to the financing from trade credit.

payment within a specified period. It was mentioned previously that cash discounts often exceed the rate of interest at which the buyer can borrow. If he borrows and takes the cash discount, the period during which accounts payable remain on the books is reduced. The effective length of credit is influenced by the size of discounts offered. Cash discount is to be distinguished from trade discount, which is a deduction from list price to all customers of a certain class—such as distributor versus wholesaler versus retailer.

Illustrative credit terms. Credit terms typically express the amount of the cash discount and the date of its expiration, as well as the final due date. Probably the most frequently encountered terms are 2/10, net 30. In other words, if payment is made within ten days of the invoice date, a 2 percent cash discount is allowed. If the cash discount is not taken, payment is due 30 days after the date of invoice. The cost of not taking cash discounts can be substantial. To illustrate:

Credit Terms	*Cost of Credit If Cash Discount Not Taken*[4]
1/10, n/20	36.36%
1/10, n/30	18.18%
2/10, n/20	73.47%
2/10, n/30	36.72%

Credit terms are expressed in different forms, depending upon the circumstances of the purchase. These circumstances fall into three groups.

1. *Individual order terms.* When terms 2/10, n/30 are quoted, the point of reference is the date of the invoice. When the purchaser is located at a distance from the seller, the credit terms may be expressed as 2/10, n/30 AOG (arrival of goods) or ROG (receipt of goods). If the purchaser does not avail himself of the cash discount, the full price is due 30 days after the arrival of the goods.

2. *Lumped-order terms and billing.* When purchases are repeated a number of times during a month, they are all lumped and billed at one time during the month. Credit terms for all sales are deemed to begin on a certain date. The following expressions are used to describe lumped-order credit terms:

EOM (end of month). The cash discount or credit period begins at the end of the month.

---

[4] The following equation may be used for calculating the cost of not taking discounts:

$$\text{cost} = \frac{\text{discount percent}}{(100 - \text{discount percent})} \times \frac{360}{(\text{final due date} - \text{discount period})}$$

To illustrate, we compute the cost of not taking a discount when the terms are 2/10, net 30.

$$\text{Cost} = \frac{2}{98} \times \frac{360}{20} = 0.0204 \times 18 = 36.72\%$$

10th prox. (proximo, or the next). The cash discount period ends on the tenth day of the following month; the full amount is due on the 30th.

MOM (middle of month). The cash discount or credit period dates from the 15th or the first. MOM arrangements cut the credit period to one half that available under EOM terms.

The first two expressions are equivalent. For example, if a hardware retailer bought a number of items during September on terms of 2/10 EOM, n/30 or 2/10 prox., n/30, a 2 percent cash discount would be allowed if payment were made by October 10. Full payment would be due by October 30.

Lumped-order terms enable a financial manager to lengthen the terms of credit. Purchases made early in September would not be billed on EOM or proximo terms until after September 30, and full payment would not be due until the end of October. The financial manager can thereby obtain almost 60 days of credit under what appears to be 30-day terms. The amounts of financing involved may be substantial. Suppose a firm's purchases are $10,000 per day. Doubling the average payment period from 30 to 60 days will double the average accounts payable. The need to obtain $300,000 from other sources is avoided.

Lumped-order billing presents an even further opportunity for lengthening the terms of credit. If billing were at the end of the month, the buyer would postpone placing orders until after the first of the month so that he would not have to make payment by the tenth or the 30th. Thus, to continue the above example, August 25 may be considered the end of August to encourage orders near the end of the month. Purchases on August 26 would not be billed until early October and would not be due on a net basis until October 31. Thus terms of ostensibly 30 days may be stretched to as much as 65 days.

3. *Dating.* In the apparel field and other lines of business with a strong seasonal or style factor, the practice of extra dating or season dating is followed. Assume that extra dating terms of 7/10–60 are used in the sale of lace and silk goods. The date from which the ten-day discount period is calculated on a purchase of goods on April 1 would be May 31. If payment were made by June 10, the cash discount is taken. If the cash discount is passed, final payment is due on July 30.

Season dating may be obtained by a buyer of summer sports shirts. He places his order in October for delivery in January under terms of 2/10–60, May 1 dating. The buyer has until May 10 for discount payment, or July 1 for net payment.

Season or extra dating is advantageous to both buyer and seller. The buyer is certain of delivery, and if he sells some of the goods during preseason sales, he has the use of extra funds. The seller benefits by reducing the risks of style or price changes. If the seller is the manufacturer, the early orders and deliveries encouraged by season dating may enable him to spread his production and shipping more evenly.

Only a few combinations of credit terms have been described. The variety of possibilities challenges the ingenuity and the resourcefulness of the financial manager in employing trade credit to provide the maximum amount of low-cost financing.

Employment of Trade Credit

Trade credit has double-edged significance for the firm. It is a source of credit for financing purchases and a use of funds by which a firm finances credit sales to customers. For example, if a firm sells on the average $3,000 of goods per day with an average collection period of 40 days, it will have accounts receivable at any balance sheet date of approximately $120,000.

If the firm buys $2,000 worth of materials per day and the balance is outstanding for 20 days, accounts payable will average $40,000. The firm is extending net credit of $80,000, the difference between accounts receivable and accounts payable.

It is important, therefore, that the firm make the maximum use of trade credit as a source of funds, but at the same time minimize the extent to which its own funds are tied up in accounts receivable.

Advantages of Trade Credit as Source of Financing

Trade credit, a customary part of doing business in most lines of activity, is convenient and informal. A firm that does not qualify for credit from a financial institution may receive trade credit because previous experience has familiarized the seller with the credit-worthiness of his customer. As the seller knows the merchandizing practices of the line of business, he is usually in a good position to judge the capacity of his customer and the risk of selling on credit to him. The amount of trade credit fluctuates with the buyers' purchases subject to any credit limits that may be operative.

Whether trade credit costs more or less than other forms of financing is a moot question. Sometimes trade credit can be surprisingly expensive to the buyer. The user often does not have other alternative forms of financing available, and the costs to the buyer may be commensurate with the risks to the seller. But in some instances trade credit is used simply because the user may not realize how expensive it is. In such circumstances careful financial analysis may lead to the substitution of alternative forms of financing for trade credit. At the other extreme, trade credit may represent a virtual subsidy or sales promotion device offered by the seller.[5]

---

[5] For numerous examples, see Robert P. Hungate, "Inter-business Financing" (Unpublished Ph.D. dissertation, University of California, Los Angeles, January 1961).

SHORT-TERM FINANCING BY COMMERCIAL BANKS

Commercial-bank lending is second in importance to trade credit as a source of short-term financing. Commercial-bank loans appear in the balance sheets of borrowers as notes payable. Also, the notes payable account sometimes contains notes due sources other than banks. In spite of the large total amount of bank credit outstanding, it should be observed that a substantial number of firms do not have a notes payable account on their balance sheets, indicating that no bank debt is owing.

Commercial banks occupy a pivotal position in the short-term and intermediate-term money markets. The influence of commercial banks is greater than appears from the dollar amounts they lend, because the banks provide marginal funds. As a firm's financing needs grow, the banks are called upon to provide the additional funds. On the other hand, when the rate of business activity levels off or declines, bank loans also decline.

Characteristics of Loans from Commercial Banks

The main characteristics of commercial-bank lending patterns are briefly described.

Forms of loans. A single loan obtained from a bank by a business firm is not different in principle from a loan obtained by an individual. In fact, it is often difficult to distinguish between a bank loan to a small business and a personal loan. A single loan is obtained by signing a conventional promissory note. Repayment is made in a lump sum at maturity (when the note is due) or in installments throughout the life of the loan.

A *line of credit* is a formal or an informal understanding between the bank and the borrower concerning the maximum loan balance the bank will allow the borrower. For example, a bank-loan officer may indicate to a financial manager that the bank regards his firm as "good" for up to $80,000 for the forthcoming year. Subsequently, the manager signs a promissory note for $15,000 for 90 days. The amount is credited to the firm's checking account at the bank. At maturity, the checking account will be charged for the amount of the loan. Interest may be deducted in advance or paid at the maturity of the loan. Before repayment of the $15,000, the firm may borrow additional amounts up to $65,000.

A more formal procedure may be followed if the firm is quite large. To illustrate, Chrysler Corporation arranged a line of credit for over $100 million with a group of banks. The banks were formally committed to lend Chrysler the funds if they were needed. Chrysler, in turn, paid a commitment fee of approximately ¼ percent on the unused balance of the commitment.

Size of loans. Banks make loans of all sizes. The bulk of loans from commercial banks by dollar amount is obtained by firms with total assets of $5 million and more. But, by number of loans, firms with total assets of $50,000 and less obtain about 40 percent of bank loans.[6]

Maturity. Commercial banks concentrate on the short-term lending market. Short-term loans make up 66 percent of bank loans by dollar amount, whereas term loans (loans with maturities longer than one year) make up only 34 percent.

Security. If a potential borrower is a questionable credit risk or if his financing needs exceed the amount which the loan officer of the bank considers to be prudent on an unsecured basis, some form of security is required. More than one half the dollar value of bank loans is secured. The forms of security are described in Chapter 15. In terms of the number of bank loans two thirds are secured or endorsed.

Minimum balance. Banks typically require that a regular borrower maintain a minimum checking account balance of 15 to 20 percent of either the line of credit or the actual amount outstanding. These balances, which are commonly called *compensating balances,* are a method of rationing funds to borrowers and raising the effective interest rate. They represent an indirect method of raising interest rates whose consequences are not fully understood by borrowers who are unfamiliar with financial matters.[7]

Repayment of bank loans. Because the bulk of bank deposits is subject to withdrawal on demand, commercial banks seek to prevent firms from using bank credit for permanent financing. A bank may therefore require its borrowers to "clean up" their bank loans at least one month each year. If a firm is unable to become free of bank debt for at least part of each year, it is using bank financing for permanent needs and should develop additional sources of long-term or permanent financing.

In summary, the typical bank loan is generally small in amount, secured, and short term, involves a compensating balance, and should be fully extinguished within a year. These characteristics limit the degree to which loans from commercial banks can meet the financing needs of firms. Such loans from banks are most appropriate for meeting the seasonal and fluctuation financing needs of business. Or they may be used as a temporary financing source while more permanent sources and forms of financing are being developed. An attempt to use loans from commercial banks for permanent financing may cause problems for both the borrowers and the banks.

---

[6] From surveys reported in "Member Bank Lending to Small Business, 1955–57," *Financing Small Business,* Report by the Federal Reserve System, April 11, 1958 Washington, D.C.: U.S. Government Printing Office, 1958), p. 375.

[7] Note, however, that if the compensating balance is set as a minimum monthly average, and the firm would maintain this average anyway, the compensating balance requirement does not entail higher rates.

Cost of commercial-bank loans. Loans from commercial banks average about 4 to 6 percent at simple interest. However, the effective rate paid will depend upon the characteristics of the firm. If the firm can qualify as a "prime risk" because of its size and financial strength, the rate of interest will be one half to three quarters of 1 percent above the rediscount rate charged by federal reserve banks to commercial banks. On the other hand, a small firm with less than average financial ratios may be required to provide collateral security and to pay an effective rate of interest of 10 percent or more.

Determination of the effective or true rate of interest on a loan depends upon the stated rate of interest and the method of charging interest by the lender. If the interest is paid at the maturity of the loan, the stated rate of interest is the effective rate of interest. If the bank deducts the interest in advance (discounts the loan), the effective rate of interest is increased. On a $10,000-loan for one year at 5 percent, the discount is $500 and the borrower obtains the use of only $9,500. The effective rate of interest is

$$\frac{\$500}{\$9,500} = 5.3 \text{ percent}$$

If the loan is repaid in 12 monthly installments, the effective rate of interest is even higher. In this event the borrower pays $500 for the use of about one half the amount he receives. The amount received is $10,000 or $9,500, depending upon the methods of charging interest. If interest is paid at maturity, the effective rate would be approximately

$$\frac{\$500}{\$5,000} = 10 \text{ percent}$$

Under the discounting method, the effective cost of the installment loan would be approximately

$$\frac{\$500}{\$4,750} = 10.53 \text{ percent}$$

In order to compare the costs of financing from alternative sources and under different methods of charging interest, the effective rate of interest must be calculated.

Choice of Bank or Banks

Banks have close relations with their borrowers. Since there is considerable personal contact over the years, the business problems of the borrower are frequently discussed; thus the bank often provides informal management counseling services. A potential borrower seeking bank relations should recognize the important differences among banks as potential sources of funds. These differences can be summarized into the following five points.

1. Banks have different basic policies toward risk. Some banks are inclined to follow relatively conservative lending practices. Other banks are engaged in what are properly termed creative banking practices. The policies partly reflect the personalities of officers of the bank, and partly the characteristics of the bank's deposit liabilities. Thus a bank with fluctuating deposit liabilities in a static community will tend to be a conservative lender. A bank whose deposits are growing with little interruption may follow "liberal" credit policies. A bank with broad diversification over geographical regions or among industries served can obtain the benefit of combining and averaging risks. Thus, marginal credit risks that might be unacceptable to a small bank or a specialized unit bank can be pooled by a branch banking system to reduce the over-all risks of a group of marginal accounts.

2. Some bank-loan officers are active in providing counsel and in stimulating development loans with firms in their early and formative years. Certain banks have distinct departments to make loans to firms expected to become growth firms. The personnel of these departments provide considerable counseling to customers.

3. Banks differ in the extent to which they will support the activities of the borrower in bad times. This characteristic is referred to as the degree of loyalty of the banks. Some banks may put considerable pressure on a business to liquidate its loans when the firm's outlook becomes clouded, whereas others will stand by the firm and work diligently to help it attain a more favorable condition.

4. The fourth characteristic by which banks differ is the degree of deposit stability. Instability arises not only from fluctuations in the level of deposits but also from the composition of deposits. Deposits can take the form of demand deposits (checking accounts) or time deposits (savings accounts, certificates of deposit, Christmas clubs, etc.). Total deposits tend to be more stable when time deposits are substantial. Differences in deposit stability go a long way toward explaining differences in the extent to which the banks are willing or able to help the borrower work himself out of difficulties or even crises.

5. Banks differ greatly in the degree of loan specialization. Larger banks have separate departments specializing in different kinds of loans, such as real estate, installment loans, commercial loans, among others. Within these broad categories there may be specialization by line of business, such as steel, machinery, textiles. The strengths of smaller banks are likely to reflect the nature of the business and economic environment in which the banks operate. They tend to become specialists in specific lines,

such as oil, construction, and agriculture, to name a few. The borrower can obtain more creative cooperation and more active support if he goes to the bank that has the greatest experience and familiarity in his loan area. The financial manager should therefore choose his bank with care. A bank that is excellent for one kind of business or need may be unsatisfactory for another firm.

6. Size of bank may be an important characteristic. Since the maximum loan a bank can make to any one customer is generally limited to 10 percent of capital accounts (capital stock plus surplus accounts), it will generally not be appropriate for large firms to develop borrowing relationships with small banks.

7. With the heightened competition between commercial banks and other financial institutions, the aggressiveness of banks has increased. Modern commercial banks now offer a wide range of financial and business services. Most large banks have business development departments which provide counseling to firms and serve as an intermediary on a wide variety of business requirements of a firm.

COMMERCIAL PAPER

Nature

Commercial paper consists of promissory notes of large firms that are sold primarily to other business firms, insurance companies, investment and pension funds, and small banks.[8] Approximately two thirds of the volume of commercial paper is placed directly by the issuer (usually a large finance company) with the investors.[9] Though the amounts of commercial paper outstanding are less than 5 percent of commercial-bank loans outstanding, this form of financing is important to particular lines of business. About one third of the volume of commercial paper is sold through commercial-paper dealers, who function primarily as note brokers.

Maturity and Cost

Maturities of commercial paper vary from two to six months, with an average of about five months. The rates on prime commercial paper vary, but are generally about ½ percent below the prime business loans.

Use

The use of the open market for commercial paper is restricted to a comparatively small number of concerns that are exceptionally good

---

[8] Small banks purchase large quantities of commercial paper, because the size of the notes does not tax their lending limitations and the paper provides a temporary outlet for funds at relatively attractive interest rates. Large banks find it advantageous to deal directly with the borrower and prefer to lend in larger units.
[9] Five large finance companies account for three fourths of the total paper outstanding.

credit risks. Dealers prefer to handle the paper of concerns with a net worth of $500,000 or more, and rarely that of concerns with a net worth of less than $250,000. Dealers shun as unprofitable companies which borrow less than $200,000 a year, because handling of their notes usually involves a disproportionately high expense.

Appraisal of Use

A number of advantages are claimed for the commercial-paper market. (1) It effects the broadest and most advantageous distribution of paper. (2) It provides more funds at lower rates than do other methods. (3) The borrower avoids the inconvenience and expense of financing arrangements with a number of institutions each of which requires a compensating balance. (4) Publicity and prestige accrue to the borrower as his product and his paper become more widely known. (5) Finally, the commercial-paper dealer frequently offers valuable advice to his clients.

There are several disadvantages in the use of commercial paper. For one, the commercial-paper house is usually bombarded with requests for information from prospective lenders. Furthermore, the open-market debtor who is in temporary financial difficulty receives little consideration, because commercial-paper dealings are impersonal.

From the standpoint of the banks, commercial paper is advantageous. It offers the bank the opportunity to carry a portfolio that is diversified both by industries and by geographical sections. In practice, however, diversification is tempered by the tendency of banks to favor the paper of well-known industries in their own vicinities. A second advantage is provided by the liquidity of commercial paper. Since it is almost always paid promptly at maturity without requests for extension or renewal, commercial paper constitutes an excellent secondary reserve. Finally, from the standpoint of the banks, the net yield of open-market paper compares favorably with the return banks can obtain from most alternative investments.

With regard to the nation's economy, the commercial-paper system makes possible fuller and more effective utilization of the country's productive capacities by redistributing funds and equalizing regional credit conditions. Thus, from the standpoint of the financial manager of business firms in regions that would otherwise face capital shortages, the commercial-paper systems improve the opportunities of obtaining financing under less onerous conditions.

SUMMARY

The most important source of short-term financing is trade credit. It is a natural source of financing, which arises out of the ordinary business transactions of the firm. A firm may obtain trade credit when it might not qualify for financing from a financial institution. Trade credit is expensive to the buyer if he loses cash discounts. Sometimes a seller uses trade credit as a virtual subsidy or sales promotion device.

Commercial banks are specialists in meeting the fluctuating short-term financing needs of business firms. Bank financing takes the form of relatively small, short-term, unsecured loans. Interest cost is related to the risk quality of the borrower and whether or not security is required for the loan. The borrower should choose a bank with experience and policies related to the needs of the borrower.

Commercial paper is an American institution involving wide distribution of promissory notes of large firms with exceptionally high credit ratings. It is a valuable impersonal source of funds at costs below the prime rate on bank loans.

SELECTED REFERENCES

Agemian, Charles A., "Maintaining an Effective Bank Relationship," *Financial Executive* (January 1964), pp. 24–28.

The Bank-Corporate Relationship, American Management Association, Management Bulletin 61, 1965.

"Business Credit Demands—Problems of Interpretation," *Monthly Review* (July–August 1962), Federal Reserve Bank of Kansas City.

Cagel, C. H., "Credit Lines and Minimum Balance Requirements," Federal Reserve Bulletin, 42 (June 1956), pp. 573–579.

Financing Small Business (Washington, D.C.: Federal Reserve System, 1958).

Lent, G. E., *The Changing Structure of Commercial Banking*, Tuck Bulletin 24 (Hanover, N.H.: Dartmouth College, 1960).

"Member Banks Lending to Small Business, 1955–57," *Federal Reserve Bulletin*, 44 (April 1958), pp. 393–411.

"Prime Commercial Paper," *Monthly Review* (July 1964), Federal Reserve Bank of Richmond.

"Rebound in Use of Bankers' Acceptances," Federal Reserve Bank of Cleveland, *Monthly Business Review* (January 1961), pp. 5–10.

Selden, Richard T., *Trends and Cycles in the Commercial Paper Market* (New York: National Bureau of Economic Research, 1963).

Stewart, William C., "How Business Picks Banks," *Burroughs Clearing House*, 44 (January 1960), pp. 33–35, 80.

Williams, Emory, "A Corporate Treasurer Views Bank Relationships," *Burroughs Clearing House*, 48 (February 1964), pp. 33–110.

QUESTIONS

14–1 It is inevitable that firms will obtain a certain amount of their financing in the form of trade credit simply because, to some extent, trade credit is a free source of funds. What are some other factors that lead firms to use trade credit?

14–2 "Commercial-paper interest rates are always lower than bank loan rates to a given borrower. Nevertheless, many firms perfectly capable of selling commercial paper employ higher-cost bank credit." Discuss the statement, indicating (a) why commercial paper rates are lower than bank rates and (b) why firms might use bank credit in spite of its higher cost.

14–3 "Trade credit has an explicit interest rate cost if discounts are available but not taken. There are also some intangible costs associated with the failure to take discounts." Discuss.

14–4 What are some of the reasons that lead firms to offer high cash discounts?

14–5 A large manufacturing firm had been selling its products on a 3/10, n/30 basis and changed its credit terms to 1/20, n/90. What changes might be anticipated on the balance sheets of the manufacturer and its customers?

14–6 The availability of bank credit is more important to small firms than to large ones. Why is this so?

14–7 What factors should a firm consider in selecting its primary bank? Would it be feasible for a firm to have a primary deposit bank (the bank where most of its funds are deposited) and a different primary loan bank (the bank where it does most of its borrowing)?

PROBLEMS

14–1 What is the equivalent annual interest rate that would be lost if a firm failed to take the cash discount under the following terms?

1) 1/15, n/30	4) 2/10, n/40
2) 2/10, n/60	5) 1/10, n/40
3) 3/10, n/60	

14–2 If a firm buys merchandise on June 26, what would be the last day for taking the cash discount, and when would the full payment be due, under each of the following terms?

1) 2/10, n/30, E.O.M. invoicing with June 25 regarded as end of current month
2) 1/10, n/60, December 1 dating
3) 2/10, n/60, A.O.G. on July 1

14–3 Given below is the balance sheet of the Commercial Credit Corporation as of December 31, 1964 (figures are altered slightly to facilitate computations).

COMMERCIAL CREDIT CORPORATION
BALANCE SHEET
December 31, 1964
(in millions of dollars)

Cash	$ 60	Bank loans	$ 220
Net receivables	2,280	Commercial paper	775
Marketable securities	120	Others	335
Repossessions	3	Total due within a year	$1,330
Total current assets	$2,463	Long-term debt	940
Other assets	137	Total shareholders' equity	330
Total assets	$2,600	Total claims	$2,600

1. Calculate:
   a) Commercial paper as a percent of short-term financing
   b) Commercial paper as a percent of total-debt financing
   c) Commercial paper as a percentage of all financing
2. Why do finance companies such as Commercial Credit use commercial paper to such a great extent?
3. Why do they use both bank loans and commercial paper?

14–4 The Morgan Corporation has a total asset turnover into sales of 1.5 times. Its sales have been growing at a 3 percent rate per year, yielding a 2 percent return after taxes on total assets.

Although its terms of purchase are 30 days, its accounts payable represent 60 days' purchases. Roger Morgan, the president of the company, is seeking to increase the company's bank borrowings in order to become current in meeting trade obligations.

MORGAN CORPORATION
BALANCE SHEET
December 31, 1966

Cash	$ 20,000	Accounts payable	$ 200,000
Accounts receivable	100,000	Bank loans	200,000
Inventory	480,000	Accruals	100,000
Current assets	600,000	Current debt	500,000
Land and buildings	200,000	Mortgage on real	
Equipment	200,000	estate	200,000
		Common stock, par	
		10 cents	100,000
		Retained earnings	200,000
		Total liabilities and	
Total assets	$1,000,000	net worth	$1,000,000

1. How much bank financing is needed to become current on trade credit?
2. Would you as a bank loan officer make the loan?

Chapter **15**

Forms of Secured Short-Term Financing

The major sources of short-term financing (trade credit, commercial-bank credit, and the commercial-paper market) were discussed in the previous chapter. If lenders are unwilling to make loans without security, the borrower may utilize accounts receivable financing or inventory financing. These are short-term forms in the sense of duration, but continuous in the sense that an operating business normally generates receivables and inventories which provide a basis for the financing.[1] Commercial banks and finance companies are the major institutions that process secured loans, although interbusiness lending other than trade credit is quite common. This chapter will describe the nature and uses of these two major forms of secured financing: accounts receivables financing and inventory financing.

FINANCING ACCOUNTS RECEIVABLE

Accounts receivable financing involves either the pledge or the sale of receivables as a basis for financing.

The pledging of accounts receivable is called accounts receivable discounting. The process is characterized by the fact that the lender takes the receivables but has recourse to the borrower (seller), and the buyer of the

---

[1] Short-term loans are those with durations under 1 year. This is an arbitrary distinction from long-term loans. However, short-term (temporary) financing requirements vary in duration according to the nature of the firm's production cycle.

goods is not ordinarily notified about the discounting of the receivables. The three largest finance companies, CIT Financial Corporation (CIT), Commercial Credit Corporation (CCC), and General Motors Acceptance Corporation (GMAC), purchased 52 percent of the $40 billion receivables bought by the 100 largest finance companies in the United States during 1960.[2]

Factoring, the second basic type of receivables financing, is the purchase of accounts receivable by the lender without recourse to the borrower (seller). The buyer of the goods is notified of the transfer and makes payment directly to the lender. The factoring firms perform credit-checking services for the seller of the goods.

Procedure for Financing Accounts Receivable

The financing of accounts receivable is initiated by a legally binding agreement between the seller of the goods and the financing institution. The agreement sets forth in detail procedures that will be followed and legal obligations of both parties. Once the working relation has been established, the seller will periodically take a batch of invoices to the financing institution. On receipt of invoices, it reviews them. A credit appraisal of the buyer is made. Invoices of companies that do not meet the credit standards of the lender will not be accepted for discounting. The financial institution seeks to protect itself at every phase of the operation. Selection of sound invoices is the essential first step in safeguarding the financial institution. If the buyer of the goods does not pay the invoice, the bank still has recourse against the seller of the goods. However, if many buyers default, the seller would doubtless be unable to meet his obligation to the bank.

Accounts receivable financing is, to a considerable extent, a mass financing operation, with handling of large numbers of invoices or accounts receivable. However, the smaller the average size of the invoice, the greater the administrative work for the financing institution. Before World War II, the average loan balance outstanding for approximately half the borrowers using accounts receivable financing was less than $100,-000, indicating that firms using accounts receivable financing were typically small firms. The development of accounts receivable financing has therefore contributed to the financing of small business. Receivables financing is also, of course, employed by large firms.

Factoring

The procedure for factoring is somewhat different from that for discounting. Again, an agreement between the seller and the factor is made

---

2 *American Banker*, 76 (May 31, 1961), p. 9.

to specify legal obligations and procedural arrangements. When the seller receives an order from a buyer, a credit approval slip is written and immediately sent to the factoring company for a credit check. If the factor does not approve the sale, the seller will generally refuse to fill the order. This procedure informs the seller prior to the sale about the buyer's creditworthiness and acceptability to the factor. If the sale is approved, shipment is made and the invoice is stamped to notify the buyer to make payment directly to the factoring company.

The factor performs three functions in carrying out the normal procedure as outlined above. They are the credit-checking, lending, and risk-bearing functions. The seller can select various combinations of these functions by changing provisions in the factoring agreement. For example, a small or a medium-sized firm can avoid establishing a credit department. The factor's service is less costly than a department which may have excess capacity for the firm's credit volume. At the same time, if the firm uses part of the time of a noncredit specialist to perform credit checking, lack of education, training, and experience may result in excessive losses.

The seller may utilize the factor to perform the credit-checking and risk-taking functions, but not the lending function. The following procedure would be carried out on receipt of a $10,000 order. The factor checks and approves the invoices. The goods are shipped on terms n/30. Payment is made to the factor, who remits to the seller. But assume that the factor has received only $9,500 by the end of the credit period. He must still remit $10,000 to the seller (less his fee, of course). If the remaining $500 is never paid, the factor sustains a $500 loss.

Now consider the situation in which the factor makes payment in advance of collection. The goods are shipped and, even though payment is not due for 30 days, the factor immediately makes funds available to the seller. If $10,000 of goods is shipped, the factoring commission is $250, and the interest expense is $65, the seller's accounting entry will read as follows:

Cash	$9,185	
Interest expense	65	
Factoring commission	250	
Due from factor on collection of accounts receivable	500	
Accounts receivable		$10,000

The $500 "Due from factor on collection of accounts receivable" entry is a reserve established by the factor to cover disputes between sellers and buyers on damaged goods, goods returned by the buyers to the seller, and the failure to make outright sale of goods. The amount is ultimately paid to the seller firm.

Factoring is normally a continuous process instead of the single cycle described above. The seller of the goods receives orders; he transmits the purchase orders to the factor for approval; on approval, the goods are shipped; the factor advances the money to the seller; the buyers pay the factor when payment is due; and the factor periodically remits any excess reserve to the seller of the goods. Once a routine is established, a continuous circular flow of goods and funds takes place among the seller, the buyers of the goods, and the factor.

Cost of Receivables Financing

Accounts receivable discounting and factoring services are convenient and advantageous, but they can be costly. The credit-checking commission is $\frac{1}{2}$ to 2 percent of the amount of invoices accepted by the factor. The cost of money is reflected in the interest rate of 6 to 8 percent charged on the unpaid balance of the funds advanced by the factor. Where the risk to the factor is excessive, he purchases the invoices (either with or without recourse) at discounts from face value.

Evaluation of Receivables Financing

It cannot be said categorically that accounts receivable financing is always a good or a poor method of raising funds for an individual business. Among the advantages is, first, the flexibility of this source of financing. As its sales expand and the firm as a consequence needs more financing, a larger volume of invoices is generated automatically. Because the dollar amounts of discounted invoices vary directly with sales, the amount of readily available financing increases. Second, receivables or invoices provide security for a loan which a firm might otherwise be unable to obtain. Third, in some instances it can be shown that accounts receivable financing is a cheaper method of financing than available alternative methods. Fourth, factoring provides the services of a credit department that might otherwise be available to the firm only under much more expensive conditions.

Accounts receivable financing also has disadvantages. First, when invoices are numerous and relatively small in amount, the administrative costs involved may render this method of financing inconvenient and expensive. Second, the firm is using a highly liquid asset as security. For a long time accounts receivable financing was frowned upon by most trade creditors. In fact, accounts receivable financing was regarded as confession of a firm's unsound financial position. It is no longer regarded in this light; many sound firms engage in receivables discounting or factoring. However, the traditional attitude causes some trade creditors to refuse to sell on credit to a firm which is discounting its receivables on grounds that to do so removes from the trade creditor a possible source of repayment.

Economically, the increased use of receivables financing has represented a substantial contribution to the financing of small businesses. It makes possible the financing of smaller firms and marginal credit risks for which other financing might not be available.

INVENTORY FINANCING

A relatively large volume of financing has taken place on inventory financing. If a firm is a relatively good credit risk, the mere existence of the inventory may be a sufficient basis for receiving an unsecured loan. If the firm is a relatively poor risk, the lending institution may insist upon security, which often takes the form of a chattel mortgage on the inventory.

Chattel Mortgage Security

The chattel mortgage gives the lending institution a lien against property of the borrower. The chattel mortgage is inconvenient if the lending institution is really worried about the credit position of the borrowing firm, because, in order to establish a valid chattel mortgage, a meticulous description of the items and recordation with the county recorder are required. Inventory description and legal control are difficult if the inventory is fluid. For example, a canner of vegetables has inventory on hand from which he makes sales and into which additional inventories flow as the canning process takes place. In order to maintain the continuous legal validity of the chattel mortgage, a change in the inventories items requires a change in the description of the inventory. Furthermore, in some jurisdictions a chattel mortgage on stock in trade is invalid.

Trust Receipts

Because of the weaknesses of the chattel mortgage, another type of security is used—the trust receipt. A trust receipt is an instrument acknowledging that the borrower holds the goods in trust for the lender. When trust receipts are used, the borrowing firm, on receiving funds from the lender, conveys a trust receipt for the goods. The goods can be stored in a public warehouse or held on the premises of the borrower. The trust receipt provides that the goods are held in trust for the lender, or are segregated in the borrowers' premises on behalf of the lender and transmitted to the lender at the end of each day.

One defect of trust receipt financing is the requirement that a trust receipt must be issued for specific goods. For example, if the security were bags of coffee beans, the trust receipts would have to indicate the bags by number. In order to validate its trust receipts, the lending institution would have to send a man to the premises of the borrower to see that the bag numbers were correctly listed. Furthermore, complex legal requirements of trust receipts require the attention of a bank officer. Problems are compounded if borrowers are widely separated geographically from the lender. To offset these inconveniences, field warehousing is coming into wide use as a method of securing loans with inventory.

Field Warehouse Financing

Like trust receipt and chattel mortgage financing, warehouse financing uses inventory as security. A public warehouse represents an independent third party engaged in the business of storing goods. Sometimes a public warehouse is not practical because of the bulkiness of goods and the expense of transporting them to and from the borrower's premises. Field warehouse financing represents an economical method of inventory financing in which the warehouse is established at the place of the borrower. To provide inventory supervision, the lending institution employs a third party in the arrangement—the field warehousing company. This company acts as the control (or supervisory) agent for the lending institution.

A field warehouse can be illustrated very simply. Suppose that a potential borrower has stacked iron in an open yard on his premises. A field warehouse could be established if a field warehousing concern places a temporary fence around the iron and erects a sign which says "This is a field warehouse supervised and conducted by the Smith Field Warehousing Corporation." These are minimal conditions, of course.

The example illustrates the two elements in the establishment of a warehouse: (1) public notification of the field warehouse arrangement and (2) supervision of the field warehouse by a custodian of the field warehouse concern. When the field warehousing operation is relatively small, the second condition is sometimes violated by hiring an employee of the borrower to supervise the inventory. This practice is viewed as undesirable by the lending institution, because there is no control over the collateral by a person independent of the borrowing concern.

The field warehouse financing operation is described best by a specific illustration. Assume that a tomato canner is interested in financing his operations by bank borrowing. The canner has sufficient funds to finance 15 to 20 percent of his operations during the canning season. These funds are adequate to purchase and process an initial batch of tomatoes. As the cans are put into boxes and rolled into the storerooms, the canner needs additional funds for both raw materials and labor.

Because of the credit rating of the canner, the bank decides that a field warehousing operation is necessary to secure its lending. The field warehouse is established, and the custodian notifies the lending institution of the description by number of the boxes of canned tomatoes in storage and under his control. Thereupon the lending institution establishes for the canner a deposit on which he can draw. From this point on, the bank finances the operations. The canner needs only enough cash to initiate the cycle. The farmers bring more tomatoes; the canner processes them; the cans are boxed, and the boxes are put into the field warehouse; field warehouse receipts are drawn up and sent to the bank; the bank establishes further deposits for the canner based on the receipts; the canner can draw on the deposits to continue the cycle.

Of course, the canner's ultimate objective is to sell the canned tomatoes. As the canner receives purchase orders, he transmits them to the bank and the bank directs the custodian to release the inventories. It is agreed that, as remittances are received by the canner, they will be turned over to the bank. These remittances by the canner pay off the loans made by the bank.

Typically, a seasonal pattern obtains. At the beginning of the tomato harvesting and canning season, the canner's cash needs and loan requirements begin to rise and reach a maximum by the end of the canning season. It is hoped that, just before the new canning season begins, the canner has sold a sufficient volume to have paid off the loan completely. If for some reason the canner has had a bad year, the bank may carry him over another year to enable him to work off his inventory.[3]

Acceptable Products

In addition to canned foods, which account for about 17 percent of all field warehouse loans, many other product inventories provide a basis for field warehouse financing. Some of these are miscellaneous groceries, which represent about 13 percent; lumber products, about 10 percent; coal and coke, about 6 percent.

These products are relatively nonperishable and are sold in well-developed, organized markets. Nonperishability protects the lender, should he have to take over the security. For this reason a bank would not make a field warehousing loan on such perishables as fresh fish. However, fresh-frozen fish, which can be stored for a long time, can be field-warehoused. An organized market aids the lender in disposing of an inventory which it takes over. Banks are not desirous of going into the automobile or the fish business. They want to be able to dispose of an inventory within a matter of hours and with the expenditure of a minimum amount of time.

Cost of Financing

The fixed costs of a field warehousing arrangement are relatively high; this type of financing is therefore not suitable for an extremely small firm. If the field warehouse company sets up the field warehouse itself, it will typically set a minimum charge of about $350 to $600 per year, plus

---

[3] As the credit position of the firm improves, the financial institution may put the firm on an unsecured credit basis.

about 1 or 2 percent of the amount of credit extended to the borrower. In addition, the financing institution will charge from 6 to 10 percent interest. The minimum size of a field warehousing operation requires an inventory of about $20,000.

Appraisal

There are several advantages in the use of field warehouse financing as a source of funds for business firms. First, the amount of funds available is flexible, because the financing is tied to the growth of inventories, which in turn is related directly to financing needs. Second, the field warehousing arrangement increases the acceptability of inventories as loan collateral. Some inventories without a field warehousing arrangement would not be accepted by a bank as security. Third, the necessity for inventory control, safekeeping, and the use of specialists in warehousing has resulted in improved warehouse practices. The services of the field warehouse companies have often saved money for the firm in spite of the costs of financing mentioned above. The field warehouse company may suggest inventory practices which reduce the labor that the firm has to employ, and reduce inventory damage and loss as well.

The major disadvantage of a field warehousing operation is the fixed cost element, which reduces the feasibility of this form of financing for small firms.

SUMMARY

Receivables and inventory financing are useful devices in meeting short-term and intermediate-term credit needs. Since they provide security for loans, they increase the ability of firms with low credit ratings to obtain financing. These forms, however, are often relatively expensive, compared with the best financing sources for all firms. Nor do they encompass the full range of financing requirements of small firms. However, officers of a number of large and well-established firms have stated that receivables and inventory financing helped them grow and develop through their formative stages.

SELECTED REFERENCES

Addison, Edward T., "Factoring: A Case History," *Financial Executive*, 31 (November 1963), pp. 32–33.

Margolin, Leo J., "Factoring Re-discovered," *Long Island Daily Commercial Review* (August 3, 1964).

Phelps, C. W., *Accounts Receivable Financing as a Method of Business Finance* (Baltimore: Commercial Finance Company, 1957).

Rogers, R. W., "Warehouse Receipts and Their Use in Financing," Bulletin of the Robert Morris Associates, 40 (January 1958), pp. 105–113.

Seidman, Walter S., *Accounts Receivable and Inventory Financing* (Ann Arbor, Mich.: Masterco Press, 1957).

Silbert, T. H., "Financing and Factoring Accounts Receivable," *Harvard Business Review*, 30 (January–February 1952), pp. 39–54.

QUESTIONS

15–1 Indicate whether each of the following changes would raise or lower the cost of accounts receivable financing, and why:

1) The firm eases up on its credit standards in order to increase sales.
2) The firm institutes a policy of refusing to make credit sales if the amount of the purchase (invoice) is below $100. Previously, about 40 percent of all invoices were below $100.
3) The firm agrees to give recourse to the finance company for all defaults.
4) The firm, which already had a recourse arrangement, is merged into a larger, stronger company.
5) A firm without a recourse arrangement changes its terms of trade from net 30 to net 90.

15–2 Would a firm that manufactures specialized machinery for a few large customers be more likely to use some form of inventory financing or some form of accounts receivable financing? Why?

15–3 "A firm that factors its accounts receivable will look better in a ratio analysis than one that discounts its receivables." Discuss.

15–4 Why would it not be practical for a typical retailer to use field warehousing?

15–5 For each of the following, list one industry, together with your reasons for including it, that might be expected to use each type of credit:

1) Field warehousing
2) Factoring
3) Accounts receivable discounting
4) Trust receipts
5) None of these

PROBLEMS

15–1 The Thompson Plastic Company has been growing at a 20 percent rate per year. However, it is suffering from insufficient working capital, and it has therefore become slow in paying its bills. Of its total accounts payable, $100,000 is overdue. This threatens the relation with its main supplier of powders used to manufacture various kinds of insulation materials for aircraft and missiles. Over 80 percent of its sales are to six large defense contractors. Its balance sheet, sales, and net profit for the year ended December 31, 1966, are shown here.

THOMPSON PLASTICS
BALANCE SHEET
December 31, 1966

Cash	$ 30,000	Trade credit	$ 250,000
Receivables	450,000	Bank loans	200,000
Inventory:		Accruals	50,000
Raw material . . $ 40,000		Total current	
Work-in-process . 200,000		debt	500,000
Finished goods . 60,000	300,000	Chattel mortgages . .	300,000
Total currents assets . . .	780,000	Capital stock	100,000
Equipment	220,000	Surplus	100,000
Total assets	$1,000,000		$1,000,000

Sales	$2,050,000
Profits after taxes	100,000

1. If the same ratio of sales to total assets continues and if sales increase by $500,000, how much will financing requirements increase?
2. The bank is reluctant to loan Thompson Plastics more than $150,000 to $200,000 on an unsecured basis. Why?
3. Could Thompson Plastics obtain more funds by use of inventory financing? Explain.
4. Would receivables financing be a possibility for Thompson Plastics? Explain.
5. Assuming the facts listed below, on the average what total amount of receivables are outstanding at any time? How much cash does the firm actually receive by factoring the average amount of receivables? What is the average duration of advances based on 360 days per year? What is the total cost of the financing? What is the effective annual interest rate paid on the money received?
   a) Receivables turn over five times a year.
   b) Cash sales amount to $50,000.
   c) The factor requires an 8 percent reserve for returns and disputed items.
   d) The factor also requires a 2 percent commission to cover the costs of credit checking.
   e) There is a 6 percent annual interest charge based on receivables less any reserve requirement or commission. This payment is made at the beginning of the period and is deducted from the advance.

15-2 The following data were taken from the financial statements of the respective companies for the year ended December 31, 1966. Assuming that the three companies are about to liquidate, prepare a comparison of the working-capital position of the three companies.

	Raymond Co.	Goodman Co.	Warner Co.
Cash	$18,000	$17,000	$ 5,000
Accounts receivable	27,000	15,000	18,000
Inventories	15,000	8,000	17,000
Current liabilities	25,000	25,000	25,000

Ratio Analysis	Raymond Co.	Goodman Co.	Warner Co.
Current ratio	_____	_____	_____
Quick ratio	_____	_____	_____
Inventory to current assets	_____	_____	_____
Cash to current assets	_____	_____	_____
Accounts receivable to current assets	_____	_____	_____
Inventory to working capital	_____	_____	_____

Compare the three companies for working-capital position.

15-3 The Karalus Company is a producer of building materials. The demand for its products is highly seasonal, concentrated in the spring and summer months. Its own production is therefore highly uneven.

Karalus would profitably allow a 10 percent trade discount to distributors if they would be willing to accept deliveries during the slack season. The 10 percent concession would be advantageous to the distributors. However, as the distributors were generally underfinanced, they could not accept deliveries without outside financing.

Outline a program of field warehousing to provide the financing for distributors.
15–4 The Collins Company manufactures plastic toys. It buys raw materials, manufactures the toys in the spring and summer, and ships them to department stores and toy stores by the late summer or early fall. Collins factors its receivables. If it did not, the following would be its situation. For example, in October 1965, the balance sheet of Collins would have looked like this:

COLLINS COMPANY
BALANCE SHEET
October 31, 1965

Cash	$ 100,000	Accounts payable . . .	$3,000,000
Receivables	3,000,000	Notes payable	2,000,000
Inventory	2,000,000	Accruals	200,000
Total current assets	5,100,000	Total current debt . .	5,200,000
		Common stock	500,000
Fixed assets	2,000,000	Mortgages	1,000,000
		Retained earnings	400,000
Total assets	$7,100,000	Total claims	$7,100,000

Collins provides season dating on its sales; thus its receivables are not due for payment until January 1966. However, Collins would have been overdue on some $2 million of its accounts payable.

Collins has an agreement with a factoring company which factors the receivables. The factoring company charges a flat commission of 2 percent and 6 percent per year interest and deducts a reserve of 8 percent for returned and damaged materials. Interest is paid in advance.

1. Show the balance sheet of Collins on October 31, 1965, giving effect to the purchase of all the receivables by the factoring company and the use of the funds to pay accounts payable. The base used for calculating the interest is the receivable amount less commission and reserve.

2. If the $3 million is the average level of receivables that are outstanding for a total of 90 days in the year before payment is received by the factor, what is the total cost of financing the amount?

15–5 Prepare a comparison of the working-capital position of Doral Chemical Company and Johnson Drug Company. Both companies should be judged as "going concerns" in the drug industry. The following data were taken from the annual reports of the respective companies for the year ended 1966. The norm used for each of the ratios was obtained from Dun & Bradstreet, Inc. (1963), where available.

FINANCIAL RATIOS

		Doral	Johnson	Norm
1.	Current ratio $\left(\dfrac{CA}{CL}\right)$	_____	_____	3.1
2.	$\dfrac{Cash}{Sales}$	_____	_____	5.8*
3.	Average collection period			
	$\dfrac{Net\ sales}{360} = S/day$			
	$\dfrac{A/R}{S/day} = $ Collection period	_____	_____	43 days
4.	$\dfrac{Sales}{Inventory}$	_____	_____	5.8
5.	$\dfrac{Sales}{Total\ assets}$	_____	_____	1.3*
6.	$\dfrac{Sales}{Inventory\ plus\ total\ assets}$	_____	_____	2.3*
7.	$\dfrac{Total\ debt}{Net\ worth}$	_____	_____	47.6
8.	$\dfrac{Fixed\ assets}{Net\ worth}$	_____	_____	37.9
9.	$\dfrac{Net\ profit\ after\ taxes}{Sales}$	_____	_____	4.4
10.	$\dfrac{Net\ profit\ after\ taxes}{Net\ worth}$	_____	_____	11.1

* Assumed.

BALANCE SHEETS
December 31, 1966

	Doral Chemical	Johnson Drugs
Cash	$ 10,000	$ 8,000
Accounts receivable	30,000	38,000
Inventories	30,000	62,000
Fixed assets	70,000	50,000
Other assets	20,000	10,000
Total assets	$160,000	$168,000
Accounts payable	$ 30,000	$ 40,000
Long-term debt	40,000	33,000
Common Stock	70,000	80,000
Earned surplus	20,000	15,000
Total liabilities and net worth	$160,000	$168,000

INCOME STATEMENTS
For Year Ended 1966

	Doral Chemical	Johnson Drugs
Net sales	$240,000	$260,000
Cost of goods sold	210,000	220,000
Gross profit	30,000	40,000
General selling and administrative expenses	15,000	20,000
Net income before federal income taxes . . .	$ 15,000	$ 20,000
Federal income taxes	6,000	6,000
Net income	$ 9,000	$ 14,000
Terms		
Sales	net 40	net 30
Purchases	net 60	net 60

Chapter 16

Intermediate-Term Financing

Receivables and inventory financing, discussed in the preceding chapter, are short term in the sense that the credit turns over within a relatively short period. They represent continuous financing in that the primary operations of the business give rise to receivables and inventories, providing the security for the borrowing. This type of financing therefore represents a transition to intermediate-term financing, treated in this chapter.[1]

Equipment financing is the subject matter of the major portion of the chapter. The discussion begins with installment equipment financing by conditional sales contracts. An extended treatment of equipment lease financing follows. Next comes a description of railroad equipment financing, a special form of lease financing. Finally, the intermediate term lending activities of the Small Business Administration are summarized.

INSTALLMENT EQUIPMENT FINANCING
Nature

Installment equipment financing is a type of secured short-to-intermediate-term borrowing for income-producing equipment or machinery. The debt on installment equipment credit is amortized in prescheduled regular installment payments based on the expected additional income from the equipment. In the most common arrangement the financing

---

1 Term loans are also intermediate loans; however, some are long term. Also, as they are similar in nature and significance to direct placement of securities, the two are discussed together in Chapter 24.

agency holds title to the equipment, usually in the form of a conditional sales contract. A conditional sales contract is essentially a chattel mortgage with a different name in order to avoid the connotation of mortgage and also to avoid being subject to usury laws. Other names for conditional sales contracts are "special budget plans" or "easy payment plans."

Procedure

Assume that a dentist needs a high-speed drill and that he has 30 percent of the purchase price. He makes the arrangements for the purchase from the manufacturer, and he agrees to finance the remaining 70 percent of the purchase price through a finance company or a bank. The dentist signs a conditional sales contract, which schedules payments based on the income he expects to earn.

The conditional sales contract may be signed with the manufacturer, who sells it to a finance company or a bank. The financing institution usually requires a recourse agreement from the manufacturer for several reasons. The vendor (manufacturer) wants his money when the equipment leaves his factory. If the equipment is returned or repossessed, however, the manufacturer is in a better position than the financing institution to recondition and sell it. A financing institution cannot be expected to recondition a wide variety of specialized equipment. However, it is usual for a conditional sales contract to require that the financing institution repossess and return the equipment to the manufacturer within 60 days after the first default.

Products, Terms, and Appraisal

Products.   Many kinds of equipment purchases are financed under conditional sales contracts. In descending order of frequency they are factory equipment, hotel and restaurant fixtures, equipment for beauty and barber shops, equipment for buses and trailers, medical equipment, diners and dining equipment, and bowling alley equipment. Studies of the credit positions of firms using installment equipment financing reveal that a high proportion of them are small firms with low credit ratings.

Terms.   The terms of installment equipment financing are influenced mainly by the length of life of the equipment purchased. The down payment runs around one third of the equipment purchase price, and the maturity runs from two to three years. The cost of equipment financing has been relatively moderate—usually 6 percent discounted on the face amount of the contract. This is an effective rate of interest of 14 or 15 percent. On heavy machinery purchased by prime credit risks the rate may run as low as $3\frac{1}{2}$ percent per year with an effective rate running to 7 to 8 percent. Sometimes loading or special fees are assessed, which make the effective rate of interest higher. Fees may arise from recordation, documentation, and insurance.

Appraisal. Equipment financing has several important advantages. First, costs are low, relative to other financing alternatives. Second, the loan is self-liquidating from extra income produced by the equipment. Third, smaller firms are able to buy equipment they could not otherwise finance. The major negative feature of installment equipment financing is that it is limited to the financing of only a few kinds of fixed assets.

LEASE FINANCING

One important new development in financing in the past decade has been the emergence of lease financing as a major form by which firms may obtain the use of assets. Leasing is best understood, and was most frequently encountered in the early days of its use, in connection with real estate. Now, however, it is possible to lease virtually any kind of fixed asset—land, plant, or equipment—that a firm may require.

Lease financing can take place in two ways. First, a firm may simply transact for the use of another party's property by paying a rental. Second, a firm that already owns property may sell the property and then lease it back for its continued use (sale and leaseback).

Some of the examples of the use of sale and leasebacks can be traced as far back as 1936. Safeway Stores was an initiator of such leases in the mid-1930s. It did this on the judgment that it was in business as a chain store operator and that its strength was in the effective conduct of a grocery chain store operation. Sears-Roebuck was another important user of leaseback; beginning in 1946 it sold some Wisconsin stores to the Northwestern Mutual Insurance Company and leased them back. Other users of the lease financing arrangement may be found in the ownership and financing of Fruehauf trailers, service stations, Greyhound bus terminals, Crucible Steel warehouses, new plants for the Continental Can Company, restaurants for the Howard Johnson franchises, as well as in a wide variety of firms for the financing of trucks, auto fleets, and machinery.

Internal Revenue Requirements for a Lease

In the immediate post-World War II period, leases had special tax advantages, which have since been restricted by the Internal Revenue Service. Now that the major characteristics of lease financing have been stabilized somewhat, the following are the major requirements of bona fide lease transactions from the standpoint of the Internal Revenue Service.

(1) The term must be less than 30 years. Otherwise the lease is regarded as a form of sale. (2) The rent must represent a reasonable return to the lessor. This return should average from 6 to 10 percent on the investment. (3) The renewal option must be bona fide, and this require-

ment can best be met by giving the lessee the first option to meet an equal bona fide outside offer. (4) There shall be no repurchase option or, if there is, the lessee should merely be given parity with an equal outside offer.

Thus, in a sale and leaseback transaction, the original sale must represent an arm's-length transaction between the seller and the purchaser. The property should consist of real estate, land, or equipment used in the business conducted by the lessee. The price should represent a reasonable negotiated price related to fair market value.

Cost Comparison

To understand the possible advantages and disadvantages of lease financing, the cost of leasing must be compared with the cost of ownership. It is possible to set up a transaction in which, from a financial standpoint, there is clearly no benefit to leasing or owning. Table 16–1 shows the comparison between leasing and buying. Here it is assumed that the firm is purchasing a piece of machinery costing $1,000, and that it has the choice of borrowing the $1,000 at 5 percent to be repaid in ten annual installments of $130 each, or of leasing the machine for $130 per month. (Under the lease arrangement the firm is paying a 5 percent implicit interest rate; this is the rate the lessor is earning.)

The first nine columns of the table are used to calculate the annual cash flow resulting from the decision to borrow, buy the machine, and depreciate it. Column 10 gives the after-tax cost of leasing—the lease payment less the tax saving resulting from the fact that the lease payment is deductible. Subtracting column 9 from column 10 gives the net advantage to owning in each year—in the example there is a *disadvantage* to leasing in the first five years and an advantage in the last five. The last column puts the net advantage figures on a present value basis, discounting them at the firm's over-all cost of capital. Here it has been assumed the cost of capital is equal to the borrowing rate; ordinarily, as was seen in Chapter 12, the cost of capital exceeds the rate on loans.

When the figures in column 13 are totaled, a positive sum indicates that owning is advantageous; a negative sum, that it is disadvantageous.

The example shows that leasing has a disadvantage of $7.33 per $1,000 principal amount involved. Some rounding of figures was employed, so the actual difference could be one or two dollars per $1,000 higher or lower than the $7.33. However, it is clear that with zero salvage value, straight line depreciation, and an implicit interest rate on the lease equal to the borrowing rate, leasing has a net disadvantage. The reason can be readily understood from the pattern of data in Table 16-1.

When the equipment is owned, the tax expense is not the cash outflow: it is interest plus depreciation expense. *Under the assumptions of this illustration,* both the lease payments and the loan expenses are level.

TABLE 16-1

COMPARISON OF THE COST OF LEASING VERSUS BUYING

(1) Year	(2) Cash Flow	(3) Interest	(4) Repayment	(5) Balance	(6) Depreciation	(7) (3)+(6) Tax Expense	(8) ½(7) Tax Saving	(9) (2)-(8) Net Cost of Owning	(10) Lease Cost after Tax	(11) (10)-(9) Advantage to Owning	(12) 5% Present Value Factor	(13) (11)×(12) Present Value of Advantage to Owning
1	$ 130	$ 50	$ 80	$920	$ 100	$ 150	$ 75	$ 55	$ 65	10	0.952	9.52
2	130	46	84	836	100	146	73	57	65	8	0.907	7.26
3	130	42	88	748	100	142	71	59	65	6	0.864	5.18
4	130	38	92	656	100	138	69	61	65	4	0.823	3.29
5	130	34	96	560	100	134	67	63	65	2	0.784	1.57
6	130	28	102	458	100	128	64	66	65	(1)	0.746	(.75)
7	130	23	107	351	100	123	62	68	65	(3)	0.711	(2.13)
8	130	18	112	239	100	118	59	71	65	(6)	0.677	(4.06)
9	130	13	117	122	100	113	56	74	65	(9)	0.645	(5.80)
10	130	8	122	—	100	108	54	76	65	(11)	0.614	(6.75)
Totals	$1300	$300	$1,000	—	$1,000	$1300	$650	$650	$650			7.33

Assumptions:

1) The firm can borrow $1,000 at 5% to be repaid in 10 equal annual installments. The annual payments are computed as:
   a) Interest factor for 10 year, 5% annuity = 7.772 (Table A-4)
   b) Required annual payment = $1,000 ÷ 7.722 = $130

2) The firm can arrange to finance its $1,000 equipment purchase under a 10-year lease plan calling for an annual rental of $130.

3) The equipment is worthless at the end of ten years.

4) The firm's average cost of capital is 5-percent.

But the loan payments represent interest and repayments. At the beginning, when the loan balance is high, interest expense is a higher proportion, and repayments are a lower proportion, of the total payment. Toward the end of the life of the loan, the reverse is true. Thus the higher interest expense at the beginning of the loan period makes the tax deduction higher during the earlier part of the loan period and lower during the later part of the period. The total tax expense ($1,300) under owning and borrowing is exactly the same as under leasing. But the time pattern of the tax expense provides for larger deductions under the owning arrangement. Column 12 shows that the present value factors are higher in the earlier years. As a consequence (under the assumptions of the illustration), the present value of the advantage of owning is $7.33. The discounted costs of owning are lower by $7.33 per $1,000 than the discounted costs of leasing.

What would happen to the relative cost of leasing versus owning if the example was modified to allow for accelerated depreciation? Accelerated depreciation would produce a higher tax shield, hence lower taxes, in the early years. This would reduce the net cost of leasing (column 9) in the early years and raise it later on. Since the lease cost after tax (column 10) is unaffected, the result would be to increase the advantage to owning (column 11) in the early years and raise it in the later years. When the analysis is carried through to the present value column, the final result of accelerated depreciation would be to make owning relatively more attractive than it already is.

Raising the cost of capital factor (column 12) would have the same effect as switching to accelerated depreciation. The advantage of leasing comes in the later years, which are the ones that would be penalized most heavily by a higher cost of capital factor. The net result would be to increase the advantage of owning.

However, a table similar to Table 16-1, constructed from the lessor's point of view, would show that leases provide higher returns than loans, other things the same, because under a lease the lessor can take advantage of the accelerated depreciation. In such a situation the lessor is permitted some profit flexibility in setting lease terms, one of the variations that may reduce the costs of leasing.

It may be useful to summarize some of the variations and their implications for the evaluation of owning versus leasing; this is done in Table 16-2. The material in the table summarizes frequently encountered arguments about advantages and disadvantages of leasing. Each assumed condition is subject to substantial qualification or error. Each will be considered in turn.

Use of accelerated depreciation. It is often argued that because of the ability to use accelerated depreciation methods, owning must therefore

TABLE 16-2

VARIATIONS IN ASSUMED CONDITIONS AND THEIR
IMPLICATIONS FOR COSTS OF OWNING VERSUS LEASING

Assumed Conditions	*Consequences*
Use of accelerated depreciation	Costs of owning lower
Implicit interest rates higher in leasing	Costs of leasing higher
Large residual values	Costs of owning lower
Rapid obsolescence	Costs of leasing lower

be less expensive than leasing. Such an argument does not take into account the competitive aspects of the money and capital markets. Competition will force tax advantages, such as accelerated depreciation, to be shared between lessor and lessee. This relates to the point made just above. The payments pattern under leasing can be quite flexible. Thus, any opportunities available to equipment owners will have to be reflected in the competitive system of rates charged by leasing companies.

Implicit interest rates higher in leasing. The statement is frequently made that leasing always involves higher interest rates. This argument is of doubtful validity. First, when the nature of the lessee as a credit risk is considered, there may be no difference. Second, it is difficult to separate the money costs of leasing from the other services that may be embodied in a leasing contract. If, because of its specialist operations, the leasing company can perform the nonfinancial services[2] at a lower cost than the lessee or some other institution could perform them, the effective cost of leasing may be lower than for funds obtained from borrowing or other sources. The efficiencies of performing specialized services may thus enable the leasing company to operate by charging a lower total cost than the lessor would have to pay for the package of money plus services on any other basis.

Large residual values. Superficially, it would appear that where residual values are large, owning will be less expensive than leasing. However, even this obvious advantage of owning is subject to substantial qualification. On leased equipment, the obsolescence factor is likely to be so large that it is doubtful whether residual values will be of a great order of magnitude. If residual values appear favorable, competition among leasing companies and other financial sources and competition among leasing companies themselves will force leasing rates down to the point where the potentials of residual values are fully recognized in the leasing contract rates. Thus, the existence of residual values on equipment is not likely to result in materially lower costs of owning. On the other hand, in connec-

---

2 For example, maintenance of the equipment.

tion with decisions whether to lease or to own land, the obsolescence factor is not involved except to the extent of deterioration in areas with changing population or use patterns. In a period of optimistic expectations about land values, there may be a tendency to overestimate rates of increase in land values. As a consequence, the current purchase of land may involve a price so high that the probable rate of return on owned land may be relatively small. Under this condition, leasing may well represent a more economical way of obtaining the use of land than owning. Conversely, if the probable increase in land values is not fully reflected in current prices, it will be advantageous to own the land.

Thus it is difficult to generalize whether current residual values or increases in the value of the land are likely to make the present cost of leasing higher or lower than the cost of owning. Generalization is impossible—the results depend on whether the individual firm has opportunities to take advantage of overoptimistic or overpessimistic evaluations of future value changes by the market as a whole.

Rapid obsolescence. Another fallacy is that leasing costs will be lower because of the rapid obsolescence of some kinds of equipment. If the obsolescence rate on equipment is high, leasing costs must reflect such a rate. Thus, in general terms, it might be argued that neither residual values nor obsolescence rates can basically affect the cost of owning versus leasing.

In connection with leasing, however, it is possible that certain types of leasing companies may be better equipped to handle the obsolescence problem. For example, the Clark Equipment Company is a manufacturer, reconditioner, and specialist in materials handling equipment and has its own sales organization and system of distributors. This may enable Clark to write favorable leases for equipment. If the equipment becomes obsolete to one user, it may still be satisfactory for other users with different materials handling requirements, and Clark is ably situated to locate these other users.

Similarly, Management Assistance, Inc., provides an integrated operation in connection with the leasing of IBM electronic accounting machine equipment; it reconditions and maintains the equipment, in addition to providing a lease finance service. Electronic accounting machine equipment that is obsolete for one firm may represent the most efficient (least cost) method of performing accounting functions in another firm. The active sales organization of Management Assistance, Inc., can thus shift the equipment to the user to whom it represents the most efficient method of performing the tasks required.

These illustrations indicate how the leasing company, by combining lending with other specialized services, may reduce the social costs of obsolescence and increase effective residual values. By such operations the total cost of obtaining the use of such equipment is reduced. Possibly other institutions that do not combine financing and other specialist functions, such as manufacture, reconditioning, servicing, and sales, may in conjunction with financing institutions perform the over-all functions as efficiently and at as low cost as do integrated leasing companies. However, this is a factual matter depending upon the relative efficiency of the competing firms in different lines of business and different kinds of equipment. To determine which combination of methods results in the lower costs, an analysis along the lines of the pattern outlined in Table 16-1 is required. Aside from the strictly quantitative considerations that would be reflected in such a table, it is useful to consider some of the possible qualitative advantages of leasing.

Possible Advantages of Leasing

Tax deductions. One factor that shows up clearly in the cost calculation is tax deduction differentials between leasing and buying. If the lease is written for a relatively short period, it will have very large, *deductible* payments in the early years and smaller renewal payments in later years. In a sense, this amounts to a very rapid write-off, which is advantageous. However, the Internal Revenue Service rightly disallows as deductions lease payments under leases (1) that call for a rapid amortization of the lessor's costs and (2) that have a relatively low renewal or purchase option.

Investment tax credit. The investment tax credit is computed as a percentage of the initial cost of long-term assets, but is limited by the firm's computed taxes. Many companies are finding that their rapid rate of asset expansion, their low profits, or a combination of the two makes it impossible to use the entire amount of their tax credit. In these instances it may be possible to lease from a large bank or other supplier of lease funds, letting the lessor take the tax credit as purchaser of the asset. The lessee obtains a low implicit interest rate on the lease in return for giving up the investment tax credit. United Airlines undertook such an arrangement in 1964, when it leased some $25 million worth of jet engines from a group of six major banks.

If this advantage is present and is of sufficient importance, it will be brought out in the cost calculations.

Increased credit availability. Two possible situations may exist to give leasing an advantage to firms seeking the maximum degree of financial leverage. First, it is frequently stated that firms can obtain more money for longer terms under a lease arrangement than under a secured loan agreement for the purchase of a specific piece of equipment. Second, leasing may not have as much of an impact on future borrowing capacity as borrowing and buying of equipment. This point is illustrated by examining the balance sheets of two hypothetical firms, A and B. Initially, the two firms' balance sheets are identical, and they both have debt ratios of 50 percent. Next, they each decide to acquire assets costing $100. Firm A borrows $100 to make the purchase, so an asset and a liability go on its balance sheet and its debt ratio is increased to 75 percent. Firm B leases the equipment. The lease may call for as high or even higher fixed charges, and the obligations assumed under the lease can be equally or more dangerous to other creditors, yet the fact that the debt ratio of firm B is lower may enable it to obtain additional credit from other lenders. The amount of the annual rentals is shown as a note to the financial statements, but all available evidence suggests that credit analysts give less weight to firm B's lease than to firm A's loan.[3]

Before Asset Increase, Firms A and B			After Asset Increase					
			Firm A			Firm B		
Total	Debt	50	Total	Debt	150	Total	Debt	50
assets 100	Equity	50	assets 200	Equity	50	assets 100	Equity	50
Totals 100		100	Totals 200		200	Totals 100		100

LEASING AS AN ADDITIONAL FINANCING ALTERNATIVE

The advantages and disadvantages of leasing from the standpoint of both lessee and lessor have been catalogued. That leasing is being used increasingly does not necessarily mean that it is superior to all other forms of financing. The fundamental reason for the growth of leasing is that the changed economic and tax environments have made it a new, useful financing alternative. Leasing is likely to be employed with other forms of financing by managers in developing a balanced capital financing portfolio for business.

With the background of leasing in general, it will be worthwhile to review the use of this method of financing transportation equipment. Leasing of railway equipment has been used since well before the turn of the century in conjunction with the use of equipment certificates.

---

[3] The accounting profession has given serious thought to capitalizing leases and showing them as both an asset and a liability on the balance sheet. The likelihood of this actually being done in the near future is remote, however. Cf. J. Myers, *Reporting of Leases in Financial Statements* (New York: American Institute of CPA's, 1961).

EQUIPMENT FINANCING BY TRANSPORTATION INDUSTRY

Railroad equipment certificates are securities issued with railroad rolling stock or other railroad equipment as collateral. The main method of financing is leasing in conjunction with equipment trust certificates.

Philadelphia Lease Plan

In recent years practically all equipment trust obligations sold publicly have been sold under the Philadelphia lease plan, which is essentially an ordinary lease arrangement. However, the institutional arrangements are somewhat unique. The parties to the contract are the manufacturer of the equipment, a trustee, and the railroad which is the purchaser of the equipment. The railroad negotiates directly with the equipment manufacturer and directs the equipment manufacturer to sell the equipment to a designated trustee, typically a commercial bank or an investment banker.

The trustee receives from the railroad an initial deposit amounting to, on the average, about 15 to 20 percent of the purchase price. The trustee purchases the equipment, receives title to it, and sells certificates of interest to the public through investment bankers. These certificates of interest, or equipment certificates, are purchased by the public, and the proceeds are used to pay the manufacturer. The manufacturer is now completely paid.

The trustee then leases the equipment to the railroad in return for the deposit which the railroad had initially made to the trustee and for annual rentals. These rentals pay the interest on the obligations and liquidate the principal at a rate much more rapid than the estimated depreciation on the equipment itself.

The Philadelphia lease plan is, in essence, little different from an ordinary mortgage or a conditional sales contract, except for the two following considerations.[4] (1) The laws of the state of Pennsylvania do not permit conditional sales contracts. They could not be used in connection with transactions occurring in that state. (2) The lease arrangement gives the lender of the money a much stronger legal position than does any other kind of contractual arrangement. Under the lease arrangement the lender *owns* the equipment. Until the equipment has been fully paid off by the rentals and the equipment certificates retired, the railroad has no claim to the property.

---

[4] The New York plan is a conditional sales contract, and was most popular in the first quarter of the century. It has no major weaknesses, but has lost out to the popularity of the lease arrangement.

Investment Quality of Equipment Certificates

Equipment certificates are prime investment quality securities, even when they are issued by a railroad company in financial distress. In fact, since the middle 1930s, railroads in process of reorganization and even facing bankruptcy have been able to sell equipment certificates at prime rates of interest. The reasons for this are as follows:

1. The equipment is indispensable to railroad operation generally and therefore has ready resalability. Resalability is enhanced by the fact that in their normal operations the railroads interchange their equipment.

2. Railroad rolling stock is durable and has a very low obsolescence rate. Railroad rolling stock apparently neither wears out nor is replaced by more modern equipment at a very fast rate.

3. The form of the obligation is such that in bankruptcy or reorganization the equipment certificate is a direct claim on the property and is not commingled with other claims.

Equipment Financing by Insurance Companies

Since the mid-1950s large insurance companies with substantial amounts of funds to invest have become interested in railroad equipment financing. At this time insurance companies had a plethora of funds, but the railroads were in a relatively tight working-capital position. The insurance companies sought to achieve a competitive advantage by developing an arrangement which avoided the 20 percent down payment. The Equitable Insurance Company pioneered in buying equipment directly from the manufacturer. The insurance company leases the equipment to the railroad for 15 years, with no down payment required. At the end of 15 years the railroad has the option of returning the equipment to the insurance company or of taking an additional lease of ten years at 20 cents a day per boxcar or passenger car. The Equitable Life Insurance Company planned to write off the equipment in 15 years, so that if the railroad had no interest in the equipment at the end of 15 years, the company would suffer no loss.

From the standpoint of the insurance company the following risks were involved: the demand for railroad equipment might fall off greatly; the railroad might default; there might not be a potential buyer for the resale of the equipment. Since the insurance company retains ownership in the equipment and there is no provision for the sale of the equipment to the railroad company at the expiration of the 15-year period, to the extent that the general price level rises or that prosperity returns to the railroad industry, the insurance company will own very valuable property.

Equipment Certificates for Airlines

The use of equipment certificates by railroads has frequently raised the question of financing air transportation equipment in the same way.

Air transport companies, even the large ones, have had a real financing problem, and only within recent years have they reached sufficient maturity to move from dependence upon relatively short-term bank financing to longer term loans or debenture financing.

Equipment financing has not been used in aircraft financing to the same extent that it has been used in railway equipment financing for the following reasons: (1) Airline equipment has a very high obsolescence rate. Certainty as to its resale value is not high. (2) The interchangeability of aircraft equipment is not so great as that of railroad equipment. (3) Accident costs are relatively high, and the legal position of the owner of the equipment is not certain in the case of accident. These equipment obligations are written so that the lender is the legal owner of the equipment, to protect his rights in the event of bankruptcy of the borrowing company; as the owner, however, he faces potential losses from accidents.[5]

GOVERNMENT LENDING PROGRAMS TO SMALL BUSINESS

Since one of the important needs of small business is intermediate financing, it is appropriate to conclude this chapter with a description of the Small Business Administration's financial programs.[6]

Scope of Operations

The SBA helps small business firms in a number of ways. It seeks to aid them in obtaining a fair share of government contracts. It also emphasizes assistance to small business in management and production problems. These two objectives recognize that a substantial number of small business firms need management counseling and assistance. In addition, the SBA actively aids small firms with their financial problems; this aspect of SBA operations will be emphasized here.

For business loans, the SBA defines a small business as one that is independently owned and operated and nondominant in its field. Specific standards depend upon the industry of the firm. Any manufacturing concern is defined as small if it employs 250 or fewer persons; it is defined as large if it employs more than 1,000 persons. Within this range the SBA has particular standards for individual industries. The wholesale concern

---

[5] Though it was not written as an equipment trust certificate, the United Airlines example cited above demonstrates that the accident liability problem can be overcome. This particular lease was for engines, not the entire aircraft, but there have been numerous instances of entire aircraft leases. The lessor simply obtains adequate insurance coverage.

[6] The Small Business Administration has a number of other functions. However, this discussion will be focused on SBA business lending programs. The relationship of the SBA to small business investment corporations (SBIC) will best be understood and therefore is described after the discussions in Chapters 17–24 on long-term financing.

is classified as small if its yearly sales are $5 million or less. Most retail businesses and service trades are defined as small if their total annual receipts do not exceed $1 million. A business operating under a franchise may obtain a loan if the SBA can be assured that the firm is not a large business through its affiliation with the franchiser. The Department of Commerce estimates that as of the end of 1964 some 4.91 million firms were in existence. Of these, 4.66 million, or 95 percent of the total, were classified as small businesses.

Loan Policies and Types

By law, the SBA makes loans to small business concerns only when financing is not available to them on reasonable terms from other sources. The SBA loans are of two types: direct and participation. In a direct loan, there is no participation by a private lender—the loan is made directly by the SBA to the borrower. In participation loans, the SBA joins with a bank or other private lending institution in making a loan to a small business firm.

A participation loan may be made either under a loan guarantee (deferred) or on an immediate basis. A participation loan on a guarantee basis provides that the SBA, on 90 days' default as to principal or interest, will purchase its guaranteed portion of the outstanding balance of the loan. When the SBA participates in a loan on an immediate basis, it purchases immediately a fixed percentage of the original principal amount of the loan. The SBA may not enter into an immediate participation if it can do so on a guarantee (deferred) basis.

Terms of Loans

The maximum amount the SBA may have outstanding to any one borrower is $350,000. This maximum applies equally to a direct loan or the SBA's portion of a participation loan. Thus, on a participation basis, the amount of financing facilitated by the SBA could be substantially more than $350,000. The maximum SBA portion of a participation loan is 90 percent. If the loan is made to a corporation formed by a pool or a group of small business concerns, the maximum is $250,000 multiplied by the number of small businesses participating in the group corporation loan.

SBA business loans are repayable in regular monthly installments, which include part of the principal plus interest on the unpaid balance. Loans for working capital are usually limited to six years; loans for construction purposes may have a maturity of ten years plus the estimated time required to complete construction; and loans to syndicates of small businesses for constructing facilities may have maturities extending up to 20 years.

The interest rate on SBA direct business loans is 5½ percent. The maximum interest rate on the SBA share of the participation loan is also 5½ percent. However, private lending institutions may charge a rate higher than 5½ percent on their share of a participation loan and also on the SBA portion of a guaranteed loan until such time as the SBA purchases its guaranteed portion. Whenever possible, the SBA seeks to have loans secured by collateral.

The above general lending program is supplemented by two specialized programs known as (1) the Small Loan Program and (2) Loans to Very Small Business. In the Small Loan Program, emphasis is placed on the character and future business prospects of the applicant. Less emphasis is placed on adequate collateral. A qualified small firm may obtain up to $15,000 for direct SBA loans or bank participation loans where the SBA portion is not more than $15,000. Small loan maturities may not exceed six years plus additional time needed for construction work where required. Interest rates are the same as for larger loans.

The Loans to Very Small Business has been called the "Six by Six" program. Loans of up to $6,000 are made for as long as six years. This program has placed an emphasis on aid to minority groups. The emphasis is on character and ability rather than collateral. This program has been included in the activities of the Office of Economic Opportunity to aid poverty areas.

Record of Operations

Since the enactment of the Small Business Act of 1953, the SBA has extended over 50,000 loans for a total of almost $2.5 billion. Table 16-3

TABLE 16–3

TYPES OF SBA LOANS, 1953–1964, CUMULATIVE
(dollars in millions)

	Direct	Immediate Participations by SBA	Deferred Participations by SBA	Total
Number of loans . . .	20,075	24,105	6,574	50,754
Percent of number . .	39.6	47.5	12.9	100.0
Dollar amount . . .	$685.9	$1,453.5	$301.5	$2,440.9
Percent of amount . .	28.1	59.5	12.4	100.0

Source: 1964 Annual Report, Small Business Administration (Washington, D. C.), p. 16.

shows the distribution, broken down by direct loans, immediate participations, and deferred participations. By number and amount, the immediate participations by the SBA have predominated.

During 1964, banks participated with the SBA in over 5,000 loans representing approximately 49 percent of all business loans approved by the SBA in 1964. Participation loans accounted for over $300 million, or 73 percent of the total dollar amount of loan approvals. Since this rate is well above the 47.5 percent 12-year average, it indicates that in recent years there has been a trend toward increased participation by commercial banks in SBA lending activity.

Through June 30, 1964, the SBA had incurred a loss on 803 business loans and had charged off a total of $9 million of unpaid principal. The SBA has estimated that, taking into account expected losses on loans made in recent years that have not yet matured to a point where loss experience has developed, an ultimate loss of 2.5 percent of total disbursements will be involved. In 1964, the operating loss of the SBA on its business loans was approximately $14 million.

Operating losses should be evaluated in the light of the fact that the SBA extends substantial counseling and training services. In addition, loan applications that are rejected still incur investigation expense. The indirect benefits of the SBA program, both to individual firms and to economic activity, are difficult to measure but should be considered. The cumulative number of loans granted, 50,754, is relatively small compared to the total of 4.66 million small business firms in existence at the end of 1964.[7]

Significance of the SBA for the Financial Manager

Although the SBA has not provided a large volume of financing, it has performed an important function for small business. Its counseling activities have been of immeasurable value. Often a small business has need of guidance rather than funds. Aid in starting and operating a business has often meant the difference between success and failure for some small firms. Furthermore, when the prospects for a small firm have appeared favorable, but it has been unable to obtain private financing, particularly because of lack of operating experience or a financial background, SBA financing may fill an important gap.

Since more than 90 percent of the 4.9 million firms in the United States may qualify as small business, the potential role of the SBA is significant. This discussion of financing small business is therefore relevant for most of the firms in the United States. The SBA may be an important

---

[7] For additional information on the material in this section, see the following publications of the Small Business Administration: *Small Business Administration—What it is —What it does; SBA Business Loans: How an SBA Loan Can Help Your Business; SBA's Small Loan Programs;* Small Business Administration *1964 Annual Report.* All of these can be obtained from the Office of Public Information, Small Business Administration, Washington, D.C., or from local offices of the SBA located in many cities of the United States.

point of contact and consultation for a firm, even though financing may not be directly obtained from this government agency. Not only does good financial management involve obtaining funds from outside sources; it also means augmenting the flow of funds by increased profits and effectively conserving and utilizing the funds that are in its possession.

SUMMARY

Conditional sales contracts continue to be a major method by which firms obtain the use of equipment. An important reason why this method of intermediate financing is favored by firms is that it represents a definite program leading to ownership of the asset.

Leasing has long been used in connection with the acquisition of equipment by railroad companies. In recent years it has been extended to a wide variety of equipment. In the absence of major tax advantages, whether or not leasing is advantageous turns primarily on the firm's ability to acquire funds by other methods. Leasing has the advantage of a smaller down payment and increased opportunities for tax savings, and it probably increases the over-all availability of nonequity financing to the firm.

On the other hand, a leasing contract is very close to a straight-debt arrangement and uses some of the firm's debt-carrying ability. Also, the rental is a fixed obligation. Because of the importance of residual value, it will generally be advantageous to a firm to own its land and buildings. Because of the obsolescence factor, the residual value considerations may be less important in connection with the acquisition of equipment. Leasing of equipment is therefore likely to continue to grow in importance.

The Small Business Administration program supplements equipment finance importantly by providing financing for the acquisition of current assets. The loans have averaged five years in duration and have been primarily for working capital financing. The SBA seeks to provide aid on management and production problems and to provide financing when normal sources are not available to the firm.

SELECTED REFERENCES

Brigham, E. F., "The Impact of Bank Entry on Market Conditions in the Equipment Leasing Industry" *National Banking Review*, 2 (September 1964), pp. 11–26.

Cary, W. L., "Corporate Financing through the Sale and Leaseback of Property," *Harvard Law Review*, 62 (November 1948), pp. 1–41.

————, "Sale and Leaseback of Corporate Property," *Harvard Business Review*, 27 (March 1949), pp. 151–164.

Cohen, A. H., *Long-term Leases—Problems of Taxation, Finance and Accounting* (Ann Arbor, Mich.: Bureau of Business Research, University of Michigan, 1954).

Gant, D. R., "Illusion in Lease Financing," *Harvard Business Review*, 37 (March-April 1959), pp. 121–142.

Griesinger, Frank K., "Leasebacks and Leasing," *Credit and Financial Management*, 61 (February 1959), pp. 13, 20–21.

————, "Pros and Cons of Leasing Equipment," *Harvard Business Review*, 33 (March-April 1955), pp. 75–89.

Hamel, Henry G., "Another Look at Leasing," *Business Management Record,* 14 (November 1963), pp. 47–52.

Keller, I. W., "Shall We Lease or Buy Equipment?" *N.A.C.A. Bulletin,* 35 (September 1953), pp. 34–47.

Knutson, Peter H., "Leased Equipment and Divisional Return on Capital," *N.A.A. Bulletin,* Vol. XLIV, No. 3 (November 1962), pp. 15–20.

Law, Warren A., and M. Colyer Crum, *Equipment Leasing and Commercial Banks* (Chicago, Ill.: Association of Reserve City Bankers, 1963).

Linderman, W. H., "Shall We Sell the Building and Lease It Back?" *N.A.C.A. Bulletin,* 35 (September 1953), pp. 50–59.

Rickey, Kenneth R., "Including All Leases in the Balance Sheet—A First," *N.A.A. Bulletin,* 40 (December 1959), pp. 51–60.

Schaff, David, "When Is a Lease a Sale for Tax Purposes?" *Controller,* 27 (February 1959), pp. 70–72.

Shillinglaw, Gordon, "Accounting for Leased Property by Capitalization," *N.A.A. Bulletin,* 39 (June 1958), pp. 31–45.

Simon, Sidney I., "The Lease-Option Place—Its Tax and Accounting Implications," *Journal of Accountancy,* Vol. 113, No. 4 (April 1962), pp. 38–45.

Smith, Charles J., "Shall We Own or Lease Our Automobiles and Trucks?" *N.A.A. Bulletin,* 40 (September 1959), pp. 65–74.

Street, Donald MacQueen, *Railroad Equipment Financing* (New York: Columbia University Press, 1959).

Vancil, R. F., and R. N. Anthony, "The Financial Community Looks at Leasing," *Harvard Business Review,* 37 (November-December 1959), pp. 113–130.

Yuille, E. C., "A Comparison of Financing Inventory—Warehouse Receipts Versus Trust Receipts," *Credit Executive of Southern California,* Vol. XVIII, No. 3 (November 1962), pp. 4–12.

QUESTIONS

16-1 "The type of equipment that is best suited for leasing has a long life in relation to the length of the lease; is a removable, standard product that could be used by many different firms; and is easily identifiable. In short, it is the kind of equipment that could be repossessed and sold readily. However, we would be quite happy to write a ten-year lease on paper towels for a firm such as General Motors." Discuss the statement.

16-2 On the basis of the factors that make leasing a desirable means of financing and your knowledge of the characteristics of different industries, give three industries that might be expected to use lease financing. Explain your answer.

16-3 Leasing is often called a hedge against obsolescence. Under what conditions is this actually true?

16-4 Is leasing in any sense a hedge against inflation for the lessee? for the lessor?

16-5 What qualities of railroad equipment certificates make them prime investment securities?

16-6 One of the alleged advantages of leasing is that it keeps liabilities off the balance sheet, thus making it possible for a firm to obtain more leverage than it otherwise could. This raises the question of whether or not both the lease obligation and the asset involved should be capitalized and shown on the balance sheet. Discuss the pros and cons of capitalizing leases and the related assets.

PROBLEMS

16–1 The Johnson Department Store is considering a sale and leaseback of its major property, consisting of land and a building, because it is 35 days late on 80 percent of its accounts payable. The recent profit record and the balance sheet of Johnson are shown below. Profit before taxes in 1966 is $25,000.

Year	Profits after Taxes
1961	$40,000
1962	50,000
1963	30,000
1964	40,000
1965	60,000
1966	14,000

JOHNSON DEPARTMENT STORE
BALANCE SHEET
December 31, 1966
(in thousands of dollars)

Cash	$ 200	Accounts payable	$1,000
Receivables	1,000	Bank loans, 6%	1,000
Inventories	1,300	Other current liabilities	500
Total current assets	2,500	Total curent debt	2,500
Net fixed assets	1,500	Common stock	1,000
		Retained earnings	500
Total assets	$4,000	Total claims	$4,000

The book value of the net fixed assets consists of the following:

Land	$ 800,000
Building	500,000
Fixtures and equipment	200,000
Total	$1,500,000

Annual depreciation charges are $40,000 a year on the building and $50,000 a year on the fixtures and equipment.

The land and building could be sold for a total of $2.3 million. The annual net rental will be $170,000.

1. How much capital gains tax will Johnson pay if the land and building are sold?

2. Compare the current ratio before and after the sale and leaseback if the net proceeds are used to "clean up" the bank loans and to reduce accounts payable and other current liabilities.

3. If the lease had been in effect during 1966, what would Johnson's profit for 1966 have been?

4. What are the basic financial problems facing Johnson? Will the sale and leaseback operation solve them?

16–2 The Town Department Store has been growing rapidly. Management estimates that it will need an additional $4 million during the next two years. Because of its weak current position, the store is considering the sale and lease-back of its land and building for $9 million. The annual net rental would be

$800,000. The immediate use of the sales' proceeds will be to retire bank loans and mortgages. The current balance sheet and recent earnings are shown below.

TOWN DEPARTMENT STORE
BALANCE SHEET
December 31, 1966
(in millions of dollars)

Cash	$1	Accounts payable	$5
Receivables	7	Bank loans, 5%	5
Inventories	6	Other current debt	1
Total current assets	$14	Total current debt	$11
Land	$1	Mortgage on property, 5%	3
Buildings	4	Common stock	2
Equipment and fixtures	1	Retained earnings	4
Net fixed assets	6		
Total assets	$20	Total claims on assets	$20

Year	Profit before Taxes (in dollars)
1959	$400,000
1960	400,000
1961	450,000
1962	500,000
1963	500,000
1964	600,000
1965	800,000
1966	800,000

Annual depreciation charges are $200,000 on the building and $400,000 on the equipment and fixtures.

1. How much capital gains tax will Town pay if the land and building are sold?

2. If the lease had been in effect during 1966, what would Town's profit after taxes have been? (Assume a 50 percent tax rate.)

3. If the firm uses the net proceeds of the sale to reduce the bank loan and accounts payable instead of the mortgage, what will be its new current ratio?

4. List some advantages and disadvantages of the sale-and-leaseback operation, and recommend whether or not the firm should adopt the proposal.

16-3 The Altman Co. is faced with the decision whether to purchase a new fork-lift truck or to lease one. The truck can be leased on a five-year contract for $1,000 a year or it can be purchased for $4,000. The lease includes maintenance and service. The salvage value of the truck five years hence is $1,000. The company uses the sum-of-the-years'-digits method of depreciation. If the truck were owned, service and maintenance charges would be $250 per year. The company requires a 10 percent return after taxes.

Answer the following questions under each set of assumptions:

a) The firm borrows the $4,000 at an interest rate of 6 percent and this same 6 percent is used as the discount factor in comparing the costs of leasing versus owning.

b) The firm borrows the $4,000 at an interest rate of 6 percent which is used in computing the interest costs of owning; but the firm's 10 percent cost of capital is used in calculating the present values of the cash flows involved in leasing versus owning.

1. Which method of acquiring the use of the equipment should the company choose?

2. What factors could alter the results indicated by the quantitative analysis based on the above facts?

3. Discuss the use of 6 percent versus 10 percent as the discount factor.

Part V

Long-Term Financing

Chapter 17

Equity Funds

The major forms of financing may be summarized into the following principal categories:

1. Equity funds
   a) Original ownership investment by founders plus retained earnings
   b) Funds from sources external to the firm
2. Debt funds
   a) Short-term financing
   b) Intermediate-term financing
   c) Long-term financing

Equity is the amount of funds contributed by the owners of the business; debt is the amount owed to the creditors. The funds supplied by the original owners of a firm are the first source of funds of a new firm. Hence our discussion of long-term financing will begin with an analysis of common stock.

Since short- and intermediate-term financing have already been described, the following chapters take up preferred stock and long-term debt financing. With the background of concepts developed in discussions of external financing, the significance of policy decisions regarding internal financing and dividend policy, which are taken up next, can be analyzed more meaningfully. Finally, because of the widespread use of rights, warrants, and convertible securities in recent years, the nature and significance of these three forms of options offered to investors are discussed in the concluding two chapters of this section.

APPORTIONMENT OF INCOME, CONTROL, AND RISK

The nature of equity ownership depends upon the form of the business organization. The central problem revolves around an apportionment of certain rights and responsibilities among those who have provided the funds necessary for the operation of the business.

The rights and responsibilities attaching to equity consist of positive considerations—income potential and control of firm—and negative considerations—loss potential and responsibility and liability.

General Rights of Holders of Common Stock

The rights of holders of common stock in a business corporation are established by the laws of the state in which the corporation is chartered and by the terms of the charter granted by the state. The characteristics of the charter are relatively uniform on many matters.

Collective rights. Certain collective rights are usually given to the holders of this stock. Some of the more important rights are (1) to amend the charter with the approval of the appropriate officials in the state of incorporation; (2) to adopt and amend bylaws; (3) to elect the directors of the corporation; (4) to authorize the sale of fixed assets; (5) to enter into mergers; (6) to change the amount of authorized common stock; (7) to issue preferred stock, debentures, bonds, and other securities.

Specific rights. In addition, holders of common stock have specific rights as individual owners. (1) They have the right to vote in the manner prescribed by the corporate charter. (2) They may sell their stock certificates, their evidence of ownership, and in this way transfer their ownership interest to other persons. (3) They have the right to inspect the corporate books.[1] (4) They have the right to share residual assets of the corporation on dissolution, but the holders of common stock are last among the claimants to the assets of the corporation.

Apportionment of Income

There are two important positive considerations involved in equity ownership: income and control. The right to income carries risks of loss. Control also involves responsibility and liability. In an individual proprietorship, using only funds supplied by the owner, the owner has a 100-percent right to income and control, loss and responsibility. As soon as the proprietor incurs debt, however, he has entered into contracts which

---

[1] Obviously, a corporation cannot have its business affairs disturbed by allowing every stockholder to go through any record that he would like to inspect. A corporation could not wisely permit a competitor who happened to buy shares of its common stock to look at all the corporation records. There must be, and there are, practical limitations to this right.

place limitations on his complete freedom to control the firm and to apportion the firm's income.

In a partnership, these rights are apportioned among the partners in an agreed manner. In the absence of a formal agreement, a division is made by the laws of the locality. But the more significant issues arise concerning the rights of the owners of a business corporation.

Apportionment of Control

Through the right to vote, holders of common stock have legal control of the corporation. As a practical matter, however, in many corporations the principal officers constitute all, or a majority of, the members of the board of directors. In such circumstances the board of directors may be controlled by the management, rather than vice versa. Management control, or control of a business by others than its owners, results. However, numerous examples demonstrate that stockholders can reassert their control when dissatisfied. In recent years, frequent proxy battles with the aim of altering corporation policies have occurred.

As receivers of residual income, holders of common stock are frequently referred to as the ultimate entrepreneurs in the firm. They are the ultimate owners and they have the ultimate control. Presumably the firm is managed on behalf of its owners, the holders of common stock; but there has been much dispute about what actually obtains. The point of view has been expressed that the corporation is an institution with an existence separate from the owners; that the corporation exists to fulfill certain functions for stockholders as one among other important groups, such as workers, consumers, and the economy as a whole.

Apportionment of Risk

The fact that, on liquidation, holders of common stock are last in the priority of claims signifies that the portion of capital they contribute provides a cushion for creditors should losses occur on dissolution. The equity-to-total-assets ratio indicates the percentage by which assets may shrink in value on liquidation before creditors will incur losses.

For example, compare two corporations, A and B, with these balance sheets:

BALANCE SHEETS

Corporation A			Corporation B		
	Debt	$ 20		Debt	$ 60
	Equity	80		Equity	40
Total assets $100	Total claims	$100	Total assets $100	Total claims	$100

The ratio of equity to total assets in corporation A is 80 percent. Total assets would therefore have to shrink by 80 percent before creditors would lose money. By contrast, in corporation B, the extent by which assets may shrink in value on liquidation before creditors lose money is only 40 percent.

Since the average equity-to-total-assets ratio for all manufacturing is approximately two thirds, a substantial equity cushion ordinarily exists. For some industries, such as airline transport and aircraft manufacturing, however, the equity cushion is only about one third of total assets.

COMMON STOCK FINANCING

Before undertaking an evaluation of common stock financing it is desirable to describe additional important characteristics. These topics include (1) the nature of voting rights, (2) the nature of the pre-emptive right, (3) the significance of par value, and (4) variations in the forms of common stock.

Nature of Voting Rights

For each share of common stock owned, the holder has the right to cast a vote at the annual meetings of stockholders of the corporation or at such special meetings as may be called.

Proxy. Provision is made for the temporary transfer of this right to vote by an instrument known as a proxy. A proxy is defined as a transfer of the right to vote. The transfer is limited in its duration, typically for the specific occasion, such as the annual meeting of stockholders.

The Securities and Exchange Commission supervises the use of the proxy machinery and issues frequent rules and regulations seeking to improve its administration. SEC supervision is justified for several reasons. First, if the proxy machinery is left wholly in the hands of management, there is a danger that the incumbent management will be self-perpetuated. Second, if it is made easy for minority groups of stockholders and opposition stockholders to oust management, there is danger that small groups of stockholders may gain control of the corporation for temporary advantages or to place their friends in management positions. Sometimes, the minority may be seeking prizes that go along with controlling the corporation, for example, income from real estate.

Eligibility to vote. In certain situations there may be some doubt about who has the right to vote. For example, in a *hypothecation of securities* (where securities are pledged as collateral for a loan), does the pledger or the lender have the right to vote? The law provides that in a simple hypothecation situation the pledger of the stock, rather than the lender, retains the right to vote. In a trust situation, where the donor has placed the stock in the hands of a trustee to be controlled for the benefit of the beneficiary, three possible parties might have the right to vote: the donor, the trustee, and the beneficiary. The law provides that the trustee shall have the right to vote.

Proxies may be mailed to stockholders of record of a specified date—for example, April 10. The voting may relate to an annual meeting to be held one month later, May 10. In the interim the stock may be sold. Who has the right to the proxy: the stockholder of record on April 10 or the new stockholder? Technically, the stockholder of record has the right to vote. He has the proxy and he may keep it. However, the new buyer may, and should, request the proxy from the seller.

Cumulative voting. A method of voting which has come into increased prominence is cumulative voting.[2] Cumulative voting for directors is required in 22 states, including California, Illinois, Pennsylvania, Ohio, and Michigan. It is permissive in 18, including Delaware, New York, and New Jersey. Ten states make no provision for cumulative voting.

Cumulative voting permits multiple votes for a single director. For example, six directors are to be elected. The owner of 100 shares can cast 100 votes for each of the six openings. Cumulatively, then, he has 600 votes. When cumulative voting is permitted, the stockholder may accumulate his votes and cast 600 votes for *one* director, instead of 100 each for *six* directors. Cumulative voting is designed to enable a minority group of stockholders to obtain some voice in the control of the company by electing at least one director to the board.

The nature of cumulative voting is illustrated by use of a well-known formula:

$$r = \frac{d \times S}{D + 1}$$

r = number of shares required to elect a desired number of directors

d = number of directors stockholder desires to elect

S = total number of shares of common stock outstanding and entitled to vote[3]

D = total number of directors to be elected

The formula may be made more meaningful by an example. The

---

[2] For an excellent discussion of all aspects of cumulative voting, see Charles M. Williams, *Cumulative Voting for Directors* (Boston: Graduate School of Business Administration, Harvard University, 1951).

[3] An alternative that may be agreed to by the contesting parties is to define S as the number of shares *voted*, not authorized to vote. This procedure, which in effect gives each group seeking to elect directors the same percentage of directors as their percentage of the voted stock, is followed perhaps most frequently. When it is followed, a group that seeks to gain control with a minimum investment must estimate the percentage of shares that will be voted, then obtain 51 percent of that number.

ABC company will elect six directors. There are 15 candidates and 100,000 shares entitled to a vote. If a group desires to elect two directors, how many shares must it have?

$$\frac{2 \times 100,000}{6 + 1} = 28,571$$

Observe the significance of the formula. Here, a minority group wishes to elect one third of the board of directors. They can achieve their goal by owning less than one third the number of shares of stock.

The question may be put in another way. Assuming that a group holds 40,000 shares of stock in this company, how many directors would it be possible for the group to elect, following the rigid assumptions of the formula? The formula can be used in its present form or can be re-expressed, solving for d.

$$d = \frac{r(D + 1)}{S}$$

Inserting the figures, the calculation would be

$$2.8 = \frac{40,000 \times 7}{100,000}$$

The 40,000 shares could elect 2.8 directors. Since directors cannot exist as fractions, the group can elect only two directors.

As a practical matter, suppose that in the situation above the total number of shares is 100,000. Hence 60,000 shares remain in other hands. The voting of all the 60,000 shares may not be concentrated. Suppose the 60,000 shares (cumulatively, 360,000 votes) are distributed equally among ten candidates, 36,000 shares per candidate. If the other 40,000 votes are distributed equally for each of six candidates, the minority group could elect all six directors.

In actuality, it is difficult to make assumptions about how the opposition votes will be distributed. What is shown here is a good example of game theory. One rule involved in the theory of games is to assume that your opponents will do the worst they can do to you, and counter with actions to minimize the maximum loss. This is the kind of assumption followed in the formula. If your opposition concentrates its votes in the optimum manner, what is the best you can do to work in the direction of your goal? Other plausible assumptions can be substituted if one has sufficient facts to support alternative hypotheses about the behavior of his opponents.

Pre-emptive Right

The pre-emptive right gives holders of common stock the first option to purchase additional issues of common stock. In some states the pre-emptive right is made a part of every corporate charter. In other states it is necessary specifically to insert the pre-emptive right in the charter.

The purpose of the pre-emptive right is twofold. First, it protects the power of control of present stockholders. Were it not for this safeguard, the management of a corporation under criticism from stockholders could prevent stockholders from removing it from office by issuing a large number of additional shares at a very low price and purchasing these shares itself. Management would thereby secure control of the corporation to frustrate the will of the current stockholders.

The second, and by far the more important, protection that the pre-emptive right affords stockholders regards dilution of value. An example may clarify this. Assume that 1,000 shares of common stock with a market value of $100 are outstanding, making the total market value of the firm $100,000. An additional 1,000 shares are sold at $50 per share, or for $50,000, thus raising the total market value of the firm to $150,000. When the total market value is divided by the new shares outstanding, a value of $75 per share is obtained. Thus, selling common stock at below market value will dilute the price of the stock and be detrimental to present stockholders and beneficial to those who purchased the new shares. The pre-emptive right prevents such occurrences.

Par Value versus No-Par Value

Some distinctions. Some distinctions need to be made among different concepts of value. *Par value* is the nominal value of common stock; it is the value arbitrarily stated on the shares. *Book value,* the concept that has been used here, is the historical value of the common stock. Book value per share is calculated by adding the balance sheet value of the common stock, plus surplus, plus any earmarked surplus accounts such as contingency reserves, and dividing this sum by the number of shares outstanding. If there is a goodwill account on the left-hand side of the balance sheet, the analyst may or may not deduct the goodwill item, depending upon whether superior earning power exists.

Market value, as explained in Chapter 12, is the prevailing price paid for a share of common stock as registered in transactions between buyers and sellers of common stock.

Intrinsic value, or economic value, is not an objective amount. It was seen to represent a judgment of the long-run value of the common stock as determined by fundamental economic forces.

These distinctions facilitate analysis of the use of par value, the trend toward no-par value, and the reversal of that trend. Originally, the purpose of a par value was to protect creditors. It was to ensure that the full amount of payment for common stock had actually been received by the company. By stating a par value clearly on the balance sheet, the creditors of the company have the assurance that, if the full amount has not been paid in, they have the right to levy a deficiency judgment against the present holders of common stock.

For example, A buys a $100 par value stock *from the company* for $65. He is liable up to $35 to a subsequent assessment by creditors upon insolvency. This deficiency assessment right obtains even though A may have subsequently sold his stock. For example, B purchases the stock from A for $115, an amount that exceeds par value by $15. The deficiency assessment liability of $35 is acquired by B, because the company had never received the full par value of the stock. The deficiency provision follows stock ownership.

No-par stock. Because of deficiency assessments and other reasons, no-par stock was developed. No-par stock was first permitted by a New York State statute in 1912. When no-par stock is issued, it is carried on the balance sheet at the price at which the stock is sold or at some other stated value. Sometimes when no-par stock is sold, a paid-in surplus is created. For example, assume 1,000 shares are sold at $10 a share, a total of $10,000. The stated value of the common stock sold may be $8,000 with a paid-in surplus of $2,000.

No-par stock has several advantages. First, it avoids the problem of deficiency assessments. Second, it avoids misleading the investor who may feel that par value has some significance. The fact that par value is stated on the common stock certificate may lead some unwary and uninformed investors to feel that somehow the intrinsic worth of the stock is represented by its stated par value. Third, it may increase the marketability of the stock, since the company can sell additional shares of common stock at any time at whatever price the stock will bring.

Some possible disadvantages of no-par stock should be examined also. First, it is sometimes said that no-par stock may lead to possible manipulation of the accounts. Stock may be sold at $10 per share and carried on the books at $8, with a paid-in surplus for the difference. However, creation of surplus can also occur with par stock. For example, a company may sell stock at $8 per share; it may establish a par value of $5 per share, showing the difference of $3 as paid-in surplus. Whether stock is par value or no-par value thus has little fundamental influence on possible manipulation.

Second, if stock is sold at a price below the present stated value or book value of no-par stock, the value of the old stock may be diluted. But the book value of par stock can also be diluted if it is sold at less than book value. Typically, par value is less than book value; if a company has earned surplus, the book value of its stock will be greater than the par value.

For some years, no-par stock was taxed at $100 value for stock transfer tax purposes. This resulted in a trend toward the use of low-par stocks of $1 to $5. However, the stock transfer tax now is based on market prices. Hence no general advantage for the use or nonuse of a nominal value for common stock exists.

Forms of Common Stock

Classified common stock. Classified common stock was used extensively in the late 1920s, sometimes in ways that misled investors. During that period "Class A" common stock was usually nonvoting. "Class B" was typically full voting. Thus promoters could control companies by selling large amounts of Class A stock while retaining Class B stock.

In more recent years there has been a revival of Class B common for sound purposes. It is used by a small, new company seeking to acquire funds from outside sources. Common stock A is sold to the public, and typically pays dividends of a consistent amount; it has full voting rights. Common stock B, however, is retained by the organizers of the company, but dividends are not paid on it until the company has established its earning power. By the use of the classified stock the public can take a position in a conservatively financed growth company without sacrificing income.

Founders' shares. Founders' shares are somewhat like Class B stock except that they carry *sole* voting rights. Class A stock does not carry voting rights, but founders' shares do not have the right to dividends for a number of years. Thus the organizers of the firm are able to maintain complete control of the operations in the crucial initial development of the firm. At the same time, other investors are protected against excessive withdrawals of funds by owners.

EVALUATION OF COMMON STOCK AS A SOURCE OF FUNDS

The chapter has covered the main characteristics of common stock, frequently referred to as equity shares in the company. By way of a summary of the important aspects of common stock, common stock financing will be appraised from the standpoint of the issuer and as opposed to debt financing.

Advantages

First, common stock does not entail fixed charges. If the company generates the earnings, it can pay common stock dividends. However, in contrast to bond interest, there is no legal obligation to pay dividends.

Second, common stock carries no fixed maturity date.

Third, since common stock provides a cushion against losses for creditors, the sale of common stock increases the credit worthiness of the firm.

Fourth, common stock may at times be sold more easily. Common stock may appeal to certain investor groups for two reasons: (1) it typically carries a higher yield than does preferred stock or debt, and (2) it provides the investor with a better hedge against inflation than do straight preferred stock and bonds, because it represents the ownership in the firm. If the firm is in a net monetary debtor position, its common stock will increase in value when the value of real assets rises during an inflationary period.

Disadvantages

First, the sale of common stock extends voting rights or control to the additional stock owners who are brought into the company. For this reason, among others, additional equity financing is often avoided by small and new firms. The owner-managers may be unwilling to share control of their companies with outsiders.

Second, common stock gives new owners the right to share in income. The use of debt may enable the firm to utilize funds at a fixed low cost, whereas common stock gives equal rights to new stockholders to share in the net profits of the firm.

Third, the costs of underwriting and distributing common stock are usually higher than those for underwriting and distributing preferred stock or debt. Flotation costs for selling common stock are characteristically higher because, although certain investor groups may be interested in common stock, the broadest market for securities is for debt securities. Insurance companies, savings banks, and other investing institutions place a large proportion of their assets in debt; the potential market for debt securities is therefore greater than that for common stocks.

Fourth, common stock typically must be sold on a higher expected return basis than debt. When anticipated earnings or dividends are related to the price at which common stock is sold, the indicated yield is higher than the interest rate the firm would have to pay on debt.[4]

Fifth, common stock dividends are not deductible as an expense for calculating the corporations' income subject to the federal income tax, but bond interest is deductible.

Other Aspects of Equity Financing

Common stock also should be considered from a social standpoint. Common stock is a desirable form of financing because it renders firms,

---

[4] In an economy experiencing inflation, bond yields may be higher than stock yields. The reasoning is that the prices of common stock may be bid up to high levels because such stock is regarded as an effective inflation hedge.

hence a major segment of the economy, less vulnerable to the consequences of declines in sales and earnings. If sales and earnings decline, common stock financing involves no fixed charges, the payment of which might force the firm into reorganization or bankruptcy.

However, there is another aspect of common stock financing that may have less desirable social consequences. Common stock prices fall in recessions, and this causes a rise in the cost of equity capital. The rising cost of equity raises the over-all cost of capital, which in turn reduces investment. This reduction further aggravates the recession. On the other hand, an expanding economy is accompanied by rising stock prices, and with rising stock prices comes a drop in the cost of capital. This, in turn, stimulates investment and may be adding to a developing inflationary boom. In summary, a consideration of its effects on the cost of capital suggests that stock financing may tend to amplify cyclical fluctuations.

Just how these opposing forces combine to produce a net effect is unknown, but the authors believe that the first is the stronger; that is, stock financing tends to stabilize the economy.

DECISION MAKING IN COMMON STOCK FLOTATIONS

So far a number of characteristics of common stock financing have been presented. The advantages and disadvantages of external equity financing, compared with the use of preferred stock and debt, have been described. The purpose of the descriptive and background material has been to provide a basis for making sound decisions when financing by common stock is a possible alternative.

Chapters 11 and 12 have already provided a framework for analyzing the advantages and limitations to the use of debt financing versus equity financing. The more specific aspects influencing financing decisions will now be considered. Among the numerous factors involved, eight have particular importance:

1. Patterns of sales and profits
2. Growth rate of sales and profits
3. Existing financial position
4. Age of firm
5. Control considerations
6. Cash flow requirements
7. Costs
8. Restrictions associated with the financing agreement

An important factor influencing financing decisions is the industry of the firm. In part, a firm's industry determines many of the above characteristics. The industry characteristics will strongly influence the asset structure, which in turn will influence the extent to which the firm will have collateral or meet other requirements of particular forms of financing.

With respect to the eight factors listed, some favor common stock financing, others favor other forms. The influence of each factor will now be discussed.

If sales and profit patterns are highly volatile, such as in the durable-goods industries, common stock financing is favored. Rarely will firms with serious profit instability employ significant amounts of long-term debt. The risks of having to meet fixed charges will be too large.

The existing financial position of the company in relation to its optimal or "target" capital structure will be another crucial factor determining whether common stock will be employed. If the maximum debt ratio considered safe for the line of business is 50 percent and the firm already had a ratio of 60 percent, common stock financing will be indicated.

If the firm is new, it may have difficulty finding creditors willing to lend large sums on long term. The age of the firm may make equity financing the only available source. If the firm is established and its existing common stock is widely held, common stock financing will not raise problems of maintaining control of the company.

The absence of fixed interest or rental payments and the fact that there are no maturity and no sinking fund requirements will make future cash flows more stable with common stock financing. Although common stock is expected to pay dividends at some time, dividend payments are ordinarily not legally required, particularly if the earnings of the firm have been small.

The relative costs of common stock financing may be favorable at a particular point in time. If both stock prices and interest rates appear to be high, stock financing may be indicated. The converse is also true, of course, and Chapter 30 deals specifically with the timing of debt and equity issues.

Finally, debt financing may carry important disadvantages, such as loan agreements with restrictions on the management, including the requirement to maintain the current ratio at some prescribed level. Debt financing may call for collateral that is not available in the required amount or kind.

This discussion of eight factors important for decisions whether to use common stock financing when long-term funds are required may be regarded as a check list. Some factors will favor the use of common stock, but all need not be present to justify the selection of common stock. When some, but not all, of the conditions favoring common stock are present, the financial manager must exercise judgment in making the final decision. Differences in recommendations may arise because the decision, in part, depends upon such uncertain factors as the future level of the firm's sales and profits.

SUMMARY

Equity capital provides the foundation of a firm's operations, since it is the basis for obtaining other forms of financing. Equity funds carry the ultimate risk as well as the ultimate control and claim to the residual income of the business enterprise.

The main advantages of common stock from the point of view of the issuer are: it carries no maturity date, does not require payment of fixed charges, and increases the firm's base for obtaining other kinds of funds. The disadvantages are: present owners must share voting rights, and dividends are not deductible as an expense for tax purposes, as is bond interest.

Another useful method of summarizing the role of common stock is to identify the conditions that favor its use. Circumstances favoring the use of common stock are:

1. The firm's sales and profits fluctuate widely.
2. Profit margins do not cover the cost of debt.
3. The firm already has a high debt-equity ratio in relation to the prudent maximum for its line of business.
4. The firm is new, lacking access to debt financing.
5. Dilution of control of the firm is not a problem.
6. Cash flow considerations are important.
7. The relative costs of common stock financing are favorable.
8. Debt financing available would carry onerous loan-agreement restrictions.

SELECTED REFERENCES

Anderson, C. J., "Trends in the Supply of Equity Capital," *Harvard Business Review*, 28 (September 1950), pp. 79–89.

Baker, John C., "Stock Options at the Crossroads," *Harvard Business Review*, 41 (January-February 1963), pp. 22–31.

Butler, W. F., and R. P. Ulin, "Business Needs for Venture Capital," *Harvard Business Review*, 28 (July 1950), pp. 52–65.

Guthmann, H. G., "Dilution and Common Stock Financing," *Harvard Business Review*, 23 (Winter 1945), pp. 246–252.

Stevenson, Harold W., *Common Stock Financing* (Ann Arbor: University of Michigan, 1957).

QUESTIONS

17–1 By what percentage could total assets shrink in value on liquidation before creditors incurred losses in each of the following cases:

    1) Equity-to-total-asset ratio, 50 percent
    2) Debt-to-equity ratio, 50 percent
    3) Debt-to-total-asset ratio, 40 percent

17–2 Distinguish between stated value and par value.

17–3 What factors, if any, are relevant to the decision to use par-value common stock versus no par stock?

17–4 List several advantages to having a company's stock listed on a major stock exchange.

17–5 What difficulties do small firms encounter in raising equity capital?

17–6 What characteristics of a new common stock issue would make its purchase more attractive to prospective investors?

17–7 How many shares must a minority group possess in order to assure election of two directors if nine new directors will be elected and there are 200,000 shares outstanding? Assume cumulative voting exists.

17–8 Does the pre-emptive right entitle stockholders to purchase convertible bonds before they are offered to outsiders?

17–9 Each month the Securities and Exchange Commission publishes a report of the transactions by the officers and directors of listed firms in their own companies' equity securities. Why do you suppose the SEC makes this report?

17–10 The SEC forbids officers and directors to sell short the shares of their own company. Why do you suppose this rule is on the books? (A "short sale" involves the following sequence of events: (1) shares are borrowed from a broker and sold, (2) subsequently, shares are bought and repaid to the broker. The transaction is profitable if the shares are bought at a lower price than was received at the time of the short sale. For this to happen, the price of the stock must decline.)

PROBLEMS

17–1 The Green Giant Company is principally engaged in the business of growing, processing, and marketing a variety of canned and frozen vegetables and is a major company in this field. High-quality products are produced and marketed at premium prices.

During each of the past several years the company's sales have increased and the needed inventories have been financed from short-term sources. The officers have discussed the idea of refinancing their bank loans with long-term debt or common stock. A common stock issue of 310,000 shares, if sold in relation to the present market price of $24 per share, would yield $7.0 million after expenses. This same sum could be raised by selling 12-year bonds with an interest rate of 6½ percent and a sinking fund to retire the bonds over their 12-year life. (See ratios for canning industry in Appendix B at end of book).

1. Should Green Giant refinance the short-term loans? Why?

2. If the bank loans should be refinanced, what factors should be considered in determining which form of financing to be used?

GREEN GIANT COMPANY
CONSOLIDATED BALANCE SHEET
March 31, 1965
(in millions of dollars)

Current assets	$47	Accounts payable	$ 4	
Fixed plant and equipment	19	Notes payable	12	
Other assets	4	Accruals	5	
		Total current liabilities		$21
		Long-term debt, 5%		21
		Preferred stock	3	
		Common stock*	4	
		Retained earnings	21	
		Net worth		28
Total assets	$70	Total claims on assets		$70

* Stated value $2.

GREEN GIANT COMPANY
CONSOLIDATED STATEMENT OF INCOME
Year Ended March 31, 1965
(in millions of dollars)

	1962	1963	1964	1965
Net Sales	$75.0	$78.2	$97.6	$115.7
Cost of goods sold	48.7	52.2	65.1	76.8
Gross Profit	26.3	26.0	32.5	38.9
Other expenses	20.6	22.0	27.0	29.5
Operating Income	5.7	4.0	5.5	9.4
Other income (net)	(1.1)	(1.4)	(1.9)	(3.1)
Earnings before tax	4.6	2.6	3.6	6.3
Taxes	2.4	1.1	1.8	3.2
Net profit	2.2	1.5	1.8	3.1
Preferred dividend	0.1	0.1	0.1	0.1
Earnings available to common stock	$ 2.1	$ 1.4	$ 1.7	$ 3.0
Earnings per share	$ 1.05	$ 0.70	$0.85	$ 1.50
Cash dividends per share	0.43	0.48	0.53	0.60
Price range for common stock: H . .	22.00	23.00	22.00	27.00
L . .	10.00	14.00	17.00	21.00

17-2   Delta Air Lines, Inc., provides transcontinental service across the southern United States between Georgia and California. In 1962 Delta's domestic services were fifth in size among airlines of the United States. The company was seeking to raise $10 million for general corporate purposes. Relevant financial information is given below. The data have been altered slightly.

DELTA AIRLINES, INC.
BALANCE SHEET
June 30, 1961
(in millions of dollars)

Cash	$ 13.0	Accounts payable	$ 14.0
U. S. Government securities	4.0	Notes payable	6.0
Receivables	15.0	Accruals	10.0
Supplies	2.0	Total current	30.0
Other current assets	1.0	Long-term debt	90.0
Total current	35.0	Total debt	120.0
Net property	113.0	Common stock, par $3:	
Other assets	2.0	Outstanding: 1.5 million	
		shares	4.5
		Capital surplus	15.0
		Retained earnings	10.5
		Net worth	30.0
Total assets	$150.0	Total claims on assets . .	$150.0

INCOME DATA
(in millions of dollars)

	1961	1960	1959	1958
Sales	$150	$120	$104	$88
Earnings after tax available to common . .	4.5	3.0	4.0	1.0
Earnings per share	3.00	1.80	2.70	0.60
Dividends per share	0.90	0.90	0.45	0.70

Common stock could be sold for $45 per share. Sinking fund debentures (ten-year life) could be sold to yield 6 percent. Flotation costs would not be sufficient to affect the decision.

Which form of financing should Delta Air Lines use to raise the $10 million?

17–3 Pitney-Bowes has been practically the sole manufacturer of postage meters, which it leases or sells outright. Postage meters accounted for half of all the United States postage used by 1959. In addition, the company makes and sells a variety of mailing and business machines.

A few years ago the company incurred $6 million in short-term bank loans because of the expansion of its Stamford plant and offices. The officers of Pitney-Bowes discussed the desirability of refinancing the bank loans with long-term debt or common stock. Underwriters informed them that 20-year, 5½ percent sinking fund debentures or 200,000 shares of common stock could be sold to raise the desired funds. As the common stock was selling above $40 per share; the company could receive about $8,000,000 net from the sale of 200,000 shares. Financial data are shown below.

PITNEY-BOWES, INC.
CONSOLIDATED BALANCE SHEET
December 31, 1959*
(in millions of dollars)

Current assets $21	Accounts payable . . . . $ 4		
Fixed plant and equipment . . 29	Notes payable 6		
	Income taxes payable . . 3		
	Other accruals 2		
	Total current liabilities . . $15		
	Prepaid rental income (net) . . 7		
	Promissory notes, 3¾%, due in 1967 4		
	Cumulative preferred stock, $50 par, 4¼% 1		
	Common stock, $2 par value 8		
	Capital surplus 4		
	Retained earnings 11		
	Net worth 23		
Total assets $50	Total claims on assets . . . $50		

* The balance sheet and income statement figures have been altered to simplify the calculations.

PITNEY-BOWES, INC.

CONSOLIDATED STATEMENT OF INCOME
Years Ended December 31
(in millions of dollars)

		1956		1957		1958		1959
Sales (net)		17		17		20		22
Rental and service income . . .		26		29		31		33
Operating income		43		46		51		55
Cost of products sold	7		7		9		9	
Depreciation on rental equipment .	2		3		3		3	
Selling, administrative, and other expenses	26		27		30		33	
		35		37		42		45
Net operating income		8		9		9		10
Income taxes		4		5		5		5
Net profit for the period		4		4		4		5
Earnings per share of common . .		1.00		1.00		1.00		1.25
Cash dividends per common share .		0.50		0.52		0.53		0.60
Price range for common stock: H .		24		24		33		45
L .		15		15		18		35

1. Should Pitney-Bowes have refinanced the short-term bank loan? Why?

2. If you were to refinance the short-term loan, what factors would enter into your consideration of the two alternatives?

3. Indicate which means of refinancing you would suggest.

4. From Pitney-Bowes latest annual report or from Moody's, prepare a balance sheet and an income statement. (a) Discuss the changes in Pitney-Bowes' financial situation that have occurred since the financing took place in 1959. (b) What have been the major financing activities by Pitney-Bowes during the intervening period? (c) In the light of the events following 1959, which of the alternatives available to Pitney-Bowes in 1959 should have been selected?

Chapter 18

Preferred Stock

NATURE OF PREFERRED STOCK

Preferred stock has claims or rights ahead of common stock. The preference may be a prior claim on earnings; it may take the form of a prior claim on assets in the event of liquidation; or it may take a preferential position with regard to both earnings and assets.

Hybrid Form

The hybrid nature of preferred stock becomes apparent when one tries to classify it in relation to bonds and common stock. The priority feature and the (generally) fixed dividend indicate that preferred stock is similar to bonds. The stipulated dividend or limited share of income that accrues to the preferred stock is like interest, except that the dividends are not tax deductible and do not have to be paid when earnings are insufficient to meet them. The latter characteristic makes preferred stock similar to common stock, because failure to pay the stipulated dividend does not cause default of the obligation, as does failure to pay bond interest.

Debt and Equity

In some kinds of analysis preferred stock is treated as debt. For example, if the firm is considering the earnings fluctuations induced by fixed-charge securities, preferred stock would be treated as debt. But suppose the problem is analysis of the vulnerability to *failure* brought on by declines in sales or in income. Since the dividends on preferred stock are not a fixed charge in the sense that failure to pay them would represent a default of an obligation, preferred stock is not treated as debt. From the viewpoint of bondholders, preferred stock represents a cushion; it provides an additional equity base. Preferred stock may therefore be treated either as debt or as equity, depending on the nature of the problem under consideration.

MAJOR PROVISIONS OF PREFERRED STOCK ISSUES

The possible characteristics, rights, and obligations connected with any specific security vary widely, and a point of diminishing returns is quickly reached in a descriptive discussion of different kinds of securities. One need only look at the main terms and characteristics in each case and examine the possible variations in relation to the kinds of situations or circumstances in which they could occur.

As economic circumstances change, new kinds of securities are manufactured. The possibilities are numerous. The kinds and varieties of securities are limited chiefly by the imagination and ingenuity of the managers formulating the terms of the security issue.

It is not surprising, then, that preferred stock can be found in a variety of forms. The nature of these variations is analyzed by reference to the three pivotal provisions of security contracts: risk, income, and control.

Preferred Stock Provisions That Limit Risk

Priority in assets and earnings. Many provisions in a preferred stock certificate are designed to reduce risk to the purchaser relative to the risk carried by the holder of common stock. Preferred stock usually has priority with regard to earnings and assets. Two provisions designed to prevent undermining these preferred stock priorities are often found. The first states that, without the consent of the holders of the preferred stock, there can be no subsequent sale of securities that have a prior or equal claim on earnings. The second provision seeks to hold earnings in the firm. It requires a minimum level of retained earnings before common stock dividends are permitted. In order to assure the availability of liquid assets that may be converted into cash for the payment of dividends, the maintenance of a minimum current ratio may also be required.

Sinking fund requirements. Another risk limiting provision may be the requirement of a sinking fund. The sinking fund is usually used to facilitate an orderly retirement of the preferred stock. Since complex technical relations may be involved, a somewhat extended discussion of the use of sinking funds will be helpful in understanding their effective use.

With any type of so-called "fund," both a reserve and a fund may be created. If only a reserve is used, the accounting entry would be a debit to surplus and a credit to reserve for retirement of preferred stock. The reserve for sinking fund is earmarked surplus. By earmarking surplus funds, a company avoids stockholder pressure for payment of additional dividends when there is a large amount of surplus. A reserve for sinking fund, in itself, does not provide actual cash for retiring obligations either currently or at the maturity of the security itself. To retire obligations, an actual cash fund must be provided. If an actual cash fund is provided, the accounting entry is a debit to sinking fund and a credit to cash.

The funds from the sinking fund may be used to buy and retire the preferred stock. Typically the firm has the right (1) to call a certain percentage of the stock each year at a stated price, the actual shares to be determined by a lottery, or (2) to buy shares in the open market. The firm will do whichever results in the greatest reduction of shares for a given total of expenditures. When the securities are purchased, the securities or the obligation outstanding are debited and the sinking fund is credited. At the same time, a reversing entry is made debiting reserve for sinking fund and crediting surplus. The amount is the par or stated value of the preferred stock retired, with any necessary adjusting entries for any premiums or discounts that may be involved.

A cash fund has two advantages: (1) it gives some assurance that the obligations will be met, and (2) when the cash fund is used to buy the preferred stock, this provides a continuing market for the securities and at the same time reduces the floating supply of securities. Thus the cash fund is likely to have a buoyant influence on the market price of the securities so purchased.

On the other hand, it must be recognized that the call privilege associated with the fund may at times work to the detriment of preferred stockholders. If, for example, the stock carries a 7 percent dividend and if yields on similar securities are 4 percent, the stock will sell for well above par. A call at par would thus disadvantage preferred stockholders greatly. On balance, however, securities that provide for a cash fund and continuing redemption are likely to sell on a lower yield basis than do securities without such a fund. Sinking funds in this way provide additional protection to the potential investor, and the cost to the issuer of obtaining funds is therefore likely to be lower.

The disadvantage of a sinking fund requirement to the firm is that it constitutes a cash drain which may partially or substantially defeat the very purposes of financing. For this reason the best protection for holders of preferred stock and for bondholders may be the earning power of the firm. It is sufficient to use a reserve that earmarks surplus but not a cash fund that freezes cash.

If a security issue does contain a sinking fund requirement, it is better that it not be an inelastic requirement. The amount to be deposited to the sinking fund should be based on the gross revenue or the net earnings of the firm rather than be a fixed amount. If the amount deposited to the sinking fund is based on the income of the firm, it is related to the ability of the firm to set aside cash for the sinking fund. Even so, when the earnings of the firm are increasing because of increased sales, sometimes its capital needs may also be increased. Therefore even sinking fund payments based on sales or net income can constitute an embarrassing cash drain for the firm.

Preferred Stock Provisions Relating to Income

Participating. Some preferred stock is called participating preferred, because it shares in income with the common. For example, a preferred issue may carry a stipulated dividend rate of $6. The certificate also may provide that earnings in excess of the stipulated dividend will be shared among holders of preferred and common stock. If the firm earned $14 per share of preferred stock, the remaining $8 would be shared in some proportion by the two classes of stockholders. Some issues provide that after common stock has received a specified amount of dividends, the preferred stock will become participating. Participation, however, is not common— a very small percentage of preferred stocks is participating.

Cumulative. A high percentage of preferred stock dividends are cumulative—past and current preferred dividends not paid are payable before common dividends may be paid. The cumulative feature is therefore a protective device. If the preferred stock was not cumulative, preferred and common stock dividends could be passed by for a number of years. The company could then vote a large common stock dividend but only the stipulated payment to preferred stock. Suppose the preferred stock with a par value of $100 carried a 7 percent dividend. Suppose the company does not pay dividends for several years, so that it accumulates an amount which would enable it to pay in total about $50 in dividends. It could pay one $7 dividend to the preferred stock and a $43 dividend to the common stock. Obviously, this device could be used to evade the preference position that the holders of preferred stock have tried to obtain. The cumulative feature prevents such evasion.[1]

An illustrative list of preferred stocks and their arrearages is presented in Table 18–1. Such arrearages may develop because of poor earnings by the firm. Arrearages on preferred stock would make it difficult to resume dividend payments on common stock for a long time. To avoid

---

[1] Note, however, that compounding is absent in most cumulative plans. In other words, the arrearages themselves earn no return.

TABLE 18-1

LISTED DOMESTIC PREFERRED STOCK ISSUES IN ARREARS
As of January 1, 1961*

Issue	Approximate Arrearage Per Share	Approximate Arrearage Amount	Market Price 12/30/60	Cash Dividends Paid in 1960
Dividends Accrued for Less Than 10 Years				
Case (J. I.) Co.—7% pfd. . . .	$ 1.75	$ 162,586	$ 73¼	$7.00
Case (J. I.) Co.—6½% 2nd pfd.	0.11	131,878	3⅞	0.46
Chicago & Eastern Illinois—A	2.00	150,000	18½	nil
Erie-Lackawanna R.R.—5% A pfd.	6.25	782,000	26½	nil
N. Y., New Haven & Hartford —5% A	5.00	2,457,700	5½	nil
U. S. Hoffman Machinery—5% cum.	0.63	38,764	17	1.88
Van Norman Inds.—Cv. Pfd. .	0.57	88,523	28½	2.10
Dividends Accrued for 10 Years or More				
International Rys. of C.A.—5% cum.	$59.75	$ 5,975,000	$ 56¾	nil
Reis (Robt.) & Co.—$1.25 pfd.	15.00	1,241,700	12	nil
Virginia-Carolina Chem.—6% Part.	85.50	18,215,946	111	nil

* Includes all dividend declarations made in 1960.
Source: Exchange, 22 (March 1961), p. 16.

delays in resuming common stock dividend payments, a compromise arrangement with the holders of common stock is likely to be worked out.

A package offer is one possibility; for example, a recapitalization plan may provide for an exchange of shares. The arrearage will be wiped out by the donation of common stock with a value equal to the amount of the preferred stock arrearage; the holders of preferred stock are thus given an ownership share in the corporation. Whether this ownership share is worth anything depends on the future earnings prospects of the company. In addition, resumption of current dividends on the preferred may be promised.

The advantage to the company of substituting common stock for dividends in arrears is that it can start again with a clean balance sheet. If earnings recover, dividends can be paid to the holders of common stock without making up arrearages to the holders of preferred stock. The original common stockholders, of course, will have given up a portion of their ownership of the corporation.

Control

Voting. The third major feature of preferred stock is the control aspect. Preferred stock may be voting or nonvoting. Even when it is non-voting, the right to vote usually is given when the corporation does not pay preferred dividends for a specified number of quarters or years. Also, holders of preferred stock are sometimes given the right to vote if the firm does not comply with certain restrictions; for example, if the current ratio falls below some specified level or if debt rises to a certain amount in absolute terms.

Convertibility. One way of obtaining voting power over time is through convertibility. Convertibility conveys more than a potential right to vote; it also conveys an interest in the income accruing to common stock by permitting the conversion of preferred stock to common, thereby giving holders of preferred stock a share in any rise in the market value of the common stock. In the middle 1930s, when the SEC *Survey of American Listed Corporations* was made, only about one fourth of the outstanding preferred stocks was convertible. In recent years, however, the convertibility feature has become much more popular. The nature of convertibility is discussed in Chapter 22.

SUMMARY OF PREFERRED STOCK PROVISIONS

Preferred stock represents an attempt to combine the benefits of two forms of securities. It possesses some of the priorities of a senior security form without the fixed requirement on earnings possessed by debt instruments. Although the possible variations in preferred stock characteristics are wide, a limited set of provisions predominates in practice. These are listed in summary form in Table 18–2.

TABLE 18–2

USUAL PROVISIONS OF PREFERRED STOCK

1. Nonparticipating
2. Nonvoting
3. Claim to assets in liquidation prior to common stock
4. Cumulative
5. No maturity
6. Callable
7. No sinking fund

1. Preferred stock is ordinarily nonparticipating; that is, holders of preferred stock are entitled to their stipulated dividend but do not ordinarily share in the residual income of the enterprise. Exceptions to this

generalization can be found in which the preferred stock receives a stipulated dividend, and after the common stock has received an equal dividend, any further dividend will be received in predetermined amounts by the two forms of financing.

2. Preferred stock is usually nonvoting by provision. Often, however, the preferred stock certificate will provide that in the event preferred stock dividends are missed for a specified number of quarters (for example, if six to eight quarterly payments are missed), the holders of preferred stock may elect a substantial portion of the directors of the corporation. This provision is for the purpose of permitting participation for the preferred stockholders in policy changes that may correct the conditions which have caused the inability to meet dividend payments.

3. Usually preferred stock has a priority over the common in earnings and in assets on liquidation.

4. The customary status is for preferred stock to be cumulative.

5. Typically, the preferred stock has no maturity, but is usually callable.

6. Callability must be provided for explicitly if it is to obtain.

7. Although sinking funds are probably found in less than 50 percent of the new issues of preferred stock, they are often provided for in industrial preferred issues to lend strength to the issue. They are less frequently found in issues of utility companies. Of course, explicit provision must be made for sinking funds.

In summary, preferred stock customarily has a prior claim on earnings and assets. Dividends on preferred stock typically cumulate, if unpaid, but are usually nonparticipating. Preferred stock does not ordinarily carry a maturity, but is callable and often provides for a sinking fund.

EVALUATION OF PREFERRED STOCK AS A SOURCE OF FINANCING

Appraisal from Standpoint of Issuer

Advantages. An important advantage of preferred stock from the standpoint of the issuer is that, in contrast to bonds, the obligation to make fixed interest payments is avoided. Also, a firm wishing to expand because its earning power is high may obtain higher earnings for the original owners by selling preferred stock with a limited return rather than by selling common stock.

By selling preferred stock the financial manager avoids the provision of equal participation in earnings that the sale of additional common stock would require. Preferred stock also permits a company to avoid sharing control through participation in voting. In contrast to bonds, it enables the firm to conserve mortgageable assets. Preferred stock is often sold on a lower yield basis than is common stock. Since preferred stock typically has no maturity, it is more flexible than bonds. Since it can be called, it is more flexible than common stock.

Disadvantages. There are several disadvantages associated with preferred stock. Characteristically, it must be sold on a higher yield basis than that for bonds. Preferred stock dividends are not deductible as a tax expense, a characteristic which makes their cost differential very great in comparison with that of bonds. Suppose that a corporation subject to a 50 percent tax is seeking to raise $10 million. If it is assumed that bonds could be sold at 4 percent, the annual interest cost on the bonds would be $400,000. If the preferred stock could be sold at 5 percent, the cost of the preferred stock would be $500,000. Since bond interest is an expense for tax purposes, it reduces income subject to taxes by $400,000. If the firm is to pay preferred stock dividends of $500,000, it must earn $1 million before taxes. After it pays the 50 percent tax, it has income of $500,000 available for preferred stock dividends. To pay $400,000 bond interest, the firm need earn only $400,000 before taxes. After payment of the bond interest, the firm has no income subject to tax. Thus the 5-to-4 ratio in preferred dividends to bond interest is magnified to a 10-to-4 ratio of required before-tax income.

Appraisal from Standpoint of Investor

In fashioning securities, the financial manager needs to consider the investor's point of view. Frequently it is asserted that preferred stocks have so many disadvantages both to the issuer and to the investor that they should never be issued. Nevertheless, preferred stock is issued in substantial amounts. In fact, between 1930 and 1950, more preferred stock was issued and sold than common stock.

From the standpoint of the investor, preferred stock provides the following advantages. (1) Preferred stocks provide reasonably steady income of a higher amount than do bonds. (2) Numerous examples can be cited where the prior-preference position of holders of preferred stock saved them from losses incurred by holders of common stock. (3) Many corporations (for example, insurance companies) like to hold preferred stocks because 85 percent of the dividends received on these shares are not taxable.

There are also some disadvantages. (1) Although the holders of preferred stock bear a substantial portion of ownership risk, their returns are limited. (2) Price fluctuations in preferred stock are far greater than those in bonds; yet yields from bonds are only moderately lower than those from preferred stock. (3) There is no legally enforceable right to dividends. (4) Accrued dividend arrearages are seldom settled in cash comparable to the amount of the obligation that has been incurred.

Preferred stocks are sold because, from the standpoint of the purchaser, they carry a higher yield. From the standpoint of the issuer, they enable the issuer to obtain funds on which a limited dividend is paid, without incurring the risk of default in periods of low earnings.

Because of the nondeductibility of preferred stock dividends as a tax expense, many companies have retired their preferred stock. Often debentures or subordinated debentures will be offered to preferred stockholders in exchange. The interest on the debentures is deductible as a tax expense, while preferred stock dividends are not deductible.

When the preferred stock is not callable, the company must offer terms of exchange that are sufficiently attractive to induce the preferred stockholders to agree to the exchange. Characteristically, the offer on the part of the company to induce stockholders to exchange their preferred stock is along the following lines. Debentures or other securities in an amount something over the recent value of the preferred stock will be issued in exchange. Sometimes debentures equal in market value to the preferred stock will be issued, plus cash or common stock to provide an extra inducement to the preferred stockholders. Sometimes the offer will be debentures or subordinated debentures equal to only a portion of the current market value of the preferred with an additional amount, represented by cash or common stock, that will bring the total amount offered to the preferred stockholders to something over its market value as of a recent date.

The replacement of its 7 percent preferred stock by U.S. Steel in 1965 illustrates one of the above exchange patterns. U.S. Steel proposed that its 7 percent preferred stock be changed into 4⅝ percent 30-year debentures at a rate of $175 principal amount of debentures for each preferred share. On August 17, 1965, when the plan was announced, the preferred stock had sold at $152. By September 29, 1965, when it was announced that the plan would be submitted to stockholders of record of October 8, 1965, at a special meeting on November 24, 1965, the preferred stock sold at $170. U.S. Steel announced also that the conversion would increase earnings available to common stock by $10 million yearly, or 18 cents a share at 1965 federal income tax rates.

These trends have reduced the use of preferred stock. But a countertrend has been the use of convertible preferred stock in mergers.[2] The principal reasoning here involves two considerations. First, the owners of the acquired firm frequently are willing to sell out because they are seeking to get away from the worries associated with ownership and management. Consequently, they can be more easily induced to sell out if they are

---

[2] Convertibles are discussed in detail in Chapter 22 and financial aspects of mergers in Chapter 27.

offered a fixed income security. Second, if bonds (or cash) are offered for the shares of the acquired firm, then the selling stockholders must pay a capital gains tax on any proceeds received in excess of their cost basis. Frequently this would involve a heavy capital gains tax liability. If the exchange is convertible preferred stock of the acquiring company for common stock of the acquired firm, the exchange can qualify for exemption on the capital gains liability. In this manner the stockholders of the acquired firm can receive a fixed income security, avoid an immediate capital gains liability, and receive additional benefits from the conversion feature if the price of the acquiring firm's common stock rises.

DECISION MAKING ON USE OF PREFERRED STOCK

The circumstances favoring the use of preferred stock can now be distilled from the foregoing analysis. As a hybrid security type, the use of preferred stock is favored by conditions that fall between those favoring the use of common stock and those favoring the use of debt.

When a firm's profit margin is high enough to more than cover preferred stock dividends, it will be advantageous to employ leverage. However, if the firm's sales and profits are subject to considerable fluctuations, the use of debt with fixed interest charges may be considered unduly risky. Preferred stock may offer a happy compromise. The use of preferred stock will be strongly favored if the firm already has a debt ratio that is heavy relative to the reference level maximum for the line of business.

Issuing preferred stock enables utility companies to increase the degree of leverage employed, but limits the amount of fixed interest charges. The tax disadvantage of preferred stock is less applicable for utility companies, since rate-making procedures result in allowable rates of return after taxes.

Relative costs of alternative sources of financing are always important considerations. When the price-earnings ratios of common stocks are relatively low, the costs of common stock financing are relatively high. The costs of preferred stock financing follow interest rate levels more than common stock prices. When the costs of income instruments such as preferred stock are low and the costs of variable value securities such as common stock are high (price-earnings ratios are low), the use of preferred stock is favored.

Preferred stock may also be the desired form of financing when the use of debt would involve excessive risk and the issuance of common stock might result in problems of control for the dominant ownership group in the company.

SUMMARY

The characteristics of preferred stock vary with the requirements of the situation under which it is issued. However, certain patterns tend to obtain. Preferred stocks usually have priority over common stocks with respect to earnings and claims on assets in liquidation. Preferred stocks are usually cumulative; they have no maturity but are callable. They are typically nonparticipating and have only contingent voting rights.

The advantages to the issuer are limited dividends and no maturity. These advantages may outweigh the disadvantages of higher cost and the nondeductibility of the dividends as an expense for tax purposes. But their acceptance by investors is the final test of whether they can be sold on favorable terms.

Preferred stocks are sold by utility companies because rate-making procedures take into consideration requirements for preferred stock dividends. Industrial companies sell preferred stock when they seek the advantages of trading on the equity, but fear the dangers of the fixed charges on debt in the face of potential fluctuations in income. If debt ratios are already high or if the costs of common stock financing are relatively high, the advantages of preferred stock will be reinforced.

SELECTED REFERENCES

Donaldson, Gordon, "In Defense of Preferred Stock," *Harvard Business Review,* 40 (July-August 1962), pp. 123–136.

Fergusson, D. A., "Preferred Stock Valuation in Recapitalizations," *Journal of Finance,* 13 (March 1958), pp. 48–69.

——, "Recent Developments in Preferred Stock Financing," *Journal of Finance,* 7 (September 1952), pp. 447–462.

Wilsey, H. L., "The Use of Sinking Funds in Preferred Stock Issues," *Journal of Finance,* 2 (October 1947), pp. 31–42.

QUESTIONS

18–1 If preferred stock dividends are passed for several years, the preferred stockholders are frequently given the right to elect several members of the board of directors. However, this same situation does not hold true in the case of bonds that are in default on interest payments. Why do you suppose this difference exists?

18–2 Preferred stocks are found in almost all industries, but one industry is the really dominant issuer of preferred shares. What is this industry, and why are firms in it so disposed to use preferred stock?

18–3 From the point of view of the issuing firm, what are some of the advantages of preferred stock?

18–4 If the corporate income tax was abolished, would this raise or lower the amount of new preferred stock issued?

18–5 Investors buying securities have some expected or required rate of return in mind. Which do you suppose is higher, the required rate of return (before taxes) on preferred stocks or on common stocks for (1) individual investors and (2) corporate investors (for example, insurance companies)?

18–6 Do you think the before-tax required rate of return is higher or lower on very high-grade preferred stocks or on bonds for (1) individual investors and (2) corporate investors?

18–7 Discuss the pros and cons of a preferred stock sinking fund from the points of view of (1) the issuing corporation and (2) a preferred stockholder.

18–8 For purposes of measuring a firm's leverage, should preferred stock be classified as debt or as equity? Does it matter if the classification is being made by (1) the firm itself, (2) creditors, or (3) equity investors?

PROBLEMS

18–1 In late 1963 the Brockton Edison Company of Massachusetts sought to raise $4 million to refinance present preferred stock issues at a lower rate. The company is a member of the Eastern Utilities Associates Holding Company System. The company could sell additional debt at 5 percent, preferred stock at 4.64 percent, or common stock at $40 per share. How should the company raise the money? Relevant financial information is provided below.

BROCKTON EDISON COMPANY
BALANCE SHEET
July 31, 1963
(in millions of dollars)

Cash	$ 0.5	Current Liabilities		$ 2.0
Receivables	1.0	Long-term debt (3.5%)		18.0
Material and supplies	0.8	Preferred stock (5.60%)		4.0
Total current	2.3	Common stock—par value $25.		7.5
Net property	37.7	Premium on common		4.4
		Earned surplus		4.1
Total assets	$40.0	Total claims		40.0

BROCKTON EDISON COMPANY
INCOME STATEMENT
For Year Ended July 31, 1963
(in millions of dollars)

Operating revenues	$12.6
Operating expenses (incl. taxes)	10.5
Net operating income	2.1
Interest deductions	0.6
Net income	1.5
Earnings per share	5.0

18–2 Genesco, Inc., is a manufacturer of apparel and footwear. Although principally a manufacturer of shoes, it has in recent years acquired a number of companies that make men's and women's apparel.

The company seeks to retire its 4.5 percent unsecured notes due in 1963 and its outstanding 5 percent notes due in 1969. A substantial amount of funds ($10 million) from new financing is earmarked for additions to working capital and retirement of short-term bank notes as they mature. Genesco can issue new debt at 5½ percent, a cumulative preferred stock issue at 4.5 percent, or common stock at $30 per share. Total new financing is expected to be $20 million. How should the company raise the money? Relevant financial data are given below. Some data have been slightly changed.

GENESCO, INC.
CONSOLIDATED BALANCE SHEET
July 31, 1962
(in millions of dollars)

Current assets	$150	Current liabilities	$ 40
Plant and equipment (net)	28	Long-term debt	60
Other assets	22	Preferred stock ($4.50)	10
		Common stock ($1 par value)	3
		Paid-in capital	42
		Retained earnings	45
Total assets	$200	Total claims	$200

GENESCO, INC.
CONSOLIDATED INCOME STATEMENT
For Year Ending July 31, 1962
(in millions of dollars)

Net sales and other income	$400
Cost of sales and expenses	381
Earnings before interest and taxes	19
Taxes and interest ($3)	10
Net income	9
Earnings per share	3
Dividends	2

Chapter 19

Long-Term Debt

DEBT VERSUS EQUITY FINANCING

In Chapters 11 and 12 the major factors determining the extent to which a firm will trade on the equity (utilize debt) were set out. It was noted that the use of debt magnifies gains and losses. Up to a range that varies with the characteristics of the firm's line of activity, additional debt is likely to provide advantageous financial leverage. Beyond that point, the use of debt is likely to be hazardous or expensive, or both.

Since every firm is likely to employ debt to some degree, it is useful to examine the various forms and characteristics of debt so that the financial manager may employ it most effectively. Section IV has already analyzed the use of some forms of debt financing. The present chapter deals with types and forms of long-term-debt securities.

INSTRUMENTS OF LONG-TERM-DEBT FINANCING

To understand long-term forms of financing, some familiarity with technical terminology is necessary. However, the presentation will be limited to only that descriptive material necessary to analyze important problems and to formulate financial policies. The discussion of long-term debt therefore begins with an explanation of several important instruments.

Six Key Concepts

Bond. Most people have had some contact with an ordinary promissory note, which is usually a short-term note. A bond is a long-term promissory note.

Mortgage. The word mortgage is derived from the French: *mort,* dead; *gage,* pledge. This conveys the idea of a legal claim (also called *lien*) on specified assets. A mortgage represents a pledge of designated property for a loan. Under a mortgage bond the corporation pledges certain real assets as security for the promise made in the bond. A mortgage bond is therefore secured by real property.[1] The pledge of security is a condition of the loan.

Debenture. A *debenture* is long-term debt that is unsecured in the sense that it lacks any specific pledge of property. However, like other general creditor claims, it is secured by any property not otherwise pledged.

Funded debt. Funded debt is simply long-term debt. When a firm is said to be planning to "fund" its floating debt, it will replace short-term securities by long-term securities. Funding does not imply placing money with a trustee or other repository. Funding means long term.

Indenture. Since a bond is a long-term promissory note, a long-term relation between borrower and lender is established. When it is a matter of an ordinary 60- or 90-day promissory note, few new developments are likely to occur in the life or affairs of the borrower to endanger repayment. The lender looks closely at the borrower's current position, because current assets are the main source of repayment. But a bond is a contractual relation between the issuer of the bond and the bondholders for a long duration.

In the ordinary common stock or preferred stock certificate or agreement, the details of the contractual relation can be summarized in a few paragraphs. The bond indenture, however, may be a document of several hundred pages and is considered a part of the single-page bond certificate actually received by the bondholder.

The indenture covers a large number of factors that will be important to the contractual parties. It discusses the form of the bond and the instrument. It provides a complete description of property pledged. The authorized amount of the bond issue is specified. Protective clauses or covenants are detailed. These include the following: (1) a pledge to keep the property in good repair; (2) a pledge to pay taxes on the property so that the pledged property is not taken by the government and therefore lost as security; (3) limits on indebtedness; (4) restrictions on dividends; (5) sometimes a minimum current-ratio requirement during the bonded indebtedness; (6) a sinking fund provision; (7) sometimes provisions for redemption or call privileges.

Not only is the bond of long duration, but the issue is also likely to be of substantial size. Before the rise of the large aggregations of savings

---

[1] There are also *chattel mortgages,* which are secured by personal property, but these are intermediate-term instruments.

through insurance companies or pension funds, no single buyer was able to buy an issue of such size. Bonds were therefore issued in denominations of $1,000 each and sold to a large number of purchasers. To facilitate communication between the issuer and the numerous bondholders, another device was utilized—the trustee.

Trustee. The trustee is the representative of the bondholders. He is presumed to act at all times for their protection and on their behalf.

Any legal person is considered competent to act as a trustee. Typically, however, the duties of the trustee are handled by a department of a commercial bank. It is interesting to observe that the trustee is usually appointed by the corporation before the bonds are sold. There is something of an anomaly here. Although the trustee is supposed to represent the bondholders, he is actually appointed by the issuer. The would-be bondholder can, however, veto the issuer's choice, if it is a bad one, by simply refusing to purchase the bonds. This tends to ensure the selection of competent trustees.

The trustee has three main responsibilities. (1) The trustee certifies the issue of bonds. This duty involves making certain that all the legal requirements for drawing up the bond contract and the indenture have been carried out. (2) The trustee polices the behavior of the corporation in its performance of the responsibilities set forth in the indenture provision. (3) The trustee is responsible for taking appropriate action on behalf of the bondholders if the corporation should default on payment of interest or principal.

In the large number of corporate bond defaults in the early 1930s, it is said that trustees did not act in the best interests of the bondholders. The trustees did not conserve the assets of the corporation effectively. Often they did not take early action, so that corporation executives continued their salaries and disposed of assets under favorable conditions for themselves but to the detriment of bondholders. Assets pledged as security for the bonds were sold; specific security was thus no longer available. The result in many instances was that holders of mortgage bonds found themselves more in the position of general creditors than secured bondholders.

As a consequence of such practices, the Trust Indenture Act of 1939 was passed in order to give more protection to bondholders. The Act of 1939 provides that trustees must be given sufficient power to act on behalf of bondholders. The indenture must fully disclose rights and responsibilities and not be deceptive. There is provision for changes in the indenture at the option of the bondholders. A specific requirement of prompt, protective action on the part of the trustees for bondholders on default is made. Provision is made for making certain that an arm's-length relation between the issuing corporation and the trustee exists. The obligor may not own more than 10 percent of the common stock of the trustee, nor the trustee more than 5 percent of the voting stock of the obligor. Finally, the corporation must make periodic reports to trustees to enable them to carry out their protective responsibilities.

CLASSIFICATION OF SECURED LONG-TERM DEBT

Long-term debt may be classified according to (1) the priority of claims, (2) the right to issue additional securities, and (3) the scope of lien.

Priority of Claims

1. A senior mortgage is a mortgage with prior claims on assets and earnings. Senior railroad mortgages have been called the mortgages next to the rail, implying that they have the first claim on the land and assets of the railroad corporations. An underlying mortgage is typically a first mortgage with a lien prior to other claims. An underlying mortgage is equivalent to a senior mortgage.

2. A junior mortgage is a subordinate lien, such as a second or a third mortgage. It is a lien or claim junior to others.

3. Subordinated debt is unsecured debt junior to other general or unsecured debt, generally bank credit.

Right to Issue Additional Securities

Mortgage bonds may also be classified with respect to the right to issue additional obligations pledging already encumbered property.

In the case of a *closed-end mortgage* a company may not sell additional bonds, beyond those already issued, secured by the property specified in the mortgage. For example, assume a corporation with plant and land worth $5 million has a bond of $2 million on these properties. If the mortgage is closed end, no more bonds having first liens on this property may be issued. Thus a closed-end mortgage provides greater security to the bond buyer. The ratio of the amount of the senior bonds to the value of the property will not be increased by subsequent issues.

If the bond indenture is silent on this point, it is called an *open-end mortgage*. Its nature may be illustrated by the facts of the example cited. Against property worth $5 million, bonds of $2 million are sold. If an additional first-mortgage bond of $1 million is subsequently sold, the property has been pledged for a total of $3 million bonds. If, on liquidation, the property sold for $2 million, the original bondholders would receive 67 cents on the dollar. If the mortgage had been closed end, they would have been fully paid.

Most characteristic is the *limited open-end mortgage*. Its nature may be indicated by continuing the example. A first-mortgage bond issue of $2 million is sold secured by the property worth $5 million. The indenture provides that an additional $1 million worth of bonds—or an additional amount of bonds up to 60 percent of the original cost of the property—may be sold. Thus the mortgage is open only up to a certain point.

These are some of the ways in which the limited feature of an open-end mortgage may be expressed. The limited open-end mortgage is flexible in that it provides for the issuance of additional securities. At the same time it limits this right; thus the original bondholder is protected.

Scope of the Lien

Bonds may also be classified with respect to the scope of their lien. When it is a matter of a *specific lien,* the security for a first mortgage or a second mortgage is a specific designation of property. A lien is granted on certain described property. On the other hand, a *blanket mortgage* pledges all real property currently owned by the company. The definition of real property is land and those things affixed thereto. Hence it would not be a mortgage on cash, accounts receivables, or inventories, but only on real property. Inventories are regarded as personal property. A blanket mortgage gives more protection to the bondholder than a specific mortgage, because it provides a claim on all real property owned by the company.

An even stronger claim is provided by a blanket mortgage with an *after-acquired-property clause.* The after-acquired-property clause provides that the bond will be a lien not only against all real property currently owned, but also against all real property subsequently acquired. In order to sell bonds at lower cost, corporations will sometimes provide an after-acquired-property clause in the bond indenture. If the corporation later needs to sell additional bonds, it would be difficult to do so, because the existing bonds already have a first lien on all property owned and subsequently acquired by the company.

Avoiding After-Acquired Property Clause

Several methods have been developed to avoid the after-acquired property clause.

Lease. One way is to lease additional property. Under a lease arrangement the corporation has the use of the property, but does not own it. Hence the company is able to have the use of resources without the necessity of financing its acquisition. Additional financing would be difficult because of the after-acquired-property clause in the existing mortgage.

Subsidiary. The corporation may avoid the after-acquired-property clause by creating a subsidiary company. A separate company may be formed by ownership of 100 percent or less of the common stock. The after-acquired property clause of the current company would not apply to the property of the subsidiary even if it is 100 percent owned by the mortgaged corporation.

Purchase-money mortgage. The purchase-money mortgage differs from an ordinary mortgage in two respects: first, the lender is likewise the vendor of the property. In other words, the mortgage is held by the person who sold the property. Second, the mortgage encumbers the property before it comes into the possession and into the equitable ownership of the purchaser and borrower; thus the property comes to the borrower already encumbered with the mortgage. An existing mortgage which may contain an after-acquired-property clause will at best have a second-mortgage claim on the encumbered portion of the property acquired with a purchase-money mortgage.

Refinancing. A fourth method of avoiding the after-acquired-property clause would be to engage in a refinancing operation. The corporation might call in the outstanding bonds, retire them, and then issue another set of bonds, larger in amount and without the after-acquired-property clause.

Merger. A fifth method of avoiding the after-acquired property clause is through merger or consolidation. Typically, the after-acquired-property clause is written so that it is not effective on merger or consolidation. The new mortgage covenants written for the firm which arise out of the merger or consolidation can omit the after-acquired-property clause.

Since the promises of the after-acquired-property clause are far-reaching, the financial manager should avoid using it. Since its provisions can be easily avoided, the investor should not attach much value to the promises.

These remarks end the discussion of characteristics of secured bonds. The variables mentioned determine the amount of protection given to the creditor. Therefore differences in the form of the indenture and in the scope of the lien will influence the rate of interest that will have to be paid by the issuing firm. These protective provisions also influence the rating which the bond receives from agencies such as Moody's or Standard and Poor's.

UNSECURED BONDS

Debentures

The debenture is an unsecured bond, and as such provides no lien on specific property as security for the obligation. Debenture holders are therefore general creditors whose claim is protected by property not otherwise pledged. The advantage from the standpoint of the issuer is that he leaves his property unencumbered for subsequent financing. However, in practice, the use of debentures appears to be a matter of style for certain industries.

If the credit positions of the leading companies in the industry are exceptionally strong, the firms may be able to issue debentures. Sometimes when the credit position of companies is unusually weak, they will have no alternative to issuing debentures. This is something of a paradox. The rate of interest on debentures sold by a strong company will be close to the prime rate of interest. In the opposite situation, the rate of interest will be very high.

American Telephone & Telegraph's vast financing program since the end of World War II has been mainly through debentures, both convertible and straight debentures. AT&T is such a strong institution that it does not have to provide security for its debt issues.

Debentures are also often issued by companies in industries where it would not be practicable to provide a lien through a mortgage on fixed assets. Such an industry would be the large mail order houses, which characteristically do not have large fixed assets in relation to their total assets. The bulk of their assets are in the form of inventory, which is not satisfactory security for a mortgage lien.

Subordinated Debentures

Debentures may be subordinated to designated notes payable—usually bank loans—or to all other debt. In the event of liquidation or reorganization the debentures cannot be paid until senior debt as named in the indenture has been paid. Senior debt typically does not include trade accounts payable. How the subordination provision strengthens the position of senior-debt holders is shown by Table 19–1.

Where $200 is available for distribution, the subordinated debt has a claim of one half of $100, or $50. However, this claim is subordinated to the senior debt and is added to the $100 claim of the senior debt. As a consequence, 75 percent of the original claim of the senior debt is satisfied.

Where $300 is available for distribution, the $75 allocated to the subordinated debt is broken into two parts: $50 goes to the senior-debt holders and the other $25 remains for the subordinated-debt holders. In this situation, the senior-debt holders are fully paid off, 75 percent of other debt is paid, and the subordinated debt receives only 25 percent of its claim.

Subordination has long been required. Alert credit managers or commercial-bank loan officers typically will insist upon subordination, particularly where debt is owed to the principal stockholders or officers of a company.

The wide use of subordinated securities was initiated by finance companies in the mid-1930s and developed greatly since that time because they perform a particularly useful role for a finance company. A rough rule of thumb is that commercial banks will lend finance companies three times the amount of the finance company's own capital. Thus, if the

TABLE 19-1

ILLUSTRATION OF LIQUIDATING PAYMENTS TO SENIOR DEBT,
OTHER DEBT, AND SUBORDINATED DEBT

Capital Structure	Claim	Initial Allocation Amount	Actual Payment	Percentage of Original Debt Satisfied
$200 available				
Bank debt	$200	$100	$150	75%
Other debt	100	50	50	50
Subord. debt. . . .	100	50	0	0
Net worth	300	0	0	0
	$700	$200	$200	
$300 available				
Bank debt	$200	$150	$200	100%
Other debt	100	75	75	75
Subord. debt. . . .	100	75	25	25
Net worth	300	0	0	0
	$700	$300	$300	

Source: Robert W. Johnson, "Subordinated Debentures: Debt That Serves as Equity," *Journal of Finance,* 10 (March 1955), p. 3.

finance company has $10 million of its own capital, it may obtain $30 million in loans through commercial paper issues and commercial bank loans. Wide use of equity funds by finance companies would lower their return on net worth, because they operate with a small margin between what money costs them and what they can earn with it.

Preferred stock, in comparison to subordinated debt, suffers from the disadvantage that preferred stock dividends are not deductible as an expense for tax purposes. The interest on subordinated debentures is an expense for tax purposes. Some people have referred to subordinated debentures as preferred stock, the dividends on which are deductible as an expense for tax purposes. Subordinated debt has therefore been a rising percentage of the total financing of finance companies.

The reasons for the use of subordinated debentures are clear. They offer a considerable tax advantage over preferred stock, and yet they do not inhibit the ability of the borrower to obtain senior debt to a degree that would obtain if all debt sources were on an equal basis.

The amount of subordinated debt that may be employed is limited, as is the amount of any form of debt. In the finance industry, there appears to be a requirement that net worth be 150 to 200 percent of subordinated debt. The rule of thumb employed by investment bankers in connection with industrial issues of subordinated debentures appears to be closer to the upper ratio of net worth to subordinated debt of 200 percent rather than the lower one.

Subordinated debentures are further stimulated by periods of tight money, when commercial banks may require a greater equity base for short-term financing. Subordinated debentures provide a greater equity cushion for loans from commercial banks or other forms of senior debt. The use of subordinated debentures also illustrates the development of hybrid securities which emerge to meet changing situations that develop in the capital market.

Income and Adjustment Bonds

Income and adjustment bonds typically arise from corporate reorganizations. Such bonds characteristically pay interest only if income is actually earned by the company, because the company, having gone through reorganization, has been in difficult financial circumstances. Interest is not a fixed charge; the principal, however, must be paid when due.

Income bonds are like preferred stock in that management is not required to pay interest if it is not earned. However, they differ from preferred stock in that if interest has been earned, management is usually required to pay it. In recent years, income bonds have been increasingly used as a source of ordinary financing.[2]

The main characteristic and distinct advantage of the income bond is that interest is payable only if the company achieves some earnings. Since earnings calculations are subject to differing interpretations, the indenture of the income bond carefully defines income and expenses. If it were not to do so, long-drawn-out litigation might ensue.

Some income bonds are cumulative for a limited number of years; others are noncumulative for the first three to five years, after which time they become cumulative. Some issues are fully cumulative.

Income bonds usually contain sinking fund provisions to provide for their retirement. The payments to the sinking funds range between $\frac{1}{2}$ and 1 percent of the face amount of the original issue. Because the sinking fund payments are typically dependent on earnings, a fixed-cash drain on the company is avoided.

Sometimes income bonds are convertible. There are sound reasons for their being convertible if they arise out of a reorganization. Creditors who receive income bonds in exchange for defaulted obligations have a less desirable position than they had before. Since they have received something based on an adverse and problematical forecast of the future of the company, it is appropriate that if the company should prosper, income

---

[2] See Sidney M. Robbins, "A Bigger Role for Income Bonds," *Harvard Business Review*, 33 (November–December 1955), pp. 100–114.

bondholders should be entitled to participate. When income bonds are issued in situations other than reorganization, the convertibility feature is a "sweetener" likely to make the issue more attractive to prospective bond buyers.

Typically, income bonds do not have voting rights when they are issued. Sometimes bondholders are given the right to elect one, two, or some specified number of directors if interest is not paid for a certain number of years.

Income bonds have been used instead of preferred stock in situations other than reorganization. Armour & Company has made repeated use of such bonds.[3] In 1943, Armour used subordinated income bonds to substitute for a preferred stock issue. At the close of 1954, Armour replaced convertible preferred stock with dividend arrearages by 5 percent cumulative income bonds subordinated to other debt, with a warrant to buy common stock. The replacement of preferred stock by income bonds resulted in a substantial tax saving for the company.

CHARACTERISTICS OF LONG-TERM DEBT

From Viewpoint of Holder

A critical framework for analyzing the position of any security holder in a corporation includes aspects of risk, control, and income.

Risk. Debt is favorable to the holder because it gives him priority in earnings and priority in liquidation. Debt also has a definite maturity and is protected by the covenants of the indenture.

Income. The bondholder has a fixed return; it is not contingent on the level of earnings of the company. On the other hand, debt does not participate in any superior earnings of the company, and gains are limited in magnitude. Frequently long-term debt is callable. If bonds are called, the investor receives funds which must be reinvested to be kept active.

Control. The bondholder typically does not have the right to vote. Yet there are periods when a substantial portion of bonds sold are convertible bonds. If bonds are convertible into common stock, under certain conditions the bondholder may obtain the position of an equity holder rather than a debt holder.

An over-all appraisal of the characteristics of long-term debt would therefore show that it is strong from the standpoint of risk, it has limited advantages with regard to income, and it is weak with respect to control.

From Viewpoint of Issuer

Advantages. (1) The cost of debt is definitely limited. Bondholders do not participate in superior profits if earned. (2) Not only is the cost

---

3 *Ibid.,* p. 106.

limited, but it is typically lower than the cost of common stock or preferred stock. (3) The owners of the corporation do not share control of the corporation when debt financing is used. (4) The interest payment on debt is deductible as a tax expense. (5) Flexibility in the financial structure of the corporation may be achieved by inserting a callable provision in the indenture of the debt. (6) The risk of loss of asset values is shifted to the holders of long-term debt.

This last point involves something of a paradox. The higher the debt-equity ratio, the greater the risk both to the creditors and to the owners, but only when the owner is a conservative investor. A person more inclined to engage in speculative activity finds it advantageous to operate with an extremely high debt-equity ratio. If the owner operates with a high debt ratio, he places a very small portion of his own assets in an individual company. If the company turns out to be successful, he gains a considerable amount because of the tremendous leverage. For example, take a corporation financed 90 percent by debt and 10 percent by equity. Assume that the corporation earns 8 percent on total assets when total assets are $100,000. This represents an $8,000 return. Suppose the corporation pays an average of 5 percent on debt; 5 percent of $90,000 is $4,500. This leaves $3,500 as the return on $10,000, that is, a 35 percent return on the investment of the holders of common stock.

A high rate of return is gained from relatively modest productivity on total assets. If the owners of the corporation can contribute to the financing of the firm only to this very small extent, the possible rate of return on their investment is tremendous. On the other hand, if the enterprise fails, the owners have lost little, because they have committed so little to the operation.[4]

Thus it is advantageous for the owners of the firm to obtain an extreme amount of debt if they can induce creditors to support this position. This possibility points to a factor of great significance for the use of the corporation. Since the corporation is a device whereby owners can obtain credit more easily than otherwise, the corporation becomes a great engine for shifting the risk of loss from the owners to the creditors.

Disadvantages. 1. Debt is a fixed charge; there is greater risk if the earnings of the company fluctuate, because the corporation may be unable to meet these fixed charges.

2. As was seen in Chapter 12, higher risk brings higher capitalization rates on equity earnings. Thus, even though leverage is favorable and

---

[4] "Little" is, of course, a relative thing. If a person puts up $100,000, his entire personal net worth, and borrows $900,000, then it is true that his loss is less than that of the creditors if the firm should prove valueless. But it might be difficult to convince him that he has suffered less.

raises earnings per share, the higher capitalization rates attributable to leverage may drive the common stock value down.

3. Debt usually has a definite maturity date. Because of the fixed maturity date, the financial officers must make provision for repayment of the debt or its refunding.

4. Since long-term debt is typically a commitment for a long period, it involves risk because the expectations and plans on which the debt was issued may change. The debt may prove to be a burden, or it may prove to have been advantageous. For example, if income, employment, and the price level fall greatly, the assumption of a large amount of debt may prove to have been unwise financial policy. The railroads are always pointed to as an example in this regard. They were able to meet their ordinary operating expenses during the 1930s, but were unable to meet the heavy financial charges they had undertaken earlier when the prospects for the railroads looked more favorable than they turned out to be.

5. In a long-term contractual relation, the indenture provisions are likely to be much more stringent than they are in a short-term credit agreement. Hence the firm may be subject to much more disturbing and crippling restrictions in the indenture of a long-term debt arrangement than it would be if it had borrowed on a short-term basis or had issued common stock.

6. There is a limit to the extent to which funds can be raised through long-term debt. Some of the generally accepted standards of financial policy dictate that the debt-equity ratio shall not exceed certain limits. These standards of financial prudence set limits or controls on the extent to which funds may be raised through long-term debt.

DECISIONS ON USE OF LONG-TERM DEBT

The foregoing discussion of the various forms of debt illustrates an important principle in business finance: any form of financing arrangement is likely to be developed as the economic environment and the needs of firms require. The only limitations are the imagination of the issuers and investment bankers and the needs of investors—and these permit a wide degree of variation in securities forms.

The foregoing review of the different kinds of equity and debt forms is purely *illustrative* of some of the readily explained types that have emerged. The future will doubtless see many new forms of hybrid securities as the economic environment changes, as the needs of issuers are altered, and as the education of investors and the advantages that they in turn may derive from some of the new provisions of securities are discerned.

The conditions favoring the use of long-term debt when a number of alternative methods of long-term financing are under consideration include the following:

1. Sales and earnings are relatively stable, or a substantial increase in sales and earnings is expected in the future, providing substantial benefit to trading on the equity.

2. A substantial rise in the price level is expected in the future, making it advantageous for the firm to incur debt as a part of a program to become a net-monetary debtor.

3. The existing debt-to-net-worth ratio is relatively low for the line of business.

4. Management thinks the price of the common stock is temporarily depressed relative to bond prices.

5. Sale of common stock would involve problems of maintaining the existing control pattern in the company.

SUMMARY

A bond is a long-term promissory note. A mortgage bond is secured by real property. An indenture is an agreement between the firm issuing a bond and the numerous bondholders, represented by a trustee.

Secured long-term debt differs with respect to (1) the priority of claims, (2) the right to issue additional securities, and (3) the scope of the lien provided. These characteristics determine the amount of protection provided to the bondholder by the terms of the security. Giving the investor more security will induce him to accept a lower yield, but will restrict the future freedom of action of the issuing firm.

The main forms of unsecured bonds are (1) debentures, (2) subordinated debentures, and (3) income bonds. Holders of debentures are unsecured general creditors. Subordinated debentures are junior in claim to bank loans. Income bonds are similar to preferred stock in that interest is paid only when earned.

The characteristics of long-term debt determine the circumstances under which it will be used when alternative forms of financing are under analysis. The cost of debt is limited, but it is a fixed obligation. Bond interest is an expense deductible for tax purposes. Debt carries a maturity date and may require sinking fund payments to prepare for extinguishing the obligation. Indenture provisions are likely to include restrictions on the freedom of action of the management of the firm.

The nature of long-term debt encourages its use under the following circumstances:

1. Sales and earnings are relatively stable.
2. Profit margins are adequate to make trading on the equity advantageous.
3. A rise in profits or the general price level is expected.
4. The existing debt ratio is relatively low.
5. Common stock price-earnings ratios are low relative to the levels of interest rates.
6. Control considerations are important.
7. Cash flow requirements under the bond agreement are not burdensome.
8. Restrictions of the bond indenture are not onerous.

SELECTED REFERENCES

Cohan, Avery B., "Yields on New Underwritten Corporate Bonds, 1935–58," *Journal of Finance*, 27 (December 1962), pp. 585–605.

Davis, Felix T., "The Case for Registered Bonds," *Banking* (June 1964), pp. 53–54, 98–102.

Donaldson, Gordon, "New Framework for Corporate Debt Policy," *Harvard Business Review*, 40 (March-April, 1962), pp. 117–131.

Foster, L. O., *Corporate Debt and the Stockholder* (Hanover, New Hampshire: Amos Tuck School of Business Administration, 1956).

Hickman, W. B., *Corporate Bonds: Quality and Investment Performance*, Occasional Paper 59 (New York: National Bureau of Economic Research, Inc., 1957).

Johnson, Robert W., "Subordinated Debentures: Debt That Serves as Equity," *Journal of Finance*, 10 (March 1955), pp. 1–16.

Robbins, Sidney M., "A Bigger Role for Income Bonds," *Harvard Business Review*, 33 (November-December 1955), pp. 100–114.

Walter, J. E., "The Use of Borrowed Funds," *Journal of Business*, 28 (April 1955), pp. 138–147.

Winn, Willis J., and Arleigh Hess, Jr., "The Value of the Call Privilege," *Journal of Finance*, 14 (May 1959), pp. 182–195.

Weston, J. Fred (ed.), *Financial Management in the 1960s: New Challenges and Responsibilities* (New York: Holt, Rinehart and Winston, Inc., 1966), selection "Is A.T.&T. Playing It Too Safe?"

QUESTIONS

19-1 There are many types of bonds: for example, mortgage, debentures, collateral trust, and varying maturities for each type. What are some factors that determine the particular type bond a company should use?

19-2 The alternative ways of setting up sinking funds are (1) the corporation makes annual payments to the trustee, who invests the proceeds in securities (frequently government bonds) and uses the accumulated total to retire the bond issue upon maturity; (2) the trustee uses the annual payments to retire a portion of the issue each year, either calling a given percentage of the issue by a lottery and paying a specified price per bond or buying bonds on the open market, whichever is cheaper. Discuss the advantages and disadvantages of each procedure from the standpoint of both the firm and the bondholders.

19-3 Why is a financial institution such as a bank a better choice for a bond trustee than an individual?

19-4 Since a corporation often has the right to call bonds at will, do you believe individuals should be able to demand repayment at any time they so desire?

19-5 What are the relative advantages and disadvantages of issuing a long-term bond during a recession versus during a period of prosperity?

19-6 On September 24, 1965, Missouri Pacific 4¾ percent income bonds due in 2020 were selling for $770, while the company's 4¼ percent bonds due in 2005 were selling for $845. Why would the bonds with the lower coupon sell at a higher price? What is the computed yield to maturity for each issue? (If you do not have access to a bond table, simply set up the equation for determining the bonds' yields.)

19-7 When a firm sells bonds, it must offer a package acceptable to potential buyers. Included in this package of terms are such features as the issue price, the coupon interest rate, the term to maturity, any sinking fund provisions, and other features. The package itself is determined through a bargaining process between the firm and the investment bankers who will handle the issue. What particular features would you, as a corporate treasurer, be especially interested in, and which would you be most willing to give ground on, under each of the following conditions:

1. You believe that the economy is near the peak of a business cycle.

2. Long-run forecasts indicate that your firm will have heavy cash inflows in relation to cash needs during the next five to ten years.

3. Your current liabilities are presently low, but you anticipate raising a considerable amount of funds through short-term borrowing in the near future.

19–8 Bonds are less attractive to investors during periods of inflation because a rise in the price level will reduce the purchasing power of the fixed-interest payments and also the principal. Discuss the advantages and disadvantages to a corporation of using a bond whose interest payments and principal would increase in direct proportion to increases in the price level (an inflation-proof bond).

PROBLEMS

19–1 In 1966, the Raymond Instrument Corporation sought to raise an additional $100 million for financing plant additions and working-capital growth. Raymond manufactures precision instruments and tools.

Through investment bankers the company could sell common stock (at a market price of $25.60 per share) to net $25, or it could sell sinking fund debentures to yield 4 percent. Costs of flotation would be slightly higher for common stock but not enough to influence the decision.

Below are the balance sheet and the income statement of Raymond Instrument at the time the financing took place.

1. Assuming that net income before interest and before taxes remains at 10 percent of sales, calculate earnings per share at sales of $200, $400, $600, $800, and $1,000 million, when financing is with common stock in contrast to debt.

2. Make a break-even chart for the earnings under 1.

3. Using a price-earnings ratio of 20 times, calculate the market value per share of common stock.

4. Make a break-even chart of the market value per share of the company for 3.

5. If the use of debt caused the price-earnings ratio on common stock to fall to 12.5, or an earnings-price ratio of 8 percent, what would the market value per share of common stock become under the range of sales suggested in 1?

6. Make a break-even chart for 5.

7. Using the data and assumptions set out, which form of financing should Raymond adopt and why?

RAYMOND INSTRUMENT CORPORATION
BALANCE SHEET
March 31, 1966
(in millions of dollars)

Current assets	$250	Accounts payable . . .	$20
Investments	25	Notes payable to banks	80
Net fixed assets	125	Taxes	40
		Other current liabilities	35
		Total current liabilities . .	$175
		Long-term debt	100
		Common stock, par $1	25
		Earned surplus	100
Total assets	$400	Total claims	$400

RAYMOND INSTRUMENT CORPORATION
INCOME STATEMENT
March 31, 1966
(in millions of dollars)

Sales	$700
Net income before taxes, 10%	70
Interest on debt	6
Net income subject to tax	64
Tax, 50%	32
Net income after tax	32

19-2 The Frontier Steel Company is planning a capital improvement program to provide greater efficiency and versatility in its operations. It is estimated that by mid-1967 the company will need to raise $50 million. Frontier is a leading steel producer with an excellent credit rating.

You are asked to set up a program for obtaining the necessary funds. Using the following information, indicate the best form of financing. Some of the items you should include in your analysis are profit margins, relative costs, control, cash flows and ratio, and *pro forma* analysis.

Frontier's common stock is selling at $80 per share. The company could sell debt (25 year) at 4.5 percent or preferred stock at 5 percent.

FRONTIER STEEL COMPANY
CONSOLIDATED BALANCE SHEET
December 31, 1966
(in millions of dollars)

Assets

Current	$190
Other investments	35
Properties (net)	285
Deferred assets	10
Total assets	$520

Liabilities

Current	$ 80	
Long-term debt (4.44%)	45	
Total liabilities		$125
Common stock, $10 par	80	
Capital surplus	75	
Retained income	220	
Reserves	20	
Total net worth		395
		$520

FRONTIER STEEL CORPORATION
CONSOLIDATED INCOME STATEMENT
For Years Ended December 31, 1964, 1965, and 1966
(in millions of dollars)

	1964	1965	1966
Sales	$610	$455	$540
Other income	5	5	5
Total	615	460	545
Costs and expenses	530	400	480
Income before taxes	85	60	65
Federal income tax	43	30	32
Net income	42	30	33
Cash dividends	23	23	23
Interest on long-term debt	1.0	1.3	2.0
Depreciation	20	16	17
Shares outstanding (widely held) . .		7,850,000	

19-3 The Dow Chemical Company is a leading manufacturer of industrial chemicals, plastics, and metals. During 1963 the company sought to raise $100 million in order to retire short-term obligations of $50 millions and add to working capital for further growth.

The alternatives available to the company were 25-year 4.35 percent sinking fund debentures or the sale of common stock at $60 per share. In both cases a 1 percent underwriting charge will be incurred. Under the debenture financing the firm was obligated to provide for the retirement of $4 million of principal annually starting in 1968. Relevant balance sheet and income statement data are listed below. Assume a 50 percent tax rate.

Which financing alternative should Dow Chemical have chosen?

DOW CHEMICAL COMPANY
BALANCE SHEET
June 30, 1963
(in millions of dollars)

Cash	$ 60		Accounts payable . . .	$70
Net receivables . . .	150		Notes payable, 4.5% . .	80
Inventories	190		Accruals	50
Total current assets . .		$ 400	Total current liabilities .	$ 200
Investments		50	Long-term debt, 4.4% . . .	100
Net property		550	Common stock, par $5 . . .	150
			Capital surplus	450
			Retained earnings	100
Total assets		$1,000	Total claims on assets . .	$1,000

DOW CHEMICAL COMPANY
CONSOLIDATED STATEMENT OF INCOME
Years Ended June 30, 1961, 1962, and 1963
(in millions of dollars)

	1961	1962	1963
Sales (net)	$820	$900	$970
Rental and service income	15	20	20
Total income	835	920	990
Cost of products sold	610	685	720
Depreciation	90	95	100
Selling, administrative, and other expenses . . .	15	20	20
Total expenses	715	800	840
Net operating income (average 18% of sales) . . .	120	120	150
Interest	10	10	8
Income taxes	45	50	62
Net profit for period	$ 65	$ 60	$ 80
Earnings per share of common	2.00	2.50	2.70
Cash dividends per common share	1.40	1.50	1.60
Price range for common stock: H	84	71	70
L	69	40	54

Chapter 20

Dividend Policy and Internal Financing

IMPORTANCE OF DIVIDEND POLICY

Dividend policy determines the division of the corporate earnings between payments to stockholders and retained earnings. Retained earnings are one of the most significant sources of financing the growth of enterprises.

Data on Internal Financing

Table 20–1 sets forth the relationship between corporate internal sources of funds and total uses of funds during the post-World War II period. For the 19-year period between 1946 and 1964, the total uses of funds by corporations was $736 billions. Internal sources financed almost two thirds of the total uses, depreciation accounted for 41 percent, and retained earnings some 22 percent. If depreciation charges are deducted from gross total uses, net total uses of funds in the amount of $433 billions is obtained. Retained earnings financed 38 percent of the net total uses of corporate funds—the firms' growth—during the 19-year period.

Significance of Internal Financing

Comprehensive studies of trends in capital formation and their financing underscore the important role of internal financing. In commenting on the progress report of a National Bureau of Economic Research

TABLE 20–1

CORPORATE INTERNAL SOURCES AS PERCENT OF TOTAL USES, 1946–1964
(in billions of dollars)

Year	Total Uses	Retained Earnings	Percentage of Retained Earnings to Total Uses	Depreciation	Percentage of Depreciation to Total Uses	Total Internal Sources	Percentage of Total Internal Sources to Total Uses
1946	19.5	7.2	36.9	4.2	21.5	11.4	58.4
1947	28.2	11.4	40.4	5.2	18.4	16.6	58.8
1948	27.0	12.4	45.9	6.2	23.0	18.6	68.9
1949	16.8	7.6	45.2	7.1	42.3	14.7	87.5
1950	36.5	12.4	34.0	7.8	21.3	20.2	55.3
1951	36.4	9.1	25.0	9.0	24.7	18.1	49.7
1952	27.3	6.4	23.4	10.4	38.1	16.8	61.5
1953	28.6	7.9	27.6	11.8	41.3	19.7	68.9
1954	23.8	6.3	26.5	13.5	56.7	19.8	83.2
1955	50.6	10.9	21.5	15.7	31.0	26.6	52.6
1956	45.0	10.5	23.4	17.3	38.4	27.8	61.8
1957	40.3	8.9	22.1	19.1	47.4	28.0	69.5
1958	35.3	5.7	16.1	20.3	57.5	26.0	73.6
1959	52.1	9.5	18.2	21.6	41.5	31.1	59.7
1960	43.8	6.2	14.1	22.9	52.3	29.1	66.4
1961	48.8	5.6	11.5	24.1	49.4	29.7	60.9
1962	54.4	7.7	14.2	27.5	50.5	35.2	64.7
1963	58.4	8.0	13.7	28.8	49.3	36.8	63.0
1964	63.3	10.4	16.4	30.5	48.2	40.9	64.6
1946–1954	244.1	80.7	33.1	75.2	30.8	155.9	63.9
1955–1960	267.1	51.7	19.3	116.9	43.8	168.6	63.1
1961–1964	224.9	31.7	14.1	110.9	49.3	142.6	63.4
1946–1964	736.1	164.1	22.3	303.0	41.2	467.1	63.5

project on "Long-term Trends in Capital Formation and Financing,"[1] Professor Eli Shapiro has called attention to the significance of internal financing effectively.

Indeed, it may be stated categorically that one of the most important features of all three papers is the stress placed on internal financing of capital formation over the first half of the twentieth century. The presence of the dominance of internal financing of capital formation is hard to rationalize in the light of the disproportionate space devoted to the role of financial institutions in the so-called business or corporate finance textbooks published as recently as the late forties or early fifties.

Because of the great importance of internal financing, dividend policy, which determines the division of corporate earnings between outflows and retained earnings, must be recognized as one of the central decision areas for financial managers.

Patterns in Dividend Payouts

Studies of dividend patterns over extended periods beginning from 1870 indicate that, over all, corporations have paid in dividends two thirds of their earnings after taxes. Table 20–2 shows that immediately following World War II dividend payout dropped to about 40 percent. This decrease was due partly to the "overstatement" of earnings because of the use of historical methods of costing during a period of rising price levels. More importantly, it was due to the rapid growth of firms and their need for funds to finance inventories and fixed assets at higher price levels.

In the early 1950s, dividend payouts reached about 50 percent of earnings. Writers in the mid-fifties observed that, of corporate earnings before taxes, one half was paid to the government. Of the remainder, one half was distributed to the stockholders. Thus, if a corporation earned $20 million, the corporate income tax would take $10 million, corporate dividends would be $5 million, and retained earnings would be $5 million.

By the end of the 1950s, dividend payouts ranged from 55 to 65 percent, suggesting that corporations might be returning to their long-term historical pattern of two thirds of net earnings, and this level was, in fact, reached during the 1960s.

Cash Flows as Determinant of Payouts

Cash flows are earnings plus depreciation and depletion charges. When dividends are related to cash flows rather than to earnings, the payout patterns appear to show two changes. One, the payout percentages drop to lower levels. For all manufacturing corporations, the payout

---

1 Eli Shapiro, "Discussion of Long-term Trends in Capital Formation and Financing," *Journal of Finance*, 10 (May 1955), p. 281.

TABLE 20-2

CORPORATE PROFITS AND DIVIDENDS, 1929-1964
(dollars amounts in billions)

Year	Corporate Profits after Tax	Dividends	Payout Percentage
1929	$ 8.3	$ 5.8	70
1930	2.5	5.5	220
1931	−1.3	4.1	0
1932	−3.4	2.6	0
1933	−0.4	2.1	0
1934	1.0	2.6	260
1935	2.2	2.9	132
1936	4.3	4.5	105
1937	4.7	4.7	100
1938	2.3	3.2	139
1939	5.0	3.8	76
1940	6.5	4.0	62
1941	9.4	4.5	44
1942	9.5	4.3	45
1943	10.5	4.5	43
1944	10.4	4.7	45
1945	8.3	4.7	57
1946	13.4	5.8	43
1947	18.2	6.5	36
1948	20.5	7.2	35
1949	16.0	7.5	47
1950	22.8	9.2	40
1951	19.7	9.0	46
1952	17.2	9.0	52
1953	18.1	9.2	51
1954	16.8	9.8	58
1955	23.0	11.2	49
1956	23.5	12.1	51
1957	22.3	12.6	56
1958	18.8	12.4	66
1959	24.5	13.7	56
1960	22.0	14.5	66
1961	21.9	15.2	69
1962	25.0	16.5	66
1963	26.7	18.0	67
1964	31.6	19.8	63
1929–1939	25.2	41.8	166
1940–1945	54.6	26.7	49
1945–1950	99.2	41.0	41
1950–1955	117.6	57.4	49
1955–1960	134.1	76.5	57
1960–1964	127.2	84.0	66

Source: Economic Report of the President, (Washington D. C.: U. S. Government Printing Office, 1965) p. 266.

appears to drop from the two-thirds ratio to a one-third ratio. The ratio would be expected to drop, but it is of interest that it dropped to almost precisely the complement of the payout ratio related to earnings.

Two, the payout ratio appears to be more stable when dividends are related to cash flows rather than to earnings. If dividends were tied more directly to cash flows than to earnings, it would suggest that cash flows may be the determinants of dividends rather than of earnings. However, the apparent increased stability in the dividend-to-cash-flow ratio may be an arithmetical accident. rather than a cause-and-effect relation. For example, consider the following data:

Year	Earnings	Dividends	Payout Percentage	Depreciation	Cash Flows	Payout Percentage
1	20	10	50	20	40	25
2	15	10	67	20	35	29
3	10	10	100	20	50	33
4	30	10	33	20	50	20

The payout percentage based on cash flows is clearly more stable than the payout based on earnings. But this result flows from adding a constant figure to the earnings. The greater stability may simply come about because of the larger denominator, resulting from adding a relatively fixed amount to earnings. Cash flows may have a greater influence on dividend policy than heretofore recognized. However, to discover the nature of the relation will require more exhaustive studies than have been made to date.

FACTORS INFLUENCING DIVIDEND POLICY

The economic patterns described above indicate the great significance of retained earnings in financing the growth of firms. This poses the fundamental question: "What determines the extent to which a firm will pay out dividends compared with retention of earnings as a source of financing?" This question may be answered by a consideration of the factors influencing dividend policy. First, the major influences on dividend policy will be described. Second, this check list will be used to attempt to explain differences in dividend patterns observed among different industries and among different firms in the same industry.

Legal Rules

The state statutes and court decisions governing dividend policy are complicated in their application, but their essential nature may be stated briefly. The legal rules provide that dividends be paid from earnings, either from the current year's earnings or from past years' earnings as reflected in earned surplus. State laws emphasize three rules: (1) the net profits rule, (2) the capital impairment rule, and (3) the insolvency rule.

The *net profits* rule provides that dividends may be paid from past and present earnings. The *capital impairment* rule protects shareholders and creditors by forbidding the payment of dividends from capital. Paying dividends from capital would be distributing the investment in the company rather than its earnings.[2] The *insolvency* rule provides that corporations may not pay dividends while insolvent. Insolvency is here defined in the bankruptcy sense that liabilities exceed assets.

Legal aspects are significant. They provide the framework within which dividend policies can be formulated. However, within these boundaries important financial and economic factors will have a major influence on policy.

Cash Position

Profits held as retained earnings (which show up in the right-hand side of the balance sheet in the surplus or retained earnings account) may be invested in assets required for the conduct of the business. Thus, although a firm has had a record of earnings, its liquidity position may not enable it to pay cash dividends. Indeed, it was seen above that a growing firm, even a very profitable one, typically has a pressing need for funds. In such a situation the firm may elect to pay dividends in some form other than cash. These alternatives will be considered later in the chapter.

Need to Repay Debt

When a firm has sold obligations in order to finance expansion or to substitute for other forms of financing, it is faced with two alternatives: it can refund the debt at maturity by replacing it with another form of security, or it can make provision for paying off the debt. Since the retained earnings of a growing firm are likely to be tied up in operating assets, it will not be able to liquidate assets. Therefore, a debt obligation implies that the firm is planning either retention of earnings to pay off the debt or new external financing in the future.

Rate of Asset Expansion

The more rapid the rate at which the firm is growing, the greater will be its needs for financing asset expansion. A fast-growing firm will see a substantial need for funds in the future. The greater the future need for funds, the more likely the firm is to retain earnings rather than to pay them out.

---

[2] It is possible, of course, to return stockholders' capital, but when this is done it must be clearly stated as such.

Profit Rate

The profit rate of a firm is a highly important variable. The profitability with which the firm employs funds will determine the relative attractiveness of paying out earnings in the form of dividends to stockholders who will use them elsewhere, compared with the productivity of their use in the present enterprise. The internal profitability rate of the firm provides a basis for comparing the productivity of retained earnings to the alternative return which could be earned elsewhere.

Stability of Earnings

If earnings are relatively stable, a firm is better able to predict what its future earnings will be. It is therefore more likely to pay out a higher percentage of its earnings in dividends than is a firm with fluctuating earnings. The latter firm is not certain that in subsequent years the hoped-for earnings will be realized, and is more likely to retain a high proportion of earnings in order to maintain dividends if earnings should fall off in the future.

Access to the Capital Markets

Large, well-established firms with a record of profitability and some stability of earnings will have easy access to capital markets and other forms of external financing. On the other hand, the small, new, or venturesome firm has a greater amount of risk for potential investors. Its ability to raise equity funds or debt from capital markets is restricted, and it must therefore retain more earnings to finance its operations. A well-established firm is likely to have a higher dividend payout rate than is a new or small firm.

Control

Another important variable is the effect of alternative sources of financing on the control situation in the firm. Some corporations, as a matter of policy, will expand only to the extent of their internal earnings. This policy is defended on the grounds that raising funds by selling additional common stock dilutes the control of the dominant group in the company. At the same time, selling debt increases the risks of fluctuating earnings to the present owners of the company. Reliance on internal financing in order to maintain control reduces the dividend payout.

Tax Position of Stockholders

The tax position of the owners of the corporation will greatly influence the desire for dividends. For example, a corporation closely held by a few taxpayers in high income tax brackets is likely to pay out a relatively low dividend. The owners of the corporation are interested in taking their income in the form of capital gains rather than in ordinary dividends, which are subject to higher personal income tax rates.

On the other hand, the stockholders in a large, widely held corporation may be interested in a high-dividend payout. At times there is a conflict of interest in large corporations between stockholders in high income tax brackets and stockholders in low income tax brackets. The former will prefer to see a low dividend payout and a high rate of earnings retention in the hope of an appreciation of the capital stock of the company. The lower income stockholder will prefer a relatively high dividend payout rate.

Corporate Tax Liabilities

In order to prevent wealthy stockholders from using the corporation as an incorporated pocketbook by which to avoid the high rates of personal income tax, tax regulations applicable to corporations provide for a special surtax on improperly accumulated income. This was the subject of the famous Section 102 of the Internal Revenue Code, which is now Section 531 of the 1954 law. The Revenue Act of 1954 placed the burden of proof on the Internal Revenue Service to justify penalty rates for accumulation of earnings. That is, earnings retention is justified unless the Internal Revenue Service can prove otherwise. This is a salutory change in that it reduces somewhat the uncertainty with regard to the propriety of earnings retention.

The ten factors outlined above influence corporations to different degrees, depending upon the particular situation. The effects of these factors result in different dividend patterns from industry to industry and from company to company. How these forces influence dividend policy will be indicated in the following sections.

DIFFERENCES IN DIVIDEND PATTERNS

A sampling of industries carried in Standard and Poor's *Industry Surveys* reveals considerable variation in dividend practices among different industries. Table 20–3 sets forth a summary of dividend payouts for four periods, 1947–1950, 1949–1953, 1954–1959, and 1960–1964.

Low Payout Industries

The explanations for the lowest dividend payout industries differ. The low payouts observed in the automobile and the rubber industries are due primarily to the instability of earnings. Payouts are low and retentions high in order to provide a cushion for years in which earnings decline. Further, because of their cyclical instability, firms in the automobile and the rubber industries have been reluctant to use debt financ-

TABLE 20-3

INDUSTRY DIVIDEND PATTERNS
1947–1950, 1949–1953, 1954–1959, 1960–1964

	Average Dividend Payout*			
	1947–1950	1949–1953	1954–1959	1960–1964
1. Tobacco	68	72	61	52
2. Paper	34	41	55	63
3. Building materials	42	51	54	61
4. Chemicals	47	54	54	61
5. Textiles	43	49	51	39
6. Liquor	32	46	50	59
7. Banking	44	46	50	47
8. Oil	36	43	49	59
9. Machinery	43	43	48	60
10. Steel	36	44	47	70
11. Meat and dairy products . . .	37	33	46	54
12. Containers	35	45	46	55
13. Food products	47	52	43	63
14. Rubber	34	39	40	48
15. Office equipment	41	49	39	38
16. Automobiles	27	30	30	66
17. Air transport	0	5	21	96

* For 1947–1959, calculated by taking the medians for the companies listed in Standard and Poor's *Industry Surveys* and calculating the arithmetic means of the medians for the individual years. For 1960–1964, industry composites averaged for the years.

Source: Calculated from Standard and Poor's *Industry Surveys.*

ing. Thus, during the postwar expansion, the financing of these industries was done largely with equity, and since new equity is more expensive than retained earnings, earnings retention has been high. The air transport and the office equipment industries are not so opposed to debt, but their rates of expansion have been so rapid that equity bases have had to increase steadily to keep the debt ratios in line. Again, this situation has led to high levels of retained earnings.

High Payout Industries

The high payouts found among firms in the textile industry in the first three periods and the air transport industry in the last one are special cases. They represent situations where an industry has suffered a decline in earnings during the period encompassed by the data. As a consequence, there has been some attempt to maintain dividends in the face of declining earnings. A high dividend payout among textile companies has also been the consequence of an attempt to ward off company raiding and mergers because of stockholders' dissatisfaction. In addition, the rate of return at which earnings in this industry, and also in the tobacco and paper products industries, could be reinvested has been low. This situation naturally has stimulated payout.

Characteristic Patterns

The remainder of the industries fall within a relatively narrow range of dividend payouts. Nearly half the industries are in the payout range of from 49 to 55 percent for the period 1954–1959. These include the paper, chemicals, building materials, and banking industries.

Dividend Patterns in Individual Firms

The time pattern of dividend payouts and the amount of dividends per share paid by different companies in the same industry and in different industries is suggested by Tables 20–4a and 20–4b for the liquor and

TABLE 20–4a

LIQUOR INDUSTRY

	National Distillers & Chemical Corp.			Distillers Corp. Seagrams, Ltd.			Brown-Foreman Distillers		
	Earn-ings*	Divi-dends*	Per-cent-age Pay-	Earn-ings*	Divi-dends*	Per-cent-age Pay-	Earn-ings*	Divi-dends*	Per-cent-age Pay-
Year	(in dollars)		out	(in dollars)		out	(in dollars)		out
1948	3.37	2.00	59	3.12	0.30	10	0.60	0.11	18
1949	3.03	2.00	66	1.98	0.45	23	0.49	0.08⅓	17
1950	3.45	2.00	58	2.39	0.57½	24	0.74	0.08⅓	11
1951	2.86	2.00	70	2.47	0.85	34	0.37	0.10	27
1952	1.13	1.75	155	2.12	0.85	40	0.51	0.12½	25
1953	1.18	1.00	85	2.16	0.85	39	0.43	0.12½	29
1954	1.38	1.00	72	2.04	0.85	42	0.39	0.12⅝	32
1955	1.60	1.00	62	1.77	0.85	48	0.45	0.12⅝	28
1956	2.11	1.00	47	1.31	0.85	65	0.37	0.14½	39
1957	2.05	1.00	49	1.45	0.85	59	0.35	0.14½	41
1958	1.76	1.00	57	1.46	0.85	58	0.54	0.13	24
1959	2.23	1.10	49	1.54	0.85	55	0.71	0.18	25
1960	1.92	1.20	63	1.62	0.85	52	0.75	0.24	32
1961	1.67	1.20	72	1.77	0.85	48	1.05	0.25	24
1962	1.76	1.20	68	1.80	0.85	47	1.16	0.26	22
1963	1.67	1.20	72	1.95	1.00	51	1.28	0.29¾	23
Average, 1948–1953			82			28			21
Average, 1954–1959			56			55			33
Average, 1960–1963			69			50			25

* Earnings and dividends are on an adjusted per share basis.

TABLE 20–4b

OIL INDUSTRY

	Sun Oil Company			Gulf Oil Company			Standard Oil Company (New Jersey)		
	*Earn-ings**	*Divi-dends**	*Per-cent-age Pay-*	*Earn-ings**	*Divi-dends**	*Per-cent-age Pay-*	*Earn-ings**	*Divi-dends**	*Per-cent-age Pay-*
Year	*(in dollars)*		*out*	*(in dollars)*		*out*	*(in dollars)*		*out*
1948	2.64	0.28	11	1.55	0.50	32	2.03	0.32	16
1949	1.52	0.31	21	1.02	0.23	23	1.49	0.67	45
1950	2.22	0.34	16	1.12	0.46	41	2.25	0.83	37
1951	2.77	0.36	13	1.42	0.46	32	2.91	1.37	47
1952	2.62	0.40	16	1.44	0.46	32	2.86	1.42½	50
1953	2.76	0.44	16	1.77	0.48	27	3.20	1.50	47
1954	2.47	0.48	19	1.85	0.50	27	2.98	1.52	51
1955	2.95	0.57½	20	2.20	0.58	27	3.61	1.75	49
1956	3.48	0.63	18	2.68	0.67½	25	4.11	2.10	51
1957	2.93	0.67	23	3.37	0.70½	21	3.96	2.25	57
1958	1.98	0.70	36	3.13	0.74	24	2.62	2.25	86
1959	2.64	0.72½	28	2.76	0.92	33	2.91	2.25	77
1960	3.05	0.75	25	3.14	0.95	30	3.18	2.25	71
1961	3.09	0.80½	26	3.21	1.08	34	3.50	2.30	66
1962	3.29	0.85	26	3.27	1.45	44	3.88	2.50	64
1963	3.85	0.90	23	3.56	1.60	45	4.74	2.75	58
Average, 1948–1953			15			31			41
Average, 1954–1959			23			26			62
Average, 1960–1963			25			38			65

* Earnings and dividends are on an adjusted per share basis.

the oil industries. In the liquor industry some of the companies pursue a "typical" dividend policy, raising dividends per share only when earnings increase substantially and then maintaining that dividend through temporary declines in earnings. This policy was clearly portrayed by Distillers Corporation-Seagram's, Ltd., whose dividend went from 30 cents a share in 1948, when the company earned over $3 per share, to 85 cents in 1951, when earnings were $2.47 per share. Although earnings in 1956 had dropped to $1.31 per share, dividends were maintained at 85 cents, the 1951–1959 per share level. Then, as earnings rose in the early 1960s, the payout fell. To bring this ratio back to "normal," the dividend was raised in 1963.

In contrast, the National Distillers and Chemical Corporation raised its dividend to $2 in 1947, when its earnings were $4.57 per share, and maintained this dividend through 1951, when its earnings dropped to

$2.86 per share. But when earnings continued to decline below $2 per share in 1953, the dividend rate was dropped to $1 per share. Some stability in dividend payments is exhibited in that dividends per share were $1 from 1953 to 1958.

Diverse patterns are observed in the oil industry. The Sun Oil Company, for example, pays a dividend of about 25 percent. In sharp contrast is the Standard Oil Company of New Jersey, with a dividend payout about three times higher. Differences in company size, ownership patterns, and rate of growth are important variables explaining these differences in dividend policies among companies in the same industry.[3]

RECENT THEORETICAL DEVELOPMENTS

The Walter Formula

Professor Walter has suggested a framework as an aid in understanding dividend policies.[4] The nature of his contribution may be indicated by his formula suggesting the fundamental factors influencing the market value of a firm's common stock. Operating on the objective of maximizing the wealth position of the common stockholder, the appropriate dividend payout is suggested by the following formula:

$$Vc = \frac{D + \dfrac{Ra}{Rc}(E-D)}{Rc}$$

where:

Vc = market value of the firm's common stock
Rc = market capitalization rate
Ra = productivity of retained earnings
E = earnings per share
D = dividends per share

Each of the factors in the formula can be measured by available data. Vc represents the market value of the firm's common stock. Market prices of stocks, with the earnings per share and dividends per share, are widely available. Rc, the market capitalization rate, can be measured by taking the earnings-price ratio for any of the widely used indexes of common stock prices, for example, Standard and Poor's index of 500 stocks. Ra, the productivity of retained earnings of the firm, may be measured by taking the change in earnings per share of an individual firm divided by the

---

[3] In addition, one encounters serious problems in measuring earnings in the oil industry. Different accounting treatments can produce radically different reported earnings figures for two firms whose cash flows are actually quite similar. Thus one must be especially careful when interpreting any earnings-based ratio for this industry.
[4] James E. Walter, "Dividend Policies and Common Stock Prices," *Journal of Finance,* 11 (March 1956), pp. 29–41.

change in book value per share over a convenient time interval, such as three to five years.

Illustrations of the application of the formula will provide a basis for explaining its significance. The first illustration begins with a situation in which the productivity of earnings retained by the firm is larger than the rate the funds could earn generally, the market capitalization rate. In Table 20–5, in situation I earnings per share are $6 and dividends per

TABLE 20–5

APPLICATION OF THE WALTER FORMULA

Situation I	Situation II	Situation III
1. $Rc = 10\%$ $Ra = 15\%$ $E = \$6$ $D = \$4$	4. $Rc = 10\%$ $Ra = 8\%$ $E = \$6$ $D = \$4$	7. $Rc = 10\%$ $Ra = 10\%$ $E = \$6$ $D = \$4$
$Vc = \dfrac{4 + \dfrac{0.15}{0.10}(2)}{0.10}$	$Vc = \dfrac{4 + \dfrac{0.08}{0.10}(2)}{0.10}$	$Vc = \dfrac{4 + \dfrac{0.10}{0.10}(2)}{0.10}$
$= \dfrac{4 + 1.5\,(2)}{0.10}$	$= \dfrac{4 + 4/5\,(2)}{0.10}$	$= \dfrac{4 + 1\,(2)}{0.10}$
$= \$70$	$= \$56$	$= \$60$
2. $D = \$2$	5. $D = \$2$	8. $D = \$2$
$Vc = \dfrac{2 + \dfrac{0.15}{0.10}(4)}{0.10}$	$Vc = \dfrac{2 + \dfrac{0.08}{0.10}(4)}{0.10}$	$Vc = \dfrac{2 + \dfrac{0.10}{0.10}(4)}{0.10}$
$= \$80$	$= \$52$	$= \$60$
3. $D = \$5$	6. $D = \$5$	9. $D = \$5$
$Vc = \dfrac{5 + \dfrac{0.15}{0.10}(1)}{0.10}$	$Vc = \dfrac{5 + \dfrac{0.08}{0.10}(1)}{0.10}$	$Vc = \dfrac{5 + \dfrac{0.10}{0.10}(1)}{0.10}$
$= \$65$	$= \$58$	$= \$60$

share are $4, a realistic payout of two thirds. Putting these figures into the formula gives the stock a market value of $70 per share. If the dividend payout is increased to $5 per share, the market value will drop to $65. If it decreases to $2, the market price rises to $80.

The illustrative results accord with common sense. If the firm can employ funds more profitably than the industry generally, the firm ought to retain the earnings rather than pay them out. On this basis a high dividend payout results in a lower indicated market price than does a low dividend payout.[5]

In situation II the market rate is above the profitability rate with which the firms may employ funds. In this situation the higher dividend payout results in the higher indicated market price for the stock. Again, this result accords with common sense. If the firm cannot employ the funds as profitably as they can be used elsewhere, they ought to be paid out in dividends.

In situation III, full equilibrium in the economic system has been reached, and the productivity of retained earnings in the firm is equal to the productivity of funds elsewhere in industry. In this situation it makes no difference whether the firm has a high dividend payout or a low dividend payout. The indicated market price for the stock will be $60 regardless of the dividend policy.

This formulation is helpful in explaining dividend practices. As Professor Walter suggests in his article, a growth firm is one in which profitability is likely to be very high. The productivity of retained funds is likely to exceed the productivity of investment generally. As a consequence, the growth firm is one in which a low dividend payout is to be expected.

In contrast, mature companies whose earning power is on the decline cannot utilize earnings as effectively as other firms. Hence, they should have a high dividend payout. Firms that are relatively stable in their rate of growth but have not reached maturity and earn about as much as industry on the average could pay out either a very high or a very low dividend. For this category, differences in dividend policy are not likely on a priori grounds to have much effect on the market price of the firm's stock.

Harkavy Study

These relations throw light on another question frequently raised with regard to dividend policy: From the standpoint of the investor is it better for the firm to retain its earnings or to pay them out in dividends? Will the investor receive more if the firm has a high dividend payout or if it has a low dividend payout? Evidence on this question was obtained by taking pairs of companies in the same industry, holding other variables constant, and varying the payout percentages and therefore the percentages of earnings retained.[6] The findings are set out in Table 20–6.

---

[5] In strict logic, under the Walter formula a firm should therefore have either a 100 percent dividend payout or a zero payout. But since R_a undoubtedly falls as the level of investment (retained earnings) rises, a point is reached where $R_a = R_c$. This point is simply at a higher level of retained earnings (low payout ratio) for a "growth" company with good investment opportunities than for a "nongrowth" firm with poor opportunities. This has led to the development of theories that make R_a a function of the payout ratio, and a discussion of them is included in the appendix to this chapter.

[6] Oscar Harkavy, "The Relation between Retained Earnings and Common Stock Prices for Large Listed Corporations," *Journal of Finance*, 8 (September 1953), pp. 283–297.

TABLE 20-6

TOTAL REALIZABLE BY STOCKHOLDERS FOR SELECTED PAIRS OF "SIMILAR" COMPANIES, 1931–1950

Company	Earnings Retained, in-Percentages	Total Dividends Paid (in dollars)	Increase in Market Price (Average, in dollars)	Total Realizable by Stockholders as Percentage of Average 1931 Price
General Baking	28	17.10	-6.90	58
Purity Baking	20	34.30	-3.00	95
American Chicle	27	36.03	31.60	142
Wm. Wrigley	7	74.00	16.60	131
Schenley	80*	15.12*	22.00*	379
Nat'l Distillers	58*	14.62*	15.60*	359
Freeport Sulphur	39	45.01	40.40	303
Texas Gulf Sulphur	15	57.25	43.00	273

* 1934–1950 used, as prerepeal statistics considered irrelevant.

Source: Oscar Harkavy, "The Relationship between Retained Earnings and Common Stock Prices for Large, Listed Corporations," *Journal of Finance,* 8 (September 1953), p. 295.

Comparing General Baking and Purity Baking, both in the same industry, General Baking had a higher percentage of retained earnings and a lower dividend payout rate. The total gain for the stockholders of General Baking, however, was lower than for the stockholders of Purity. This is the case where the lower payout resulted in the lower realizable gains.

In contrast is the second pair in the table, American Chicle and William Wrigley and Company. American Chicle in this case had the lower dividend payout; it retained the higher proportion of earnings. In this case, however, the total realizable in the form of dividends and stock-price appreciation by stock owners was greater for the low payout company than for the high payout company.

These and other examples establish that is is not possible to generalize whether low dividends and high retained earnings will result in a high combined dividend and increase in market price for the stock owners, or whether the reverse will obtain. The results depend, as the Walter formula indicates, upon whether the profitability of a company is high compared to the average for industry as a whole. If so, to retain earnings will be advantageous to the company and to the stock owners. If the profitability of retained earnings is low, dividend payouts should be higher.

Reconciliation of Theory with the Check List

In describing the factors influencing dividend policy an important influence was assigned to the following factors:

1. Cash position of the firm
2. Need to repay debt
3. Rate of asset expansion
4. Level of profits; size of profit margins; returns on new investments
5. Stability of earnings
6. Access to capital markets
7. Control position in the firm
8. Tax position of the stockholders and the corporation

It is interesting to observe that most of these factors are positively associated with the factors to which Walter and Harkavy assign central importance—the prospective profitability of retained earnings. A firm which is growing rapidly is likely to be in a high profit line business with high profit potentials. Its rate of asset expansion will be high; it has heavy financing needs, or debts to be repaid. Its cash position will be tight. Any incipient instability of earnings will be swamped by the upward thrust of the growth of earnings. Access to the capital markets will be limited in relation to needs.

In short, most of the factors making for a low dividend payout will be associated with a high profitability of retained earnings. These are all reinforcing factors making for a low dividend payout and high percentage of retained earnings, resulting in the financing of a substantial proportion of net capital formation of the firm by retained earnings, as observed in studies of capital formation and its financing.

The indicated pattern would be quite clear for a strong growth situation. However, for gradations of growth and profitability, individual factors influencing dividend policy will be present in varying degrees. Weighing and combining the influence of these factors to arrive at dividend decisions are important responsibilities of financial managers.

STABILITY OF DIVIDEND POLICY

Another relation observed in dividend policy is the widespread tendency of corporations to pursue a relatively stable dividend policy. Profits of firms fluctuate considerably with changes in the level of business activity. Figure 20–1 shows that dividends are more stable.

As Professor Linter has observed, corporations seek to maintain a target amount of dividends paid.[7] Dividends increase with a lag as a step-

---

[7] For an excellent discussion providing a foundation for understanding dividend policy, see John Lintner, "Distribution of Incomes of Corporations among Dividends, Retained Earnings and Taxes," *American Economic Review*, 46 (May 1956), pp. 97–113.

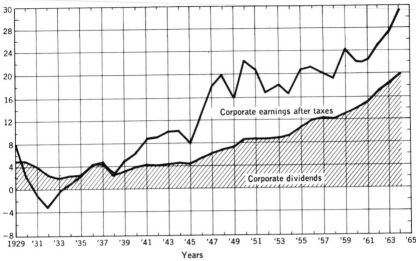

Fig. 20–1.   Corporate Earnings after Taxes and Dividends
(billions of dollars)

function of earnings. Only after an increase in earnings appears clearly sustainable and relatively permanent are dividends increased. When dividends have been increased, strenuous efforts are made to maintain the dividend. If earnings decline, until it is clear that an earnings recovery will not take place, dividends will be maintained.

The foregoing also explains the practice of firms of declaring dividend extras during the final quarter of their fiscal year. As earnings of the firm increase, at first the customary quarterly dividend will not be altered. Year-end "extras," however, will be declared. This explains why in Figure 20–1 the amount of dividends will rise moderately in years when earnings increase sharply. Only after it is clear that earnings have risen to a new plateau will the "customary" amount of dividends be increased.

We may now evaluate this practice of following a stable dollar amount of dividends policy. First, consider the stable dividend policy from the standpoint of the stockholders as owners of a company. Their acquiescence with the general practice must imply that stable dividend policies lead to higher stock prices on the average than do alternative dividend policies. Is this a fact? Does a stable dividend policy maximize security values for a corporation? As there has been no systematic empirical study on this question, on a factual basis there is really no answer to the question.

On a priori grounds, however, it would be expected that a stable dividend policy would lead to higher stock prices. A stable dividend policy is likely to lead to higher stock prices because investors will value more highly dividends they are certain to receive. If dividends fluctuate, invest-

TABLE 20–7

DIVIDEND STABILITY AND STOCK PRICE FLUCTUATIONS

Twenty Selected Common Stocks with Long, Unbroken Quarterly Cash Dividend Records	*Quarterly Payment Began*	*Price Range, August, September, and October 1957 (in dollars)*				*Maximum Decline from High to Low*	
		Open	*High*	*Low*	*Close*	*Points (in dollars)*	*Percentage*
Allied Chemical & Dye Corp.	1903	90	90½	72¾	73¾	17¾	19.6
American Can Co.	1923	44⅞	44⅞	38⅝	39⅛	6¼	13.9
American Tel. & Tel. Co.	1882	173⅜	174⅝	160	165	14⅝	8.4
Consolidated Edison Co.	1891	42¾	43¼	40½	42	2¾	6.4
Dow Chemical Co.	1912	60½*	60½*	49	54⅜	11½	19.0
duPont de Nemours (E. I.) & Co.	1905	199½	201¾	160¾	175¼	41	20.3
Eastman Kodak Co.	1902	108¾	109	86¼	96⅝	22¾	20.9
General Electric Co.	1899	69⅝	70	56	60⅜	14	20.0
General Foods Corp.	1922	48	49⅜	43	45	6⅜	12.9
General Motors Corp.	1923	45	45⅛	36⅝	38⅞	8½	18.8
Int. Business Machines	1916	335	341	270½	298½	70½	20.7
Int. Harvester Co.	1910	34¾	35⅜	29⅝	30⅞	5¾	16.3
Liggett & Meyers Tobacco Co.	1912	63¾	68	62¼	65⅞	5¾	8.5
Minnesota Mining & Mfg. Co.	1916	89¾	91½	74	77¼	17½	19.1
National Lead Co.	1906	128	129	86⅝	94⅜	42⅜	32.8
Pacific Gas & Electric Co.	1919	47⅞	48¼	43¾	45½	4½	9.3
Procter & Gamble Co.	1898	49¾	51½	47½	49	4	7.8
Texas Co.	1903	74¼	75	58⅝	64½	16⅜	21.8
Union Carbide Corp.	1918	121¼	121¾	96¾	97½	25	20.5
Woolworth (F. W.) Co.	1913	42	42¼	39	39¼	3¼	7.7

Twenty Selected Common Stocks Having Either Brief Quarterly Dividend Longevity Records or None

Longevity Records or None	Quarterly Payment Began	Price Range, August, September, and October 1957 (in dollars)				Maximum Decline from High to Low	
		Open	High	Low	Close	Points (in dollars)	Percentage
American Airlines, Inc.	1954	19¾	19⅞	14⅛	16¼	5¾	28.9
Carrier Corporation	1948	52⅝	52⅝	33½	37¾	19⅛	36.3
Case (J. I.) Co.	—	18	18	12⅜	13⅛	5⅝	31.3
Detroit Steel Corp.	1955	16¼	16¾	10⅜	11½	6⅜	38.1
Dresser Industries, Inc.	1948	50⅞	52¼	37¼	39¾	15	28.7
Federal Paper Board Co.	1948	35⅛	35⅛	32	32⅛	3⅛	8.9
General Cable Corp.	1951	39½	40½	30	32¾	10½	25.9
General Portland Cement Co.	1947	66½	66⅞	49	52¼	17⅞	26.7
International Paper Co.	1946	102¾	102¾	83½	86	19¼	18.7
Jefferson Lake Sulphur Co.	1948	46⅛	46⅛	26⅛	26⅛	20	43.4
Lockheed Aircraft Corp.	1949	37⅞	38	26	33⅛	12	31.6
Long Island Lighting Co.	1951	21¼	21¾	19¼	19¾	2½	11.5
Minute Maid Corp.	—	7	8¾	6	6⅛	2¾	31.4
National Supply Co.	1947	47⅜	47¾	32½	37¼	15¼	31.9
Niagara Mohawk Power Corp.	1950	20½	29⅞	26¼	27¾	3⅝	12.1
Owens-Corning Fiberglas Corp.	1954	57¾	57¾	36¾	41⅜	21	36.4
Pacific Finance Corp.	1947	39⅝	40⅞	35¼	37½	5⅝	13.8
Schering Corporation	1952	41¾*	43⅛*	31¼	34	11⅞	27.5
Spencer Chemical Co.	1946	57⅛	57½	46½	47¾	11	19.1
Vanadium Corp. of America	1950	43½	43½	26⅛	28½	17⅜	39.9

* Adjusted for stock dividends or splits.
Source: Exchange, 18 (December 1957), pp. 6–7.

ors may discount, with some percentage probability factor, the likelihood of receiving any particular amount of dividends. That is, the same average amounts of dividends received under a fluctuating dividend policy are likely to have a higher discount factor applied to them than to dividends under a stable dividend policy.

Another advantage of a stable dividend from the standpoint of a corporation and its stock owners is the requirement of legal listing. Legal lists are lists of securities in which state governments, mutual savings banks, pension funds, insurance companies, and other fiduciary institutions are permitted to invest. One of the criteria for placing a stock on the legal list is an uninterrupted payment of dividends. Thus legal listing encourages pursuance of a stable dividend policy.

A third argument for a stable and unbroken cash dividend policy is that the stock of such companies is subject to little decline in a fluctuating market. This is illustrated by the data set out in Table 20–7. Some other factors could, of course, influence the degree by which stock prices fall in a bear market. It is significant that the average pattern of decline among companies using a stable dividend policy was much lower than the average pattern of decline for the companies with more fluctuating dividend practices. Of course, another important variable is the degree of fluctuation in underlying earnings, which may be more important than the dividend practices themselves. Dividends are often a proxy variable for expected future dividends; therefore the influence of payout on stock values may become difficult to discern.

STOCK DIVIDENDS AND STOCK SPLITS

One of the significant issues of dividend policy in which the financial manager plays an important policy formulation role is that of stock dividends and stock splits. A stock dividend is paid in additional shares of stock instead of cash, and simply involves the transfer of surplus to the capital stock account.[8]

An interesting example of the use of stock dividends is the case of the Commonwealth Edison Company. In October 1958 it announced that practically all the annual earnings would be distributed each year in the

---

[8] One point that should be made in connection with stock dividends is that the transfer from earned surplus to the capital stock account must be based on market value. In other words, if a firm's shares are selling for $100 and it has 1 million shares outstanding, then a 10 percent stock dividend requires the transfer of $10 million (100,000 × $100) from earned surplus to capital stock. Quite obviously, stock dividends are thus limited by the size of earned surplus. The rule was put into effect to prevent the declaration of stock dividends unless the firm has had earnings. This is another in a long series of rulings designed to prevent investors from being fooled by the practices of unscrupulous firms.

form of cash and stock dividends. The company would continue to pay the regular 50 cents per share quarterly cash dividend, plus one annual dividend in stock, equivalent to the difference between the amount earned on common stock in that year and the $2 cash dividend paid. This device gives investors a combination of both cash and stock dividend.

In a stock split, on the other hand, there is no change in the total capital account or surplus. A larger number of shares of common stock are issued. In a two-for-one split, each stockholder would have two shares for each one previously held. Book value per share would be cut in half. The par, or stated, value per share of common stock is similarly changed.

From a practical standpoint there is little difference between a stock dividend and a stock split. The New York Stock Exchange considers any distribution of stock totaling 24 percent or less of outstanding stock to be a stock dividend. Any distribution of stock of 25 percent or more is regarded as a stock split. Though the two are similar, the issues outlined below are often discussed in connection with both stock dividends and stock splits.

Stock Dividends

In connection with stock dividends, two basic policy questions have been raised: price effects and effects on extent of ownership.

Price effects. The results of a careful empirical study of the effects of stock dividends are now available and can be used as a basis for observations on the price effects of stock dividends.[9] The findings of the study are presented in Table 20–8. When stock dividends were associated with a cash dividend increase, the value of the company's stock six months after the ex-dividend date had risen by 8 percent. On the other hand, where stock dividends were not accompanied by cash dividend increases, stock values fell by 12 percent during the subsequent six-month period.

These data seem to suggest that stock dividends are seen for what they are—simply additional pieces of paper—and that they do not represent true income. When they are accompanied by cash dividend increases, investors bid up the value of the stock. On the other hand, when stock dividends are not accompanied by cash dividend increases, investors are disappointed and the price of the stock drops. The fundamental determinant is underlying earnings trends, which also explains the good performance of the firms paying no cash dividends.

Effects on extent of ownership. Table 20–9 shows the effect of stock dividends on common stock ownership. Large stock dividends resulted in the largest percent increases in stock ownership. The use of stock dividends increased ownership by 25 percent on the average. For companies and industries that did not offer stock splits or stock dividends, the percent

---

[9] C. Austin Barker, "Evaluation of Stock Dividends," *Harvard Business Review*, 36 (July–August 1958), pp. 99–114.

TABLE 20–8

PRICE EFFECTS OF STOCK DIVIDENDS

| | Price at Selected Dates (in percentages) | | |
	Six Months Prior to Ex-dividend Date	At Ex-dividend Date	Six Months after Ex-dividend Date
Cash Dividend Variable			
1. Cash dividend increase	100	109	108
2. No cash dividend increase	100	99	88
3. No cash dividend	100	110	121

Year	Cash Dividend Differential Associated with Stock Dividends (in percentages)	Real Gain after Six Months (in percentages)
1951	13	9
1952	13	7
1953	14	6
1954	28	10
1951–1954	17	8

TABLE 20–9

EFFECTS OF STOCK DIVIDENDS ON STOCK OWNERSHIP

	Percentage Increase in Stockholders, 1950–1953
Stock dividend, 25% and over	30
Stock dividend, 5–25%	17
All stock dividends	25
No stock dividends or splits	5

Source: C. Austin Barker, "Evaluation of Stock Dividends," *Harvard Business Review,* 36 (July–August 1958).

increase in ownership was only 5 percent. Furthermore, the degree of increase in ownership increased with the size of the stock dividend.

This evidence suggests that stock dividends increase share ownership. Regardless of the effect on market price, the use of stock dividends effectively increases stock ownership by lowering the unit price at which shares are traded to a more popular range.

Stock Splits

Since stock splits and stock dividends are similar phenomena, this discussion of stock splits will be brief and will focus on two questions: the effect of stock splits on stock prices and on ownership. Again C. A. Barker has contributed two definitive studies. One covers a market in which stock prices moved relatively sidewise, and another a period in which stock market prices were moving up relatively sharply.[10]

These findings are summarized in Table 20–10. In the 1951–1953 period, stock splits associated with a dividend increase resulted in an increase in the market price of stocks by an average of 15 percent. Stock

TABLE 20–10

EFFECTS OF STOCK SPLITS ON STOCK PRICES

Period	Cash Dividend Variable	Price Index at Selected Dates, (in percentages)		
		One Year before Split	At Split Date	Six Months after Split
Level market, 1951–1953	Dividend increase	100	115	115
	No dividend increase	100	106	100
Bull market, 1954–1955	No dividend increase	100	105	92
	Dividend increase	100	118	118

splits not associated with effective dividend increases resulted in a 6 percent rise at the stock split date, but six months later stock prices fell back to their previous level. During the bull market of 1954–1955, the results were even more dramatic, as shown by the data in the table.

The effect of stock splits on breadth of ownership was consistent with the findings in the stock dividend study. These are summarized in Table 20–11. On all stock splits, ownership increased by 30 percent over the period covered. Again, the percent of increase was larger where stock splits were associated with increased dividends. In companies in which no splits had occurred, the increase in stock ownership was only 6 percent, representing one fifth of the percentage increase in stock ownership where splits occurred.

It is of interest to note the range of stock prices resulting after the stock splits had taken place and had resulted in an increase in stock own-

---

10 The first article was C. Austin Barker, "Effective Stock Splits," *Harvard Business Review*, 34 (January–February, 1956), pp. 101–106. The second was "Stock Splits in a Bull Market," *Harvard Business Review*, 35 (May–June 1957), pp. 72–79.

TABLE 20-11

EFFECT OF STOCK SPLITS ON NUMBER OF STOCKHOLDERS

Split Stocks	Percentage Increase in Ownership
With increased dividends	32
No dividend increases	28
Total splits	30
No splits	6

ership. The $20 to $50 category was the most popular. Some 82 percent of the splits resulted in prices in this range during the 1951–1953 period, and for the 1954–1955 period the corresponding percent was 80.

It was found also that the $18-to-$25 price range resulted in an even better performance in increasing stock ownership. For the earlier period, 25 percent of the stock splits resulted in the stocks' selling in this price range; and during the 1954–1955 period, 17 percent of the stock ended in this area.

SUMMARY

Dividend policy determines the extent of internal financing by a firm. The financial manager decides whether or not to release corporate earnings from the control of the enterprise. Because dividend policy affects the financial structure, the flow of funds, corporate liquidity, stock prices, and investor satisfaction—to list a few ramifications—the manager exercises a high degree of judgment in establishing a dividend pattern.

As a guide to boards of directors responsible for dividend policy, the following check list summarizes the major economic and financial factors influencing dividend policy and the direction of the influence.

1. *Rate of growth and profit level.* Economic theory suggests that high growth rates are associated with higher profit opportunities and lower growth rates with smaller profit margins. The higher the growth rate and the larger the prospective margins, the lower the dividend payout is likely to be.

2. *Stability of earnings.* If earnings are relatively stable from the standpoint of both long-term growth and cyclical fluctuations, the dividend payout is likely to be higher.

3. *Age and size of firm.* A well-established, large firm has better access to the capital markets than has a new and small firm. Hence the dividend payout, other things being equal, will be higher for the larger and older firm.

4. *Cash position.* The stronger a firm's cash or liquidity position in relation to its prospective future need for funds, the higher the probable dividend payout.

5. *Need to repay debt.* A firm that has incurred heavy indebtednesses has implicitly committed itself to a relatively high rate of earnings retention unless it seeks to prepare the markets for a common stock or debt refunding issue.

6. *Control.* If maintenance of existing control is an important consideration, the dividend payout may be lower to permit financing from retained earnings. The procedure avoids issuance of additional securities, which would involve

dilution of ownership or the increased risks of debt. On the other hand, if a struggle for control of the firm with opposition groups is in progress or threatened, the dividend payout may be higher to appeal to stockholder goodwill.

7. *Maintenance of a target dividend.* The objective of a stable dividend policy will make for low payouts when profits are temporarily high and high payouts when profits are temporarily depressed; and will cause dividends to lag behind profit growth until the establishment of new earnings levels is strongly assured.

8. *Tax position of stockholders.* Corporations closely held by a few taxpayers in high income tax brackets are likely to have a lower dividend payout. Corporations widely held by small investors will tend to have higher dividend payouts.

9. *Tax position of the corporation.* Potential penalties for excessive accumulation of retained earnings may cause dividend payouts to be higher than economic and financial considerations alone would indicate.

Of the factors listed, some make for higher dividend payouts, some for lower. It is not possible to provide a formula which can be used to establish the proper dividend payout for a given situation. This is a task requiring the exercise of judgment. The considerations summarized above provide a check list for guiding dividend decisions.

Empirical studies indicate a wide diversity of dividend payout ratios not only among industries but among firms in the same industry. Studies also show that dividends are more stable than earnings. Firms are reluctant to raise dividends in years of good earnings, and they resist dividend cuts as earnings decline.

The Walter formula spotlights the return on retained earnings relative to the average market rate of return on investment as a critical determinant of dividend policy. A high rate of return on retained earnings indicates a low payout ratio, whereas a low rate relative to the market average indicates the desirability of a high payout ratio to increase the price of the common stock. The Harkavy study is inconclusive with regard to the effect on market price of payout ratios alone. However, stable dividends, whether high or low, tend to increase stock prices by reducing the uncertainty facing an investor.

Neither stock splits nor stock dividends alone exert a fundamental influence on prices. The fundamental determinant of the price of the company's stock is the company's earning power compared with the earning power of other companies. However, both stock splits and stock dividends can be used as an effective instrument of financial policy. They are useful devices in reducing the price at which stocks are traded, provide a method for conserving cash, and provide a means of shifting ordinary income for tax purposes to capital gains.

SELECTED REFERENCES

Barker, C. A., "Are Stock Dividends Effective?", *Harvard Business Review,* 36 (July–August 1958), pp. 99–114.

————, "Effective Stock Splits," *Harvard Business Review,* 34 (January–February 1956), pp. 101–106.

————, "Stock Splits in a Bull Market," *Harvard Business Review,* 35 (May–June 1957), pp. 72–79.

Boness, A. James, "Elements of a Theory of Stock-Option Value," *Journal of Political Economy,* 72 (April 1964), pp. 163–175.

470 Long-Term Financing

Boorstin, Robert L., "A Rational Dividend Policy for Savings and Loan Companies," *Financial Analysts Journal*, 19 (July–August 1963), pp. 33–46.

Brigham, Eugene F., "The Profitability of a Firm's Purchase of Its Own Common Stock," *California Management Review*, 7 (Winter 1964), pp. 69–76.

Dhrymes, Phoebus J., and Mordecai Kurz, "On The Dividend Policy of Electric Utilities", *Review of Economics and Statistics*, pp. 46, 76–81.

Dobrovolsky, S. P., "Economics of Corporate Internal and External Financing," *Journal of Finance*, 13 (March 1958), pp. 35–47.

Ellis, Charles D., "Repurchase Stock to Revitalize Equity," *Harvard Business Review*, (July–August, 1965), pp. 119–128.

Harkavy, Oscar, "The Relation Between Retained Earnings and Common Stock Prices for Large Listed Corporations," *Journal of Finance*, 8 (September 1953), pp. 283–297.

Lintner, J., "Distribution of Incomes among Dividends, Retained Earnings, and Taxes," *American Economic Review, Proceedings*, 46 (May 1956), pp. 97–113.

Merjos, Anna, "Reverse Stock Splits", *Barron's* (May 1962), p. 9.

———, "Stock Split Timing", *Barron's* (April 1960), pp. 9–20.

Miller, Merton H., and Franco Modigliani, "Dividend Policy, Growth and the Valuation of Shares", *Journal of Business*, 34 (October 1961), pp. 411–432.

Porterfield, J. T. S., "Dividends, Dilution, and Delusion," *Harvard Business Review*, 37 (November–December 1959), pp. 56–61.

———, *Investment Decisions and Capital Costs* (Englewood Cliffs, New Jersey: Prentice-Hall, Inc. 1965).

Sosnick, Stephen H., "Stock Dividends are Lemons, Not Melons," *California Management Review*, 3 (Winter 1961), pp. 61–82.

Walter, James E., "Dividend Policy: Its Influence on the Value of the Enterprise", *Journal of Finance*, 18 (May 1963), pp. 280–291.

———, "Dividend Policies and Common Stock Prices," *Journal of Finance*, 11 (March 1956), pp. 29–41.

Weston, J. Fred (ed.), *Readings in Finance From Fortune* (New York: Holt, Rinehart and Winston, Inc., 1958), selection 24.

QUESTIONS

20–1 Discuss the merits and demerits of each of the following dividend policies:
1) Constant payout ratio
2) Constant dollar dividend per share
3) Constant regular quarterly dividend plus a year-end extra when earnings are sufficiently high or corporate investment needs are sufficiently low.

20–2 How would each of the following changes probably affect aggregate payout ratios? Explain your answer.
1) An increase in the personal income tax rate
2) A liberalization in depreciation policies for federal income tax purposes
3) A rise in interest rates
4) An increase in corporate profits
5) A decline in investment opportunities

20–3 Aggregate dividend payout ratios have been increasing since the end of the second World War. Why?

20–4 Discuss the pros and cons of having the directors formally announce what a firm's dividend policy will be in the future.

20–5 What purpose do stock dividends and stock splits accomplish?
20–6 What is the difference between a stock dividend and a stock split? As a stockholder, would you prefer to see your company declare a 100 percent stock dividend or a two-for-one split?
20–7 "The cost of retained earnings is less than the cost of new outside equity capital. Consequently, it is totally irrational for a firm to sell a new issue of stock and, during the same year, pay dividends." Discuss this statement.

PROBLEMS

20–1 Listed below are pertinent financial data for the common stocks of Cerro Corp., Polaroid, and National Fuel Gas. Cerro is a leading producer of copper, zinc, and lead, whose product demand is quite cyclical. Polaroid manufactures cameras and film. National Fuel Gas is an integrated gas system serving the Northeastern United States.

CERRO CORPORATION

Year	Earnings	Dividends	Price Range	Payout	Price-Earnings* Ratio
1964	$4.59	$1.14	46–19	25%	10–4
1963	2.25	0.73	21–12	32	9–5
1962	0.99	0.69	21–11	70	18–10
1961	0.87	0.66	27–18	76	25–17
1960	2.01	0.58	24–15	29	11–7
1959	1.73	0.54	27–19	31	14–9
1958	0.95	0.46	25–13	48	20–10
1957	1.11	0.79	29–12	71	22–9
1956	2.19	0.75	37–26	34	12–8
1955	2.78	0.64	28–16	23	7–4

POLAROID

Year	Earnings	Dividends	Price Range	Payout	Price-Earnings* Ratio
1964	$1.16	$ .06	46–32	5%	40–28
1963	0.71	.05	53–30	7	88–32
1962	0.63	.05	55–20	8	115–85
1961	0.52	.05	60–44	10	116–72
1960	0.56	.05	65–41	9	68–35
1959	0.69	.05	47–24	7	59–23
1958	0.47	.05	27–11	11	37–18
1957	0.36	.04	13–6	11	30–13
1956	0.22	.03	7–3	14	21–11
1955	0.13	.02	3–2	15	23–15

NATIONAL FUEL GAS

Year	Earnings	Dividends	Price Range	Payout	Price-Earnings* Ratio
1964	$2.17	$1.36	34–31	63%	16–14
1963	2.29	1.30	37–29	57	16–13
1962	2.15	1.23	31–23	57	14–11
1961	1.84	1.20	33–24	65	18–13
1960	1.86	1.20	24–22	64	13–12
1959	1.74	1.15	25–21	66	14–12

1958	1.78	1.10	24–17	62	13–10
1957	1.30	1.10	20–16	85	15–13
1956	1.58	1.03	22–19	65	14–12
1955	1.57	1.00	23–20	64	15–12

* Price-earnings ratios are the high and low for the year according to *Standard & Poor's Reports.*

   1. What differences are revealed by the data on the dividend policy of the three firms? What explanations can be given for these differences?
   2. What is the relation of dividend policy to the market price of the stock?
20–2 In the following table, earnings and dividend data are shown for AT&T and Sun Oil Company, a closely held, growing firm.
   Explain the difference in the percentage of dividends paid out by each.

AMERICAN TELEPHONE AND TELEGRAPH

Year	Earnings	Dividend	Payout	Average Price
1964	$3.24	$1.95	60%	70
1963	3.03	1.80	59	64
1962	2.90	1.80	62	59
1961	2.76	1.73	63	60
1960	2.77	1.65	60	47
1959	2.61	1.58	60	40
1958	2.34	1.50	64	33
1957	2.17	1.50	69	28
1956	2.20	1.50	68	30
1955	2.19	1.50	68	30

SUN OIL COMPANY

Year	Earnings	Dividend	Payout	Average Price
1964	$4.30	$0.95	22%	59
1963	3.85	0.90	23	46
1962	3.29	0.85	26	41
1961	3.09	0.81	26	43
1960	3.05	0.75	25	37
1959	2.64	0.73	28	44
1958	1.98	0.70	35	46
1957	2.93	0.67	23	50
1956	3.48	0.63	18	49
1955	2.95	0.58	20	44

20–3 Using Walter's formula, calculate the value of stock under the following sets of facts:

	E equals	D equals	Ra	Rc	Vc
A	$8	$5	10%	6%	
B	8	3	10	6	
C	8	5	5	10	
D	7	5	12	10	
E	8	3	12	10	

   What generalizations may be drawn from the use of Walter's theory as expressed by his formula?
20–4 Union spokesmen have made arguments similar to the following:

"Corporations such as General Foods retain about one half their profits—that is, they do not pay them out in dividends. Therefore, their profits are too high, because if they financed by selling common stock instead of by retained earnings, their prices or profits would not need to be so high."

Evaluate the statement.

20–5 Select a pair of companies in problems 1 and 2 and calculate dividend payout based on cash flows. Would your previous explanation of dividend policies be affected by the cash flow payout patterns? The following financial data are appropriately scaled: Totals are in millions of dollars.

Year	Net Income*	Depreciation and Depletion*	Year	Net Income*	Depreciation and Depletion*
	CERRO CORPORATION			AMERICAN TELEPHONE & TELEGRAPH	
1964	26.00	8.78	1964	1,658.6	1,469.4
1963	12.69	8.83	1963	1,479.5	1,332.1
1962	5.53	8.98	1962	1,388.2	1,219.0
1961	4.94	8.18	1961	1,284.6	1,099.9
1960	9.38	7.56	1960	1,213.0	1,007.8
1959	8.00	6.95	1959	1,113.2	930.0
1958	3.97	6.27	1958	952.3	834.0
	POLAROID CORPORATION			SUN OIL COMPANY	
1964	18.32	5.24	1964	68.51	57.71
1963	11.22	4.39	1963	61.22	62.19
1962	9.96	3.41	1962	53.19	57.12
1961	8.11	3.75	1961	49.79	65.60
1960	8.81	2.87	1960	49.27	63.33
1959	10.74	2.18	1959	42.84	52.81
1958	7.21	1.58	1958	32.06	56.42
	NATIONAL FUEL GAS				
1964	11.05	4.64			
1963	11.66	4.65			
1962	10.96	4.60			
1961	9.35	4.20			
1960	9.16	3.96			
1959	8.56	3.95			
1958	8.78	3.90			

* In millions of dollars.

Theoretical Material on Dividend Policy

Dividend policy in practice tends to be rather pragmatic and to follow "traditional practices" and rules of thumb. However, there has been a considerable amount of theoretical work on dividend policy in recent years. The first section of this appendix presents a graphic model which, at a rather intuitive and nonrigorous level, integrates the cost of capital concepts developed in Chapter 12 with the capital budgeting concepts discussed in Chapter 7. Following this, some of the more advanced theoretical works of recent years are analyzed in detail.

A GRAPHIC MODEL OF DIVIDEND POLICY

A rational, knowledgeable stockholder should prefer to have the firm reinvest earnings if the return on reinvestment exceeds the rate of return the investor could himself obtain. Since dividends are subject to the personal income tax, the required internal investment rate is somewhat lower than the outside investment rate; this was demonstrated in Chapter 12 in connection with the discussion of the cost of retained earnings capital. Assuming that investors are knowledgeable and rational, how should corporate dividend policy be determined? To answer this question, it is necessary to indicate the interrelationships between (1) investment opportunities, (2) corporate debt policy, (3) cost of capital, and (4) size of the capital budget.

As a first step, it is useful to draw on the concepts developed in Chapter 12 and its appendixes to derive a marginal cost of capital schedule. Recall that in Chapter 12 the cost of equity capital was shown to be constant until depreciation and retained earnings have been used up; after this, the cost of equity rises as the firm begins to use the more expensive new outside equity capital. This situation was shown in Figure 12C–1. For simplicity, it is assumed that additional increments of debt can be obtained at a constant rate so long as the debt is supported by additional increments of equity; that is, so long as the debt ratio remains constant.

Next, recall that the firm is assumed to have an optimal debt ratio, or a ratio that will produce a minimum average cost of capital. At this minimum, the average and marginal costs of capital must be equal.[1] To illustrate, refer to Chart A of Figure 20A–1. First, the curve labeled ACD is the average cost of debt capital; the curve ACE_1 is the average cost of equity so long as only depreciation and retained earnings are used; and the curve ACC_1 is the average cost of all capital, debt, and equity, based on ACE_1 and ACD. The minimum point on ACE_1 denotes the cost of capital at the optimum capital structure, assumed to be 50 percent in the example. Since the marginal cost of capital is equal to the average at the minimum point, the marginal cost of capital curve (MCC) can be constructed as shown in Chart B of Figure 20A–1. If depreciation charges

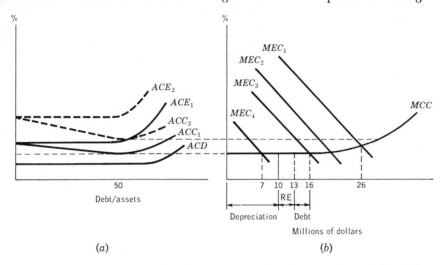

(a)   (b)

Fig. 20A–1. Graphic Model of Interrelationship between Cost of Capital, Investment Opportunities, and Dividend Policy

amount to $10 million and total earnings to $5 million, then the MCC curve is constant up to $20 million—$10 million of depreciation funds, $5 million of retained earnings, and $5 million of debt to match the $5 million addition to equity capital.

At higher levels of capital acquisition, the firm is forced to go to the outside equity capital market, hence it has a higher average cost of equity funds. This higher average cost of equity, when averaged in with the (assumed) constant average cost of debt funds, produces a higher over-all average cost of capital. There are, in effect, a family of higher and higher equity cost curves, hence a family of higher over-all cost curves. One such set (in addition to the minimum cost set), designated ACE_2 and

---

[1] This is proved in elementary economics textbooks. For example, see P. A. Samuelson, *Economics*, 5th edition (New York: McGraw-Hill, 1961), pp. 522–528.

ACC_2, has been indicated. The minimum point on ACC_2 is another point on the MCC curve shown in Chart B of the figure. If all the possible sets of ACE and ACC curves were plotted, the minimum points of the ACC's would trace out the MCC curve.

The MEC curves in Chart B are schedules showing the marginal rates of returns on investment. At any one time, a firm will be faced with but one such MEC; MEC_1 would indicate relatively many investment opportunities, while MEC_4 would indicate that good investment opportunities are relatively scarce.

Now suppose that, at a particular point in time, the hypothetical firm actually faces MEC_3. Given its MCC curve, the firm should have a gross investment of $16 million. Of this amount, $10 million represents the replacement of worn-out assets, so the net increase in (capital) assets is $6 million. To maintain the optimum capital structure, the net increase in assets must be financed by $3 million of equity and $3 million of debt. Since retained earnings are considerably cheaper than new outside equity, retained earnings should be used.

Total earnings available to the common stockholders was assumed to be $5 million. If $3 million is retained, then $2 million is available for distribution to stockholders in the form of dividends.

If MEC_1 was the appropriate investment opportunity schedule, the firm should make a gross investment of $26 million and a net investment of $16 million. Under the present assumptions, half the latter figure, or $8 million, should be equity. Logically, the firm should retain the entire $5 million of earnings in order to minimize its requirements for expensive outside equity capital.

At the other extreme, a firm faced by MEC_4 should not even spend all its depreciation funds on new assets. This firm should invest only $7 million. Now if it is to maintain the 50 percent debt ratio, this firm would have (1) to spend $7 million of depreciation funds on new assets, (2) to distribute the entire $5 million earnings to stockholders, and (3) to distribute 50 percent of the remaining $3 million cash flow to stockholders and 50 percent to creditors by retiring debt. Assuming the distribution to stockholders is in the form of cash dividends,[2] this firm would pay dividends of $6.5 million against earnings of only $5 million, or a payout of 130 percent.

If a firm should be in the expanding phase of its operations, and thus be faced with an MEC_1-type investment schedule, it is likely to retain 100 percent of its earnings. If it is an intermediate position, such as the firm with MEC_3, then it will pay out a portion of its earnings and retain a

---

[2] An alternative form would be the retirement of stock by open market or other forms of purchase. See Eugene F. Brigham, "The Profitability of a Firm's Purchase of Its Own Common Stock," *California Management Review*, 7 (Winter 1964), pp. 69–76.

portion. Finally, if it is actually declining, as is the firm with MEC_4, the payout should exceed earnings. It is impossible to obtain precise measures of the *MEC* and the *MCC* schedules; thus it cannot actually be *proved* that firms behave in the manner the theory would suggest. However, there is much evidence that firms with good investment opportunities in relation to their cash flows have low payout ratios, and vice versa.

The above analysis *assumes* that investors are indifferent between dividends and retained earnings so long as the firm has profitable investment opportunities. However, if this is not true—for example, if investors *prefer* to receive dividends rather than capital gains—then dividend policy can have a direct effect on the cost of capital and alter the conclusions reached above. The following section deals with some of the research that has been conducted on this subject.

INFLUENCE OF DIVIDEND POLICY ON THE VALUE OF A FIRM'S COMMON STOCK

Considerable literature on dividend policy has appeared since the Walter and the Harkavy articles of the mid-1950s. The present discussion will be focused on the central questions of whether "dividends really matter at all"—whether dividend policy can affect the price of a company's common stock.

It is useful to begin with the presentation by Ezra Solomon, which provides a foundation for comparing other formulations. The Solomon materials are summarized in Table 20A–1, which contains an explanation of the symbols employed.

Solomon distinguishes between simple expansion, or "growth," and dynamic models. In the expansion model, the firm reinvests a constant dollar amount (this implies that the dividend payout percentage is declining). Solomon presents the results in the three formulas listed in Table 20A–1 under the Growth Model caption. Equation (20A–1) is in Solomon's words, "a dividend and capital gains version of valuation."[3] Equation (20A–3) expresses value entirely in terms of net earnings data. Solomon concludes that valuation can be expressed either in terms of dividends or earnings and "the two models come to exactly the same thing."[4]

The same conclusion applies to Solomon's dynamic model, which is equation (20A–4). Another presentation of formulation of the dynamic model was set forth solely in terms of dividends by Gordon and Shapiro. Their results are set forth in Table 20A–2.

---

[3] Ezra Solomon, *The Theory of Financial Management* (New York: Columbia University, 1963), p. 60.
[4] *Ibid.*, p. 60.

TABLE 20A–1

SOLOMON MODEL
No Debt; No Outside Equity Financing

"Growth" model—firm can reinvest a constant dollar amount $= bE_o$
"Dynamic" model—firm can reinvest at a constant ratio which is an
increasing absolute amount $= bE(t)$

Growth Model

$$V = \frac{D}{k_e} + \frac{Ebm}{k_e} \qquad \text{[Solomon equation (5.5), page 60]} \qquad (20A\text{–}1)$$

$$V = \frac{E(1-b)}{k_e} + \frac{Ebm}{k_e} \qquad \text{[Solomon equation (5.4), page 60]} \qquad (20A\text{–}2)$$

$$V = \frac{E}{k_e} + \frac{bE(m-1)}{k_e} \qquad \text{[Solomon equation (5.6), page 60]} \qquad (20A\text{–}3)$$

Dynamic Model

$$V = \frac{D}{k_e} + Vbm \qquad \text{[Solomon equation (5.12), page 65]} \qquad (20A\text{–}4)$$

Where:

$V =$ market value of the firm

$D =$ dividend in initial period

$E =$ net operating income

$b = \dfrac{E - D}{E} =$ retention rate for internal investments

$r =$ return on reinvestment opportunities

$k_e =$ expected yield on common stock which stockholders can achieve without any further net investment

$m = \dfrac{r}{k_e}$, where $r > k_e$

Source: Ezra Solomon, *The Theory of Financial Management,* (New York: Columbia University Press, 1963).

TABLE 20A–2

GORDON AND SHAPIRO MODEL
No Debt; No Outside Equity Financing (Growth is assumed in the model)

$$V = \frac{D_o}{k_e - g} \qquad \text{[Gordon-Shapiro equation (7), page 105]}$$

Where:

V = market value of the firm

D_o = initial dividend

E = net operating income

$b = \dfrac{E - D}{E}$ = retention rate for internal investments

r = expected return on reinvestments = ρ of Miller-Modigliani

$g = br$ = growth rate of dividends and market value of the firm

k_e = expected yield on common stock which stockholders can achieve without any further net investment

Source: Myron J. Gordon and Eli Shapiro, "Capital Equipment Analysis: The Required Rate of Profit," *Management Science,* III (October 1956), pp. 102–110.

Solomon's equation for his dynamic model is equivalent to the Gordon and Shapiro equation. The reconciliation between the two is shown in Table 20A–3. By the indicated algebraic processes, the two equations are shown to be the same.

TABLE 20A–3

RECONCILIATION OF SOLOMON'S DYNAMIC MODEL WITH THAT OF GORDON AND SHAPIRO

$$V = \frac{D}{k_e} + Vbm \qquad \text{[Solomon equation (5.12), page 65]}$$

$$V = \frac{D}{k_e} + \frac{rbV}{k_e}$$

$$k_e V - rbV = D$$

$$V = \frac{D}{k_e - rb}$$

$$V = \frac{D_o}{k_e - g} \qquad \text{[Gordon-Shapiro equation (7), page 105]}$$

Where:

$$m = \frac{r}{k_e}$$

$g = br$ = growth rate of dividends and market value of the firm

V = market value of the firm

$D_o = D$ = initial dividend

E = net operating income

$$b = \frac{E - D}{E} = \text{earnings retention rate}$$

r = expected return on reinvestments

k_e = expected yield on common stock which stockholders can achieve without any further net investment

$r > k_e$

Sources: Ezra Solomon, The Theory of Financial Management (New York: Columbia University Press, 1963).

Myron J. Gordon and Eli Shapiro, "Capital Equipment Analysis: The Required Rate of Profit," *Management Science*, III (October 1956), pp. 102–110.

Miller and Modigliani have also analyzed the issues under discussion here. Their formulations are shown in Table 20A–4.

TABLE 20A–4

MILLER-MODIGLIANI DIVIDEND AND GROWTH MODEL
Alternative Sources of Financing in Cases I, II, III below
(Investment is a function of earnings.)

I. *Earnings Approach*

$$V(0) = \frac{X(0) \, (1 - k)}{\rho - k \, \rho^*} \qquad \text{[Miller-Modigliani equation (23), page 421]}$$

II. *Dividends Approach*

$$V(0) = \frac{X(0) \, [1 - k_r]}{\rho - g} \qquad \text{[Miller-Modigliani equation (24), page 422]}$$

Setting (23) = (24) and solving for g;

$$g = k \, \rho^* \frac{1 - k_r}{1 - k} - k_e \rho \frac{1}{1 - k} \text{[Miller-Modigliani equation (25), page 423]}$$

III. *All External Financing* $(k = k_e)$

$$V(0) = \frac{X(0) \, (1 - k)}{\rho - \left(\dfrac{k \rho^* + k \rho}{1 - k} \right)} \text{ Substituting (25) into (23)}$$

Where:

$X(0) = $ current net operating income

$V(0) = $ current market value of the firm

$k = $ ratio of annual investment by firm to annual earnings

$k_r = $ fraction of total profits retained in each period $= (E - D)/E$

$k_e = $ amount of external capital raised per period expressed as a function of earnings $= [I - (E - D)]/E$

$k = k_e + k_r$

$g = $ rate of growth of dividends and market value of the firm

$\rho = $ expected yield on common stock which stockholders can achieve without any further net investment $= k_e$ of Solomon and R_c of Walter

$\rho^* = $ expected return on investment opportunities $= r$ of Solomon and R_a of Walter

Source: Merton H. Miller and Franco Modigliani, "Dividend Policy, Growth, and the Valuation of Shares," *Journal of Business*, XXXIV (October 1961), pp. 411–433.

Their conclusions are emphatic:

Like many other propositions in economics, the irrelevance of dividend policy, given investment policy, is "obvious, once you think of it." It is, after all, merely one more instance of the general principle that there are no "financial illusions" in a rational and perfect economic environment. Values there are determined solely by "real" considerations—in this case the earning power of the firm's assets and its investment policy—and not by how the fruits of the earning power are "packaged" for distribution.[5]

It is clear that Miller and Modigliani's dividend approach provides exactly the same valuation formula as Gordon and Shapiro. The numerator is dividends; the denominator is the capitalization factor less the retention rate multiplied by the profitability rate on new investment by the firm.[6]

Next are considered the implications of the alternative formulations of the influence of dividends on stock prices in the Walter formula presented in Chapter 20. To begin with, it is useful to recognize that the Walter formula is the same as Solomon's simple expansion model, shown in Table 20A–5. By substitution of the equivalent symbols, the equations are shown to be the same.

The dynamic models of valuation imply the same dividend policy as does the Walter formula. This may be illustrated by using any of the equations of Miller and Modigliani in Table 20A–4. If ρ^* is greater than ρ (with the constraint that the denominator must not be negative), the lower the dividend (so long as it is some positive quantity), the higher the value of the firm's common stock. If ρ^* is less than ρ, a near-100 percent dividend payout is implied.

It is concluded that all the approaches to dividends result in the same policy implications as the Walter formulation.

But, of course, dividend payouts are neither zero nor 100 percent. The profitability of the firm's investment is not certain as to its level or duration. These models, which imply the existence of supernormal profits for an extended period, are probably overoptimistic. The higher the rate of retained earnings and investment, the more difficult it will be for the firm to achieve high profit rates. A larger retention rate and a higher investment rate are likely to make it difficult to find investment opportunities of high profitability. In short, the higher the investment rate, the more likely that it will be difficult to find investments that offer high profit rates. But if a firm invests only in response to attractive profit opportunities, the amount of investment is likely to be smaller than if the firm starts with a target investment rate.

Hence the uncertainty of internal profitability rates, their duration, and the profitability of alternative uses of funds prevent the zero or 100

---

[5] Merton H. Miller, and Franco Modigliani, "Dividend Policy, Growth, and the Valuation of Shares," *Journal of Business*, University of Chicago, Vol. XXXIV, 4 (October 1961), p. 414.
[6] *Ibid.*, p. 44.

TABLE 20A-5

RECONCILIATION OF SOLOMON'S SIMPLE, EXPANSION GROWTH MODEL WITH WALTER'S MODEL

$$V = \frac{D}{k_e} + \frac{Ebm}{k_e} \qquad \text{[Solomon equation (5.5), page 60]}$$

$$V_c = \frac{D + \frac{r}{k_e}(E - D)}{k_e}$$

$$V_c = \frac{D + \frac{R_a}{R_c}(E - D)}{R_c} \qquad \text{[Walter equation (1), page 32]}$$

Where:

Solomon = Walter

$V =$ $V_c =$ market value of firm

$D =$ $D =$ current dividend

$E =$ $E =$ net operating income

b $= \dfrac{E - D}{E} =$ earnings retention rate

$k_e =$ $R_c =$ Expected yield on common stock which stockholders can achieve without any further net investment

$r =$ $R_a =$ expected return on investment opportunities

$m = \dfrac{R_a}{R_c} = \dfrac{r}{k_e}$

Sources: Ezra Solomon, The Theory of Financial Management (New York: Columbia University Press, 1963).
James E. Walter, "Dividend Policies and Common Stock Prices," *Journal of Finance,* XI (March 1956), pp. 29–41.

percent dividend payout implications of the formulas from being carried out fully. Dividend policy in practice is influenced by the nine factors listed in the text of Chapter 20.

It should be recognized also that tax factors have an important influence on dividend policy. Chapter 3 indicates that personal income tax rates rise much more rapidly than the corporate tax rates. If the corporation needs funds for expansion, its dividend payments are likely to be reduced because of the personal income tax factor. If the firm paid out its earnings in dividends and then sought to raise funds to finance expansion, the funds available from the dividends paid out would have been reduced by the amount of personal income taxes paid. The average personal income tax rate on dividends received has been variously estimated at from 30 to 40 percent.

It is concluded that the higher profit rates of growth firms result in lower dividend payouts. The lower internal profit rates of mature firms make for higher dividend payouts. The uncertainty of continued high profits and their duration make for high dividend payments for most mature firms. The effect of the tax structure is to reduce these payouts somewhat. On balance the factors discussed in the text determine whether payouts will be above or below the 50 percent level.

Using the symbols suggested by Solomon, some logical dividend payouts based on long-term stable relationships can be suggested.[7] The following symbols are employed:

E = net income available to common stock

D = dividends paid out

b = dividend payout ratio, $\dfrac{D}{E}$

T = sales to total operating asset turnover

R = sales

K = total operating assets

I = investment or change in total operating assets per year

M = profit margin on sales

g = growth rate of sales, assets, and profits, $\dfrac{I}{K}$

B = debt

S = stock

$L = \dfrac{B + S}{S}$ = leverage factor

For 100 percent equity financing ($L = 1.0$), it follows that

$$E = TMK$$

because when these terms are expressed as ratios, they cancel to E.

$$E = \frac{R}{K} \cdot \frac{E}{R} \cdot \frac{K}{1}$$

---

[7] These relations are presented in another form in James E. Walter, *The Valuation of Cash Dividends*. (Mimeographed manuscript, August 26, 1965) Section III, "Alternative Cash Distribution Policies."

The dividend payout, b, can be inferred from the firm's retention requirements, which are given by the following expression:

$$(1 - b) = g \div (TM)$$

$$(1 - b) = \frac{I}{K} \div \left(\frac{R}{K} \cdot \frac{E}{R}\right)$$

$$= \frac{I}{K} \cdot \frac{K}{E}$$

$$= \frac{I}{E}$$

Both these expressions may be illustrated by a numerical example. Let T, M, and K have the following values:

$T = 2$ times
$M = 5$ percent
$K = \$100,000$

Then:

$E = TMK$
$E = 2(0.05)(\$100,000)$
$E = \$10,000$

If the firm is growing 8 percent per year, g has the value of 8 percent. The retention rate would be calculated as follows:

$$(1 - b) = g \div (TML)$$
$$= 0.08 \div 2(0.05)$$
$$= \frac{0.08}{0.10}$$
$$= 0.8 = 80\%$$

If the growth rate dropped to 4 percent, the required retention rate would drop to 40 percent. If M were 8 percent, the required retention rate would drop to 50 percent.

If the firm employs no external equity financing but utilizes debt financing, the retention rate is reduced by the leverage factor. Thus if a firm has a debt-to-equity ratio of 60 percent, the leverage factor as defined becomes 1.6, or 160 percent. The required retention rate then becomes:

$$(1 - b) = g \div (TML)$$
$$= 0.08 \div [2(0.05)(1.6)]$$
$$= 0.08 \div 0.16$$
$$= 50\%$$

Thus the use of outside debt financing reduces the earnings retention rate required to achieve the target rate of growth. In the present example, the retention rate was reduced from 80 percent to 50 prcent. If the target rate of growth declined to 4 percent, the required retention rate would drop to 25 percent or a dividend payout of 75 percent. These formulations depend on the stability relations and target growth factors postulated in the examples.

PROBLEMS

20A–1 (1) To verify the relation between the Solomon formulas for expansion and the Walter formula in the text, apply the data of situation I in Table 20A–5 to any one of the three Solomon expansion formulae.

(2) Now utilize the same numerical examples in the Solomon dynamic model. Why do you obtain a different result?

(3) Now use the same numbers in the Gordon and Shapiro model and in the Miller and Modigliani formulas. Comment on your results.

20A–2 The Miller and Modigliani formulas under continuous discounting can be expressed as linear relations for earnings and dividends as follows:

For all internal financing

Total earnings	$\ln X(t) = \ln X(0) + k\rho^* t$
Total dividends	$\ln D(t) = \ln X(0)(1 - k) + k\rho^* t$
Earnings per share	$\ln x(t) = \ln x(0) + k\rho^* t$
Dividends per share	$\ln d(t) = \ln x(0)(1 - k_r) + k\rho^* t$

The following values and financing assumptions are given.

General Symbols: *Illustrative Values*

$X(0) =$ total initial earnings of firm	$=$	\$1,000
$D(0) =$ total initial dividends of firm	$=$	600
$N =$ total number of shares of common stock	$=$	100
$x(0) =$ initial earnings per share	$=$	\$ 10
$d(0) =$ initial dividends per share	$=$	\$ 6
$\rho =$ market rate of return	$=$	10%
$\rho^* =$ internal rate of return	$=$	20%
$t =$ time	$=$	10 years
$k =$ ratio of investment to total earnings in time (t)	$=$	0.4
$k_e =$ investment financed from external sources		
$k_r =$ investment financed from internal sources		

1. Evaluate each formula in the matrix below.

2. Comment on the values at the end of ten years of total earnings, total dividends, earnings per share, and dividends per share under the alternative methods of investing at a rate equal to 40 percent of the firm's annual earnings. Graph these relations on semilog paper with time on the horizontal axis.

3. What is the value of the firm under the alternative financing assumptions?

	1. All Internal Financing $k = 0.4 \quad k_e = 0 \quad k_r = 0.4$	2. All External Financing $k = 0.4 \quad k_e = 0.4 \quad k_r = 0$	3. Mixed Financing $k = 0.4 \quad k_e = 0.1 \quad k_r = 0.3$
A. Total earnings	$\ln X(t) = \ln X(0) + k\rho^* t$	Same as 1A	Same as 1A
B. Total dividends	$\ln D(t) = \ln X(0)(1 - k_r) + k\rho^* t$	$\ln D(t) = \ln X(0)(1 - k_r) + k\rho^* t$	$\ln D(t) = \ln X(0)(1 - k_r) + k\rho^* t$
C. Earnings per share	$\ln x(t) = \ln x(0) + gt$ $g = k\rho^*$	$\ln x(t) = \ln x(0) + gt$ $g = \dfrac{k(\rho^* - \rho)}{1 - k}$	$\ln x(t) = \ln x(0) + gt$ $g = k\rho^* \dfrac{1 - k_r}{1 - k} - k_e\rho \dfrac{1}{1 - k}$
D. Dividends per share	$\ln d(t) = \ln x(0)(1 - k_r) + gt$ g = same as 1C	$\ln d(t) = \ln x(0)(1 - k_r) + gt$ g = same as 2C	$\ln d(t) = \ln x(0)(1 - k_{r_t}) + gt$ g = same as 3C
E. Value of firm	$V(0) = \dfrac{X(0)(1 - k)}{\rho - \rho^* k}$	Same as 1E	Same as 1E

Chapter 21

Use of Rights in Financing

A *right* is an option to buy a security at a specified price during a designated period. Thus a right is a form of a "call" in the sense that the holder can exercise his option to "call" on the issuing corporation for shares of stocks at the specified price during the period in which the rights may be exercised. Warrants and convertibles, other forms of stock purchase options, are discussed in the following chapter.

In a number of companies, new issues of securities must first be offered to existing holders of common stock as "privileged subscriptions." When a company offers a new issue to existing stockholders, it usually issues stock purchase warrants, generally referred to as "rights." These rights must generally be exercised within a relatively short period, usually not more than 30 days. When corporations are required to offer new issues to holders of common stock, this legal requirement is referred to as the "pre-emptive right."

About 40 percent of all new issues of securities (by number of issues) and approximately two thirds of new issues of common stock are sold through privileged subscriptions, most of which involve the use of rights.[1] Thus rights perform a highly important role in the financing of corporations. Despite their widespread use, the significance of rights is often misunderstood by both the issuers and the investors. For these reasons, the use of rights is analyzed in this chapter. Aspects of rights will be discussed in the following order: the pre-emptive right, technical procedures, theoretical relations, patterns in practice, and advantages and limitations.

---

[1] Securities and Exchange Commission, *Volume and Nature of Corporate Securities Offerings* (Washington, D.C.: U.S. Government Printing Office, July 1957), p. 14.

PRE-EMPTIVE RIGHT

The pre-emptive right gives stockholders the first opportunity to purchase additional issues of the company's securities. The concept of rights grows out of the common-law doctrine that a stockholder should have the opportunity to preserve his pro rata share in the earnings, ownership, and surplus of a company.

Legal Requirements

Provisions with respect to pre-emptive rights vary among the individual states. The situation in the 50 states plus the District of Columbia is summarized in Table 21–1.

TABLE 21–1

TREATMENT OF PRE-EMPTIVE RIGHT IN STATE LAWS

Provisions of State Law	Number	Percentage
Pre-emptive right required	2	4
Pre-emptive right provided unless specifically denied in corporate charter	36	71
Pre-emptive right denied unless specifically granted in the corporate charter	5	10
No statutory provision	8	15
Total	51	100

Source: J. R. Nelson, "Rights" (Unpublished Ph.D. dissertation, University of California, Los Angeles, 1961), p. 29. Computed from Commerce Clearing House, *Corporation Law Guide,* 1960.

Only two states require that pre-emptive rights be carried by corporate charters. However, the dominant practice, found in almost three fourths of the states, provides that the pre-emptive right obtains unless specifically denied in the corporate charter. A survey of the first 100 companies listed in the 1958 *Fortune* directory of the 500 largest United States industrial corporations shows that 55 percent denied the pre-emptive right to their stockholders.[2]

Purpose

If a group of stockholders owns, for example, 10 percent of the stock of a company and is permitted to subscribe to new shares of stock, it will be able to maintain its 10 percent ownership of the company. Preservation of values of the stock owner's pro rata portion of retained earnings was explained in Chapter 17.

---

[2] Unpublished study by the authors.

TECHNICAL PROCEDURES

A number of technical procedures are involved in connection with rights offerings. Since the rights typically may be exercised during a relatively short period, the timing aspects are of particular importance. The dates of interest are the filing of the registration statement, the record date, and the trading period. As with any new issue of stock, registration with the Securities and Exchange Commission must first take place. After a 20-day waiting period, the securities may be sold publicly if the SEC interposes no stoppage. The record date for determining who shall be entitled to rights follows the effective date of registration. The trading period begins shortly after the date of record.

These relations will be made clearer by an example. After a clarification of the technical points, the characteristic general patterns of practice will be indicated.

On January 27, 1961, the American Telephone & Telegraph Company filed a registration statement with the SEC covering 11,225,000 shares of common stock. The company proposed to sell such stock on the basis of one new share for each 20 shares, rights to be received by stockholders of record on February 23, 1961. On February 15, 1961, the directors of AT&T set a subscription price of $86 on the stock, which was then selling at approximately $116. In a letter to share owners dated February 24, 1961, Mr. Kappel, the president of the company, advised that warrants (rights) would be mailed on March 10, 1961, and the rights would be valueless after April 14, 1961. Thus the trading period was between March 10 and April 14, approximately 35 days. Trading in the rights also takes place earlier on a when-issued basis.

These relations for the AT&T issue can be placed against a broader perspective. A study was made of 387 issues of securities listed on the New York Stock Exchange and sold through rights during the period 1946–1957.[3] Of the 387 issues, the length of time between the registration date and the beginning of the trading period was 10 to 15 days in 65 percent of the issues; it was between 15–20 days in an additional 18 percent. Thus the length of the trading period was between 10 to 20 days in 83 percent of the issues. The somewhat longer trading period for the AT&T issues described above may be due to the relatively large size of the issue, the large number of shareholders involved, and the fact that no investment banker was used in connection with the offering.

The number of rights needed to buy one new share at the subscription prices varies. In 29 percent of the cases, ten rights were required, and in 16 percent, five rights. The range of four to ten rights required encom-

---

[3] J. R. Nelson, "Rights" (Unpublished Ph.D. dissertation, University of California, Los Angeles, 1961).

passed 81 percent. However, the number of rights required is a function of the amount of funds raised and the relation between the existing market price of the stock and the subscription price placed on the new issue. These matters are taken up in the following section.

THEORETICAL RELATIONS

In formulating an issue of securities with the use of rights, the financial manager will confront a number of considerations. Among these are (1) number of rights that will be required to purchase the new security, (2) value of rights, (3) effect on the market price of the existing securities, (4) effects on the shareholders of the company, (5) tax aspects, and (6) effects on the costs of floating the issue. Each of these will be analyzed.

Basically, the value relations are determined by the relative size of the new issue and the subscription price discount from the existing market price of securities. These generalizations can be made most meaningful by an example of the characteristic relations based on Table 21–2.

TABLE 21–2

SOUTHEAST COMPANY
Balance Sheet before Rights Offering

	Total debt, 5% . . .	$ 40,000,000
	Common stock . . .	10,000,000
	Retained earnings . .	50,000,000
	Total liabilities and	
Total assets $100,000,000	capital	$100,000,000

If the par value of the common stock is $10, the number of shares outstanding is one million. It follows that the book value per share is $60. If the firm earns 10 percent on total assets, its earnings before charges and taxes will be $10 million. Earnings and price per share (assuming a price-earnings ratio of 25) will be:

Total earnings	$10,000,000
Interest on debt	2,000,000
Income before taxes	8,000,000
Taxes (50% assumed)	4,000,000
Earnings after taxes	4,000,000
Earnings per share	$ 4
Market price of stock (price-earnings ratio of 25 assumed)	$100

Two factors jointly determine the number of rights that will be required: the amount of new funds to be raised and the subscription price at which the new shares are to be sold. Suppose the amount of new funds to be raised is $10 million. If the subscription price is set at $10, the number of new shares to be sold will amount to 1,000,000. If the subscription price is $50, the number of new shares to be raised will be one fifth of the previous figure, or 200,000.

Since the original number of shares outstanding was 1,000,000, if an additional 1,000,000 shares are to be sold, one right will be required to subscribe to each new share. If only 200,000 shares are to be sold, five rights will be required to subscribe to a new share. Thus the number of rights that will be required to subscribe to a new share is the ratio of existing shares outstanding to the number of new shares that will have to be sold.

Value of a Right

As a foundation for developing some guidelines for policy decisions on the amount of the discount from market price, certain basic relations need to be understood. The nature of these relations may be explored by assuming for illustrative purposes that the subscription price is $10.

The 1,000,000 shares of stock outstanding before the new issue had a market value of $100 per share or a total market value of $100 million. When the additional 1,000,000 shares are sold at $10 per share, $10 million are added to the total market value of the stock outstanding. The total market value of $110 million divided by 2,000,000 shares of stock gives a market price per share of $55. Thus, when the rights may be exercised and the shares are sold ex-rights, the new value of the shares will be $55. Since the rights carried the option to buy a share of stock for $10 initially worth $100, but whose value will be $55, the value of the right will theoretically be $45.

The relations can be set forth clearly in a series of formulas:[4]

$$\frac{\text{Value of one}}{\text{right}} = \frac{\text{Market value of stock ex-rights} - \text{Subscription price}}{\text{Number of rights required to purchase one share}}$$

$$R = \frac{M_e - S}{N} \qquad (21\text{-}1)$$

$$\frac{\text{Value of one}}{\text{right}} = \frac{\text{Market value of stock, rights on} - \text{Subscription price}}{\text{Number of rights required to purchase one share plus 1}}$$

$$R = \frac{M_o - S}{N + 1} \qquad (21\text{-}2)$$

---

[4] Formula (21-1) follows directly from the verbal explanation. Formula (21-2) can be derived from formulas (21-1) and (21-3) as follows:

1. Substitute (21-3) into (21-1), obtaining

$$R = \frac{M_o - R - S}{N} \qquad (21\text{-}4)$$

Market value of
stock, ex-rights $= $ (Market value of stock, rights on) $-$ (Value of one right)

$$M_e = M_o - R \qquad (21\text{-}3)$$

The use of these relations can be illustrated by the data of the example given.

Using formula (21-1), the value of a right:

$$R = \frac{\$55 - \$10}{1} = \$45$$

Using formula (21-2) gives the same result:

$$R = \frac{\$100 - \$10}{1 + 1} = \$45$$

The relation between the value of the stock, ex-rights, and the right itself is shown by formula (21-3):

$$M_e = \$100 - \$45 = \$55$$

Effects of Incremental Earnings

The results set forth above are correct so far as they go, but they should be used by the financial manager with caution in planning new issues with rights offerings. The above analysis does not take into account the earning power of the additional funds obtained by the firm. If the earnings on the addition to assets is greater than the cost of the incremental funds, the market value of the firm's stock may receive an upward stimulus. The converse may also obtain.

The crucial role of the earnings on the additional assets and the effects of this on the price-earnings ratio of the firm's stock may substantially modify the relation suggested by the above formulas. The nature of

---

2. Simplify (21-4) as follows, ending with (21-3); this completes the derivation.

$$R = \frac{M_o - S}{N} - \frac{R}{N}$$

$$R + \frac{R}{N} = \frac{M_o - S}{N}$$

$$R\left(\frac{N + 1}{N}\right) = \frac{M_o - S}{N}$$

$$R = \frac{M_o - S}{N} \cdot \frac{N}{N + 1}$$

$$R = \frac{M_o - S}{N + 1} \qquad (21\text{-}3)$$

these effects is suggested by Problem 21–6 and the excellent article by Professor G. H. Evans cited in the references at the end of this chapter. The profitability of the incremental investment financed through the rights offering will influence the relations between the market values of the stock with and without rights, thereby affecting investor decisions to invest in the company through the rights or by buying the stock directly.

Effects on Position of Stockholders

The effects of the new financing on earnings and the price-earnings relations will also determine whether the stockholders benefit from the rights offering. If the relation suggested by the formulas obtain, the stockholders will neither benefit nor lose by the rights offering. This statement may be made clear by considering the position of an individual stockholder.

An individual stockholder had ten shares of stock before the rights offering. The ten shares had a market value of $100 per share; thus the total market value of his ten shares was $1,000. If he exercises his rights, he will be able to purchase ten additional shares at $10 a share, a new investment of $100; his total investment is now $1,100. He now owns 20 shares of his company's stock, which, after the rights offering, has a value of $55 per share. The value of his stock is $1,100, exactly what he invested in it.

Alternatively, if he sold his ten rights, which have a value of $45 per right, he would receive $450. He would now have his original ten shares of stock plus $450 in cash. But his original ten shares of stock now have a market price of $55 per share. The $550 market value of his stock now and of $450 in cash is the same as the original $1,000 market value of stock with which he began. From a purely mechanical or arithmetical standpoint, the stockholder neither benefits nor gains from the sale of additional shares of stocks through rights.

Why, then, is there either enthusiasm in connection with new issues of stocks through rights or, as is sometimes the case, criticism by stockholders of rights offerings? Before the rights offering, when the Southeast Company was earning $4 per share, let us assume that it was paying 50 percent of its earnings in dividends. Therefore the dividends per share before the rights offerings were $2 per share. If the company stock was selling at $100 per share, it sold on a 2 percent dividend yield basis.

After the company sells an additional 1,000,000 shares of stock through rights, the company has 2,000,000 shares of stock outstanding. It has engaged in a 2-for-1 split of its stock, except that it obtained $10 million in the process. If this had been a stock split of 2 for 1 or a stock dividend of 100 percent, the earnings per share would have dropped to $2. But because of the additional $10 million, on which it is assumed the company will earn the same rate that it has been earning on total assets, the earnings per share are $2.25.[5] If the company maintains the same dividend policy as before, this company would be expected to pay out $1.25 in dividends.

But if the company maintained its same dividend per share of $2, the dividend payout would be approximately 89 percent. Under such circumstances, the market price of the stock may rise, because stockholders are now receiving a higher dividend in relation to their investment.

An illustration of this is the American Telephone and Telegraph Company (AT&T), which repeatedly, from 1946 on, has sold additional issues of convertible debentures through rights to its holders of common stock. Some concessions in the price were offered to existing stockholders. Until the stock split in 1959, the same $9 dividend was maintained. Thus, in effect, AT&T was increasing its dividend, since some element of stock split is involved when an offering of securities is made through rights.

For this reason there is often excitement over a new issue of stocks through a rights offering. For example, International Business Machines (IBM) sold a privileged subscription in 1957 through rights. They offered 1,050,000 shares at $220 per share when the market price of its stock was about $228. During the subscription period the market price of its stock rose to $337. The rights' value also rose. The rights represented an effective dividend increase. Of course, in this instance the sale of stock took place during 1957, when sales of computers of the type that IBM produced were increasing at a rate of about 50 percent per annum, and IBM profits were increasing at a correspondingly high rate. Thus the stock sale was regarded by stock owners as an indication that IBM was going to continue to expand and that its profits would continue to increase.

Rights offerings as such may leave the stockholders in exactly the position they occupied before. However, the rights offering may be associated with an effective increase in the dividend payout. Or the offering may call attention to the company's past and prospective favorable growth rates. As a consequence, the rights offering may result in improvement in the earnings, dividends, and market price of the stock. The reverse may also result if the effects of the new financing on earnings and dividends are negative.

---

[5]

Total assets	$110,000,000
Total earnings	11,000,000
Interest on debt	2,000,000
Income before taxes	9,000,000
Taxes (50%)	4,500,000
Earnings after taxes	4,500,000
Earnings per share (2,000,000 shares)	$2.25

Relation between Market Price and Subscription Price

We are now able to investigate the factors influencing the level of the subscription price that will be designated. The size of the concession from the market price offered by the subscription price is determined by the nature and costs of distribution of the new issues of securities desired. A continuation of the example will illustrate the principle involved.

Let us assume that the articles of incorporation of the Southeast Company permit it to use rights or not, depending on whether or not it judges their use to be advantageous to the company and its stockholders. The financial vice-president of the company is considering three alternative methods of raising the additional sum of $10 million.

ALTERNATIVE I:

Sale of additional shares through investment bankers to the public at approximately $100 per share, the company netting approximately $96 per share; thus it would need to sell 105,000 shares.

ALTERNATIVE II:

Sale of additional shares through rights with investment bankers in stand-by capacity only, with a commission of 1 per cent on the original issue plus ¾ percent on all shares unsubscribed and taken over. Allowing for the usual market pressure attending sales of common stock through rights, the new shares would be sold at a 15 percent discount, or at $85. Thus 125,000 additional shares would be offered through rights. With eight rights, an additional share could be purchased at $85.

ALTERNATIVE III:

Sale of additional shares through rights at $10 per share. Investment bankers would not be employed at all. The number of additional shares of common stock to be sold would be 1,000,000. For each right held, existing holders of common stock would be permitted to buy one share of the new common stock.

Under alternative I, investment bankers are used. Rights would not be utilized at all. In this circumstance the underwriting commission is assumed to be approximately 4 percent. In alternative II, where rights are used with a small discount, the underwriting commission is reduced, since the investment bankers are used in stand-by capacity only. The underwriting commission consists of two parts—1 percent on the original issue for operating in a stand-by capacity; an additional ¾ of 1 percent commission is offered when the bankers take over unsubscribed shares and sell them. Thus the actual commission will range somewhere between 1 percent and 1¾ percent.

Under alternative III, the subscription price is assumed to be $10 a share. With such a large concession, it might not be necessary to use investment bankers at all, because the rights would be certain to have value and would be either exercised or sold.

Which of the three alternatives is superior may now be analyzed. Alternative I provides for wider distribution of the securities sold, as well as the certainty that the company will receive the $10 million involved in the new issue. The company pays for these services in the form of underwriting charges.

Under alternative II, by utilizing rights, underwriting expenses are reduced. There is also a reduction in the unit price per share. Because underwriting services are not utilized fully, the distribution is likely to be less wide.

Alternative III involves no underwriting expense, but it results in a substantial decrease in the unit price of shares. Initially, the shares will be less widely distributed. Furthermore, the issue is equivalent to a forced levy on the stockholders. The rights must be sold to prevent substantial losses. Consequently, alternative III places pressure on stockholders and will not be advantageous to them unless it is associated with some form of dividend increase. If this takes place, the stock owners may be compensated for the inconvenience of the rights offering. Note also that alternative III, with its large stock-split effect, will result in a much lower final stock price per share. Many people feel that there is an optimal stock price—one that will produce a maximum total market value of the shares—and that this price is generally in the range of $30–$60 per share. If this is the feeling of Southeast's directors, they may feel that alternative III permits them to reach this more desirable price range while at the same time reducing flotation costs on the new issue.

To summarize:

	Advantages	*Disadvantages*
Alternative I	1. Wider distribution 2. Certain of receiving funds	1. Underwriting costs
Alternative II	1. Smaller underwriting costs 2. Lower unit price of shares	1. Narrower distribution
Alternative III	1. No underwriting costs 2. Substantial decrease in unit price of shares	1. Rights must be exercised; pressure on owners 2. Narrower distribution of shares

The alternative that is most advantageous depends upon the company's needs. If the company is strongly interested in a wider distribution of its securities, alternative I is preferred. If it is most interested in reducing the unit price of its shares and is confident that the lower unit price will induce wider distribution of its shares, alternative III will be preferred. If the company's needs are moderate in both directions, alternative II may offer a satisfactory compromise. Whether rights will be used and the level of the subscription price depend upon the needs of the company at a particular time.

Tax Aspects of Rights

Any tax matter is always a function both of general principles and of the particular situation of a taxpayer, as well as of the particular facts of a given situation. There are two bases for determining the tax position of rights. The rights can be treated as having a cost basis of zero, and no adjustment in the cost basis for the common stock is made. If the rights are sold, the proceeds would be a capital gain for income tax purposes. The holding period would begin on the date the common shares on which the rights were issued were acquired. The holding period ends with the date on which the rights were sold. These dates would determine whether the capital gain would be long term or short term.

The second method is an allocation of the cost basis determined by dividing the market price of the right by the market price of the common stock. This method establishes the percent of the market price of the common stock represented by the value of rights. This percentage is applied to the cost basis of the common stock to determine the cost basis of each right. The cost basis of each right is deducted from the original cost basis of the common stock. When either the rights or the stocks are sold, the market values are related to the cost basis to determine the capital gain or loss.

How these principles would work out in specific instances may, however, be modified by special circumstances. The above explanation is purely for the purpose of indicating the basic pattern of tax treatment of rights.

PATTERNS IN PRACTICE

The foregoing illustrative materials and analysis have suggested that the price results of rights offerings reflect technical relations, and future earnings and dividend prospects. Accordingly, it is of significance to observe how these patterns may actually work out in practice.

Exercise of Rights

Interestingly enough, it is expected that a small percentage of stockholders may neglect to exercise their rights or to sell them. In an offering in 1955, the holders of $1\frac{1}{2}$ percent of the shares of General Motors common stock did not exercise their rights.[6] The loss involved to these stock-

---

6 Eldon A. Grimm, "The Money You Save May Be Your Own," *Exchange*, 16 (December 1955), pp. 17–20.

holders was $1.5 millions. The holders who failed to exercise their rights in a number of offerings during 1955 varied from 1.5 to 2.75 percent of the shares of stock outstanding. In an AT&T issue in that year, the loss to shareholders who neglected to exercise their rights was $960,000.[7]

As a consequence of the failure of a small percentage of shareholders to exercise their rights, the financial manager must increase slightly the size of the new security issue to compensate for the nonexercise of rights.

Market Price and Subscription Price[8]

Measured from the registration date for the new issue of the security, the average percentage by which the subscription prices of the new issues were below their market prices was 22.8 percent during the years 1946–1947 and 15.3 percent during the years 1956–1957. Examples of price concessions of 40 percent or more were observed in a small percentage of issues. The most frequently encountered discount is from 10 to 20 percent.

Effect on Subsequent Behavior of Market Price of Stock

It is often stated that new issues of stock through rights will depress the price of the existing common stock of the company. To the extent that a subscription price in connection with the rights offering is lower than the market price there will be a "stock split effect" on the market price of the common stock. If the prevailing market price of a company's stock is $100 and the subscription price is $10, the new market price will probably drop to $55.

But the second question is whether, because of the rights offering, the actual new market price would be $55 or lower or higher. Again, empirical analysis of the movement in stock prices during rights offerings indicates that generalization is not practicable. What happens to the market prices of the stock ex-rights and after the trading period depends upon the prospects of the issuing company.

Price Behavior of Rights

There is much literature on rights that sets forth the slogan of "sell early and buy late" during the rights trading period. This slogan implies that the value of rights is high during the early part of the trading period and low during the latter part. The explanation for this difference might be that stockholders reach their decisions slowly because they are not aware of the value of rights during the early part of the trading period or because they are waiting to see how values will develop. At any rate, they do not exercise their rights or sell them during the early part of the period

---

[7] *Ibid.*
[8] The data for this section and the following are from Nelson, *op. cit.*

but wait until later. Thus, in the latter part of the period for trading the rights, the supply is augmented relative to the supply of rights during the early part of the period, and the price declines.

A study of the price behavior of rights during the trading period for the years 1955–1956 showed that the number of cases where the rights value was higher during the second half of the trading period was almost equal to the number of cases where the rights were higher in the first half of the period.[9] These data were adjusted for movements in the Dow-Jones industrial average as a whole.

These findings suggest that the value of the rights is determined primarily by prospects of the individual company as judged by investors during the rights trading period. Where the company's outlook is strong, there will be a vigorous rise in the rights value during the rights trading period, although the rise is influenced by the degree of speculative exuberance about the outlook for the company during the rights trading period. Sometimes, on the first day of trading, rights will be pushed up to an extremely high level; later, as the true prospects of the company are more soberly assessed, the rights may decline in price. It appears that no generalization can properly be made.

In view of the uncertain price behavior and investor interest in rights during the trading period, underwriters have performed a more active role. Rights behavior during the trading period will be influenced by the action of underwriters who may be supporting the market in one way or another. Where investment bankers are used in a rights offering, they watch the market and purchase rights during the period of offering to stockholders. They exercise these rights, and from time to time prior to the expiration of the rights, offer the stock publicly at a price in line with the prevailing market. In this manner the underwriters reduce their risks substantially, and stockholders who are unable to exercise their rights have a better opportunity to realize on them by selling them. Furthermore, the possibility of a large block of unsubscribed securities demoralizing the market after the expiration date for trading in the rights is greatly reduced.

This plan differs from the old method of handling the rights. Formerly, underwriters would merely stabilize the stock or the rights, or both. It was the custom among underwriters not to make any offering of the securities until after the amount of subscription was known, and often it was too late to remedy the consequences of an unsuccessful offering. Under the old method the distribution machinery of the underwriters was immobilized for from ten days to three weeks while their capital was committed. Under the new method the value of the rights is stabilized and

---

9 *Ibid.*

the investment bankers begin selling securities during the period when the trading in rights has directed attention to the company's securities.

SIGNIFICANCE OF RIGHTS BEHAVIOR

To this point the material on rights has sought to develop an understanding of the nature and behavior of rights and their values. Much of this may have appeared to be from the standpoint of the investor. But such an approach is necessary to uncover the basic properties of rights. With this understanding as a background, it is now possible to focus directly on the significance of the use of rights in formulating financing policies. This material may be conveniently organized in terms of advantages of, and limitations to, the use of rights.

Advantages of Use of Rights in New Financing

It has been seen that the pre-emptive right gives the shareholders the protection of preserving their pro rata share in the earnings and surplus of the company. The firm also benefits. By offering new issues of securities to the existing stockholders, it increases the likelihood of a favorable reception for the stock. By their ownership of common stock in the company, these investors have already indicated a favorable evaluation of the company. They may be receptive to the purchase of additional shares, particularly when the additional reasons indicated below are taken into account.

The shares purchased with rights are subject to lower margin requirements. For example, margin requirements since November 1963 have been 70 percent; in other words, a person buying listed stocks must have at least $70 of his own funds for every $100 of securities purchased. However, if shares of new issues of stocks are purchased with rights, only $25 per $100 of common stock purchased must be furnished by the investor himself; he is permitted by law to borrow (if feasible) up to 75 percent of the purchase price. Furthermore, the absence of a clear pattern in the price behavior of the adjusted market price of the stocks and rights before, during, and after the trading period may enhance interest in the investment possibilities of the instruments.

These factors may offset the tendency toward a downward pressure on the price of the common stock occurring at the time of a new issue.[10] But with the increased interest and advantages afforded by the rights offering, the "true" or "adjusted" downward price pressure may actually be avoided.

---

[10] The downward pressure develops because of the augmentation of the supply of securities without a necessarily equivalent increase in the demand.

A related advantage is that the flotation costs to an issuer associated with a rights offering will be lower than the costs of a public flotation. Costs referred to here are cash costs. For example, the flotation costs of industrial issues of common stock in 1955 were 9 percent on public issues compared with 3.8 percent of the proceeds to the company on privileged issues.[11] Underpricing on privileged issues increases their "costs" to 20.6 percent. However, the underpricing is not a cash outlay.

Indeed, the financial manager may obtain benefits from underpricing. Since a rights offering is a stock split to a certain degree, it will cause the market price of the stock to fall to a level lower than it otherwise would have been. But stock splits will increase the number of shareholders in a company by bringing the price of a stock into a more attractive trading level. Furthermore, because a rights offering is an indirect stock split, it may be associated with a dividend increase.

Finally, the total effect of the rights offering may be to stimulate an enthusiastic response from stockholders and the investment market as a whole, with the result that opportunities for financing become more attractive to the firm. Thus the financial manager may be enabled to effect common stock financing at lower costs and under more favorable terms.

Limitations on Use of Rights in New Financing

The use of a rights offering to avoid or reduce underwriting expenses will also lose the benefits of underwriting services. For example, the breadth of distribution of securities may be reduced.

The risks of an unsuccessful offering are increased to the degree that the services purchased from investment bankers are reduced. Some of the risks are inherent in the nature of the rights offering procedure. Since a trading period in the rights is involved, the sale of the new issue is exposed to substantial adverse market developments over a more extended period than if a straight public underwriting had been used.

Finally, the rights offering may be a kind of forced levy on the stockholder. If the subscription price is set close to the market value, the value of rights will be so small that it constitutes a nuisance for the existing owners of small and medium holdings of shares. If the subscription price is set substantially below the existing market price, the rights are certain to have substantial value. But if there is no general market interest in the securities, the value may be less than the expected or theoretical value. If this is so, a loss results for the existing shareholders, which may adversely affect future financing opportunities available to the financial manager.

---

[11] H. W. Stevenson, *Common Stock Financing* (Ann Arbor: University of Michigan, 1957), p. 61.

SUMMARY

This summary focuses on the key decisions confronting the financial manager with regard to a rights offering and indicates the major features bearing on such decisions.

Rights offerings may be used effectively by financial managers to increase the goodwill of shareholders. If the new financing associated with the rights represents a sound decision resulting in improved earnings prospects for the firm, a rise in stock values will probably ensue. The use of rights will permit shareholders to preserve their positions or to improve them. On the other hand, if the new financing is not well advised, the rights offering may represent a forced levy on the shareholders.

Because the rights offering is directed to existing shareholders, it may be possible to reduce the costs of flotation of the new issue. However, these savings are possible only if the benefits of broadened distribution of the securities and protection against adverse price developments during the flotation period either are not needed or are required to a reduced degree.

A major decision for financial managers in a rights offering is to set the subscription price or the amount of the concession from the existing market price of the stock. Formulas reflecting the static effects of a rights offering indicate that neither the stockholders nor the company benefits or loses from the price changes. The rights offering has the effect of a stock split. The level set for the subscription price will to a great degree reflect the objectives and effects of a stock split.

The subsequent price behavior of the rights and the common securities in the associated new offering will reflect the earnings and dividends prospects of the company as well as the underlying developments of securities markets. The new financing associated with the rights offering may be an indicator of prospective growth in the sales and earnings of the company. The stock-split effects of the rights offering may be used to alter the company's dividend payments. The effects of these developments on the market behavior of the rights and the securities before, during, and after the rights trading period will reflect the expectations of investors toward the outlook for earnings and dividends per share.

SELECTED REFERENCES

Barry, Eugene P., *The Financing of Stock Issues with Preemptive Rights* (New York: Shields & Company, March 1948).

Evans, G. H., Jr. "The Theoretical Value of a Stock Right," *Journal of Finance,* 10 (March 1955), pp. 55–61. See comments on this article by Stephen H. Archer and by William Beranek in *Journal of Finance,* 11 (September 1956), pp. 363–370.

"1958 Rights Financing Profitable to Share Owners," *Exchange,* 20 (March 1959), pp. 8–9.

QUESTIONS

21–1 It is frequently stated that the primary purpose of the pre-emptive right is to allow individuals to maintain their proportionate share of the ownership and control of a corporation. Just how important do you suppose this consideration is for the average stockholder of a firm whose shares are traded on the New York or American stock exchanges? Is the pre-emptive right likely to be of more importance to stockholders of closely held firms?

21-2 How would the success of a rights offering be affected by a declining stock market?

21-3 What are some of the advantages and disadvantages of setting the subscription price on a rights offering substantially below the current market price of the stock?

21-4 Is a firm likely to get a wider distribution of shares if it sells new stock through a rights offering or directly to underwriters? Why would a company be interested in getting a wider distribution of shares?

21-5 Why do corporations often sell convertibles on a rights basis?

PROBLEMS

21-1 The common stock of the Industrial Research Company is selling for 99 on the market. The stockholders are offered one new share at a subscription price of 75 for every three shares held. What is the value of each right? Prove your answer.

21-2 Lewis has 20 shares of Northwood Industries. The market price per share is $70. The company now offers stockholders one new share to be purchased at $40 for every five shares held.

1. Determine the value of each right and prove your answer.
2. Assuming that Lewis uses 15 rights or he sells 15 at the market price you have calculated, prepare a statement showing the changes in his position under the above two assumptions.

21-3 The Marfield Manufacturing Company's capital consists of 8,000 shares of common stock and 4,000 warrants, each good to buy one share of common at $80. The warrants are protected against dilution. The company issues rights to buy one new share at $40 for every two shares held. With the stock selling with rights at $60, compute:

1. The theoretical value of the rights before the stock sells ex-rights
2. The new subscription price of the warrant after the rights issue.

21-4 National Appliance Company common stock is priced at $43 per share on the market. Notice is given that stockholders may purchase one new share at a price of $25 for every five shares held. You hold 80 old shares at the time of notice.

1. At approximately what price will each right sell on the market?
2. Why will this be the approximate price?
3. What effect will the issuance of rights have on the original market price? Why?

21-5 The Broadway Company is financed solely with common stock. Its balance sheet is given below:

BROADWAY COMPANY
BALANCE SHEET
End of year, 1966

		Common stock $3 par	$ 30,000
		Surplus	120,000
Total assets	$150,000		$150,000

Earnings available to common stock after taxes are $30,000. The price-earnings ratio is 16.

The company sells an additional 10,000 shares at $25 per share with a rights offering whereby one new share can be purchased for each old share held.

NEW BALANCE SHEET

		Common stock $3 par	$ 60,000
		Capital surplus	220,000
		Surplus	120,000
Total assets	$400,000	Total claims	$400,000

After the rights offering, earnings available to common stock after taxes are $90,000.
  1. Using the formulas provided, what is the value of each right?
  2. What will be the new market price of the stock when it goes ex-rights if the market falls by the value of one right?
  3. What will be the new market price of the stock if the same price-earnings ratio prevails before and after the rights offering?
  4. Is there a difference between your result in parts 2 and 3? Explain.

21–6 The Wilson Company has the following balance sheet and income statement.

THE WILSON COMPANY
BALANCE SHEET BEFORE RIGHTS OFFERING

		Total debt (5%)	$ 500,000
		Common stock (par value $2)	200,000
		Retained earnings	300,000
Total assets	$1,000,000	Total liabilities and capital	$1,000,000

Earnings rate: 10% on total assets

Total earnings	$100,000
Interest on debts	25,000
Income before taxes	75,000
Taxes (40% rate assumed)	30,000
Earnings after taxes	$ 45,000

Earnings per share	$0.45
Dividends per share (56%)	$0.25
Price-earnings ratio	20X
Market price per share	$9.00

The Wilson Company seeks to raise an additional $400,000 in a rights offering. The additional funds will continue to earn 10-percent. The price-earnings ratio is assumed to stay at 20 times, and dividend payouts will be 56-percent. Assume a 40 percent tax rate.
  1. Assuming the subscription price is set at $2 per share.
     a) How many additional shares of stock will have to be sold?
     b) How many rights will be required to purchase one new share?
     c) What will be the new earnings per share?
     d) What will be the new market price per share?

  e) A stock dividend of what percentage would have the same effect on earnings per share?

  f) A stock split of what degree would have the same effects on earnings per share?

  g) What will be the new dividend per share if the dividend payout ratio is maintained?

 2. Assume that the subscription price is set at $5; answer questions a to g in part 1.

 3. What is the significance of the result in part 1 as compared with part 2?

Chapter 22

Warrants and Convertibles

In the preceding chapter the nature of rights, one of the forms of common stock purchase options, was discussed. The formulation of the terms of options and their potential effects pose many challenging issues for financial managers. Similar complexities are involved in the additional forms of options treated in the present chapter—warrants and convertibles.

Rights are options issued to aid new financing and are of limited duration. Though warrants and convertibles also facilitate new financing, their duration extends well beyond the period in which new securities are initially distributed.

The use of warrants and convertibles increases during a period of rising stock prices and a mixed economic outlook. The offerings of bonds with conversion privileges rose to almost $1 billion in 1929, and bonds with warrants were offered in the amount of $365 million during that year. After a decline in the use of options during the depressed thirties and the war period of the forties, security offerings involving the use of conversion provisions or warrants again became of increased importance.[1]

Because of the increased use of warrants and convertibles in post-World War II financing, their potentials and limitations need to be fully understood by financial managers. Their possibilities are particularly significant for managers of small- and medium-sized firms, because options

---

[1] W. Braddock Hickman, *Statistical Measures of Corporate Bond Financing since 1900*, A Study by the National Bureau of Economic Research (Princeton, N.J.: Princeton University Press, 1960), pp. 210–211.

facilitate the access of such firms to the capital markets. Because of the high risks of investments in small firms, such firms may be unable to sell debt or preferred stock unless convertible or warrant privileges are attached. In view of these securities' large and increasing significance, full consideration of these options is developed in the present chapter. The discussion starts with warrants, because of their relation to rights analyzed in the previous chapter.

WARRANTS

Definition

A warrant is a long-term option to purchase a stated number of shares of a specified security, for a stipulated period, at a stated price or prices. Warrants are typically issued by operating companies as a "bonus" in connection with the sale of a new issue of bonds in order to make the bonds more attractive to prospective buyers.

Significant differences exist between the rights previously discussed and warrants. A warrant typically involves a longer option period than does a right. The option price at the time of issuance of the warrant is usually at or above the market price of the stock which will be purchased, whereas the subscription price for a right is typically below the prevailing market price of the stock. The option price on a warrant is likely to vary over time, whereas the short-term option price of a right is fixed.

The purpose of the use of the warrant differs from that of a right. Rights offerings are associated with a specific and immediate financing need of the company. Warrants are associated with both present and future financing operations.

Customary Provisions

The nature of warrants may be further understood by examining a number of the provisions encountered, some of which are customarily found, while others may occur only infrequently.

1. The stated price at which warrants may be exercised may be fixed or may progress. If progressive, the price customarily increases as time goes on or as the number of warrants exercised increases.

2. Some warrants are of value as long as the corporation is in existence. These are known as perpetual warrants. Other warrants are exercisable only for a stated number of years.

3. Warrants may be detachable or nondetachable. A nondetachable warrant may be separated from the bond only when the bondholder wishes to exercise his right to purchase the stock. Detachable warrants may be sold separately. A detachable warrant will give greater value to a bond than will a nondetachable warrant. If the warrants are immediately

detachable and the bonds are sold ex-warrant, their market price may decline substantially (representing the value of the warrant plus speculative possibilities).

4. Warrants carry no voting rights and do not receive interest, dividends, or payments on account of principal.

An illustrative list of warrants is set forth in Table 22–1.

TABLE 22–1

ILLUSTRATIVE LIST OF WARRANTS LISTED ON THE AMERICAN STOCK EXCHANGE

	Recent Price		*Option to Purchase Common Shares*		
Name of Company	*Common*	*Warrants*	*No.*	*Price*	*Date Option Expires*
Alleghany Corporation	11⅜	8	1	$ 3.75	Perpetual
Atlas Corporation	2⅞	1	1	6.25	Perpetual
First National Realty & Construction	3	1	1.15	6.00	12/31/71
General Acceptance Corporation	20¼	5½	1	20.00	11/1/69
Hilton Hotels Corporation	15¼	3¼	1	46.00	10/15/71
Jefferson Lake Petrochemicals	7⁹⁄₁₆	3¼	1	8.00	6/1/71
Mack Trucks	37⅜	17¼	1.4	50.00	9/1/66
Martin Marietta (1956)	19⅜	19⅝	2.73	45.00	11/1/68
McCrory	10⅝	2¼	1	20.00	3/15/76
Pacific Petroleum	10⅞	5⅝	1.1	19.00	3/13/68
Rio Algom. Mines, Ltd., Series A	11¾	⁵⁄₁₆	0.13	22.23	12/31/66
Sperry Rand	19⅛	8⅞	1.08	28.00	9/15/67
Textron, Inc.	40¼	15⅞	1	30.00	5/1/84
Trans World Airlines	33⅝	17⅜	1	22.00	12/1/73
Tri-Continental Corporation	45¾	35¾	1.27	17.76	Perpetual
Universal American (1962 Series)	6	1¼	1	13.75	3/31/67
Uris Buildings	18¼	9¾	1.06	12.50	5/1/75

Source: "Speculative Vehicles; Stock Warrants Can Give Holders a Fast Ride—Up and Down," *Barron's* (February 17, 1964), p. 9.

Use of Warrants

Warrants are most widely used as a"sweetener" for the issue of senior securities. Using warrants enables corporations to sell debt at lower rates of interest than they would otherwise have to pay. The use of warrants by smaller companies makes possible the sale of debt which might not otherwise have a market.

The extent to which the warrants will provide an inducement for the sale of debt and the extent to which they themselves will have market value depend upon the following factors: (1) duration of the option, (2) stated price at which the option may be exercised in relation to the present market value of the common stock, (3) number of warrants outstanding relative to the common stock issue, (4) speculative possibilities of the related common stock, (5) restrictions on stock market purchases, such as margin requirements that will give an advantage to the use of warrants —the higher the margin requirements, the greater the advantage to the use of warrants, (6) type of warrant—detachable or nondetachable.

Another use of warrants arises when refinancing occurs. In late 1952 the Alleghany Corporation proposed an exchange to holders of their Series A preferred stock; these stockholders were entitled to $100 per share in liquidation and to accumulated dividends of $113. For each share of preferred stock, they were offered a $100 principal, 5 percent debenture bond, plus 20 perpetual warrants, with a stated option price of $3.75 per share of common stock. The common stock was then selling at approximately $3.

Formula Value of Warrants

The theoretical or formula value of a warrant is obtained as follows:

$$
\begin{array}{c} \text{Formula value} \\ \text{of} \\ \text{warrant} \end{array} = \left(\begin{array}{c} \text{Market price} \\ \text{of} \\ \text{common stock} \end{array} \ less \ \begin{array}{c} \text{Option} \\ \text{price} \end{array} \right) \times \begin{array}{c} \text{Number of shares each} \\ \text{Warrant entitles owner} \\ \text{to purchase} \end{array}
$$

For example, a Tri-Continental Corporation warrant entitles the holder to purchase 1.27 shares of common stock at $17.76 per share. If the market price of the common stock is $27.76, the formula price of the warrant may be obtained as follows:

$$(\$27.76 - \$17.76)1.27 = \$12.70$$

At times a warrant may sell above its formula price if the prospects for the common stock are good. On the other hand, arbitrage operations will prevent the price of the warrant from falling below its theoretical value.

To this point the discussion of warrants may appear to have been from an investment standpoint. Our main interest is in the use of warrants in financing, although the two are interrelated. A warrant may be associated with losses as well as gains. A most dramatic example of this was the creation of warrants for more than 7,000,000 shares of common stock of the American and Foreign Power Company. At their peak value of $175 in 1929, the warrants had an indicated market value of over $1 billion. In the recapitalization plans for American and Foreign Power presented in 1944 and 1950, the warrants were to be wiped out completely as having no value, despite the fact that the company remained solvent.

The fact is that the use of warrants introduces volatility in both directions, particularly if the value of the warrant is small in relation to the associated common stock. The hypothetical cases in the table below illustrate this point.

SOURCE OF LEVERAGE IN THE PRICE OF WARRANTS

	Company	
	I	*II*
Option price of common through exercise of warrant	$50	$ 5
Common stock market price	$52	$55
Theoretical value of one warrant	$ 2	$50
If common rises to	$54	$60
Warrant will rise to	$ 4	$55
Gain for common stock	4%	9.09%
Gain for warrant	100%	10.00%

In these examples, when the common stock grows in value by a dollar, the warrant also does, because the market price of common is above the stated option price. Hence the theoretical value of the option rises by the same absolute amount as that of the common stock. The same absolute dollar amount of gain on the warrant results in a much higher percentage gain or loss. When the stock is selling below the option price, this 1-for-1 relation will not obtain. In situations where the price of the warrant is small in relation to the value of the common stock, and the common stock is near the stated option price, the price movements of the warrants will be highly volatile.

Use of Warrants in Financing

The use of warrants in financing may best be portrayed by means of a specific example.

The Genisco Company (Table 22–2) illustrates how a relatively small company was able to raise $340,000 when its debt ratio on September 30, 1956, before the financing, was just under 50 percent. The firm sold 10,000 shares of stock to net $70,000. Then it raised an amount of money equal to approximately three fifths of its existing net worth by selling debt with warrants. A substantial portion ($220,000) of the proceeds was used to retire current debt; the remainder was used to purchase equipment and to increase its cash in readiness for further growth. The debt ratio, after the sale of debentures and stock, rose to almost 50 percent. However, the debt ratio dropped to the 44 percent level after the exercise of warrants.

TABLE 22–2

Balance Sheet
GENISCO, INCORPORATED
(in thousands of dollars)

	Sept. 30, 1956 (before financing)	Pro Forma (after Debentures and Stock)	Warrants Exercised
Assets			
Current assets	800	890	1030
Plant and equipment	100	160	160
Total assets	900	1,050	1,190
Liabilities			
Current	420	200	200
Long-term debt	20	320	320
Total liabilities and long-term debt	440	520	520
Equity			
Common stock, $1 par, 500,000 authorized			
Outstanding, 178,000	178	178	188
New stock sold, 10,000 . . .		10	
Warrants, 18,000 shares at $7.75*			18
Paid-in surplus		60	182
Retained earnings	282	282	282
Total equity	460	530	670
Total liabilities and equity .	900	1,050	1,190

* Warrants to purchase 18,000 shares at $7.75, of which $6.75 is credited to paid-in surplus.

On September 30, 1956, the three principal stockholders owned 79 percent of the common stock of the company. After the company sold 10,000 new shares and one of the stockholders disposed of 23,000 shares, the three principal stockholders held 63 percent of the common stock. Options to purchase additional shares of stock were granted to underwriters and key employees. If the warrants issued by the company to purchase 18,000 new shares were exercised by the holders and if the underwriters exercised their options, the common stock interest of the three principal stockholders would still be more than 52 percent, sufficient to maintain control of the company.

This example illustrates how warrants may be used to facilitate the sale of debt by a company. In this example, the options were granted for purchase of the stock at the price at which the additional shares of common stock were sold at the time of the debenture issue. This is an example of the use of warrants to enable the firm to sell debentures under favorable terms. The debentures bore an interest rate of 6 percent, which was reasonably low for a small company financing in late December 1956, when the long-term capital markets were quite tight.

Warrants and Dilution

It is generally argued that the use of warrants in financing may be disadvantageous to the stockholders because warrants dilute earnings, the market price, and the book value of common stock. Table 22–3 provides data for analysis of dilution effects of warrants.

The illustration is divided into three parts. Under balance sheet 1,

TABLE 22–3

USE OF WARRANTS IN FINANCING GROWTH

A. Before sale of warrant.

Balance Sheet 1

	Debt at 5%	$ 20,000
	Common stock (par $5) . .	50,000
	Retained earnings	30,000
Total assets $100,000	Total	$100,000

B. Sell 100 debentures at $1,000 at 5 percent, with 20 warrants each to buy common stock at $10, which is $1 above the market price now prevailing. Earning power on assets increased to 15 percent.

Balance Sheet 2

	Debt at 5%	$120,000
	Common stock (par $5) . .	50,000
	Retained earnings	30,000
Total assets $200,000	Total	$200,000

C. Warrants exercised at $10.

Balance Sheet 3

	Debt at 5%	$120,000
	Common stock (par $5)* . .	60,000
	Paid in surplus†	10,000
	Retained earnings	30,000
Total assets $220,000	Total	$220,000

* $50,000 + 2,000 at $5 = $60,000.
† 2,000 × $5 = $10,000.

before the sale of warrants, earnings on assets are assumed to be 10 percent, or $10,000. Since 10,000 shares of stock are outstanding, after debt interest is paid, earnings per share on common stock is 90 cents. With a price-earnings ratio of 10, the market price of the stock is $9. The book value per share is $80,000 divided by 10,000, or $8 per share (Table 22–4).

TABLE 22–4

FINANCIAL RESULTS IN THE USE OF WARRANTS

	Balance Sheet 1	Balance Sheet 2	Balance Sheet 2	Balance Sheet 3	Balance Sheet 3
Earnings on assets after taxes . . .	10%	15%	10%	15%	10%
Earnings on assets .	$10,000	$30,000	$20,000	$33,000	$22,000
Debt interest . . .	$ 1,000	$ 6,000	$ 6,000	$ 6,000	$ 6,000
Earnings for common stock	$ 9,000	$24,000	$14,000	$27,000	$16,000
Number of shares of common stock . .	10,000	10,000	10,000	12,000	12,000
Earnings per share of common stock . .	$0.90	$ 2.40	$ 1.40	$ 2.25	$ 1.33
Price-earnings ratio .	10	10	10	10	10
Market price of stock	$9.00	$24.00	$14.00	$22.50	$13.33
Book value per share .	$8.00	$ 8.00	$ 8.00	$ 8.33	$ 8.33

In part B, debentures are sold at $1,000 each, bearing a 5 percent interest rate. Each of the debentures carries 20 warrants to buy common stock at $10 per share, a price $1 above the prevailing market price. It is assumed that by doubling the size of the company its earning power on assets will be increased to 15 percent. Similar results would be obtained if the earning power were maintained at 10 percent. The gain, however, would not have been so spectacular. Under balance sheet 2 the market price of the shares rises to $24. If earning power remains at 10 percent, the market price per share rises to $14.

Under part C the warrants are exercised at $10 per share of common stock. In balance sheet 3, it is assumed that one half the purchase price of the stock at $10 is divided into par value and one half into paid-in surplus. Under the assumption of earnings on assets at a 15 percent rate or a 10 percent rate, earnings per share, market price, and book value are all improved, compared with the initial situation.

Table 22–3 and Table 22–4 illustrate how the use of warrants may be advantageous, even though dilution may occur when the warrants are exercised. They have still performed the function of selling both debt and additional shares of stock on favorable terms.

Appraisal

The primary advantage of warrants is that they allow balanced financing by a combination of debt and equity. The warrants aid the sale of the debentures and allow a sale of equities at a higher future price.

A possible disadvantage in the use of warrants is that the firm may not be able to control the time when the warrants are exercised. This disadvantage, however, is not likely to be a real one, because the firm, if it experiences the expected growth in the volume of business, will need additional financing. Thus growth in the volume of business itself will cause a continuing demand for new funds, and when the warrants are exercised the additional funds can undoubtedly be put to good use.

From the standpoint of the investor, warrants present an opportunity for magnifying both gains and losses. Because the investment community has a tendency to over-react to the prospects of both gains and losses, there is a tendency for speculative fervor to develop in the use of warrants. The use of warrants during the late 1920s has been judged by some competent investment analysts to have been undesirable. Whether their use in the bull market of the late 1950s turns out to have been advantageous or disadvantageous remains to be seen.

From the standpoint of their use as a financing device, warrants aid in the sale of both debt and equity securities. Compared with convertibles, which provide for the sale of common stock at a somewhat higher future price, warrants may be regarded as less favorable from the standpoint of the issuing company. However, this disadvantage may be offset by the fact that warrants may be exercised, if detachable, without converting the debt into equity. Thus the firm is able to continue to use leverage and in this way increase the earnings per share available to common stock.

CONVERTIBLES[2]

Definition

Convertible securities are bonds or preferred stock that is exchangeable, at the option of the holder, for common stock, under specified terms and conditions. The *conversion price* is the price at which the shares received are valued. The *conversion ratio* is the number of shares that will be received. For example, a $100-par preferred stock is convertible into common stock at 2, the number of shares that will be received on conversion. The conversion price is $50, because 2 into $100 value equals $50.

Characteristically, when a convertible security is issued, the conversion price is set above the prevailing market price of the common stock. If

---

[2] A more rigorous treatment of convertible securities is contained in the appendix to this chapter.

the prevailing price of the common stock is $46 at the time the convertible preferred stock is issued and the conversion price set on the common is $50, there is a premium of $4 of the conversion price over the prevailing price of the common stock. This premium of about $4 represents not quite 10 percent of the prevailing price of the common stock. Sometimes the premiums are set somewhat higher than 10 percent, or sometimes, after the convertible security is sold, the price of the common stock declines so that a larger premium is involved when an investor buys the convertible on the open market. Brunswick Corporation, for example, sold convertible debentures with a conversion price of $51 at a time when the common was selling for $47. Subsequently, the common fell to $7, establishing a very high premium.

Investors who buy preferred stock or bonds for their senior position may not necessarily convert into common stock as the common stock rises above the conversion value, because the preferred stock (or bonds) would rise in value parallel to the rise in value of the common stock. For example, if the common stock in our previous illustration, which was selling at $46 when the convertible preferreds were issued, now rises to $60, the convertible preferred will probably sell for around $120 to $125. The preferred will not sell any lower than $120, because the convertible preferred represents the equivalent of two shares of common stock, which are worth $120.

Relative Use of Convertibles

A study made by Professor C. James Pilcher, of the University of Michigan, of the use of convertibles during the period of 1933 through 1952 found that approximately 20 percent of all public offerings of senior securities during this period contained convertible features. The use of convertibles has increased greatly, particularly since the end of World War II. In 1951, for example, 60 percent of all public offerings were convertibles. By 1964, however, this figure had fallen back to the 20 percent found in the earlier period.

There have been clear and definite advantages to investors who bought convertibles in the post-World War II period. The post-World War II period was one of great uncertainty. Many forecasts of a major postwar recession were made; others forecast an unprecedented boom. The use of convertibles permits the investor to hedge against both. In the event of a postwar collapse, he had the protection of his senior position. But if a boom and inflation caused common stock prices to soar, the convertible would rise with the price of the common stock. Thus convertibles offer the investor both lower risk and speculative potentialities; a hedge against deflation and inflation. Note, however, that the coupon interest rate on a convertible is always lower than the interest rate of an equivalent risk straight bond. Hence, an investor who buys a convertible gives up interest income in the hope of a capital gain.

A sampling of the price behavior of convertibles issued in 1952 shows that by 1955 the market price of a common stock was approximately 150 percent of the conversion price. In other words, the market price of the stock rose approximately 50 percent above its market price at the time the convertibles were issued. Correspondingly, through 1955 there were marked profits for people who bought convertible issues at the time they were originally sold. Note also, though, that profits would have been even greater had the holders of these convertibles purchased the common stock for which they were exchangeable.

Convertibles as Sweeteners

From the standpoint of the issuing corporation, the use of convertibles also has distinct advantages. Convertibles enable a firm to sell future issues of common stock at a higher price than the price at which its common stock is selling when the convertibles are issued. For example, if a company whose common stock is selling at $45 were to sell a new issue of common stock, characteristically the stock would be priced somewhat below the current market, at about $42 to $43. Price pressure results, because an additional issue of common stock augments the quantity of the stock available and does not change the demand conditions. If the firm had sold a convertible preferred issue as a means of selling common stock in the future, the conversion price of the common stock would have been set around $50, so that the common stock would be sold $7 per share (or 17 percent) higher than otherwise.

Characteristically, convertibles contain a provision that gives the issuer the opportunity to call the convertible at specified prices. If the common stock rises to $60, the preferred stock, with a conversion rate of 2, would rise to $120 or more. The call price on the preferred stock would probably be around $105. If the company called the preferred (giving the usual notification of 20 days) at 105, stock owners could convert or sell. By converting into common they would obtain $120 for their preferred rather than $105. The use of a call provision would give the company a method of forcing conversion.

Convertibles in Financing Growth

Another advantage from the standpoint of the issuer is that a convertible issue may be used as a temporary financing device. During the years 1946 through 1957, American Telephone & Telegraph Company sold $10 billion of convertible debentures. By 1959 about 80 percent of these convertible debentures had been converted into common stock. AT&T could not have sold straight debt in this amount because their financial structure would have been unbalanced. On the other hand, if AT&T had simply issued large amounts of common stock periodically, there would have been price pressure on its stock, because the market is slow to digest large blocks of stock.

By using convertible debentures, however, which provided for a lag of some six to nine months before they were converted into common stock, AT&T received relatively cheap money to finance growth. Transmission lines and telephone exchange buildings must first be built to provide the basis for ultimately installing phones. While AT&T is installing transmission lines and telephone exchange buildings, these investments are not earning any money. Therefore it was important to AT&T to minimize the cost of money while these installations were being made. After six to nine months had elapsed and these installations were translated into telephones that were bringing in revenues, AT&T was better able to pay the 6 percent common stock dividend. Thus convertibles provide for stages in financing by a firm.

Disadvantages

No form of financing is without its disadvantages. From the standpoint of the investor, the price of convertibles may contain a large speculative premium. If the common stock is selling at 40, the conversion price is 50, and the preferred stock is selling for around 120 (as it may very well be because of the speculative interest in convertibles), a substantial premium is paid for the common stock if it is bought via the convertible preferred stock route.

From the standpoint of the issuer, convertibles have a possible disadvantage. Although the convertible stock gives the issuer the opportunity to sell the common stock at a price 15 to 20 percent higher than it could otherwise be sold, if the common stock greatly increases in price the issuer may find that he would have been better off if he had waited and simply sold the common stock. Further, if the company truly wants to raise equity capital, and if the price of the stock declines after the bond is issued, then it is stuck with debt. In the case of Brunswick, cited above, there is very little likelihood that the bonds will be exchanged for stock.

But the plain fact of the matter may well be that the company has no alternative, especially if it is a small and growing company. A sufficient investment demand in the company's debt securities or preferred stock may not be present. For this reason the company may be virtually forced to use convertibles. In this kind of situation the convertibles perform a very useful function in that they enable management to raise additional debt and equity money and maintain control in the company.

DECISIONS ON USE OF WARRANTS AND CONVERTIBLES

The nature of decisions on the use of convertibles and warrants in the financing of firms may be described by an illustration that highlights their characteristics. The Jensen Corporation has the following balance sheet:

BALANCE SHEET 1
Original Situation

Current assets	$ 50,000	Current debt	$ 30,000
Net fixed assets	50,000	Common stock, par $2 . .	10,000
		Earned surplus	60,000
Total assets	$100,000	Total claims	$100,000

The book value per share is $70,000 divided by 5,000 shares, which is $14 per share. The market value per share, based on a price-earnings ratio of 20 times, is determined from the earnings per share. The company earns 20 percent on total assets before taxes.

Total earnings	$20,000
Taxes at 50%*	10,000
Earnings after taxes	$10,000
Earnings per share	$ 2.00
Market price of stock	$40.00

* A tax rate of 50 percent is used for ease of computation.

In the following few years, sales are expected to double and the financing needs of the firm will double. The firm decides to sell $50,000 debentures to meet a portion of its financing needs. It is undecided, however, whether to sell convertible debentures or debentures with warrants. The new balance sheet would appear as follows:

BALANCE SHEET 2
Debentures Sold

Current assets	$100,000	Current debt	$ 50,000
Net fixed assets	100,000	Debentures	50,000
		Common stock, par $2 . .	10,000
		Earned surplus	90,000
Total assets	$200,000	Total claims	$200,000

The convertible debentures would pay a 6 percent interest rate and be convertible into 20 shares of common stock for each $1,000 debenture.

The debentures with warrants would carry a 6 percent coupon and would entitle each holder of a $1,000 debenture to buy 20 shares of common stock at a price of $40. Carl Jensen owns 62 percent of the Jensen Corporation before the financing.

If convertible debentures are sold and are later all converted, the balance sheet would appear as follows:

BALANCE SHEET 3
Debentures Converted

		Current debt	$ 50,000
		Debentures	0
		Common stock	12,000
		Paid-in surplus	48,000
		Earned surplus	90,000
Total assets	$200,000	Total claims	$200,000

The debentures are converted into common stock at a ratio of 20. The 50 debentures are converted into 1,000 shares of common stock of par value of $2, resulting in a total addition to the common stock account of $2,000. The $2,000 deducted from the total $50,000 transferred from the debenture account is paid-in surplus.

If the debentures with warrants had been sold, the warrants also carry the right to purchase 20 shares of common stock. Again 1,000 additional shares of common stock will be issued but will bring in $40 per share, a total of $40,000. The par value of common stock added is $2,000, resulting in a paid-in surplus of $38,000. The new balance sheet would appear as follows:

BALANCE SHEET 4
Warrants Exercised

		Current debt	$ 50,000
		Debentures	50,000
		Common stock	12,000
		Paid-in surplus	38,000
		Earned surplus	90,000
Total assets	$240,000	Total claims	$240,000

Finally, the alternative may be considered of Carl Jensen's selling 1,400 shares of common stock directly at $36 to net $50,000 after flotation costs.[3] The balance sheet would appear as follows.

---

[3] Because of the conversion, or warrant "sweetener," flotation costs in the sale of the debentures is considered small compared with the cost of selling common stock directly.

BALANCE SHEET 5
Common Stock Sold

	Current debt	$ 50,000
	Common stock	12,800
	Paid-in surplus	47,200
	Earned surplus	90,000
Total assets $200,000	Total claims	$200,000

The consequences of each course of action may now be examined. For each balance sheet situation, the effects on earnings per share, control by Carl Jensen, and the financial structure can be compared. The details for calculations of earnings per share with a 20 percent return on total assets are first shown:

	(1) Original Situation	*(2)* Debentures Sold	*(3)* Debentures Converted	*(4)* Warrants Exercised	*(5)* Common Stock Sold
Total earnings	$20,000	$40,000	$40,000	$48,000	$40,000
Debenture interest	0	3,000	0	3,000	0
Earnings before tax	20,000	37,000	40,000	45,000	40,000
Tax at 50%	10,000	18,500	20,000	22,500	20,000
Earnings after tax	10,000	18,500	20,000	22,500	20,000
Number of shares	5,000	5,000	6,000	6,000	6,400
Earnings per share	$2.00	$3.70	$3.33	$3.75	$3.125
Percentage control	62%	62%	52%	52%	48%
Debt to total assets	30%	50%	25%	42%	25%

The control position of Carl Jensen is determined by relating his ownership of 3,100 shares to the number of shares shown in the above tabulation. The debt-to-total-asset percentages are calculated from the five balance sheets presented.

Some principles of business finance in connection with the use of convertibles and warrants may now be set forth. The earnings per share are increased by the expanded operations under all forms of financing. Balance sheet 2 may be taken to represent the situation in which straight debentures are sold. The use of straight debentures would result in favorable earnings per share and maintain Carl Jensen's present percentage of control, but would give the highest debt ratio. A small company may be unable to sell straight debt.

As contrasted with the sale of common stock directly, the use of both convertible debentures and debentures with warrants maintains over 50 percent control for the principal stockholder and provides greater earnings per share. The use of warrants results in the same percentage control but provides greater earnings per share. The greater earnings per share result from the larger total assets resulting from the new money raised when the warrants are exercised to buy common stock. Also, the debt ratio is higher in the debentures-with-warrants form of financing.

The nature of the alternative methods of financing are illustrated in general terms by the above example. The power of both convertibles and warrants to contribute to increased earnings per share while preserving control of the company is shown. The resulting debt-to-total-asset ratios demonstrate that convertibles are more likely to be used when the existing debt ratio of the firm is already high. The subsequent conversion of the debt or preferred stock will augment the equity base with a corresponding reduction in the amount of senior securities outstanding. The exercise of warrants, however, will still leave the senior securities on the balance sheet. Hence lower initial debt ratios will encourage the use of senior obligations with warrants.

SUMMARY

Like rights, both warrants and convertibles are forms of options used in financing business firms. The use of long-term options such as warrants and convertibles is encouraged by an economic environment combining prospects of both boom or inflation and depression or deflation. The senior position of the securities protects against the latter. The option feature offers the opportunity for participation in rising stock prices.

Both the convertibility privilege and warrants are used as "sweeteners." The option privileges they grant may make it possible for small companies to sell debt or preferred stock which otherwise could not be sold. For large companies, the "sweeteners" result in lower costs of the securities sold. In addition, the options provide for the sale of the common stock in the future at prices higher than could be obtained at the time. The options thereby permit the delayed sale of common stock at more favorable prices.

The exercise of convertibles by their holders does not ordinarily bring additional funds to the company. The exercise of warrants will provide additional funds to the company.[4] The conversion of securities will result in reduced debt ratios. The exercise of warrants will strengthen the equity position but still leave

---

[4] An outstanding exception is the convertible debentures issued by AT&T since the end of World War II. For each $100 principal amount of debentures an additional $35 to $45 (varying with the issue) was required to obtain one share of common stock.

the debt or preferred stock on the balance sheet. In comparing the use of convertibles with senior securities carrying warrants, a firm with a high debt ratio should choose convertibles. A firm with a moderate or low debt ratio may employ warrants.

SELECTED REFERENCES

Armour, Lawrence A., "Safety Plus Growth," *Barron's* (July 1965), p. 9.

Broman, Keith L., "The Use of Convertible Subordinated Debentures by Industrial Firms 1949–59," *Quarterly Review of Economics and Business,* 3 (Spring 1963), pp. 65–75.

Fried, Sidney, "The Speculative Merits of Common Stock Warrants" (New York: R. H. M. Associates, 1961).

Guthmann, H. G., "Measuring the Dilution Effect of Convertible Securities," *Journal of Business,* 11 (January 1938), pp. 44–50.

Pease, Fred, "The Warrant—Its Power and Its Hazards," *Financial Analysts Journal* 19 (January–February 1963), pp. 25–32.

Pilcher, C. J., *Raising Capital with Convertible Securities* (Ann Arbor: Bureau of Business Research, University of Michigan, 1955).

Rosenberg, Joseph, "Convertibles Preferred," *Barron's* (August 1965), p. 5.

Skelly, William S., *Convertible Bonds—A Study of Their Suitability for Commercial Bank Bond Portfolios* (New York: Salomon Bros. & Hutzler, 1959).

QUESTIONS

22–1   Why do warrants typically sell at prices greater than their theoretical values?

22–2   Why do convertibles typically sell at prices greater than their theoretical values (the higher of the conversion value or straight debt value)? Would you expect the percentage premium on a convertible bond to be greater or less than that on a warrant? (The percentage premium is defined as the market price minus the theoretical value, divided by the market price.)

22–3   What effect does the trend in stock prices (subsequent to issue) have on a firm's ability to raise funds through (1) convertibles and (2) warrants?

22–4   If a firm expects to have additional financial requirements in the future, would you recommend that it use convertibles or bonds with warrants? Why?

22–5   How does a firm's dividend policy affect each of the following:

    1)   The value of long term warrants

    2)   The likelihood that convertible bonds will be converted

    3)   The likelihood that warrants will be exercised

22–6   Evaluate the following statement: "Issuing convertible securities represents a means by which a firm can sell common stock at a price above the existing market."

PROBLEMS

22–1   The Baker Electronics Corporation was planning to finance an expansion in the summer of 1966. The principal executives of the company were agreed that an industrial company of this type should finance growth by means of common stock rather than debt. However, they felt that the price of the company's common stock did not reflect its true worth, so they were desirous of selling a convertible security. They considered a convertible debenture but feared the burden of fixed interest charges if the common stock did not rise in price to make conversion attractive. They decided on an issue of convertible preferred stock.

The common stock was currently selling at $60 per share. Budgeted earnings were $4 per share and were expected to grow at a rate of 8 percent per year. It was agreed by the investment bankers and the management that the common stock would sell at 20 times earnings.

1) What should be the conversion price set by the issuer?

2) Should the preferred stock include a call-price provision? Why?

22–2 (Fill in the indicated blanks.)

1. Baker Electronics, Inc., has the following balance sheet:

BALANCE SHEET 1

Current assets	$ 50,000	Current debt	$ 20,000
Net fixed assets	50,000	Common stock, par value,	
		$2	20,000
		Earned surplus	60,000
Total assets	$100,000	Total claims	$100,000

The firm earns 20 percent on total assets before taxes (50 percent tax rate). What are earnings per share? ————————————— (ONE)

If the price-earnings ratio for the company's stock is 20 to 1, the market price of the company's stock is ————————————— (TWO)

The book value of the company's stock is ————————————— (THREE)

2. In the following few years, sales are expected to double and the financing needs of the firm will double. The firm decides to sell debentures to meet its financing needs. It is undecided, however, whether to sell convertible debentures or debentures with warrants. The new balance sheet would appear as follows:

BALANCE SHEET 2

Current assets	$100,000	Current debt	$ 40,000
Net fixed assets	100,000	Debentures	60,000
		Common stock, par value,	
		$2	20,000
		Earned surplus	80,000
Total assets	$200,000	Total claims	$200,000

3. The convertible debentures would pay 5 percent interest and be convertible into 25 shares of common stock for each $1,000 debenture. The debentures with warrants would carry a 6 percent coupon and entitle each holder of a $1,000 debenture to buy 20 shares of common stock at $40. Richard Baker owns 80 percent of Electronics before the financing.

4. Assume that convertible debentures are sold and are later all converted. Show the new balance sheet figures in the blanks.

BALANCE SHEET 3

	Current debt ——————— (FIVE)	
	Debentures ——————— (SIX)	
	Common stock, par value,	
	$2 ——————— (SEVEN)	
	Paid-in surplus ——————— (EIGHT)	
	Earned surplus ——————— (NINE)	
Total assets ——————— (FOUR)	Total claims ——————— (TEN)	

5. Complete the firm's income statement after the debentures have all been converted:

Net income after all charges except debenture interest and before
   taxes (20% of total assets) ——————————— (TEN A)
Debenture interest ——————————————— (ELEVEN)
Federal income tax, 50% ——————————— (TWELVE)
Net income after taxes ——————————— (THIRTEEN)
Earnings per share after taxes ——————— (FOURTEEN)

6. Now, instead of convertibles, assume that debentures with warrants were issued. Assume further that the warrants were all exercised. Show the new balance sheet figures in the blanks.

BALANCE SHEET 4

	Current debt ——— (SIXTEEN)	
	Debentures ——— (SEVENTEEN)	
	Common stock, par	
	value, $2 ——— (EIGHTEEN)	
	Paid-in surplus ——— (NINETEEN)	
	Earned surplus ——— (TWENTY)	
Total assets ———————	Total claims ——— (TWENTY-ONE)	
(FIFTEEN)		

7. Complete the firm's income statement after the debenture warrants have all been exercised.

Net income after all charges except debenture interest and
   before taxes $50,000
Debenture interest ——————————————— (TWENTY-TWO)
Federal income tax ——————————————— (TWENTY-THREE)
Net income after taxes ——————————— (TWENTY-FOUR)
Earnings per share after taxes ——————— (TWENTY-FIVE)

22–3 The Dixon Company has grown rapidly during the past five years. Recently its commercial bank has urged the company to consider increasing permanent financing. Its bank loan had risen to $200,000, carrying 6 percent interest. Dixon has been 30 to 60 days late in paying trade creditors.

Discussions with an investment banker have resulted in the suggestion to raise $400,000 at this time. Investment bankers have assured Dixon that the following alternatives will be feasible (flotation costs will be ignored):

Alternative 1: Sell common stock at $8.

Alternative 2: Sell convertible bonds at a 6 percent coupon, convertible into common stock at $10.

Alternative 3: Sell debentures at a 6 percent coupon, each bond carrying 100 warrants to buy common stock at $10.

Additional facts are as follows:

DIXON COMPANY
BALANCE SHEET
December 31, 1966

		Current liabilities	$350,000
		Common stock, par $1.00. .	100,000
		Retained earnings	50,000
		Total liabilities and capital	$500,000
Total assets	$500,000		

DIXON COMPANY
INCOME STATEMENT
December 31, 1966

Sales	$1,000,000
All costs except interest	900,000
Gross profit	100,000
Interest	12,000
Profit before taxes	88,000
Taxes at 50%	44,000
Profits after taxes	44,000
Shares	100,000
Earnings per share	$0.44
Price-earnings ratio	20X
Market price of stock	$8.80

E. E. Bradley, the president, owns 80 percent of the common stock of Dixon Co. and wishes to maintain control of the company.

1. Show the new balance sheet under each of the alternatives. For 2 and 3 show the balance sheet after conversion of the debentures or exercise of warrants. Assume that one half the funds raised will be used to pay off the bank loan and one half to increase total assets.

2. Show Bradley's control position under each alternative, assuming he does not purchase additional shares.

3. What is the effect on earnings per share of each of the alternatives, if it is assumed that profits before interest and taxes will be 20 percent of total assets?

4. What will be the total debt-equity ratio under each alternative?

5. Which of the three alternatives would you recommend to Bradley and why?

Some Theoretical Aspects of Convertible Securities[1]

The essential features of a convertible bond may be described by reference to Figure 22A–1. While the figure may be given either an *ex post* or *ex ante* interpretation, at this point it is more convenient to think of it *ex post*. In other words, the conditions described are assumed to have occurred.

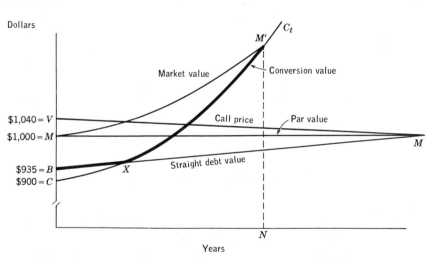

Fig. 22A–1. Hypothetical Model of a Convertible Bond

The hypothetical bond was sold for M dollars in year t_o, and this initial price was also the par (and maturity) value. The bond was callable at the option of the corporation, with the call price originating at V, somewhat above par, and declining linearly over the term to maturity to equal M at maturity.

---

[1] For a somewhat more detailed treatment of the theory of convertibles, see Eugene F. Brigham, "An Analysis of Convertible Debentures: Theory and Some Empirical Evidence," *Journal of Finance* (March 1966). The appendix is based on the article.

527

The original conversion value (C) was established by multiplying the market price of the stock at the time of issue by the number of shares into which the bond may be converted (the conversion ratio). The stock price grew at a constant rate (g), causing the conversion value curve (CC_t) to rise at this same rate. This established the curve CC_t, which shows the conversion value at each point in time. All of this is expressed by equation (22A–1),

$$C_t = P_o(1 + g)^t R \qquad (22A–1)$$

where:

$C_t =$ conversion value at time t
$P_o =$ initial price of the common stock $=$ \$45 per share
$g =$ rate of growth of the stock's price $= 4\%$
$R =$ conversion rate, or number of shares received on conversion $= 20$

The initial conversion value of the bond, when $t = 0$, is simply \$45 $\times$ 20, or \$900. One year later it is \$45(1.04)(20) = \$936; after two years it has risen to \$973.44; and so on. Had growth turned out to be zero, CC_t would have been a horizontal line; had it been negative, CC_t would have declined; and had growth been uneven, CC_t would not have been a smooth curve, and equation (22A–1) would have been more complicated.

In addition to its value in conversion, the bond also had a straight-debt value, or the price at which the bond would sell if it did not have the conversion option, at each point in time that was determined by the following equation:

$$B_t = \sum_{K=1}^{(T-t)} \frac{I}{(1 + i)^K} + \frac{M}{(1 + i)^{(T-t)}} \qquad (22A–2)$$

where:

$B_t =$ convertible bond's value as a straight debt instrument at time t
$T =$ original term to maturity, 20 years
$i =$ market rate of interest on equivalent risk, pure debt issues, $4\frac{1}{2}\%$
$I =$ dollars of interest paid each year, \$40 $= 4\%$ of M
$M =$ bond's redemption value at maturity, \$1,000, the par value

If $I = iM$, then $B_t = M$; but in the illustrative case, as is typically true, $I < iM$ with the consequence that $B_t < M$ prior to the maturity date. In Figure 22A–1, the values of B_t are shown by the line BM; B_o is seen to be \$935 in the illustrative case.

Note that the conversion value and the straight debt value combine to establish a lower bound for the price of the bond. Logically, the bond could not sell for less than its value as straight debt (BM), and if it should fall below the conversion value (CC_t) arbitragers would enter the market, short the stock, and cover their short positions by buying and converting bonds. This latter process would continue until the market price of the bond is driven up to its conversion value. The higher of these two floors dominates, with the discontinuous curve BXC' forming the effective market value floor.

The curve designating the market value (MM') lies above the line of basic value (BXC_t) over most of the range but converges with BXC_t in year N. The rationale behind this price action is developed in the following two subsections.

Why the Market Value Exceeds the BXC_t Floor

The spread between MM' and BXC_t, which represents the premium marginal investors[2] are willing to pay for the conversion option, may be explained by several factors. First, since the convertible bond may be converted into common stock if the company prospers and the stock price rises, it usually commands a premium over its value as straight debt (that is, the right of conversion has a positive value). Second, the convertible bond usually commands a premium over its conversion value because, by holding convertibles, an investor is able to reduce his risk exposure. To illustrate, suppose someone buys the hypothetical bond for $1,000. At the time, it is convertible into 20 shares of stock with a market price of $45, giving a conversion value of $900. If the stock market turns sharply down and the stock price falls to $22.50 per share, a stock investor would suffer a 50 percent loss in value. Had he held a convertible bond, its price would have fallen from $1,000 to the bond value floor, BM in Figure 22A–1, which is at least $935. Hence, holding the convertible entails less risk than holding common stock, and this also causes convertibles to sell at a premium above their conversion value.

Why the Market Value Approaches the Conversion Value

The MM' curve in Figure 22A–1 rises less rapidly than the CC_t curve, indicating that the market value approaches the conversion value as the conversion value increases. This empirically validated fact is caused by three separate factors. First, and probably most important, the bondholders realize that the issue is callable, and if it is in fact called, they have the option of either surrendering for redemption or converting. In the former case they receive the call price, while in the latter they receive stock with a value designated by C_t. If the market price of the bond is above either of these values, the holder is in danger of a potential loss in

---

[2] Marginal investors, often called "the market," are defined as those just willing to hold the bond at its going price. These investors are, in fact, the ones who actually determine the level of the bond's price.

wealth in the event of a call, and this fact prevents wide spreads between MM' and BXC_t whenever the market value exceeds the call price.

The second factor driving MM' toward CC_t is related to the loss protection characteristic of convertibles. Barring changes in the interest rate on the firm's straight debt securities, the potential loss on a convertible is equal to the spread between MM' and BM. Since this spread increases at high conversion values, the loss potential also increases, causing the premium attributable to the loss protection to diminish.

The third factor causing the gap between MM' and CC_t to close has to do with the relationship between the yield on a convertible and that on the common stock for which it may be exchanged. As was seen in Chapter 12, the yield on most common stocks consists of two components—a dividend yield and a capital gain yield. In the next section it is shown that convertibles also have two yield components, one from interest payments and one from capital gains. After some point, the expected capital gain is the same for both instruments, but the current yield on the bond declines vis-à-vis that on the common stock because dividends on growing stocks typically rise while interest payments are fixed. This causes the gap between MM' and CC_t to close, and eventually would lead to a negative premium except for the fact that voluntary conversion occurs first.

Convertible Yields

The actual rate of return earned on a convertible is found by solving equation (22A–3) for k, the internal rate of return:

$$M = \sum_{t=1}^{N} \frac{I}{(1+k)^t} + \frac{T.V.}{(1+k)^N} \qquad (22A-3)$$

where:

M = price paid for bond
I = dollars of interest received per year
T.V. = terminal value of bond: call price if surrendered on call; maturity value if redeemed; conversion value if converted; or market price if sold
N = number of years bond was held
k = internal rate of return

The equation is purely definitional; it simply states that if one paid M dollars for a convertible bond, held it for N years, and received a series of interest payments plus a terminal value, then he has received a return on his investment equal to k.[3]

---

[3] Three simplifications are made in this analysis. First, taxes are ignored. Second, the problem of reinvestment rates is handled by assuming that all reinvestment is made at the internal rate of return. Third, it is assumed that the bondholder does not hold stock after conversion; he cashes out, as would be true of an institutional investor precluded from holding common stock.

The *ex ante* yield on a convertible (k^*) is probabilistic—it is dependent upon a set of variables subject to probability distributions; hence it must itself be a random variable. It is possible, however, to define each of the determinants of k^* in terms of its mean expected value; $E(g)$, for example, is the expected value of the growth rate in the stock's price over N years. For simplicity, $E(g)$ and other random variables are shortened to g, T.V., and so on. With the variables defined in this manner, it is possible to work sequentially through two equations to find the expected rate of return on a convertible bond.

Remembering that bondholders are assumed to cash out in year N, presumably reinvesting the terminal value received in some other security, the determinants of T.V. may be established: (1) the corporation's policy in regard to calling the bond to force conversion; or (2) the investor's decision to hold the bond until it is called, to sell it, or to voluntarily convert.

Corporation's call policy. It will be shown in the empirical section that corporations issuing convertible bonds generally have policies regarding just how far up the CC_t curve they will allow a bond to go before calling to force conversion. These policies range from calling as soon as they are "sure" conversion will take place (this generally means a premium of about 20 percent over the call price) to never calling at all. If the policy is never to issue a call, however, the firm generally relies on the dividend-interest differential to cause voluntary conversion.

It is apparent that call policy has a very direct influence on the T.V. figure used in equation (22A–3). Naturally, therefore, expectations about call policy influence the expected rate of return on a convertible bond.

Investors' Cash-Out Policy. This factor is similar to the corporate call policy in that it sets a limit on how far up the CC_t curve an investor is willing to ride. The decision is influenced by the interest-dividend relationship, by the investor's aversion to risk (recall that risk due to a stock price decline increases as one moves up the CC_t curve), and by his willingness to hold securities providing low current yields. To simplify, it is assumed that investors are willing to ride higher up CC_t, given the dividend interest relationship, than the firm is willing to let them ride; hence, corporate call policy supersedes investor cash-out policy.

Years the Bond Is Held

As was seen, the path of the conversion value curve is traced out by equation (22A–1).

$$C_t = P_o(1 + g)^t R \qquad (22A–1)$$

Recognizing that $R = M/P_c$, where P_c is defined as the conversion price of the shares, equation (22A–1) may be rewritten:

$$C_t = \frac{P_o}{P_c}(1 + g)^t M \qquad (22A–4)$$

Setting equation (22A–4) equal to the T.V. defined by corporate policy (for example, $1,200 if a 20 percent premium is used), one finds:

$$T.V. = \frac{P_o}{P_c} (1 + g)^N M \qquad (22A\text{–}5)$$

Now, converting to logarithmic form and solving for N, one obtains:

$$N = \frac{(\log P_c - \log P_o) + (\log T.V. - \log M)}{\log (1 + g)} \qquad (22A\text{–}6)$$

Equation (22A–6) may be interpreted as follows. First, an inspection of equation (22A–3), which was used to find the realized internal rate of return (k), reveals that for given values of M, I, and T.V., smaller values of N produce larger values of k. In other words, for a given interest component and a given capital gains component, the faster the capital gain is realized, the larger the internal rate of return. From equation (22A–6) it is seen that N is smaller as the differentials between $\log P_c$ and $\log P_o$, and between $\log$ T.V. and $\log M$ decline, and the larger the rate of growth.[4] P_o, P_c, and M are all known with certainty at $t = 0$, while T.V. (defined by corporate policy), g, and N are expected, probabilistic values.

With these definitions and equations, consider how an investor might look upon *ex ante* convertible bond yields. The following is the calculating sequence. First, the investor (or potential investor) has expectations about the variables on the right side of equation (22A–6). Specifically, he *knows* P_c, P_o and M, and he has expectations about the values of T.V. and g.[5] This information may be used to solve equation (22A–6) for N. With N estimated, the potential investor has all the data necessary to solve equation (22A–3) for k^*, the expected yield on the bond.

---

[4] Since $\log X - \log Y$ is equal to X/Y, these log differentials could be expressed as ratios of the absolute values. In other words, N is smaller as the ratios P_c/P_o and T.V./ M become smaller.

[5] A word about T.V. and g is in order. In a later section it is shown that corporations do have policies with regard to calling to force conversion, and investors are able to make forecasts about the *minimum* conversion value at which the bond is likely to be called. Further, somewhat strong institutional constraints tend to prohibit firms from calling bonds until this minimum value has been reached.

The growth rate of the common stock is much less predictable, but it, too, can be estimated. One approach is simply to extrapolate past share price growth, adjusted in whatever manner the investor thinks appropriate. Alternatively, one can recognize that stock price growth is dependent upon earnings and dividend growth and that these are dependent upon retained earnings, the rate of return at which retained earnings can be invested, and the amount of leverage employed by the firm (among other things). In this appendix no attempt is made to specify the manner in which investors measure expected growth.

Market Equilibrium

When convertible bonds are initially offered to the public, they are typically priced at par (usually $1,000).[6] If the terms of the issue, in combination with investor expectations about the other key variables, produce an expected rate of return just equal to the marginal investor's required rate of return on investments with this degree of risk (his opportunity cost, in a sense), then the bond will just clear the market. The price will not run up in the manner of a "hot issue," nor will it fall after underwriters have ceased stabilization. In the unlikely event that investor expectations are borne out exactly, the conversion value will follow a predicted CC_t curve, the market price will follow a predicted MM' curve, the firm will call the bond at the predicted T.V., and investors will realize a yield $k*$.

An Illustrative Case

To illustrate the material in this and the subsequent section, it is useful to present an example. Suppose that a firm's stock price has been rising and is expected to continue rising by 4 percent per year; that the firm is known to have called convertibles in the past when the conversion value exceeded the par value by 20 percent; and that its common stock is currently selling for $45 per share. If the firm then offers a debenture that pays 4 percent interest and is convertible into 20 shares of stock for sale at par, $1,000 (the conversion price is thus $50, or $1,000/20), a potential investor could calculate the years to conversion by substituting the expected values in equation (22A–6). He would find N approximately equal to eight years.[7] With this estimate of the years the bond will remain outstanding, the investor could then substitute in equation (22A–3) and solve for $k*$. For the values in the example, this would be approximately 6 percent.[8] If this *ex ante* yield is equal to or greater than the investor's required rate of return on investments with the same (estimated) risk, then he would buy the bonds. If the marginal investor's opportunity cost is just met, the issue price will be stable.[9]

---

[6] It must be made very clear that the discussion at this point is related to publicly offered bonds, not to those offered through rights to existing stockholders. There are quite fundamental differences, which are discussed later, between rights offerings and issues sold to the general public.

[7]

$$N = \frac{(\log \$50 - \log \$45) + (\log \$1200 - \log \$1000)}{\log (1.04)} \approx 8$$

[8]

$$\$1,000 = \sum_{t-1}^{8} \frac{\$40}{(1 + k*)^t} + \frac{\$1200}{(1 + k*)^8} \text{ when } K* = 6\%.$$

[9] In the case of rights offerings, bonds are generally underpriced; consequently, they sell at a premium over par immediately after issue.

Trade-Offs between Interest and Capital Gains

When the corporation negotiates with investors (actually investment bankers, who anticipate the market's reaction to the issue) prior to selling convertible bonds, six key determinants of k^* come into play:

Predetermined Variables	$M =$ issue price of bond (usually $1,000)
	T.V. $=$ terminal value at which the firm is expected to force conversion
	$P_0 =$ current market price of shares
	$g =$ expected growth rate of prices
Decision Variables	$P_c =$ conversion price
	$I =$ coupon interest rate

Predetermined variables are defined as those not subject to negotiations. Obviously, the price of the bond could be subject to negotiation, but typically it is not; if the issue price differs from par it does so by a small amount and reflects underwriting costs. The terminal value, here defined to be determined by the corporation's call policy, could likewise be settled in the indenture, but normally it is not. Similarly, it would be possible to put g at least partially in the decision variable category by limiting the dividend payout, but this is not done. Note that N is not included in the list; it is itself dependent upon the other variables, hence including it would be redundant.

The decision variables—conversion prices and coupon interest rates —are the terms actually negotiated in the pre-issue meetings between the corporation and the underwriters. Equations (22A–3) and (22A–6) may be studied to gain insights into the way in which different combinations of I and P_c interact with the predetermined variables to influence k^*. This, in turn, provides insights into rational trade-offs between the two decision variables.

One way to consider the relationships between the decision variables is illustrated in Figure 22A–2. Here, the vertical axis measures the ratio of straight debt interest to the coupon rate on the convertible issue, while the horizontal axis gives the ratio of the conversion price to the initial market price of the stock. Limits of 1.0 are set for both ratios on the assumptions (1) that convertible interest yields can never exceed equivalent risk straight debt yields (if they did, this would indicate that the value of the option to convert was *negative*), and (2) that the conversion price is never set lower than the stock's market price at time of issue.[10] The curves

---

[10] This latter assumption has, to the authors' knowledge, always held true for nonrights offerings. There have been occasions—most notably AT&T's 1949 issue—when stockholders were offered convertibles with the conversion price lower than the initial market price.

are the locus of a set of isoyield points for given growth (and other) expectations.

Points *A* and *B* on the 4 percent growth rate curve illustrate the construction of the isoyield curves. At point *A* straight debt and convertible coupon rates are 4.5 percent and 4.0 percent, respectively, giving a ratio of 1.125, while the conversion price to market price ratio is $50/$45 = 1.100.

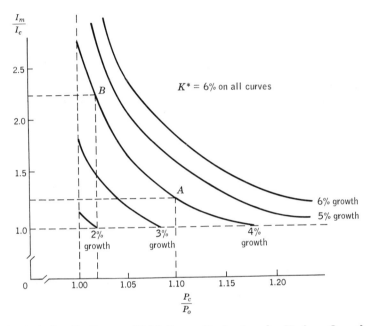

Fig. 22A-2.   Six Percent Yield Curves Derived under Various Growth,
Interest Rate, and Price Combinations
*All curves assume that the issuing corporation will
call when bonds have a conversion value of $1,200*
I_m = Straight debt interest
I_c = Convertible debt interest
P_o = Initial market price of stock
P_c = Conversion price

These values were found in the example above to produce a 6 percent expected yield on the convertible bond. At point *B,* the convertible interest rate is only 2 percent, so the yield ratio becomes 4.5/2.0 = 2.250. In order to obtain the 6 percent expected return, given the 4 percent growth rate, conversion must occur faster; specifically, by working through equation (22A-3), one finds that it must occur in five years rather than eight. Solving equation (22A-6) for the conversion price that allows conversion in five years yields a figure of $46, or a P_c/P_o ratio of $46/$45 = 1.02. This completes the derivation of point *B*. Other points on the curves are determined in a similar manner: by arbitrarily setting a convertible coupon rate, then working through the equations to find a conversion price that produces a 6 percent yield.

The expected yield on a convertible bond has two components—an interest yield known with relative certainty and a yield from capital gains that is considerably less certain. Consequently, the average investor would probably think of a convertible as being less risky than common stock but more risky than straight bonds.

Assuming that investors are risk averters, expected yields on convertibles should lie between those on stocks and those on nonconvertible debt. This suggests that market forces will drive a firm's convertible bonds to a point along an appropriate isoyield curve. However, this is not necessarily correct. Suppose, for example, that investors' require an 8 percent return on the company's common stock, $4\frac{1}{2}$ percent on its straight debt and 6 percent on its convertibles. This would mean that the firm could set a 2 percent coupon and a \$46 conversion price (point *B*), a 4.0 percent coupon and a \$50 conversion price (point *A*), or any other combination along the 6 percent yield curve. Intuition suggests, though, that the first situation is more risky than the second. With the coupon set at 4 percent, most of the return is from interest, while with a 2 percent coupon the expected yield is derived largely from capital gains. In general, the higher up the vertical axis on any yield curve, the more dependent the yield is on capital gains, and, consequently, the greater the risk of not attaining the indicated yield.

This leads to the conclusion that the firm's trade-off opportunity curve is something other than an isoyield curve, and such a situation is illustrated by Figure 22A–3. Equations (22A–3) and (22A–6) are used to construct a set of yield curves, all under the assumption that the stock will grow at 4 percent per year and that the bond will be called when its conversion value is \$1,200. If the coupon rate on the convertible is set close to the straight debt interest rate, the yield ratio is close to 1.0. In this case the convertible is very much like a regular bond, and the bond could be sold on an expected yield basis just above the 4.5 percent straight bond yield. On the other hand, if a very low coupon is set, the bondholder is relying primarily on capital gains. Under such circumstances, he may require a yield close to the 8 percent return on common stock. The hypothetical trade-off opportunity curve shown in Figure 22A–3 incorporates this hypothesis.[11]

All the curves in Figure 22A–3 are drawn on the assumption of a 4

---

[11] An alternative hypothesis would be that investors are indifferent between interest and capital gains, hence the trade-off curve should lie exactly on the isoyield curve appropriate to the firm's risk class. Still another hypothesis would be that investors prefer capital gains because of their tax advantage, hence the trade-off curve should be *steeper* than any single yield curve.

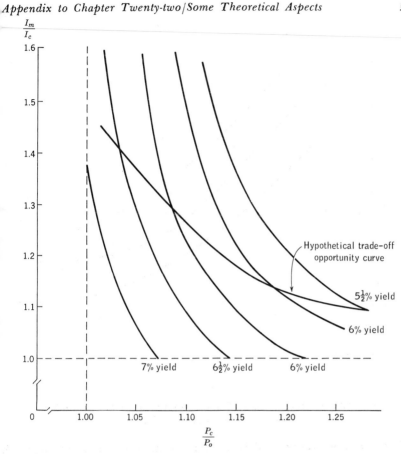

Fig. 22A–3. Hypothetical Trade-off Opportunity Curves for
4 Percent Growth Rate
All curves assume a 4 percent rate.

percent growth rate. At higher growth rates, the yield curves are shifted to the right, and this, in turn, leads to higher trade-off curves. Figure 22A–4 shows hypothetical trade-off curves under various growth assumptions; note that at higher growth rates the curves are higher.

Actually, of course, trade-off opportunity curves can be derived only empirically, but there is evidence indicating that, in fact, they do take the shape suggested by the model. The theory suggests that, other things held constant, a scatter diagram of I_m/I_o against P_c/P_o ratios should be approximated by a downward sloping curve that is somewhat flatter than any isoyield curve which could be constructed. That this condition does in fact hold is shown by Figure 22A–5, where the ratios of groups of growth and nongrowth companies are compared. The fits are by no means perfect, but this is to be expected because "other things" are not held constant. Credit ratings differ; some of the bonds have stepped-up conversion prices;

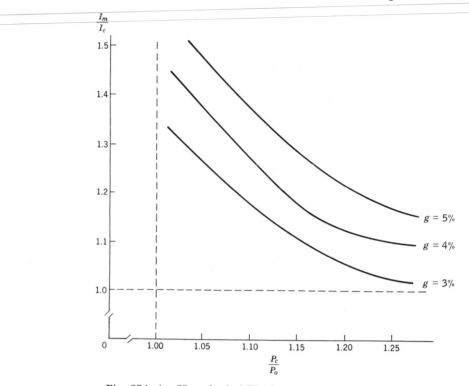

Fig. 22A–4. Hypothetical Trade-off Opportunity Curves under
Various Growth Assumptions

their remaining lives are widely different; and, most important, the stock prices of the different companies, even within the growth and nongrowth categories, are not expected to grow at the same rates. All in all, the fits are reasonably good, and the curves do have the postulated shapes and positions.

EMPIRICAL DATA ON CONVERTIBLE BOND USAGE

To gain insights into the corporate planning that lies behind the decision to issue convertibles, as well as to determine the characteristics of convertible bonds themselves, a sample of issues was examined and a detailed questionnaire was sent to the issuing firms. During the period 1961 to 1963, 215 publicly offered convertible bonds having a value of $1,080 million were sold to the public.[12] Of this total, $820 million, or 76 percent, were sold by 42 listed companies; these 42, shown in Table 22A–1,

---

[12] "Corporate Financing Directory," *Investment Dealers' Digest* (February 1965).

TABLE 22A–1

LIST OF COMPANIES IN SAMPLE

1. Air Reduction Company
2. Allied Stores Corp.
3. American Distilling Company
4. American Machine and Foundry Company
5. Armour and Company
6. Ashland Oil and Refining Company
7. Automatic Canteen Company of America
8. Baxter Laboratories, Inc.
9. Belco Petroleum Corp.
10. Berman Leasing Company
11. Brunswick Corporation
12. Canada Dry Corp.
13. Chock Full O'Nuts Corp.
14. City Products Corp.
15. Collins Radio Company
16. Continental Baking Company
17. Control Data Corp.
18. Crowell-Collier Publishing Company
19. FMC Corp.
20. General Acceptance Corp.
21. Holly Sugar Corp.
22. Hunt Foods and Industries, Inc.
23. International Silver Company
24. Interstate Department Stores
25. Keystone Steel and Wire Company
26. Lafayette Radio Electronics Corp.
27. Litton Industries
28. McCall Corp.
29. National Airlines, Inc.
30. Nopco Chemical Company
31. Northern Indiana Public Service Company
32. Occidental Petroleum Corp.
33. Ryder System, Inc.
34. Stokely-Van Camp, Inc.
35. Stouffer Foods Corp.
36. Symington Wayne Corp.
37. Thor Power Tool Company
38. Union Oil Company of California
39. United Aircraft Corp.
40. U. S. Freight Company
41. Vornado, Inc.
42. Xerox Corp.

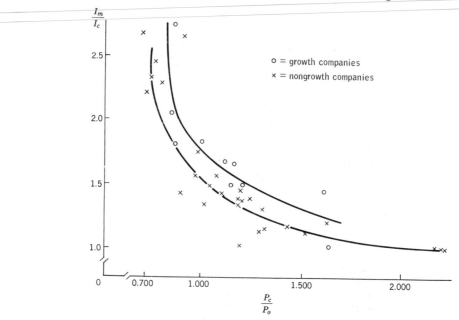

Fig. 22A–5. Relationship between I_n/I_c and P_c/P_n on Outstanding Bonds

A. Growth companies were selected as follows:

1. The Standard and Poor's list of 200 growth companies, dated February 22, 1965, was scanned and compared with the list of firms contained in *Moody's Convertible Bonds*. All companies on both lists (twenty) were initially included in the sample.

2. The value for I_c becomes very small, or even negative, when the market price of the bond is very large. (I_c is the yield to maturity on the bond). Ten of the growth companies were deleted from the sample because their ratios either became negative or "exploded" as I_c approached zero.

B. Nongrowth companies were selected as foilows:

1. The first 35 companies in *Moody's Convertible Bonds* not designated as growth companies by Standard and Poor were chosen as the basic sample.

2. Companies with negative or very large yield ratios were deleted, as in the growth company sample.

C. The curves were fitted free-hand.

were chosen for the sample.[13] Because of the selection process, the remarks in this section refer only to the use of convertibles by large corporations.

Statistics on the Sample

Table 22A–2 gives information on the sample companies and on the characteristics of the bonds themselves. Panel A shows that the issues

---

[13] One firm, Crowell-Collier, had two convertible issues during the period, so there are actually 43 bonds in the sample. Twenty-two firms, or 52 percent, completed the questionnaire.

TABLE 22A–2

STATISTICS ON THE SAMPLE OF CONVERTIBLE BONDS

	Dollars	Issues	
		Number	Percent
A. Size of Issue	(millions)		
	2.5– 4.9	3	7
	5.0– 9.9	16	37
	10.0–19.9	11	26
	20.0–29.9	5	12
	30.0–39.9	4	9
	40.0–60.0	4	9
B. Category		Number	Percent
	Industrial	37	86
	Transportation	4	9
	Public utility	1	2
	Finance	1	2
	Years to		
C. Maturity	Maturity	Number	Percent
	15	5	12
	20	25	58
	21	1	2
	22	2	5
	25	7	16
	30	3	7
D. Quality Rating	S & P Rating	Number	Percent
	A	3	7
	BBB	11	26
	BB	20	46
	B	9	21
E. Coupon Rate		Number	Percent
	$3\frac{1}{8}$–$3\frac{1}{2}$	2	5
	$3\frac{5}{8}$–4	4	9
	$4\frac{1}{8}$–$4\frac{1}{2}$	17	40
	$4\frac{5}{8}$–5	16	37
	$5\frac{1}{8}$–$5\frac{1}{2}$	2	5
	$5\frac{5}{8}$–$6\frac{1}{2}$	2	5
		Number	Percent
F. Rights Offering	Offered to stockholders	23	53
	Not offered to stockholders	20	47
		Number	Percent
G. Stepped-up	Price stepped up	8	19
Conversion Price	Not stepped up	35	81
		Number	Percent
H. Sinking Fund	Sinking fund	38	88
Provision	No sinking fund	5	12
	Number of		
I. Underwriting	Underwriters	Issues per Underwriter	
Data	13	1	
	5	2	
	2	3	
	1	5	
	1	9	

ranged in size from $2.5 million to $60 million, with the majority falling in the $5 million to $20 million classes. Industrial firms predominated; the fact that convertibles were not used to any extent by utilities, which have been doing much new financing, is significant. Section C of the table shows that maturities ranged from 15 to 30 years, with 20 and 25 years being most frequent.

The bond ratings ranged from A to B, with 67 percent falling below BBB, the lower limit of "investment-grade" securities.[14] However, the fact that the convertible issues were generally rated low *should not* be interpreted as meaning that the firms' straight debt was also low rated. All but two of the convertible issues were subordinated—generally to all existing and future long- and short-term debt. This clearly caused the convertibles to be rated well below the straight debt issues of the same companies.

About one half of the issues were sold through rights offerings; 19 percent employed a stepped-up conversion price; and 88 percent had a sinking fund provision.[15] It is not shown in the table, but all the bonds had essentially the same call provisions—they were callable immediately after issue with the call premium starting at the coupon interest rate and declining by $\frac{1}{4}$ percent per year to par. Relatively high concentration was found from the underwriting data, with Lehman Brothers acting as principal underwriter for nine issues, and Eastman Dillon, Union Securities for five.

Reasons for Using Convertibles

When a firm sells convertibles, it does so for one of two primary reasons: (1) it wants equity capital and believes that convertibles are an expedient way of selling common stock, or (2) it desires debt but finds that by adding the convertible feature interest costs are reduced substantially. Of the firms replying to the questionnaire, 73 percent were primarily interested in obtaining equity, while 27 percent used convertibles to sweeten debt issues. The bonds of this latter group generally carried the lower ratings, which was to be expected.[16]

---

[14] BB bonds "are regarded as lower medium grade. They have only minor investment characteristics." *Standard & Poor's Bond Guide.*

[15] The typical sinking fund provision does not commence for some ten years after issue; it requires the corporation to deliver funds to the trustee, who uses the funds to acquire bonds by lottery at par or through open market purchase, whichever is cheaper; and it gives the firm the right to deliver bonds acquired in conversion rather than money. Generally, the sinking fund amortizes from 50 to 80 percent of the total amount of bonds.

[16] Recall that the firms in the sample are large, all listed on either the New York Stock Exchange or the American Stock Exchange. Had the sample been extended to smaller, financially weaker companies, it is likely that a larger percentage would have indicated that convertibles were used to sweeten debt issues.

Financing Alternatives

To check the consistency of the responses to question 1, as well as to gain insights into other sources of funds and their costs, the following question was asked: "At the time you decided to use convertibles, what alternatives were available for raising *the same amount of funds as was obtained from selling convertibles?*" All companies indicated that common stock could have been sold at net prices ranging from 2 to 5 percent below the market price, the larger discounts being applicable to small firms and to those needing large sums of money relative to the value of their outstanding shares. It is worth noting that neither in the questionnaire responses nor in subsequent interviews with selected firms was a fear indicated that a common stock issue would have brought on the danger of a break in the market price of the stock. The feeling seemed to hold that the market could absorb a stock issue the size of the convertible debenture offering. All but two respondents indicated that straight debt could have been sold. When rates on straight debt were mentioned, they ranged from $\frac{1}{2}$ to 1 percent above those on the convertible issue.

In summary, the relatively large, listed corporations in the sample were by no means forced to use convertibles. They generally had the opportunity of selling either straight debt or stock, both at "reasonable" costs, but they deliberately chose to employ convertibles.

Conversion Policy

It was pointed out in the preceding sections that a firm's policy with regard to forcing conversion by calling the issue is one of the vital determinants of the rate of return to bondholders. In order that something might be learned about this factor, the firms were asked about their conversion policy on the questionnaire, and the sample of bonds was examined to see when conversion actually was forced.

The question and the responses to it are shown in Table 22A-3. Almost a quarter of the companies stated that their policy was to force conversion as soon as the conversion value exceeded the call price by about 20 percent. Another 23 percent indicated that they would encourage voluntary conversion by raising dividends.[17] The remaining 54 percent of

---

[17] One of these firms returned a schedule showing the way voluntary conversion occurred in its case. In September 1964, the common dividend was raised by 25 percent. At this point bondholders would receive about 15 percent more income from dividends on conversion than in interest on the bonds. The conversion value was approximately equal to the market value and exceeded the call price by about 30 percent. Between the time of the dividend increase and the record date of the next quarterly dividend, some 50 percent of the bonds were converted voluntarily, and the company indicated that these conversions were continuing as additional bondholders recognized the income differential.

TABLE 22A–3

CONVERSION POLICIES

"Which of the following most nearly reflects your company's policy with regard to conversion?"

	No.	Percent
1. Force conversion by calling as soon as you are "sure" the bonds will actually be converted, not redeemed. (Please indicate by how much conversion value must exceed call price.)	5	23
2. Encourage conversion by increasing common stock dividends, thus making the yield on common higher than that on bonds.	5	23
3. Have not encouraged conversion at all, but would force conversion prior to selling a new debt issue.	2	9
4. Do not plan to force or encourage conversion at all.	7	31
5. Other. (Please explain.)	3	14
	22	100

Note: The three companies checking "other" have no established conversion policy.

the respondents either did not plan to force conversion at all or else had no clearly defined policy.

These responses have been borne out reasonably well by actual experience. Of the 43 bonds in the sample, 20 had reached the point where the conversion value exceeded the call price by at least 20 percent. Six of these bonds, or 30 percent, had been called by March 1965.

Institutional Factors Making Convertibles Attractive

Questionnaire responses and interviews suggested that two strictly institutional phenomena may serve to make convertibles a relatively attractive form of financing. First, a number of institutional investors—life insurance companies, certain pension funds, and banks, for example—are severely restricted in their ability to hold common stocks. The investment officers of many of these institutions are thought to feel that it would be desirable to have more equities than regulations permit. Convertible bonds provide these intermediaries with a method of indirectly holding more equities than the law permits.

The second institutional factor has to do with margin requirements. Stockbrokers suggest that there exists a class of investors who desire to obtain more leverage than is available under current margin requirements. Many convertible bonds can be bought on a 20 percent or lower margin versus one of 70 percent on listed common stocks.

To the extent that high-leverage investors and restricted institutions are important factors in the market, it is possible that this might, in effect, shift to the right the supply curve for funds placed in the convertible market, thus lowering the cost of capital of convertibles. This is, in fact, what many advocates of convertibles suggest.[18] Although it may be true, there is no reason whatever to suppose that the supply shift could not be matched by an equal demand shift on the part of corporate borrowers, thus eliminating the supposed advantage attributed to convertibles. Indeed, is it not possible that corporations could be "oversold" on the use of convertibles, thus causing them to demand an excessive amount of funds through such issues and making the cost of convertible capital relatively more expensive than other types? This condition is completely speculative, of course. There is no evidence to indicate whether these institutional factors create a favorable or unfavorable situation for convertibles. The institutional effects are probably favorable on balance but decidedly of second order importance.

IMPACT OF CONVERTIBLES ON STOCKHOLDER RETURNS

Given its trade-off possibility curve, what particular coupon rate/conversion price combination should a firm select, or should it use convertibles at all? The answer to this question is probabilistic—it depends upon what actually happens after the fact, but the material developed in this appendix does permit some tentative suggestions.

Since the desirability of using convertibles is probabilistic, thus necessarily subjective, it is difficult to reach any very general conclusions. It is, however, possible to describe specific circumstances under which using convertibles appears to be advantageous *ex ante,* and conversely. Fortunately, the basic assumptions seem to apply to most of the firms that returned the questionnaire.

Target debt/equity ratio. The first assumption is that the firm has a long-run target debt/equity ratio, and that this target ratio is independent of the decision to use or not to use convertibles. Further, when convertibles are used, they are classified as debt until converted, at which point they are classed as equity for purposes of calculating the target debt ratio.

Financial alternatives. The firm is assumed to be capable of obtaining funds in the desired mix; that is, it is able to borrow or sell stock in whatever amounts are necessary to maintain its target debt ratio.

---

18 For example, see W. S. Skelly, *Convertible Bonds: A Study of Their Suitability for Commercial Bank Bond Portfolios* (New York: Salomon Bros. & Hutzler, 1959), *passim.*

Further, market conditions are assumed to be such that it may deviate, within the limits of its annual outside financing needs, from the target ratio at any time. In other words, it can finance with debt one year and with equity the next, oscillating about the target ratio rather than maintaining it exactly. The decision to use debt or equity in any given year will depend upon conditions in the security markets and on the relationship between the actual and the target debt/equity ratios.

While the questionnaire responses and interviews suggested that this assumption is approximately correct for the large, listed firms in the sample, it is probably not true for smaller companies. For small, nonlisted businesses the flotation costs of stock are probably substantially higher than the costs of selling bonds. Further, it may be that the convertibles of small companies sell in a broader market than their common stock and therefore reduce the fear of loss of control. Finally, if a small firm sells a block of stock, there is more likelihood that it will cause a subsequent break in the market price than if a sale is made by a larger firm whose stock sells in a broader market. These possibilities must be explored in greater detail before the analysis may be applied to small firms.

Capital budget. It is further assumed that the firm has determined its capital budget. This decision is not presumed to be made independently of the over-all cost of capital, but it is presumed to be made independently of the method of financing during the current year. In other words, using or not using convertibles will have no impact on the level of investment (other than whatever secondary effects convertibles might have on future investment through their impact on the cost of capital).

Required rate of return. The "marginal investor" is assumed to have a required rate of return which he expects to earn on the firm's shares (and convertibles). This return varies over time, and at any given time it varies among firms in accordance with their "riskiness," which is defined as the variance of the expected rate of return. The required rate of return on shares is expected to be realized from the dividend yield plus a capital gain, while that on convertibles is expected to come from interest payments plus capital gains.

Various conditions. Suppose a firm's long-run plans indicate that new outside funds—both debt and equity—will be required in each future year as far ahead as has been forecast. The necessary equity capital can be raised (1) by the sale of common stock, (2) by the sale of debt now, and a refund later with an equity issue (this will cause a temporary deviation from the target debt ratio), or (3) by the sale of convertibles which, when converted, will provide the required equity. If convertibles are sold, they may be used in either of two ways. First, the firm can sell both straight and convertible debt in the current year, and thus have more debt than is called for by the target ratio, with this situation being rectified when conversion occurs. Alternatively, it can sell both common stock and debt in the current year to maintain the target debt ratio, but make part of the debt convertible. This current issue of convertible debt, when converted, will thus provide for part of the future equity requirements. (The converted debt will, of course, be replaced to maintain the target debt ratio.)

Operating within the assumptions specified above, which choice is best? For firms interested in their stockholders, the best choice is that which maximizes the wealth of existing shareholders. This amounts to selecting the financing package that (consistent with the target debt ratio) minimizes the number of new shares that must be given up, *ex ante,* to raise the necessary equity funds. This, in turn, depends upon management's judgment versus that of the market about the "proper level" of share prices.

Stock "fairly priced." If the firm's management and the "market" are in agreement (1) about the firm's prospects for growth and (2) about its appropriate risk class, then they must also be in agreement about the current price of the stock. Under such circumstances, there is no reason to think that any one of the choices is clearly superior to any other. The institutional factors discussed above—the demand for convertibles generated by margin requirements and limitations on institutional holdings of common stocks—may be sufficient to create an advantage for convertibles, but this is not at all clear. Aside from this possible point, the use or nonuse of convertibles would appear to be a matter of indifference when the stock is thought to be fairly priced.

Stock undervalued. If management deems its stock to be undervalued—presumably because it thinks the market is overly pessimistic about the firm's growth prospects or risk class, or is simply undervaluing all equities at the particular time—then the best financing decision is to issue debt. Later on, when the stock price has risen, sufficient equity will be issued to return to the target debt ratio. Convertibles are a better choice than common stock, but using them is still not as good as using straight debt. That component of the convertible's expected return which investors plan to receive from the common stock is, presumably, undervalued. This means the firm must set the conversion price relatively low or the coupon rate relatively high, in order to sell the bonds.

If the decision is made to issue convertibles, perhaps because of a belief that the institutional factors offset the undervaluation of the stock, then the firm should move to the right side of its trade-off opportunity curve. In other words, more emphasis should be placed on the interest component, which bond purchasers are evaluating correctly, than on the capital gains component, which they are undervaluing.

Stock overvalued. If the stock is overvalued, exactly the reverse holds true. Financing should be with common stock, but convertibles are a better choice than straight debt. If convertibles are to be used regardless, then a position on the left side of the trade-off opportunity curve should be selected.

Simulating the Effect of Convertibles on Shareholder Returns

Management may be reluctant to pit its judgment against that of the market, deeming stock market forecasting to be out of its province. Since this suggests that an indirect approach may be useful, a simulation model was developed in order to observe the way expected rates of return to existing shareholders are altered by introducing convertibles into the capital structure.[19]

The program starts from specific assumptions about the target debt ratio, the forecast capital budget, the target dividend payout ratio, the expected return on investment, and so on. From these inputs it calculates earnings and dividends per share, a projected market price per share, and the firm's financing requirements for a ten-year period. Given the dividends, the ending price of the stock, and an assumed personal tax rate for stockholders, the program calculates the after-tax return to the initial stockholders.

The data used were obtained from a large electric utility, and for firms in this industry the long-term capital budget, the rate of return on investment, and so on, can be estimated with reasonable accuracy. The firm's management was sincerely interested in the outcome of the simulation study, so their estimates were developed quite carefully. The program called for convertibles to be used to raise equity capital that would be needed in the future; that is, the debt-equity ratio was maintained at the target level (60 percent) at all times. A flotation cost equal to 0.5 percent was assessed against convertible bond issues, and one of 2 percent was assessed against common stock offerings. These figures, as well as the trade-off opportunity curve applicable to convertible issues, were obtained from investment bankers.

The simulation was run under a variety of different trade-offs, but the outcomes were always the same—using convertibles lowered the rate of return to stockholders over what it would have been had the firm financed by straight debt and equity issues. The differences, however, were too small for much significance to be attached to them; the estimated annual rate of return was 6.5 percent when convertibles were not used versus about 6.4 percent when convertibles were used.

---

[19] The basic program employed was developed by Professor John P. Shelton from the Consolidated Telephone Company (B) case in Masson, Hunt, and Anthony, *Cases in Financial Management* (Homewood, Ill.: Irwin, 1960), pp. 247–250.

It is assumed in the program that present stockholders continue to hold their stock for a ten-year period.

SUMMARY

The major findings of this appendix may be summarized as follows. First, the graphic model showed that a convertible bond has a market value floor which is set by the higher of its straight debt or conversion value. Typically, the bond will sell above this floor because (1) of a capital gains potential coupled with a degree of protection against losses due to a drop in stock prices and (2) of institutional constraints against the purchase of stock.

A convertible's *ex ante* yield is dependent upon expectations about the following: (1) growth rates, (2) firm's policy on calling to force conversion, (3) conversion ratio, (4) price of the shares at time of issue, and (5) coupon interest rate. If this *ex ante* yield, as computed by marginal investors, differs from their required rate of return, the bond will go to a premium or a discount immediately after issue.

To gain insights into the actual usage of convertible debentures, a questionnaire was sent to each of the 42 listed firms that had a public offering from 1961 through 1963. While it would be redundant to present a detailed description of the sample statistics, it is interesting to note (1) that 73 percent of the responding firms indicated that they were mainly interested in raising equity capital when they sold convertibles and (2) that essentially all these (large, listed) firms seemed to have had the ability to finance with straight debt or common stock at the time they issued convertibles.

The *ex ante* desirability of using convertibles depends on management's views about impending movements in the price of its stock vis-à-vis the market's views. If management believes its stock to be relatively overpriced, then financing with stock is best, convertibles second best, and straight debt worst. Just the reverse holds if the stock is thought to be undervalued. If management agrees with the market (or refuses to take a stand), the choice of financing under a set of reasonable assumptions turns out to be immaterial. Note, however, that *ex post* a firm using convertibles will always have intermediate financing results. Since convertibles lie between debt and equity, a firm using them is "hedging its bets."

There are, however, some perhaps important institutional factors that might render convertible financing advantageous in a more positive sense. To the extent that certain investors who really want to make equity commitments are able to buy convertibles but not common stock, the demand curve for convertibles may be shifted to the right. This shift, in turn, would lower the cost of convertible capital vis-à-vis directly sold common stock. The extent of this phenomenon was not investigated, but it may well be important at times. In addition, the conclusions stated apply only to larger, publicly owned corporations. The use of convertibles by smaller firms was not investigated, but there are reasons for believing that convertible securities might offer special advantages to smaller companies with less financial flexibility than to the large firms in the sample studied.

Part VI

Capital Market
Institutions

Chapter *23*

Investment Banking

NATURE OF INVESTMENT BANKING

In the American economy, saving is performed by one group of persons while investing is performed by another. ("Investing" is used here in the sense of actually putting money into plant, equipment, and inventory, not "investing" in the sense of buying securities.) Thus savings are placed with financial intermediaries who in turn make the funds available to firms wishing to acquire plant and equipment and to hold inventories.

One of the major institutions which perform this channeling role is known as investment banking. Some of the larger investment bankers are listed in Table 23–1. The rank of an investment banking firm by size of capital will not necessarily coincide with the volume of business that the firm conducts.

The term "investment banker" is somewhat misleading in that investment bankers are neither investors nor bankers. That is, they do not invest their own funds permanently, nor are they repositories for individuals' funds, as are commercial banks or savings banks. What, then, *is* the nature of investment banking? In defining any set of institutions a functional rather than a descriptive definition is required; for example, an elephant is best defined in terms of appearance, but a shovel is best defined in terms of what it does. Investment banking is best defined in terms of what investment bankers do.

The many activities of investment bankers may be described first in general terms and then with respect to specific functions. The historical and traditional function of the investment banker has been to act as the

TABLE 23-1

LARGEST TEN INVESTMENT BANKERS MEASURED BY AMOUNTS OF TOTAL CAPITAL

	Date of Report	Total Capital
1. Merrill Lynch, Pierce, Fenner & Smith, Inc., New York (C)*	12/25/64	$114,988,116
2. Equitable Securities Corp., Nashville (C)	12/31/64	49,883,501
3. Allen & Company, New York (P)	7/31/64	45,070,543
4. Francis I. du Pont & Co., New York (P)	12/31/64	41,861,996
5. Bache & Co., New York (C)	12/31/64	41,762,994
6. Eastman Dillon, Union Securities Co., New York (P)	8/30/64	30,353,889
7. Lehman Brothers, New York (P)	4/30/64	29,412,206
8. Dean Witter & Company, San Francisco (P)	12/31/64	29,134,018
9. Blyth & Co., Inc., New York (C)	12/31/64	28,917,624
10. Shelby Cullom Davis & Company, New York (P)	7/31/64	27,734,480

* C = corporation; P = partnership.
Source: "Net Worth of the Leading Underwriters," *Finance* (March 1965).

middleman in channeling driblets of savings and funds of individuals into the purchase of business securities, primarily bonds. The investment banker does not do this by acting as the banker, but by purchasing and distributing the new securities of individual companies. Specifically, the investment banker has the following functions.

Underwriting

Underwriting is the insurance function of bearing the risks of adverse price fluctuations during the period in which a new issue of securities is being distributed. The nature of the underwriting function of the investment banker can best be conveyed through an example. A business firm needs $10 million. It goes to an investment banker, conferences are held, and the decision is made to issue $10 million of bonds. An underwriting agreement is drawn up, and on a specific day the investment banker will present the company with a check for $10 million (less commission). In return, the investment banker will receive bonds in denomination of $1,000 each, which he sells to the public.

The company receives the $10 million before the investment banker has sold the bonds. Between the time the investment banker pays the firm the $10 million and the time at which the investment banker has sold the bonds, the latter bears all the risk of market price fluctuations in the bonds. Conceivably, it can take the investment banker 10, 20, 30 days, 6 months, or longer to sell bonds. If in the interim the bond market collapses, the investment banker will be carrying the risk of loss in the sale of the bonds. There have been dramatic instances of bond market collapse within one week after an investment banker has bought $50 million or $100 million of bonds.

But the individual firm does not need to be concerned about the risk of market price fluctuations while the investment banker is selling the bonds. The firm has received its $10 million. One fundamental economic function of the investment banker, then, is to underwrite the risk of market price fluctuations between the time the investment banker transmits the money to the firm and the time the bonds are placed in the hands of their ultimate buyers. For this reason, the investment banker is often called an underwriter: he is an underwriter of risk during the distribution period.

Distributing

The second function of the investment banker is securities marketing. The investment banker is a specialist who has a staff that distributes securities. The investment banker can therefore perform the physical distribution function more efficiently and more economically than could an individual corporation. Sporadically, whenever it wished to sell an issue of securities, each corporation would find it necessary to establish a marketing or a selling organization. This procedure would be a very expensive and ineffective method of selling securities. The investment banker has a permanent, trained staff continuously available to distribute the securities. In addition, his staff builds up a broad clientele over a period, further increasing the ease with which he can sell securities.

Advice and Counsel

Since the investment banker is engaged in the origination and sale of securities, through experience he becomes an expert in advising about terms and characteristics of securities that will appeal to investors. The advice and guidance of the investment banker in determining the characteristics and provisions of securities so that they will be successfully marketed may be almost invaluable. Furthermore, as a seller of the securities, the reputation of the investment banker depends upon the subsequent performance of the securities. Therefore he will often sit on the board of directors of firms whose securities he has sold. In this way he is able to provide continuing financial counsel and to increase the firm's probability of success.

Source of Funds

A fourth function performed by the investment banker is that of serving as a source of funds to the issuing concern during the distribution or selling period. During the interim period, between the time the investment banker purchases the corporation securities and the time the investment banker receives the funds from their sale, the investment banker must provide the funds to carry the securities. The investment banker in turn procures a substantial amount of the funds from the commercial banking system on short-term loans during the distribution period. Nevertheless, the investment banking firm must bear the risk connected with the use of the funds.

Such, then, are the main economic functions provided by investment bankers. The investment houses engage in a wide variety of activities to provide many other services to business firms, but the other activities will best be understood after a more complete description of the investment banking operation.

INVESTMENT BANKING OPERATION

To understand clearly the investment banking function it is useful to trace the history of a new issue of securities by a corporation. Since the firm has sold securities before, typically through an investment banker, it will tend to continue to use the same investment banker. The historical investment banker has become familiar with the background of the corporation; he will therefore be in an advantageous position to handle the current issue.

Pre-underwriting Conferences

First, the members of the issuing firm and the investment banker hold pre-underwriting conferences. At these conferences they discuss the amount of capital to be raised, the type of security to be issued, and terms.

Memorandums will be written by the treasurer of the issuing company, describing alternative proposals suggested at the conferences. Meetings of the board of directors of the issuing company will be held to discuss the alternatives and to attempt to reach a decision.

At some point the issuer enters an agreement with the investment banker that a flotation will take place. The investment banker will then begin to conduct what is called an underwriting investigation. If the company is proposing to purchase additional assets, the underwriter's engineering staff will make an engineering analysis of the proposed asset acquisition. A public accounting firm will be called upon to make an audit of the issuing firm's financial situation. In addition, the public accounting firm will aid in the preparation of the registration statements for the Securities and Exchange Commission (SEC) in connection with these issues.

A firm of lawyers will be called in to give interpretations and judgments about legal aspects of the flotation. In addition, the originating underwriter, who will be the manager of the subsequent underwriting syndicate, will make an exhaustive investigation of the prospects of the company.

When the investigations are completed but before registration with the SEC, an underwriting agreement will be drawn up by the investment banker. Terms of the tentative underwriting agreement may be modified through discussions between the underwriter and the issuing company. Finally, agreement will be reached on all underwriting terms except the actual price of the securities.

Registration Statement

A registration statement will then be filed with the SEC. The commission requires a 20-day waiting period, during which time its staff analyzes the registration statement to determine whether there are any omissions or misrepresentations of fact. The SEC may file exceptions to the registration statement or ask for additional information from the issuing company or the underwriters during the 20-day waiting period. During this period the underwriting investment bankers are not permitted to offer the securities for sale. However, they may print preliminary prospectuses with all the information customarily contained in a prospectus except the offering price.

Setting the Price of the Securities

The actual price the underwriter pays the issuer is not generally determined until the close of the registration period. There is no universally followed practice, but one frequently followed arrangement when a new issue of stock is involved calls for the investment banker to buy the securities at a set number of points below the closing price on the last day of registration. For example, suppose the shares of the XYZ Company, with a current price of $38, have sold in a range of $35 to $40 per share during the previous three months. The firm and the underwriter agree that the investment banker will buy 200,000 new shares at $2.50 below the closing price on the last day of registration. If the stock closes at $36 on the day the SEC releases the issue, then the firm will receive $33.50 per share. Typically, such agreements have an escape clause that provides for the contract to be voided if the price of the securities ends below some predetermined figure. In the illustrative case, this "upset" price might be set at $34 per share. Thus if the closing price of the shares on the last day of registration is $33.50, the issuing firm will have an option of withdrawing from the arrangement.

The Underwriting Syndicate

The investment banker with whom the issuing firm has conducted its discussions will not typically handle the purchase and distribution of the issue by himself. Because the money amounts involved are large and the risk of price fluctuation substantial, the investment banker forms a syndicate, in an effort to minimize the amount of risk he carries. A syndicate is a temporary association for the purpose of carrying out a specific objective. The nature of the arrangements for a syndicate in the underwriting and sale of a security through an investment banker may best be understood with the aid of Figure 23–1.

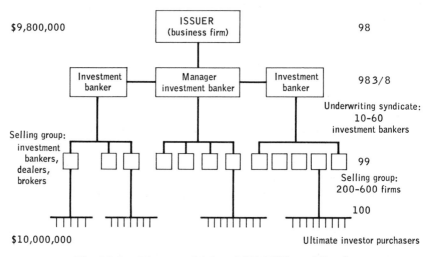

Fig. 23–1. Diagram of Sales of $10 Million of Bonds
through Investment Bankers

The managing banker invites other investment bankers on the basis of their knowledge of the particular kind of offering to be made and on the basis of their strength and dealer contacts in selling securities of the type involved in the issue.

Each investment banker has business relations with other investment bankers and dealers; thus each investment banker has a selling group consisting of himself and other investment bankers and dealers. Some firms combine all these characteristics. For example, the firm of Merrill Lynch, Pierce, Fenner and Smith, Inc., underwrites some issues and manages the underwriting of others. On still other flotations it will be invited by the manager to join in the distribution of the issue. It also purchases securities as the dealer and carries an inventory in these securities. It publishes lists of securities it has for sale. In addition to being a dealer, Merrill Lynch, of course, carries on substantial activity as a broker. An individual investment firm may carry on all these functions, just as a department store sells all kinds of merchandise.

But there are also firms with a narrower range of functions—specialty dealers, specialty brokers, and specialty investment counselors. Thus in the financial field there is specialization of financial functions as well as a department store type of operations. A dealer purchases securities outright, holds them in inventory as a grocery store would, and sells them at whatever price he can get. He may benefit from price appreciation or he may suffer a loss on declines, as any merchandiser does. A broker, on the other hand, takes orders for purchases and transmits them to the proper exchange; his gain is the commission he charges for the service.

Syndicates are used in the distribution of securities for three reasons. (1) A single investment banker may be financially unable to handle a large issue alone. (2) The originating house may desire to spread the risk even if it is financially able to handle the issue alone. (3) The utilization of several selling organizations as well as other underwriters permits an economy of selling efforts and expense, and encourages broader, nationwide distribution.

The participating underwriters and dealers are provided with full information on all phases of these financing transactions. They share in the underwriting commission. To show how the underwriting commission is shared, let us illustrate how a two-point spread would be divided. An investment banker buys $10 million worth of bonds to be sold at par, or $1,000 each. If the investment banker receives a two-point spread, he will buy the bonds from the issuer at 98; thus he must pay the issuer $9.8 million for the issue of $10 million. Typically, on a two-point spread, the manager-underwriter will receive the first $\frac{3}{8}$ of 1 percent for originating and managing the syndicate. Other underwriters will receive from $\frac{5}{8}$ to $\frac{3}{4}$ of 1 percent. For the purposes of the illustration, let us assume that they receive $\frac{5}{8}$ of 1 percent. Members of the selling syndicate or group receive from $\frac{7}{8}$ of 1 percent to 1 percent.

If the manager of the underwriting group makes a sale to an ultimate purchaser of the securities, he will receive the $\frac{3}{8}$ percent as manager, $\frac{5}{8}$ percent as underwriter, and 1 percent as the seller—the full 2 percent. If he wholesales some of the securities to members of the selling group who make the ultimate sale, the latter will receive the 1 percent selling commission, and the manager will receive the other 1 percent for managing and underwriting the issue. If the issue is managed by one firm, underwritten by a second, and sold by a third, the 2 percent commission is divided, with 1 percent going to the selling firm, $\frac{5}{8}$ percent to the underwriter, and $\frac{3}{8}$ percent to the manager of the underwriting group.

Syndicate Operations

Purchase-group syndicates are of two types—unlimited syndicates and divided syndicates. Divided-syndicate agreements for underwriters are most generally used. In the divided-syndicate agreement, the liability of each member is limited to the amount of his participation. His liability at the dissolution of the syndicate would be his participation less his performance. Performance is the securities he has sold or taken. Divided responsibility therefore means that each underwriter is responsible for his own share of the participation and no more.

In an undivided syndicate, an accounting is made at the termination of the syndicate agreement. Any unsold securities are divided among the participants in relation to their participation, regardless of their performance. For example, in an undivided syndicate the firm may have agreed to take one million shares of ten million, and it may have sold one million. But if two million shares remain unsold at the termination of the syndicate agreement, the underwriting firm is responsible for one tenth of the two million, or 200,000 shares, even though it has sold its full one million. It is easy to see why underwriters prefer the divided agreement.

The Selling Group

The selling group is formed primarily for the purpose of distributing securities; it consists of dealers who take relatively small participations from the members of the buying group. The underwriters act as wholesalers; members of the selling groups act as retailers. The number of houses in a selling group depends partly upon the size of the issue. A selling group may have as many as 300 to 400 dealers; for example, the one for Communications Satellite Corporation consisted of 385 members.

The operation of the selling group is controlled by the selling group agreement, which usually covers the following major points:

1. *Description of the issue.* The selling group letter, in addition, refers to an enclosed prospectus which gives the full description of the issue and issuer.

2. *Concession.* Members of the selling group subscribe to the new issue at a public offering price less the concession given to them as a commission for their selling service.

3. *Handling repurchased securities.* The selling group agreement provides that no member of the selling group be permitted to sell the securities below the public offering price. The syndicate manager invariably pegs the quotation in the market by placing orders to buy at the public offering price continuously. A careful record is kept of bond numbers so that repurchased bonds may be identified with the member of the selling group who sold them. General practice is to cancel the commission on such bonds and add brokerage costs incurred in the repurchase. Repurchased bonds are then placed with other dealers for sale.

4. *Duration of selling group.* The most common provision in selling group agreements is that the group have an existence of 30 days, subject to earlier termination by the manager. The agreement may be extended,

however, for an additional 80 days by members representing 75 percent of the selling group.

Offering and Sale

After the selling group has been formed, the actual offering proceeds. Publicity in advance of the offering date is developed. Advertising material for release as soon as permissible is prepared. The actual day of the offering is chosen with a view to avoiding temporary congestion in the security market and other unfavorable events or circumstances.

The formal public offering is called "opening the books," an archaic term which reflects ancient customs of the investment banking trade. When the books are opened, the manager accepts subscriptions to the issue from both selling group participants and outsiders who may wish to buy.

If the demand for the issue is great, the books may be closed immediately. An announcement is then made that the issue is oversubscribed. On the other hand, when the reception is not strong, the book may remain open for an extended period.

Market Stabilization

During the period of the offering and distribution of securities, the manager of the underwriting group typically stabilizes the price of the issue. The duration of the price-pegging operation is usually 30 days. The price is pegged by placing orders to buy at a specified price in the market. The pegging operation is designed to prevent a cumulative downward movement in the price if it should soften. A downward price shift would result in losses for all members of the underwriting group. As the manager of the underwriting group has the major responsibility, he assumes the task of pegging the price.

This discussion raises the question of pricing the new issue. If the issue is simply more shares of an already outstanding stock, then the price of the existing stock is the main determinant of the price of the new shares. If the issue is a new one, the main guides to pricing it are the prevailing prices of similar outstanding issues. During the underwriting conferences, comparisons are made with other companies who have recently issued similar securities, and the prices and yields of these securities are analyzed. The new issue is priced to yield about what competitive securities yield.

The investment banker will have an easier job if the issue is priced low, with a high yield. The issuer of the securities naturally wants as high a price and as low a yield as possible. Some conflict of interest on price therefore arises between the investment banker and the issuer. If the issuer is financially sophisticated and looks to comparisons with similar issues of securities, the investment banker is forced to price pretty close to the market.

If the market deteriorates during the offering period, the investment banker carries a rather substantial risk. For this reason the pegging operation may not be sufficient to protect the underwriters. Such risks may be considerable. In the Pure Oil Company issue of $44 million convertible preferred stocks of September 3, 1937, at 100, only $1 million of shares were sold by the underwriters. At the conclusion of the underwriting account, initial trading took place at 74. Not until 1941 did the stock again sell as high as 90. In the $48 million issue of Bethlehem Steel Corporation convertible debentures ($3\frac{1}{2}$ percent) offered at 100 in 1937, stockholders took only $4 million of the debentures. By October 15, the debentures sold as low as 85. By the end of 1938, however, they had risen to 100 again.

It has been charged that pegging the price during the offering period constitutes a monopolistic price-fixing arrangement. On the other hand, investment bankers reply that not to peg the price would increase the risk and therefore the underwriting cost to the issuer. On balance, it appears that the pegging operation is a socially useful function. The danger of monopolistic pricing is avoided, or at least mitigated substantially, by competitive factors. If an underwriter attempts to set a monopolistic price on a particular issue of securities, the investor can turn to thousands of other securities that are not involved in price-pegging operations. The degree of control over the market by the underwriter in a price-pegging operation is therefore negligible.

Three additional aspects of investment banking remain for discussion. The first concerns cost of flotation, the second is competitive bidding, and the third is the new role of the investment banker.

COSTS OF FLOTATION

The cost of selling new issues of securities can be put into perspective by Table 23–2. The table summarizes in a general way the data on cost of flotation developed over the years through 1955 by the Securities and Exchange Commission. Important generalizations can be drawn from it.

1. The cost of flotation for common stock is greater than for preferred stocks, and the costs of both are greater than the cost of flotation for bonds, regardless of the size of issue.

2. The costs of flotation as a percentage of the gross proceeds are greater for small issues than for large issues.

What are the reasons for these relations? The explanations are found in the amount of risk involved and the physical job of distribution. There is a broader market for debt, particularly among institutional investors, than for preferred stock or common stock. For this reason the distribution job is greater for common stock, and the expenses of marketing it are greater.

The explanation for the variation in cost with the size of issue is also easily found. In the first place, certain fixed expenses are associated with any distribution of securities. Four items of expense account for 85 percent of the cost of flotation. Many of these expenses are fixed expenses, such as the underwriting investigation, the preparation of the registration statement, legal fees, and so forth. Since they are relatively large and relatively fixed, their percentage of the total cost of flotation runs high on small issues.

Second, small issues are typically those of relatively less well-known firms. The underwriting expenses may be larger than usual, because the

TABLE 23-2

COSTS OF FLOTATION, 1951-1955
(costs expressed as percentage of gross proceeds)

| *Size of Issue (in millions of dollars)* | *Debt* | | | *Preferred Stock* | | | *Common Stocks* | | |
	Underwriting Commission	*Other Expenses*	*Total Costs*	*Underwriting Commission*	*Other Expenses*	*Total Costs*	*Underwriting Commission*	*Other Expenses*	*Total Costs*
Under 0.5	—	—	—	—	—	—	21.0	6.0	27.0
0.5– 0.9	7.5	4.0	11.5	8.7	4.0	12.7	17.1	4.6	21.8
5.0– 9.9	1.0	0.8	1.8	2.9	0.8	3.7	5.3	0.9	6.2
20.0–49.9	0.8	0.5	1.3	2.8	0.4	3.2	5.0	0.4	5.4
50.0 and over	0.9	0.3	1.2	2.1	0.4	2.5	—	—	—

Source: Securities and Exchange Commission, *Cost of Flotation of Corporate Securities,* 1951-1955 (Washington, D.C.: U.S. Government Printing Office, June 1957).

danger of omitting vital information is greater for a small firm. Furthermore, the selling job is greater. A larger number of salesmen must exert greater effort to sell the securities of a less well-known firm. For these reasons the underwriting commission, as a percentage of the gross proceeds, is relatively high for small issues.

It has been charged that the expenses of flotation have become high since the advent of the SEC in 1933. An analysis of the costs of flotation has been made, breaking them down into costs associated with registration and those not affected by registration. Underwriting commissions account for about 65 percent of the total cost of flotation. Registration expenses account for about 30 percent, and expenses not affected by registration account for the remainder, or about 5 percent. Registration expenses as a percentage of the gross proceeds are relatively minor and do not vary greatly with the cost of flotation. Costs partly affected by registration— printing, engraving, legal, accounting, and engineering costs—do increase somewhat in percentage as the size of flotation decreases. The other costs are relatively minor.

These data demonstrate convincingly that the high percentage costs of flotation on small issues are not caused by discrimination against small issues. The fixed expenses of flotation are large when expressed as a percentage of the proceeds on small issues.

In addition to the factors discussed above, flotation costs are also influenced by whether or not the issue is a rights offering, and if it is, by the extent of the underpricing. If rights are used and if the underpricing is substantial, then the investment banker bears little risk of inability to sell the shares. Further, very small selling effort will be required in such a situation. These two factors combine to enable a company to float new securities to its own stockholders at a relatively low cost.

COMPETITIVE BIDDING

Another significant issue that has been raised in connection with investment banking is the proposal that competitive bidding be required on all new issues of corporate securities. One of the factors stimulating this proposal was the adoption by the Securities and Exchange Commission of Rule U–50 in 1941 requiring competitive bidding for utilities securities under the Holding Company Act of 1935. A similar rule for railroad bonds was enacted by the Interstate Commerce Commission in 1944, and the rule has also been promulgated by the Federal Power Commission and several state power commissions.

As a consequence of the adoption of these rules, the high-grade bond business was divided into two major parts. One sector concerns bonds sold by direct placement to institutions. The other, which includes most of the very high-grade bond business remaining after direct placement, concerns bonds sold under compulsory competitive bidding.

The main arguments that have been offered for extending competitive bidding to industrial issues are the following:

1. It is said that there is undue concentration in the investment banking business. Data in Table 23–3 show the largest firms by volume of management activity.[1] During the mid-thirties six firms managed more than 57 percent of total registered issues. During the period 1948–1951, however, this percentage dropped to 40.

2. As a consequence of concentration in the investment banking business, informal understandings have developed among investment bankers so that they do not compete actively for business. When it is understood

---

[1] This list for volume of management activity can be compared with that for size according to the amount of capital (see Table 23–1).

TABLE 23-3

CONCENTRATION IN INVESTMENT BANKING

Investment Banking Firms	Percentage of Total Registered Issues Managed	
	Jan. 1934– June 1939	1948–1951
Morgan Stanley & Co.	23.2%	13.1%
The First Boston Corp.	10.7	12.6
Dillon Read & Co., Inc.	7.4	3.5
Kuhn, Loeb & Co.	6.7	2.5
Smith, Barney & Co.	5.1	2.1
Blyth & Co., Inc.	4.2	5.9
Total	57.3%	39.7%

Source: Paul L. Howell, "Competition in the Capital Markets," Harvard Business Review, 31 (May–June 1953), p. 88.

that a firm has dealt with a particular investment banker in the past, other investment bankers do not "poach on his preserves."

3. It is argued that because the investment banker "carries water" on both shoulders when he is formulating the terms of a security issue, the lack of competitive bidding leads to advantageous pricing for him. The implication is that it is to the advantage of the investment banker to price the issue low (1) because it will be easier to sell initially and (2) because subsequently the issue will rise in price if it has been priced too low initially. A reputation for handling issues that later rise in price will make the sale of subsequent issues easier for the investment banker.

The arguments against competitive bidding are these:

1. The changed nature of the securities market since the early 1930s makes the protection by competitive bidding on industrial issues unnecessary. Two major forces have changed the capital market: (1) Firms now utilize internal financing to raise more than 50 percent of their total financing; in other words, the availability of internal financing has reduced the dependence of business firms on external financing. (2) The rise in direct placement, which accounts for a substantial amount of financing, gives the issuer many alternatives to dealing with the investment banker.[2] In other words, if the issuer is not happy with the deal offered to him by his historical investment banker in the preliminary discussions, he can call on an insurance company, or possibly a commercial bank if he needs the

---

Direct sale of an issue, or a direct loan obtained by the firm from an insurance company, pension fund, or other source, without the use of investment banker as underwriter and distributor. Direct placement is discussed in the following chapter.

money for a shorter period. The availability of these easy alternatives has been suggested as an argument, therefore, against the need for competitive bidding.

2. Though competitive bidding on public utility issues has been in force since 1941, competitive bidding on industrial issues would be much more difficult to carry out and would be much less satisfactory. Utility issues are typically high-grade, large issues from well-known companies. Industrial issues require more investigation and tailoring to the needs of the particular issuer. The need for consultation between investment banker and issuer is much greater for industrial issues than for public utility flotations. As a consequence, much duplication of expense would be involved in making the requisite analysis in order to submit bids on an industrial issue.

On balance, the changed structure of the capital market appears to have rendered unnecessary the requirement of competitive bidding on new issues of corporate securities by industrial firms. There are ample market alternatives to the issuer. If competitive bidding were required on industrial issues, the main consequences would be to raise the cost of issuing securities and probably to drive more security flotations into the private placement fold.

As a practical matter, from time to time, when money market conditions become easy, as they did during the recession of 1954, large, well-established industrial firms may actually put some of their issues out at competitive bids. This is a function of whether the money market is a buyer's or a seller's market.

NEW ROLE OF THE INVESTMENT BANKER

In the immediate postwar period, the investment banking business was looked upon as a declining industry. Internal financing cut off the need for a great deal of external financing. The rise of insurance company and many other specialized sources of direct financing apparently left investment bankers with a dwindling share of the capital financing business.

The shrinking role of the investment banker in part reflected the absence of vigor in plant and equipment expansion which characterized the 1930s. But a respectable body of economists suggested that a lower rate of growth in the American economy was an inevitable result of economic maturity. The end of the frontier, the slowing of the rate of population growth, meant that the American economy would stagnate. The opposite, however, took place in the post-World War II period. The economy resumed its vigorous and rapid growth, with the result that outside financing and business for investment bankers were stimulated.

But even more important, the investment banking business itself reassessed its functions. The investment banker of the 1950s has brought to fruition the forecast for investment banking that was made in an article that appeared in *Fortune* in September 1939, entitled "The Investment Banker: 1939." After discussing the situation of the investment banker at the end of the 1930s, the article concluded:

> While the investment banker cannot control the forces of capital formation, he may stimulate them, just as he stimulated the processes of integration in the twenties. He may do this in various ways. He may travel and inquire. He may take a flier now and then. And he may take every opportunity to spread a doctrine, not of recrimination against the present restrictions, but of excitement in the possibilities of a new America. For it is safe to say that what integration was to the twenties, technological development *must* be to the forties, if private enterprise is to survive.

This article provided a good forecast of what in fact occurred. A subsequent article in *Fortune* in 1957, by T. A. Wise, entitled "The House of Lehman," described the activities of a modern investment banker, Lehman Brothers. Here is the picture of an investment banker not only handling the traditional new issues of companies but also multiplying its activities in many ways so that it can be of service to firms in all their financial operations.

One most dramatic example of the new role of investment bankers is the sponsorship of new venture companies. For example, in February 1954 one of the partners of Lehman Brothers, Joe Thomas, helped Litton Industries raise $1.5 million. Lehman Brothers rounded up the money for Litton before the electronic business took on the romantic aura it achieved a few years later. In return, Lehman received 75,000 shares of Litton common stock priced at from 10 cents to $1 a share. Lehman Brothers' profit on the Litton financing at the end of 1957 was $1 million, and of course since then the Litton stock has risen manifold. So the modern investment banker is a true creator. He brings into being small firms and does a creative job of selling the securities.

But the investment banker does many other things. The investment banker acts as a finder in direct placements. Because of his knowledge of the financial markets, the investment banker has organized investment trusts, receiving remuneration as manager and adviser to them.

The investment banker is active as a middleman in mergers and consolidations. As an independent third party, he suggests the terms on which mergers may be made. He makes an analysis of advantages and disadvantages of the union, works out the preliminary basis for the merger, and receives a fee for doing so.

In connection with rights offerings the investment banker now undertakes a number of trading activities to keep up the value of the stock during the rights trading period. In connection with rights offerings, he will contract either on a risk basis or on a best-effort basis.

In short, the investment banker has looked afresh at the capital market. He has cultivated increased activities to which a group with financial acumen and experience could contribute. No longer can investment banking be regarded as a declining element in the financial world. The investment banker is now a revitalized, creative force in the capital markets.

SUMMARY

The investment banker provides middleman services to both the seller and the buyer of new securities. He helps plan the issue, underwrites it, and handles the job of selling the issue to the ultimate investor. The cost of the service to the issuer is related to the magnitude of the total job the banker must perform to place the issue. The investment banker must also look to the interests of the investor, because if the investor is not satisfied with the banker's products he will deal elsewhere.

Today the role of the investment banker has broadened widely beyond the traditional role of underwriter and distributor of securities. He has extended his activities to the procurement of risk capital for new enterprises, to the organization and administration of investment companies, to participation in merger negotiations, and to related activities.

SELECTED REFERENCES

Howell, Paul L., "Competition in the Capital Markets," *Harvard Business Review,* 31 (May–June 1953), pp. 89–93.

Investment Bankers Association of America, *Fundamentals of Investment Banking* (Englewood Cliffs, N.J.: Prentice-Hall, Inc., 1949).

Nair, Richard S., "Investment Banking: Judge Medina in Retrospect," *The Financial Analysts Journal* (July–August 1960).

———, "Pricing a Corporate Bond Issue," *Federal Reserve Bank of New York* 43 (October 1961) pp. 172–176.

Waterman, M. H., *Investment Banking Functions* (Ann Arbor: Bureau of Business Research, University of Michigan, 1958).

J. Fred Weston (ed.), *Financial Management in the 1960s: New Challenges and Responsibilities* (New York: Holt, Rinehart and Winston, Inc., 1966); selections "The Biggest Broker in the West" and "Wherever You Look, There's Loeb, Rhoades."

QUESTIONS

23–1 Suppose two firms were each selling $10 millions of common stock. The firms are identical—that is, they are of the same size, in the same industry, have the same leverage, and have other similarities—except that one is publicly owned and the other is closely held. Would their costs of flotation be the same? If different, state the probable relationships. Had the issue been $10 millions of bonds, would your answer have been the same?

23–2 Define these terms: brokerage firm, underwriting, selling group, and investment banker.

23–3 Prior to 1933 investment banking and commercial banking were both carried on by the same firm. In that year, however, the Banking Act required that these functions be separated. Based on your knowledge of investment banking and commercial banking, discuss the pros and cons of this forced separation.

23–4 Before entering a formal agreement, investment bankers investigate quite carefully the companies whose securities they underwrite; this is especially true of the issues of firms going public for the first time. Since the bankers do not themselves plan to hold the securities, but to sell them to others as soon as possible, why are they so concerned about making careful investigations? Does your answer to the question have any bearing on the fact that investment banking is a very difficult field to "break into"?

23–5 If competitive bidding was required on all security offerings, would flotation costs be higher or lower? Would the size of the issuing firm be material in determining the effects of required competitive bidding?

23–6 Since investment bankers price new issues in relation to issues outstanding, should a spread exist between the yields on the new and the outstanding issues? Discuss this matter separately for stock issues and bond issues.

PROBLEMS

23–1 Listed below are salient facts on the terms of sale of several securities sold through investment bankers in recent years. All facts are taken from prospectuses issued in connection with the sales. Explain the differences in underwriting costs between the issues.

		Securities Issued		
Company Name, Business, Industry Characteristics	Date	Size (in millions of dollars)	Unit Price to Public (in dollars)	Under-writing Cost (in percent-age)
I. *Bonds*				
A. *Nonconvertible*				
1. General Motors Acceptance Corporation. Organized 1919. Finances distribution of new cars and dealers' installment sales of General Motors products. Industry is competitive, discount rates fluctuate depending on competitive factor. 4½%, due 1985	Nov. 1, 1963	$150.00	$ 995.00	0.875
2. The Western Union Telegraph Company. Organized 1851. Furnishes communication services throughout United States.				

| Company Name, Business, Industry Characteristics | Date | *Securities Issued* | | |
		Size (in millions of dollars)	*Unit Price to Public (in dollars)*	*Under-writing Cost (in percent-age)*
Provides the only public telegraph message service. Competitive with telephone and mail. 5%, due 1992	Mar. 1964	75.00	1,005.00	1.46
3. The Maston Company, Inc. Organized in 1923. Provides commercial and industrial loans of up to three years. 5½%, due 1977	Apr. 1962	5.00	1,000.00	2.29
B. *Convertible: with rights* 1. Litton Industry, Inc. Organized 1953. Manufacturing and sales business, commercial and military electrical equipment and systems. Industry is highly competitive and subject to changes in defense budget. 3½%, due 1987. Market price: $137.75; conversion price: $160 until 1972, thereafter $170	Apr. 1962	50.70	1,000.00	1.70*
2. Brunswick Corporation. Organized 1907. Principal products are bowling supplies. Company is one of the two leading manufacturers in its field. 4½%, due 1981. Market price: $46.75; conversion price: $51	Jan. 1961	25.60	1,000.00	2.06*
3. Chock Full O'Nuts. Organized 1932. Operates a chain of counter-service restaurants. Restaurants principally located in the Borough of Manhattan, New York City. 4½%,				

		Securities Issued		
Company Name, Business, Industry Characteristics	Date	Size (in millions of dollars)	Unit Price to Public (in dollars)	Under-writing Cost (in percent-age)
due 1981. Market price: $26; conversion price: $28.50	Aug. 1961	7.00	1,000.00	4.07*
C. *Convertible: nonrights* 1. Union Oil Company of California. Organized 1890. Engaged in substantially all branches of oil industry. The oil industry is characterized by intensive competition. 4¼%, due 1991. Market price: $54.88; conversion price: $65	June 1961	60.00	1,000.00	1.26
2. Baxter Laboratories, Inc. Organized 1931. One of the leading pharmaceutical companies in the manufacture and sale of parenteral solutions. Industry is extremely competitive. 4%, due 1982. Market price: $31; conversion price: $38	Apr. 1962	10.00	1,020.00	2.29
3. Standard Motor Products, Inc. Organized 1926. Engaged in the manufacture and sale of replacement parts for electrical and fuel systems, mainly for motor vehicles. Primary market is the automobile industry. 4¾%, due 1984. Market price: $13.13; conversion price: $15	Apr. 1964	3.00	1,000.00	4.27

II. *Nonconvertible Preferred Stock*
 1. Brockton Edison Company. Organized 1883. An electric utility in Massachusetts serving an aggregate population of

| | | Securities Issued | | |
| | | Size (in millions of dollars) | Unit Price to Public (in dollars) | Under-writing Cost (in percent-age) |
Company Name, Business, Industry Characteristics	Date			
about 200,000. Is a member of the holding company system of Eastern Utilities Associates. No competition within its territory. 4.64%	Oct. 1963	6.00	1,019.78	1.64

III. *Common Stock*
  A. *With Rights*

1. Bank of America. Organized 1904. Provides banking services in the state of California. Operates the largest system of branch banks in the nation. Market price: bid, $65.88, ask, $69.75; subscription price: $59	Nov. 1961	94.4	59.00	1.19*
2. The Western Casualty and Surety Company. Organized 1924. Engaged in the underwriting of all major types of insurance except life. In 1960, ranked forty-seventh among 115 leading insurance company groups of all types. Market price: bid, $60.50, ask, $62; subscription price: $57	Mar. 1962	10.7	57.00	1.96*
3. The Akron-Dime Banks. Organized in 1960 from the consolidation of the Dime Banks and the Bank of Akron. The Dime Bank was organized in 1900 and Bank of Akron Company in 1918. Bank has 11 offices serving Summit County, Ohio. Is the second largest of six commercial banks in the country.				

		Securities Issued		
Company Name, Business, Industry Characteristics	Date	Size (in millions of dollars)	Unit Price to Public (in dollars)	Under-writing Cost (in percent-age)
Market price: bid, $34, ask, $35; subscription price: $26	June 1965	1.7	26.00	1.92*
B. *Nonrights* 1. Communications Satellite Corporation. Organized 1963. Plans to establish and operate a global commercial communication satellite system. Authorized by the Communication Satellite Act of 1962, but not an agency of U.S. Government. No previous market price	June 1964	200.00	20.00	2.3
2. Delta Air Lines, Inc. Organized 1930. Engaged in transportation of persons, property, and mail by air. Industry is regulated by the government. Market price: $38	Apr. 1962	7.6	37.25	6.38
3. Hudson Wholesale Groceries, Inc. Organized 1918. Engaged primarily in the procurement, warehousing, and sale of groceries and nonfood items to supermarkets, discount stores, and neighborhood grocery stores. No previous market price	May 1962	0.8	8.00	19.25

* These figures represent the minimum cost of financing, assuming that the subscription is fully subscribed. This cost would increase if the underwriter were required to buy any unsubscribed stock. In general the subscription price is sufficiently below the market price to insure complete subscription.

23–2 Excerpts from prospectuses, with particular focus on the underwriter agreements, are given below.

1. What differences do you find in the underwriting costs and agreements?

2. How do you explain the differences?

A summary of the financial information on the companies follows:

	(A) Speedee Mart, Inc.	(B) Spiegel, Inc.	(C) Beckman Instruments, Inc.
Total assets, end 1960	$2.3*	$291.3*	$39.0*
Net worth, end 1960	0.7	64.2	19.5
Sales			
1958	0.097	152.7	39.8
1960	0.253	268.8	54.3
Net income after taxes			
1958	0.018	5.0	(0.946)
1960	0.023	11.8	3.1

* Dollar amounts in millions.

A. Speedee Mart, Inc.   *90,000 shares, common stock, without par value:*

	Price to Public	Underwriting Discounts and Commissions	Proceeds to Company
Per share	$ 6	$ 0.60	$ 5.40
Total	$540,000	$54,000.00	$486,000.00

Description of Business

Speedee Mart, Inc. (the "company"), whose principal offices are located at 7988 Normal Avenue, La Mesa, California, was incorporated in California on April 10, 1956. It is engaged in the business of enfranchising others (franchisees) to manage and operate retail food stores under the name "Speedee Mart." From October 2, 1960, 51 franchised stores have been doing business under franchises as herein described and the company was in varying stages of establishing 33 additional stores.

Speedee Mart markets are located primarily to provide convenient neighborhood food-shopping facilities away from metropolitan shopping centers. In a sense, these convenience markets, which are open from 7 A.M. to 11 P.M. seven days a week, are in competition with several national supermarket chain store organizations, local chain stores, and large independent food stores, as well as other neighborhood markets. However, the Speedee Mart stores do not purport to compete for the large weekly shopping trade, but rather to provide a convenient place for customers to make purchases for daily needs. The company believes that it meets supermarket prices on items comprising a majority of its sales volume.

Underwriting

The underwriter, J. A. Hogle & Company, 132 South Main Street, Salt Lake City, Utah, has made a firm commitment, subject to the terms and conditions of the underwriting agreement (a copy of which is filed as an exhibit to the registration statement), to purchase all the shares of the company offered hereby. The company has been advised by the underwriter that the common stock is proposed to be offered by the underwriter for sale initially at the public offering price set forth on the cover page of this prospectus. Concessions to selected dealers may be allowed in an amount not exceeding 35 cents per share, of which 15 cents per share may be reallowed to other dealers, provided such reallowance is retained. The public offering price and the concessions and reallowances to dealers may be changed by the underwriter after the initial public offering by reason of changes in market conditions.

Source: Prospectus, J. A. Hogle & Company, January 31, 1961.

B. Spiegel, Inc. *$40,000,000, 5¼% debentures, dated April 1, 1961; due April 1, 1983:*

	Price to Public	Underwriting Discounts and Commissions	Proceeds to Company
Per unit	100%	1.5%	98.5%
Total	$40,000,000	$600,000	$39,400,000

Description of Business

The company is engaged, and intends to continue to engage, in the sale of merchandise by mail. Customers are offered three ways to buy: cash with order, 30-day charge, and monthly payment. The company is believed to sell a substantially larger proportion of its total volume on the monthly payment plan than any other national retailer of general merchandise does.

The company expects to continue to concentrate its efforts in the specialized techniques of catalogue credit promotion, credit acceptance, collections, and credit finance. Experience has demonstrated that monthly payment selling is more profitable than selling for cash. Monthly payment customers tend to buy more frequently and in larger amounts than do cash customers. In addition, after being charged with the company's total interest expense, the servicing of the credit accommodation now contributes materially to consolidated profit.

Underwriting

Subject to the terms and conditions set forth in the underwriting agreement, the company has agreed to sell to each of the underwriters named below, and each of the underwriters for whom Wertheim & Company is acting as representative, has severally agreed to purchase, at the price set forth on the cover page of this prospectus, the principal amount of debentures set opposite its name.

The nature of the underwriting commitments is such that the several underwriters are obligated, subject to certain conditions, to purchase all the debentures offered hereby. In the event of default by any underwriter, the underwriting agreement provides that in certain circumstances other underwriters may be substituted or the agreement terminated.

The company has been advised by Wertheim & Company, representatives of the underwriters, that in connection with the sale of the debentures by the underwriters, concessions may be allowed to other dealers not in excess of 0.25 percent.

Source: Prospectus, Wertheim & Company, April 12, 1961.

C. Beckman Instruments, Inc. *69,933 shares, common stock, par value $1 per share:*

The company hereby offers to the holders of its common stock the right to subscribe for additional shares of its common stock at the rate of one additional share for each 20 shares held of record on the close of business on March 28, 1961, all as more fully set forth herein.

	Subscription Price	Underwriting Commissions		Proceeds to Company	
Per share . . .	114*	Min.	2.00*	Max.	112.00*
		Max.	5.40	Min.	108.60
Total . . .	7,972,362	Min.	139,866.00	Max.	7,832,496.00
		Max.	377,638.20	Min.	7,594,723.80

* In dollars.

Description of Business

The company and its subsidiaries are engaged in the business of designing, developing, manufacturing, and selling precision instruments for scientific, industrial, medical, and laboratory use.

Underwriting

In the underwriting agreement, the several underwriters, represented by Lehman Brothers, have agreed, subject to the terms and conditions therein set forth, to purchase from the company all the shares of common stock offered hereby not purchased upon exercise of rights, at the subscription price set forth on the cover page of this prospectus. For their respective commitments the underwriters are to receive compensation as set forth below and on the cover page of this prospectus. Reference is made to the underwriting agreement filed as an exhibit to the registration statement.

The company has agreed to pay the underwriters $2 per share with respect to each share of common stock offered hereby, plus $3.40 per share on all shares (herein called the "unsubscribed stock") not purchased upon the exercise of rights or which are purchased by the underwriters upon the exercise of rights purchased by them. The minimum underwriting commissions and maximum proceeds to the company shown on the cover page of this prospectus are based on the assumption that all shares of common stock offered hereby will be subscribed for by other than the underwriters, and the maximum underwriting commissions and minimum proceeds to the company are based on the assumption that none of such shares will be so subscribed for.

If the aggregate sales price of all unsubscribed stock sold by the several underwriters during the period of the subscription offer and within 30 days thereafter is in excess of the aggregate subscription price of the unsubscribed stock, the underwriters will pay to the company 50 percent of such excess. Such excess is to be computed after deducting all costs and expenses (including selling concessions, brokerage commissions, and transfer taxes) and any losses paid or incurred, directly or indirectly, by the underwriters in connection with the distribution of the unsubscribed stock, the purchase of rights (whether or not exercised), stabilization operations, overallotments, short sales and related transactions. For the purpose of this paragraph unsubscribed stock not sold or contracted to be sold by the underwriters on the date upon which such 30-day period terminates will be deemed to have been sold on such date of termination at the weighted average of the sales prices of the common stock of the company on the New York Stock Exchange on such date.

Name	Percentage to Be Purchased
Lehman Brothers	20.00
A. C. Allyn and Company, Inc.	6.00
Ball, Burge & Kraus	2.00
J. Barth & Company	2.00
Bear, Stearns & Company	8.00
Blyth & Company, Inc.	8.00
Burnham and Company	2.00
Eastman Dillon, Union Securities & Company	8.00
Goodbody & Company	2.00
Hayden, Stone & Company	4.50
Hornblower & Weeks	4.50
Paine, Weber, Jackson & Curtis	4.50
Paribas Corporation	8.00
Peltason, Tenebaum Company	2.00
Shearson, Hammill & Company	4.50
Stein Bros. & Boyce	2.00
Sutro & Company	2.00
Wagenseller & Durst, Inc.	2.00
Dean Witter & Company	8.00
Total	100.00

Lehman Brothers, as representative of the underwriters, has advised the company that the underwriters may offer shares of common stock as set forth on the cover page of this prospectus, that initially they may allow concessions not in excess of $2.50 per share to certain dealers, and that the underwriters and such dealers initially may reallow concessions not in excess of 50 cents per share to other dealers. Such concessions to dealers may be changed by the representative.

Source: Prospectus, Lehman Brothers, March 28, 1961.

Chapter 24

Financial Markets and Direct Placement

The activity of investment banking, discussed in the preceding chapter, has been greatly influenced by two major institutional developments. One is the rise of direct placement, which bypasses in some degree the use of the investment banker. The other is a form of competition that results from the operation of the markets for "used," or already issued, securities. These institutions are also in competition with each other. Direct placement of financing not only reduces the use of the investment banker in the original flotation but also obviates subsequent public trading in the instruments if they continue to be privately held. Because of these interrelations, the two sets of institutions are discussed together in the present chapter.

TERM LOANS AND DIRECT PLACEMENT

One of the important changes in the operation of capital markets since the early 1930s has been the bypassing of investment bankers through the rise of term lending and direct (private) placement, in which the number of purchasers is small. A *term loan* is a direct business loan with a maturity of more than one year but less than 15 years, with provision for systematic repayment (amortization) during the life of the loan. *Private placements* are direct business loans with a maturity of more than 15 years.[1]

---

[1] This is the dividing line drawn by N. H. Jacoby and R. J. Saulnier, *Term Lending to*

Approximately 50 percent of private placements are in the form of long-term promissory notes.[2] The private placement differs from the term loan only in an arbitrary maturity length, which becomes even more fuzzy when we find that some "private placements" call for repayment of as much as 20 percent of the principal within five years and nearly 60 percent in ten years, "exclusive of repayments from optional and contingent sinking funds."[3] Thus term loans and private placements represent about the same kind of financing arrangements.

Because term loans and private placements "straddle" the medium-term and long-term business credit markets and because both "short-circuit" investment bankers, they will be treated together in this discussion of developments in the capital markets.

Development

Term loans have been growing in total amount. A 1937 survey indicated that term loans at commercial banks amounted to only $827 million, something less than $1 billion. By November 1946 term loans amounted to $4.6 billion, representing 34 percent of all bank business loans. Another survey made by the Board of Governors of the Federal Reserve System in October 1957 found that term loans represented about 38 percent of the business loans by commercial banks and at that date totaled $15.4 billion.[4]

The importance of direct placements increased steadily from 1934 to about 1948, at which time they represented 44 percent of *all issues* and 50 percent of *all debt issues* (see Table 24–1). Since that time both percentages have been rather volatile, with the percentage of total debt ranging from 34 percent in 1958 to 58 percent in 1951, and private placements as a percent of all kinds of issues ranging from 30 percent in 1957 and 1958 to 52 percent in 1963.

The reasons for the development of these types of longer term financing can be analyzed in relation to demand-and-supply factors.

Demand Factors

1. Borrowers are certain to have their money over an extended period. During both the 1921 recession and the recession of 1929–1932, demand loans were called by commercial banks or straight loans were not renewed. Therefore, longer term financing developed because firms

---

Business (New York: National Bureau of Economic Research, 1942), pp. 10–14, and Appendix B, pp. 143–147. See also the analysis in Avery B. Cohan, *Private Placements and Public Offerings* (Chapel Hill: School of Business Administration, University of North Carolina, 1961), pp. 2–5.

2 E. Raymond Corey, *Direct Placement of Corporate Securities* (Cambridge, Mass.: School of Business Administration, Harvard University, 1961), pp. 115–116.

3 *Ibid.*, pp. 120–121.

4 *Federal Reserve Bulletin*, 45 (April 1959), p. 353.

wanted to avoid being caught in a situation where short-term loans would be cut off.

2. Term loans and private placements were given a stimulus after 1934 by the increased cost and time involved in a public offering. The Securities Acts of 1933 and 1934 required that new financing go through the registration process and the 20-day waiting period. The expenses of developing data for the SEC registration statements increased the cost of public flotations, particularly for issues of less than $1 million, because the fixed costs are spread over small amounts.

3. A public offering takes time to prepare—there are registration statements to be written, underwriting agreements to be made, and two to three months may be required for the public offering. A private placement or term loan, especially where there may be a continuing relation between the insurance company or bank and the borrower, can be consummated in a matter of hours.

4. If the securities of a public offering are widely held, it is more difficult to negotiate a modification in the indenture (loan agreement) provisions. If some of the terms of a direct loan have turned out to be onerous and not in the best interests of the borrower, the borrower can negotiate directly with the bank or the insurance company. It is much more difficult to contact thousands of bondholders to obtain agreement about modifying indenture provisions of the bond issue.

5. Direct-lending volume was also stimulated by the refunding operations inaugurated in the middle 1930s. Many industrial concerns had sold long-term debt during the 1920s at interest rates running from 5 to 8 percent. In the 1930s, when interest rates were much lower, these concerns were able to negotiate term loans at 2 to 4 percent.

6. The increased rates of corporate taxation in the 1930s made it more difficult for small and medium sized firms to finance their growth with internal funds. For this reason it became necessary for them to turn to external sources; direct longer term loans represented one of the available external sources.

7. The postwar period of reconversion and expansion made term financing necessary. Metal-product manufacturers and many other war contractors needed medium term funds for reconversion and replacement purposes. Individuals organizing new retail and service establishments needed medium term financing.

Supply Factors

1. In the early 1930s there was a phenomenal increase in the excess reserves of commercial banks. Simultaneously, there was a decrease in the supply of corporate bonds, because the pace of economic activity had slowed down, the rate of growth of individual firms was dampened, and

the amount of external financing required therefore was reduced.[5] Both insurance companies and commercial banks found themselves with excess funds available for investment. As outlets for these funds, they began to compete in making direct, medium, and long-term loans to business firms.

2. Inauguration in 1933 of deposit insurance by the Federal Deposit Insurance Corporation reduced the likelihood of widespread runs by depositors on banks. The result was greater stability in the deposits of small banks, as well as greater stability of their own deposits with the larger correspondent banks. Greater stability of deposits made it feasible for business firms to make longer term loans.

3. A third factor stimulating the supply of monies available for term loans is the method of evaluation of marketable securities. Bank and insurance examiners typically value securities at cost or market, whichever is lower. Therefore, if the market falls below purchase costs, the difference is regarded as an estimated loss and is required to be written off. The procedure places the capital position of a lender subject to temporary fluctuations in the market prices of bonds which he holds in his investment portfolio. Direct loans, on the other hand, have no quoted market value. Therefore a term loan, payment on which is being made and which will be fully paid off by maturity, presents no problem in terms of a write-off, if interest rates should rise, during which time a downward pressure is placed on the value of marketable securities.

Given the demand factors listed previously and given these new supply factors, it is not difficult to see why the volume of term loans grew from less than $1 billion to the level of $14 billion over a 20-year period.

Characteristics of Direct Loans

Size of loan. The typical term loan is a small loan in terms of its dollar amount. Most commercial bank term loans are from $100,-000 to $250,000. About 50 percent of life insurance loans run from about $1 million to $5 million. Commercial banks typically make the smaller and shorter term loans; life insurance companies make larger and longer term loans on the average, although they also make short-term loans. For a period, the Reconstruction Finance Corporation (RFC) and the federal reserve banks were making term loans under special government-lending programs. Most of their loans were very small, less than $5,000.

Size of borrowers. It has been estimated that 90 percent of the term loans made by commercial banks are to small firms with assets of less than $5 million. Most of the term and direct loans made by insurance com-

---

5 This condition occurred during the early development of term loans. Later, after 1946, the increased needs for external financing increased the use of term financing.

TABLE 24–1

SUMMARY OF CORPORATE SECURITIES PUBLICLY OFFERED AND PRIVATELY PLACED FROM 1934 THROUGH JUNE 1964
(amounts in millions of dollars)

Calendar Year	Total			Public Offerings			Private Placements			Private Placements as Percentage of Total	
	All Issues	Debt Issues	Equity Issues	All Issues	Debt Issues	Equity Issues	All Issues	Debt Issues	Equity Issues	All Issues	Debt Issues
1934	397	372	25	305	280	25	92	92	0	23.2	24.7
1935	2,332	2,225	108	1,945	1,840	106	387	385	2	16.6	17.3
1936	4,572	4,029	543	4,199	3,660	539	373	369	4	8.2	9.2
1937	2,309	1,618	691	1,979	1,291	688	330	327	3	14.3	20.2
1938	2,155	2,044	111	1,463	1,353	110	692	691	1	32.1	33.8
1939	2,164	1,979	185	1,458	1,276	181	706	703	4	32.6	35.5
1940	2,677	2,386	291	1,912	1,628	284	765	758	7	28.6	31.8
1941	2,667	2,389	277	1,854	1,578	276	813	811	2	30.5	33.9
1942	1,062	917	146	642	506	136	420	411	9	39.5	44.8
1943	1,170	990	180	798	621	178	372	369	3	31.8	37.3
1944	3,202	2,670	532	2,415	1,892	524	787	778	9	24.6	29.1
1945	6,011	4,855	1,155	4,989	3,851	1,138	1,022	1,004	18	17.0	20.7
1946	6,900	4,882	2,018	4,983	3,019	1,963	1,917	1,863	54	27.8	38.2
1947	6,577	5,036	1,541	4,342	2,889	1,452	2,235	2,147	88	34.0	42.6
1948	7,078	5,973	1,106	3,991	2,965	1,028	3,087	3,008	79	43.6	50.4
1949	6,052	4,890	1,161	3,550	2,437	1,112	2,502	2,453	49	41.3	50.2

Calendar Year	Total			Public Offerings			Private Placements			Private Placements as Percentage of Total	
	All Issues	Debt Issues	Equity Issues	All Issues	Debt Issues	Equity Issues	All Issues	Debt Issues	Equity Issues	All Issues	Debt Issues
1950	6,362	4,920	1,442	3,681	2,360	1,321	2,680	2,560	120	42.1	52.0
1951	7,741	5,691	2,050	4,326	2,364	1,962	3,415	3,326	88	44.1	58.4
1952	9,534	7,601	1,933	5,533	3,645	1,888	4,002	3,957	45	42.0	52.1
1953	8,898	7,083	1,815	5,580	3,856	1,725	3,318	3,228	90	37.3	45.6
1954	9,516	7,488	2,029	5,848	4,003	1,844	3,668	3,484	184	38.5	46.5
1955	10,240	7,420	2,820	6,763	4,119	2,644	3,477	3,301	176	34.0	44.5
1956	10,939	8,002	2,937	7,053	4,225	2,827	3,886	3,777	109	35.5	47.2
1957	12,884	9,957	2,927	8,959	6,118	2,841	3,925	3,839	86	30.5	38.6
1958	11,558	9,653	1,906	8,068	6,332	1,736	3,490	3,320	170	30.2	34.4
1959	9,748	7,190	2,558	5,993	3,557	2,436	3,755	3,632	122	38.5	50.5
1960	10,154	8,081	2,073	6,657	4,806	1,851	3,497	3,275	221	34.4	40.5
1961	13,165	9,420	3,745	8,143	4,700	3,443	5,022	4,720	302	38.1	50.1
1962	10,705	8,969	1,735	6,064	4,440	1,624	4,640	4,529	112	43.3	50.5
1963	12,237	10,872	1,364	5,823	4,714	1,109	6,413	6,158	255	52.4	56.6
1964*	7,350	5,160	2,190	4,394	2,299	2,094	2,957	2,861	96	40.2	55.4

* January–June.

Source: Securities and Exchange Commission, *30th Annual Report,* fiscal year ended June 30, 1964, p. 179.

panies were to larger firms. The RFC and the federal reserve banks loaned mainly to medium sized firms.

Industry of the borrower. Earlier surveys indicated that nearly 40 percent of term loans were confined to two major industry groups: (1) transportation, communication, and other public utilities and (2) petroleum, coal, chemicals, and rubber. These two groups also showed the highest ratio of term-to-total bank borrowing. This reflects the large proportion of their assets having relatively long service lives. By contrast, the smaller users of term credit were commodity dealers and sales finance companies, which have small fixed investment. A 1957 survey showed that the greatest relative increase in term loans was in trade, construction, and real estate—small firms growing rapidly.

Maturity. For commercial banks, the term loan runs five years or less, typically three years. For insurance companies, the most typical maturities have been 10 to 20 years. This difference reflects the fact that commercial banks are stronger in the short-term field, and insurance companies in the medium and long-term field.[6] Most federal reserve bank and RFC loans were for less than three years.

Collateral. Commercial banks have required security on about 60 percent of the volume and 90 percent of the number of term loans made. They have taken as security mainly stocks, bonds, machinery, and equipment. Insurance companies also have required security on nearly a third of their direct loans. Their main collateral has been real estate.

In recent years institutional investors have increasingly taken compensation in addition to fixed interest payments on directly negotiated loans. The most popular form of additional compensation is an option to buy common stock, "the option being in the form of detachable warrants permitting the purchase of the shares at stated prices over a designated period."[7]

Use of funds by borrowers. During the earlier period, more than 50 percent of direct loans were used to refund outstanding bonds sold originally at higher interest rates. More recently, direct loans have provided primarily working capital, and, secondarily, plant and equipment financing.

Sinking fund or repayment provisions. More than three quarters of term loans by number and more than half of them by amount are repayable in equal installments. Only a small percentage of the loans have any balloon segment of repayment at the end. Term loans are geared specifi-

---

6 On occasion, banks and insurance companies cooperate in their term lending. For example, if a firm (usually a large one) seeks a 20-year term loan, a bank may take the loan for the first five to ten years, an insurance company for the last 10 to 15 years.
7 C. M. Williams and H. A. Williams, "Incentive Financing," *Harvard Business Review*, 38 (March–April 1960), p. 124.

cally to the ability of the firm to meet a certain repayment or amortization schedule. Direct loans by insurance companies have generally made it necessary to use sinking fund payments to retire outstanding obligations, paralleling the amortization requirements of bank term loans.

Terms of Loan Agreements

The direct, or term, loan assures funds to the borrower; he will not be faced with the inability to renew his loan if his needs for funds continue. Offsetting the advantages of giving the firm the assurance of the use of funds for from 3 to 20 years is a set of disadvantages that grow out of the inherent nature of the term loan. On a 90-day loan, where the commercial bank has the option to renew, it can take the occasion to re-examine the situation of the borrower. If it has deteriorated unduly, the loan officer simply does not renew the loan. On a term or direct loan, however, the bank or insurance company has tied itself up for a period of years. Thus there are certain restrictive provisions in the loan agreement to protect the lender for the duration of the loan. These restrictive provisions typically are as follows.

1. The current ratio must be maintained at some specified level—$2\frac{1}{2}$ to 1, 3 to 1, $3\frac{1}{2}$ to 1, depending upon the borrower's line of business. Net working capital must be maintained at some minimum.

2. There are restrictions on the amount of additional fixed assets that may be purchased by the borrower in the future. The lender seeks to protect himself against the borrower's sinking his funds excessively in fixed investments.

3. Typically, there are prohibitions against incurring additional long-term indebtedness except with the permission of the lender. Furthermore, the lender does not permit the pledge of assets without the permission of the lender. Also, the loan agreement prohibits the borrower from assuming any contingent liabilities, such as guaranteeing the indebtedness of a subsidiary.

4. The loan agreement may require that any major changes in management personnel, or its composition, must be subject to the approval of the lender. The loan agreement will require life insurance on the principals of the business, especially if they are key personnel. In addition, the loan agreement may provide for the creation of a voting trust or a granting of proxies for a specified period to ensure that the management of the company will be under the control of the group upon which the lender has relied in making the loan.

5. The lender will require adequate records and financial budgets for three to six months in advance.

This list does not exhaust all the kinds of terms found in loan agreements, but it is illustrative. It will serve to indicate the kind of protective provisions the bank or insurance company will seek to embody in the loan agreement.

Cost of Term Loans

Another major aspect of term lending is its cost. As with other forms of lending, the interest rate on term loans varies with the size of the loan and the quality of the borrower. On term loans, surveys show that on loans of less than $500 the interest rate may run up to 10 percent. On loans of $1 million and above, term loan rates have been close to the prime rate. The size of the loan often reflects the quality of the borrower as well as the fixed cost involved in making small loans.

The interest rate may be related to the Federal Reserve rediscount rate. Often the loan agreement will specify that the interest rate will be based on the average of the rediscount rate in that Federal Reserve district during the previous three months, generally ½ percent to 1 or 2 percent above the rediscount rate. In other words, the loan rate can fluctuate during the life of the loan and is often tied to the rediscount rate. It may also be geared to the published prime rate charged by the New York City banks.

Some costs of registration statements and expenses associated with preparing details for registration statements are also avoided. However, this does not appear to be a dominant factor according to others who have studied the problem. Nor is a substantial cost saving achieved on the average. The expenses that are saved may be absorbed by expert bargaining on the part of the supplier of funds. The lender is aware of the possible savings to the borrower by direct placement, and he may seek to obtain all or a portion of these savings in the form of a higher yield.

With regard to direct placement, the investment banker often performs the role of finder or agent in arranging for the placement. The investment banker may bring the borrower together with one or more sources of funds. The fees of the investment banker as agent or finder in bringing the user and sources of funds together are smaller than his underwriting and distribution commissions.

On balance, then, with all factors considered, the costs of direct financing are likely to be somewhat lower than the costs of public financing. The basic reason for this result is that some of the services required for security distribution have been eliminated because of funds assembled by financial institutions such as insurance companies and pension funds. Insurance companies, pension funds, and so on, also incur costs in the assembly of funds. But their costs of assembling funds may be low, because the funds are pooled primarily for purposes other than to invest in a new issue of securities.

APPRAISAL OF DIRECT FINANCING

From the Standpoint of Lender

From the standpoint of the lender, the advantages of direct financing are as follows:

1. Direct lending provides a new outlet for the lender's funds; it represents an invasion of a new funds market.

2. It enables the lender (insurance company, bank) to put his funds to work at relatively higher rates of interest.

From the standpoint of the lender, there are the following disadvantages:

1. There is greater risk because the circumstances of the borrower may change over the extended period of the loan.

2. Investigation costs are higher than on short-term loans. Since the term of the loan is longer, the lender has to be certain that adverse circumstances are not likely to develop during the term of the loan.

3. There is a disadvantage to some extent from the standpoint of the commercial bank in that the bulk of its liabilities are demand deposits. If assets are tied up in term loans, the bank is tying up its assets for long periods, whereas its liabilities are of shorter duration.

From the Standpoint of Borrower

The advantages to the borrower are as follows:

1. Much seasonal short-term borrowing can be dispensed with. The danger of nonrenewal of loans is thereby avoided.

2. The private borrower avoids the expenses of Securities and Exchange Commission registration and investment bankers' distribution.

3. Less time is required to complete arrangements for obtaining a loan than is involved in a bond issue.

4. Since only one lender is involved rather than many bondholders, it is possible to modify the loan indenture expeditiously.

The possible disadvantages of direct long-term loans to a borrower are as follows.

1. The interest rate may be higher on a term loan than on a short-term loan, because the lender is tying up his money for a longer period. He does not have the opportunity to review the lender's status periodically, as he does with the short-term loan.

2. The cash drain is large. Since the loans provide for regular amortization or sinking fund payments, the company experiences a continuous cash drain. From this standpoint direct loans are less advantageous than equity money, which never has to be repaid, or a preferred stock without maturity, or even a bond issue without a sinking fund requirement.

3. Since the loan is a long-term commitment, the lender will employ higher credit standards; that is, he will insist on the borrower's being in a stronger financial position: having a better current ratio, a lower debt-equity ratio, better activity ratios, and better profitability ratios.

4. Furthermore, the loan agreement will have restrictions that would not be found in a 90-day note. The reasons for the restrictions and their nature have already been explained.

5. Investigation costs may be high. The lender makes a more elaborate investigation than he would for a short-term note. The lender stays with the company for a longer period; therefore the longer term outlook for the company must be looked into. For this reason the lender may set a minimum on a loan (for example, $50,000); otherwise he cannot charge a rate of interest high enough to recover his costs of investigating the applicant.

The positive advantages of public distribution or public offerings of securities in contrast to private placement are the following:

1. The firm is enabled to establish its credit and achieves publicity by having securities publicly and widely distributed. In this way the firm is able to engage in future financing at lower rates.

2. The wide distribution of debt or equity might enable its repurchase on favorable terms at some subsequent date if the market price of these securities should fall.

3. Owners or managers of the firm avoid detailed restrictions found in term loans or private placement agreements. Indentures, of course, also contain restrictions, but some hold the view that the restrictions in term loans or private placements are even more stringent.

Economic Aspects of Long-Term Loans

Finally, it is useful to comment on several aspects of the broader economic significance of long-term loans.

1. The long-term loan may make the economy less vulnerable to forced liquidation. Since the loan is not subject to renewal every 90 days, there is less danger of forced liquidation of loans accumulating during a depression when lenders become pessimistic and the financial position of the borrower deteriorates.

2. It brings insurance companies into direct lending to business. Before the 1930s, insurance companies invested in business primarily by buying bonds. In such a situation the insurance company was simply one among other bondholders. But now the relation is direct. The insurance company has considerable liability stability. The flow of cash into an insurance company is highly predictable, and the danger of a wave of cash

surrenders of life insurance policies during a recession has proved historically to be very small. The insurance company therefore is in a position to allow an extension to a borrower if he gets into difficulties. This arrangement makes the economy less vulnerable to forced liquidation or to a continuous chain of liquidation in one area which forces liquidation in another, causing a downward spiral in the economy.

3. Term loans increase the availability of longer term debt for smaller businesses. However, it does not solve the small-business financing problem, because it does not represent equity funds (the funds are not left in the business permanently). Since amortization of the loan on a systematic basis is required, the small firm has the money only for a limited period and must have substantial cash throw-off ability in order to handle the term loan.

The term loan extends the period over which the small business firm can grow by plowing back earnings. Funds to repay the loan over its three- or five-year period must come fundamentally from retained earnings unless business engages in additional outside equity financing.

In the discussion of the development of direct, long-term lending at the beginning of the chapter, the important impact of capital market changes and the role of government were indicated. More complete understanding of the factors referred to can be obtained from the following discussion of securities markets and their regulation.

SECURITIES MARKETS
Organized Security Exchanges

The organized security exchanges represent an important capital market mechanism used to facilitate financing. The best known is the Big Board, the New York Stock Exchange. Second in importance is what used to be known as the "Curb," but is now the American Stock Exchange. There are also regional stock exchanges, the Midwest and the Pacific Coast, for example.

An indication of the magnitude of values involved is provided by a table of the market values of stocks and bonds listed on the New York Stock Exchange since 1924 (Table 24–2). At the end of 1964, the total values involved were more than $600 billion—$474 billion in common stocks alone. Thus a fluctuation of 1 percent in common stock prices represents values of more than $4.7 billion.

The security exchanges have great significance for the corporate financial manager in at least three ways.

1. Security exchanges facilitate the investment process because they provide a market place in which to conduct transactions efficiently and

relatively inexpensively. Investors are thus assured that they will have a place in which to sell their securities, if they decide to do so. Many persons regard the securities exchanges as a very complicated set of market mechanisms. In their basic concept, exchanges are simply a place for facilitating the buying and selling of securities by channeling purchase and sale orders to one central location.

2. By providing a market, exchanges create an institution in which transactions taking place continuously test the values of securities. The purchases and sales of securities record judgments on the values and prospects of companies and their securities. Companies whose prospects are

TABLE 24–2

MARKET VALUE OF STOCKS AND BONDS LISTED ON THE NEW YORK STOCK EXCHANGE
End of Indicated Year
(dollars in billions)

Year	All Listed Stocks	All Listed Bonds
1924	$ 27	$ 34
1929	65	47
1933	33	35
1939	46	50
1949	76	128
1953	117	100
1954	169	107
1955	208	105
1956	219	99
1957	196	106
1958	277	106
1959	308	105
1960	307	108
1961	388	105
1962	346	111
1963	411	118
1964	474	128

Source: New York Stock Exchange, *Fact Book,* 1965, pp. 36–37.

judged favorable by the investment community will have higher values, facilitating new financing and growth.

3. Security prices are relatively more stable because of the operation of the security exchanges. Organized markets provide liquidity and continuous markets, which make for more frequent, but smaller, price changes. In the absence of organized markets, price changes would be less frequent but more violent.

The securities markets aid in the digestion of new securities issues and facilitate the successful flotation of subsequent issues. Two practices said to contribute to effectively functioning securities markets may be briefly noted.

Margin trading involves the buying or selling of securities on credit. When margin requirements, for example, are 40 percent, a buyer or seller of securities can buy $20,000 worth of stocks with only $8,000 in cash, and borrow the other $12,000, on which he pays interest. The stock broker lends the margin purchaser the funds, retaining custody of the stock as collateral.

Short selling is the selling of a security that is not owned by the seller at the time of sale. It is usually performed in anticipation of a decline in the market price. For example, a stock selling at $40 may be sold short. Suppose that in two months the market drops to $30. The short seller can buy at $30 and make delivery on stock which he sold at $40. The seller borrows the stock from his broker; in general, the broker has the stock because others of his customers have purchased it on margin.

Insofar as margin trading and short selling provide for a more continuous market, they encourage stock ownership and have two beneficial effects. (1) They broaden the ownership of securities by increasing the ability of people to buy securities. (2) They provide for a more active market; more active trading makes for narrower price fluctuations. A qualification has to be stated. When a strong speculative psychology grips the market, margin trading can be a fuel which feeds the speculative fervor. Short selling can also aggravate pessimism on the downside. However, there are restrictions on short selling which provide that a short sale may not be made at a price lower than the previously recorded price. Current rules on short selling limit speculative and manipulative practices. Similarly, flexible margin requirements have had salutary effects on the use of credit in stock market transactions.

Over-the-Counter Markets

Of much importance among the institutions that facilitate absorption of new issues of securities by firms are the over-the-counter markets. In fact, these markets handle the bulk of all security transactions. They account for most of the transactions in corporate bonds and preferred stock and at least one third the total market activity in common stocks.[8] The over-the-counter market provides the main outlet for securities being offered to the public for the first time.

Over-the-counter markets are all facilities that provide for security transactions not conducted on organized stock exchanges. They consist

---

[8] Federal Reserve Bank of Richmond, "Trading 'Over-the-Counter,'" *Monthly Review* (April 1959), pp. 8–10.

primarily of the thousands of broker-dealer firms which take positions in, and make markets in, individual issues of securities.

An important question facing the financial manager regarding the over-the-counter markets in relation to the organized exchanges is whether or not to list his company's securities. Listing requirements relate to size of company, number of years in business, information on profit and loss, and financial statements. Typical barriers are age, size, and some history of earnings. If the firm is small and does not meet the requirements of one of the organized exchanges, it has no alternative.

After a firm's stock has been seasoned in over-the-counter trading and has become eligible for listing on an exchange, it will usually take steps to be listed. Often this is associated with publicizing the firm and getting brokers and dealers who have become interested in the security to dramatize the listing.

REGULATION OF SECURITY TRADING

The operations of investment bankers, the exchanges, and the over-the-counter markets described in the previous sections of this chapter are significantly affected by a series of federal statutes enacted during and after 1933. The financial manager is affected by these laws for several reasons. (1) Corporate officers are subjected to additional liabilities. (2) The laws affect the ease and costs of financing. (3) They also affect the behavior of the money and capital markets in which the corporations' securities are sold and traded. (4) Investors' willingness to buy securities is influenced by the existence of safeguards provided by these laws.

Securities Act of 1933

The first of the securities acts followed Congressional investigations after the stock market collapse of 1929–1932. The reasons motivating the Act were (1) the large losses to investors, (2) the failures of many corporations on which little information had been provided, and (3) the misrepresentations to investors.

The basic objective of the Securities Act of 1933 is to provide both for *full disclosure* of relevant information and a *record of representations.* It seeks to achieve these objectives by the following means.

1. It applies to all interstate offerings to the public (some exemptions are government bonds and bank stocks) in amounts of $300,000 or more.

2. Securities must be registered at least 20 days before they are publicly offered. The registration statement provides financial, legal, and technical information about the company. A prospectus summarizes this

information for use in selling the securities. If information is inadequate or misleading, the SEC will delay or stop the public offering.

3. After the registration has become effective, the securities may be offered if accompanied by the prospectus. Preliminary or "red herring" prospectuses may be distributed to potential buyers during the waiting period.

4. Any purchaser who suffers a loss may sue for damages if the registration statement or prospectus contains misrepresentations or omissions of material facts. Liabilities and severe penalties may be imposed on the issuer, its officers, directors, accountants, engineers, appraisers, underwriters, and others who participated in the preparation of the registration statement.

The act provides for full disclosure. It also has resulted in a procedure for obtaining a record of representations.

Securities Exchange Act of 1934

The Securities Exchange Act of 1934 extends the disclosure principle as applied to new issues by the act of 1933 to trading in already issued securities (the "secondhand" securities market). It seeks to accomplish this by the following measures.

1. It establishes a Securities and Exchange Commission (the Federal Trade Commission had been administering the Act of 1933).

2. It provides for registration and regulation of national securities exchanges. Companies whose securities are listed on an exchange must file reports similar to registration statements with both the SEC and the stock exchange, and provide periodic reports as well.

3. It provides control over corporate "insiders." Officers, directors, and major stockholders of a corporation must file monthly reports of changes in holdings of the stock of the corporation. Any short-term profits from such transactions may have to be paid to the corporation, if stockholders take legal action.

4. The act gives the SEC the power to prohibit manipulation by such devices as pools (aggregation of funds in order to affect prices artificially), wash sales (sales between members of the same group to record artificial transaction prices), and pegging the market. "Put-and-call" transactions were made subject to regulation.

5. The SEC is given control over the proxy machinery and practices.

6. Control over the flow of credit into security transactions is established by giving the Board of Governors of the Federal Reserve System the power to control margin requirements.

It will be noted that these powers extend only to listed securities. Many feel that the powers should be extended also to unlisted securities.

Maloney Act of 1938

The Maloney Act provides for self-regulation of brokers and dealers. It resulted in the formation in 1939 of the National Association of Securities Dealers (NASD), which now includes more than 3,000 of the 4,000 registered securities firms in the country. The NASD has operated effectively to raise the standards of securities practices by the development of a moral code, which has a stronger influence than would detailed legal rules.

Bankruptcy Act of 1938

The Bankruptcy Act provides for general revision of the federal bankruptcy laws applicable to the reorganization of corporations. It provides that the supervising court ask for an advisory opinion from the SEC on reorganization plans submitted to it in cases in which the listed liabilities are more than $3 million. The court may invite opinions in other cases. The SEC has issued many reports on the fairness and feasibility of proposed plans. (The issues involved here will be discussed in Chapters 28 and 29.)

Investment Company Act of 1940

Though many sound investment companies were in operation during the late 1920s, many unsound companies were also created. Abuses primarily involved (1) excessive debt and preferred stock leverage, (2) speculative investments, and (3) excessive salaries and fees. The act of 1940 provides several protections for investors. Investment companies are required to register with the SEC and to file a recital of investment policies. Stringent regulations regarding stock ownership by the investment company were developed. (The investment company cannot own more than 10 percent of the voting stock of a company in which it invests.) Restrictions are placed on borrowing by investment companies, and provisions are made for relatively simple capital structures. Uniform accounting methods and periodic reports to stockholders are prescribed.

Investment Advisers Act of 1940

The Investment Advisers Act of 1940 seeks to provide protection to the public who buy the services of expert advisers on the purchase of securities. It requires that investment advisers who receive fees for their services must register with the SEC. Fees must be based not on profits or appreciation in the market values, but rather on the size of assets administered; or the fee may be a flat fee. Advisers must make full disclosure in writing of their investment interest in companies.

APPRAISAL OF REGULATION OF SECURITY TRADING

Why should security transactions be regulated? If a valid answer exists, it is found in the argument that a great body of relevant knowledge is necessary for an informed judgment of the value of a security. The individual investor confronts large corporations and must receive protection to level the odds. Security values are subject to great gyrations which influence sentiment and business conditions generally. Hence social well-being requires that orderly markets be promoted.

The objectives of the regulation may therefore be summarized into three points:

1. To protect the amateur investor from fraud and to provide him with a basis for more informed judgments
2. To control the volume of bank credit to finance security speculation
3. To provide orderly markets in securities

Progress has been made on all three counts. There has been some cost in the increased time and expense involved in new flotations by companies. Though these burdens have not been as large as some persons have claimed, room for improvement exists. The regulations are powerless to prevent investors from investing in unsound ventures or to prevent stock prices from skyrocketing during booms and falling greatly during periods of pessimism. But requirements for increased information have been of great value.

From the standpoint of the financial manager, regulation has twofold significance. It affects the costs of issuing securities and also the effectiveness of the operation of the securities markets. With regard to the first, the data on costs of flotation reviewed in the previous chapter indicate that the costs of flotation have in fact been increased by regulation requirements. The increase, however, appears to have been only moderate except for smaller issues. The enactment of the regulatory acts of the 1930s returned public confidence in the securities markets and paved the way for renewed wide public participation in the securities markets with the post-World War II recovery in spending power. The net effect of regulation has therefore been to facilitate the raising of capital by business.

However, the effectiveness of the functioning of the securities markets is still subject to dispute and is under constant study. From April 3, 1963, to August 8, 1963, four volumes of a *Report of Special Study of Securities Markets of the Securities and Exchange Commission* were published. A summary report of the special study group was published on September 17, 1963. The five parts of the special study committee report covered the following topics: (1) qualifications of persons in the securities industry, (2) activities and responsibilities of broker-dealers and investment advisors, (3) primary and secondary distributions to the public, (4) trading markets, (5) exchange markets, (6) over-the-counter markets, (7) regional exchanges and off-the-exchange trading, (8) obligations of issuers of publicly held securities, (9) securities credit, (10) open-end investment companies (mutual funds), and (11) pattern of regulation including self-regulation. A number of issues were raised particularly with regard to the operations of the floor trader and the specialist and the conduct of odd-lot operations.

One of the consequences of the special study report was the introduction of House Resolution 6789, House Resolution 6793, and Senate Bill 1642, representing bills to amend the Securities Act of 1933 and the Securities Exchange Act of 1934. The purpose of the bills was to extend disclosure requirements to issuers of additional publicly traded securities, to provide for improved qualification and disciplinary procedures for registered brokers and dealers, and for a number of other purposes. Hearings were held on these bills on April 3, 1963, November and December 1963, and January and February 1964. These hearings resulted in the passage of the Securities Act Amendment of 1964, which modified somewhat the role of the floor trader and provided for certain qualification and disciplinary procedures for registered brokers and dealers.

The voluminous reports of the special study report indicate that many unresolved issues still remain in connection with the operation of the securities markets.[9] It is too early to sift the recommendations of the study group and to evaluate the legislative changes that have taken place. However, this remains an area of great importance not only for the operation of security markets but also for the mechanisms that facilitate the work of the financial manager in utilizing the public markets for raising funds.

SUMMARY

Direct placement has expanded because of the trend to saving through institutions. The function of assembling driblets of savings has been taken over to a great degree by the insurance companies, pension funds, and commercial banks. Thus these institutions, because they hold large pools of funds, may buy an issue of securities from a company directly. However, there are some offsetting advantages for public flotations and subsequent public trading that have kept private

---

[9] See, for example, George J. Stigler, "Public Regulation of the Securities Markets," *Journal of Business*, 37 (April 1964), pp. 117–142; Sidney Robbins and Walter Werner, "Professor Stigler Revisited," *Journal of Business* 37 (October 1964), pp. 406–413; George J. Stigler, "Comment" *Journal of Business*, 37 (October 1964), pp. 414–422; Roland I. Robinson and Robert Bartell Jr., "Uneasy Partnership: SEC/NYSE," *Harvard Business Review* 43 (January–February 1965), pp. 76–88.

placements at less than one half of all debt issues and about one third of all equity issues.

A continuing market for a firm's securities is provided through securities markets. The securities exchanges are organized markets for securities trading. However, the bulk of trading as measured by volume takes place on the over-the-counter markets. From the standpoint of the financial manager, listing on exchanges seems advantageous for seasoned issues. The over-the-counter market may aid in the seasoning process until the security can meet the requirements for listing.

The financial manager should be familiar with the federal laws regulating the issuance and trading of securities, because they influence his liabilities and affect financing methods and costs. Regulation of securities trading seeks (1) to provide information which investors can utilize as a basis for judging the merits of securities, (2) to control the volume of credit used in securities trading, and (3) to provide orderly securities markets. The laws, however, do not prevent purchase of unsound issues or wide price fluctuations. They increase somewhat the costs of flotation but have probably decreased the costs of the use of funds by restoration of public confidence in the securities markets.

SELECTED REFERENCES

Conklin, George T., "Direct Placements," *Journal of Finance,* 6 (June 1951), pp. 85–123.

Corey, E. R., "Corporate Financing by Direct Placement," *Harvard Business Review,* 38 (November 1950), pp. 67–76.

Federal Reserve Bank of Kansas City, "Taxes and Term Structure of Yields," *Monthly Review,* (December 1960), pp. 3–14.

Federal Reserve Bank of Richmond, "Trading Over the Counter," *Monthly Review,* (April 1959), pp. 8–10.

Fraine, H. G., "Direct Sale of Security Issues," *Journal of American Association of University Teachers of Insurance* (March 1949), pp. 40–56.

Freund, William C., and Edward D. Zinbarg, "Application of Flow of Funds to Interest-Rate Forecasting," *Journal of Finance* 18 (May 1963), pp. 231–248.

Friend, Irwin, G. W. Hoffman, and W. J. Winn, *The Over-the-Counter Securities Market* (New York: McGraw-Hill, Inc., 1958).

McFerrin, John B., "The Structure of the American Capital Market," *Southern Economic Journal,* 21 (January 1955), pp. 247–260.

Pawley, F. R., "Directly Placed Finance Company Paper," *Federal Reserve Bulletin,* 40 (December 1954), pp. 1245–1252.

Ritter, Lawrence S., "An Exposition of the Structure of the Flow-of-Funds Accounts" *Journal of Finance,* 18 (May 1963), pp. 219–230.

Soldofsky, Robert M., "The Size and Maturity of Direct-Placement Loans," *Journal of Finance,* 15 (March 1960), pp. 32–44.

Taylor, Stephen, "Uses of Flow-of-Funds Accounts in the Federal Reserve System," *Journal of Finance,* 18 (May 1963), pp. 249–263.

Walter, J. E., *The Role of Regional Security Exchanges* (Berkeley: Bureau of Business and Economic Research, University of California, 1957).

Weston, J. Fred, "A Closer Look at Interest-Rate Relationships," *The Morgan Guaranty Survey,* (April 1961), pp. 2–8.

———, "Flows Through Financial Intermediaries," *Federal Reserve Bulletin,* 50 (May 1964), pp. 549–557.

————, (ed.), *Financial Management in the 1960s: New Challenges and Responsibilities* (New York: Holt, Rinehart and Winston, Inc., 1966); selections "New Forces in the Stock Market" and "Wall Street's Main Event: SEC v. the Specialists."

QUESTIONS

24-1 Do you think that an increase in the institutionalization of savings (an increase in the importance of financial institutions) would stimulate or retard the development of private placements as opposed to public offerings? Explain your position.

24-2 Table 24-1 shows that private placements generally constitute over one half of all debt offerings, but only a very small percentage of equity offerings. What is the explanation for this situation?

24-3 Would you expect to find larger or smaller firms doing a greater percentage of their debt financing as private placements versus public offerings?

24-4 How would you expect a firm's cost of capital to be affected if it changed its status from an over-the-counter stock to one listed on the New York Stock Exchange?

24-5 Evaluate the following statement: "Short selling is fundamentally a form of gambling; it is simply betting that a stock's price will decline. Buying stocks, on the other hand, is more in the nature of truly investing; stock is purchased in order to receive a dividend return on the invested capital. Consequently, if we do not wish to see Wall Street turned into an eastern Las Vegas, all short selling should be forbidden."

24-6 Evaluate the following statement: "The fundamental purpose of the federal security laws dealing with new issues is to prevent investors, principally small investors, from sustaining losses on the purchase of stocks."

PROBLEMS

24-1 Suggest the form and source of financing for the following situations:

1) A manufacturer, after a long search for a particular type of equipment he needed, finally found it. The seller demanded cash in full or the deal was off, but the manufacturer had only enough cash for 20 percent of the total required.

2) A hardware dealer saw profits ahead if he could immediately stock up on certain items at favorable prices. He needed additional funds of $2,500 to take advantage of the opportunity.

3) A neighborhood dealer had recently moved to larger quarters. He needed $2,000 to finance additional inventory to handle increased business.

4) The growing business of a retail butcher on a busy thoroughfare warranted the cost of modernizing for customer convenience and more attractive display. The owner needed $3,000 to pay in full for items not eligible under FHA Title I financing.

5) An established partnership needed to purchase a heavy crane with special attachments which would increase earnings about $200 per month. The partnership was in the contracting business. It was able to make a one-third down payment, but did not have the balance of $4,000.

6) An automobile mechanic purchased a service station at a relatively low cost because of its previous poor earnings record. He had saved about $5,000, which he invested in the business and which mostly represented payment for

equipment acquired. Increased volume necessitated employment of two men, and the owner required an additional $3,000 to carry inventory and meet payrolls.

7) A small manufacturer in the woodwork business with a record of stable earnings needed $5,000 to buy additional productive equipment to handle orders for houseware items that had become in short supply. The mortgage on his plant had been partially paid off.

24-2 The Custom Company produces precision instruments and is growing rapidly. To date, the company's increased financing needs were met by short-term loans. Recently, because of a sharp increase in demand for its products, the company has had to stretch its production capacity and has been forced to subcontract to a great extent.

To alleviate the shortage in production capacity, the board of directors at its last meeting authorized an expansion program and requested the treasurer of the company to draw up a financing plan.

Edward May, the treasurer, accordingly set out to formulate a long-range expansion plan. For this purpose, May had his assistant prepare a *pro forma* income statement and cash plan for the period 1967–1971 on the basis of short-term bank financing.

Talks with banks revealed that the company could secure a term loan amounting to $4 million maximum at 4½ percent to be amortized over a five-year period. There were indications that the bank might ask for provisions concerning current ratio and additional bank borrowing. Assume the short-term interest rate equals that of the term loan.

At the end of December 1966, May was still wondering about a better financing mode, his alternatives being a short-term bank loan or a term loan. Pertinent financial data are shown on the next three pages.

Custom Company
ACTUAL AND PRO FORMA BALANCE SHEET
Year End 1964–1971
(in thousands of dollars)

	1964	1965	1966	1967	1968	1969	1970	1971
Assets								
Current assets	$2,900	$3,100	$3,300	$3,600	$4,200	$5,000	$5,100	$5,600
Fixed assets	2,000	2,200	2,500	5,000	5,000	5,000	5,000	5,000
Total assets	4,900	5,300	5,800	8,600	9,200	10,000	10,100	10,600
Liabilities								
Notes payable	2,600	2,310	1,970	4,000	3,200	2,900	1,800	1,000
Accounts payable	1,000	1,060	1,170	1,100	1,560	1,640	1,700	1,750
Provision for taxes and other accounts	300	330	360	400	440	460	500	550
Current	3,900	3,700	3,500	5,500	5,200	5,000	4,000	3,300
Common stock	500	500	500	500	500	500	500	500
Retained earnings	500	1,100	1,800	2,600	3,500	4,500	5,600	6,800
Total net worth	1,000	1,600	2,300	3,100	4,000	5,000	6,100	7,300
Total claims	$4,900	$5,300	$5,800	$8,600	$9,200	$10,000	$10,100	$10,600

CUSTOM COMPANY

INCOME STATEMENT

1964–1971

(in thousands of dollars)

	1964	1965	1966	1967	1968	1969	1970	1971
Sales	$10,000	$11,000	$12,100	$13,200	$14,500	$16,000	$18,000	$20,000
Costs of sales	7,500	8,100	8,875	9,030	10,000	11,150	12,750	14,350
Gross profit	2,500	2,900	3,225	4,170	4,500	4,850	5,250	5,650
Operating expenses	1,000	1,140	1,200	1,320	1,450	1,600	1,800	2,000
Depreciation	500	560	625	1,250	1,250	1,250	1,250	1,250
Profit from operations	1,000	1,200	1,400	1,600	1,800	2,000	2,200	2,400
Provision for taxes	500	600	700	800	900	1,000	1,100	1,200
Retained earnings	$ 500	$ 600	$ 700	$ 800	$ 900	$ 1,000	$ 1,100	$ 1,200

Custom Company
CASH PLAN
1967–1971

Cash Inflow		Depreciation	Retained Earnings	Total
1967	. . . . .	1,250	800	2,050
1968	. . . . .	1,250	900	2,150
1969	. . . . .	1,250	1,000	2,250
1970	. . . . .	1,250	1,100	2,350
1971	. . . . .	1,250	1,200	2,450

1. Prepare *pro forma* balance sheets for 1967–1971 under the assumption that a term loan is used for expansion with an amortization schedule of $800,000 per year beginning in 1967. Total assets will remain as shown on the balance sheet.

2. Calculate for the years 1967–1971 the following ratios for the balance sheets as given, compared with the balance sheets if a term loan is used.

    a) Current assets to current liabilities
    b) Short-term debt to net worth
    c) Long-term debt to net worth
    d) Total debt to net worth

3. a) What do you think of a provision in the term loan agreement limiting the company from further bank borrowing for the duration of the term loan?

    b) How about a current ratio of 2 to 1 at all times as a provision in the term loan agreement?

    c) Recommend the mode of financing you consider best for the Custom Company. Discuss the advantages and the disadvantages of both the short-term loan and the term loan.

Chapter 25

Comparison of Sources
of Financing

Investment bankers, exchanges, and over-the-counter markets are "facilitating institutions" in the process of financing business. They are not ultimate sources of funds, but merely bring together the ultimate lender and
borrower. By way of summary and to tie together many threads, a comparison is now made of the characteristics of the major sources of financing for firms.

VARIABLES IN NATURE OF SOURCES

In analyzing financing sources, the financial manager considers certain important characteristics that form the basis of his appraisal of the relative
attractiveness of alternative sources of funds. The important characteristics of sources of financing may be summarized into eight factors:

1. Duration of need for funds
2. Form of financing supplied
3. Degree of risk taken by source of funds
4. Stability of supply of funds
5. Facilities for mass financing
6. Cost of funds
7. Nature of contact
8. Amount of management counsel

1. The *duration* of the use of funds refers to the kinds of financing
provided, whether they are short-term, medium-term, or long-term sources,
or sources on a continuing basis.

2. The *form* of financing supplied refers to whether the financing is in the form of debt, equity, or some intermediate type of credit.

3. The *degree of risk* taken by the supplier of funds varies widely. Does the lender limit himself to blue-chip securities or blue-chip customers, or is he willing to undertake a substantial amount of risk?

4. How *stable* is the source of funds? Is the source of funds subject to changes over the business cycle? When business turns down, does the source of funds tend to dry up? Or will the source of funds stay with the firm and help it during periods of financial difficulty?

5. What is the degree to which *mass financing* can be handled by the lender? For example, accounts receivable financing involves handling large batches of invoices. Unless the lender is organized to handle a large number of papers at low cost, this method of financing will be too expensive.

6. The *cost of funds* varies in accordance with several factors. One is the extent of risk exposure faced by the supplier. Another is the volume of paper work to be performed. A third is money and capital market conditions.

7. What is the *degree of contact* between the lender and the borrower? Is it a personal relation? Is it close and direct? Is the contact sufficiently direct so that terms of the agreement can be modified if such changes benefit both parties?

8. How much *management counsel* is provided by the source of funds? Where there is close and direct contact, the lender often provides considerable management counsel. Indeed, management counsel may be more valuable than the funds themselves and may be more important than the variations in the cost of funds.

INTERNAL FINANCING

In Chapter 20 it was seen that internal sources provide more than two thirds of total sources of funds. Depreciation charges represent 40 percent of total sources; retained earnings provide about 28 percent.

Internal financing accounts for such a substantial proportion of financing for a number of reasons. First, it is an inexpensive method of *acquiring* funds. Though the costs of *using* internal funds should be considered no different from the costs of externally acquired equity funds, the costs of *acquiring* internal funds is negligible. Second, plowing back earnings avoids the taxation leakage that would occur if dividends were paid to stockholders, if personal income taxes were paid, and if the corporation then sought to sell additional securities to the stockholders. Third, in a growing, profitable company, the market price of its stock does not appear to be adversely affected by nonpayment of dividends or by very low dividend payouts.

Probably the most important reason for a low dividend payout is the combination of a high growth rate in the demand for the firm's products, resulting in a substantial need for additional financing, coupled with a high profit rate. The high profit rate makes the firm an attractive place in which to invest funds. Stockholders would have difficulty finding better alternatives, and this consideration is reinforced by the tax advantages of leaving the funds in the business. The high earning power will result in increased earnings per share resulting from the plowback, and the price of the stock will rise, offering opportunities for capital gains.

If the growth rate of the firm's sales and profits is less spectacular, the dividend payout rate will doubtless be higher. But firms typically follow the policy of paying a stable dollar amount of dividends, with an increase following an increase in earnings and lagging behind until the higher earnings level appears well established. This practice will also result in a substantial proportion of retained-earnings-to-financing needs. Stockholders' satisfaction with such a policy is likely because of their familiarity with the company and their confidence in its outlook as indicated by their ownership of its common stock.

For all the above reasons, historical studies of the growth and development of industries have demonstrated the pre-eminent role of internal financing of capital formation. However, external financing also performs a substantial role. Furthermore, because external financing is the incremental financing, it is likely to represent a critical and strategic element in facilitating the healthy growth of business firms. Appraisal of the important variables determining the characteristics of outside financing is therefore essential for sound management of finances of the firm. An analysis of the many forms of external financing potentially available to the financial manager now follows.

MAJOR PRIVATE INSTITUTIONS PROVIDING EXTERNAL FINANCING

The characteristics of the alternative sources of financing are summarized in Table 25–1. This summary will serve as a guideline to the discussion.

Commercial Banks

Commercial banks have total assets of approximately $325 billion, consisting primarily of business loans, consumer loans, and investments in government securities. The American banking system is characterized by unit banks—more than 13,500 banks, most of which are relatively small. Many are small businesses run on a personal basis by individuals, though

TABLE 25-1

SUMMARY OF CHARACTERISTICS OF MAJOR SOURCES OF FUNDS

A. *Commercial Banks*

1. Close direct contact
2. Relatively high credit risks
3. Limited mass financing
4. Short- and medium-term, no equity financing
5. Sources of funds subject to seasonal, cyclical, and secular changes
6. Limited management counsel
7. Operations change total money supply

B. *Investment Banks*

1. Close relation
2. Intermediary institution
3. No mass financing
4. Most adapted to handle large issues of nationally known companies
5. Greatly influenced by cyclical changes in market's receptivity to new issues
6. Some management counsel on financing

C. *Life Insurance Companies*

1. More centralized
2. High credit rating
3. No mass financing
4. Medium- and long-term credit, limited equity financing
5. Sources of funds subject to little cyclical variability, strong continued secular growth
6. Limited management counsel

D. *Finance Companies*

1. Very direct contacts
2. May take greater credit risks
3. Specialists in mass financing
4. Short and continued financing, no equity financing
5. Sources of funds subject to variations in commercial bank policy
6. More management counsel

E. *Equity Markets*

1. Impersonal
2. Not a large segment favorably disposed to bearing great risks
3. No mass financing
4. Mainly national markets
5. Great cyclical variations in availability of funds
6. No management counsel

F. *Other Business Firms*

1. Close relation
2. Will take greater risks
3. No mass financing
4. Long-term debt; source usually related to tie-in sales or purchase relation
5. Great cyclical and random variations
6. Some management counsel

G. *Investment Development Companies*

1. Very close relation to management
2. May take great credit risks
3. No mass financing
4. Long-term and equity financing
5. Sources of funds little influenced by cyclical and secular changes
6. Considerable management counsel

TABLE 25–1 *(Continued)*

H. Community Development Companies

1. Close relation	5. Sources of funds may be limited in total and appreciably altered by cyclical influences
2. May take great risks	
3. No mass financing	
4. Long-term and equity financing	6. Some management counsel

I. *Friends and Relatives*

1. Close relation	5. Great cyclical and random variations in availability
2. Great risks taken	
3. No mass financing	6. Varied management counsel
4. Long-term debt and equity financing; special situations and circumstances	7. Frequently a major portion of control must be shared

some are extremely large institutions. Historically, commercial banks have concentrated mainly in the short-term lending field, but in recent years they have entered the medium-term debt field to a greater degree.

Although, by and large, banks serve the high-quality, low-risk borrower, many now have new business development divisions, and a few even have their own SBIC's, which do essentially equity financing. Their activities encourage small and growing businesses where prospects are favorable. In these areas, banks expose themselves to a larger degree of risk.

Because the operation of commercial banks changes the total money supply, the reserve positions of commercial banks, which determine the volume of their lending potential, are subject to increases and decreases, reflecting Federal Reserve policy. Hence the stability of the availability of funds of commercial banks is not as great as that of institutions whose lending ability is less subject to policy changes of the Federal Reserve.

Facilities for mass financing are limited primarily to the larger banks where a division of labor can be successfully organized and put into operation. Only the larger banks provide receivables financing, which involves handling of large batches of invoices. Because banks limit themselves to higher quality risk and because the amount of mass financing by other than the largest banks is limited, the cost of bank financing is moderate.

The contacts between the financial manager and the bank lending officer may be frequent. A good financial manager makes it his duty to become well acquainted with bank lending officers, to have lunch with them occasionally, or perhaps to meet them at professional meetings. Many aspects of financing are on a very personal basis.

Commercial bank lending officers provide a limited amount of management counsel. But their volume of operations is such that they cannot counsel customers at great length or in detail. However, over a period of years bank lending officers develop much practical business experience and judgment. They convey this judgment to the borrowers to the extent that it is feasible to do so, and to the degree that borrowers are receptive and avail themselves of it.

Life Insurance Companies

Life insurance companies hold assets of about $160 billion. In their investment policies, life insurance companies are subject to legal restrictions of the states in which they operate. The very nature of their business is more centralized than that of commercial banks, and a relatively small number of insurance companies account for a large proportion of insurance activity in the United States.

Insurance companies restrict themselves to financing mostly high credit quality firms. They do not engage in mass financing. They specialize in the medium- and long-term credit market. Unlike commercial banks, they provide limited equity financing. In recent years, insurance companies have purchased the warrant-carrying or convertible debt issues of small businesses. Warrants give insurance companies the right to buy common stock of the small firms; thus the companies are enabled to take a residual equity position.

The funds of life insurance companies represent a source subject to little cyclical variation. In fact, life insurance companies have shown a strong secular growth. Their assets have continually increased; they are therefore not likely to be pressured to liquidate loans, as are the commercial banks.

The largest insurance companies are not in a position to have close contact with the borrowers. In selling insurance policies, insurance companies are highly decentralized, with agency systems spread far and wide throughout the country. In making real estate loans, insurance companies use correspondents who help them develop business and service the loans. But in their business lending activity, insurance companies are still relatively centralized.

Some companies, like the Prudential Life Insurance Company, have attempted to regionalize their activities. An increasing amount of regional business lending is made by insurance companies that have decentralized.

The large insurance companies have been sensitive to the complaint that their money has not been available to small business to the degree desired. They have attempted, within the limitations of their organization structures, to make loans to small firms.

Because insurance companies are centralized, their ability to provide a firm with management counsel is generally less than that of commercial banks. However, on individual term loans or direct placements, discussions between insurance company officers and the financial manager of a firm may provide considerable guidance.

Finance Companies

Finance companies provide continuing financing to business. They will finance lower quality risks. A unique and important characteristic of finance companies is their ability to handle mass financing. Their organization is set up to do this, and by tradition and training they are specialists in mass financing.

Finance companies are a source of considerable management counsel. As their customers are often smaller firms, their clients need both money and counsel.

Because they undertake greater risk exposure, handle mass financing, and provide a great deal of management counsel, the costs of funds obtained from finance companies are somewhat higher (running to 10 to 12 percent) than those obtained from commercial banks. However, finance companies engaging in receivables financing or factoring have argued that their money is less expensive than that of commercial banks, if certain variables are taken into account. One of these variables is the requirement of commercial banks that the borrower maintain a compensating balance of 15 to 25 percent of the amount borrowed, depending upon the tightness of the money market. Because interest is paid on the total amount borrowed, the effective cost of the amount actually used is much higher than the nominal interest rate stated. In addition, the commercial bank charges for the total outstanding loan, although the borrower may accumulate large amounts in his deposit account in anticipation of repayment. The finance company charges on a daily basis, on the average amount of money borrowed outstanding each day. Because of these considerations, the cost of funds from finance companies for comparable risks may be no higher than that of funds from other sources.

Interestingly enough, in view of the competition between finance companies and commercial banks, finance companies rely heavily upon commercial banks as a source of funds. Often a rule of thumb followed in commercial bank lending is that a finance company may borrow three times the amount of its own equity money. Thus, during tight money periods, when commercial banks must restrict the volume of their lending, these restrictions will be in turn transmitted to finance companies, who will become more selective in their own lending policies.

Mutual Savings Banks

Mutual savings banks, with over $50 billion in assets, are found mainly in the Northeast. They invest primarily in home mortgage loans and government securities and hold nominal amounts in corporate bonds and stocks. Most of their business investment is made indirectly in high-grade corporate bonds. They are relatively minor sources of business financing.

Fire and Casualty Insurance Companies

Fire and casualty insurance companies are aggressive investors with approximately $25 billion in assets. In many ways they are a type of investment company that also conducts an insurance business. Nearly one third of their investment is in common stock. They look for special situations and are willing to buy other than just blue-chip stock.

Investment Companies

There are some 450 investment companies (also called mutual funds or investment trusts and closed-end funds) in the United States. Such companies have grown rapidly in recent years until they now hold assets of more than $35 billion. More than 90 percent of their assets are in corporate common stocks. In general, the bulk of their investments is in relatively blue-chip common stocks. The amount of their funds has become so large in recent years that there are not enough blue stocks for them to buy at attractive prices; they have therefore turned more and more to "light blue-chip stocks," taking a somewhat higher risk.

Pension Funds

Among the fastest growing sources of financing are corporate pension funds and trusts administered by commercial banks. Corporate pension funds amount to more than $30 billion. About one third of their assets is in common stock and about 45 percent in corporate bonds. Some pension funds invest in the securities of the companies with which they are associated; the profit-sharing or pension funds of Sears Roebuck and General Motors are cases in point. The amount they invest in the stock of their own companies is an important factor in maintaining a continuous segment of demand in the market for these securities.

Trust funds administered by commercial banks are substantial. In the *Journal of Finance* of March 1959, Goldsmith and Shapiro estimated personal trust accounts to be about $50 billion. These funds are invested heavily in common stock, but since they are invested by hired managers for someone else's benefit, the managers tend to be conservative in their purchases.

Pension fund and investment fund purchases of common stock push the prices of blue chips up so high that the secondary issues become relatively more attractive. Consequently, the flow of funds from individual investors moves more in the direction of secondary issues, augmenting the total demand for common stocks and thereby increasing the availability of common stock financing for business firms.

Savings and Loan Associations

Savings and loan associations now have assets of over $100 billion. Except for liquidity reserves held as cash and government securities, practically all their money is invested in home mortgages. They may represent a source of funds for small business in that their home mortgage loans may free the funds of individuals for business uses.

Educational and Religious Funds

Assets of college and university endowment funds amount to over $5 billion. More than 50 percent of their investments is in common stocks. Income from endowment money is used primarily to finance maintenance and expenses of university buildings. In a period of rising price levels, universities are forced to invest in equities in order to protect the purchasing power of their endowments. College endowment funds have therefore put an increasing portion of their funds into equities and have invested less heavily in corporate bonds.

Investment Development Companies

Investment development companies, such as the American Research and Development Company (which was formed on December 31, 1949), the Rockefeller Brothers (New York City), and the J. H. Whitney & Company (formed in February 1946 with a seven-man partnership) are specialized sources of funds.

Method of operation. The method of operation of investment development companies can best be understood by beginning with an example. A new business venture makes an application for financial assistance. If the proposed project is within the scope and interests of the particular investment development company, it receives a rigorous examination. Some companies use their own staff for this investigation, while others, like the American Research and Development Corporation, depend upon a board of technical advisers acting in a consultative capacity. A high percentage of applications is rejected. If the application is approved, money is loaned or equity securities are bought. Investment development companies generally take an equity position in the firms they finance, but they may also extend loan capital. They seek to avoid mortgage bonds, since security in the form of a mortgage reduces the credit available from banks and other credit agencies.

Investment development companies perform a continuing and active role in the enterprise. Typically, they do not require voting control, but they usually have a member on the board of directors of the new enterprise. The matter of control has not been one of the crucial considerations in the investment company's decision to invest. If the investment development company owns 20, 30, or 40 percent of the stock so that it can participate in the income, the management of the company should be sufficiently strong to effectively make the organization and policy decisions of the firm. The investment company does maintain continuous contact and provides a considerable amount of management counsel.

The essential and distinctive contribution of the investment development company is that typically it is formed and financed by a small number of wealthy persons. For tax reasons, wealthy individuals are interested in receiving their income in the form of capital gains rather than current income. They are therefore in a position to take larger risks. If they lose on the venture, assuming they are in a 70 percent personal income tax bracket, the net loss is only 30 percent of the investment. If they gain, they will take the gain in the form of capital gains and therefore they pay only a 25 percent tax. The odds are shifted in favor of making this form of investment.

In addition to their ability to take increased risks, members of the development companies generally have considerable business experience. They are in a position to make an informed evaluation of the prospects of a company. Thus the investment development corporations can perform a unique, high-quality function as a source of funds and management counsel to firms.

Under the Investment Company Act of 1940, investment development companies are described as closed-end, nondiversified investment companies of the management type. As closed-end companies they are under no obligation to buy back the shares they have issued. Among the stockholders of the American Research and Development Corporation, for example, are several registered investment companies. The American Research and Development Corporation has secured modifications in state laws to permit investment by investment companies and insurance companies in the investment development companies themselves. This change permits diversification on the part of investment companies and insurance companies that broadens the potential role of the investment development companies. It widens the scope and source of their financing.

The economic significance of the investment development companies and their possible contribution to the American economy are considerable. (1) They may broaden the scope of institutional investment. (2) They provide a superior credit-and-risk appraisal. (3) They broaden the sources of equity capital investment. (4) They provide a significant, important, and informed kind of management counsel. (5) The arrangement provides for continued financial assistance which often will be essential in financing the new and growing enterprise. The rise of government-sponsored, small business investment corporations reflects the application of the same principles, with other advantages that will enable them to take over a large share of the potential growth of the investment development companies. It will be useful, therefore, to describe the nature of the small business investment corporations at this point.

SMALL BUSINESS INVESTMENT CORPORATIONS

The Small Business Investment Company Act of 1958 empowers the Small Business Administration to license and regulate small business investment corporations (SBIC's) and to provide them with financial assistance. These SBIC's receive their corporate charters from their own states, not from the Small Business Administration. Private capital of a minimum amount of $300,000 is required for the formation and licensing of a small business investment corporation. This can be matched by SBA's purchase of subordinated debentures (bearing 5 percent interest) in a like amount. Such purchases can now go as high as $700,000 to match the private investment. The maturity is 20 years. The SBA also may lend SBIC's, under Section 303(b) of the Act, up to 50 percent of their paid-in capital and surplus or $4 million, whichever is less. Thus, $700,000 private capital can obtain $700,000 subordinated debenture proceeds and a $700,000 operating loan.

No more than 20 percent of the statutory capital of a small business investment corporation may be invested in one company. A $700,000 private capital company with $700,000 subordinated debenture money has statutory capital of $1.4 million, and a 20 percent limit of $280,000. Before the 1964 amendments to the Small Business Investment Act, the lesser of 20 percent of paid-in capital and surplus or $500,000 could be invested in a single small business. This maximum absolute dollar amount has now been removed. In addition, Special Discretionary Portfolio investments by SBIC's can be made, using a limited percentage of their assets. Within the limitation, SBIC's will be permitted to purchase the securities of small firms either on the market or by negotiation. With these investments they can finance small insurance companies and leasing companies, and can make loans with rapid amortization provisions.

By the end of 1964, some 700 SBIC's were in actual operation.[1] Their total capital was over $750 million. Of this total, over $500 million was loaned out to over 10,000 small business firms.

In their principles of operation small business investment corporations have followed two policies similar to the characteristics of the investment development corporations. First is their emphasis on investment in convertible securities and obligations with warrants, giving the SBIC a residual equity position in the companies to which funds are provided. Second is emphasis on the provision by the SBIC of management counsel, for which a fee is charged.

---

[1] Small Business Administration, *Annual Report to the President and Congress* (Washington, D.C.: U.S. Government Printing Office, 1965) p. 30. The empirical data in this section and the legislative changes of 1964 are summarized from information provided in Section V of the 1964 Report of the SBA entitled, "Strengthening Free Enterprise by Providing Capital for Small Business."

Three main types of small business investment corporations have been in operation—vertical, horizontal, and captive. A vertical small business investment corporation, such as the Electronics Capital Corporation of San Diego, California, specializes by line of business. A horizontal corporation, such as Growth Capital, Inc., of Cleveland, Ohio, invests in diversified lines of business. A captive small business investment company is organized by an operating business, usually for the purpose of providing longer term or equity financing to its customers, but there are restrictions on the use of such financing for the purchase of inventory from the operating business or for bailing out previous debts. A subdivision of the captive type is the bank-owned SBIC. More than 20 commercial banks have established SBIC subsidiaries, and about 200 other banks own stock in SBIC's.

In view of the growth and development of the small business investment corporations, a brief summary of their advantages is in order. Dividends received by the small business investment corporations from their small business investments are 100 percent deductible from the SBIC's income, compared with 85 percent for ordinary corporations. Losses from convertible debentures or the stocks into which these are converted can be treated as losses chargeable against ordinary income, not against capital gains. SBIC's are exempt from penalties for improper accumulation of income if they meet certain requirements set forth in the regulations. Investors in small business investment corporations may treat their own stock losses as ordinary losses chargeable against ordinary income. SBIC's may also obtain certain exemptions from personal holding company treatment, and public companies may qualify as regulated investment companies under subchapter M.

In 1964 additional tax advantages were obtained. These include (1) Issuance of rulings by the Internal Revenue Service allowing SBIC's, through 1968, to set aside reserves for bad debts equal to at least 10 percent of appropriate investments. After 1968 an experience factor will be determined and (2) issuance by the Internal Revenue Service of a proposed ruling, for discussion purposes, which would provide special tax treatment of options acquired by SBIC's solely as part of an investment package consisting of equity securities with warrants attached.[2]

The small business investment corporations benefit from the aura of government sponsorship and access to long-term subordinated funds on attractive terms. The emphasis on charging for management counseling and services enhances the income of the small business investment corporations and probably stimulates the payer to give more attention to the advice. These factors, coupled with the excitable expectations of investors in the bull market, which has predominated since 1958, provided a recep-

---

[2] 1964 Annual Report of the Small Business Administration, *ibid.*, p. 15.

tive environment for the public flotations of the small business investment corporations—until 1961. Beginning in that year, investor reaction to SBIC securities plunged drastically. The stock of Electronics Capital, the largest of the publicly owned SBIC's, dropped from a 1961 high of 66½ to a 1964 low of 5. Others reacted similarly. Most authorities feel, however, that it is still too early to judge the long-term impact of SBIC's on the general economy.

INDIVIDUALS AND NONFINANCIAL BUSINESS SOURCES OF FINANCING

Thus far the main institutional sources of financing of business have been discussed. An analysis of some of the other classes of sources of funds is now discussed.

Employees

Many firms run a significant program to enable employees to purchase stock. In one form the program may give stock options to key executives to encourage them to identify with the interest of the company, but stock purchase programs may be extended to employees at all levels. Because the program usually sells the stock to the employees at a price somewhat below the current market, it is a form of extra compensation as well. Such programs primarily seek to encourage the employee to identify himself with the well-being of the company. His stock, its value, and the earnings from it will be tied to the success of the company as a whole.

There are disadvantages to employee stock ownership plans, too. (1) For the rank-and-file employee the amount provided may be too small to have any effect on him. (2) If the amount is of any significance, fluctuations in stock prices may cause ill-will during times when stock prices are depressed.

The main disadvantage from the standpoint of the employee is that he may be putting too many of his financial eggs in one basket. His own job security is tied to the future welfare of the company. If his savings are also dependent upon the future welfare of this company, a reversal in the fortunes of the company may bring disaster to him. In any event, sale of stock to employees has never been a major source of business financing.

Customers

The sale of preferred stock or nonvoting common stock to customers was conducted on a large scale by the public utilities in the 1920s. To a considerable extent the utility companies' regular employees merchandized the securities to anyone with whom they dealt. There were two main reasons for selling stock to customers. (1) Since the customer had frequent association with the utility because he paid his bills periodically, it was an economical and efficient method of utilizing a source of funds. (2) By placing part of the ownership of the utilities in the hands of customers, the utilities hoped that the pressure for government ownership would be mitigated. Customers who also were stockholders might be less critical of rate increases.

The main disadvantage of sales of securities to customers is that the ordinary customer is not in a position to assume the risks of common stock ownership. In addition, he is unfamiliar with the intricacies of the financial markets. As a consequence, the stock market crash of 1929 and the large losses that followed led to the Securities Act of 1933 and the Public Utilities Holding Company Act of 1935, both of which contained prohibitions against the sale of stock to customers by public utilities by the methods used during the 1920s.

At present there appears to be some interest on the part of industrial firms to encourage ownership of stock among customers. This policy tends to tie customers to the seller of a particular product; also, it is an additional merchandising device. The big risk of stock ownership by customers is that, in a declining market, customers may become disaffected and the company may incur their ill-will.

Equity Markets

The equity markets, in relation to individual purchases of securities, represent a vast impersonal market. The 1956 census of shareholders conducted by the New York Stock Exchange found that almost nine million persons held stock in public corporations, about one in every 12 adults. With the continued rise in security prices, the number of stockholders had probably increased to 20 million by the end of 1965.

Interbusiness Financing[3]

Mercantile and commercial credit. On the average, Department of Commerce and Census data suggest that approximately 90 percent of manufacturing sales and more than 92 percent of wholesale sales are made on credit rather than for cash. This relatively large volume of sales on credit results in over $100 billion of outstanding receivables of nonfinancial firms. By contrast, the business loans of all commercial banks approximate $45 billion. Thus it appears that trade credit is more than double the size of business credit obtained from commercial banks.

Equity and long-term debt financing. American businesses have extensively financed independent (non-affiliated) customer or supplier

---

[3] See also the section on management of accounts receivable in Chapter 6.

businesses on an equity or long-term loan basis. Numerous examples of this can be cited.

On July 1, 1948, Bethlehem Steel Corporation held 30 percent of the common stock of the Rheem Manufacturing Company, a fabricator of steel drums. Bethlehem Steel Corporation sold steel to the Rheem Manufacturing Company.

In 1951, General Motors loaned $28 million to Jones and Laughlin Steel Corporation, which provided a portion of the steel requirements of General Motors Corporation.

Barium Steel in 1955 borrowed $5 million from the General Electric Company, one of its major customers, to pay its taxes and to improve its working-capital position.

In 1957, Lukens Steel Corporation made arrangements to borrow $39 million, including $15 million from General Electric, to finance the construction of new facilities in order to increase its ingot-steel capacity from 0.75 million tons to 1.1 million tons.

These examples indicate the wide variety and large magnitude that interbusiness financing of this kind can represent. They indicate the variety of the relations and the extent to which the characteristics of the loan transaction can be tailored to the circumstances of the lender and to the needs of the borrower.

Equipment financing. As a consequence of increasing mechanization of the American economy, a rapidly growing form of financial assistance to business customers has been financing of machinery and equipment by the manufacturer. Usually such financing is on an installment payment term basis extending more than one year. American business has provided financing of this kind in order to expand the market for its products. The products sold are generally of large-unit value and are frequently sold to smaller businesses which are not well supplied with funds or able to pay cash. Often the manufacturer will not only perform the initial financing but will also continue to carry the receivables for the following reasons:

1. It will enable the manufacturer to earn the financing charge.
2. It eliminates the possibility that a financial institution will injure relations with the customers by its collection procedures and attitudes.
3. It enables the manufacturer to maintain a continuing relation with the business customer in order to cultivate future orders.
4. It enables the manufacturer to supply merchandise on credit to business customers whose credit ratings are not acceptable to a bank or finance company. The manufacturer, because of his intimate knowledge of the business and his frequent and close contacts with the buyers, is in a better position to evaluate the credit risk.

Interbusiness financing is a field in which the dollar magnitude of the items involved is large. The potential role of interbusiness financing is important both for the operations of business and for the nature, level, and characteristics of economic activity as well.

GOVERNMENT AND QUASI-GOVERNMENT CREDIT PROGRAMS

Federal Credit Programs

Two federal credit programs for business have already been described. The small-business loan program of the Small Business Administration was discussed in Chapter 16. The SBIC program was discussed in a previous section of the present chapter. The number of the programs and the areas they serve are broad indeed.[4] Four major types of federal credit programs are in operation. (1) Direct government loans provide credits directly to private borrowers, as in the loans to small business by the SBA. (2) Loans are also made by federally sponsored credit institutions, as in the mortgage loans to agribusiness made by the Federal Land Bank System. (3) Guarantees of private loans are negotiated, as in the guaranty for equipment and property loans of railroads or the guaranty of loans for small airline companies. (4) Insurance of private loans is made, as in the insurance of maritime construction loans or residential mortgage loans of the Federal Housing Administration.

Though this discussion of federal credit programs is brief, it encompasses the four major types of programs in the major areas of coverage: agriculture, housing, business, and international. The programs relate to business finance directly in the latter two areas. However, in both agriculture and housing, small business is likely to benefit from funds made available to agribusiness and housing. For example, more liberal mortgage terms available for home financing may free more of an individual's funds for his small-business operations.

The magnitude of the federal credit programs is significant.[5] By mid-1960, direct federal loans outstanding had reached $23 billion. Private loans partly or completely insured or guaranteed by federal agencies totaled $67 billion, representing 12 percent of total private debt outstanding. A total of new credits of $20 billions per year is being extended in the form of direct, insured, or guaranteed loans.

Because of the significance of these programs, each is described briefly. The most important activities are grouped under the four areas of agriculture, housing, business, and international in the following summary:[6]

---

[4] Commission on Money and Credit, *Money and Credit: Their Influence on Jobs, Prices and Growth* (Englewood Cliffs, N.J.: Prentice-Hall, 1961), pp. 185–87.

[5] *Ibid.*, pp. 182–183.

[6] This summary is based on an unpublished memorandum prepared for the Commission on Money and Credit by J. Fred Weston and David A. Snell, *Analysis of Technical Components of Federal Credit Programs*, pp. 528.

A. *Agriculture*
1. Federal Land Banks (FLB) and National Farm Loan Associations (NFLA). These two function together. The federal land banks sell tax-exempt bonds secured by the mortgages made by the national farm loan associations to the individual farmers. The federal land banks borrow directly in the capital market.
2. Federal Intermediate Credit Banks and Production Credit Bank System. These two also function together. The production credit associations borrow from the federal intermediate credit banks.
   The federal land banks and the national farm loan associations have the objectives primarily of providing for the mortgage borrowing of farmers. Their function was to meet the needs of the farmers for long-term mortgage credit on real property. The basis for their operation was the theory that there was a chronic gap in the availability of mortgage credit to the agricultural sector. In contrast, the objective of the production credit associations was to meet the short-term and intermediate-term working-capital needs of the farmers.
3. Banks for Cooperatives
   a) Banks for cooperatives sell their own debentures and make loans to cooperative production and marketing institutions.
   b) The objective is to encourage a particular form of marketing institution in the agriculture sector. The reason for this organization is the theory that there were excessive costs and charges in the distribution mechanism from the time crops left the farm until they reached the ultimate consumer.
4. Rural Electrification Administration
   Established in 1935, REA made loans for power and telephone systems for rural areas. The funds were borrowed from the Treasury at its average cost of borrowing, and, in turn, loans were made to both public agencies and private power companies and telephone companies.
5. Farmer's Home Administration
   The Farmer's Home Administration is a government agency whose activities overlap with the first and second group of lending agencies in that it provides direct loans to meet the mortgage loans and intermediate-term financing. Besides providing credit, it provides considerable counseling.
6. Commodity Credit Corporation
   a) In its operation, the agency makes crop loans on commodities. If the loan is not repaid, the agency takes over the commodity.
   b) When the loan is made initially, it is never intended that the loan be paid. The operations of the Commodity Credit Corporation represent an outright subsidy to the farmers.

B. *Housing*
1. The Federal Housing Administration (FHA) insures loans made by private lenders against default, and charges a small insurance fee for the service.
2. The Veterans Administration (VA) guarantees loans made to veterans, but, unlike the FHA, does not insure loans. It also makes direct grants to borrowers.
3. The Federal National Mortgage Association (FNMA) has the primary

function of providing a secondary market by buying and selling home mortgages.

4. The Federal Home Loan Bank System provides advances and other services for the savings and loan associations. It operates the Federal Savings and Loan Insurance Corporation, which insures deposits of savings and loan associations.

5. The Urban Renewal Administration provides federal subsidies for programs initiated by individual cities, together with private developers, to raze blighted areas and replace them with new developments.

6. The Community Facilities Administration provides loans on very favorable terms mainly to colleges and universities for dormitory and faculty housing programs.

7. Public Housing Program. The Public Housing Administration is part of the FHA. The PHA constructs public housing facilities rented below cost to persons in low-income groups.

C. *Business*

1. The Reconstruction Finance Corporation (RFC) was established in early 1932 primarily to make loans to railroads and financial institutions during the depression. It was terminated in 1953. Its later function of making direct loans to small business was taken over by the Small Business Administration.

2. The War and Defense Production programs provided for V or VT loans to firms that had government contracts. At present, loans are guaranteed by individual defense agencies acting through the federal reserve banks.

3. The Maritime Commission makes long-term loans secured by mortgages to shipping companies for the construction and purchase of vessels. The major current program involves government insurance of private loans to ship operators for vessel construction and reconversion, under Title XI of the Merchant Marine Act of 1936.

4. The Civil Aeronautics Board is authorized to guarantee any lender against loss of interest and 90 percent of principal on loans for aircraft purchases, up to a total of $5 million for each borrower, to serve short-haul airlines.

5. The Transportation Act of 1958 authorizes the Interstate Commerce Commission to guarantee loans to railroads to acquire equipment and property.

6. The Small Business Administration (1) seeks to help small firms obtain federal contracts, (2) provides management counseling, (3) makes direct loans or participating loans to provide funds to small business, and (4) makes disaster loans. The Small Business Administration provides funds for local, state, and regional development companies. The SBA also charters and makes long-term loans to small-business investment companies, which in turn provide long-term financing for small business.

7. The Federal Deposit Insurance Corporation (FDIC) provides insurance for commercial bank deposits up to $10,000 per account.

D. *International Financing*

1. The Export-Import Bank of Washington (EXIMBANK)
   a) The Export-Import Bank makes intermediate and long-term loans to American business and to foreign governments and business.
   b) The loans are mostly "tied" loans in that the money must be spent in the United States.

c) In addition, it will insure short-term financing of sales of goods against certain kinds of political risks.

2. The International Cooperation Administration (ICA) is a politically oriented program under the supervision of the State Department. It makes grants and loans primarily for the purpose of giving military and economic aid to countries threatened by the USSR.

3. The Development Loan Fund (DLF) was established in 1957. Its purpose has been to supplement the lending activity of both the intergovernmental agencies and the ICA. Loans are to be made on specific projects which demonstrate their prospective return, but the credit standards and credit terms to be employed were relatively lenient.

In 1961 Congress approved the establishment of the Agency for International Development (AID) to take over and consolidate the activities of the ICA and DLF, with emphasis on placing the economic aid program on a long-term basis.

4. The International Bank for Reconstruction and Development (IBRD) has centered on large capital loans primarily to underdeveloped countries. The loans are made on a business basis and repaid in hard currency.

5. The International Finance Corporation (IFC) invests in private firms whose expanded activities will stimulate the economic development of the area. It seeks private investment partners and sells portfolios, when seasoned, to private investors.

6. The International Development Association (IDA) is an affiliate of the IBRD and makes loans on the basis of developmental priority. Terms of loans are favorable with low interest, long maturities, and repayments in soft currencies.

7. The Inter-American Development Bank (IDB) operates on the same pattern as IDA, but specializes in loans to Latin-American countries.

The federal credit programs are presumed to supplement the private lending agencies. The government programs are supposed to fill certain credit gaps caused by inadequate competition in certain areas, to provide funds for high-risk areas, and to provide funds for activities that yield high social returns. These purposes may be illustrated by the business financing programs.

The Reconstruction Finance Corporation was established because of the drying up of funds during the recession of 1929–1932. The V or VT loans have the social purpose of aiding firms in defense activities. The maritime, small airline, and railroad credit programs are to provide funds for high-risk areas. The Small Business Administration loans are to provide funds for the high-risk area of small business, justified by some on grounds of aiding a segment of business, justified by some on grounds of aiding a segment of business with a social priority. The insurance of bank deposits represents the insurance principle of combining risks and thereby reducing the over-all risk.

The impact of the programs has been described in the following terms.[7]

---

[7] R. J. Saulnier, H. G. Halcrow, and N. H. Jacoby, *Federal Lending and Loan Insur-*

1. Most of the agencies arose to serve emergency needs or to serve special sectors of the economy, such as agriculture and housing. The programs that were established to serve emergency needs have frequently been put on a permanent basis.
2. The operations of the agencies were in part complementary to private lending sources insofar as loan insurance provisions made it possible for private lenders to enter relatively risky fields. Once having had experience in these high-risk fields, the lending firms were sometimes able to continue to lend in these areas without receiving the protection of the government insurance program.

   Government lending also broadened the areas of business lending by developing new techniques of lending, which subsequently were adopted by private agencies. Some of these techniques were the use of term lending to business firms and the development of techniques of collateralizing loans to marginal borrowers in order to reduce the risk of lending.
3. The Reconstruction Finance Corporation (now defunct) and the Federal Reserve Bank, under the so-called Section 13-B program, provided working-capital loans to business. However, the loans were of relatively short duration and did not meet the longer term financing requirements of small business.
4. Because of the restricted area in which the public agencies loaned to business, the complete financing needs of business, particularly small business, were not met. The public agencies tend to require relatively high credit standards.

The broader philosophical implications of these programs are beyond the scope of this study. Suffice it to conclude that the dollar magnitudes involved are large and that many segments of business have made use of the financing provided by the federal credit programs.

Development Credit Corporations

Development credit corporations are quasi-governmental organizations established to attract industry to a local area. They have been organized on a state-wide, regional, or city basis. Sometimes a portion of their funds and direction come from government sources. Other development credit corporations are established by civic-minded groups of businessmen. Development credit corporations were organized by regions in the early 1940s. The state-wide corporations were first organized in New England in 1949. It has been estimated that there are almost 4,000 local development companies in the United States.[8]

Basic concept. A group of civic-minded leaders forms a development credit corporation to attract new firms. The capital for the corporation is contributed by existing local business or individuals, sometimes with government contributions. An impetus to the activity of the develop-

---

ance (Princeton, N.J.: Princeton University Press, 1958), pp. 145–146. This study is part of a series of the National Bureau of Economics Financial Research Program.
8 Small Business Administration, *Capital for Community Growth*, brochure dated April 1961 (Washington, D.C.: U.S. Government Printing Office, 1961).

ment credit corporations may come from financing by the Small Business Administration of local and state development corporations. The SBA may lend a local development corporation up to $250,000 for each small business to be assisted under specified conditions.

The basic concept of the development credit corporations is to subsidize venture firms by providing them with a preferred form of financing. The development corporation will give preference to firms contributing to the economic development of the area. Development corporations are quasi-governmental agencies. Their owners consist primarily of the financial institutions and firms that provide the leadership to promote the economic development.

The bulk of the loans of development credit corporations, nearly 70 percent, is for the construction of new or expanded plants. About 20 percent of the loans is used to finance machinery and equipment purchases. Thus some 90 percent of development credit lending is in the direction of financing the acquisition of plant and equipment that will place the firms in the area permanently. The management of the development credit corporation screens applicants carefully for the purpose of stimulating the formation and expansion of firms whose operations fit into or stimulate the economic base of the region.

Operating experience. The operating experience of the development credit corporations has been relatively good thus far. Reported losses have been a small percentage of their outstanding volume. Their profits have not been large, because they have not competed with other lenders. They have sought to turn loans over to others when borrowers have developed sufficiently to become satisfactory credit risks for conventional financial institutions.

Development credit corporations charge lower than the market rate of interest. Most development corporations, despite low rates of interest, which represent a subsidy, have reported profits from their operations. In part, this has been made possible because the managements of member firms have contributed free time in credit analysis and management counsel. Typically, the corporation does not pay dividends because of the public-service aspect of its activity.

Future prospects. It is not likely that development credit corporations will expand to represent a substantial source of financing for business. They exist primarily to meet the needs of a marginal type of firm. When the firm qualifies for a regular kind of credit, it is characteristically turned over to conventional lenders. Since the main financial need of small business is for permanent working-capital financing, development credit corporations do not meet the needs of a substantial segment of small-business and venture-capital financing requirements.

TABLE 25-2

SUMMARY OF CHARACTERISTICS OF ALTERNATIVE SOURCES OF FINANCING

Source of Funds	Duration of Use of Funds	Form of Financing Supplied	Degree of Risk Taken by Source of Funds	Stability of Availability of Funds	Facilities for Mass Financing	Cost of Funds	Nature of Contact	Amount of Management Counsel
A. Commercial banks	Mainly short term, some medium	Debt	High quality	Cyclical variations	Limited	Moderate	Close	Moderate to considerable
B. Life insurance companies	Medium to long term	Mostly debt	High quality	Secular growth	Limited	Moderate	Limited but direct	Small to moderate
C. Finance companies	Continuing	Debt	Considerable	Cyclical	Considerable	Somewhat high	Close	Small to considerable
D. Mutual savings banks	Long term	Debt	Secured by real estate	Stable	None	Low	Indirect	None
E. Fire and casualty insurance companies	Long term	Debt and equity	Moderate	Variable	None	Moderate	Indirect	Small
F. Investment companies	Long term	Debt and equity	High quality	Variable	None	Small	Indirect	None
G. Pension funds	Long term	Debt and equity	High quality	Stable	None	Moderate	Indirect	None
H. Savings and loan associations	Long term	Debt	Medium to low	Stable	None	Moderately high	Direct	None
I. Educational and religious funds	Long term	Debt and equity	High quality	Variable	None	Moderate	Indirect	None

Source of Funds	Duration of Use of Funds	Form of Financing Supplied	Degree of Risk Taken by Source of Funds	Stability of Availability of Funds	Facilities for Mass Financing	Cost of Funds	Nature of Contact	Amount of Management Counsel
J. Investment development companies	Long term	Debt and equity	Moderate to high	Stable	None	Moderate to high	Direct and close	Considerable
K. Development credit corporations	Long term	Debt	Moderate to high	Stable	None	Low	Direct and close	Small to large
L. Federal lending and loan insurance	Short, medium, and long	Debt	Low to moderate	Erratic	None	Low	Direct	Small to large
M. Employees	Long term	Mostly equity	Moderate to high	Erratic	None	Moderate	Direct	None
N. Customers	Long term	Debt and equity	Moderate to high	Erratic	None	Low	Indirect	None
O. Equity markets	Permanent	Equity	Full range	Erratic	None	Varies	Indirect	None
P. Interbusiness	Short, medium, and long	Debt and equity	Continuing low to high	Variable	Small	Moderate	Close and direct	Small to considerable

SUMMARY

The financial manager has a wide variety and range of sources of financing available to him. Each form of financing has comparative advantages and disadvantages. This chapter has examined many sources of funds differing according to the nature of the financing offered by each. The cost of funds, the duration of use, the degree of risk the source of funds is willing to undertake, the dependability of the source, and the amount of management counsel provided with the funds are some of the more important characteristics to consider. A summary of significant characteristics of alternative sources of funds is set forth in Table 25-2.

The experienced financial manager will use multiple sources to meet a combination of needs. He will shift in his relative use of the different sources as the financing needs of his firm and its ability to obtain different forms of financing change. In addition, the financial manager will adapt to changes in the characteristics and policies of the financing sources, as well as to the changes in the broader economic and financial environment.

SELECTED REFERENCES

Andrews, Victor L., "The Supply of Loanable Funds from Non-Insured Corporate, State-, and City-Administered Employee Pension Trusts," *Journal of Finance, XVI* (2, May 1961), pp. 328–350.

———, "Interest Rates, Liquidity, and the Financing of Captive Finance Companies," *National Banking Review* (2, June 1965) Number 4, pp. 461–481.

Badger, S. C., "Funds in the Stock Market," *Harvard Business Review*, 34 (July–August 1956), pp. 21–34, 162–166.

Dauten, Carl A., and M. T. Welshans, "Investment Development Companies," *Journal of Finance*, 6 (September 1951), pp. 276–290.

Fergusson, D. A., "The Industrial Development Bank of Canada," *Journal of Business*, 21 (October 1948), pp. 214–238.

Hickman, W. Braddock, *Corporate Bonds: Quality and Investment Performance,* Occasional Paper 59 (New York: National Bureau of Economic Research, Inc., 1957).

Neenan, W. B., "Review of Institutional Activity in the Equity Market, 1951–54)," *Journal of Finance*, 12 (December 1957), pp. 468–488.

Silberman, C. E., "The Big Corporate Lenders," *Fortune*, 54 (August 1956), pp. 111–114.

QUESTIONS

25-1 It is reasonable for a firm to extend credit to its customers, but why should a company lend money to its own suppliers?

25-2 What is there about the nature of insurance companies that causes them to make, on the average, (1) longer term loans, and (2) larger loans, than commercial banks?

25-3 What problems are raised by the increasing purchases of equities by institutional investors?

25-4 Why do small businesses often find capital available but fail to reach an agreement with the potential suppliers of funds?

25-5 What would be the main sources of financing available to a manufacturing business just starting operations? Why are the sources limited?

25-6 Are there any reasons to believe that there will be a shortage of equity capital during the next decade?

PROBLEM

25-1 Match each firm in list 1 with the most appropriate source of financing found in list 2, and set forth the key factors determining your choice.

List 1

a) Firm selling a large volume of small- and medium-sized orders to numerous medium-sized firms. Working-capital position and ownership investment relatively small.

b) Medium-sized firm producing plastic toys. Profitability good, but dependent on independence of action by two owners. Growth good, requiring substantial investment in inventories of specialized packaging materials.

c) Medium-sized firm in growing industry. Needs a 15-to-20 year loan of $2 million; needs funds quickly; professional, financial, and business analysis indicates that the firm's outlook is promising.

d) Two scientists with strong technical competence have an idea to develop a product. Only technical experts could appraise the soundness of the idea. Need management guidance and encouragement as well as financing.

e) Large, highly reputable firm in the steel industry with expansion needs. Good credit rating with a 60 percent debt-to-equity ratio. Fairly high price-earnings ratio.

f) Firm has large seasonal needs for funds in the autumn of each year.

g) Textile firm with declining profits because of competition of lower labor costs in other regions of the United States. Considering relocation in low-cost labor areas in cities interested in attracting new industry.

List 2

1. Commercial bank
2. Investment bank
3. Life insurance company
4. Finance companies
5. Equity markets
6. Suppliers
7. Investment-development companies
8. Community-development companies
9. Friends and relatives

Part VII

Financial Strategies for Growth

Chapter 26

Mergers and Holding Companies

Growth is vital to the well-being of a firm. Without growth a firm is unable to attract able management and technical talent, because it cannot give them recognition in promotions or challenging creative activity. Without able executives, the firm is likely to decline and die.

Much of the material in the previous chapters on analysis, planning and control, and financing has direct bearing on the potential contribution of financial management to the growth of a firm. However, because of the central importance of the growth requirement, the present section is focused on strategies for promoting it.

Because merger activity plays such an important part in the growth of firms in the United States, financial management is required both to appraise the desirability of a prospective purchase or merger and to participate directly in the valuation of the respective companies involved in a merger. Consequently, it is important that the subject matter of financial management encompass material which will provide the background necessary for effective participation by financial managers in merger negotiations and decisions.

To begin with, it is important to settle matters of terminology. The combinations taking place between firms take many forms and are sometimes given special names. If firm A acquires firm B, absorbing it so that firm B disappears, what is often called a *merger* results. This might also meaningfully be called an *acquisition*. When firms A and B join to form a new firm C, what results is often called a *combination* or *consolidation*.

Many methods and techniques of bringing about interfirm relations have been employed. Though there is no general agreement on termi-

631

nology, two distinctions are generally followed. A merger is the acquisition of one firm by another in which at least one firm disappears. A consolidation occurs when, in corporate combinations, none of the constituent companies survives and a completely new company is established. This general terminology is followed in the discussion.

In dealing with financial aspects of acquisitions and mergers, the technical accounting distinction between *purchase* and *pooling of interests* will be observed. A purchase involves the acquisition by a large company of a much smaller one, with the complete absorption of the smaller into the larger. A pooling of interests is a combination involving two companies, not widely different in size, in which the identity of managements of the constituent firms is preserved and they continue to carry on important functions in the resulting firm.[1]

Financial managers need to be aware also of the broader significance of mergers. Despite the heightened merger activities in the 1920s and again after World War II, no recent merger movement has approached the order of magnitude and consequences of the mergers that took place from 1890 to 1905. The first major merger movement occurred at the turn of the century, when more than 200 combinations took place, involving amounts totaling $10 billion, a tremendous sum for the size of the economy at that time. Privately produced production in 1900 has been estimated to have been about $15 billion, only 3 percent of the $500 billion economy in 1960. The wave of mergers that took place at the turn of the century encompassed a large number of industries. Moody found that 78 of the 92 mergers he studied gained control of 50 percent or more of the output of the market. The mergers at that time gave to American industry its characteristic pattern of concentration. Regardless of the business objectives and motives of merger activity, the social and the economic consequences must also be taken into account.

BUSINESS COMBINATIONS
Large-Scale Operations

One of the objectives of the growth of firms, either by external acquisitions or by internal development, is large size for the purpose of achieving economies of large-scale operations. But it has been argued by some economists that large-scale operations achieved by mergers, resulting in multiplant and multiproduct companies, are not likely to provide economies of scale. It is said that such an operation represents activity that could be carried on as well by a number of firms as by one firm. It is sug-

---

[1] A more detailed discussion of purchases and pooling of interests is set out in the following chapter.

gested further that such mergers probably have, as their objective, market control rather than economies of scale.

Evidence on these matters is not conclusive, and more information on factual matters is needed. Nevertheless, explanations have been offered to demonstrate how multiplant and multiproduct operations may still confer significant economies of scale of operations. These are derived from the following five factors.

1. Research. Especially crucial are research activities. The large firm can finance large-scale research which may benefit a great number of its diverse operations. But suppose a large firm is broken into ten units. Could not the ten units each contract to hire research from a research organization? It is true that research in the large firm is often conducted by executives hired on a salary basis. In addition, independent research firms sell their services on a fee basis. There are some kinds of research, however, that are the unique contribution of the large firm.

Suppose a large firm that spends $50 million a year on research is divided into ten firms, each of which could allocate $5 million a year for research. If each of these ten firms hires the services of a research organization, each would attempt to buy $5 million worth of research, which would give it a competitive advantage over its nine rivals and any other firms in the industry. It seems reasonable that certain kinds of research could not effectively be purchased by the $5 million per year but could be achieved by the $50 million budget.

Modern large-scale business organizations represent the combination of centralized and decentralized decisions. Research is an activity performed most efficiently when centralized. Although the amounts of money spent on research are relatively small, their significance is critical for the progress of the firm.

2. Top-management skills. Related to indivisibility of research expenditures is the value of the highly able executive. The very competent individual is another one of the indivisible factors that make for an advantage of large-scale operations. It cannot be denied that many decisions are decentralized and that for many matters delegation of authority to committees and subordinates take place. On the other hand, some of the centralized decisions and the catalytic process of a great mind on policy matters are of pervasive and powerful influence on the growth pattern and performance of an organization.

3. Operating economies. Often there are other economies of multiproduct operations. Lower salary ratios may be achieved by consolidating certain departments (accounting, marketing, advertising, switchboard, clerical); marketing costs may be lowered by consolidating salesmen covering the same territory for several companies, thus reducing the total number of salesmen required; production savings may come from the ability to utilize by-products and other items.

4. Risk reduction. Still another important factor is the risk reduction of multiplant operations, which is heightened by the tax structure. If a new firm attempts an innovation or a new product line and fails, the loss may force it out of business completely. On the other hand, if an established firm attempts a change or an innovation, any loss can be offset against assured income from other sources. The higher the tax rate, the higher the proportion of the innovation costs borne by taxes. This is another reason why multiproduct and multiplant firms confer economic advantages, not only on the firm itself but also on the economy as a whole in terms of the potential rate of economic progress.

5. Market capitalization rates. While it is not strictly an operating economy, the fact that the earnings of larger economic units are capitalized at lower rates and hence produce higher market values has stimulated many mergers. Larger firms have better marketability, are more able to diversify and thus reduce risks, and are generally better known. All these factors cause them to sell at higher price-earnings ratios. As a result, it may be possible to consolidate firms and have the resulting market value greater than the sum of their individual values, even though there is no increase in aggregate earnings. To illustrate, three companies may each be earning $100 and selling at 10 times earnings, for a total market value of ($100)(10)(3) equals $3,000. When these companies combine, the new company may obtain a Stock Exchange listing or take other actions to improve the price of its stock. If so, the price-earnings ratio may rise to 15, in which case the market value of the consolidated firm would be $4,500.

These five factors provide a plausible rationale for the existence and operation of larger multiproduct and multiplant enterprises. Merger activity in recent years has pursued the objectives of both larger size and diversification. Since the potential benefits of large-scale operations have already been discussed, the motives and effects of diversification are now examined.

Purposes of Diversification Activity

Numerous reasons have been given for diversification activity by business. For example, one writer has cited 43 reasons for diversification activity, grouped under six major categories.[2] The many motives given for mergers can be summarized into a number of major factors.

1. Adverse secular trends. One major reason for diversification ac-

---

[2] Thomas A. Staudt, "Program for Product Diversification," *Harvard Business Review,* 32 (November–December 1954), pp. 122–123.

tivity has been evolutionary changes in the development of the economy that have brought into being new industries and have rendered some older industries obsolete. For example, the rise of the automobile and the airplane industries has had adverse effects on the growth of the railroad industry. As a consequence, the railway equipment industry suffered a substantial decline in growth. In companies such as Baldwin-Lima-Hamilton new product diversification was sought in more attractive areas. The textile industry is another example of an industry adversely affected by technological developments: the rise of synthetic materials produced adverse effects on the cotton and wool textile business.

2. **Opportunities for greater growth.** Regardless of its existing product-market areas, a firm is likely to view with envy the tremendous growth rates of the newer industries. The rise of the electronics, nuclear energy, and plastics industries has stimulated many firms to seek participation in attractive growth areas.

3. **Reduction of cyclical instability.** The capital goods or durable goods industries are subject to considerable cyclical instabilities. The capital goods area is the most volatile of all the segments in the American economy. As a consequence, companies in these areas have sought diversification into more stable lines. For example, Excello Corporation, which formerly had concentrated on machine tools, diversified into the production of machines for making milk cartons. Since milk cartons are related to the consumer nondurable industries, it was hoped that the demand for products of this kind would make the total sales of the firm more stable.

4. **Economies of purchase or distribution.** Often by rounding out product lines a firm may achieve savings by adding items that can conveniently be obtained by the same set of purchasing agents. Or economies of distribution may be achieved by adding items to lines that are already carried by salesmen in meeting the same types of customers.

5. **Vertical integration.** As an industry approaches maturity, its growth rate is likely to level off. Furthermore, because of the unfavorable developments in the relation between growth and capacity, profit margins are likely to narrow. With narrowing profit margins, a firm may seek to obtain more profits by vertical integration, either forward toward the consumer or backward by making some parts that it formerly purchased from suppliers. A clear example of the latter is the backward integration by automobile companies in recent years. This trend has had an adverse affect on manufacturers of auto parts, forcing them to seek product diversification to offset their declining automobile markets. Examples of the latter are Borg Warner and Bendix Aviation Company.

6. **Taxes.** Our tax laws have encouraged diversification activity. For example, if a firm has stable income from its existing lines of business, it is better able to bear risks of entering new areas of activity. Any losses

on the new area can be offset against the assured income from the stable areas. Thus, on any new risky activity, a company with stable income can shift half the cost of a risky venture to the corporate income tax. An example is Kern County Land, a company with a large, stable income coming from oil royalties. Kern County has made major investments in J. I. Case, a farm-machinery manufacturer; Walker Products, an auto-parts manufacturer; and other similar high-risk firms.

7. **Technological change.** A great increase in the amount of expenditures for research and development has occurred. The rise, stimulated in part by the emphasis on advanced technology in the defense program and in part by a desire to keep pace with the USSR in technological developments, has heightened the pace of technological change and of shifts between industries in the United States. As a consequence, most American firms, whether large, medium, or small, have been giving increased attention to strategies of diversification in recent years.

All diversification decisions involve allocation of funds of the firm from one area to another. Since the financial manager is responsible for handling resource application in the firm, he is expected to participate effectively and usefully in these decisions. If he is not able to do so, his role in significant top-management decisions in the firm will be diminished. It is therefore important that the financial manager understand which forms of diversification are likely to lead to successes and which forms are likely to lead to failure. He should be able to participate effectively in such analysis.

Mergers versus Internal Growth

Many of the objectives of diversification may be achieved either through internal growth or by external growth through acquisitions and mergers. In the post-World War II period considerable diversification was achieved by many firms by the external acquisition route. The reasons for utilizing external acquisition instead of, or together with, internal growth to achieve diversification may be briefly indicated.

1. **Speed.** New facilities may be acquired more quickly through mergers. New products, new processes, new plants, and new productive organizations can be purchased in their full development through acquisition or through merger. The postwar shortages gave an incentive to expansion through mergers in that acquiring firms could obtain capacity more quickly by buying individual firms than by building new plants or other facilities. This motive was undoubtedly a factor in the postwar mergers that took place in the whiskey-distilling industries.

2. **Cost.** The desired facilities may be obtained more cheaply by purchasing the ownership stock of each existing company. For many reasons the securities of a company may be selling below the replacement

costs of the firm's assets. For example, stock market prices were relatively depressed from 1946 to 1953. The market values of common stock were low in relation to earnings levels. A basis was provided for developing favorable merger terms. The stock of a company could be acquired without causing a precipitous rise in price.

Mergers in the steel industry in the period immediately following 1946 are good examples of this influence. A steel company could add new capacity much more cheaply by buying another company than by building new plants to achieve the same increase in capacity. Furthermore, the speed factor mentioned above was important here. The duration of the seller's market in steel was unknown. The sooner a steel company could acquire additional facilities and get them into operations for making sales, the more likely it would be to benefit from the favorable market conditions.

Related to the above is the objective of obtaining the services of desired personnel. Sometimes the inducement of higher compensation to attract an outstanding individual or management group might be either unduly expensive or useless. Simply buying the company that employs these people may prove to be the most effective means of obtaining their services. In such circumstances a merger may be the only practicable method of obtaining the kind of superior management talent or technical skill that the acquiring firm is seeking to obtain.

3. Financing. Sometimes it is possible to finance an acquisition when it is not possible to finance internal growth. A large steel plant, for example, involves a large investment. Steel capacity may be acquired in a merger through an exchange of stock more cheaply than it can be obtained by buying the facilities themselves. Sellers may be more willing to accept the stock of the purchaser in payment for the facilities sold than would investors in a public distribution. The use of stock reduces cash requirements for the acquisition of assets.

4. Risk. The desired new product, new process, or new organization may be developed with less uncertainty of investment loss. The purchased facility may already have demonstrated its revenue-yielding capacity. By obtaining new products and new processes through merger, the company may be able to obtain qualities that have been established as revenue-producing sources.

5. Stabilizing effects. A merger may represent the most effective method of achieving stability and progress at a given stage of industrial development. It may represent the most efficient method of combining facilities and disposing of obsolete and inefficient properties, as was probably true at some stages in the development of industries such as railroad transport, air transport, banking, agricultural implements, and steel.

6. Taxes. Without question, the high level of taxation was a factor in the postwar period. A study by a Harvard group indicated that taxes were important in the sale of about one tenth the total number of selling companies and of one fourth of these companies with total assets of more than $1 million.[3] Taxes appear to have been a major reason for the sale of about one fourth the *assets* of all companies sold and of one third the total assets of all acquired companies with assets over $1 million. Tax considerations were of less consequence in the motives of the purchaser.

7. Competitive advantages. The development of new products and market areas may be accomplished through mergers. Firms in the early stages of development can in this way avoid combating difficult competition. Market control may be obtained more rapidly and with less risk through mergers than by internal expansion. The merger of two large firms may result in market dominance by the combined firms. Coordinated price and output policies that might be illegal in separate firms may be achieved legally by a single, consolidated enterprise.

Regardless of the motives or objectives of mergers from a business standpoint, the consequences of the market-control position of the acquiring company may lead to intervention by governmental regulatory agencies. A list of mergers to which the Federal Trade Commission has raised objections during the period 1950 through 1957 is given in Table 26–1. Many of the firms involved are very large. But the significant factor is that one or more of the firms involved had a market position that was significantly influenced by the proposed merger.

Hence it is not enough for the financial manager to consider only the business aspects of the merger. He must also consider the effects on market control. If the merger will have potentially adverse affects on competition, there is a strong likelihood that government action will be interposed against the merger.

FORMS OF PURCHASE AND OWNERSHIP

The actual procedures for bringing about a corporate combination involve a number of variables. The principal variables are whether assets or stocks will be purchased, whether money or stock will be used in payment of the purchase, and, finally, whether all or part of the acquired company will be involved. The combination of the variables that have had the most significance in the history of corporate combination activity is now discussed.

[3] J. K. Butters, J. Lintner, and W. L. Cary, *Effects of Taxation: Corporate Mergers* (Boston, Mass: Division of Research, Graduate School of Business Administration, Harvard University, 1951).

TABLE 26–1

PERCENTAGE OF GROWTH IN ACQUIRER SALES

Acquirer	Acquired	Sales Acquirer	Sales Acquired	Percentage Growth in Sales
Scott Paper		$ 97		Total 78.35
	Soundview Pulp & Paper		$ 23	23.71
	Detroit Sulphite Pulp		13	13.40
	Hollingsworth & Whitney		40	41.24
Hilton Hotels	Statler Hotels	97	67	69.07
Vendo	Vendorlator	21	11	52.38
A. G. Spaulding	Rawlings Manufacturing	23	11	47.83
Brown Shoe	G. R. Kinney Co.	138	46	33.33
Bethlehem Steel	Youngstown	2,097	617	29.42
Owens-Illinois	National Container	370	95	25.68
Continental Can	Robert Gair	666	160	24.02
Union Bag & Paper	Hankin's Container	106	24	22.64
Pillsbury Mills		201		Total n.a.
	Ballard & Ballard		30	14.23
	Duff's Baking Mix Div.		n.a.	n.a.
International Paper	Long Bell Lumber	796	106	13.32
American Radiator & Sanitary Corp.	Mullins Manf.	400	51	12.75
Schenley	Park & Tilford Distilleries	421	53	12.59
Continental Can	Hazel Atlas Glass	666	80	12.01
Brillo	Williams Company	11	1	7.27
Gulf Oil	Warren Petroleum	1,896	100	5.27
Crown Zellerbach	St. Helens Pulp	253	9	3.56
General Shoe	Delman, Inc.	135	3	2.22
Scovill Manufact.	DeLong Hook & Eye	110	2	1.82
Beatrice Foods	(131 Companies)	205	n.a.	
Borden	(80 Companies)	613	n.a.	
Erie Sand & Gravel	Sandusky Div. of Kelley Island Co.	n.a.	n.a.	
Farm Journal	Better Farming	n.a.	n.a.	
Foremost Dairies	(30 Companies)	48	n.a.	
Fruehauf	Carter Manufacturing	223	n.a.	
	Brown Equipment		n.a.	
	Hobbs Mfg. & Hobbs Trailer		n.a.	
	Strict Plastic		n.a.	
	Independent Metal Products		n.a.	
Luria Brothers	Pueblo Compressed Steel	n.a.	n.a.	
	A. M. Wood & Company		n.a.	
	Lispett Inc.		n.a.	
	Apex Steel		n.a.	
	Cermack-Laflin Corp.		n.a.	
Maryland & Virginia Milk Producers	Green Spring Milk		n.a.	
Minute Maid	Snowcrop Div. of Clinton Foods	37	n.a.	
National Dairy	(39 Companies)	906	n.a.	

n.a. = not available.

Source: J. Fred Weston, "Criteria for Judging Mergers," *Proceedings of the Thirty-Second Annual Conference of the Western Economic Association,* 1957.

Purchase of Assets versus Purchase of Stock

Prior to 1950 there were strong inducements for a company to acquire the assets rather than the stock of the acquired company. The reasons for this require a brief legal and administrative background. In 1913 the Clayton Act was adopted. Sections 7 and 11 of the Clayton Act empowered the Federal Trade Commission to prohibit the acquisition by one company of the stock of another company if adverse effects on competition were likely. However, the prohibition against acquisition of other companies could effectively be avoided by purchasing the assets of a company directly or by first acquiring control of the company by purchases of stock and then subsequently arranging for purchase of assets of the acquired company. Although control of a company through stock acquisitions might be illegal, the courts held that if the acquired stock was used to absorb the assets of the company before the Federal Trade Commission could file a complaint or complete proceedings under a complaint, the acquisition was not subject to the prohibitions of the Clayton Act.[4] This loophole in the Clayton Act virtually prevented any commission controls over mergers.

After many years of effort to change Sections 7 and 11 of the Clayton Act, a law amending the sections was approved December 29, 1950. Under the amendment the Federal Trade Commission now has equal power over both kinds of acquisitions; hence, from the legal standpoint, there is no advantage to purchase of assets.

Under present circumstances, either kind of purchase (of assets or of stock) has its particular advantages. For example, if the acquiring company seeks to obtain a portion of the assets or specific assets particularly valuable or useful to the acquiring company, it can do so by the purchase of assets, but not by the purchase of stock. In addition, from a technical, legal standpoint, the acquiring company avoids all the liabilities of the sellers except encumbrances such as mortgages that may exist on the specific assets acquired by the acquiring company.

It must be recognized that the selling company will continue in existence even though a portion of its assets may have been sold. This being the case, the surviving firm may offer competition to the acquiring company, precisely in the areas where assets were acquired by the buying firm. In addition, any purchase of a significant portion of the selling company will typically require stockholder approval. Stockholders disapproving of the sale or of any of the terms of the sale may bring suit against the action taken in connection with the sale of the assets.

The advantages of purchase of the stock of a company are somewhat

---

[4] *Thatcher Mfg. Co. v. Federal Trade Commission and Swift & Co. v. Federal Trade Commission* (1926), 272 U.S. 554; *Arrow-Hart and Hegeman Electric Co. v. Federal Trade Commission* (1934), 291 U.S. 587.

different. In the first place, no formal agreement will be necessary with the company whose stock is being purchased. A firm, by buying in the open market, can simply begin to buy up the stock of the company in which it has an interest. The purchasing can proceed gradually, and perhaps without the knowledge of the company whose stock is being bought. Furthermore, after a sufficient portion of the shares of the company has been obtained, the acquiring company may gain a seat on the board of directors of the second company and subsequently complete its purchase.

Both the purchase of the assets of a company and the acquisition of the stock may proceed on a relatively informal basis. However, where more formal procedures are followed, they are referred to as a statutory merger or a statutory consolidation. The nature of these procedures is first briefly described. The nature of the holding company form of operation is then described in some detail, because it involves a significant extension of the technique of financial leverage previously described in discussions of financial structure and forms of financing.

Statutory Merger

A statutory merger or statutory consolidation results in the legal cessation of the separate existence of the participating corporations. In a statutory merger only the surviving corporation continues. In a statutory consolidation a new corporation is created. The statutory procedure provides that the surviving corporations enjoy the rights and privileges held by the constituent companies, including liabilities for their debts. The statutory procedure thus facilitates the orderly conveyance of the rights and obligations of the constituent companies.

The procedure in a statutory merger or a statutory consolidation is as follows. Typically, the major officers of the companies concerned will meet in initial discussion. They will arrive at a preliminary agreement. This agreement must be ratified by the directors of both companies. After ratification by the directors, it will be submitted to the stockholders. Typically, a two-thirds majority of common stockholders' shares will be required for ratification of the agreements.[5]

After ratification by the stockholders, the merger or consolidation becomes effective on the filing of the agreement in the office of the secretary of state of the states involved. Recording in appropriate counties of these states establishes the effective date of merger or consolidation. A certificate

---

[5] In connection with ratification of such agreements by stockholders, prospectuses are developed by the participating companies. The above discussion is based in part on the prospectuses issued in connection with the "Agreement of Merger, dated as of the 25th day of April, 1955, of Stromberg-Carlson Company with and into General Dynamics Corporation," and the "Agreement of Consolidation, dated as of April 12, 1955, between Sperry and Remington Rand."

of merger or consolidation is issued, and the terms of the agreement are thereby put into effect. No instruments of conveyance are needed, and the securities of the surviving corporation or new corporation are exchanged for those of the constituent corporations, following the terms of the agreement.

Rights of creditors. Ratification by creditors of the constituent companies is not required in order to effectuate the agreement. By and large, the rights and privileges of the creditors, however, are continued onto the surviving corporation. Some technical claims such as an after-acquired property clause or conversion privileges may, however, be modified as a consequence of the merger. Sometimes the statutes of the individual states provide for a complete carryover of the rights and privileges of creditors into the new securities issued by the new or surviving corporation.

Minority stockholders. A minority of stockholders may object to the merger on a number of grounds, often to the price set on their shares of stock. If a voluntary agreement on valuation cannot be reached, a claim will be filed in the courts, where formal procedures will be followed to arrive at a valuation of the dissenting shareholders' stock. After the courts have arrived at a value, a cash payment will be made to the dissenting stockholders. If the number of dissenting stockholders is large, the cash payment requirements may be so heavy that the consummation of the intended merger or consolidation is blocked.

The requirement of meeting the claims of dissenting stockholders is one of the barriers to complete fusion of the type described under statutory mergers and statutory consolidations. This is one among several reasons for preferring a holding company relation in which control may be obtained by investment in only a portion of the ownership shares of the controlled corporation. The nature and consequences of this form of purchase and ownership are explored in the following section.

HOLDING COMPANIES

In 1889 New Jersey became the first state to pass a general incorporation law permitting corporations to be formed for the sole purpose of owning the stocks of other companies. This law was the origin of the holding company. The Sherman Act of 1890, which prohibits combinations or collusion in restraint of trade, gave an impetus to holding company operations as well as to outright mergers and complete amalgamations, because companies could do as one company what they were forbidden to do, by the terms of the act, as separate companies.

Many of the advantages and disadvantages of holding companies are no more than the advantages and disadvantages of large-scale operations, already discussed in connection with mergers and consolidations. Whether a company is organized on a divisional basis or with the divisions kept as separate companies does not affect the basic reasons for conducting a large-scale multiproduct, multiplant operation. However, the holding company form of large-scale operations has different advantages and disadvantages from those of completely integrated divisionalized operations.

Advantages

Control with fractional ownership. Through the holding company operation a firm may buy 5, 10, or 50 percent of the stock of another corporation. Such fractional ownership may be sufficient to give the acquiring company effective working control or substantial influence over the operations of the company in which stock ownership has taken place. An article in the *New York Times* of November 16, 1958, makes this point clearly.

Working control is often considered to entail more than 25 percent of the common stock, but it can be as low as 10 percent if the stock is widely distributed. One financier says that the attitude of management is more important than the number of shares owned, adding that "if they think you can control the company, then you do." In addition, control on a very slim margin can be held through friendship with large stockholders outside the holding company group.

Sometimes holding company operations represent the initial stages of the transformation of an operating company into an investment company, particularly when the operating company is in a declining industry. When the sales of an industry begin to fall off permanently and the firm begins to liquidate its operating assets, it may use these liquid funds to place the investments of its stockholders in industries having a more favorable growth potential. An illustration of this is provided by the same *New York Times* article.

Former investment banker, Gordon W. Wattles, who holds many corporate directorships, is the architect of the pyramid built on Century Investors and Webster Investors. The former was once an aviation investment concern, while the latter began as a cigar maker.

Another advantage of obtaining control through partial ownership is the leverage that may be developed thereby, representing trading on the equity to a magnified degree. For illustration, an equity capital of some $8.4 million in Century and Webster Investors controls possibly $450 million in operating companies. Thus $1 of capital in the two top concerns may control as much as $50 in operating assets, amounting to 2 percent of the dollar value of assets controlled. In the utility holding companies in the 1920s, the degree of leverage was even greater.

Isolation of risks. Because the various operating companies in a holding company system are separate legal entities, the obligations of any one unit are separate from the obligations of the other units. Catastrophic losses incurred by one unit of the holding company system are therefore not transmitted as claims on the assets of the other units.

Though this is the customary generalization of the nature of a holding company system, it is not completely valid. In extending credit to one of the units of a holding company system, an astute financial manager or credit manager will look through the holding company veil and require a guarantee or a claim on the assets of all of the elements in a complete holding company system. Therefore, to some degree, the assets in the various elements of a holding company are joined. The advantage remains to the extent that unanticipated catastrophies which may occur to one unit in a holding company system will not be transmitted to the other units.

Approval not required.   If a holding company group is seeking to obtain effective working control of a number of companies, it may quietly purchase a portion of the stock of the companies in which it is interested. This is a completely informal operation; the permission or approval of the stockholders of the acquired company or companies is not required. Thus the guiding personalities in a holding company operation are not dependent upon negotiations and approval of the other interest groups, in order to obtain their objectives.

Disadvantages

Partial multiple taxation.   Provided the holding company owns at least 80 percent of a subsidiary's voting stock, it is permitted to deduct the entire amount of dividends received from the affiliate. However, if less than 80 percent stock is owned, only 85 percent of the dividends may be deducted. With a tax rate of 48 percent, this means that the effective tax on intercorporate dividends is 7.2 percent. This partial double taxation somewhat offsets the benefits of holding company control with limited ownership, but whether the penalty of 7.2 percent of dividends received is sufficient to offset other possible advantages is a matter that must be decided in individual situations.

Risks of excessive pyramiding.   While pyramiding magnifies profits if the operations are successful, as was seen in the trading-on-the-equity analysis, it also magnifies losses. The greater the degree of pyramiding, the greater the degree of risk involved for any degree of fluctuations in sales or earnings of the company. This is one of the potential disadvantages of pyramiding operations through holding companies.

Ease of legal dissolution.   In a holding company operation that falls into disfavor with the Department of Justice of the United States Government, it is relatively easy to require dissolution of the relation by disposition of stock ownership. A clear case in point is the recent requirement that du Pont dispose of its 23 percent stock interest in General Motors Corporation. The acquisition took place in the early 1920s. Because there was no fusion between the corporations, there were no difficulties, from an operating standpoint, in requiring the separation of the two companies.[6] On the other hand, if complete amalgamation had taken place, it would have been much more difficult to break up the company after years had elapsed.

PUBLIC UTILITY HOLDING COMPANIES

No discussion of holding companies would be complete without a review of the use of holding companies by public utilities. Many of the lessons, advantages, and dangers of holding company operations are exhibited in an exaggerated form in the public utility area.

Advantages

The original conception of holding companies in the public utility field was sound. The public utility area was one in which the technology was advancing rapidly during the 1920s. A public utility holding company could obtain distinct advantages.

Operating economies. By the use of staffs of top engineers and highly qualified experts in the legal and operating areas, the parent holding company can provide very valuable services to the operating company. In addition, by integrated operations, the peak-load problems of one area can be met from the resources of other divisions of the holding company system; thus the volume of operations can be regularized.

Facility in financing. The parent holding company, because of its large size and because it is well known, is able to obtain financing for all the members of the holding company system on terms that are more favorable than any single operating unit can obtain. There are economies of scale in financing. Furthermore, a body of experts can be assembled to analyze the capital market and to develop forms of securities that can be successfully marketed.

Capital gains associated with growth. The 1920s were a period of rapid growth for the utility industry. Operating companies purchased in the early 1920s increased in value greatly with the growth of the industry, with substantial gains to controlling interests. These profits led to vigorous competition in bidding, driving up the price of operating companies to the point where many years of future growth were represented in the purchase prices.

The utility holding company systems were originally based on the sound business concept that the parent company could bring together ex-

---

6 Complex problems arose from the ruling that proceeds from the divestiture of shares would be taxed to du Pont shareholders as ordinary income.

pert engineers, lawyers, and others, who could effectively serve all members of a system. The overbidding on stock and properties created unsound conditions, which resulted in numerous abuses.

Abuses

The nature of abuses in the public utilities holding company field may be summarized briefly.[7]

Properties overvalued. Since the parent company purchased the assets of the operating company by using its own common stock, preferred stock, or bonds, arbitrary values could be set on both the assets and the securities. Much "watering" of securities consequently took place.

Excessive charges made for advisory services. The basic theory of the holding company operation of providing specialized technical services to operating companies was distorted. The charges made did not always meet the test of the market place in setting prices and were sometimes so high that they reduced the normal profits of the operating companies.

Excessive intercompany profits taken on construction activities. The operating companies established to provide construction services were not required to compete with independent outsiders. They made excessive charges to other members of the holding company system.

Excessive "upstream" loans made. One of the advantages of a holding company system is that the parent, because it is large and well known, may be able to float securities under more favorable terms than those the individual operating companies would be able to command. However, one of the ways in which high values on securities could be established was by the payment of cash dividends by the parent company. Since the parent company sometimes did not in fact achieve profits, dividends were sometimes paid by means of liquid assets acquired through borrowings by the parent companies from the operating companies. This was the process of milking the operating companies by means of loans made "upstream" from the operating company to the holding company.

Excessive leverage used in capital structures. Small profits of operating companies could result in tremendously high rates of return for the parent holding company. However, since high debt-leverage ratios were employed, even a temporary decline in operating profits would be magnified into substantial losses at the higher levels of the holding company system. Since the operating companies were often bought at substantial premiums over book or current reproduction values, the earning on the inflated values would be small initially and vulnerable to complete erosion, if the extreme leverage factor moved adversely.

---

[7] See selections 2, "Ivar Kreuger," and 27, "Through the Wringer with A. G. & E.," appearing in *Readings in Finance from* Fortune (New York: Holt, Rinehart and Winston, 1958), pp. 3–6, 91–95.

Leverage in Holding Companies

The problem of excessive leverage is worthy of further note. An illustration of the nature of leverage is set forth in Figure 26–1, which illustrates the chain of control by the Insull interests, December 31, 1930. A numerical analysis of these relations is set forth in Table 26–2.

TABLE 26–2

EQUITY IN OPERATING COMPANY AT BOTTOM OF PYRAMID OWNED BY SUCCESSIVE HOLDING COMPANY ABOVE IT

(Based on Book Values of Securities of the Specified Companies as of December 31, 1930*)

Company or Interest	Percentage of Total Securities of Specified Company Constituted by Its Voting Stock	Percentage of Voting Stock of Specified Company Owned by Company Next above It	Percentage of Total Securities of Specified Company Owned by Company Next above It	Percentage of Total Securities of Operating Company at Bottom of Pyramid Owned by Specified Company†
Insull Interests‡				0.05
Corporation Securities Co. of Chicago and Insull Utility Investments, Inc. . . .	69.7	66.0§	46.0	.10
Middle West Utilities Co. . . .	80.4	28.1	22.6	.45
National Electric Power Co. . .	19.1	99.0	18.9	2.40
National Public Service Corporation	7.9	93.0	7.3	32.90
Seaboard Public Service Co. . .	72.3	100.0	72.3	45.5
Florida Power Corporation . .	45.5	100.0	45.5	100.00
West Florida Power Co.	100.0	100.0	100.0	

* *Source:* Utility Corporation 72A, Securities and Exchange Commission, p. 160.

† Product of figures in columns 3 and 4 carried to the company next above. The figures in this column represent the equity in the bottom company owned at each level.

‡ Insull family: Insull companies, their officers and directors, and Halsey Stuart & Co.

§ Insull interests as of November 21, 1931, owned 62 percent and 69.3 percent, respectively, of the total number of shares of voting stock of Utility Investments, Inc., and Corporation Securities Company of Chicago. The percentage given in the table (66.0) was computed from combined totals for the two companies.

Source: Hiram L. Jome, *Corporation Finance* (New York: Holt, Rinehart and Winston, 1948), p. 644. (Out of print).

This analysis shows that the Insull interests controlled operating companies at the bottom of the pyramid by a $\frac{1}{20}$ of 1 percent investment. As

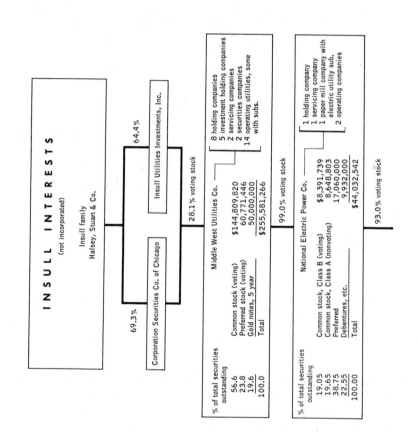

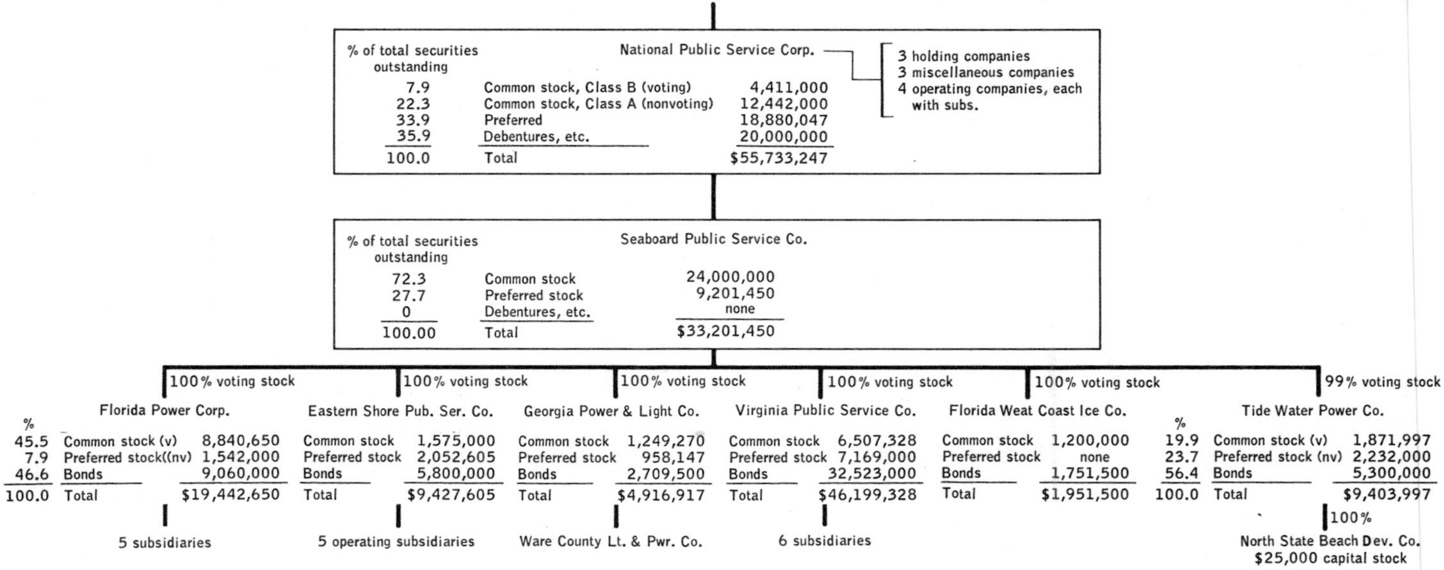

National Public Service Corp.

% of total securities outstanding		
7.9	Common stock, Class B (voting)	4,411,000
22.3	Common stock, Class A (nonvoting)	12,442,000
33.9	Preferred	18,880,047
35.9	Debentures, etc.	20,000,000
100.0	Total	$55,733,247

3 holding companies
3 miscellaneous companies
4 operating companies, each with subs.

Seaboard Public Service Co.

% of total securities outstanding		
72.3	Common stock	24,000,000
27.7	Preferred stock	9,201,450
0	Debentures, etc.	none
100.00	Total	$33,201,450

Tide Water Power Co. — 99% voting stock

	%	
Common stock (v)	19.9	1,871,997
Preferred stock (nv)	23.7	2,232,000
Bonds	56.4	5,300,000
Total	100.0	$9,403,997

North State Beach Dev. Co. — 100%
$25,000 capital stock

Florida Weat Coast Ice Co. — 100% voting stock

Common stock	1,200,000
Preferred stock	none
Bonds	1,751,500
Total	$1,951,500

Virginia Public Service Co. — 100% voting stock

Common stock	6,507,328
Preferred stock	7,169,000
Bonds	32,523,000
Total	$46,199,328

6 subsidiaries

Georgia Power & Light Co. — 100% voting stock

Common stock	1,249,270
Preferred stock	958,147
Bonds	2,709,500
Total	$4,916,917

Ware County Lt. & Pwr. Co.

Eastern Shore Pub. Ser. Co. — 100% voting stock

Common stock	1,575,000
Preferred stock	2,052,605
Bonds	5,800,000
Total	$9,427,605

5 operating subsidiaries

Florida Power Corp. — 100% voting stock

%		
45.5	Common stock (v)	8,840,650
7.9	Preferred stock((nv)	1,542,000
46.6	Bonds	9,060,000
100.0	Total	$19,442,650

5 subsidiaries

Fig. 26–1. Holding Company System of Insull Interests, December 31, 1920

Source: Hiram L. Jome, *Corporation Finance,* pp. 642–643. (New York: Holt, Rinehart and Winston, 1948.)

a ratio, this represents $\frac{1}{2000}$. In other words, $1 of capital at the top holding company level controlled $2,000 of assets at the operating level. To put it another way, $100,000 of assets at the holding company level controlled $200 million worth of assets at the operating level. A similar situation obtained in the railroad field. It has been stated that Robert R. Young, with an investment of $254,000, obtained control of the Allegheny system consisting of total operating assets of $3 billion.

The nature of leverage in a holding company system and its advantages and disadvantages are set forth by the hypothetical example developed in Table 26–3. As in the previous examples, although this is a

TABLE 26–3

LEVERAGE IN A HOLDING COMPANY SYSTEM

Holding Company 2			
Common stock B of holding company 1	5,000	Debt	2,000
		Preferred stock	1,000
		Common stock A* . . .	1,000
		Common stock B	1,000
Holding Company 1			
Common stock B of operating company	100,000	Debt	50,000
		Preferred stock	10,000
		Common stock A* . . .	30,000
		Common stock B	10,000
Operating Company			
Total assets	2,000,000	Debt	1,000,000
		Preferred stock	150,000
		Common stock A* . . .	650,000
		Common stock B	200,000

* Common stock A is nonvoting.

hypothetical case, it is chosen to illustrate, by the use of rounded numbers, actual situations. Further leverage could, of course, have been postulated in this situation by setting up a third company to own the common stock B of holding company 2 and, in turn, to sell securities in order to finance its ownership.

Table 26–4 shows the results of holding company leverage on gains and losses of the controlled group. In the first column it is assumed that the operating company earns 12 percent on its $2 million of assets before taxes of 50 percent, while in the second column it is assumed that the return on assets is 8 percent.

A return of 12 percent on the operating assets of $2 million gives a

TABLE 26–4

RESULTS OF HOLDING COMPANY LEVERAGE ON GAINS AND LOSSES

Assume that each company pays:	4% on debt
	5% on preferred stock
	8% on common stock A

	Earnings before Taxes	
Operating Company	*12%*	*8%*
Amount earned	240,000	 160,000
Less: Tax*	100,000	 60,000
Available to meet fixed charges . .	140,000	 100,000
Debt interest	40,000	 40,000
Preferred stock	7,500	 7,500
Common stock A	52,000	 52,000
Total charges	99,500	 99,500
Available to common B	40,500	 500
Dividends to common B	40,000	 500
Holding Company 1		
Amount earned	20,000	 250
Less: Tax (0.5 × 0.15 × $18,000)*	1,350	 0
Available to meet fixed charges . .	18,650	 250
Debt interest	2,000	 2,000
Preferred stock	500	 500
Common stock A	2,400	 2,400
Total charges	4,900	 4,900
Available to common B	13,750	loss
Dividends to common B	10,000	
Holding Company 2		
Amount earned	5,000	
Less: Taxes (0.5 × 0.15 × $4,920)*	369	
Available to meet fixed charges . .	4,631	
Debt interest	80	
Preferred stock	50	
Common stock A	80	
Total	210	
Available to common B	4,421	
Percent return on common B . . .	442%	

* Tax computed on earnings less interest charges at a 50% rate.

profit of $240,000. The debt interest of $40,000 would be deductible from this amount, and the 50 percent rate would be applied to the remainder. The amount available to common stock after payment of debt interest, preferred stock interest, and an 8 percent return to the nonvoting common stock A is $40,500. Assuming a $40,000 dividend payout, the amount earned on the assets of holding company 1 would be $20,000. If the same kind of analysis were followed through, the amount available to the common stock B in holding company 2 would be $4,421. This return is on an investment of $1,000, representing a return on the investment in common stock B of holding company 2 of about 440 percent. The power of leverage in a holding company system was indeed great.

On the other hand, if, because of a decline in revenues, the pretax earnings dropped to 8 percent of the total assets of the operating company, the results would be disastrous. The amount earned under these circumstances is $160,000. After deducting the bond interest, the amount subject to tax is $120,000, resulting in a tax of $60,000. The aftertax earnings would be $100,000. The total prior charges would be $99,500, leaving $500 available to common stock B. If all earnings were paid out in dividends to common stock B, the earnings of holding company 1 would be $250. This would not be enough to meet the debt interest. The holding company system would be forced to default on the debt interest of holding company 1.

This example, which is based on the prototype of the Midwest Utilities system, illustrates the potentiality for tremendous gains in a holding company system. It also illustrates how a small decline in earnings on the assets of the operating companies would be disastrous. Because of the resulting large losses in security values in the upper layers of the holding company system, considerable investor losses actually did take place, resulting in a widespread feeling that fraud had been involved.

The trial of Samuel Insull, Sr., for example, took place because of complaints that fraud had been perpetrated. The verdict of the trial, however, concluded that though business mistakes may have been made, fraud was not involved. As long as the sales and revenues of the operating companies were high, the profits at all levels of operations were favorable. The depression of 1929–1932 interrupted the underlying growth trend in revenues with resulting disaster in the utility holding systems.

Although holding companies offer the potential opportunity of controlling other companies with only partial ownership, in a high percentage of industrial companies the parent company owns virtually all the stock of the subsidiary. One of the reasons for the high percentage of ownership is the legal requirement that the parent own at least 80 percent of the stock of the subsidiary, to be permitted to receive dividends without being taxed on them. Unless the subsidiary is at least 80 percent owned, the parent must pay a 7.2 percent tax on dividends received.

Public Utility Holding Company Act of 1935

The public utility holding company operations generally did not involve outright fraud; nevertheless, abuses were involved. These abuses led to the enactment of the Public Utility Holding Company Act of 1935, which provided for the following:

1. Ownership of 10 percent or more of the voting stock of an operating electric or retail gas utility company by another corporation constitutes holding company status, requiring registration with the SEC. All business methods and financial transactions of registrants are regulated by the SEC, including approval by the SEC of all security issues.

2. The "death sentence" clause provided for integrated geographic operations. Each system was to be in a single, unified area and not so large as to "impair the advantages of localized management."

3. Simplification of capital structures was provided for, and the "grandfather clause" limited the corporate levels to three. An operating company could have a "father" and a "grandfather" but not a "great-grandfather."

Companies with assets totaling more than $15 billion were affected by the subsequent administration of the act by the SEC. To achieve integrated operations and simplified capital structures required transfers of securities and property worth approximately $12 billion. The adjustments involved in transfers of this magnitude were not accomplished painlessly; they resulted in complaints and recriminations by companies affected.

BANK HOLDING COMPANY ACT OF 1956

A recent piece of legislation affecting the operation of holding companies has been applied to the banking business. Activities in this area led to the Bank Holding Company Act of 1956. It contained the following leading provisions:

1. No bank holding company may own nonbanking assets.

2. Existing bank holding companies that hold bank assets may continue to do so. However, the formation of new bank holding companies owning 25 percent or more of two banks requires a permit from the Board of Governors of the Federal Reserve System.

3. A merger or consolidation of any two bank holding companies requires prior consent from the Board of Governors of the Federal Reserve System.

4. Bank holding companies may no longer hold stock in banks located outside the state in which the bank holding company conducts its main operations. Thus a bank holding company may no longer cross state lines unless the state in which it seeks to go has specifically granted these powers. To date, no state has acted affirmatively.

5. The act prohibits a bank holding company from borrowing funds from the subsidiary bank (upstream lending). It also prohibits a subsidiary bank from

lending to another subsidiary in the same system (horizontal lending). However, it does not forbid borrowing of funds by the subsidiary from the parent bank.

The enactment of the Bank Holding Company Act of 1956 is much too recent to enable an evaluation on the basis of experience. The potential abuses of intersystem lending between nonbank and bank elements in a bank holding system are easy to visualize. It was because of these potential abuses that the act was passed. However, it appears that little evidence existed that the abuses feared had actually occurred in banking operations.

SUMMARY

Some distinctions in terminology were noted. In a merger, firm A acquires firm B, absorbing B, so that only firm A remains. When firm A joins firm B, forming a new firm C, the combination is referred to as a consolidation. From the standpoint of financial treatment, the distinction is between a purchase and a pooling of interests. A purchase is the acquisition by a large company of a smaller one; the larger company completely absorbs the smaller. Pooling of interests is a combination of companies of comparable size in which the managements continue to carry on important functions.

Business combinations may lead to large sized firms, which in turn may provide economies of operations. Or combinations can be used to achieve diversification, with possible advantages. Mergers, rather than internal development, may be used to achieve diversification for a number of reasons: greater speed, lower cost, less cash required, less risk, avoidance of duplicate facilities, reduction of number of competitors, and tax advantages.

External acquisitions may take a number of forms. The purchase of assets permits obtaining specific assets sought. It avoids all legal liabilities of the selling firm except encumbrances attached to the specific assets acquired. Formal approval of the selling firm is required.

Stock purchases may be accomplished on the open market without formal agreement with the acquired company. A statutory merger results in legal cessation of the separate existence of the constituent corporations. Stock purchases without the statutory procedures will continue the separate existence of the companies, sometimes in a holding company relation.

The holding company form has advantages and disadvantages. It permits control of an operating entity with only fractional ownership. In this way it permits increased financial leverage and isolates risks of the operations of the individual entities. It results in partial multiple taxation. Tendencies toward excess pyramiding may also result. The strengths and weaknesses of holding companies were exhibited in an exaggerated form in the public utility field, resulting in the Public Utility Holding Company Act of 1935, which regulates the nature and forms of holding company operations in the field. More recent legislation has reflected concern about holding company operations combining ownership of both banking and nonbanking companies.

SELECTED REFERENCES

Ansoff, H. Igor, and J. Fred Weston, "Merger Objectives and Organization Structure" *Quarterly Review of Economics and Business* (August 1962), pp. 49–58.

Austin, Douglas V., "A Defense of the Corporation Pirate," *Business Horizons* (Winter 1964), pp. 51–58.

Bock, Betty, *Mergers and Markets* (New York: National Industrial Conference Board, Inc., 1962, 1964).

Bonbright, J. C., "Holding Companies," *Encyclopedia of the Social Sciences*, 7, pp. 403–409.

Butters, J. Keith, John Lintner, William L. Cary, and Powell Niland, *Effects of Taxation: Corporate Mergers* (Boston: Division of Research, Graduate School of Business Administration, Harvard University, 1951).

"A Case Study in Corporate Acquisition," Financial Management Series, No. 115 (New York: American Management Association, 1957).

Cook, P. W., Jr., "Trends in Merger Activity," *Harvard Business Review*, 37 (March–April 1959), pp. 15–18.

Drayton, Clarence I., Jr., Craig Emerson, and John D. Griswold, *Mergers and Acquisitions: Planning and Action* (New York: Financial Executives Research Foundation, Inc., 1963).

Federal Trade Commission, *Report on Corporate Mergers and Acquisitions* (Washington, D.C.: U.S. Government Printing Office, 1955).

Gort, Michael, *Diversification and Integration in American Industry* (Princeton, N.J.: Princeton University Press, 1962).

Integration Policies and Problems in Mergers and Acquisitions, Financial Management Series, No. 113 (New York: American Management Association, 1957).

Kaplan, A. D. H., "The Current Merger Movement Analyzed," *Harvard Business Review*, 33 (May–June 1955), pp. 91–98.

"Legal, Financial and Tax Aspects of Mergers and Acquisitions," Financial Management Series, No. 114 (New York: American Management Association, 1957).

Lintner, John, and J. Keith Butters, "Effect of Mergers on Industrial Concentration, 1940–47," *Review of Economics and Statistics*, 32 (February 1950), pp. 30–48.

Mace, Myles L., and George G. Montgomery, Jr., *Management Problems of Corporate Acquisitions* (Boston: Harvard University, 1962).

Tincher, William R., "Yardsticks for Evaluating Corporate Acquisitions," *Management Review* (October, 1964), pp. 33–45.

Weston, J. Fred, "The Recent Merger Movement," *Journal of Business*, 25 (January 1952), pp. 31–38.

———, *Planning for Corporate Merger* (Los Angeles: Division of Research, Graduate School of Business Administration, University of California, Los Angeles, 1963).

———, *The Role of Mergers in the Growth of Large Firms* (Berkeley: University of California Press, 1953).

——— (ed.), *Financial Management in the 1960s: New Challenges and Responsibilities* (New York: Holt, Rinehart and Winston, Inc., 1966); selections "The Chief Shows Them How at Indian Head," "Textron: How to Manage a Conglomerate," "Under Marion Harper's Big Tent," and "The Unfinished Job at W. R. Grace."

QUESTIONS

26-1 The number of mergers tends to fluctuate with business activity, rising as GNP rises and falling when production falls. Why does this relationship exist?

26–2   A large firm has certain advantages over a smaller firm. What are some of the *financial* advantages of large size?

26–3   What are some of the potential benefits that can be expected by a firm which merges with a company in a different industry?

26–4   What particular abuses led to the formation of the Public Utility Holding Company Act of 1935?

26–5   Mergers can often be important to rapidly growing firms. How?

26–6   Distinguish between holding companies and operating companies. Give an example of each.

26–7   Which appears to be more risky, the use of debt in the holding company's capital structure or debt in the operating company? Why?

26–8   Is the public interest served by an increase in merger activity? Give arguments both pro and con.

PROBLEMS

26–1   Given the following balance sheets:

H COMPANY

CONSOLIDATED BALANCE SHEET

Cash	$ 800	Borrowings	$ 600
Other current assets	600	Common stock	1,000
Net property	1,000	Surplus	800
Total assets	$2,400	Total claims on assets . .	$2,400

A COMPANY

BALANCE SHEET

Current assets	$200	Net worth	$400
Net property	200		
Total assets	$400	Total net worth . . .	$400

1. The holding company, H, buys the operating company, A, with "free" cash of $400. Show the new consolidated balance sheet for H after the acquisition.

2. Instead of buying A, H Company now buys operating company B with free cash of $600. The balance sheet of B Company follows:

B COMPANY

BALANCE SHEET

Current assets	$ 400	Borrowings	$ 400
Net property	600	Net worth	600
Total assets	$1,000	Total claims in assets . .	$1,000

Show the new consolidated balance sheet for H after the acquisition.

3. What are the implications of your consolidated balance sheets for measuring the growth of firms resulting from acquisitions?

26–2   H Company is a holding company owning the entire common stock of Minor Company and Operating Company. The balance sheet as of December 31, 1966, for each subsidiary is identical with the following one.

BALANCE SHEET
December 31, 1966

Assets		*Liabilities*	
Current assets	$2,400,000	Current liabilities . . .	$ 600,000
Fixed assets, net	3,600,000	First mortgage bonds	
		(4%)	2,000,000
		Preferred stock (5%) . .	1,000,000
		Common stock (par	
		$10)	2,000,000
		Surplus	400,000
Total assets	$6,000,000	Total claims on assets	$6,000,000

Each company earns $660,000 annually before taxes and before interest and preferred dividends. A 50 percent tax rate is assumed.

1. What is the annual rate of return on each company's net worth (common stock plus surplus)?
2. You are to construct a balance sheet for H Company based on the following assumptions. The common stocks of Minor and Operating are the only important assets of H Company. These are carried at par value. The holding company should earn 16 to 20 percent on its common stock outstanding. Debt pays 4 percent; preferred stock pays a 6 percent dividend. What will the firm's rate of return be based on your balance sheet?
3. How could the rate of return in part 2 be increased?
4. What investment is necessary to control the three companies under the assumptions of the initial conditions?

26-3 "The average percentage growth in the assets of the acquiring company per acquisition was regularly and substantially smaller for larger buyers than for smaller buyers.
"The disproportionately small relative contribution of mergers to the assets of large acquiring companies was highly regular, not only for all manufacturing and mining, but for all durable and nondurable manufacturers separately and for each of the 10 major manufacturing groups in which 80 or more mergers occurred during the period. Moreover, this same relation is found in equally regular and dramatic form within the 1,000 largest manufacturing companies, and it is found quite consistently when this list is broken down into the separate industry groups listed above. Manifestly, the average acquisitions made by larger firms were much less important to them, in terms of relative assets, than the average acquisitions of smaller companies."[8]

Evaluate the conclusions drawn in the last sentence.

---

[8] Butters, J. Keith, John Lintner, William L. Cary, and Powell Niland, *Effects of Taxation: Corporate Mergers* (Boston: Division of Research, Graduate School of Business Administration, Harvard University, 1951), pp. 263–264.

AVERAGE PERCENTAGE GROWTH PER ACQUISITION
IN ASSETS OF ACQUIRING COMPANIES
(by industry and size class, acquiring company)*

| | Asset-Size Class of Acquirer (millions of dollars) | | | | | | |
Industrial Group	Over 100	50–100	10–50	5–10	1–5	Under 1	All Sizes Combined
Manufacturing and mining	0.5%	4.0%	7.8%	17.8%	34.7%	122.4%	1.8%
Manufacturing	0.5	4.0	7.9	18.0	34.7	124.3	1.8
Durable manufacturing . .		1.1%	7.7	18.9	33.4	†	2.2
Primary metals		0.6	9.8	24.5%		†	0.9
Fabricated metals . . .		1.1	6.6	17.7		†	3.2
Nonelectrical machinery		0.9	4.3	21.5		†	4.1
Electrical machinery . .		1.7	16.1	34.7		†	5.0
Transportation equipment		2.9	9.5	34.3		†	4.4
Other durables		1.1	3.6	18.1		†	2.9
Nondurable manufacturing		0.6	8.1	17.3	36.1	†	1.5
Foods		0.6	7.5	20.4		†	1.3
Textiles		4.5	8.0	38.4		†	8.1
Paper		1.1	7.2	14.7		†	4.2
Chemicals		1.2	4.6	11.9		†	1.9
Petroleum and coal . .		0.3	22.7	32.5		†	0.6
Other nondurables . .		1.1	9.3	23.0		†	5.8
Mining		4.0	3.0	21.7		†	4.8

* The assets of acquiring companies were taken from the most recent balance sheet as of the date of each individual acquisition.
† Not significant because of small number of reported cases.

Chapter 27

Financial Aspects of Mergers

The previous chapter presented the nature of, the motives behind, and some effects of, various types of business combinations. The present chapter centers on the financial terms and consolidation procedures involved in these combinations.

TERMS OF MERGERS

For every merger actually consummated, a number of other potentially attractive combinations fail during the negotiating stage. In some of these cases, negotiations are broken off when it is revealed that the companies' operations are not compatible. In others, tangible benefits would result, but the parties are unable to agree on the merger terms. Of these terms, the most important is the price paid by the acquiring firm for the firm acquired, or the percentage distribution of shares when a consolidation takes place. Factors that influence this important aspect of a merger are now considered.

A merger carries potentialities for either favorable or adverse effects on earnings, market prices of shares, or both. Previous chapters have shown that investment decisions should be guided by the effects on market values and that these effects should in turn be determined by the effects on future earnings and dividends. These future events are difficult to forecast, however, so stockholders as well as management give considerable weight to the immediate effects of a contemplated merger on earnings per share. Directors of companies will often state, "I do not know how the merger may affect the market prices of the shares of my company, because so many forces influencing market prices are at work. But the effect on earnings per share can be seen directly."

An example will illustrate the effects of a proposed merger on earnings per share and suggest the kinds of problems that are likely to arise. Assume the following facts for two companies:

	Company A	Company B
Total earnings	$20,000	$50,000
Number of shares of common stock	5,000	10,000
Earnings per share of stock	$ 4.00	$ 5.00
Price-earnings ratio per share	15X	12X
Market price per share	$ 60.00	$ 60.00

Suppose the firms agree to merge, with B acquiring the shares of A by a one-for-one exchange of stock, the exchange ratio being determined by the respective market prices of the two companies. Assuming no increase in earnings, the effects on earnings per share are shown in the following tabulation:

		Earnings per Share	
	Shares of Company B Owned after Merger	Before Merger	After Merger
A's stockholders	5,000	$4	$4.67
B's stockholders	10,000	5	4.67
Total	15,000		

Since total earnings are $70,000 and a total of 15,000 shares will be outstanding after the merger has been completed, the new earnings per share will be $4.67. Earnings will increase by 67 cents for A's stockholders, but they will decline by 33 cents for B's.

The effects on market values are less certain. If the combined companies sell at the 15 times price-earnings ratio of company A, the new market value per share of the new company will be $70. In this case shareholders of both companies will have benefited. This result comes about because the combined earnings are now valued at a multiplier of 15, whereas prior to the merger a portion of the earnings was valued at a multiplier of 15 and a portion valued at a multiplier of 12.

If, on the other hand, the earnings of the new company are valued at the multiplier of 12 of company B, the indicated market value of the shares will be $56. The shareholders of both companies will have suffered a $4 dilution in market value.

Because the effects on market value per share are less certain than those on earnings per share, the impact on earnings per share tends to be given greater weight in merger negotiations. The following analysis will also emphasize effects on earnings per share, while recognizing that maximizing market value is the valid rule for investment decisions.

If the merger takes place on the basis of earnings, neither earnings dilution nor earnings appreciation will take place. This follows from the results shown below:

	Shares of Company B Owned after Merger	Earnings per Old Share Before Merger	Earnings per Old Share After Merger
A shareholders[1]	4,000	$4	$4
B shareholders	10,000	$5	$5
Total	14,000		

It is clear that the equivalent earnings per share after the merger are the same as before the merger. The effects on market values will depend upon whether the 15-times multiplier of A or the 12-times multiplier of B obtains.

Of the numerous factors affecting the valuation of the constituent companies in a merger, all must ultimately be reflected in the earnings per share or market price of the companies. Hence, all the effects on the earnings position or wealth position of stockholders are encompassed by the foregoing example. The discussion may, therefore, turn to a consideration of the factors that will influence the terms on which an acquisition or a merger is likely to take place. Both quantitative and qualitative factors receive consideration.

Quantitative Factors Affecting Terms of Merger

Five factors have received the greatest emphasis in arriving at merger terms:

Earnings	Market values
Dividends	Book values
Net current assets	

Analysis is typically based on the per share values of the foregoing factors. The relative importance of each factor and the circumstances under which each is likely to be the most influential determinant in arriving at terms will vary. The nature of these influences is now described.

Earnings. Earnings are important in determining the values that

---

1 Based on earnings, the exchange ratio is 4:5; that is, company A's shareholders receive four shares of B's stock for each five shares of A stock they own. Earnings per share of the merged company is $5, but since A's shareholders now own only 80 percent of the number of their old shares, their equivalent earnings per *old* share is the same $4.

will be established in a merger, because the future income from an asset determines its present worth. An estimate of earnings and the determination of an appropriate capitalization factor are needed. The analysis must necessarily begin with historical data on earnings achieved by the firm. In the evaluation of these earnings, their past growth rate, their future trend, and their variability are all important factors that will influence the capitalization factor or multiplier to be employed.

A clear illustration of how the analysis of earnings must be focused into an estimate of future growth rates and of how these affect the multiplier that will be employed can be illustrated by an extension of the preceding example. In previous chapters it has been shown that price-earnings ratios are related to expected growth rates. Since company A had the higher P/E ratio, it is reasonable to assume that its earnings may be expected to grow more rapidly than those of company B.

Suppose A's expected growth rate is 10 percent and B's five percent. Looking at the proposed merger from the point of view of company B and its stockholders and assuming that the exchange ratio is based on present market prices, it is seen that B will suffer a dilution in earnings when the merger occurs. However, B will be acquiring a firm with more favorable growth prospects; hence its earnings after the merger should increase more rapidly than before. In fact, the new growth rate turns out to be a weighted average of the growth rates of the individual firms, weighted by their respective total earnings before the merger. In the example, the new expected growth rate is 6.43 percent.

With the new growth rate it is possible to determine just how long it will take company B's stockholders to regain the earnings dilution; that is, how long it will take earnings per share to be back to where they would have been without the merger. This can be determined graphically from Figure 27–1.[2] Without the merger, B would have initial earnings of $5 per share, and these earnings would have grown at a rate of 5 percent per year. With the merger, there is an initial earnings dilution to $4.67 per share, but the rate of growth increases to 6.43 percent. Under these conditions the earnings dilution is overcome after five years; from the fifth year on, earnings will be higher, assuming the merger is consummated.

This same type of relationship could be developed from the point of view of the faster growing firm. Here there would be an immediate earnings increase but a reduced rate of growth. Working through the analysis would show the number of years before the earnings accretion had been eroded.

---

[2] The calculation could also be made algebraically by solving for N in the following equation: $E_1(1 + g_1)^N = E_2(1 + g_2)^N$. Where E_1 = earnings before the merger, E_2 = earnings after the merger, g_1 and g_2 the growth rates before and after the merger, and N the break-even number of years.

It is apparent that the critical variables are (1) the respective rates of growth of the two firms, (2) their relative sizes, which determine the actual amount of the initial earnings per share dilution or accretion as well as the new weighted average growth rate, (3) the firms' P/E ratios, and (4) the exchange ratio. These factors interact to produce the resulting pattern of earnings per share for the surviving company. It is possible to generalize the relationships somewhat,[3] but here it is necessary simply to note that in the bargaining process the exchange ratio is the variable that must be manipulated in efforts to reach a mutually satisfactory earnings pattern.

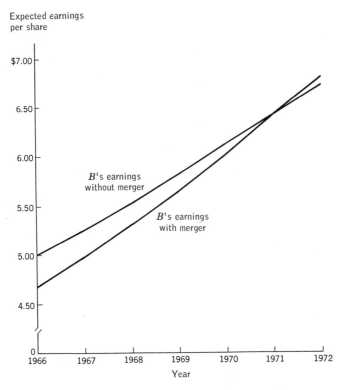

Fig. 27-1. Effect of Merger on Future Earnings

Dividends. Dividends, because they represent the actual income received by stockholders, may influence the terms of merger. However, recent developments in the theory of dividend policy have shown that the traditional emphasis of investment books on the importance of dividends in determining market prices of stock is of doubtful validity. As the mate-

---

[3] For a generalization, as well as for a more detailed examination of the interrelations, see D. F. Folz and J. Fred Weston, "Looking Ahead in Evaluating Proposed Mergers," *N.A.A. Bulletin* (April 1962).

rial in Chapter 20 indicates, dividends are likely to have little influence on the market price of companies with a record of high growth and high profitability. For example, companies such at Litton Industries have not yet paid cash dividends, but command market prices representing a high multiplier of current earnings. At the end of 1964, Litton was selling at a multiplier of approximately 40 times.

However, for utility companies with their special circumstances and for companies and industries where growth rates and profitability have declined, the dollar amount of dividends paid may have a relatively important influence on the market price of their stock. Dividends may therefore influence the terms on which these companies would be likely to trade in a merger.

Table 27–1 summarizes material from a study made by Professor Chelcie Bosland covering acquisitions during the first half of the decade of the 1950s and from a study, compiled by the authors, of selected mergers following the end of Bosland's study.

A number of companies had neither earnings nor dividends in some years. The purchase must therefore have been based on something other than current or recent earnings or dividends. The multipliers on the latest years' earnings for the Bosland study through the mid-1950s were in some cases under 10 times. Where the multipliers were higher for the earlier years, these levels were sometimes due to depressed earnings rather than to a high market price. In more recent mergers, many of which took place during strong bull markets, multipliers generally averaged higher than they did for the earlier period. Whereas a 10-to-12 P/E multiplier range was characteristic for the earlier period, a range of 18 to 25 for the later period could be considered more characteristic. In the earlier period, multipliers did not change greatly when averaged over five years. For the sample for the later years, the multipliers tended to increase greatly when related to an average of either earnings or dividends. This was because of a strong growth factor in recent years, which makes the average lower than the figure for the latest year. To diminish the influence of this factor, the authors calculated the average earnings and average dividends over a three-year period rather than a five-year period, as did Professor Bosland.

The dividend multipliers demonstrate wide variability. For the distress companies covered by Professor Bosland's earlier study, dividends were low because either earnings were depressed or the earnings outlook was uncertain. For the later period a number of the acquired firms were growth companies, which characteristically have low dividend payouts.

It must therefore be concluded, from this analysis of the actual terms on which purchases have taken place, that neither past earnings nor past dividends alone provide an adequate explanation of the terms of purchase actually employed. Other possible influences are now considered.

Market values. Neither historical earnings nor dividends provide a satisfactory explanation of terms of mergers, but prospective growth rates in earnings and dividends are probably most influential. Current market prices of stocks are supposed to reflect stockholders' expectations of future earnings and dividends and should therefore strongly influence merger terms.

Let us examine the facts in this connection. Table 27–2 presents detailed data on selected mergers and averages for a total of 130 mergers which took place during the period 1955–1964. Based on the most recent prices, an average premium of 10 percent was paid by the purchasing company for the purchased company. The authors also made calculations based on market prices as of two quarters previous to the merger date. The aim was to select prices before the announcement of the merger or before rumor of the merger, so that market prices would not reflect the rumored merger terms. However, they sought a time period not too far removed from the actual merger date, so that the market prices could have some relationship to the merger transaction. Based on prices two quarters earlier, the premium averaged 20 percent. For the earlier Bosland study, the average premium paid over market price was 43 percent. But his sample of companies included a heavy weighting of companies in the textile and the automobile industries, with depressed earnings immediately prior to the merger.

One could predict in advance that the value placed on a company in an acquisition is likely to exceed its current market price for a number of reasons. (1) If the company is in a depressed industry, stockholders are likely to overdiscount the dismal outlook for the company evidenced in a very low current market price. (2) The prospective purchaser may be interested in acquiring the company for the contribution that it may make to the acquiring company. Thus the acquired company is worth more to an informed purchaser than it is in the general market. (3) Unless stockholders are offered more than current market prices for their stock, they may have no inducement to sell.

The value placed on the company in an acquisition or a merger is likely to be above its current market price for the reasons indicated. However, whether the value is above or below the current market price, the exchange price is likely to be *different* from the market price. The reason for this difference is that the current market price of a security reflects the value placed on it by stockholders, who are holding the stock from an investment or a speculative standpoint. In a merger the stock of a company is valued in terms of its business and operating contributions in a joint operation. The operations value of the acquired or the merged company is therefore likely to be different from the value placed on it from a purely financial standpoint. Another way of expressing this same point

TABLE 27–1

CAPITALIZATION FACTORS IN SELECTED MERGERS

Date	Companies Purchased	Companies Purchasing	Approx. Equivalent Amount Paid	P/E (amount paid ÷ latest year's earnings)	P/E (amount paid ÷ average earnings)	Amount paid ÷ latest year's dividends	Amount paid ÷ average dividends
Apr. 1953	Willys-Overland	Kaiser Motors	$17.00	8	11	—	—
May 1954	Robbins Mills	J. P. Stevens & Co.	13.75	—	9	46	13
June 1954	American Woolen Co.	Textron, Inc.	25.00	—	—	—	12
July 1954	Pacific Mills	Burlington Mills	50.00	20	14	36	23
July 1954	Goodall-Sanford	Burlington Mills	20.00	27	10	18	29
Dec. 1953	Taylor-Wharton I & S	Harrisburg Steel Corp.	50.00	8	9	17	19
Dec. 1953	Russel-Miller Milling	F. H. Peavey & Co.	36.00	17	15	22	26
June 1954	Birdsboro Steel Foundry & Machine Co.	F. W. Richmond	20.00	8	9	17	18
Aug. 1954	Hotels Statler, Inc.	Hilton Hotels, Corp.	50.00	18	18	50	45
Aug. 1954	Follansbee Steel	F. W. Richmond	20.00	9	8	16	14
Aug. 1954	Fabricon Products	Eagle-Picher	33.00	8	7	15	20

Date	Companies Purchased	Purchasing	Approx. Equivalent Amount Paid	P/E (amount paid ÷ latest year's earnings)	P/E (amount paid ÷ average earnings)	Amount paid ÷ latest year's dividends	Amount paid ÷ average dividends
Feb. 11, 1959	Sylvania Electric	General Telephone	60.00	17	15	30	30
Mar. 1, 1961	Nickel Plate	Norfolk & Western Railway	50.00	17	17	25	25
Oct. 27, 1961	Philco	Ford Motor	20.00	43	22	—*	—*
Oct. 12, 1963	Yale & Towne	Eaton Mfg.	30.00	14	15	30	24
Nov. 20, 1963	Virginia Carolina Chemical	Socony Mobil Oil Co.	80.00	15	20	—*	—*
July 28, 1964	Haveg Industries	Hercules Powder	50.00	38	47	83	106
June 21, 1965	Strong Cobb Arner	Foremost Dairies	7.75	12	14	39	116
July 2, 1965	Pure Oil	Union Oil	60.00	19	20	38	38

* No dividends paid.

Source: Chelcie C. Bosland, "Stock Valuation in Recent Mergers," *Trusts and Estates*, June, July, and August, 1955, for mergers through 1954. Individual New York Stock Exchange listing statements for the mergers after 1954. Earnings and dividends averaged over five years for years through 1954 and for three years after 1954.

TABLE 27–2

PREMIUM (DISCOUNT) PAID BY PURCHASING COMPANY IN SELECTED CORPORATE MERGERS, 1955–1964

(based on market prices immediately preceding the merger and as of two quarters previous to date)

Merger Date	Companies Purchased (A)	Companies Purchasing (B)	Merger Terms*	Percentage Premium Paid by Purchaser Over the Market Price of Purchased Company	
				Based on Most Recent Prices	Based on Prices as of Two Quarters Previous to Merger Date
Jan. 26, 1955	Lane Wells Co.	Dresser Industries	4 shares of B for 5 shares of A	(10.4)	(10.1)
Jan. 27, 1955	Tennessee Products Corp.	Merrit-Chapman	1.25 shares of B for each share of A	7.2	29.3
Jan. 28, 1955	Gleaner Harvester	Allis Chalmers	1 share of B for 3½ shares of A	4.4	17.4
July 15, 1955	Byron Jackson	Borg Warner	4 shares of B for 5 shares of A	7.1	9.2
Oct. 11, 1955	D. L. Clark Co.	Beatrice Foods	1 share of B for 3½ shares of A	3.0	21.9
Nov. 22, 1955	Gaylord Container	Crown Zellerbach	Share for share	5.4	22.6
Apr. 2, 1956	Kinney & Co.	Brown Shoe	2 shares of B for 3 shares of A	18.0	15.2
June 14, 1956	Electrodata Corp.	Burroughs Corp.	Share for share	4.7	10.4

Merger Date	Companies Purchased (A)	Companies Purchasing (B)	Merger Terms*	Percentage Premium Paid by Purchaser Over the Market Price of Purchased Company Based on Most Recent Prices	Based on Prices as of Two Quarters Previous to Merger Date
June 21, 1956	York Corp.	Borg Warner	0.5 shares of B for 1 share of A	1.9	7.0
Aug. 7, 1956	Hazel Atlas	Continental Can	0.46 shares of B for 1 share of A	(9.5)	(8.5)
Nov. 8, 1957	Superior Steel	Copperweld Steel	0.75 shares of B for 1 share of A	(1.3)	(5.7)
Dec. 3, 1957	Marathon Corp.	American Can	0.8 shares of B for 1 share of A	(14.5)	14.5
Mar. 11, 1958	National Supply Co.	Armco Steel	0.85 shares of B for 1 share of A	2.8	8.3
May 2, 1958	Airborne Instrument	Cutler Hammer	Share for share	3.0	25.2
May 29, 1958	Marchant	Smith-Corona	1.25 shares of B for 1 share of A	16.1	30.6
Nov. 7, 1958	Hancock Oil	Signal Oil	Share for share	10.5	23.7
Nov. 14, 1958	Libbey-Owens-Ford Glass Fibers	Johns Manville	1 share of B for 2.5 shares of A	1.8	0.7
Jan. 27, 1959	Aircraft Radio Corp.	Cessna Aircraft	2 shares of B for 3 shares of A	4.4	25.7

(Table continued on following page.)

TABLE 27-2 (Continued)

Merger Date	Companies Purchased (A)	Companies Purchasing (B)	Merger Terms*	Percentage Premium Paid by Purchaser Over the Market Price of Purchased Company — Based on Most Recent Prices	Based on Prices as of Two Quarters Previous to Merger Date
Mar. 5, 1959	Sylvania Electric	General Telephone	Share for share	0.0	13.0
May 8, 1959	Youngstown Steel	Consolidated Freightways	1.375 shares of B for 1 share of A	58.3	33.7
June 12, 1959	South Bend Lathe Works	Amsted Industry	1 share of B for 2 shares of A	0.9	1.9
June 15, 1959	Hevi-Duty Electric Co.	Basic Products Corp.	Share for share	7.3	14.9
July 28, 1959	Nurbute Corp.	Crescent Petroleum	20 convertible (5%) shares + 5 common of (B) for every 100 shares of (A)	26.2	26.5
Aug. 28, 1959	Best Foods	Corn Products	1 share of (B) for 0.625 shares of (A)	12.1	20.6
Sept. 24, 1959	Gamewell Co.	E. W. Bliss Co.	Share for share	(12.3)	(11.2)
Jan. 25, 1960	Butler Bros.	City Products Corp.	Cash sale	20.9	9.0
Feb. 19, 1960	James Lees & Sons	Burlington Industries	2.33 shares of (B) for each share of (A)	7.7	25.9

Merger Date	Companies Purchased (A)	Companies Purchasing (B)	Merger Terms*	Percentage Premium Paid by Purchaser Over the Market Price of Purchased Company — Based on Most Recent Prices	Based on Prices as of Two Quarters Previous to Merger Date
July 12, 1960	Cuno Eng. Corp.	A. M. F.	4.4 shares of (B) for 10 shares of (A)	5.3	21.9
Oct. 28, 1960	Telemeter Magnetics	Ampex Corp.	1 share of (B) for 2 shares of (A)	3.6	12.8
Dec. 11, 1961	Philco Corp.	Ford Motor Co.	1 share of (B) for 4½ shares of (A)	0.0	(18.0)
Jan. 11, 1962	Union Texas Natural Gas Corp.	Allied Chemical	⅞ share of (B) for one share of (A)	9.6	97.2
Sept. 21, 1964	Champlin Oil	Celanese Corp.	2 shares of (B) for 3 shares of (A)	5.0	20.0
Average (mean) premium paid†				10.0%	20.1%
Median premium paid†				7.2	17.6

* Merger terms refer to the companies' common shares except when otherwise noted.
† Based on an actual merger sample of 130 mergers for the most recent price premium and 125 cases for the premium paid as of two quarters previous to the merger.

Source: Individual company prospectuses or New York Stock Exchange listing statements.

is to recognize that, though the market value placed on a company may be appropriate for the company when it operates as a separate company, its market value as part of a combined operation, as reflected in the proposed merger, is likely to be changed. It must thus be concluded that the past or current market price of a firm's stock will be only one of a number of influences on its value in a merger or an acquisition.

Book value per share. Book values are now generally considered to be relatively unimportant in determining the value of a company. Book value is said to represent merely the historical investments that have been made in the assets of the company. These historical investments may have little relation to current values or prices. One major source of differences is that either price levels may have changed since the investments were made, or the earning power or earning prospects of the company may have been altered. A second major influence is that asset values on the books of the company do not include the value of the firm as a going concern, its organizational strength, or special attributes it may have by virtue of superior location, superior executive talents, or other elements that may not be reflected on the balance sheet.

Table 27–3 analyzes the relationship between the price paid and the book value of the acquired company. For the earlier Bosland study, discounts from book value predominated. Again, this is because of the large book values of the depressed textile and automobile companies in the period studied. Market prices paid represented a large premium over current market price, but a large discount from current book values.

In the sample of companies taken for the early 1960s, premiums and discounts were about equally divided. It is not possible to generalize on whether a premium or a discount from book value will be paid. For a growth company, typically, a premium over book value will be paid. For a company in a depressed industry or whose own outlook is unfavorable, it is likely that the purchase price will represent a discount from book value.

Though book values certainly do not wholly determine merger terms, their influence should not be underestimated. When book values substantially exceed market values, they may well have an impact on merger terms. The book value is an index of the amount of physical facilities made available in the acquisition or the merger. Despite a past record of low earning power of a company, it is always possible that, under effective management, its assets may once again achieve normal earning power. If this is the case, the market value of the company will rise. Because of the potential contribution of physical properties to improved future earnings, book values may have an important influence on actual merger or acquisition terms.

Net current assets per share. In some analyses the term "net current assets" means current assets less all debt (both current and long term) divided by the number of common shares. In this analysis, however, the calculations are current assets minus only current liabilities divided by the number of common shares.

Net current assets per share are likely to have an influence on merger terms, because they represent the amount of liquidity that may be obtained from a company in a merger. In the textile mergers, net current assets per share were very high. This was one of the characteristics that made them attractive in the mergers. When the high liquidity of the textile companies was coupled with the large tax losses carried by many of them, merger possibilities became very strong. By buying a textile company, often with securities, an acquiring company was in a position to look for any other company that had stable earnings. Any company with stable earnings would have twice as much value to an acquiring company with a tax loss than it previously had for itself. Sometimes the deal could be sweetened by giving some cash as well as securities. The strong liquidity position of the textile companies made such procedures possible. Moreover, during the early period of the H. K. Porter Company acquisitions, high liquidity was also an objective for providing a means of acquiring other companies.

Because of the special circumstances in which liquidity might or might not be a need or an objective of the acquiring company, one would not expect liquidity alone, as measured by net current assets, to be a consistently dominating factor in determining the terms of mergers.

Relative Importance of Factors

An attempt will now be made to combine in an overview the relative importance of the five factors influencing the terms of mergers thus far discussed. A conspectus of these influences is set forth in Table 27–4, based on Professor Bosland's broad study of mergers in the early 1950s, augmented by the studies made by the authors for the early 1960s. Although Professor Bosland concluded that prospective earnings probably have the greatest impact on valuations placed in mergers, this belief cannot be demonstrated by the table, partly because the table presents historical earnings, whereas prospective future earnings will be the fundamental determinant of value.

It is interesting to note from Table 27–4 that, in every instance of the Bosland sample of companies for the early 1950s, the exchange ratio was bracketed by the variables influencing exchange ratios—that is to say, some of the ratios were below the exchange ratio and some were above. For the authors' sample for the early 1960s, there were two exceptions to this generalization. In the Hercules Powder acquisition of Haveg the ratios for Hercules to Haveg were, in every case, above the exchange ratio.

TABLE 27-3

PREMIUM OF DISCOUNTS FROM BOOK VALUE AND MARKET VALUE, SELECTED MERGERS

Date	Companies Purchased	Companies Purchasing	Amount Paid (in dollars)	Amount Paid Over or Under Book Value as Percentage of Book Value
Apr. 1953	Willys Overland	Kaiser Motors	17.00	(13.3)
Sept. 1953	Autocar Co.	White Motor Co.	9.00	(64.6)
July 1954	Reo Motors	Henney Motor Co.	30.00	(20.1)
May 1954	Robbins Mills	J. P. Stevens & Co.	13.75	(55.4)
June 1954	American-Woolen	Textron, Inc.	25.00	(58.2)
July 1954	Goodall-Sanford	Burlington Mills	20.00	(51.9)
July 1954	Pacific Mills	Burlington Mills	50.00	(29.6)
Aug. 1954	Wamsutta Mills	M. Lowenstein & Sons	9.50	(50.1)
Dec. 1953	Taylor-Wharton I & S	Harrisburg Steel Corp.	50.00	(38.4)
Dec. 1953	Russel-Miller Milling	F. H. Peavey & Co.	36.00	(54.8)
Feb. 1954	R.K.O. Pictures	Howard Hughes	6.00	38.2
May 1954	Kelley-Island Lime & Plaster Co.	Groups of Buyers	28.50	(15.6)
June 1954	Birdsboro Steel Foundry & Machine	F. W. Richmond	20.00	(14.2)

| Date | Companies | | Amount Paid (in dollars) | Amount Paid Over or Under Book Value as Percentage of Book Value |
	Purchased	Purchasing		
Aug. 1954	Hotels Statler, Inc.	Hilton Hotels Corp.	50.00	117.4
Aug. 1954	Chickasha Cotton Oil Co.	J. W. Ferguson, Jr.	19.00	(52.5)
Aug. 1954	Follansbee Steel	F. W. Richmond	20.00	(42.7)
Aug. 1954	Fabricon Products	Eagle-Picher	33.00	16.2
Feb. 11, 1959	Sylvania Elec.	General Telephone	60.00	54
Mar. 1, 1961	Nickel Plate	Norfolk & Western Railway	50.00	6
Oct. 27, 1961	Philco Corp.	Ford Motor	20.00	(22)
Oct. 12, 1963	Yale & Towne	Eaton Mfg.	30.00	(5)
Nov. 20, 1963	Virginia Carolina Chemical	Socony Mobil Oil Company	80.00	(9)
July 28, 1964	Haveg Industries	Hercules Powder	50.00	573
June 21, 1965	Strong Cobb Arner	Foremost Dairies	7.75	45
July 2, 1965	Pure Oil	Union Oil	60.00	22

Source: Chelcie C. Bosland, "Stock Valuation in Recent Mergers," *Trusts and Estates*, June, July, and August 1955 for mergers through 1954. Individual New York Stock Exchange listing statements for the mergers after 1954.

TABLE 27–4

RELATION BETWEEN EXCHANGE RATIOS AND VARIABLES INFLUENCING EXCHANGE RATIOS

	Exchange Ratio	Latest Year's Earnings	Average Earnings*	Latest Year's Dividend	Average Dividend	Net Current Assets per Share	Book Value per Share	Market Value per Share
Early 1950s								
Nash Kelvinator with Hudson (American Motors)	1.5	d*	2.76	2.67	1.62	0.72	0.92	1.52
Studebaker-Packard (Studebaker-Packard)	7.5	2.97	16.90	15.00	12.91	6.71	8.03	6.58
Timken-Detroit Axle with Standard Steel Spring (Rockwell Spring & Axle)	1.0	1.08	0.85	1.00	0.98	0.91	1.17	0.91
U. S. Spring & Bumper with Rheem (Rheem Mfg. Co.)	0.44	0.47	0.53	0.40	0.33	2.77	.46	0.34
Consolidated Vultee with General Dynamics (General Dynamics)	0.57	0.61	0.96	0.60	0.71	2.35	.80	0.52
Royal Typewriter with McBee (Royal McBee Corp.)	1.14	1.61	2.18	2.72	3.76	d*	1.67	1.42

	Exchange Ratio	Latest Year's Earnings	Average Earnings*	Latest Year's Dividend	Average Dividend	Net Current Assets per Share	Book Value per Share	Market Value per Share
Mathieson Chem. with Olin Indust. (Olin Mathieson Chem. Corp.)	1.05	1.29	1.06	2.00	1.43	d*	1.50	0.99
Merritt-Chapman & Scott with Marion Power Shovel (Merritt, Chapman & Scott)	0.67	1.26	0.78	10.00	d*	0.64	0.70	0.99
Early 1960s								
General Telephone with Sylvania Electric (General Telephone)	1.00	0.87	0.71	0.93	0.80	0.10	0.87	1.27
Norfolk & Western Railway with Nickel Plate (Norfolk & Western)	2.22	2.84	2.73	2.50	2.22	1.50	2.58	2.67
Ford Motor with Philco (Ford Motor)	4.50	d*	6.58	—†	—†	0.59	2.12	4.50
Eaton Mfg. with Yale & Towne (Eaton Mfg.)	1.14	1.31	1.17	1.80	1.42	0.42	0.83	1.38

(Table continued on following page.)

Table 27–4 (*Continued*)

	Exchange Ratio	Latest Year's Earnings	Average Earnings*	Latest Year's Dividend	Average Dividend	Net Current Assets per Share	Book Value per Share	Market Value per Share
Hercules Powder with Haveg Indust. (Hercules Powder)	0.83	1.32	1.58	1.25	1.53	1.03	1.88	1.13
Foremost Dairies with Strong Cobb Arner (Foremost Dairies)	2.19	1.20	1.19	3.30	5.71	2.15	1.70	1.75
Union Oil with Pure Oil (Union Oil)	0.77	0.71	0.65	0.56	0.48	0.48	0.43	0.60
Socony Mobil with Virginia Carolina Chemical (Socony Mobil)	0.83	1.00	1.23	—†	—†	0.29	0.69	1.31
Martin Co. with American Marietta (Martin Marietta)	1.30	1.86	1.54	0.85	0.90	2.17	1.23	1.17
Charles of the Ritz with Lanvin-Parfums (Lanvin-Charles of the Ritz)	1.30	1.39	1.44	1.25	0.55	3.60	2.94	1.00

* d = deficit for one or more of the companies which makes calculation of ratio meaningless.
† — = no dividend paid by one company.

Source: Chelcie C. Bosland, "Stock Valuation in Recent Mergers," *Trusts and Estates,* June, July, and August, 1955 for mergers through 1954. Individual New York Stock Exchange listing statements for the mergers after 1954. Calculations based on data from individual prospectuses and New York Stock Exchange listing applications.

And in the acquisition of Pure Oil by the Union Oil Company, in every case the ratios of Union to Pure Oil were a little below the exchange ratio.

Analysis of the data in Table 27–4 suggests that a combination of factors rather than any single influence determines what the exchange ratio in a merger will be. A limited number of combined factors may determine the actual terms of the merger. For example, in the merger between National Gypsum Company and American Encaustic Tiling Company, the exchange ratio reflected four factors, as shown in Table 27–5. The average of the ratios of book value, earnings, dividends, and market price approximates the actual exchange ratio. The averaging of four or five factors to coincide with the actual terms of the exchange may be purely accidental. Also, it may reflect the many imponderables and uncertainties in arriving at the actual terms of merger. One method of compromising the otherwise irreconcilable diverse points of view is to take an arbitrary and mechanical average of a number of the factors affecting the terms of a merger.

TABLE 27–5

NATIONAL GYPSUM AND AMERICAN ENCAUSTIC TILING MERGER

	American Encaustic (per share)	National Gypsum (per share)	Ratio
Book value	$ 9.62	$33.30	3.46–1
Earnings (3-year average) . . .	1.67	3.79	2.27–1
Dividend*	1.30	2.80	2.15–1
Market price	19.00	47.00	2.47–1
Average of ratios			2.59–1
Actual exchange ratio . . .			2.40–1

* Stock dividends computed at cash value.

The influence of an average of a number of variables influencing the exchange ratio is suggested by Table 27–6. Column A averages earnings, dividends, net current assets, and book value and market value. Both earnings and dividend figures are used when the figure is not a deficit. Averaging these factors results in a ratio close to the actual exchange ratio in the case of the merger of Nash Kelvinator with Hudson and the merger between Timken Axle and Standard Spring. Column B drops the liquidity measure from the average of the ratio. The result approximates the actual exchange ratio in the merger of U.S. Spring & Bumper with Rheem Manufacturing Company.

In column C, dividends are dropped from the average. The result is a close indicator for the Studebaker-Packard merger and the merger of

TABLE 27-6

EXCHANGE RATIOS IN MERGERS RELATED TO AVERAGES OF LEADING VARIABLES INFLUENCING EXCHANGE RATIOS

	Exchange Ratio	A*	B*	C*	D*
Early 1950s					
Nash-Kelvinator with Hudson (American Motors)	1.5	1.70	1.90	1.73	2.14
Studebaker with Packard (Studebaker-Packard)	7.5	9.87	10.4	8.6	8.82
Timken-Detroit Axle with Standard Steel Spring (Rickwell Spring & Axle Co.)	1.0	0.99	1.00	1.00	0.95
U.S. Spring & Bumper with Rheem (Rheem Mfg. Co.)	0.44	0.76	0.42	0.45	0.45
Consolidated Vultee with (General Dynamics Corp.)	0.57	0.94	0.70	0.72	0.70
Royal Typewriter with McBee (Royal McBee Corp.)	0.875	2.23	2.23	1.72	1.74
Mathieson Chem. with Olin Industries (Olin Mathieson)	0.95	1.38	1.38	1.21	1.11
Merritt-Chapman & Scott with Marion Power Shovel (Merritt, Chapman & Scott)	0.67	2.40	2.75	0.93	1.01
Early 1960s					
General Telephone with Sylvania Electric (General Telephone)	1.00	0.81	0.99	1.00	1.07
Norfolk & Western Railway with Nickel Plate (Norfolk & Western)	2.22	2.42	2.65	2.70	2.75
Ford Motor with Philco (Ford Motor)	4.50	—†	—†	4.40	5.54
Eaton Mfg. with Yale & Towne (Eaton Mfg.)	1.14	1.15	1.33	1.17	1.35
Hercules Powder with Haveg Industries (Hercules Powder)	0.83	1.32	1.40	1.44	1.23
Foremost Dairies with Strong Cobb Arner (Foremost Dairies)	2.19	5.02	1.99	1.55	1.48
Union Oil with Pure Oil (Union Oil)	0.77	0.56	0.60	0.58	0.66
Socony Mobil with Virginia Carolina Chemical (Socony Mobil)	0.83	0.82**	1.00**	1.00	1.15
Martin Co. with American Marietta (Martin Marietta)	1.30	2.43	1.28	1.42	1.52
Charles of the Ritz with Lanvin-Parfums (Lanvin-Charles of the Ritz)	1.30	5.04	1.65	1.78	1.20

(See footnotes on opposite page.)

Nash Kelvinator with Hudson, the two automobile industry mergers. Finally, column D averages earnings and market value. This is probably the least useful measure as an indicator of the actual exchange ratio.

The actual exchange ratio is generally bracketed by the ratios for the combination of factors, but not always. In some instances the actual exchange ratio is closest to one combination of variables influencing exchange ratios; in other instances it is closest to another combination. It must therefore be concluded that the circumstances of an individual merger determine which variables will have the greatest influence on the merger terms. In the acquisition of a company that is in distress because of its industry outlook or because of the recent quality of its management, the price is likely to be below book value and somewhat above market value. The price is likely to be somewhat above current market value because in the hands of the acquiring company the physical assets acquired will be expected to have greater earning power. On the other hand, when a growth company is purchased, typically it has some unique quality in the form of research capability, general management capability, location, patents, or some other factor that has produced a differentially high earnings growth rate. Because of the likelihood that the acquired growth company will contribute to a greater rate of growth for the acquiring company, an amount is paid that represents a premium not only over the book value but also over recent and current market values.

Conclusions on Relative Importance of Factors

It does not appear possible to generalize about which combination of variables influencing mergers is likely to provide the best guide to the actual exchange ratio. In some instances historical earning power may be a guide, but it is probably just a coincidence if historical earnings are also a good guide to prospective future earnings in the merger.

Book value plays an important role when it is considerably above current market value. For example, Burlington Mills purchased Pacific Mills, paying $50 per share, at a time when Pacific Mills was selling at about $25

---

* A—Average: Recent earnings, dividends, net current assets, book value, market value
　B—Average: Recent earnings, dividends, book value, market value
　C—Average: Recent earnings, book value, market value
　D—Average: Recent earnings, market value
† No dividends and deficit earnings
** Calculated excluding dividend ratio

Source: Chelcie C. Bosland, "Stock Valuation in Recent Mergers," *Trusts and Estates,* June, July and August, 1955 for mergers through 1954. Individual New York Stock Exchange listing statements for the mergers after 1954.

per share. The book value of Pacific Mills was $71 per share, and net current assets were approximately $40 per share.[4]

Another example is the purchase of American Woolen by Textron. In this bitterly fought purchase, American Woolen was obtained at a cash value of $25 per share. The book value of American Woolen was $60, but its market value was only $16 per share. Its net current assets per share, however, were $24, approximately equal to the amount paid for American Woolen by Textron.

Qualitative Influences

Quantitative factors alone, however, will never provide an adequate explanation of the basis on which the terms of merger are determined. Sometimes the most important influences affecting the terms will be qualitative factors and business considerations not reflected in historical quantitative data. A soundly conceived merger is one in which the combination yields what may be called the synergistic, or "two plus two equals five" effect. By the combination, something more results than the individual firms could achieve separately.

For example, in the 1953 merger between Merck and Company and Sharp and Dohme, it was said that each company complemented the other in an important way. Merck had a strong reputation for its research organization. Sharp and Dohme had a most effective sales organization. The combination of these two pharmaceutical companies was said to have added strength to both. Another example is the merger in late 1954 between Carrier Corporation and Affiliated Gas Equipment, Inc. The merger enables the combined company to provide a complete line of air-conditioning and heating equipment. The merger between the Hilton Hotels and the Statler Hotels was said to have led to economies in the purchase of supplies and materials. One Hilton executive estimated that the savings that would accrue simply from the combined management of the Statler Hotel in New York and the New Yorker Hotel, owned by the Hilton chain, would amount to $700,000 a year. The bulk of the saving would be in laundry, food, advertising, and administrative costs.

The qualitative factors are thus likely to reflect such influences as the following. The merger or acquisition may enable one company to obtain general-management ability that it lacks but which the other company possesses. Another factor may be the acquisition of the technical competence of the scientific or engineering staff of one of the companies. Or one of the companies may have fallen behind in the technological race; it

---

4 Some holders of preferred stock of Pacific Mills objected. They argued that Pacific Mills was worth at least $60 a share in liquidation and that the offering by Burlington was inadequate, even though it was approximately double the current market price of the stock.

needs to combine with another company if it expects to catch up at all. In such a situation the company lacking the technical competence possessed by the other firm may be willing to pay a substantial premium over previous levels of earnings, dividends, or market or book values.

Or the purpose of the merger may be that of developing a production capability which a firm does not possess. Some firms are strong in producing custom-made items with high-performance characteristics, yet these firms, on entering new markets, must make use of mass-production techniques. If the firm has had no experience in mass-production techniques, it may have to obtain it by means of a merger. Again, the firm may need to develop an effective sales organization. For example, some of the companies previously oriented to the defense market, such as the aircraft companies, in attempting to market products for the commercial field find that they have only a limited industrial sales organization.

The foregoing are the kinds of qualitative considerations that may have an overriding influence on the actual terms of merger. The values of these contributions are often difficult to quantify. The use of historical data is never likely to provide a complete guide to what the terms will be. The all-encompassing question, of course, is how these factors will affect the contribution of each company to future earnings per share in the combined operation. The historical data and the qualitative considerations described above, in addition to judgment and bargaining, combine to determine merger terms.

After merger terms have been agreed upon, the financial manager must be familiar with the principles for recording the financial results of the merger and for reflecting the initial effect on earnings per share of the merger. The following section deals with these matters.

FINANCIAL POLICIES IN CONSOLIDATIONS

In the past, books on corporation finance have frequently referred to "the scientific method" of consolidation as a basis for setting up the balance sheet of the new corporation and for determining shares of ownership of the enterprise. "The scientific method" followed a pattern that generally resulted in the allocation of securities in excess of the values of the constituent companies in the merger. Typically, the "scientific method" apportioned long-term debt for net current assets contributed by each company, preferred stock for fixed assets, and common stock for the superior earning power created by the combination of the two companies. Modern practice is distinctly different.

The consolidation of the financial statements of two or more companies that have combined must follow the regulations and supervision of the Securities and Exchange Commission. For example, for the fiscal year ended June 30, 1957, 107 corporation proxy statements contained an item relating to mergers, consolidations, acquisitions of businesses, and purchase and sale of property.[5]

The commission's requirements follow the recommendations of professional accounting societies on combinations, but interpretation of actual situations requires considerable financial and economic analysis.[6]

Both the Securities and Exchange Commission and *Accounting Research Bulletin No. 48* make a distinction between "purchase" and "pooling of interests." Three main tests must be met to establish that a "pooling of interests" has occurred:

TABLE 27-7

FINANCIAL TREATMENT OF A PURCHASE

	Mammoth Company	Petty Company	Adjustments Debit	Adjustments Credit	Pro Forma Balance Sheet
Assets					
Current assets	$ 80,000	$ 4,000			$ 84,000
Other assets	20,000	2,000			22,000
Net fixed assets	100,000	4,000			104,000
Intangible assets . . .			$54,000		54,000
Total assets . . .	$200,000	$10,000			$264,000
Liabilities and net worth					
Current liabilities . . .	$ 40,000	$ 4,000			$ 44,000
Long-term debt	20,000				20,000
Common stock	40,000	1,000	1,000	$ 4,000	44,000
Capital surplus	20,000			56,000	76,000
Retained earnings . . .	80,000	5,000	5,000		80,000
Total	$200,000	$10,000			$264,000

Explanation	*Mammoth*	*Petty*
Par value per share common stock	$ 4	$ 0.50
Number of shares outstanding	10,000	2,000
Book value per share . .	$ 14	$ 3
Total earnings	$ 30,000	$ 2,000
Earnings per share . .	$ 3	$ 1
Price-earnings ratio . .	20×	30×
Market value per share	$ 60	$ 30

---

[5] Andrew Barr, chief accountant, Securities and Exchange Commission, "Accounting Aspects of Business Combinations," *Accounting Review,* 34 (April 1959), pp. 175–181.

[6] *Ibid.* See also the official release issued by the Committee on Accounting Procedure of the American Institute of Accountants, *Accounting Research Bulletin No. 48: Business Combination, Journal of Accountancy,* 103 (February 1957), pp. 54–55.

1. The net worth of the two firms must be roughly of the same size at the time of combination.
2. The relative sizes of the two firms must be approximately equal.
3. Both managements must continue to carry on important functions in the resulting firm.

In a purchase, an important part of one or more of the ownership interests is absorbed, and the other tests of pooling of interests are not met.

In practice it is difficult to distinguish between purchase and merger, especially when combinations show characteristics of each.[7] However, the Securities and Exchange Commission spends long hours in conferences with representatives of registrants discussing the financial treatment of combinations.

The significance of the distinction between purchase and pooling of interests relates to the creation of goodwill. In a purchase, the excess over the book value of net worth purchased is set up as goodwill, and capital surplus is increased accordingly. In a pooling of interests, any premium over book value is charged against capital surplus. As a consequence, the combined total assets after the merger represent a simple sum of the asset contributions of the constituent companies. These general statements may be made more meaningful by concrete illustrations of first a purchase and then a pooling of interests.

Financial Treatment of a Purchase

The financial treatment of a purchase may best be explained by the use of a hypothetical example which seeks to generalize the treatment observed in a number of prospectuses issued by companies involved in purchases. The Mammoth Company has just purchased the Petty Company under an arrangement known as a purchase. The facts are as given in Table 27–7, which also includes the financial treatment. The illustration conforms to the general nature of a purchase. Measured by total assets, the Mammoth Company is twenty times as large as the Petty Company. Its total earnings are fifteen times as large. Let us assume that the terms of the purchase will be one share of Mammoth versus two shares of Petty, based on the prevailing market value of their shares of common stocks. Thus Mammoth is giving $30 of market value and $7 of book value for each share of Petty stock. Petty's market value per share is $30, and its book value is $3 per share. The total market value of Mammoth that is paid for Petty is $60,000. The goodwill involved may be calculated as follows:

Value given by Mammoth	$60,000
Net worth of Petty purchased	6,000
Goodwill	$54,000

[7] Barr, *op. cit.*, pp. 175–181. See also the excellent discussion by William W. Werntz, "Intangibles in Business Combinations," *Journal of Accountancy*, 103 (May 1957), pp. 46–50.

The goodwill of $54,000 will represent a debit in the Adjustment column and will be carried to the *pro forma* balance sheet. The *pro forma* balance sheet is obtained by simply adding the balance sheets of the constituent companies.

The other adjustments to round out the entry are described below.

Common stock, Petty	$ 1,000	
Retained earnings, Petty	5,000	
Goodwill	54,000	
Common stock, Mammoth		$ 4,000
Capital surplus, Mammoth		56,000

Thus a total value of $60,000 has been given by Mammoth. This represents a payment of $1,000 for the common stock of Petty, $5,000 for the retained earnings of Petty, and goodwill of $54,000. The corresponding credit is the 1,000 shares of Mammoth given in the transaction at their par value of $4 per share, resulting in a credit of $4,000. Capital surplus of Mammoth is increased by $56,000. When these adjustments are carried through into the *pro forma* balance sheet, total assets are increased from the $210,000 of the constituent companies by the $54,000 increase in goodwill; the result is new total assets of $264,000. Total tangible assets, however, still remain $210,000.

The effects on earnings per share for stockholders in each company are now shown.

Total earnings	$32,000.00	
Total shares	11,000	
Earnings per share	$	2.91
For Petty Shareholders		
New earnings per share[8]	$	1.46
Before-purchase earnings per share		1.00
Accretion per share	$	0.46
For Mammoth Shareholders		
Before-purchase earnings per share	$	3.00
New earnings per share		2.91
Dilution per share	$	0.09

Total earnings represent the combined earnings of Mammoth and of Petty. The total shares are 11,000, because Mammoth has given one share of stock for every two shares of Petty previously outstanding. The new earnings per share are therefore $2.91. The calculation of accretion or earnings dilution proceeds on the same principles as the calculations set forth earlier in the chapter. The results require two important comments, however.

---

[8] Petty shareholders, after the 1 for 2 exchange, have only half as many shares as before the merger. Therefore their earnings per *old* share are $2.91 ÷ 2 = $1.46.

It will be noted that, although the earnings accretion per share for Petty is $0.46, the earnings dilution per share for Mammoth is relatively small, only 9 cents per share. The explanation is that the size of Mammoth is large in relation to that of Petty. This example also illustrates a general principle that when a large company acquires a small one it can afford to pay a high multiple of earnings per share of the smaller company. In the present example, the price-earnings ratio of Petty is 30, whereas the price-earnings ratio of Mammoth is 20. If the acquiring company is large relative to the acquired firm, it can pay a substantial premium and yet suffer only small dilution in its earnings per share.

But it is unrealistic to assume that the same earnings on total assets will obtain after the merger. After all, the purpose of the merger is to achieve something that the two companies could not have achieved alone. When in late 1953 Philip Morris & Company purchased Benson & Hedges, maker of Parliament, a leading filter-tip brand, it was buying the ability and experience of Benson & Hedges. By means of this merger Philip Morris & Company was able to make an entry into the rapidly growing filter-cigarette business more quickly than it could otherwise have done. The combined earnings per share are likely to be higher.

In the previous illustration it will be noted that the earnings rate on the tangible assets of Mammoth are 15 percent and on the total assets of Petty are 20 percent. Let us now assume that the return on total tangible assets of the combined companies rises to 20 percent. With the same total shares of 11,000 outstanding, the new earnings per share will be $1.91. Thus there will be accretion of $0.91 for the Petty shareholders, a rise of almost a dollar per share. Here, however, there will be an accretion of 82 cents for the Mammoth shareholders as well.

Another general principle is illustrated. If the purchase of a small company adds to the earnings of the consolidated enterprise, earnings per share will increase for both participants in the merger. Even if the merger results in an initial dilution in earnings per share of the larger company, the merger may still be advantageous. The initial dilution in the earnings per share may be regarded as an investment. The investment will have a payoff at some future date in terms of increased earnings per share of the consolidated company.

Treatment of Goodwill

In a purchase, goodwill is likely to arise. Since goodwill represents an intangible asset, its treatment is subject to the exercise of judgment. It will be useful, therefore, to set out a few generalizations representing the prevailing concensus on good practice with respect to the treatment of goodwill or intangible assets.

1. When goodwill is purchased, it should not be charged to surplus

immediately on acquisition. It is preferable that the goodwill be written off against income and go through the income statement. Since goodwill is to be written off against income, it would not be appropriate to write it off entirely on acquisition, because an immediate write-off would be of such magnitude that distortion of earnings for that year would result.

2. The general view is not to write off purchased goodwill by charges to capital surplus. Purchased goodwill is supposed to represent, and to be reflected in, a future rise of income. It should be written off against income rather than against capital surplus. If goodwill is set up and capital surplus is created where no actual goodwill exists, it would be appropriate to write off such goodwill, but such writing off is more in the nature of correcting an error.[9]

3. When goodwill is purchased, an estimate should be made of its period of life. Annual charges, based on the estimated life of the goodwill, should then be made against income, to amortize the goodwill over the estimated period of the usefulness of the goodwill purchased.

4. If the life of intangibles does not appear to be limited, no systematic write-off is required. However, a conservative policy may justify a systematic write-off over a period in amounts that will not distort income.

5. Intangibles that are amortized should be periodically reviewed. If evidence of a decrease in goodwill has appeared, it should be recognized. If evidence of loss has developed, amortization should be started.

When goodwill is purchased, it should be treated as the purchase of any other valid asset. It should be written off to the extent that the value represented by any part of goodwill has a limited life, as is likely to be the situation. In a free-enterprise economy, the existence of high profits represented by superior earning power attracts resources into that line of business. The growth of capacity and the increase in competition are likely to erode the superior earning power over time.

Financial Treatment of Pooling of Interests

When a business combination is a pooling of interests rather than a purchase, the accounting treatment is simply to combine the balance sheets of the two companies. Goodwill will not ordinarily arise in the consolidation.

The financial treatment may be indicated by another example, which generalizes data from a large number of examples. (A concrete illustration is provided by the Remington Rand-Sperry Corporation merger, presented in the Appendix to this chapter.) The present illustration reflects the facts as they are set forth in Table 27–8. In order to focus on the critical issues, the balance sheets are identical in every respect. A difference in the

---

9 See the discussion in Werntz, *loc. cit.*, pp. 47–48.

amount and rate of profit (after interest) of the two companies is indicated.

Book value per share is $24. The amount of profit after interest and taxes is $40,000 for Company A and $20,000 for Company B. Earnings per share are therefore $8 and $4, respectively. The price-earnings ratio is 15 for A and 10 for B, so that the market price of stock for A is $120 and for B $40. The working capital per share is $10 in each instance. The dividends per share are $4 for A and $2 for B.

The ratios influencing the terms of mergers are the following:

	Ratio A to B
Book value	1
Earnings per share	2
Market price of stock	3
Dividends per share	2
Working capital per share	1

In this example there are no data on trends in these factors nor information on the qualitative factors previously discussed. The average of the five ratios is 1.80. However, in this situation, with the individual ratios of such wide disparity, an average is not very meaningful.

For illustration, assume that the terms of the merger would reflect either earnings or market price per share. If the terms of merger are based on earnings, 15,000 shares of stock are outstanding. Total earnings are $60,000. The number of shares of stock in the new company AB is 15,000; thus earnings per share in the company will be $4. As the owners of company A receive two shares, they are receiving the equivalent of $8 per share of stock which they had originally held. Stockholders of both A and B have experienced neither earnings dilution nor earnings accretion.

When the terms of exchange are based on market price per share, the terms of exchange will be 3 to 1. The number of shares of stock outstanding increases to 20,000, so that earnings per share become $3. The stockholders in company A now receive three shares of stock each with earnings per share of $3. Nine dollars of earnings per original share represents an accretion of $1 for the stockholders of company A. The earnings per share of $3 for the stockholders of company B represents dilution of $1 per share.

The general principle is that when terms of merger are based on the market price per share and the price-earnings ratios of the two companies are different, earnings accretion and dilution will occur. The company with a higher price-earnings ratio will attain earnings accretion; the company with the lower price-earnings ratio will suffer earnings dilution. If the sizes of the companies are greatly different, the effect on the larger company will be relatively small, whether in earnings dilution or in earnings accretion. The effect on the smaller company will be large.

TABLE 27-8

FINANCIAL TREATMENT OF POOLING OF INTERESTS

	A	B	Adjustments or Ratios	New Firm AB If Exchange Basis Is	2/1	3/1
Current assets	$100,000	$100,000			$200,000	$200,000
Fixed assets . .	100,000	100,000			200,000	200,000
Total assets	$200,000	$200,000			$400,000	$400,000
Current liabilities . . .	$ 50,000	$ 50,000			$100,000	$100,000
Long-term debt . . .	30,000	30,000			60,000	60,000
Total debt . . .	80,000	80,000			160,000	160,000
Common stock, par value $10	50,000	50,000	$ 50,000* 100,000†	$ 50,000* 100,000†	150,000	200,000
Capital surplus	60,000	60,000			70,000	20,000
Earned surplus . . .	10,000	10,000			20,000	20,000
Total claims on assets	$200,000	$200,000			$400,000	$400,000
Number of shares of stock	5,000	5,000	1.0		15,000	20,000
Book value	$ 24.00	$ 24.00				
Amount of profit after interest and taxes . .	$ 40,000	$ 20,000			$ 60,000	$ 60,000
Earnings per share . .	$8	$4	2.0		4.0	3.0
Price-earnings ratio . .	15	10	3.0			
Market price of stock .	$120	$40				

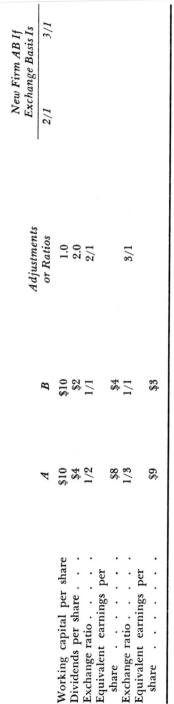

	A	B	Adjustments or Ratios	New Firm AB If Exchange Basis Is 2/1	3/1
Working capital per share . . .	$10	$10	1.0		
Dividends per share	$4	$2	2.0		
Exchange ratio	1/2	1/1	2/1		
Equivalent earnings per share	$8	$4			
Exchange ratio	1/3	1/1	3/1		
Equivalent earnings per share	$9	$3			

* = 2/1 ratio basis.
† = 3/1 ratio basis.

The material in Table 27–8 also illustrates the financial treatment of pooling of interests. Instead of increasing balance sheet values, as occurred in the "scientific method" of financial treatment of mergers, total assets in the new company will equal the sum of the total assets of the companies before the merger. Any increase in the stated value of any common stock is offset by a charge to the capital surplus of the combined companies.

SUMMARY

This chapter has focused on the financial aspects of mergers. With regard to the terms of mergers both quantitative and qualitative aspects have been considered. The quantitative aspects deal with the relative influence of earnings, dividends, market values, book values, and net current asset values. Prospective future earnings will have the greatest influence in determining the terms of merger, because the future earnings from an asset determine its present worth. This value cannot be determined from historical data. However, past levels and growth rates of earnings, as well as the rate of return on physical assets, are likely to provide guidance in making estimates of future earnings.

Dividends have an influence on exchange ratios when the earning power of the company may have been relatively low, and the ability or willingness to pay dividends may reflect favorable liquidity position of the company or management which has indicated an awareness of the needs and interests of the stockholders. Market values have influence as a presumptive indication of stockholders' expectations of the future earning power of the constituent companies. Book value is not likely to be important unless the ratio of book value to market value is high. Book values may indicate the potential level of earnings if improved management restores the normal earning power on assets. Net current assets may be an influence when liquidity needs are an important consideration from the standpoint of one or more of the companies involved in the merger.

The quantitative factors, particularly historical data, are not likely to determine the terms of merger. Important qualitative influences include contributions that one company may make to the other or that the two companies may jointly achieve in a number of areas.

The financial treatment of mergers depends upon whether the merger is treated as a purchase or a pooling of interests. In a purchase, goodwill arises if the acquirer pays more than the book value of the assets of the company acquired, so that total assets of the combined companies become greater than the sum of the assets combined. In a pooling of interests, the total assets of the combined companies will not be enlarged. Any increase in common stock resulting from the combination will be offset by a corresponding decrease in the capital surplus of the combined companies.

If the terms of merger reflect the respective earnings per share of the two companies, neither earnings dilution nor earnings accretion will result. If the exchange terms are based on the market price of the shares of the company and the prevailing price-earnings ratios of the two companies differ, earnings accretion and dilution are likely to result. Any initial earnings dilution may be offset by the improved earnings of the combined operation. After a period, appreciation of earnings per share for all the constituent companies in the merger may be achieved.

SELECTED REFERENCES

"Accounting Problems of Mergers and Consolidations," *N.A.C.A. Bulletin,* 38 (September 1956), pp. 133–138.

Barr, Andrew, "Accounting Aspects of Business Combinations," *Accounting Review,* 34 (April 1959), pp. 175–181.

Bosland, Chelcie C., "Stock Valuation in Recent Mergers: A Study of Appraisal Factors," *Trusts and Estates* (June, July, and August 1955).

Folz, David F., and J. Fred Weston, *Looking Ahead in Evaluating Proposed Mergers* (Los Angeles: Graduate School of Business Administration, University of California, Los Angeles, 1962).

Graichen, Raymond E., "Buying and Selling a Corporate Business," *Journal of Accountancy,* 107 (April 1959), pp. 43–54.

Jaenicke, Henry R., "Management's Choice to Purchase or Pool," *Accounting Review,* 37 (October 1962), pp. 758–765.

Maher, C. L., "Corporate Acquisitions—Tax Accounting Consequences," *N.A.A. Bulletin,* 46 (March 1965), pp. 50–54.

Sapienza, S. R., "An Examination of AICPA Research Study No. 5—Standards for Pooling," *Accounting Review,* 39 (July 1964), pp. 582–590.

———, "Business Combinations—A Case Study," *Accounting Review,* 38 (January 1963), pp. 91–101.

Werntz, William W., "Intangibles in Business Combinations," *Journal of Accountancy,* 103 (May 1957), pp. 46–50.

Wyatt, Arthur R., *A Critical Study of Accounting for Business Combinations* (New York: American Institute of Certified Public Accountants, 1963).

QUESTIONS

27–1 Would the book value of a company's assets be considered the absolute minimum price to be paid for a firm? Why? Is there any value that would qualify as an absolute minimum?

27–2 Discuss the situation where one firm, California Motors for example, calls off merger negotiations with another, American Space Labs, because the latter's stock price is overvalued. What assumption concerning dilution is implicit in the above situation?

27–3 Thus far, many methods by which a company can raise additional capital have been discussed. Can a merger or a purchase be considered a means of raising additional equity capital? Explain.

27–4 A particularly difficult problem regarding business combinations has been whether to treat the new company as a purchase or as a pooling of interests.

  1. What criteria can be set down to differentiate between the above forms of business combinations?

  2. Would you as a stockholder in one of the firms prefer a purchase or a pooling arrangement? Why?

  3. Which combination would you prefer if you were a high-ranking manager in one of the firms?

27–5 The previous question discusses purchases and pooling arrangements. Why is it important to make a distinction between these two combination forms?

27–6 Are the negotiations for merger or purchase agreements more difficult if the firms are in different industries or in the same industry? if they are about the same size or quite different in size? Why?

27–7 How would the existence of long-term debt in a company's financial structure affect its valuation for merger purposes? Could the same be said for any debt account regardless of its maturity?

27–8 During 1964–1965, the Pure Oil Company was involved in merger negotiations with at least three other firms. The terms of these arrangements varied from a transfer of stock to a direct cash purchase of Pure Oil. Discuss the relative advantages to a corporation of paying for an acquisition in cash or in stock.

PROBLEMS

27–1 You are given the following data on two companies:

TERMS OF MERGER ANALYSIS

	A	B	Adjustments or Ratio	Consolidated Statement
Current assets	120,000	120,000		1._____
Fixed assets	80,000	80,000		2._____
Total assets	200,000	200,000		3._____
Current liabilities	60,000	60,000		4._____
Long-term debt	40,000	40,000		5._____
Total debt* 5% . . .	100,000	100,000		6._____
			⎰1._____	
Common stock, par value $5	50,000	50,000	⎱2._____	7._____
Capital surplus	40,000	40,000	3._____	8._____
Earned surplus	10,000	10,000		9._____
Total claims on assets	200,000	200,000		10._____

			Ratios	
(1) Number of shares of stock	10,000	10,000		1._____
(2) Book value per share	_____	_____	1._____	2._____
(3) Amount of profit before interest and taxes†	65,000	25,000		3._____
(4) Earnings per share	_____	_____	2._____	4._____
(5) Price-earnings ratio	20	15		
(6) Market price of stock	_____	_____	3._____	
(7) Working capital per share	_____	_____	4._____	
(8) Dividends per share, 50% payout . . .	_____	_____	5._____	
(9) Exchange ratio . .	_____	_____	6._____(A/B)	
(10) Equivalent earning per share	_____	_____		

* Average rate on interest-bearing and noninterest-bearing debt combined.
† Assume a 50 percent tax rate.

    1. What in your judgment would be a reasonable basis for determining the terms at which shares in A and in B would be exchanged for shares in the new AB company? What exchange ratio would you recommend and why?

    2. Use the market price of stock relation as the basis for the terms of exchange of stock in the old company for stock in the new company (2 shares of AB for 1 share of A, or ½ share of AB for 1 share of B). Then complete all calcula-

tions for filling in all the blank spaces, including the adjustments for making the consolidated statement. Treat this problem as a situation which the SEC and accountants would refer to as a "pooling of interests."

27–2 The Titan Company has just purchased the Miniature Company under an arrangement known as a "purchase" (in contrast to a "pooling of interests"). The purchase was made by stock at a settlement based exactly on the indicated market prices of the two firms. The data on the two companies are given below.

1. Fill in the blank spaces and complete the Adjustments and *Pro Forma Balance Sheet* columns, and show the journal entries for the stock purchase. Give an explanation for your entries.
2. Calculate earnings dilution or accretion for both companies on the assumption that total earnings are unchanged.
3. Calculate the earnings dilution or accretion on the assumption that the return on combined tangible assets rises to 20 percent after interest and taxes.
4. Comment on your findings.

	Titan	Minia-ture	Adjust-ments	Pro Forma Balance Sheet
Current assets	$ 900,000	$14,000		
Other assets	300,000	10,000		
Fixed assets	800,000	16,000		
Intangibles				
Total assets	$2,000,000	$40,000		
Current liabilities	$ 400,000	$16,000		
Long-term debt	300,000			
Common stock	400,000	4,000		
Capital surplus	300,000			
Retained earnings	600,000	20,000		
Total claims	$2,000,000	$40,000		
Par value	$ 8.00	$ 1.00		
Number of shares				
Total earnings available to common . .	$ 250,000	$16,000		
Book value				
Earnings per share				
Price earnings ratio	10 times	25 times		
Market value per share				

27–3 Every merger agreement is subject to negotiation between the companies involved. One significant indicator of the compensation received by the acquired company is the respective market prices of the companies' stocks relating to the merger terms. The actual merger data are given below.

Calculate the percent premium or discount received by the acquired company, using market prices as the criteria. Compare the results of your calculations based on the stock prices of the two previous quarters with that of your results based on the prices immediately preceding the merger. Which is the proper measure of the actual discount or premium received: the one indicated by the earlier stock prices or the one indicated by the stock prices immediately preceding the merger? Explain.

	Companies	Date	Terms	Market Price Two Quarters before Merger		Market Price Preceding Merger	
				(A)	(B)	(A)	(B)
1	(A) Celanese Corp.	9/21/64	2 shares of Celanese for every 3 shares of Champlin	62	34	67	42
	(B) Champlin Oil						
2	(A) Cities Service Co.	6/14/63	0.9 shares (2.25 pref.) for each Tenn. Corp. share (common)	65	48	61	55
	(B) Tennessee Corp.						
3	(A) Ford Motor Co.	12/11/61	1 share of Ford for every 4½ shares of Philco	81	22	113	25
	(B) Philco Corp.						
4	(A) General Telephone	3/5/59	Share for share basis	52	46	69	69
	(B) Sylvania Elec.						

Actual Merger Cases

The text follows the practice of using simplified examples to illustrate general principles. The actual cases which follow are presented to show the realism of the generalized examples.

FINANCIAL TREATMENT OF A PURCHASE
Foremost Dairies, Inc.—Strong Cobb Arner, Inc.

The financial treatment of a purchase may be illustrated with the data for the acquisition by Foremost Dairies, Inc., of Strong Cobb Arner, Inc., pursuant to an agreement dated April 30, 1965. Foremost Dairies treated the acquisition of Strong Cobb Arner as a purchase for accounting purposes.

The financial treatment of the purchase is shown in Table 27A–1, which provides the reported financial data for Strong Cobb Arner and Foremost Dairies, with the adjustments and eliminations and the resulting *pro forma* combined statement. A *pro forma* combined summary of earnings is shown in Table 27A–2.

NOTES

(1) Adjustments and eliminations give effect to (a) the acquisition of the assets and assumption of liabilities of Strong Cobb Arner, Inc., by Foremost Dairies, Inc., for $8,567,856 in cash and $5,411,300 principal amount of convertible capital (subordinated) debentures and (b) the classification as an asset of the excess ($4,389,127) of the aforementioned consideration ($13,979,156) over the consolidated net assets ($9,590,029) of Strong Cobb Arner, Inc., as of January 31, 1965. The allocation of such excess to specific assets has not as yet been determined and is dependent upon completion of studies and allocations to appropriate asset classifications. Amounts of such excess allocated to property, plant, and equipment will be depreciated over the remaining lives of the units of property; as to the remaining excess, no determination has been made on amortization policy.

In connection with the purchase of the net assets of Strong Cobb Arner, Inc., Foremost Dairies, Inc., has agreed to assume any liability for additional federal income taxes which may become payable with respect to the former company and subsidiaries. No provision has been made; therefore, any payment ultimately required will result in an increase in the amount assigned to the excess of the initial purchase price. Acquisition costs and related expenses of Foremost will be treated similarly.

(2) The purchase price of $13,979,156 referred to above will be increased by an amount computed at the rate of 5½% per year on the aforementioned purchase price from May 15, 1965, to the date of closing under the purchase agreement. Foremost also

TABLE 27A-1

FINANCIAL TREATMENT OF A PURCHASE
PRO FORMA COMBINED CONDENSED BALANCE SHEET
(dollars in thousands)

Assets	Strong Cobb Arner, Inc., and Subsidiaries, 1/31/65	Foremost Dairies, Inc., and Subsidiaries, 12/31/64	Adjustments and Eliminations	Pro Forma Combined
Current Assets			(1)	
Cash, short-term investments, and other current assets	$ 1,396	$ 38,111	$(8,568)	$ 30,939
Receivables—net	5,435	31,632	—	37,067
Inventories	4,970	18,342	—	23,312
Prepaid expenses	139	1,074	—	1,213
Total current assets	11,940	89,159	(8,568)	92,531
Investments and Noncurrent Receivables —Net	332	9,602	—	9,934
Property, Plant and Equipment—Less Accumulated Depreciation	3,855	48,902	—	52,757
Excess of Initial Purchase Price Over Net Assets of Strong Cobb Arner, Inc. (1)(2)	—	—	4,389	4,389
Goodwill and Other Deferred Charges	129	1,989	—	2,118
Total	$16,256	$149,652	$(4,179)	$161,729
Liabilities				
Current Liabilities	$ 6,181	$ 30,296	—	$ 36,477
Long-Term Debt				
Notes payable to insurance company (4⅞%)	—	20,000	—	20,000
4½% subordinated debentures . . .	—	16,271	—	16,271
Convertible capital (subordinated) debentures (5½%)	—	—	$ 5,411	5,411
Other	485	—	—	485
Total long-term debt	485	36,271	5,411	42,167
Deferred Federal Income Tax and Other Deferred Credits	—	5,827	—	5,827
Stockholders' Equity				
4½% preferred stock	—	6,269	—	6,269
Common stock	1,803	17,084	(1,803)	17,084
Other capital	2,591	18,305	(2,591)	18,305
Retained earnings	5,196	44,963	(5,196)	44,963
Total	9,590	86,621	(9,590)	86,621
Cost of common shares reacquired . .	—	9,363	—	9,363
Total stockholders' equity . .	9,590	77,258	(9,590)	77,258
Total	$16,256	$149,652	$(4,179)	$161,729

Source: New York Stock Exchange Listing Statement A-22586, June 21, 1965, for Foremost Dairies, Inc.

has certain obligations with respect to all outstanding options for the purchase of common stock of Strong Cobb Arner, Inc.

(3) The above *pro forma* combined condensed balance sheet does not include any amounts for Pharmaceutical Laboratories, Inc., acquired by Strong Cobb Arner, Inc., in May 1965. Reference is made to "Information Concerning the Company—Recent Developments" and to Note 3 of the Notes to the Financial Statements of Strong Cobb Arner, Inc., and subsidiaries.

TABLE 27A–2

FOREMOST DAIRIES, INC., AND SUBSIDIARIES
AND
STRONG COBB ARNER, INC., AND SUBSIDIARIES

PRO FORMA FINANCIAL STATEMENTS

The following *pro forma* combined summary of earnings and preceding *pro forma* combined condensed balance sheet represent combinations, on a purchase basis, and condensations, of amounts shown in the statement of consolidated earnings of Foremost Dairies, Inc., and subsidiaries for the year ended December 31, 1964, and the statement of consolidated earnings of Strong Cobb Arner, Inc., and subsidiaries for the year ended January 31, 1965, and of the consolidated balance sheet of Foremost Dairies, Inc., and subsidiaries as of December 31, 1964, and the consolidated balance sheet of Strong Cobb Arner, Inc., and subsidiaries as of January 31, 1965, all included elsewhere in this proxy statement, adjusted as explained in the notes below. The *pro forma* financial statements, the compilation of which have been checked by Haskins & Sells as stated in their opinion in-

PRO FORMA COMBINED SUMMARY OF EARNINGS
(thousands of dollars) [1]

Net sales and other operating income—net		$386,674
Costs and expenses		
Cost of sales	284,561	
Selling, delivery and administrative expenses . . .	87,486	372,047
Profit from operations		14,627
Other income—net		2,105
Total		16,732
Interest on indebtedness (2)		2,170
Income before taxes on income		14,562
Provision for taxes on income (2)		7,360
Net income		7,202
Cash dividends—preferred stocks		303
Earnings applicable to common stock		$ 6,899
Earnings per share of 7,659,000 shares of Foremost common stock outstanding (3)		$.90

cluded elsewhere in this proxy statement, should be read in conjunction with the financial statements and notes thereto of Foremost Dairies, Inc., and subsidiaries and Strong Cobb Arner, Inc., and subsidiaries included elsewhere herein. The *pro forma* financial statements do not include Drew Chemical Corporation and its subsidiaries (see "Information Concerning Foremost—Recent Developments").

NOTES

(1) Divested units of Foremost have been excluded from the summary. No amount has been included for *pro forma* earnings on reinvestment of approximately $10,000,000 excess of the net proceeds from sale of divested units in 1965 over cash to be paid in connection with the acquisition of Strong Cobb Arner, Inc., nor has any deduction been included for depreciation or amortization (if any) of amounts of the excess of the initial purchase price over the net assets of Strong Cobb Arner, Inc. (see note 1 to *pro forma* combined condensed balance sheet) to be allocated respectively to property, plant, and equipment and to other asset classifications. The summary is not represented to be indicative of the results that would have been achieved had the proposed acquisition of Strong Cobb Arner, Inc., been effected on or prior to December 31, 1964, nor is it represented to be indicative of future results.

(2) Interest on indebtedness includes $298,000 applicable to the $5,411,000 principal amount of convertible capital (subordinated) debentures issuable by Foremost in connection with the acquisition of Strong Cobb Arner, Inc. The effect of such interest on taxable income has been reflected in the provision for taxes on income.

(3) Assuming full conversion of the debentures referred to above, earnings per share would not change significantly.

From Table 27A–1, it can be seen that Foremost Dairy paid $8,568,000 in cash plus $5\frac{1}{2}$ percent convertible subordinated debentures in the amount of $5,411,000 for Strong Cobb Arner, representing a total of $13,979,000. The book value of the net worth received on the purchase of Strong Cobb Arner was $9,590,000. This excess of initial purchase price over the net assets or book value of Strong Cobb Arner was indicated as an intangible asset. The total assets of the surviving corporation are $161,729,000. These relationships are summarized in Table 27A–3.

TABLE 27A–3

SUMMARY OF RELATION BETWEEN PURCHASE PRICE AND BOOK VALUE RECEIVED IN ACQUISITION BY FOREMOST OF STRONG COBB ARNER
(dollars in thousands)

Price paid for Strong Cobb Arner	$ 13,979
Book value received	9,590
Excess of initial purchase price over net assets of S.C.A..	4,389
Total assets of S.C.A..	$ 16,256
Total assets of Foremost	149,652
Less: Cash paid	(8,568)
Plus: Excess of initial purchase price over net assets of S.C.A..	4,389
Total assets of surviving corporation	$161,729

Philip Morris—Benson & Hedges

Some of the implications of the financial treatment of a purchase are illustrated by the material contained in the prospectus dated December 30, 1953, covering the acquisition of Benson & Hedges by Philip Morris & Company. In late 1953, Philip Morris & Company made the decision to enter the rapidly growing filter-cigarette business by buying Benson & Hedges, makers of Parliament, a leading filter-tip brand. At the time of the merger, the assets of Philip Morris amounted to some $244 million, and the assets of Benson & Hedges to $16 million.

Pro forma balance sheet. The individual balance sheets, the appropriate adjustments, and the *pro forma* balance sheet are shown in Table 27A–4. The analysis is made as a purchase.

Benson & Hedges had 438,428 shares of common stock outstanding, with a par value of $4. The total par value of this common stock on the balance sheet was $1.7 million; the total net worth was $7 million. Philip Morris purchased Benson & Hedges by giving one share of its stock for one share of Benson & Hedges stock. The approximate market value of the Philip Morris stock at the time of the acquisition was $49. The total market value paid to Benson & Hedges was therefore $21 million, but the book net worth purchased was only $7 million.

The difference between the market price paid for Benson & Hedges and the book value of its net worth is treated as an intangible asset, goodwill. Therefore the following adjustments were made in combining the two balance sheets to obtain a *pro forma* balance sheet for the combined company. First, a debit was made to intangible assets in the amount of $14 million to record the excess of market value paid over book value as the net worth of Benson & Hedges. Second, adjustments of an additional $7 million were made by a debit to the common stock, capital surplus, and earned surplus accounts of Benson & Hedges to close them out. These two sets of debits totaled the $21 million purchase price.

The common stock in the *pro forma* balance sheet was increased by $2.2 million over the $12.2 million which had existed on the books at Philip Morris. The total amount of ($5 par value) common stock on the *pro forma* combined balance sheet is therefore $14.4 million. The capital surplus of Philip Morris is credited with $18.8 million. This credit of $18.8 reflects the $21 million less the $2.2 million increase in the par value of Philip Morris common stock issued. Additional reconciliations are shown in Table 27A–4.[1]

---

[1] The publication of *Accounting Research Bulletin No. 48* by the American Institute of Certified Public Accountants in 1957 led Philip Morris to change the definition of the transaction with Benson & Hedges from a purchase to a merger. The board of directors of Philip Morris took the action of accounting for the Benson & Hedges transaction retroactively as a merger (pooling of interests). In a pooling of interests the difference between the price for an asset by a company and its book net worth is charged to the capital surplus of the acquiring company.

TABLE 27A–4

PHILIP MORRIS & CO. LTD., INCORPORATED
RECONCILIATION OF ADJUSTMENTS FOR PRO FORMA STATEMENT
Oct. 31, 1953

(dollars in millions)

	Philip Morris	Benson & Hedges	Adjustments		Pro Forma
Assets					
Current assets	$220.6	$12.8			$233.4
Investments and other assets .	2.2	0.2			2.4
Net fixed assets	21.7	2.9			24.6
Intangible assets	0	0	$14.0*		14.0
Total	$244.5	$15.9	$14.0		$274.4
Liabilities					
Current liabilities	$ 82.6	$ 6.2			$ 88.8
Long-term debt	32.0	2.7			34.7
Preferred stock—Philip Morris	30.6	0			30.6
Common stock—Benson & Hedges, 438, 428, par $4 . .		1.7	1.7†		
Common stock—Philip Morris, 2,448,121, par $5	12.2				14.4
Philip Morris payment for Benson & Hedges, 438,428, par $5				2.2‡	
Capital surplus	33.3	1.1	1.1†	18.8‡	52.1
Earned surplus	53.8	4.2	4.2†		53.8
Total	$244.5	$15.9	$7.0	$21.0	$274.4

* The $14.0 goodwill represents the excess of market value paid (to Benson & Hedges by the exchange of stock) over book value of net assets.

Benson & Hedges	Total assets . . .	$15.9	Purchase price . . .	$21.0
	Total debt . . .	8.9	Net assets	7.0
	Net assets . . .	$ 7.0	Goodwill	$14.0

† Purchase and elimination of Benson & Hedges common stock and surplus of $7 million.

‡ Common stock of Philip Morris issued in exchange for Benson & Hedges stock: 438,428 shares at $5 = $2,192,140.

Value recorded for Benson & Hedges	$21.0
Par value of common stock given in payment	2.2
Increase in Philip Morris capital surplus	$18.8
Less: Elimination of Benson & Hedges capital surplus	1.1
Net increase in Philip Morris capital surplus	$17.7

Effect on earnings. Another financial aspect of mergers may be demonstrated by the Philip Morris data. Philip Morris bought Benson & Hedges by a direct exchange of stock. According to prospectus information, Philip Morris common stock had been selling near $49 per share, and Benson & Hedges near $40. A reasonable estimate of earnings for the two companies is $12 million for Philip Morris and $1.2 million for Benson & Hedges.

TABLE 27A-5

EFFECT ON EARNINGS PER SHARE

Earnings
Philip Morris	$12,000,000
Benson & Hedges . . .	1,200,000
	$13,200,000

Total new shares
Philip Morris	2,448,121
Benson & Hedges . . .	438,428
	2,886,549

Earnings per share
New total ($13,200,000 ÷ 2,886,549)	4.57
Philip Morris before purchase ($12,000,000 ÷ 2,448,121)	4.90
Benson & Hedges before purchase ($1,200,000 ÷ 438,428)	2.74

Market-price-to-earnings ratio
Philip Morris ($49 ÷ $4.90)	10×
Benson & Hedges ($40 ÷ $2.74)	15×
($49 ÷ $2.74)	18×

The new shares outstanding were to total 2,886,549. Dividing this number into total earnings of $13.2 million gives earnings of $4.57 per share on the new total earnings. The earnings per share of Philip Morris before the purchase had been $4.90. The earning per share on Benson & Hedges common stock before the purchase had been $2.74. Hence a small dilution in earnings per share of common stock for the stockholders of Philip Morris resulted from the purchase. On the other hand, there was a large increase in the earnings per share for the holders of common stock of Benson & Hedges.

This transaction illustrates a basic principle. The transaction takes place on the basis of market prices per share. If price-earnings ratios are different, dilution occurs for stockholders of one company and appreciation for the other.

Philip Morris had a price-earnings ratio of approximately 10. Benson & Hedges had a price-earnings ratio of about 15. However, Benson &

Hedges was treated as having a price of $49, because the purchase was on a share-for-share exchange. Thus the price-earnings ratio for Benson & Hedges for purposes of the merger was 18 times. As a consequence of the purchase, the immediate earnings of Philip Morris dropped from $4.90 to $4.57. The postpurchase earnings of Benson & Hedges rose from $2.74 to $4.57 per share. This illustrates that the relative size of the two companies will determine the amount of earnings dilution or earnings appreciation resulting from the transaction. The initial earnings dilution for Philip Morris may be shortly offset by earnings improvement resulting from the advantages of the merger.

FINANCIAL TREATMENT OF POOLING OF INTERESTS

Socony Mobil Oil—Virginia-Carolina Chemical

The pooling of interests method may also be illustrated in the acquisition by Socony Mobil Oil Company of Virginia Carolina Chemical Corporation in 1963. The actual and *pro forma* balance sheets are shown in Table 27A–6. The *pro forma* adjustments in Table 27A–6 are summarized separately in Table 27A–7 for the merger transactions.

In the material in Table 27A–8, all the *pro forma* adjustments must be taken into account. Some of these relate to other financial transactions that took place at the same time as the merger. These are summarized into three accounting journal entries in Table 27A–8.

The first journal entry simply covers the issuance of $200 million of marketable securities. The second journal entry covers the issuance of notes payable, principally to banks, to retire the 5 percent prior preferred stock. The third journal entry covers the merger transaction including the pooling-of-interests treatment. In Table 27A–9 a complete reconciliation is provided. The book value of Virginia-Carolina was $66.1 million. Bank debt was issued to pay off $13.8 million 5 percent prior preferred stock, leaving $52.3 million to be accounted for. Socony Mobil issued $17.8 million par value of common stock, leaving $34.5 million. Of the $34.5 million, $31.1 million represents a transfer of retained earnings of Virginia-Carolina to the combined retained earnings. Only $3.4 million remains. Of the capital surplus of Virginia-Carolina, $6.4 million is eliminated, thus leaving $3.4 million additional capital surplus to be carried forward in the combined statement. This has the net effect of carrying forward the $17.8 million capital stock of Socony Mobil, the $31.1 million of retained earnings of Virginia-Carolina, and $3.4 million of Virginia-Carolina's capital surplus.

To put it another way, the assets and the liabilities of Virginia-Carolina are being added and the net worth is being eliminated. The net

TABLE 27A-6

SOCONY MOBIL OIL COMPANY, INC. AND SUBSIDIARIES
AND
VIRGINIA-CAROLINA CHEMICAL CORPORATION AND CONSOLIDATED SUBSIDIARIES
FINANCIAL TREATMENT OF A POOLING OF INTEREST
PRO FORMA COMBINED BALANCE SHEET (UNAUDITED)(1)
(dollars in thousands)

Assets	Mobil 12/31/62	V-C 6/30/63	Pro Forma Adjustments Add (Deduct)	Pro Forma Combined
Current Assets:				
Cash	$ 150,311	$ 7,936	$	$ 158,247
Marketable securities at amortized cost (approximating market) . . .	154,949		198,814 (2)	353,763
Accounts and notes receivable (less estimated doubtful accounts) . . .	647,552	26,476		674,028
Inventories:				
Crude oil, refined products, etc. . .	483,044	15,238		498,282
Materials and supplies	53,955	572		54,527
Total Current Assets	1,489,811	50,222	198,814	1,738,847
Investments and Long-Term Receivables (at cost less reserves)	346,099	1,716		347,815
Net Properties, Plants, and Equipment (at cost)	2,253,124	38,897		2,292,021
Prepaid and Deferred Charges	47,429	6,687	1,186 (2)	55,302
Total	$4,136,463	$97,522	$200,000	$4,433,985
Liabilities and Shareholders' Equity				
Current Liabilities:				
Notes and loans payable (principally to banks)	$ 96,489	$	$ 13,848 (3)	$ 110,337
Accounts payable	327,547	6,586		334,133
Accrued liabilities	74,696	2,808		77,504
Income, excise, state gasoline, and other taxes payable	261,846	3,259		265,105
Long-term debt maturing within one year	14,896	327		15,223
Total Current Liabilities . . .	775,474	12,980	13,848	802,302
Long-Term Debt	228,179	15,990	200,000 (2)	444,169
Deferred Credits and Reserves:				
Deferred credits	21,926	2,202		24,128
Reserve for insurance	57,000	219		57,219
Reserve for employee benefit plans	75,840			75,840
Total Deferred Credits and Reserves	154,766	2,421		157,187
Minority Interest in Subsidiary Companies	14,073			14,073

TABLE 27A–6 *(Continued)*

Liabilities and Shareholders' Equity	Mobil 12/31/62	V-C 6/30/63	Pro Forma Adjustments Add (Deduct)	Pro Forma Combined
Shareholders' Equity:				
Capital stock, par value $15 per share:				
Authorized—75,000,000 shares				
Issued—48,798,781 shares	731,982		17,757 (4)	749,739
Treasury—69,918 shares (at cost) . .	(483)			(483)
5% Prior Preferred Stock		13,848	(13,848)(3)	
5% Convertible Preferred Stock . . .		10,643	(10,643)(4)	
Common Stock		753	(753)(4)	
Treasury Common Stock		(19)	19 (4)	
Capital Surplus	630,228	9,768	(6,380)(4)	633,616
Earnings Retained in the Business . .	1,602,244	31,138		1,633,382
Total Shareholders' Equity . .	2,963,971	66,131	(13,848)	3,016,254
Total	$4,136,463	$97,522	$200,000	$4,433,985

NOTES TO THE BALANCE SHEET:

(1) The pro forma combined balance sheet has been prepared on a pooling-of-interests basis and on the assumption that the terms and conditions of the merger (explained elsewhere) will be consummated. Certain reclassifications have been made to conform Virginia-Carolina with Mobil.

(2) Sale by Mobil of $200,000,000 4¼% debentures in March 1963.

(3) Redemption of V-C's 5% prior preferred stock which has been called for redemption on October 16, 1963. Short-term loans to January 2, 1964, with provision for conversion into term loans after that date, have been arranged by V-C to effect this redemption.

(4) Issuance of 1,183,800 shares of Mobil capital stock, $15 par value, in exchange for all the outstanding common stock and 5% convertible preferred stock of V-C. The excess of the par value of the Mobil stock issued over the par values of the V-C stocks to be exchanged therefor, $6,380,000, has been charged to Capital Surplus in accordance with the pooling-of-interests concept. No provision has been made herein for any expenses in connection with the merger.

Source: New York Stock Exchange Listing Statement A-21324, November 20, 1963, for Socony Mobil Oil Company, Inc.

TABLE 27A–7

SUMMARY OF POOLING-OF-INTEREST TREATMENT FOR MERGER BETWEEN SOCONY MOBIL OIL AND VIRGINIA-CAROLINA CHEMICAL

Par value of stock issues		$17,757
Par value of stocks received:		
5% convertible preferred	$10,643	
Common stock	753	
Less: Treasury stock	(19)	11,377
Excess of par value paid over par value received and charged to capital surplus		$ 6,380

TABLE 27A–8

**JOURNAL ENTRIES FOR RECORDING PRO FORMA ADJUSTMENTS
IN SOCONY MOBIL OIL–VIRGINIA-CAROLINA CHEMICAL
COMBINED BALANCE SHEET**
(dollars in thousands)

(1) Marketable securities at amortized cost (approximating
 market) $198,814
 Prepaid and deferred charges 1,186
 Long-term debt $200,000
 (Issuance of 4¼% debentures in March 1963.)

(2) Notes and loans payable (principally to banks) . . . 13,848
 5% prior preferred stock 13,848
 (Preferred called for redemption on October 16, 1963.)

(3) 5% convertible preferred stock 10,643
 Common stock (V-C) 753
 Capital surplus (V-C) 6,380
 Treasury common stock 19
 Capital stock issued (Mobil) 17,757

(Issuance of 1,183,800 shares of Mobil capital stock $15
par value in exchange for all the outstanding common stock and 5% convertible preferred stock of
V-C. The excess of the par value of Mobil stock issued over the par value of the V-C stocks is $6,380,000,
which has been charged to capital surplus.)

TABLE 27A–9

RECONCILIATION OF ELIMINATION ENTRIES
(dollars in millions)

Book value of V-C . . . . , . . .	$66.1
Less: Redeemed 5% prior preferred	13.8
	52.3
Book value of Mobil stock issued	17.8
	34.5
Transfer of retained earnings	31.1
Amount to be transferred to the surviving corporation's capital surplus account	$ 3.4
V-C's capital surplus	$ 9.8
Less: Amount to be transferred to the surviving corporation's capital surplus account	3.4
Debit to capital surplus account	$ 6.4

worth is eliminated by adding that same amount of net worth to entries for Socony Mobil. The amount of net worth of Virginia-Carolina to be accounted for is $66.1 million. Immediately $13.8 million is eliminated through issuance of debt to retire the 5 percent prior preferred stock. The remainder, $52.3 million, is a debit that eliminates all the $52.3 million from Virginia-Carolina. A corresponding credit is needed to carry forward this amount of book value of net worth into the *pro forma* combined statement. Of the $52.3 million, $17.8 million is represented by additional common stock. An additional $31.1 million represents the carrying forward of all the retained earnings of Virginia-Carolina. Of the amount remaining, $3.4 million represents a net credit to the capital surplus of the combined company. This net credit results from debiting the capital surplus of Virginia-Carolina, $6.4 million, and as there was a balance of $9.8 million, the difference between the balance and the debit is the net remaining credit balance of $3.4 million on the *pro forma* combined statements.

Remington Rand—Sperry Corporation

Some further implications of a pooling-of-interests treatment are illustrated by the merger of the Remington Rand Corporation and the Sperry Corporation into the Sperry Rand Corporation.

The adjusting entries in Table 27A–10 are the key to understanding the consolidation. The first adjustment provides for the retirement of the Remington Rand preferred stock of $2.6 million in the creation of the new Sperry Rand stock of the same amount with the same characteristics.

TABLE 27A–10

SPERRY RAND CORPORATION
RECONCILIATION OF ADJUSTMENTS OF PRO FORMA BALANCE SHEET
December 31, 1954
(dollars in millions)

	Remington Rand	Sperry Corp.	Adjustments Dr.	Adjustments Cr.	Pro Forma
Assets					
Current	$177.0	$186.0			$363.0
Investments and other assets	7.0	1.0			8.0
Net fixed assets	76.0	37.0			113.0
	$260.0	$224.0	0	0	$484.0
Liabilities					
Current	$ 49.8	$ 99.6			$149.4
Long-term debt	100.0	19.0			119.0

TABLE 27A–10 (*Continued*)

	Reming-ton Rand	Sperry Corp.	Adjustments Dr.	Adjustments Cr.	Pro Forma
Preferred stock					
Remington Rand $4.50 dividend, $25 par, 102,269 shares outstanding . . .	2.6		$ 2.6*		
Sperry Rand: Same . . .· .				2.6*	2.6
Common stock					
Remington Rand Corp. 50 cents par; outstanding 5,200,000	2.6		2.6†		
Sperry Corp.: $1 par; outstanding 4,200,000 . . .		4.2	4.2†		
Sperry Rand Corp.: 50 cents par; outstanding, 24,000,000 shares				12.0†	12.0
Capital surplus	26.0	7.2	5.2†		28.0
Earned surplus	79.0	94.0			173.0
	$260.0	$224.0	$14.6	$14.6	$484.0

* Retirement of Remington Rand preferred stock of $2.6 million and creation of Sperry Rand preferred stock of $2.6 million.
† Replacement of Remington stock and Sperry Corporation stock by new Sperry Rand stock:

Remington Rand: 5,200,000 shares (2 new for 1 old, 10,400,000 shares created, at 50 cents per share) . . . $ 5,200,000
Sperry Corp.: 4,200,000 (includes stock dividend) shares (3¼ new for 1 old, 13,600,000 at 50 cents per share) . . $ 6,800,000

Total credits $12,000,000

Remington Rand common stock 5,200,000 at 50 cents . . . . $ 2,600,000
Sperry Corp. common stock 4,200,000 at $1 . . . . $ 4,200,000

  6,800,000
Capital surplus   5,200,000

Total debits $12,000,000

Adjustment provides for the retirement of Remington Rand stock and Sperry Corporation stock by the new Sperry Rand Corporation stock. There had been Remington Rand stock of 5,200,000 shares at 50 cents par value, totaling $2.6 million. The terms of exchange were two new shares of Sperry Rand stock for one existing share of Remington Rand. This would result in a total of 10,400,000 shares of Sperry Rand stock arising from the Remington Rand stock. At 50 cents par value, the total value of the shares amounted to $5.2 million.

Sperry Corporation had outstanding $4.2 million of shares of stock at $1 par value. These shares were exchanged at 3¼ shares new for one share old, the conversion resulting in 13,600,000 shares at 50 cents par and equaling $6.8 million. Thus the total credit to the common stock account was $12 million.

This credit was offset by the retirement of Remington Rand stock of $2.6 million plus Sperry common stock of $4.2 million, making a total of $6.8 million. Capital surplus was debited for the $5.2 million, the difference between the $12 million new Sperry Rand stock and the debit to the common stock accounts of Remington Rand and Sperry Corporation.

The point to be emphasized here is that the difference between the common stock amounts set up on the books of the new company and the

TABLE 27A-11

ANALYSIS OF EARNINGS DILUTION*

	Remington Rand	Sperry Corp.	Ratio– Rand to Sperry	Sperry Rand Pro Forma
1. Number of shares of stock	5,164,000	4,344,000		24,444,000
2. Net worth	$100,850,000	$ 99,650,000		$200,500,000
3. Book value	$19.53	$22.94	0.85	$ 8.17
4. Total assets	$260,000,000	$224,000,000		$484,000,000
5. Profit on total assets . .	$ 17,000,000	$ 28,000,000		$ 45,000,000
6. Earnings to common stock	$ 16,000,000	$ 28,000,000		$ 44,000,000
7. Earnings per share . .	$ 3.03	$ 6.23	0.49	$ 1.75
8. Total market value . .	$247,900,000	$278,000,000		$525,900,000
9. Market price per share	$48.00	$64.00	0.75	$21.51
10. Price-earnings ratio . .	15.84	10.27		
11. Dividends per share . .	$ 1.00	$ 1.64	0.61	
12. Working capital . . .	$128,000,000	$ 85,000,000		
13. Working capital per share	$24.79	$19.57	1.27	
14. Actual exchange ratio	2/1	3.25/1	0.62	
15. Equivalent earnings per share after merger . . .	3.50	5.69		

Av. of lines 3, 8, 9, 11 = 0.68

* Data differ slightly from December 31, 1954, figures in Table 27A-10. Data in Tables 27A-11 based on interim financial statements in *Proxy Statement for Special Meeting of Stockholders*, May 26, 1955, issued by the Sperry Corporation.

charge-off to the old accounts is charged to the capital surplus of the merging corporations.

An analysis of earnings dilution can be made (see Table 27A–11). A comparison of the terms of merger involves a comparison of ratios. In every case Remington Rand is the numerator and the Sperry Rand Corporation is the denominator.

The actual terms of exchange were two shares of Sperry Rand for one share of Remington Rand common stock, and 3.25 shares of Sperry Rand common for one share of Sperry Corporation common stock. This figure worked out to a ratio of 0.62 of Remington Rand to Sperry Corporation, giving almost the precise relation between the dividends per share of the two companies. It was closer to market price per share than any of the other factors except dividends.

Effect on earnings. The earnings per share on an equivalent basis after merger for Remington Rand were $3.50 compared with $3.03 before the merger. For Sperry Corporation, postmerger earnings were $5.69, in contrast to $6.23 before the merger. Remington Rand gained earnings accretion of 47 cents per share as a consequence of the merger. Stockholders at the Sperry Corporation experienced earnings dilution of 54 cents per share as a consequence of the merger. The Remington Rand price-earnings ratio was approximately 16, whereas the price-earnings ratio of Sperry Corporation had been 10. Since the trade was close to the ratio of market prices and since price-earnings ratios differed, initial earnings accretion and dilution occurred.

Chapter 28

Failure and Financial Rehabilitation[1]

Thus far the text has dealt with issues associated mainly with the growing, successful enterprise. This section of the book covers financial difficulties, remedies, and measures designed to forestall further deterioration.

This material is significant for the financial manager of successful, as well as potentially unsuccessful, firms. The successful firm's financial manager must know his firm's rights and remedies as a creditor and must participate effectively in efforts to collect from financially distressed debtors. In these matters he will need to participate fully with the firm's credit department, if the firm has one. In some firms, responsibility for collections may fall on the treasurer, the controller, or the vice-president in charge of finance. Conversely, the financial manager must know how to handle most effectively his own firm's affairs if financial difficulties arise. Often such understanding may mean the difference between loss of ownership of the firm and rehabilitation of the operation as a going enterprise.

In addition, the financial manager is responsible for setting up controls by which deterioration in the firm's performance may be detected before it is too late to apply the appropriate remedies. Effective financial controls contribute to profitable operations and sound finances. Effective

---

[1] Mr. Marion W. Engleman, member of the State Bar of California and secretary of Credit Managers Association of Southern California, Inc., reviewed the following two chapters and made valuable suggestions.

controls can help to avoid failure; they can also be employed to aid in rehabilitation activities.

The life cycle of an industry or firm is often depicted as an S-shaped curve, as shown in Figure 28–1. The sections are described as follows:

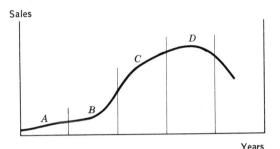

Fig. 28-1.   Hypothetical Life Cycle of a Typical Firm

A, Experimentation period: slow growth of sales and profits, introduction of new product or firm.

B, Exploitation period: rapid growth of sales; high profitability; acceptance of the product.

C, Maturity: rate of growth of sales becomes about constant; growth tied to replacement demand.

D, Decline: appearance of product substitutes; technological obsolescence; saturation of demand.

Figure 28–1 merely represents a hypothetical life cycle of a representative firm. Although it is an oversimplification, it provides a useful framework for analysis. The hypothesis represented by the four-stage life-cycle concept is based on a number of assumptions. It assumes competent management in the growth periods and insufficient management foresight prior to the decline phase. Obviously, one of management's primary goals is to prolong phase *B* and completely forestall phase *D,* and a great many firms are apparently successful in these endeavors.

If an industry experiences the period of decline, financial readjustment problems will arise affecting most firms in the industry. In addition,

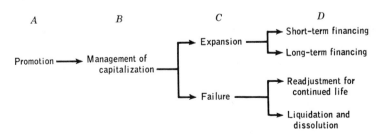

Fig. 28-2.   Financial Life Cycle

specific events may result in business failure. The life cycle of a firm in terms of a financial orientation is set out in Figure 28–2.

Financial policies and strategies for facilitating the healthy growth of a firm have been discussed previously. This chapter contains a discussion of failure and financial policies, including reorganization, for remedying failure; the next chapter continues the discussion of reorganization and also discusses liquidation when failure is complete.

FAILURE

Although failure can be defined in several ways, according to various applications of the term, it does not necessarily result in the collapse and dissolution of a firm.

Economic Failure

Failure in an economic sense usually signifies that a firm's revenues do not cover costs. Another formulation states that a firm has failed if the rate of earnings on the historical cost of investment is less than the going rate of interest. According to still another possible definition, a firm can be considered a failure if its actual returns have fallen below expected returns. There is no consensus on the definition of failure in an economic sense.[2]

Financial Failure

Failure from a financial standpoint is a less ambiguous term than the concept of economic failure. Financial failure signifies insolvency; even here, however, two aspects are generally recognized.

Insolvency in an equity sense. A firm can be considered a failure if it is insolvent in the sense that it cannot meet its current obligations as they come due, even though its total assets may exceed its total liabilities.

Insolvency in a bankruptcy sense. A firm is a failure or is bankrupt if its total liabilities exceed a fair valuation of its total assets. The "real" net worth of the firm is negative.

Failure may occur in any of the senses described above. The subsequent discussion will try to make clear the particular usage employed.

CAUSES OF FAILURE

According to data compiled regularly by Dun & Bradstreet, Inc., the yearly rate of failure per year per 10,000 firms was about 50 immediately prior to

---

[2] In still another economic sense, a firm that goes bankrupt may not be a failure at all. To illustrate, suppose someone starts a business to *attempt* to develop a product which, if successful, will produce very large returns, and if unsuccessful, will result in a total loss of invested funds. The entrepreneur *knows* that he is taking a risk, but thinks the potential gains are worth the chance of loss. If the loss in fact results, then it was expected (in a probability sense).

World War II.[3] Failure is here used to mean insolvency in either an equity or a bankruptcy sense. The failure rate was low, about 20 to 30 per 10,000 firms, in the years immediately following World War II because of the vigorous rate of business activity in making up the war postponements of production. In recent years the failure rate has risen to 60 per 10,000 firms, reflecting the resumption of stronger competition between firms.

The average liability per failure averaged about $20,000 prewar and about $45,000 postwar. The Dun & Bradstreet compilations indicate also that about 60 percent of firms fail during the first five years of their lives; another 25 percent fail during the second five years.[4]

Different studies assign the causes of failure to different factors. The Dun & Bradstreet compilations assign these causes as follows:

Cause of Failure	Percentage of Total
Neglect	3
Fraud	2
Disaster	1
Management incompetence	91
Unknown	3

A number of other studies of failures may be generalized into the following groupings:[5]

Cause of Failure	Percentage of Total
Unfavorable secular shifts	20
Management incompetence	60
Catastrophes	10

Both classifications presumably include the effects of recessions and place the resulting failures in the category of managerial incompetence. This method is logical, because managements should be prepared to operate in environments in which recessions take place, and should frame their policies to cope with downturns as well as to benefit from business upswings.

The discussion is concerned with the occurrence of insolvency either in an equity sense (inability to meet cash obligations when due) or in a bankruptcy sense (deficit in net worth). A number of financial remedies are available to management when it becomes aware of the imminence or occurrence of insolvency.

---

3 The Failure Record through 1963 (New York: Dun & Bradstreet, Inc. 1964), p. 3.
4 Ibid., p. 12.
5 See studies referred to in A. S. Dewing, The Financial Policy of Corporations (New York: Ronald, 1953), Vol. II, Chap. 28.

1. Quasi reorganization or adjustment
2. Extension
3. Composition
4. Reorganization
5. Liquidation
   a) Assignment
   b) Bankruptcy

These remedies are described in the remainder of this chapter in the order listed. The following chapter deals with the financial decisions involved in reorganization and liquidation procedures.

QUASI REORGANIZATION

Quasi reorganization is associated with previous operating losses because it is most frequently used to eliminate a deficit in retained earnings. Although retained earnings are negative, positive net worth still remains; so the firm is not insolvent in a bankruptcy sense.

The general procedure in a quasi reorganization can be stated briefly. A portion of the remaining net worth is designated "capital surplus." The deficit in retained earnings is charged against capital surplus, eliminating the deficit in retained earnings. The firm has now "cleaned up" the balance sheet and is ready to develop a positive balance in the retained earnings account with subsequent earnings. Since the common stock account is affected, stockholder approval of a quasi reorganization is generally required. But since the direct position of creditors is not affected, their approval is not required.

An example illustrates how a quasi reorganization may be used to eliminate a deficit. A company has a deficit of $100,000 which it wishes to wipe out.

BALANCE SHEET 1

Company L

		Current liabilities	$300,000
		Long-term debt	200,000
		Preferred stock	150,000
		Common stock, par value	
		$10	250,000
		Retained earnings . . .	(100,000)
Total assets	$800,000	Total claims	$800,000

The quasi reorganization is achieved through the following series of steps.

Step 1: Change the par value of the common stock from $10 to $2 per share in order to create a surplus.

ACCOUNTING ENTRY:

Common stock	$200,000	
Capital surplus		$200,000

Step 2: Eliminate the deficit in retained earnings by charging it off against the capital surplus.

ACCOUNTING ENTRY:

Capital surplus	$100,000	
Retained earnings		$100,000

As a result of these actions, the new balance sheet would appear as follows:

Company L

	Current liabilities	$300,000
	Long-term debt	200,000
	Preferred stock	150,000
	Common stock	
	Par value, $2	50,000
	Capital surplus	100,000
	Retained earnings . . .	0
Total assets $800,000	Total claims . . . $800,000

The claims of creditors are totally unaffected by these accounting adjustments at the time they are made. The position of the creditors is, however, affected in another sense. To make this clear, assume that the company earnings are $50,000 in the year subsequent to the quasi reorganization. If the balance sheet changes had not taken place, the $50,000 earnings would have had to be applied against the deficit. But as it is now, the company can show retained earnings or earned surplus of $50,000 and pay dividends therefrom if corporate liquidity and other considerations make this an appropriate action.

Quasi reorganization may also arise from downward revaluation of assets which are earning less than the going rate or less than they were when purchased. This may be illustrated by another example.

Company B has assets whose earning power has permanently declined. The company seeks a fresh start by revaluing downward its net fixed assets so that ratios of profit to total assets or to net worth will appear more attractive.

BALANCE SHEET 1

Company B

Current assets	$1,000,000	Total debt	$1,400,000
Net fixed assets	2,000,000	Common stock, par value	
		$100	2,000,000
		Retained earnings . . .	(400,000)
Total assets	$3,000,000	Total claims . .	$3,000,000

The accounting entry for the $600,000 writedown of the net property would be

    Retained earnings . . . . $ 600,000
        Net fixed assets . . . . $ 600,000

With the consent of stockholders, par value is changed to $10 per share. The accounting entry to reflect this is

    Common stock $1,800,000
        Capital Surplus $1,800,000

Now the deficit can be closed out against the capital surplus by the following entry:

    Capital surplus $1,000,000
        Retained earnings $1,000,000

As a result of these changes, the new balance sheet would appear as follows:

BALANCE SHEET 2

Company B

Current assets	$1,000,000	Total debt	$1,400,000
Net fixed assets	1,400,000	Common stock, par value	
		$10	200,000
		Capital surplus	800,000
		Retained earnings . . .	0
Total assets	$2,400,000	Total claims . . .	$2,400,000

In this illustration, the position of creditors appears to have been affected in that the total assets of the company are reduced and the cushion for creditors has been reduced from $1.6 million to $1 million. In reality, the apparent reduction in the cushion simply records a decline in values which in fact has already taken place.

Accounting Research Bulletin No. 43 (1953) approves readjustments of this kind but requires that the following conditions be met:[6]

1. There should be clear disclosure to stockholders prior to obtaining their formal approval.
2. The readjustment should seek to reflect fully the circumstances causing the revaluation.
3. Asset value should be realistic and avoid excessive writedowns in order to overstate subsequent earnings.

Quasi reorganization is a useful accounting restatement for giving th firm a fresh start and for reflecting the new actualities of a situation for firm. It presumes that the firm has been meeting its obligations to creditors and that it will now show profits for the future. Where obligations to creditors are not being met, actions involving the participation of creditors may be required. Such actions are now discussed.

EXTENSION AND COMPOSITION

Extension and composition are discussed together because they both represent voluntary concessions by creditors. Extension *postpones* the date of required payment of past-due obligations. Composition voluntarily *reduces* the creditor's claim on the debtor. The purpose is to keep the debtor in business and to avoid court costs. Although creditors absorb a temporary loss, the recovery is greater than if one of the formal procedures had been followed, and the hope is that a stable customer will have emerged.

Procedure

A meeting of the debtor and his creditors will be held. The creditors appoint a committee consisting of four or five of the largest creditors, with one or two representatives of the smaller ones. These meetings are typically arranged and conducted by adjustment bureaus associated with local credit managers' associations or by trade associations. The facts are presented in a general statement to the adjusting bureaus.

After a meeting is held at the adjustment bureau and it is judged that the case is capable of adjustment, the bureau will send investigators to make an exhaustive report. The bureau and the creditors' committee will use these facts to formulate a plan for adjustment of claims. Another meeting between the debtor and the creditors will be arranged. At this meeting an attempt will be made to work out an extension or a composition or a combination of the two. Subsequent meetings may be required to reach final agreements.

---

6 "Restatement and Revision of Accounting Research Bulletins," *Accounting Research Bulletin, No. 43* (New York: American Institute of Accountants, 1953).

Conditions Precedent

At least three conditions are typically precedent to make an extension or composition feasible.

1. Debtor is a good moral risk.
2. Debtor shows ability to effect recovery.
3. General business conditions are favorable to recovery.

Extension

An extension is preferred by creditors in that it provides for payment in full. The debtor buys current purchases on a cash basis and pays off his past balance over an extended time. In some cases, creditors may agree not only to extend time of payment but also to subordinate existing claims to new debts incurred in favor of vendors extending credit during the period of the extension. The creditors must have faith that the debtor will solve his problems. Because of the uncertainties involved, however, creditors will want to exercise controls over the debtor while waiting for their claims to be paid.

As examples of controls, the committee may insist that an assignment be executed, to be held in escrow in case of default. Or if the debtor is a corporation, the committee may require that stockholders transfer their stock certificates into an escrow until performance under the extension. The committee may also designate a representative to countersign all checks. In addition, the committee may obtain security in the form of notes, mortgage, or assignment of accounts receivable.

Composition

In a composition a pro rata cash settlement is made. Creditors receive from the debtor in cash a uniform percentage of the obligations. The cash received is taken as full settlement of the debt. The ratio may be 10 percent or higher. Bargaining will take place between the debtor and the creditors over the savings that result in avoiding certain costs associated with the bankruptcy: costs of administration, legal fees, investigators, and so on. In addition to financial considerations, the debtor gains in that the stigma of bankruptcy is avoided, and thus may be induced to part with the savings that result from avoiding bankruptcy.

Combination Settlement

Often the bargaining process will result in a compromise involving both an extension and a composition. For example, the settlement may provide for a cash payment of 25 percent of the debt and six future installments of 10 percent each. Total payment would thereby aggregate 85 percent. Installment payments are usually evidenced by notes. Creditors will also seek protective controls.

Appraisal of Voluntary Settlements

The advantages of voluntary settlements are informality and simplicity. Investigating, legal, and administrative expenses are held to a minimum. The procedure is the most economical and results in the largest dividend to creditors.

One possible disadvantage is that the debtor is left in control of his business. This situation may involve legal complications or erosion of assets still operated by the debtor. However, numerous controls are available to give the creditors protection.

A second disadvantage is that small creditors may take a nuisance role in that they may insist on payment in full. As a consequence, settlements typically provide for payment in full for claims under $50 or $100. If a composition is involved and all claims under $50 are paid, all creditors will receive a base of $50 plus the agreed-on percentage of the balance of their claims.

Significance to the Financial Manager

Substantial opportunities for asset conservation are provided by voluntary settlements. Since the formal methods are expensive, prompt action by the financial manager and a clear understanding of the potentials of working through the local credit association groups may achieve substantial savings for his firm.

REORGANIZATION

This section will outline the different kinds of reorganization statutes and the dates of their enactment. The reorganization procedures have great significance both from a social standpoint and from the standpoint of the positions of creditors and owners of a firm.

Reorganization is a form of extension or composition of the firm's obligations. However, it is more formal than the procedures thus far described. Regardless of the legal procedure followed, the reorganization processes have several features in common:

1. The firm has become insolvent in either an equity sense (unable to meet cash obligations as they come due) or insolvent in a bankruptcy sense (claims on the firm exceed assets). Hence some modifications in the nature or amount of the firm's obligations must be made. A scaling down of terms or amounts must be formulated. This procedure may represent scaling down of fixed charges or funding of short-term debt into long-term debt.

2. New funds must be raised for working capital and for property rehabilitation.

3. The operating and managerial causes of difficulty must be discovered and eliminated.

Each of the approaches to reorganization will customarily deal with these three basic matters. Reorganization procedures reflect a pattern of common-law and statutory developments as outlined below.

OUTLINE OF REORGANIZATION PROCEDURES

A. Nonrailroad
  1. Equity Receivership
  2. Chapter 77B of the Bankruptcy Act (1934)
  3. Chapter X (1938)—Corporations
  4. Chapter XI (1938)—Corporations and individuals

B. Railroad
  1. Section 77 (1933)
  2. Mahaffie Act (1948)

Because these procedures have a heavy legalistic content, their essential provisions are summarized in comparative form in Table 28–1, which distills a mass of factual information on reorganization. This table should be studied both vertically and horizontally.

Equity Procedure

The device of equity receivership developed in the United States before 1900. More than 1,000 railroad receiverships took place from 1870 on. Equity receiverships developed to prevent disruptive seizures of property by individual creditors, because any creditor with an unsatisfied claim could obtain a judgment and then take legal action to enforce his lien by seizure and sale of any property on which the lien rests. Such sales would not only take away the firm's property but disrupt its operating effectiveness. Receivership was developed to prevent these disasters. A *receiver* is an officer appointed by a court to hold and manage properties.

While the property is in the possession of a receiver, no further actions against it may be taken without the consent of the court. Therefore a receivership prevents the further dissipation of property through many individual suits. It provides a method of obtaining the maximum amount for creditors as a group by providing for sale of the business as a going firm.

The equity-receivership procedure, however, contained serious defects:

1. Protective committees were used by insiders to further their own interests.
2. The courts had little control over the development of the reorganization plan.

3. No provision was made for an independent review of the plan by a competent disinterested party.
4. Dissenters could not be forced to agree to the plan. The only alternative was to pay them off in cash. Hence no plan could be carried through unless it had the support of a large majority of the creditors.
5. It was difficult to raise new capital. The amount of cash needed depended upon the percentage of agreement (how many creditors would have to be paid off in cash) and the upset price. But acceptance depended on the plan, and the plan depended on the amount of cash needed. A stalemate resulted.
6. Considerable time elapsed during the proceedings, and the expenses were heavy.

Because of the defects of the equity-receivership process, the Bankruptcy Act was amended by Section 77B, enacted in 1934 to provide for improvements in the reorganization process. Because this section was part of a hastily developed recovery program, additional study led to further modification in 1938, when the Chandler Act was passed. The Chandler Act provided for reorganization of corporate enterprises under Chapter X and for both unincorporated and corporate firms to effect arrangements with unsecured creditors under Chapter XI. Since Section 77B was superseded by the Chandler Act, this discussion is limited to Chapters X and XI.

Chapter X of Bankruptcy Act (1938)

Chapter X made improvements in the Bankruptcy Act. It provided that:

1. Voluntary petitions could be made by the debtor.
2. A disinterested trustee control the reorganization process.
3. The trustee work with protective committees.
4. The trustee prepare the reorganization plan.
5. There be court hearings on the plan before approval is sought from the claimants.
6. An advisory opinion be given by the Securities and Exchange Commission on fairness and feasibility of the proposed plan.
7. Dissenters be bound by two-thirds (by dollar amount) majority of each class of creditors and by a majority of stockholders when they are entitled to vote.

These were desirable advances in the reorganization process. Especially important was the two-thirds rule for removing the power of the minority dissenters to profit unduly from the need to obtain 100 percent agreement. But the process remains long and drawn out. Though the fairness of plans may have been increased, speed has not been achieved.

Chapter XI of Bankruptcy Act (1938)

Chapter XI of the Bankruptcy Act, applies only to the unsecured creditors of the firm. The provisions are voluntary. The court conducts

TABLE 28–1

SUMMARY OF FINANCIAL REHABILITATION PROCEDURES

Function	*Equity Receivership and Reorganization*	Bankruptcy Act		*Section 77 (1933)*
		Chapter X	*Chapter XI*	
1. Initiation of proceedings	1. Friendly creditor *petitions* court for appointment of receiver	1. a. *Voluntary* by debtor b. *Involuntary*—3 or more creditors with claims totaling $5,000 or more	1. a. Voluntary only b. Noncorporate and corporate c. Affects only unsecured creditors	1. a. Railroads only b. Voluntary c. Involuntary by creditors representing 5% or more of total indebtedness
2. Custody of property	2. Court appoints *receiver to* a. Take title to property b. Attempt rehabilitation	2. Court appoints *disinterested trustee* (mandatory if debts over $250,000) a. Cannot be officer or employee b. Co-trustee from previous management to aid in operation	2. Court may or may not appoint receiver or trustee	2. Trustees who act as operating managers
3. Creditor protection	3. Each class of creditors forms a *protective committee* to represent it	3. *Committees* representing each class of creditors and stockholders are formed	3. Court conducts meetings; may use advisory creditors' committee	3. Committee for each class of creditor

Function	Equity Receivership and Reorganization	Bankruptcy Act		Section 77 (1933)
		Chapter X	Chapter XI	
4. Reorganization plan	4. Protective committees form a joint *reorganization committee* to formulate plan	4. a. Trustee, creditors, or creditors' committee prepares plan; confers with committees b. Court hearings on the plan c. *SEC renders advisory report* (mandatory if debts exceed $3,000,000)	4. Debtor proposes arrangement	4. Presented by a. Trustee, or b. Debtor, or c. Holders of 10% or more of each class of security
5. Court review	5. Court fixes upset price	5. *Court approves plan if* a. Fair b. Feasible	5. Court holds hearings	5. a. Hearings before Interstate Commerce Commission b. ICC submits plan to court c. Court approval
6. Reorganization plan	6. Provides for a. Foreclosure sale b. Formation of new corporation to take over property c. Raise cash to pay off dissenters	6. Provides for a. Provision for exchange of securities b. Provision for selection of new management c. Adequate means for execution of plan	6. Composition—claims of unsecured creditors scaled down, or extension in time of payment, or both	6. Same as Chapter X

(Table continued on following page.)

TABLE 28–1 (*Continued*)

Function	Equity Receivership and Reorganization	Bankruptcy Act Chapter X	Bankruptcy Act Chapter XI	Bankruptcy Act Section 77 (1933)
	d. Underwriting agreement to sell additional securities e. Voting trust to provide uninterrupted management during rehabilitation			
7. Approval	7. All claimants must approve	7. Two-thirds of each class of creditors by value; majority of stockholders (unless total liabilities exceed total assets)	7. Majority in number and amount of each class	7. Same as Chapter X
8. Execution of plan	8. Reorganization committee is usually only bidder at foreclosure sale a. Can make best utilization of assets b. May use claims at face value c. New corporation formed and receiver dismissed by court	8. Court confirms plan. Additional securities may be sold with the aid of investment bankers	8. Receiver, trustee, or disbursing agent to carry out arrangement	8. Plan executed by ICC

the meetings and may or may not utilize a trustee or a receiver. The court plan may provide for scaling down of claims or for payment in full over an extended period. The plan may also provide for the issuance of capital stock or debentures to the creditors in exchange for their claims.

The plan requires the approval of a majority by number and amount of creditors for each class. In addition to binding all unsecured creditors by the action of the majority, Chapter XI also provides the advantage of placing the assets of the debtor exclusively in the custody of the court and makes his assets immune from further actions, one of the risks of a voluntary settlement. But settlements under this chapter are likely to be more expensive and time-consuming than out-of-court settlements where such settlements are feasible.

Section 77 of Bankruptcy Act (1933)

Section 77, enacted in 1933, applies to railroads. The provisions are identical with those of Chapter X except for modifications reflected in the characteristics of the railroad industry. Because of the responsibility of the Interstate Commerce Commission over railroads, the ICC conducts the hearings on reorganization plans and submits a plan to the court. The court, however, gives final approval for the plan, after which it is executed by the ICC.

Mahaffie Act (1948)

Because of the expensive and cumbersome reorganizations under Section 77 of the Bankruptcy Act, the Mahaffie Act was passed in 1948. Like Section 77, it applies only to railroads and contains three main provisions:

1. It provides for composition of the amount of claims on any class of funded debt. The procedures are under the supervision of the ICC, and the ICC is empowered to order the execution of accepted plans.
2. The plan must be approved by 75 percent or more (by dollar amount) of each class of obligations affected.
3. Any party which considers itself adversely affected by the plan may seek court review of the ICC order that put the plan into effect.

The Mahaffie Act seeks to avoid court time and expense. Unsecured creditors are not participants but are, of course, relatively unimportant sources of railroad financing. In situations where agreements can be reached, the procedure may be flexible and inexpensive. Experience has not been sufficient to indicate whether railroad reorganizations will be fundamentally improved by the provisions of the Mahaffie Act or whether its principles are potentially transferable to other corporate reorganizations.

The preceding discussion has been descriptive mainly of legal rules.

But such rules constitute essential background for understanding the framework for financial aspects of business reorganizations. In addition, the legal requirements will often determine what financial alternatives are open. A reorganization is, in essence, a composition, a scaling down of claims. In any composition, two conditions must be met: (1) the scaling down must be fair to all parties and (2) in return for the sacrifices, the likelihood of successful rehabilitation and profitable future operation of the firm must be feasible. These are the standards of *fairness* and *feasibility* employed by the SEC and the courts, which are analyzed further in the next chapter.

SUMMARY

Problems associated with the decline and failure of a firm are the topic of this chapter. The end of a firm's life cycle must be foreseen, and, if possible, appropriate remedies applied to correct an adverse trend.

The major cause of failure is incompetent management. Bad managers should of course be removed as promptly as possible. But if failure has occurred, a number of readjustment methods may be applied to enable the company to continue profitably.

Extension (postpones the due date) and composition (reduces the amount owed) represent voluntary settlements on the basis of compromise. They are used primarily where the prospects of the debtor are still favorable and recovery is likely.

Reorganization is the formal equivalent of extension or composition. Obligations must be scaled down, and new funds or new management, or both, will be necessary to revitalize the firm.

Trustees control the reorganization and prepare a plan which, if fair and feasible, is put into operation when approved by two thirds of the creditors (by value) by class and a majority of the holders of common stock. Financial aspects of the reorganization and the liquidation process are more fully analyzed in the next chapter.

SELECTED REFERENCES

The Failure Record through 1963: A Comprehensive Failure Study (New York: Dun & Bradstreet, Inc., Business Economics Department, 1964).
Fergusson, D. A., "Preferred Stock Valuation in Recapitalizations," *Journal of Finance,* 13 (March 1958), pp. 48–69.
Michaelson, A. M., "Business Purpose and Tax-free Reorganization," *Yale Law Review,* 61 (January 1952), pp. 14–44.
Walter, James E., "Determination of Technical Solvency," *Journal of Business,* 30 (January 1957), pp. 30–43.

QUESTIONS

28–1 Discuss the relationship between size of firm and the life-cycle concept.
28–2 Discuss the relationship between diversification and the life-cycle concept.
28–3 Should a firm always attempt to forestall the declining phase of the life cycle diagram shown as Figure 28–1? What about a firm created for the purpose of exploiting a given mineral deposit, say an iron ore mine?

28–4 "A certain number of business failures is a healthy sign. If there are no failures, this is an indication (1) that entrepreneurs are overly cautious, hence not as inventive and as willing to take risks as a healthy, growing economy requires or (2) that competition is not functioning to weed out inefficient producers, or (3) that both situations exist." Discuss, giving pros and cons.

28–5 How can financial analysis be used to forecast the probability of a given firm's failure? Assuming that such analysis is properly applied, can it always predict failure?

28–6 Why do creditors usually accept a plan for financial rehabilitation rather than demand liquidation of the business?

PROBLEMS

28–1 The financial statements of the Curtis Publishing Company for 1955 were as follows:

CURTIS PUBLISHING COMPANY
BALANCE SHEET
December 31, 1955
(in millions of dollars)

Current assets	$ 40	Current liabilities	$ 14
Investments	16	Advance payments for subscrip-	
Net fixed assets	45	tions	26
Goodwill	5	Reserves	2
		$4 prior preferred stock, no par (600,000 shares, callable at $75)	
		$7 preferred stock, no par (30,000 shares, callable at $100)	
		Common stock, par value $1 (3,000,000 shares outstanding)	
		Stated capital*	30
		Capital surplus	15
		Retained earnings	19
Total assets	$106	Total claims	$106

* Except for rounding amounts, the form of the capital accounts is reproduced as shown in the annual report for 1955.

A recapitalization plan is proposed in which each share of the $4 prior preferred will be exchanged for one share of $1.60 prior preferred (stated value, $25) plus one 6 percent subordinated income debenture (stated principal, $40). The $7 preferred would be retired from cash.

1. Show the *pro forma* balance sheet giving effect to the recapitalization, showing the new prior preferred at its stated value and the common stock at its par value.

2. Present the *pro forma* income statement (in millions of dollars carried to two decimal places).

CURTIS PUBLISHING COMPANY
CONSOLIDATED STATEMENT OF INCOME AND EXPENSE
For Year Ended December 31, 1955
(in millions of dollars)

Operating income		$180.0
Operating expense		172.0
Net operating income		8.0
Other income		1.0
Other expense		0.0
Earnings before income tax		9.0
Income tax at 50 percent		4.5
Income after taxes		4.5
Dividends on $4 prior preferred stock . . .	$2.4	
Dividends on $7 preferred stock	0.2	2.6
Income available for common stock		$ 1.9

3. How much does the firm increase income available to common stock by the recapitalization?
4. How much less is the required pretax earnings after the recapitalization compared to those before the change? "Required earnings" is that amount which is just enough to meet fixed charges, debenture interest, and/or preferred dividends in this case.
5. How is the debt-to-net-worth position of the company affected by the recapitalization?
6. Would you vote for the recapitalization if you were a holder of the $4 prior preferred stock?

28–2 The Perfecto Instrument Company produces precision instruments. The company's products are designed and manufactured according to specifications set out by its customers and are highly specialized.

Declines in sales and increases in development expenses in recent years resulted in a large deficit by the end of 1966.

PERFECTO INSTRUMENT COMPANY
BALANCE SHEET
December 31, 1966
(in thousands of dollars)

Current assets	$ 500	Current liabilities		$ 600
Fixed assets	500	Long-term debt (unsecured)		300
		Capital stock		200
		Earned surplus or (deficit)		(100)
Total assets	$1,000	Total claims		$1,000

Independent assessment led to the conclusion that the company would have a liquidation value of about $600,000. As an alternative to liquidation, the management concluded that a reorganization was possible with additional investment of $300,000. The management was confident of eventual success of the company and stated that the additional investment would restore earnings to $150,000 per

PERFECTO INSTRUMENT COMPANY
SALES AND PROFITS
1963–1966
(in thousands of dollars)

Year	Sales	Net Profit after Tax before Fixed Charges
1963	$3,500	$350
1964	$3,200	300
1965	1,900	(100)
1966	1,800	(150)

year after taxes and before fixed charges. The appropriate multiplier to apply is 8 times. The management is negotiating with a local investment group to obtain the additional investment of $300,000. If the funds are obtained, the holders of the long-term debt would be given one half the common stock in the reorganized firm in place of the present claims.

Should the creditors agree to the reorganization or should they force liquidation of the firm?

Chapter 29

Financial Aspects of Reorganization and Liquidation Procedures

When a business becomes insolvent in a bankruptcy sense, a decision must be made whether to dissolve the firm through liquidation or to keep it alive through reorganization.[1] Fundamentally, this decision depends upon a determination of what the value of the firm will be if it is rehabilitated versus the value of each part if the firm is dismembered.

Liquidation values depend upon the degree of specialization of the capital assets used in the firm and hence their resale value. In addition, liquidation itself involves costs of dismantling, including legal costs. Successful reorganization also involves costs. Typically, better equipment must be installed; obsolete inventories must be disposed of; improvements in management must be made.

Net liquidation values will be compared with the value of the firm after reorganization, net of the costs of rehabilitating. The procedure that promises the higher returns to the creditors and owners will be the course of action favored. Often the greater indicated value of the firm in reorganization, compared with its value in liquidation, will be used to force a compromise agreement among the claimants in a reorganization, when they otherwise would have felt that their relative position had not been treated fairly in the reorganization plan. The principles for determining

---

[1] This discussion is based on the excellent treatment by N. S. Buchanan, *The Economics of Corporate Enterprise* (New York: Holt, Rinehart and Winston, 1940), pp. 363–388.

the relative distributions among the claimants in reorganization and bankruptcy are now analyzed.

FINANCIAL DECISIONS IN REORGANIZATIONS

In reorganizations both the SEC and the courts are called upon to determine the *fairness* and the *feasibility* of proposed plans of reorganization. In developing standards of fairness in connection with such reorganizations, both the courts and the SEC have adhered to two court decisions which established precedent on these matters.[2]

Standards of Fairness

The basic doctrine of fairness states that claims must be recognized in the order of their legal and contractual priority. Junior claimants may participate only to the extent that they have made an additional cash contribution to the reorganization of the firm.

The carrying out of this concept of fairness involves the following steps:

1. An estimate of future sales must be made.
2. An analysis of operating conditions must be made so that the future earnings on sales can be estimated.
3. A determination of the capitalization rate to be applied to these future earnings must be made.
4. The capitalization rate must be applied to the estimated future earnings to obtain an indicated value of the properties of the company.
5. Provision for distribution to the claimants must then be made.

Illustrative case. The meaning and content of these procedures may best be set out by the use of an actual example of reorganization involving the Northeastern Steel Corporation.[3]

Table 29–1 gives the balance sheet of the Northeastern Steel Corporation as of March 31, 1957. The company had been suffering losses running to $2.5 million per year. On February 1, 1957, a voluntary petition for reorganization under Chapter X of the Bankruptcy Act was filed by Northeastern in the United States District Court for the District of Connecticut. By order dated February 5, 1957, the petition was approved by the court, and J. William Hope and Richard Joyce Smith were appointed

---

[2] *Case* vs. *Los Angeles Lumber Products Co.,* 308 U.S. 106 (1939) and *Consolidated Rock Products Co.* vs. *duBoise,* 213 U.S. 510 (1940). Securities and Exchange Commission, Seventeenth Annual Report, 1951 (Washington, D.C.: U.S. Government Printing Office), p. 130.

[3] Corporate Reorganization release of the Securities and Exchange Commission numbered 107, dated August 26, 1957. Figures have been altered and rounded to make the calculations easy and for convenience of exposition.

TABLE 29–1

NORTHEASTERN STEEL CORPORATION
BALANCE SHEET
March 31, 1957
(amounts in millions)

Current assets	$ 3.50
Net property	12.50
Miscellaneous assets	0.70
Total assets	$16.70
Accounts payable	$ 1.00
Taxes	0.25
Notes payable	0.25
Other current liabilities	1.75
4½% 1st mortgage bonds, due 1970	6.00
6% subordinated debentures, due 1975	7.00
Common stock ($1)	1.00
Paid-in capital	3.45
Earned surplus	(4.00)
Total liabilities and capital	$16.70

disinterested trustees. On June 13, 1957, the trustees filed with the court a plan of reorganization, which was subsequently analyzed by the SEC.

The trustees found that the company could not be internally reorganized; they concluded that the only feasible program would be to combine Northeastern with an established producer of stainless and alloyed steel. Accordingly, the trustees solicited the interest of a number of steel companies. Late in March 1957, Carpenter Steel Company showed an interest in Northeastern. On June 3, 1957, Carpenter made a formal proposal to take over the $6 million of 4½ percent first mortgage bonds of Northeastern, to pay $250,000 taxes owed by Northeastern, and to pay 40,000 shares of Carpenter Steel common stock to the company. Since the stock had a market price of $75 per share, the value of the stock was equivalent to $3 million. Thus, Carpenter was offering this sum, plus the $6 million take-over and the $250,000 taxes, a total of $9.25 million on assets that had a net book value of $16.7 million.

Trustees' plan. The trustees' plan based on 40,000 shares at $75, equaling $3 million, is shown in Table 29–2. The total claims of the unsecured creditors equal $10 million. However, the amounts available are only $3 million. Thus each claimant would be entitled to receive 30 percent before the adjustment for subordination. Before this adjustment, holders of notes payable would receive 30 percent of their claim of $250,-000, or $75,000. However, the debentures are subordinated *to the notes*

TABLE 29–2

NORTHEASTERN STEEL CORPORATION
TRUSTEES' PLAN

Prior Claims	Amount	Receives
Taxes	$ 250,000	Cash paid by Carpenter
1st mortgage, 4½%, 1970 . . .	6,000,000	Same assumed by Carpenter

Trustees' plan for remainder of claims

Valuation based on 40,000 shares at $75 equals $3 million, or 30% of $10 million liabilities.

Claims	Amount	30 Percent × Amt. of Claim	Claim after Sub-ordination	No. of Shares of Common Stock
Notes payable	$ 250,000	$ 75,000	$ 250,000	3,333
General unsecured creditors	2,750,000	825,000	825,000	11,000
Subordinated debentures	7,000,000	2,100,000	1,925,000	25,667
	$10,000,000	$3,000,000	$3,000,000	40,000

payable, so an additional $175,000 would be transferred to notes payable from the subordinated debentures.

SEC evaluation. The Securities and Exchange Commission, in evaluating the proposal from the standpoint of fairness, made the following analysis. The SEC began with an evaluation of the prospective value of Northeastern Steel (Table 29–3). After a survey and discussion with various experts, they arrived at estimated sales of Northeastern Steel Corporation of $25 million per year. It was further estimated that the profit margin on sales would equal 6 percent, thus giving an indicated future earnings of $1.5 million per year.

The SEC analyzed price-earnings ratios for comparable steel companies and arrived at 8 times future earnings for a capitalization factor. Multiplying 8 by $1.5 million gave an indicated total value of the company of $12 million. Since the mortgage assumed by Carpenter Steel was $6 million, a net value of $6 million is left for the other claims. This value is exactly double that of the 40,000 shares of Carpenter Steel stock paid for the remainder of the company. Because the SEC felt that the value of these claims was $6 million rather than $3 million, the SEC concluded that the trustees' plan for reorganization did not meet the test of fairness. It will be noted that under both the trustees' plan and the SEC plan, the holders of common stock would receive nothing.

Table 29-3

NORTHEASTERN STEEL CORPORATION

SEC EVALUATION OF FAIRNESS

Valuation

Estimated sales of Northeastern Steel Corp.	$25,000,000 per year
Earnings at 6%	1,500,000
Price-earnings ratio of 8 (total value)	12,000,000
Mortgage assumed, $6,000,000	6,000,000
Net value	$ 6,000,000

Claims	*Amount*	*Claim*	*Claim after Subordination*
Notes payable	$ 250,000	$ 150,000	$ 250,000*
General unsecured creditors . . .	2,750,000	1,650,000	1,650,000
Subordinated debentures (subordinate to notes payable)	7,000,000	4,200,000	4,100,000*
Totals	$10,000,000	$6,000,000	$6,000,000
Total available	6,000,000		
Percentage of claims	60%		

* Notes payable must be satisfied before subordinated debentures receive anything.

Because no better alternative offer could be obtained, the proposal of Carpenter Steel was accepted despite the SEC disagreement with the valuation. This example illustrates how the implementation of the standard of fairness is actually applied in a reorganization plan.

Standards of Feasibility

The primary test of feasibility is that the fixed charges on the income of the corporation after reorganization are amply covered by earnings. Adequate coverage of fixed charges for a company in need of reorganization generally requires an improvement in earnings or a reduction of fixed charges, or both.

Policies required. Among the actions that will have to be taken to improve the earning power of the company will be the following:

1. Where the quality of management has been inefficient and inadequate for the task, new talents and abilities must be brought into the company if it is to operate successfully subsequent to the reorganization.
2. If inventories have become obsolete to a considerable degree, the useless inventory should be disposed of and the operations of the company streamlined.
3. Sometimes the plant and the equipment of the firm need to be modernized before it can operate and compete successfully on a cost basis.
4. Reorganization may also require an improvement in production, market-

ing, advertising, and other functions, to enable the firm to compete successfully and earn satisfactory profits.

5. Sometimes it is necessary to develop new product activity of the firm so that it can move from areas where economic trends have become undesirable into areas where the growth and stability potential is greater.

Application of feasibility tests. Referring again to the Northeastern Steel Corporation example, the SEC observed that the reorganization involved taking over the properties of the Northeastern Steel Corporation by the Carpenter Steel Company. It judged that the direction and aid of the Carpenter Steel Company would remedy the production and operating deficiencies that had troubled Northeastern Steel. Whereas the debt-to-equity ratio of Northeastern Steel had become unbalanced, the Carpenter Steel Company went into the purchase with only a moderate amount of debt. Table 29–4 illustrates the consolidation of Carpenter Steel with the Northeastern Steel Corporation. After the consolidation has taken place, the total debt of Carpenter Steel is approximately $17.5 million, compared with the total net worth of more than $46 million. Thus the debt-to-equity ratio of 38 percent after the reorganization was a favorable one.

The net income after taxes of Carpenter Steel had been running at a level of approximately $6 million. The interest on the debt of Carpenter Steel would run $270,000 on the long-term debt and, taking other borrowings into account, would total a maximum of $300,000 per year. The $6 million profit after taxes would therefore provide ample coverage of fixed charges.

These, then, are the two main standards of evaluating a reorganization: *fairness* and *feasibility*. Before leaving the topic of reorganization, it is desirable to comment on rival doctrines of fairness: the *relative priority doctrine* versus the *absolute priority doctrine*.

Legal Doctrines of Fairness in Corporate Reorganization

The logic used by those favoring the absolute priority doctrine is that claims should be satisfied in the order and manner in which they would have been treated if actual bankruptcy and liquidation had occurred.

Proponents of the relative priority doctrine, on the other hand, argue that, since liquidation has not actually occurred, the future value of the company is not certain. The estimate of future earnings and the appropriate capitalization rates to be employed are matters of judgment on which errors may be made. Hence, they argue that the relative priority doctrine—which gives junior claimants a contingent position—should be followed. In the event that the results of the future operations of the company may turn out to be different from those anticipated, this is said to be the fairer treatment.

Basis for relative priority doctrine. Studies of the subsequent history of reorganized companies show that inaccurate estimates of both fu-

TABLE 29-4

CARPENTER STEEL COMPANY
PRO FORMA CONSOLIDATION AFTER PURCHASE
(dollars in millions)

	Carpenter	North-eastern	Adjustments Dr.	Cr.	Pro Forma Carpenter Consolidated
Current assets	$30.8	$ 3.5		(a) 0.25	$34.05
Net property	16.7	12.5			29.2
Misc. assets		0.7			0.7
Total assets . . .	$47.5	$16.7			$63.95
Accounts payable . . .	$ 2.3	1.0	(c) 1.0		$ 2.3
Taxes	6.4	0.25	(a) 0.25		6.40
Notes payable		0.25	(c) 0.25		
Other current liabilities	2.7	1.75	(c) 1.75		2.7
Total Current Debt	11.4	3.25			11.40
1st 4½s—1970		6.0	(b) 6.0	(b) 6.0	6.0
Debentures, 1975 . . .		7.0	(c) 7.0		
Reserves	0.1				0.1
Common stock ($5) . .	4.3	1.0	(c) 1.0	(c) 0.2	4.5
Capital surplus	6.5	3.45	(c) 3.45	(c) 2.80	9.3
Earned surplus	25.2	(4.00)		(c) 4.00	25.2
Acquisition surplus . .				(c) 7.45	7.45
Total Claims . . .	$47.5	$16.7			$63.95

(a) Represents payment of taxes.
(b) Represents assumption of first mortgage by Carpenter.
(c) Issued 40,000 shares at $5 ($200,000). Adjusting entries:

Common stock, Northeastern	$ 1.00
Capital surplus, Northeastern . . . · . . .	3.45
Notes payable, Northeastern	0.25
Unsecured creditors, Northeastern	2.75
Subordinated debentures, Northeastern . . .	7.00
	$14.45
Common stock, Carpenter	$ 0.20
Earned surplus, Northeastern	4.00
Capital surplus, Carpenter	2.80
Acquisition surplus, Carpenter	7.45
	$14.45

ture earnings and capitalization rates were made.[4] Professor Calkins found that the SEC's estimate of future earnings varied from about one third to

---

[4] De Forest Billyou, "A Decade of Corporate Reorganization under Chapter X," *Columbia Law Review*, 49, No. 4 (April 1949), pp. 456–500; Francis J. Calkins, "Corporate Reorganization under Chapter X—A Post-Mortem," *Journal of Finance*, 3 (June 1948), pp. 19–28.

one seventh of the earnings actually attained four to six years subsequent to the reorganization. Sales were also underestimated by a factor of one third to two thirds. Calkins also found that the SEC's estimates of the appropriate capitalization rate were somewhat on the low side, but this is an offsetting error which has the effect of increasing the value placed on securities.

The net result of an underestimate of earnings and an underestimate of capitalization rates, according to Calkins, resulted in understatement of the true value of the company in reorganization. Because the estimates of future value have been low, the holders of common stock, and sometimes the owners of preferred stock, have been penalized, to the advantage of the holders of debt. The holders of debt as creditors of the company are given the ownership of the company, whereas the common stock interests are completely eliminated. Because of the inability to forecast the future accurately, it has been urged that holders of common stock be given a residual claim or the opportunity to obtain a residual claim by putting additional funds into the company. The relative priority doctrine provides for such a method of distribution of claims.

In the relative priority doctrine, the position of each of the claimants is somewhat scaled down. If the company is insolvent and bankrupt—that is, if total liabilities exceed total assets and the holders of common stock can have had no claim under the absolute priority doctrine—they are given a contingent participation. This grant is made particularly when the holders of common stock have made an additional contribution of funds to the company.

Application of relative priority doctrine. An illustration of how the relative priority doctrine would be put into effect and as it is employed

TABLE 29–5

RELATIVE COMPANY

BALANCE SHEET
May 20, 1966 (prior to reorganization)

Assets		*Liabilities and Capital*	
Cash	$ 200,000	Notes payable	$1,000,000
Receivables, net	1,800,000	Accounts payable . . .	3,000,000
Inventory	3,000,000	Total current liabilities	4,000,000
Total current assets . . .	5,000,000	First mortgage bonds . .	2,000,000
Fixed assets	4,000,000	Preferred stock, 6% . .	1,000,000
		Common stock	3,000,000
		Surplus	(1,000,000)
Total assets	$9,000,000	Total claims on assets . .	$9,000,000

under the equity-receivership reorganization procedure is conveyed by the use of the data in Table 29–5.

The first step in the allocation of claims in the new company is to determine a value for the company. After analysis, discussion with other companies in the same line of business, and reports of experts, a valuation is made.

RELATIVE COMPANY
VALUATION ANALYSIS

Estimated future sales*	$10,000,000
Estimated earnings on sales, 6.5%	650,000
Price-earnings ratios of similar companies . . .	10×
Capitalized value of future earnings	$ 6,500,000

* If additional cash of $500,000 is invested in the company to rehabilitate the equipment.

The estimated future sales of the Relative Company are $10 million. From comparisons with other companies, it appears that an estimated earnings on sales of 6.5 percent after taxes is reasonable. This yields $650,000 in earnings. The nature of the business suggests that a price-earnings ratio of 10 times or a capitalization rate of 10 percent is appropriate. The capitalized value of future earnings for this company is therefore $6.5 million. This sum will be the total assets of the reorganized company on its *pro forma* balance sheet, giving effect to the reorganization (Table 29–6). The assets of the company must conform to this total.

TABLE 29–6

RELATIVE COMPANY
PRO FORMA BALANCE SHEET
May 20, 1966

Assets		*Liabilities and Capital*	
Cash	$ 700,000	Income bonds, 5% . . .	$1,750,000
Receivables, net	1,800,000	Preferred stock, 6% . . .	2,000,000
Inventories	2,000,000	Common stock, $5 par . .	2,500,000
Total current assets	$4,500,000	Paid-in surplus	250,000
Fixed assets	2,000,000		
Total assets	$6,500,000	Total claims on assets	$6,500,000

Experience suggests the following purely hypothetical reductions in the values of assets. Inventories are written down by one third, from $3 to $2 million. Fixed assets are revalued to 50 percent of the present valuation, from $4 million to $2 million. The individual asset items now total $6.5 million, the same amount that was arrived at by capitalizing future earnings.

The total resources are now allocated among the respective claimants on the basis of their relative positions, including their bargaining strength. Through the process of bargaining with the committees representing the various classes of creditors and owners, the following terms are established:

Reorganization Terms

1. Holders of first-mortgage bonds have agreed to take 50 percent of their present holdings in 5 percent income bonds, and 50 percent in new $5 par-value common stock.

2. One fourth of the notes payable will be paid in the form of new $5 par-value common stock, and one half will be given in the form of 5 percent income bonds.

3. Accounts payable will be reduced by $500,000, and the remainder will be divided: $250,000 of 5 percent income bonds, $2 million of 6 percent preferred stock, and $250,000 common stock.

4. Present holders of preferred stock are to be given $350,000 in new $5 par-value common stock.

5. Present holders of common stock are to be given $400,000 in new $5 par-value common stock if they buy 50,000 shares of additional common stock of $5 par value at a price of $10 per share.

It will be noted that the only claims not reduced are those of the first-mortgage holders, but even these holders are required to take 50 percent of their claim in the form of common stock and the balance in income bonds. One fourth of the notes payable is paid in the form of new 5 percent par-value common stock, and one half is given in the form of income bonds. Thus, if any income is earned by the company, the holders of first-mortgage bonds will have a claim on the first two thirds of the income.

Accounts payable are reduced by $750,000. The accounts payable are given $2 million of preferred stock and $250,000 of common stock. Thus the accounts payable will receive income only after income has been received by the previous first-mortgage holders and by the previous holders of notes payable. The accounts payable are given a small claim in the residual equity of the company.

The $1 million claim of the holders of preferred stock is set down one stage in priority into common stock. The old holders of preferred stock will have only a residual claim on the income of the company.

The present holders of common stock retain an interest in the company only by being the source of an additional $500,000 of cash, which will be used in the rehabilitation of the equipment and in the plant and production organization of the company. The new investment of these holders of common stock is recorded as follows:

Cash	$500,000	
Common stock, 50,000 at $5		$250,000
Paid-in surplus		250,000

A number of claims on the new common stock have been allocated. These represent an allocation of the equity position in the reorganized company. The total carried on the new balance sheet for common stock is $2 million. Since the par value is $5, the total number of shares issued is 500,000. The participation of each of the claimants in the common stock interest is shown below.

Claim on Common Stock by Original Claimants	Dollar Amount	Number of Shares	Percentage of Total
First-mortgage holders	1,000,000	200,000	40
Notes payable holders	250,000	50,000	10
Accounts payable holders	250,000	50,000	10
Preferred stockholders	350,000	70,000	14
Common stockholders	650,000	130,000	26
Total	2,500,000	500,000	100

The original claims and their treatment in the reorganization may be tabulated in order of priority:

Original Claim		Receive in the Reorganization
Secured creditors		
First-mortgage holders .	$2,000,000	Income bonds of . . . . $1,000,000 plus 40 percent of the ownership
General creditors		
Notes payable	$1,000,000	Income bonds of . . . . $ 500,000 plus 10 percent of the ownership
Accounts payable . . .	$3,000,000	Income bonds of . . . . $ 250,000 plus preferred stock . . $2,000,000 plus 10 percent of the ownership
Preferred stock		
Preferred stock . . .	$1,000,000	14 percent of the ownership
Common stock		
Common stock . . .	$2,000,000	
New cash investment .	$ 500,000	26 percent of the ownership

Every claimant gives up something, in either priority of position, fixity of claim, or dollar amount of claim. No party is likely to be completely satisfied. The result must inevitably represent the result of bargaining.

This hypothetical example illustrates how the relative priority doctrine can be worked out in practice. Though the precedent of the courts and the SEC are firm on this point, there is always the possibility that the mounting experience which demonstrates that, because estimates of future sales, future earnings, and capitalization rates are so difficult to achieve accurately, both the courts and the SEC may in time modify the rigidity of the absolute priority doctrine. They may move in the direction of giving the residual claimants some contingent stake in the new company if changes in the underlying conditions affecting an industry alter the underlying earnings potential of the companies in the industry. Under circumstances such as these, to give the creditors of the company complete ownership and to wipe out completely the stake of the residual claimants appear to carry elements of inequity.

This, then, is the reorganization process with particular reference to the financial variables and implications. Reorganization applies to companies that have encountered operating difficulties resulting in financial losses. Reorganization procedures are applied when the company can be rehabilitated and again become an effective competitor in its industry. Where this possibility is not present, liquidation will take place instead. The procedures followed are those either of assignment or of bankruptcy.

LIQUIDATION PROCEDURES

Liquidation of a business takes place when the estimated value of the firm is greater "dead than alive."

Assignment is a liquidation procedure that does not go through the courts, although it can be used to achieve full settlement of claims on the debtor. *Bankruptcy* is a legal procedure carried out under the jurisdiction of special courts in which a business firm is formally liquidated and claims of creditors are completely discharged.

Assignment

Assignment as well as bankruptcy takes place when the debtor is so hopelessly insolvent and so utterly lacking in the ability to rehabilitate himself that his enterprise must be dissolved and put out of business. Assignment is a technique for liquidating a debtor and yielding a larger amount to the creditor than is likely to be achieved in bankruptcy.

Technically, there are three types of assignments:

1. Common law assignment
2. Statutory assignment
3. Assignment plus settlement

Common law assignment. The common law provides for an assignment whereby a debtor transfers his title to assets to a third person, known as an assignee or a trustee. The trustee is instructed to liquidate the assets and to distribute the proceeds among the creditors on a pro rata basis.

Typically, an assignment is conducted through the adjustment bureau of the local credit managers' association. The assignee may liquidate the assets through what is known as a bulk sale, which is a public sale through an auctioneer. The auction is preceded by sufficient advertising so that there will be a number of bids at the auction. Liquidation may also be by a piecemeal auction sale conducted on the premises of the assignor by a competent licensed auctioneer, rather than by a bulk sale. On-premises sales are particularly advantageous in the liquidation of large machine shops or manufacturing plants.

The common law assignment, as such, does not discharge the debtor from his obligations. If a corporation goes out of business and does not satisfy all its claims, there will still be claims against the corporation, but in effect it has ceased to exist. The people who have been associated with the corporation can then proceed to organize another corporation free of the debts and obligations of the previous corporation. There is always the danger, however, that the court may look through the corporate veil and hold the individuals responsible. It is therefore usually important to obtain a complete settlement.

Although a common law assignment has taken place, the assignee, in drawing up checks paying the creditors, may write on the check the requisite legal language to make the payment a complete discharge of the obligation. There are technical legal requirements for this process, which are best carried out with the aid of a lawyer, but essential is a statement that endorsement of this check represents full payment for the obligation. A common law assignment is often used by an individual debtor (a sole proprietorship) or a partnership. Following the execution of such an assignment, the assignor requests voluntarily signed releases from the creditors. Such releases are usually forthcoming in situations of "honest failures," thus avoiding the necessity of bankruptcy.

Statutory assignment. Statutory assignment is similar in concept to common law assignment. Legally, it is carried out under state statutes regulating assignment; technically, it requires more formality. The debtor executes an instrument of assignment, which is recorded. This recordation provides notice to all third parties. A court is utilized; the court appoints an assignee and supervises the proceedings, including the sale of the assets and distribution of the proceeds. As in the common law assignment, the debtor is not discharged from the balance of his obligations. He can discharge himself, however, by printing the requisite statement on the dividend check.

Assignment plus settlement. Both the common law assignment and the statutory assignment may take place with recognition and agreement beforehand with the creditors that the assignment will represent a complete discharge of obligation. Normally, the debtor will communicate with the local credit managers' association. The adjustment bureau of the local credit managers' association will arrange a meeting of all the creditors. A trust instrument of assignment is drawn up. The adjustment bureau is designated to dispose of the assets, which are sold through regular trade channels, by bulk sales, by auction, or by private sales. The creditors will, typically, leave all responsibility for the liquidation procedure with the assignee, the adjustment bureau of the local credit managers' association.

Having disposed of the assets and obtained funds, the adjustment bureau will then distribute the dividends pro rata among the creditors, with the designation on the check that this is in full settlement of the claims on the debtor. Ordinarily, a release is not agreed upon prior to the execution of the assignment. After full examination of the facts, the creditors' committee will usually make a recommendation for the granting of a release, after the execution of the assignment. If releases are not forthcoming, the assignor may, within four months of the date of the assignment, file a voluntary petition in bankruptcy. In this event, the assignment is terminated and the assignee must account and report to the trustee and the referee in bankruptcy, and deliver to the trustee all assets in the estate (usually by that time assets have been reduced to cash).

Assignment has substantial advantages over bankruptcy. Bankruptcy through the courts involves much time, legal formality, and accountant and legal expenses. An assignment saves the substantial costs of a bankruptcy proceeding, and it may save time as well.

Furthermore, an assignee usually has much more flexibility in disposing of property than does a bankruptcy trustee. He may be more familiar with the normal channels of trade. Since he takes actions much sooner, before the inventories become obsolete, he may achieve better results.

BANKRUPTCY

Though the bankruptcy procedures leave room for improvement, the Federal Bankruptcy Acts themselves represent two main achievements. (1) They provide safeguards against fraud by the debtor during liquidation and at the same time provide for an equitable distribution of the debtor's assets among his creditors. (2) Insolvent debtors may discharge all their obligations and start new businesses unhampered by a burden of prior debt.

Prerequisites for Bankruptcy

A voluntary petition of bankruptcy may be filed by the debtor. But if an involuntary petition of bankruptcy is to be filed, three conditions must be met:

1. The total debts of the insolvent must be $1,000 or more.
2. If the debtor has less than 12 creditors, any one of the creditors may file the petition if the amount owed him is $500 or more. If there are 12 or more creditors, the petition must be signed by three or more creditors with provable total claims of $500 or more.
3. Within the four months preceding, the debtor must have committed one or more of the six acts of bankruptcy.

Acts of Bankruptcy

The six acts of bankruptcy follow.

1. Concealment or fraudulent conveyance. Concealment is hiding assets with intent to defraud creditors. Fraudulent conveyance is transfer of property to a third party without adequate consideration and with intent to defraud creditors.

2. Preferential transfer. A preferential transfer is the transfer of money or assets by an insolvent debtor to a creditor, giving the creditor a greater portion of his claim than other creditors would receive on liquidation.

3. Legal lien or distraint. If an insolvent debtor permits any creditor to obtain a lien on his property and fails to discharge the lien within 30 days, or if the debtor permits a landlord to distrain for nonpayment of rent, he has committed an act of bankruptcy. In this way creditors, by obtaining a lien, may force an insolvent but obdurate debtor into bankruptcy.

4. Assignment. If a debtor makes a general assignment for benefit of his creditors, an act of bankruptcy likewise exists. Again, this enables creditors who have become distrustful of the debtor in the process of assignment to transfer the proceedings to a bankruptcy court. As a matter of practice, typical in common law assignments, creditors will require that a debtor execute a formal assignment document to be held in escrow, to become effective if informal and voluntary settlement negotiations fail. If they do fail, the assignment becomes effective and the creditors have their choice of throwing the case into the bankruptcy court.

5. Appointment of receiver or trustee. If an insolvent debtor permits the appointment of a receiver or a trustee to take charge of his property, he has committed an act of bankruptcy. In this event, the creditors may remove a receivership or an adjustment proceeding to a bankruptcy court.

6. Admission in writing. If the debtor admits in writing his inability to pay his debts and his willingness to be judged bankrupt, he has committed an act of bankruptcy. The reason for this sixth act of bankruptcy is that debtors are often unwilling to engage in voluntary bankruptcy because it carries some stigma of avoidance of obligations. When negotiations are being conducted with a debtor and they have reached an impasse, however, admission in writing is one of the methods of forcing the debtor to commit an act of bankruptcy and of moving the proceedings into a bankruptcy court, where the debtor will not be able to resist all plans for settlement.

Adjudication and the Referee

On the filing of the petition of involuntary bankruptcy, a subpoena is served on the debtor. There is usually no contest by the debtor, and the court adjudges him bankrupt. On adjudication, the case is transferred by the court to a referee in bankruptcy. A referee in bankruptcy is generally a lawyer appointed for a specified term by the judge of the bankruptcy court to act in his place after adjudication.

In addition, on petition of the creditors, the referee in voluntary proceedings, or the judge in involuntary proceedings, may appoint a receiver, who serves as the custodian of the property of the debtor until the appointment of a trustee. This arrangement was suggested because a lengthy period elapses between the date of the filing of a petition in bankruptcy and the election of a trustee at the first creditors' meeting. To safeguard the creditors' interest during this period, the court, either through the referee or the judge, may appoint a receiver in bankruptcy. The receiver in bankruptcy has full control until the trustee is appointed.

First Creditors' Meeting

At the first meeting of the creditors, a trustee is elected. Frequently, each of the different blocks of creditors will have a different candidate for trustee, making the election a drawn-out affair. Frequently, the trustee will be the adjustment bureau of the local credit managers' association. At this first meeting the debtor may also be examined for the purpose of obtaining necessary information.

Subsequent Procedure

The trustee and the creditors' committee act to convert all assets into cash. The trustee sends a letter to people owing the debtor money, warning that all past-due accounts will result in instant suit if immediate payment is not made, and if necessary he will institute such suit. Appraisers are appointed by the courts to set a value on the property. With the advice of the creditors' committee and by authorization of the referee, the merchandise is sold by approved methods. As in an assignment, auctions may be held.

Property may not be sold without consent of the court at less than 75 percent of the appraised value that has been set by the appraisers appointed by the court. If cash is received from the disposition of the property, and after all expenses associated with the proceedings of the bankruptcy have been paid, the trustee may pay the remaining funds to the claimants.

Final Meeting and Discharge

When the trustee has completed his liquidation and has sent out all the claimants' checks, he makes an accounting, which is reviewed by the creditors and the referee. After all the payments have been made by the trustee, the bankruptcy is discharged and the debtor is released from all debts.

If the hearings before the referee indicate the probability of fraud, the FBI is required to undertake an investigation. If fraud was not committed and the bankruptcy is discharged, the debtor is again free to engage in business. Since business is highly competitive in many fields, he will probably not have great difficulty in obtaining credit again. Under the National Bankruptcy Act, however, a debtor may *not* be granted a discharge more often than at six-year intervals.

Priority of Claims on Distribution of Proceeds of a Bankruptcy

The order of priority of claims is as follows:

1. Costs of administration and operating the bankrupt estate.
2. Wages due workers if earned within three months prior to the filing of the petition in bankruptcy. The amount of wages is not to exceed $600 per person.
3. Taxes due the United States, state, county, or any other governmental agency.
4. Secured creditors with the proceeds of the sale of specific property pledged for a mortgage.
5. General or unsecured creditors. This claim consists of the remaining unpaid balances to secured creditors after the sale of specific property, in addition to trade credit, bank loans, and debenture bonds.
6. Preferred stock.
7. Common stock.

To illustrate how this priority of claims works out, let us take a specific example. The balance sheet of the Bankrupt Firm is shown in Table 29–7. Assets total $90 million. The claims are those indicated on the right-hand side of the balance sheet. It will be noted that the subordinated debentures are subordinated to the notes payable to commercial banks.

TABLE 29–7

BANKRUPT FIRM

BALANCE SHEET

Current assets	$80,000,000	Accounts payable . .	$20,000,000	
		Notes payable		
Net property	$10,000,000	(due bank) . . .	10,000,000	
		Accrued wages,		
		1,400 @ $500 . . .	700,000	
		U. S. taxes	1,000,000	
		State and local taxes .	300,000	
		Current debt		$32,000,000
		1st mortgage	$ 6,000,000	
		2nd mortgage . . .	1,000,000	
		Subordinated Deben-		
		tures*	8,000,000	
		Long-term debt . . .		$15,000,000
		Preferred stock . . .	2,000,000	
		Common stock . . .	26,000,000	
		Capital surplus . . .	4,000,000	
		Earned surplus . . .	11,000,000	
		Net worth		$43,000,000
	$90,000,000	Total		$90,000,000

* Subordinated to $10 million notes payable to the First National Bank.

Now assume that the assets of the firm are sold. The following amounts are realized on liquidation:

Current assets	$28,000,000
Net property	5,000,000
Total	$33,000,000

The order of priority of payment of claims is shown by Table 29–8. Fees and expenses of administration typically are about 20 percent of gross proceeds. In this example they are assumed to be $6 million. Next in priority are wages due workers, which total $700,000. The total amount of taxes to be paid is $1.3 million. Thus far the total paid from the $33 million is $8 million. The first mortgage is then paid from the net proceeds of $5 million from the sale of fixed property, leaving $20 million available to the general creditors.

The amount therefore available to the general creditors is $20 million. The claims of the general creditors total $40 million. Since $20 million is available, each claimant receives 50 percent of his claim before the

TABLE 29-8

BANKRUPT FIRM

ORDER OF PRIORITY OF CLAIMS

Distribution of Proceeds on Liquidation

1. Proceeds of sale of assets	$33,000,000
2. Fees and expenses of administration of bankruptcy	$ 6,000,000
3. Wages due workers earned 3 months prior to filing of bankruptcy petition	700,000
4. Taxes	1,300,000
	$25,000,000
5. First mortgage, paid from net property	5,000,000
6. Available to general creditors	$20,000,000

Claims as General Creditors	Claim	Application of 50 Percent	After Subordination Adjustment	Percentage of Claims Received
Unsatisfied portion of first mortgage . . .	$ 1,000,000	$ 500,000	$ 500,000	50
Unsatisfied portion of second mortgage . .	1,000,000	500,000	500,000	50
Notes payable	10,000,000	5,000,000	9,000,000	90
Accounts payable . . .	20,000,000	10,000,000	10,000,000	50
Subordinated debentures	8,000,000	4,000,000	0	0
	$40,000,000	$20,000,000	$20,000,000	

$$\text{Percentage of payment} . \quad \frac{\$20,000,000}{\$40,000,000} = 50$$

subordination adjustment. The subordination adjustment requires that the subordinated debentures turn over to the notes to which they are subordinated all amounts received until the notes are satisfied. In this situation, the claim of the notes payable is $10 million, but only $5 million is available. The deficiency is $5 million. After transfer by the subordinated debentures of $4 million, there remains a deficiency of $1 million, which will be unsatisfied. It will be noted that 90 percent of the bank claim is satisfied, whereas only 50 percent of other unsecured claims will be satisfied. These figures illustrate the usefulness of the subordination provision to the security to which the subordination is made. Since no other funds remain, the claims of the holders of preferred and common stock are completely wiped out.

Studies of the proceeds in bankruptcy liquidations reveal that unsecured creditors receive, on the average, about 15 cents on the dollar. Consequently, where assignment for creditors is likely to yield more, assignment is to be preferred to bankruptcy. This statement is true largely because of the remaining weaknesses of the bankruptcy proceedings.

WEAKNESSES IN THE BANKRUPTCY PROCEDURE

From time to time in this and the preceding chapters, certain weaknesses in the bankruptcy law and its administration have been pointed out. Some of these weaknesses represent hazards for the financial manager, but if he is aware of these problems, he may be in a position to avoid the pitfalls.

Definition of Insolvency

Insolvency in a bankruptcy sense means that assets *at their fair and reasonable value* are insufficient to meet total debts. However, the debtor may be insolvent in the equity sense; in other words, he may be unable to meet his debts but may also be unwilling to be petitioned into bankruptcy. If the petitioning creditors attempt to place the debtor into involuntary bankruptcy, and the debtor then proves solvency in the bankruptcy sense, the case is dismissed and the petitioning creditors must bear all the expense, including the fees of the defendant's attorney.

Since the affairs of the debtor may be in an uncertain state when he has fallen into financial difficulty, some doubt may arise concerning whether he is insolvent in a bankruptcy sense. For example, the going-concern value of the special dies and fixtures of a manufacturing firm may be $250,000. Their value in liquidation may be only the value of scrap iron. If the going-concern "fair and reasonable value" of the assets of a firm establishes that it is not insolvent in a bankruptcy sense, proceedings initiated by the creditors may turn out to be very costly to them. The financial manager must be aware of such hazards. Often information regarding the true state of affairs can be obtained with a moderate amount of searching or effort. The financial manager should therefore develop wide sources of information among financial officers and credit men at all times so that, when it is necessary to obtain information of this sort, he can obtain a dependable fund of knowledge.

Cumbersome Proceedings

The bankruptcy procedure remains legalistic, time-consuming, and costly. Approximately two thirds of the bankruptcy cases are no-asset cases; that is, there are no assets from which proceeds will be developed. Provision should be made to handle such cases expediently, because the expenses involved are not justified by the possibility of any return. Though every precaution should be taken to prevent the abuse of the bankruptcy privilege, cases that can produce nothing but additional expense should be dealt with in a summary fashion.

Management of Property

Bankrupt estates are generally not administered with the efficiency and competence with which a healthy organization is conducted. In fact, such estates are generally administered with gross inefficiency unless they are closely supervised by creditor interests. One reason for this is that trustees who are appointed to liquidate the bankrupt estates for the benefit of creditors may know too little about the fundamental nature of the business and may take too long to perform their duties. Here again is an area where the financial manager must be alert to press the claims of his firm effectively and to inform himself about the nature of the operation which has gone into bankruptcy.

Fraud

Sometimes fraud or collusion will be used to the adverse interests of the creditors. Occasionally an attorney or a group of attorneys will obtain from the creditors of a bankrupt the right to proceed against him. With these proxy claims they will elect one of the colleagues as trustee, who proceeds to sell the property of the bankrupt to the ring at a low amount. The ring then sells the property at its real value, and the profits are divided among the members of the ring.

Both the financial manager and the local credit associations can be alerted to behavior of this kind. The financial manager should not permit his claims to be taken by lawyers unless he knows them to be responsible and unless he follows the proceedings on an informed basis. In this way the assets of his firm may be conserved.

Lack of Interest

The very small returns that are typically received by unsecured creditors discourages their participation in bankruptcy cases. The entire philosophy of the administration of the bankruptcy laws is, however, predicated on the active interest and participation of the creditors. As a consequence, the failure of a financial manager to maintain the interest of his firm and to press his claims may result in substantial losses. Here again is an area where time, attention, and effort of the financial manager may conserve substantial financial resources for his firm.

SUMMARY

The amount received by a creditor is dependent upon the success of a reorganization plan, which in turn depends upon the efforts of the creditors as the plan is being developed.

The application of standards of fairness and feasibility developed in this chapter are tools to determine the probable success of a particular plan of reorganization. The concept of fairness involves the estimation of sales, earnings, and a capitalization rate applied to the latter to determine the appropriate distribution to each claimant. This distribution may be on the basis of the absolute priority of each claim, just as though an actual bankruptcy and liquidation were in operation. Since an actual liquidation does not take place and the future value of the firm is largely a matter of judgment, the doctrine of relative priority is probably fairer. This doctrine provides some residual interest for all claimants.

The feasibility test examines the ability of the new enterprise to carry the fixed charges resulting from the reorganization plan. The quality of management and the company's assets must be assured. Production and marketing may also require improvement.

Finally, where liquidation is treated as the only solution to the debtor's insolvency, the creditors should attempt procedures that will net them the largest recovery. Assignment of the debtor's property is the cheaper and the faster procedure. In addition, there is more flexibility in disposing of the debtor's property and thus providing larger returns.

Bankruptcy provides formal procedures to safeguard the debtor's property from fraud and provides equitable distribution to the creditors. The procedure is long and cumbersome. In addition, the debtor's property is generally poorly managed during bankruptcy proceedings unless the trustee is closely supervised by the creditors.

SELECTED REFERENCES

"Allocation of Securities in Corporate Reorganization: Claims Measurement through Investment Value Analysis," *Yale Law Review*, 61 (May 1952), pp. 656–685.

Baldwin, W. H., "McKesson and Robbins Reorganization," *Harvard Business Review*, 20 (Spring 1942), p. 473.

Billyou, D. F., "Priority Rights of Security Holders in Bankruptcy Reorganizations: New Directions," *Harvard Law Review*, 67 (February 1954), pp. 553–590.

Blum, Walter J., "Full Priority and Full Compensation in Corporate Reorganizations," *University of Chicago Law Review*, 25 (Spring 1958), pp. 417–444.

Calkins, Francis J., "Corporate Reorganization under Chapter X: A Post-Mortem," *Journal of Finance*, 3 (June 1948), pp. 19–28.

———, "Feasibility in Plans of Corporate Reorganizations under Chapter X," *Harvard Law Review*, 61 (May 1948), pp. 763–781.

Fraine, Harold G., and Robert H. Mills, "Effect of Defaults and Credit Deterioration on Yields of Corporate Bonds," *Journal of Finance*, 16 (September 1961), pp. 423–434.

Guthmann, H. G., "Absolute Priority in Reorganization," *Columbia Law Review*, 45 (September 1945), pp. 739–754.

O'Leary, P. M., "The Role of Banking Groups in Corporate Reorganizations," *American Economic Review*, 28 (June 1939), pp. 337–344.

Watson, E. T. P., "Distribution of New Securities in Section 77 Reorganizations," *Journal of Finance*, 5 (December 1950), pp. 337–367.

Wren, H. G., "Feasibility and Fairness in Section 20b Reorganizations," *Columbia Law Review*, 52 (June 1952), pp. 715–745.

QUESTIONS

29–1 Which type of security holders—first-mortgage bondholders or common stockholders—would be more likely to favor the relative priority doctrine over the absolute priority doctrine? Why?

29–2 Would it be possible to form a profitable company by merging two companies both of which are business failures? Explain.

29–3 Distinguish between a reorganization and a bankruptcy.

29–4 Would it be a sound rule to liquidate whenever the liquidation value is above the value of the corporation as a going concern? Discuss.

29–5 Why do liquidations of all types usually result in losses for the creditors or the owners, or both? Would partial liquidation or liquidation over a period limit their losses? Explain.

29–6 Are liquidations likely to be more common for public utility, railroad, or industrial corporations? Why?

PROBLEMS

29–1[5] On September 13, 1956, a voluntary petition for reorganization under Chapter X of the Bankruptcy Act was filed by Green River Steel Corporation in the U. S. District Court for the Western District of Kentucky, Owensboro Division. The petition was approved and a trustee was named. On November 12, 1956, the trustee filed a plan for reorganization with the court.

GREEN RIVER STEEL COMPANY
BALANCE SHEET
July 31, 1956
(in thousands of dollars)

Assets			*Long-term debt*		
Current assets	$ 4,000		4½% mortgage due RFC .	$ 4,500	
Net property account . .	9,000		Deferred interest	300	
Total assets	$13,000		3½% debentures, due 1961	4,000	
			Interest accrued on 3½% debentures	18	
Current liabilities			Total long-term debt .	$ 8,818	
4½% mortgage due RFC (2,100 past due) . . .	$ 4,000				
Notes payable to banks . .	1,000				
Accounts payable	1,500		*Capital stock*		
Interest due to RFC . . .	1,000		Common (10 cents par) .	7	
Accruals	200		Paid-in surplus	80	
Total current liabilities	$ 7,700		Earned surplus (deficit) .	(3,605)	
			Total claims	$13,000	

---

[5] Based on SEC Reorganization release No. 1940. *In the matter of Green River Steel Corporation, Debtor, in proceedings for the reorganization of a corporation pursuant to Chapter X of the Bankruptcy Act* (Washington, D. C., January 24, 1957), pp. 1–25. Facts altered and rounded to facilitate calculations.

On November 22, 1950, Green River Steel was incorporated under the laws of Kentucky for the purpose of engaging in the production and sale of semi-finished steel products. In July 1953, Green River started operations. In early 1954, when the plant was ready to produce at its rated capacity, the entire industry was hit by the recession. In addition, the company lacked working capital, as shown by the balance sheet below.

All attempts to secure additional funds failed. In spite of the difficulties, there has been a steadily improving trend in both sales and net profits.

However, with the entire $4 million principal amount of one of the mortgage notes held by RFC falling due on January 1, 1957, it was obvious to the management that the company could not meet its obligations.

GREEN RIVER STEEL COMPANY
SALES AND PROFITS
1954–1956
(in thousands of dollars)

Year Ended	Net Sales	Net Operating Profit before Interest Charges	Net Profits
July 31, 1954	$ 5,413	(1,603)	(2,185)
July 31, 1955	10,790	47	575
July 31, 1956	17,270	826	204

The trustee's plan of reorganization was based on an offer by Jessop Steel Company. The trustee's plan follows:

1) The United States, as the holder of RFC notes, will receive a new first-mortgage note in the principal amount of $9 million at the date of consummation, maturing 18 years thereafter, and bearing interest rate of 3 percent per year for the first three years, and 4½ percent per year thereafter.

2) The holders of outstanding debentures will receive in exchange for each $1,000 principal amount and the interest accumulated thereon to the date of consummation, a new $1,000 income subordinated debenture note, maturing 25 years thereafter, and bearing interest, if earned and noncumulative, of 2 percent for the third through the sixth years, 2½ for the seventh and eighth years, and 3½ percent thereafter. The new debentures will be subordinate (a) to a $9 million first-mortgage note, (b) to new ten-year notes payable to Jessop in the principal amount of not less than $1.5 million, and (c) to bank loans of $3 million.

3) The holders of the common stock of the debtor will receive in exchange for each ten shares of such stock one share of common stock of Jessop. New common stock will be issued by Green River to Jessop, which will become the sole stockholder of the reorganized enterprise.

4) The trustee's plan provides for the issuance of ten-year notes to Jessop in exchange for cash advanced to the debtor in the principal amount of $1.5 million at the consummation date, maturing in ten years and bearing interest of 4 percent per year.

5) The plan also provides for sinking funds for the retirement of the first mortgage note, the ten-year note, and the new debentures.

The *pro forma* liabilities and net worth giving effect to the trustee's plan are:

Notes payable to banks	$3,000	
Accounts payable	1,500	
Accruals	200	
Current liabilities		$ 4,700
First mortgage due RFC	9,800	
10-year note to Jessop, 4%	1,500	
Subordinated income debentures	4,000	
Long-term debt		15,300
Common stock, par value, $10	3,000	
Capital surplus	1,000	
Net worth		4,000
Total claims		$24,000

The *pro forma* statement is based on continuing the accounts payable at $1.5 million, increasing the bank loans to $3 million and additional investment of $1.5 by Jessop Steel.

1. What is the value of the assets of Green River less the new capital invested in the business?
2. Using the capitalization of income method, if the sales of Green River rise to $30 million, the profit rate on sales (before interest) is 7 percent and the price-earnings ratio is 8, what is the amount of the total assets of Green River after reorganization?
3. What is the amount of total assets of Green River if sales are $25 million but all other conditions are as in (2)?
4. Assume that sales of Green River are $25 million but that the profit rate rises to 8 percent. What is the amount of total assets of Green River now?
5. Because Jessop Steel would become the sole owner of Green River, does it make any difference whether Jessop's $1.5 is treated as debt or as ownership investment?
6. What is your appraisal of the fairness of the proposed reorganization plan?
7. What is your opinion of the feasibility of the reorganization plan?

29–2 On May 10, 1965, the Simpson Company filed an involuntary petition in bankruptcy, having defaulted interest on its outstanding debt. At this date, it issued the following balance sheet.

Assets		*Liabilities and Net Worth*	
Cash	$ 10,000	Accounts payable . . .	$ 500,000
Receivables	190,000	Notes payable, 8% . . .	500,000
Inventory	800,000	First mortgage, 5% . . .	1,000,000
Machinery	2,000,000	Second mortgage, 6% . .	1,000,000
Plant	5,000,000	Debentures, 6%	2,000,000
Surplus	1,000,000	Preferred stock, 7% . . .	1,000,000
		Common stock	3,000,000
Total	$9,000,000	Total	$9,000,000

The Simpson Company, after the necessary reorganization, can earn $320,000. You have determined that 8 percent is an appropriate capitalization rate to employ.

1. State your plan of reorganization, using: (a) absolute priority doctrine, (b) relative priority doctrine.
2. Defend both your plans for (a) "fairness" in legal connotation, (b) "feasibility" in legal connotation.

29–3 The Pomona Pipe Company has suffered several years of operating losses. Because of the unfavorable outlook for the firm, it goes into bankruptcy and is dissolved. How much would each class of claimant on assets receive in liquidation?

POMONA PIPE COMPANY
BALANCE SHEET
September 30, 1965
(last balance sheet before dissolution)

Cash	$ 20,000	Accounts payable . . .	$ 1,000,000
Accounts receivable . .	100,000	Loans from banks . . .	2,000,000
Inventories	2,000,000	Property taxes	5,000
Building	10,000,000	Accrued wages* . . .	60,000
Equipment	5,000,000	Federal income taxes . .	5,000
		1st mortgage on build-ing	4,000,000
		2nd mortgage on build-ing	2,000,000
		Subordinated convertible debentures†	1,000,000
		Preferred stock	3,000,000
		Common stock	3,000,000
		Retained earnings . . .	1,050,000
	$17,120,000		$17,120,000

* Incurred during the last two months, no claim exceeds $600.
† Subordinated to bank loan only.

On liquidation, the following amounts are received from respective items:

Cash	$ 20,000
Receivables	50,000
Inventories	1,000,000
Building	5,000,000
Equipment	2,000,000

What would be the priority of payment, and how much would each class of creditor receive?

Part VIII

An Integrated View of Financial Management

Chapter 30

The Timing of Financial Policy

The previous parts of this book have dealt with the environment of financial management, financial planning and control, forms of financing, sources of financing, and financial strategies for growth. The immediately preceding topic ended with financial embarrassments and rehabilitation. This final part of the book seeks to end on a more positive note. It deals with two topics that relate to the dynamics of business enterprise. Because they involve decisions of the firm over time, the materials could not easily be integrated with the foregoing topics without making them unduly segmented. The first new topic deals with the timing of financial policy in relation to varying conditions of cost and availability of funds. The second views the firm in broad perspective to observe how the types of financing needs and the kinds of available financing change through the life history of a firm.

This chapter deals with the timing of financial policy. Variations in the relative cost and availability of funds require comparison of the changes in the cost and availability of equity money, long-term money, and short-term money over time. Fluctuations in the level of business activity produce a number of impacts on the firm. For good timing of financial policy, the financial manager must take into account prospective changes in asset requirements that will have to be financed over time. He must also consider prospective prices and return from capital assets. Finally, he must plan his needs to meet future maturing obligations.

SIGNIFICANCE TO FINANCIAL MANAGEMENT

The significance of the timing of financial policy by firms is suggested by the following:

> Since 1951, when the Federal Reserve won the right to pursue an independent monetary policy, the cost and availability of money have been a constant problem for corporate management. At times, as in the tight money squeeze of 1957, it has been a major worry.
>
> Company treasurers resented the high rates that banks charged on loans; they resented even more banks' insistence that they hold compensating balances, depriving them of the full use of their borrowed money. And because they feared that rates would go even higher and that credit might not be available at all, they stepped up their demands—which had the effect of further tightening an already tight situation.[1]

Financial managers are concerned with variations in money and capital-market conditions because changes in the cost and availability of funds that have been experienced periodically in the past and will be experienced in the future are of substantial magnitude.

Table 30–1 shows how the cost of short-term funds, as measured by the rate on three-month treasury bills, can change by more than 50 percent within one year. On long-term, high-grade corporate bonds, the changes can be 10 percent or more, measured from the peaks.

There is evidence that corporate financial managers are aware of, and concerned with, variations in the cost of money. For example, a 1956 *Fortune* article pointed out that the General Electric Company had sold an issue of $300 million, 3.5 percent debentures in May of 1956.[2] The article pointed out that if G.E. had sold the issue six months earlier, it could have saved ¼ of 1 percent in interest, or $750,000 a year. If it had raised the money three years earlier (in 1954), it probably could have saved ½ percent, or $1.5 million a year. On the other hand, if it had waited until January 1957, approximately half a year later, it probably would have paid ½ percent more in interest, or perhaps even ¾ percent more; in such an event it would have had to pay from $1.5 million to over $2 million more in yearly interest.

Another example is provided by the postwar financing of U.S. Steel, highlighted in a financial review.[3] The article explains that U.S. Steel had engaged in a $5 billion postwar expansion program, financed mainly from internal sources. However, its earnings dropped from an average of $400 million for 1955–1957 to just over $300 million for the years 1958–1960.

---

1 "Where the Credit Pinch Hurts," *Business Week*, February 27, 1960, p. 65.
2 Charles E. Silverman, "The Fine Art of Raising Capital," *Fortune*, July 1956; Reprinted in J. Fred Weston (ed.), *Readings in Finance from Fortune* (New York: Holt, Rinehart and Winston, 1958), p. 28.
3 The following material on U.S. Steel is based on "Calling the Turn?" *Forbes*, 87 (April 15, 1961), p. 28.

TABLE 30-1

DECLINES IN SELECTED INTEREST YIELDS FROM PEAKS TO LOWS DURING SELECTED PERIODS[4]

Part 1: Absolute Declines from Peak Levels (in percentage points)

3-month Treasury Bills		*Long-term U. S. Bonds*		*Moody's Corporate Aaa Bonds*		*Moody's State and Local Aaa Bonds*	
Dec. 1959–		Jan. 1960–		Jan. 1960–		Sept. 1959–	
Dec. 1960	2.24	Dec. 1960	0.49	Sept. 1960	0.36	Sept. 1960	0.51
Oct. 1957–		Oct. 1957–		Sept. 1957–		Sept. 1957–	
June 1958	2.75	Apr. 1958	0.61	June 1958	0.55	May 1958	0.74
Apr. 1953–		June 1953–		June 1953–		June 1953–	
June 1954	1.55	Aug. 1954	0.69	Apr. 1954	0.55	Aug. 1954	0.54

Part II: Percentage Declines from Peak Levels

3-month Treasury Bills		*Long-term U. S. Bonds*		*Moody's Corporate Aaa Bonds*		*Moody's State and Local Aaa Bonds*	
Dec. 1959–		Jan. 1960–		Jan. 1960–		Sept. 1959–	
Dec. 1960	49.9	Dec. 1960	11.2	Sept. 1960	7.8	Sept. 1960	14.2
Oct. 1957–		Oct. 1957–		Sept. 1957–		Sept. 1957–	
June 1958	76.8	Apr. 1958	16.4	June 1958	13.4	May 1958	21.6
Apr. 1953–		June 1953–		June 1953–		June 1953–	
June 1954	70.8	Aug. 1954	21.0	Apr. 1954	16.2	Aug. 1954	28.0

Source: "Credit Developments in 1960," *Monthly Review,* Federal Bank of Richmond, March 1961, p. 3.

Similarly, depreciation accruals are related to the level of operations, averaging $285 million a year in 1955–1957, but dropping to $205 million for 1958–1960. "So, to keep up the pace of its capital spending, without slimming dividend checks, the Corporation would have to borrow." The article then called attention to the good record of U.S. Steel in timing its bond flotations. "Where top-grade corporates had to be priced to yield 4.43 percent as recently as September 1959, Big Steel will probably have to pay no more than 4.05 percent—for a saving of some $1.2 million a year."

The consistently good timing of U.S. Steel is shown by the diagram in Figure 30–1. In commenting on the observation that U.S. Steel seemed each time to have picked the cyclical low point in high-grade industrial

---

[4] Based on monthly averages of daily figures, except in the case of state and local government obligation yields, which are based on monthly averages of Thursday figures.

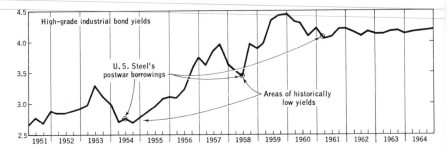

Fig. 30-1. Timing of Borrowing by United States Steel
Source: Forbes, 87 (April 15, 1961)

bond yields for bringing out its new issues, Finance Committee Chairman
Robert C. Tyson stated:

"We have no crystal balls. Any time you are going to do these things,
you look at the cost of money."

Admittedly, savings of $2 million or so are not large in relation to
profits after taxes of $400 to $500 million achieved by large companies.
However, from the standpoint of effective operation of the financial department, the sound timing of financing is a matter of great importance.
Furthermore, though any one department's operation is not likely to determine the success or failure of a company, when it is taken in conjunction with other departments, the cumulative effect can be very great.

This statement does not imply that interest rates have a determining
influence on investment activity. A difference in the impact of interest
costs on the following categories of investment must be recognized:

1. Business
    a) Heavy industries versus light industries
    b) Small firms versus large firms
2. State and local governments
3. Housing and construction activity

Lower interest rates stimulate investments in certain kinds of heavy
industries, such as the public utilities. High interest rates, in contrast, may
cause postponement of projects of relatively long duration, where the fixed
investment is high in relation to the total investment required for the
activity. Variations in interest rates therefore result in substantial variations in the cost of undertaking such projects.

The greatest influence of interest rates, however, lies in their role as
an index of the availability of financing. A period of high interest rates
reflects a period of tight money, in turn associated with tight reserve positions at commercial banks. At such times interest rates will rise, of course,
but there are conventional limits on interest rates. As a consequence, a
larger quantity of funds is demanded by borrowers than banks will make

available. Banks therefore begin to ration funds among prospective borrowers by continuing lines of credit to traditional customers but restricting loans to borrowers whose credit standards are not as strong. In other words small firms will characteristically have greater difficulty obtaining financing during periods of tight money.

Furthermore, even among large borrowers, the bargaining position of the financial institutions is stronger in a period of tight money. It is a lender's market rather than a borrower's market. As a consequence, the availability of loans is likely to be restricted. Furthermore, the restrictive conditions in term loans are likely to be more onerous when the demand for funds is high.

Interest rates are therefore of very great significance to financial managers as an index to the availability of funds. For small- and medium-sized firms, a period of rising interest rates may indicate increasing difficulty in obtaining any financing at all. Or, if financing is obtained, it will be obtained under less favorable conditions.

To summarize, then, a period of tight money will fall with particularly heavy impact on the utilities and other heavy industries, state and local governments, and the housing and construction sectors. For the heavy, long-term investments made in these areas, the impact of interest rates on profitability is likely to be very great.

For small firms a period of tight money may be associated not only with high costs of borrowing but also with virtual unavailability of financing. Even for large firms, during a period of tight money, problems may be encountered. The prospective profitability of projects available to the large firms is higher than probable variations in interest rates, and thus will not affect the investment behavior of large firms. Nevertheless, there is an impact. During periods of high interest rates, restrictions on lending agreements are likely to be more onerous.

The converse conditions to all the arrangements describing periods of tight money and high interest rates would apply during periods of easy money conditions and relatively low interest rates.

DATA ON RELATIVE COSTS OF FINANCING OVER TIME

It has been seen that the cost of money can vary widely over the business cycle. In addition, costs of different forms of financing differ, and the timing of swings in the cost of money and in the relative cost of financing by different sources changes over time. Detailed data are presented to provide a factual foundation for decision making in choosing between the alternatives available to financial managers. The data in Figure 30–2 give stock yields since 1910.

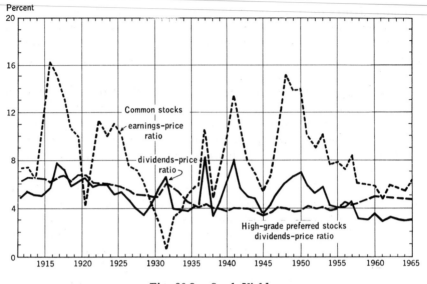

Fig. 30-2.   Stock Yields
Source: Historical Supplement to Federal Reserve
Chart Book on Financial and Business Statistics, p. 51

Cost of Equity Funds

Both the earnings-price ratio and the dividend yield on common stocks have exhibited wide fluctuations. Earnings-price ratios have been as high as 16 percent and as low as 5 to 6 percent, excluding very abnormal years. Dividend-yield ratios have also fluctuated widely, not so much because dividends have fluctuated greatly but because the price factor in the denominator has gyrated widely.

Preferred stocks' yields have shown much more moderate fluctuations. A slight downward secular trend is exhibited from 1910 until the end of World War II, when the dividend yields on preferred stocks declined from about 6 percent to a little under 4 percent. Since the end of World War II, following the upward trend in interest rates, dividend yields have returned to approximately a 5 percent level.

Relation between Long-Term and Short-Term Interest Rates

One of the important elements in the financial manager's timing decisions is an understanding of the relation between long-term and short-term interest rates. Long-term interest rates are rates on securities with maturities in excess of one year and probably more than five years. Short-term interest rates are those on securities with maturities of under one year.

Figure 30-3 sets out the data on the pattern of the relation between long-term and short-term interest rates. At some periods, short-term interest rates were higher than long-term interest rates, notably in the later 1920s and whenever the money market situation becomes extremely tight. These data refute the theory set out by some distinguished economists who argued on the basis of the evidence of the 1930s that short-term rates of interest are always lower than long-term rates. Their argument was based on the reasoning that long-term securities represented a greater degree of

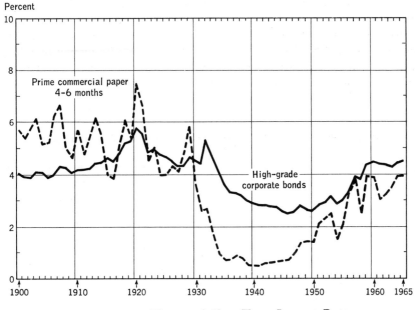

Fig. 30-3.   Long-Term and Short-Term Interest Rates
Source: Op. cit., p. 37

imperfect moneyness than did short-term securities. Because of the greater risk involved, therefore, they argued that long-term rates would always be higher than short-term rates. Their reasoning was undoubtedly sound. There is greater risk to holding long-term securities than short-term securities, but this risk is of a particular kind. The longer the maturity of the security in an uncertain economic environment, the greater the danger that the firm may not make an effective adaptation to its environment and therefore may not be able to meet its obligations in 10, 15, or 20 years.

However, many other kinds of uncertainties are faced by the firm and the investor, which may dominate this particular kind of uncertainty. One of these uncertainties is changes in supply and demand of loanable funds over time. When the supply of funds is tight relative to the demand for them at prevailing prices, there will be strong pressure for short-term interest rates to rise. Short-term interest rates reflect current supply-and-demand situations. Long-term interest rates reflect an average of supply-and-demand conditions over the life of the security. This characteristic accounts for the fact observed that short-term interest rates are much more highly volatile than long-term interest rates (Fig. 30–3).

The theory has been put forth that long-term interest rates may appropriately be regarded as an average of short-term interest rates. Thus the relation between long rates and short rates will depend upon what is happening to the future of short-term interest rates, as illustrated by Table 30–2. In section A it is assumed that short-term interest rates rise 1 percent each year, beginning at 2 percent in 1965. The corresponding interest rate in 1965 for a five-year period can be approximated by taking a simple arithmetic average of the five short-term rates, 4 percent. Thus in 1965 the long-term rate would be double the short-term rate.

TABLE 30–2

RELATION BETWEEN SHORT-TERM AND LONG-TERM INTEREST RATES

Year	A		B	
	5-Year Note	Short-Term Rates	5-Year Note	Short-Term Rates
1965	4	2	4	6
1966		3		5
1967		4		4
1968		5		3
1969		6		2

Consider, however, the situation under section B. Here, in a tight-money situation in 1965, short-term rates are 6 percent, but are expected to decline by 1 percent each year. The average of these rates would be the same as in section A, because the numbers are identical—their order is simply reversed. Now, however, the long-term rate of 4 percent lies below the short-term rate of 6 percent.

These examples do not prove the relation between short-term rates and long-term rates. They do, however, illustrate the pattern that would obtain if the only factor operating was expected changes in interest rate movements, themselves reflecting a broad group of supply-and-demand factors. However, many other uncertainty factors do operate on the market. Some of these include differences (1) in the risks of loss and failure among individual business firms, (2) in the outlook trends for different industries, (3) in the degree to which price-level changes affect different products in industries, and (4) in the impact that changes in government legislation will have on different firms in an industry.

Interest Rate Structure

The discussion now turns to an analysis of the wide range of relations between money costs in the postwar period. The basic data, on bond yields and interest rates since 1950 for ten categories of money costs, are presented in Table 30–3. The table indicates that when a person speaks of "the interest rate," he is in fact referring to an interest rate structure, or cost-of-money structure. The table includes the timing of cyclical peaks and troughs in business conditions.

The variations in money costs (and the availability of funds indicated thereby) are substantial. For example, during the trough of the business cycle during 1954, prime commercial paper carried a 1.31 percent average interest rate. At the subsequent peak of business conditions in the third quarter of 1957, the rate for prime commercial paper had risen to 4 percent. Thus this rate at the peak of 1957 was 300 percent of that in the third quarter of 1953.

The data in Table 30–3 are presented to indicate the range of variations *between* rates on different securities at any moment of time, variations in rates on a particular security over time, and changes in the structure of rates through time. It provides the basic factual background for money cost patterns that will be discussed later. Furthermore, it provides a factual foundation for evaluating the timing of financial policy of firms during the post-World War II period. Reference to the table may be made in connection with end-of-chapter problems.

As a starting point toward understanding the patterns exhibited in Table 30–3, the data are graphed in Figures 30–4 and 30–5. Figure 30–4 illustrates the relation between interest rates on 20-year treasury bonds and three-month treasury bills over the post-World War II cycles. The relative costs typically spread widely apart during a business downturn and tend to narrow during a business upswing. Not only does the spread vary over time, but the absolute level also varies over time. It will be observed also that the movements in short-term rates are much more volatile than movements in long-term interest levels.

Further aspects are presented in Figure 30–5, which presents movements over time in treasury-bill yields, Federal Reserve Bank discount rates, commercial paper rates, rates on corporate Triple A bonds, and level of gross national product. Again, the impact of general business conditions on money market rates is observed. With this abundant factual material on the movements of the cost of money, some generalizations may now be made and systematic patterns observed.

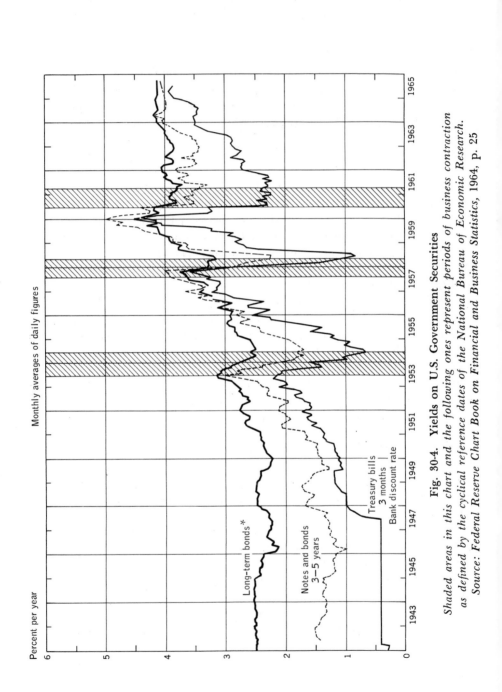

Fig. 30-4. Yields on U.S. Government Securities

Shaded areas in this chart and the following ones represent periods of business contraction as defined by the cyclical reference dates of the National Bureau of Economic Research.
Source: Federal Reserve Chart Book on Financial and Business Statistics, 1964, p. 25

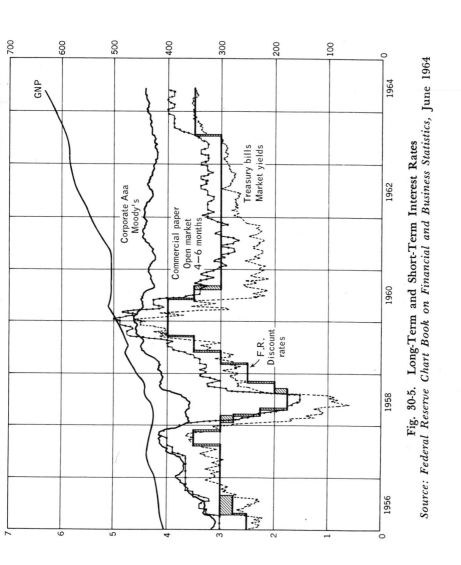

Fig. 30-5. Long-Term and Short-Term Interest Rates

Source: Federal Reserve Chart Book on Financial and Business Statistics, June 1964

TABLE 30–3

BOND YIELDS AND INTEREST RATES

Period Quarters	Three-Month Treas. Bills	Nine-to-Twelve Month Issues	Taxable Bonds	Corporate Bonds Aaa	Corporate Bonds Baa	Common Stock Dividend Yields	High-Grade Municipals	Avg. Rate Short-Term Bank	Prime Coml. Paper, 4–6 Mos.	Fed. Res. Bank Disc. Rate	
1950* 1	1.118	1.14	2.24	2.58	3.24	6.16	2.58	2.60	1.31	1.50	
2	1.166	1.19	2.31	2.61	3.28	6.17	2.62	2.68	1.31	1.50	
3	1.233	1.27	2.34	2.63	3.21	6.22	2.64	2.63	1.47	1.62	
4	1.353	1.44	2.38	2.67	3.20	6.57	2.67	2.84	1.71	1.75	
1951* 1	1.400	1.62	2.42	2.70	3.23	6.40	2.74	3.02	1.96	1.75	
2	1.532	1.84	2.61	2.90	3.49	6.55	2.94	3.07	2.20	1.75	
3	1.628	1.72	2.59	2.89	3.46	5.91	2.84	3.06	2.25	1.75	
4	1.649	1.73	2.66	2.95	3.61	5.55	3.01	2.37	2.26	1.75	
1952† 1	1.658	1.69	2.70	2.96	3.51	5.49	2.07	3.45	2.38	1.75	
2	1.700	1.74	2.61	2.94	3.50	5.45	2.10	3.51	2.31	1.75	
3	1.786	1.95	2.71	2.95	3.52	5.56	2.33	3.49	2.31	1.75	
4	2.126	2.03	2.75	2.97	3.51	5.13	2.40	3.51	2.31	1.75	
1953 1	2.082	2.04	2.89	3.12	3.57	5.34	2.61	3.54	2.36	2.00	
2	2.231	2.46	3.09	3.40	3.86	5.58	2.99	3.73	2.75	2.00	
Peak 3	1.876	2.17	2.97	3.29	3.88	5.73	2.88	3.74	2.74	2.00	July
4	1.630	1.61	2.79	3.13	3.74	5.55	2.59	3.76	2.25	2.00	
1954 1	1.053	1.02	2.51	2.86	3.51	5.14	2.38	3.72	2.00	1.75	
2	0.650	0.76	2.54	2.90	3.49	4.82	2.48	3.60	1.56	1.50	
Trough 3	1.007	0.89	2.51	2.89	3.47	4.46	2.29	3.56	1.31	1.50	August
4	1.174	1.10	2.57	2.90	3.45	4.20	2.33	3.55	1.31	1.50	

1955	1	1.335	1.49	2.78	3.02	3.48	4.21	2.45	3.54	1.69	1.50
	2	1.432	1.71	2.82	3.05	3.51	3.87	2.48	3.56	2.00	1.75
	3	2.086	2.14	2.92	3.13	3.59	3.93	2.63	3.77	2.54	2.18
	4	2.564	2.56	2.91	3.15	3.62	4.07	2.71	3.93	2.99	2.50
1956	1	2.310	2.43	2.93	3.10	3.60	3.86	2.69	3.93	3.00	2.50
	2	2.527	2.69	2.93	3.26	3.76	4.01	2.75	4.14	3.38	2.75
	3	2.850	3.17	3.21	3.56	4.07	4.24	3.07	4.35	3.50	3.00
	4	3.230	3.33	3.40	3.75	4.37	4.13	3.44	4.38	3.63	3.00
1957	1	3.140	3.35	3.26	3.66	4.43	4.35	3.32	4.38	3.63	3.00
	2	3.316	3.55	3.58	3.91	4.63	4.05	3.75	4.40	3.79	3.00
Peak	3	3.578	4.02	3.66	4.12	4.93	4.50	3.90	4.83	4.00	3.50 July
	4	3.102	3.09	3.30	3.81	5.03	4.77	3.47	4.85	3.81	3.00
1958	1	1.354	1.77	3.25	3.63	4.68	4.50	3.45	4.49	2.33	2.35
Trough	2	0.881	0.98	3.20	3.57	4.55	4.15	3.26	4.17	1.54	1.75 April
	3	2.484	2.84	3.75	4.09	4.87	3.72	3.96	4.21	2.93	1.91
	4	2.814	3.24	3.80	4.08	4.85	3.34	3.84	4.50	3.33	2.50
1959	1	2.852	3.56	3.92	4.13	4.85	3.43	3.76	4.51	3.35	2.92
	2	3.247	3.97	4.09	4.46	5.04	3.28	4.04	4.87	3.83	3.50
	3	3.998	4.80	4.26	4.52	5.18	3.34	4.13	5.27	4.63	3.83
	4	4.572	4.98	4.27	4.58	5.28	3.28	4.05	5.36	4.88	4.00
1960	1	3.439	3.93	4.08	4.49	5.25	3.59	3.87	5.34	4.49	4.00
Peak	2	2.641	3.35	3.98	4.45	5.26	3.52	3.78	5.35	3.81	3.65 May
	3	2.489	2.99	3.84	4.25	5.01	3.73	3.53	4.97	3.39	3.00
	4	2.272	2.79	3.88	4.35	5.10	3.49	3.45	4.99	3.23	3.00

* Data for 1950–1951 only available as quarterly totals; no monthly figures published.
† Not published until 1955.

(Table continued on following page.)

Table 30–3 (Continued)

Period Quarters	Three-Month Treas. Bills	Nine-to-Twelve-Month Issues	Taxable Bonds	Corporate Bonds Aaa	Corporate Bonds Baa	Common Stock Dividend Yields	High-Grade Municipals	Avg. Rate Short-Term Bank	Prime Coml. Paper, 4–6 Mos.	Fed. Res. Bank Disc. Rate
Trough 1961 1	2.420	2.86	3.78	4.22	5.02	3.15	3.38	4.97	3.03	3.00 March
1961 2	2.359	3.02	3.88	4.33	5.03	2.99	3.35	4.97	2.91	3.0
3	2.304	3.03	4.02	4.45	5.12	2.93	3.33	4.99	3.05	3.0
4	2.617	3.03	4.06	4.42	5.10	2.85	3.32	4.96	3.19	3.0
1962 1	2.719	2.99	4.01	4.39	5.04	2.95	3.03	4.98	3.25	3.0
2	2.719	3.02	3.90	4.28	5.02	3.78	3.06	5.01	3.25	3.0
3	2.792	3.00	3.94	4.32	5.03	3.60	3.01	4.99	3.34	3.5
4	2.856	2.95	3.87	4.24	4.92	3.40	2.93	5.02	3.29	3.5
1963 1	2.897	2.99	3.93	4.19	4.88	3.28	2.97	5.00	3.34	3.5
2	2.995	3.17	4.01	4.22	4.84	3.13	3.10	5.01	3.38	3.5
3	3.379	3.54	4.04	4.31	4.84	3.06	3.13	5.01	3.88	3.5
4	3.523	3.77	4.14	4.35	4.84	3.13	3.12	5.00	3.96	3.5
1964 1	3.553	3.67	4.18	4.38	4.83	3.03	3.14	4.99	4.00	3.5
2	3.478	3.83	4.13	4.41	4.85	3.05	3.10	4.99	4.00	3.5
3	3.527	3.82	4.16	4.42	4.82	3.00	3.09	4.98	3.89	3.5
4	3.856	3.96	4.14	4.44	4.81	3.05	3.01	5.00	4.17	4.0
1965 1	3.942	4.03	4.15	4.42	4.78	2.99	3.09	4.97	4.38	4.0
2	3.810	3.98	4.14	4.46	4.85	3.07	3.15	4.99	4.38	4.0

(See top of following page for sources.)

Sources for Table 30-3

1. Three-month Treasury bills	*Economic Indicators*
2. Nine-to-twelve-month issues	*Federal Reserve Bulletin,* column marked "Others"
3. Taxable bonds	*Economic Indicators*
4. Corporate securities	*Economic Indicators*
5. Common-stock yields	*Survey of Current Business,* based on Moody's 200 stocks
6. High-grade municipals	*Survey of Current Business,* consists of Standard & Poor's 15-bond index, Aaa after 1961.
7. Average-rate short-term bank loans	*Federal Reserve Bulletin,* consists of all loans for 19 large cities
8. Prime commercial paper	*Federal Reserve Bulletin*
9. Federal reserve discount rate	*Federal Reserve Bulletin*

Peaks and Troughs, National Bureau of Economic Research, *Business Cycle Indicators,* Vol. I (Princeton: Princeton University Press, 1961), Tables A 1, p. 960.

CHARACTERISTIC PATTERNS IN COST OF MONEY

The general nature of the relationships between long and short-term interest rates and between rates and GNP are shown in Figure 30-6. Short-term interest rates show the widest amplitude of swings. Long-term interest rates are not as sensitive as short-term rates. Short-term rates move more quickly than long-term rates. The costs of debt money tend generally to lag movements in general business conditions, both at the peak and at the trough. But the movements of long-term rates lag more than short-term rates.

The cost of equity funds may best be approximated by earnings-price ratios. To understand the behavior of earnings-price ratios, the behavior of both earnings and prices must be analyzed. Corporate earnings are highly volatile. They lead the business cycle both on the upturn and on the downturn. Prices of common stocks anticipate changes in corporate earnings. Prices of equities are also influenced by money market conditions. Owing to the gradual tightening in money market conditions as expansion continues, the prices of equities tend to turn down before corporate profits reach their peak. Hence price-earnings ratios level off before earnings do, and the cost of equity financing turns up. Thus price-earnings ratios will begin to drop and earnings-price ratios will begin to rise before interest rates peak and turn down. Hence, the cost of equity money will begin to rise in the latter stages of the recovery.

For effective application of these guidelines it is necessary that the financial manager know at what stage of the cyclical fluctuations he finds himself as he contemplates the timing of the acquisition of funds. A forecast of interest rate movements is therefore required. As an approach to

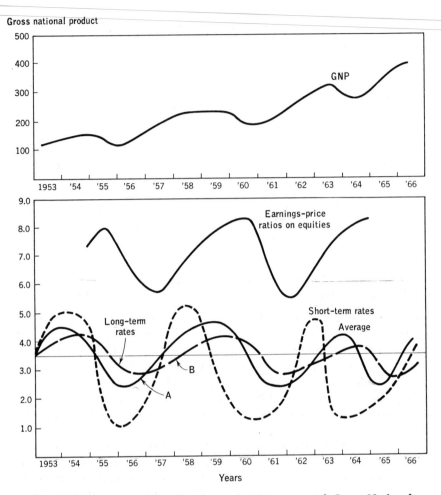

Fig. 30-6. Illustrative Relation between Movements of Gross National
Product and Interest Rates

laying a framework and foundation for forecasting interest rates, two
kinds of material are covered: first, broad trends to provide a basic foundation; second, data for short-term forecasting.

PATTERNS IN FUND FLOWS

Within the broad framework described above, the forecast of short-term
movements in interest rates must look at immediate prospects for changes
in the short-run supply and demand for funds. In the analysis of the supply and demand for funds, attention will be focused first on the supply
of savings. National savings have averaged about 13½ percent of the net

national product.[5] Personal savings account for from 70 to 75 percent of total savings, with corporate savings accounting for the remainder, twenty to 25 percent of total national savings. The share of savings by nonfarm households and by agricultural and unincorporated business enterprises related to the total personal disposable income has averaged about 12 percent. National income statistics presented on a current basis show personal savings as a percentage of disposable personal income running at about a 7 percent rate.

There has been an increase in the amount of indirect savings. Indirect savings are transmitted through a financial intermediary (banks, insurance companies, investment funds, pension funds) by the saver to the ultimate user. This percentage has risen from about 25 percent between 1900 and 1929 to about 40 percent in the 1950s. Thus a considerable portion of saving does not bring the user and the saver into direct contact.

Another aspect of saving of some significance is that contractual saving, in which the saver makes a long-term commitment to save (for example, life insurance, pensions, mortgage repayments) has risen from 10 percent of the total amount of individual savings around 1900 to 20 percent in the 1920s and well over 50 percent in the 1950s and 1960s. Savings are therefore less subject to discretionary decisions by individuals on a current basis than they were in the past.

Of the total amount of savings, averaging from $35 to $40 billion annually in recent years, about one half has come from savings institutions—commercial banks, mutual savings banks, life insurance companies, and savings and loan associations. The other half has come from nonbank sources—corporations, corporate pension funds, fire and casualty companies, state and local governments, and the United States Government. Among the savings institutions as suppliers of funds, each has supplied about $5 billion per year, except the mutual savings banks, which have supplied about one half that amount. Although the flow of nonbank funds has fluctuated greatly, it has shown an upward trend.

The principal uses of funds have been nonfinancial corporate bonds and stocks, real estate mortgages, state and local government net debt, and federal government and agency debt. These are mainly long-term funds. The principal uses of short-term funds have been consumer credit and various types of bank loans. These would be principally short-term bank loans to business. Thus the principal competitors for business uses of funds are residential real estate mortgages and federal, state, and local government borrowings.

---

[5] These data and related material are taken from the *Conference on Savings and Residential Financing, 1958 Proceedings* (United States Savings and Loan League, September 1958). The present data are taken from the paper by Raymond W. Goldsmith, "The Supply of Savings."

TABLE 30-4

**CORPORATE SECURITIES OFFERED FOR CASH SALE
IN THE UNITED STATES***
1934-1964

Year	Common Stock (Millions of dollars)	(Percentages)	Preferred Stock (Millions of dollars)	(Percentages)	Bonds and Notes (Millions of dollars)	(Percentages)	Totals (millions of dollars)
1934	19	4.8	6	1.5	372	93.7	397
1935	22	0.9	86	3.7	2,224	95.4	2,332
1936	272	6.0	271	5.9	4,028	88.1	4,572
1937	285	12.4	406	17.6	1,618	70.0	2,310
1938	25	1.2	86	4.0	2,044	94.8	2,155
1939	87	4.0	98	4.5	1,980	91.5	2,164
1940	108	4.1	183	6.8	2,386	89.1	2,677
1941	110	4.1	167	6.3	2,390	89.6	2,667
1942	34	3.2	112	10.4	917	86.4	1,062
1943	56	4.8	124	10.6	990	84.6	1,170
1944	163	5.1	369	11.5	2,670	83.4	3,202
1945	397	6.6	758	12.6	4,855	80.8	6,011
1946	891	12.9	1,127	16.3	4,882	70.8	6,900
1947	779	11.8	762	11.6	5,036	76.6	6,577
1948	614	8.7	492	7.0	5,973	84.3	7,078
1949	736	12.2	425	7.0	4,890	80.8	6,052
1950	811	12.8	631	9.9	4,920	77.3	6,361
1951	1,212	15.7	838	10.8	5,691	73.5	7,741
1952	1,369	14.4	564	5.9	7,601	79.7	9,534
1953	1,326	14.9	489	5.5	7,083	79.6	8,898
1954	1,213	12.7	816	8.6	7,488	78.7	9,516
1955	2,185	21.3	635	6.2	7,420	72.5	10,240
1956	2,301	21.0	636	5.8	8,002	73.2	10,939
1957	2,516	19.5	411	3.2	9,957	77.3	12,884
1958	1,334	11.6	571	4.9	9,653	83.5	11,558
1959	2,003	20.9	510	5.3	7,066	73.8	9,579
1960	1,644	16.2	393	3.9	8,120	79.9	10,159
1961	3,272	24.9	449	3.4	9,425	71.7	13,147
1962	1,318	12.2	436	4.0	9,016	83.8	10,770
1963	1,022	8.4	342	2.8	10,872	88.8	12,237
1964†	2,544	22.9	356	3.2	8,208	73.9	11,108

* Gross proceeds.
† January–October only.

Source: SEC Statistical Bulletin.

External long-term corporate financing can be divided into three major categories—common stock, preferred stock, and bonds and notes. Until the bull market in stocks began to surge in 1953, bonds and notes accounted for more than 80 percent of external financing (Table 30-4). In recent years, except for the recession of 1957-1958 and in 1963, common stock financing has risen to about 20 percent of external financing, and preferred stock to about 5 percent, with bonds and notes accounting for the remaining 75 percent.

FORECASTING THE LEVEL OF INTEREST RATES

Although profound and impressive studies of the theory of interest rates have been made, from the practical standpoint it is necessary mainly to assess the future behavior of the major supply-and-demand factors. The major categories of the sources and uses of funds for the economy are set out in Table 30–5. By projecting the sources and uses of funds in different categories, the direction of the pressure on interest rates can be estimated.

The table can be used in the following way. Historical patterns can be established of uses and sources of funds in relation to the growth of the economy as a whole as measured by gross national product. When in any particular year the demand for funds grows faster in relation to the supply of funds when compared to historical patterns, interest rates are likely to rise. This tendency can be illustrated from the data in Table 30–5. In 1955 the demand for investment funds increased by $3.3 billion. After the fact, the sources of funds increased by a like amount. They were so increased only by drawing on the commercial banking system, which is the pivot in the financial mechanism.

Whenever the demand for funds must be met by drawing on the commercial banking system to a greater than normal degree, characteristically, interest rates will rise. This influence is observed even more clearly when the demand for short-term funds increased from $5.7 billion in 1954, to $15.2 billion in 1955, an increase of $9.5 billion in one year. The increase in the demand for funds was met mainly by increasing the supply of funds from commercial banks by $8.3 billion. This was an increase far above the average amount by which commercial bank lending expands in a normal year. Interest rates rose in 1955. Similar patterns may be observed in other periods, especially 1958–1959. Since 1959, however, the international balance of payments problem has tended to obscure these historical relationships somewhat.

Table 30–5 illustrates also that the demand for short-term funds is much more volatile than the demand for long-term funds. The demand for long-term funds proceeds in an orderly secular-growth fashion, interrupted only moderately by changes in the pace of business activity. However, the demand for short-term funds fluctuates greatly as the level of business activity fluctuates, reflecting the liquidation and augmentation of investment in inventories by firms over the business cycle.

Additional examples may be cited of application of use of the techniques suggested by the foregoing material. The summary of the kinds

TABLE 30-5

SUMMARY OF SOURCES AND USES OF FUNDS
(in billions of dollars)

	1953	1954	1955	1956	1957	1958	1959	1960	1961	1962	1963	1964 (est.)	1965 (proj.)
Uses (funds raised)													
Investment funds (Table 2)	20.0	22.4	25.7	25.5	27.3	30.5	31.5	27.2	33.4	37.5	42.7	44.8	45.0
Short-term funds (Table 3)	5.0	5.7	15.2	10.8	7.3	7.6	15.9	14.4	10.5	19.4	23.5	25.6	27.5
U.S. Government and agency publicly held securities (Table 4)	4.2	3.2	1.6	—6.1	—	6.2	10.5	—2.7	5.9	6.0	2.5	3.0	1.8
Total uses	29.2	31.3	42.5	30.2	34.6	44.3	57.9	39.0	49.7	62.9	68.7	73.4	74.3
Sources (funds supplied)													
Life insurance companies (Table 12)	4.9	5.0	5.2	5.1	4.9	5.1	5.2	5.4	5.6	6.4	6.6	7.3	7.7
Mutual savings banks (Table 13)	1.8	2.0	2.0	2.0	1.9	2.5	1.4	1.5	2.1	3.1	3.4	4.3	3.9
Savings and loan associations (Table 14)	3.7	4.2	5.7	4.9	4.9	6.2	8.3	7.1	9.3	10.2	12.9	11.0	10.0
Fire and casualty insurance companies (Table 15)	1.3	1.2	0.9	0.5	0.8	0.9	1.6	1.1	1.3	1.2	1.3	1.3	1.3
Corporate pension funds (Table 16)	1.7	1.9	1.9	2.2	2.5	2.7	3.1	3.3	3.4	3.5	3.7	4.1	4.3
State and local government retirement funds (Table 17)	1.0	1.1	1.2	1.4	1.6	1.7	1.9	2.1	2.1	2.5	2.6	3.0	3.3
Investment companies (Tables 2 & 4)	0.4	0.5	0.8	0.9	1.0	1.5	1.5	1.1	1.4	1.5	0.8	1.1	1.5
Credit unions (Tables 2, 3, 4)	0.3	0.2	0.4	0.4	0.5	0.3	0.7	0.6	0.4	0.6	0.7	0.9	1.1
Total savings institutions	15.1	16.1	18.1	17.4	18.1	20.9	23.7	22.2	25.6	29.1	32.0	33.0	33.1
Commercial banks (Table 5)	4.0	10.3	5.0	4.3	5.0	15.2	4.2	9.3	15.9	19.4	19.8	20.5	19.0
Business corporations (Tables 2, 3, 4)	2.9	0.6	9.5	—0.9	2.0	5.1	8.9	3.1	2.8	8.1	9.2	9.8	8.5

Other investor groups

Federal agencies (Table 2)	0.1	−0.2	0.5	0.8	1.5	0.5	2.4	1.8	0.8	0.8	−0.8	0.4	0.8
Brokers and dealers (Table 3)	0.3	0.7	0.4	—	−0.3	0.9	—	−0.1	1.0	−0.1	1.4	−0.4	—
Other consumer lenders (Table 11)	0.3	0.2	0.4	0.5	0.3	0.2	0.4	0.4	0.4	0.5	0.6	0.6	0.5
State and local governments* (Tables 2 & 4)	1.5	1.7	0.6	0.9	1.0	−0.1	1.2	1.3	0.5	0.2	0.5	−0.3	0.9
Foreign investors (Tables 2, 3, 4)	0.8	0.6	1.4	0.8	0.3	−0.1	4.9	1.7	0.7	2.0	0.8	0.5	0.6
Total other investor groups	3.0	3.0	3.3	3.0	2.8	1.4	8.9	5.0	3.3	3.4	2.5	0.8	2.8
Residual: Individuals and others† (Table 18)	4.2	1.3	6.6	6.4	6.7	1.7	12.2	−0.6	2.0	2.9	5.2	9.3	10.9
Total sources	29.2	31.3	42.5	30.2	34.6	44.3	57.9	39.0	49.7	62.9	68.7	73.4	74.3

* Excluding retirement funds.
† Includes revaluation of book assets of other holders.

Source: Investment Outlook for 1965 (New York, Bankers Trust Company, 1965).

of data presented in Table 30–5 is presented in Table 30–6.[6] The analysis by *Business Week* of the major supply and demand factors for both 1958 and 1959 had indicated a rise in interest rates during these years. When the sum of demands was totaled and the sum of supplies totaled, at existing interest rates, the quantity demanded exceeded the quantity supplied. Pressure would thus be put on the banking system to supply additional funds, and the price would rise. Reference to Table 30–3 for these years shows that interest rates did in fact rise.

The following three quotations from *Business Week* also indicate the

TABLE 30–6

HOW BAD WILL THE CAPITAL SHORTAGE BE?

Money Needed (billions of dollars)

1958 Borrowers raised these amounts	for these purposes	1959 The forecasts are Bankers Trust Co.	Salomon Bros. & Hutzler
$ 9.0 .	. Domestic corporate, foreign financing . .	$ 8.0 .	. $ 7.9
14.8 .	. Real estate mortgages	15.7 .	. 13.3
5.9 .	. State and local government finance . . .	5.9 .	. 4.6
2.9 .	. U.S. Treasury bond issues	? .	. ?
$32.6 .	. Total	29.6 .	. 25.8

What Regular Lenders Supply

1958 These amounts	were supplied by these lenders	1959	
$ 6.5 .	. Savings and loan associations	6.7 .	. 5.5
2.5 .	. Mutual savings banks	2.3 .	. 2.2
5.6 .	. Life insurance companies	5.6 .	. 4.7
1.2 .	. Fire, casualty insurance companies . . .	1.7 .	. 1.3
2.9 .	. Corporate pension funds	3.2 .	. 3.3
1.6 .	. State and local gov't. retirement funds . .	1.7 .	. 1.6
8.4 .	. Other	4.2 .	. 1.0
$28.7 .	. Total	25.4 .	. 19.6

Additional Amounts Needed

$ 3.9	4.2? .	. 6.2?
	(plus Treasury's needs)	

Source: "How Bad Will the Capital Shortage Be?" *Business Week*, March 14, 1959, p. 50.

---

[6] "The Treasury Holds the Key," *Business Week*, March 14, 1959, p. 50.

effectiveness of forecasting short-term interest rate. The first quotation of March 14, 1959, properly forecasts the upturn in interest rates in the year 1959.

The next quotation, from the issue of May 14, 1960, likewise correctly forecasts the decline in interest rate during 1960. Finally, the issue of December 24, 1960, suggested an upturn in interest rates during 1961, despite the indication that government policy would be in the direction of a movement toward lower long-term interest rates with somewhat higher short-term rates. *Business Week's* analysis indicated that the strength of demand for long-term money would be so great that the effect of government policy would be to reduce the magnitude of the rise that otherwise would have taken place, rather than to result in an absolute decline in long-term interest rates.

The U.S., the world's richest nation, will be capital-hungry again this year —even hungrier than it was in 1958. In fact, the shortage of long-term funds may well turn out to be 1959's toughest financial problem.

Just how big the capital shortage will be can't be pinned down exactly as yet, and economists differ in their reading of the signs. But, as the table shows, it promises to run to at least $4.2 billion, with some forecasts raising that figure to $6.2 billion or even higher. That's without making any allowance for Treasury needs and for any attempts by the Treasury to draw funds from the long-term market.[7]

Back to Market—Now, underwriters who were pinched by the decline in volume of big corporate deals are again optimistic. They question whether business can spend at the rate projected for this year without tapping the capital market for more than it did last year—when capital spending amounted to only $32.50 billion. Besides, interest costs seem to have passed their peak. As the cost of long-term money drops, many companies will probably carry through borrowing plans postponed.[8]

Any businessman who is counting on the cost of money going down substantially next year seems likely to be disappointed. From all indications, 1961 shapes up as another year of tight—and expensive—money for most borrowers. The one situation that could produce a dramatic reduction in interest rates is a full-fledged depression, which neither lenders nor borrowers expect.[9]

These illustrations from historical data indicate a method by which financial managers may construct short-term forecasts in the cost of money. The U.S. Steel example, cited early in the chapter, indicates how successfully this may be done by the individual firm.

The procedure for making a short-term forecast of movements and interest rates must take into account not only prospective demand and supply of funds, but also the role of monetary and fiscal policy. The nature of these influences is now briefly summarized.

---

7 *Ibid.*
8 "Capital Outlays to Lift Borrowing," *Business Week,* May 14, 1960, p. 70.
9 "It Looks Like a Lenders' Market," *Business Week,* December 24, 1960, p. 30.

FEDERAL RESERVE POLICY

No discussion of interest rate behavior would be complete without an analysis of the role of the central bank, which in the United States is the Federal Reserve System. The central bank is equipped with a set of powers having a significant influence on the operations of commercial banks, whose loan and investment activities in turn have an important influence on the supply of money. Of these powers the most powerful, and hence the one used sparingly, is changing reserve requirements. The one most often used, which can be applied in a more direct and pinpointed fashion, is changing the pattern of open-market operations. Changes in the discount rates are likely to have more of a psychological influence than direct quantitative effects.

Selective controls over real estate and consumer credit have been enforced periodically, but experience with them is not sufficient to determine whether the Federal Reserve authorities can effectively utilize these instruments of selective credit control. Changes in stock margin requirements have been used to counter strong movements in stock prices and probably perform some useful role. However, the underlying influences which determine stock prices are so strong and pervasive that changes in margin requirements typically are not of sufficient power to determine the future course of stock market prices.

FISCAL POLICY

The fiscal policy of the federal government has considerable impact on the movements in interest rates. A cash budget deficit represents a stimulating influence by the federal government, and a cash surplus exerts a restraining influence from the government-spending sector of the economy. However, this generalization needs to be modified by the way a deficit is financed and by the way a surplus is used. To have the most stimulating effect, the deficit should be financed by sale of securities through the banking system, particularly the central bank. To have the most restrictive effect, the surplus should be used to retire bonds held by the banking system, particularly the central bank.

The impact of Treasury financing programs will have a different impact at different times. Ordinarily, when the Treasury needs to draw on funds from the money market, it competes with other potential users of funds; the result may be a rise in interest rate levels. On the other hand, the desire to hold down interest rates also influences Treasury and Federal Reserve policy. To ensure the success of a large new offering, Federal Reserve authorities may temporarily ease money conditions, a procedure that will tend to soften interest rates. If the Treasury encounters resistance in selling securities in the nonbanking sector, securities may be sold in large volume to the commercial banking system, which expands its reserves and thereby increases the monetary base. This change in turn tends to lower the level of interest rates.

Thus the financial manager will find it necessary and desirable to keep in close touch with federal budget developments and the nature of governmental fiscal policy, particularly interactions between fiscal and monetary policy, in order to judge trends in costs of money. This subject deserves much more detailed and analytical treatment than can be given here, but it is of great significance for sound decision making by financial managers.

IMPLICATION OF COST OF MONEY PATTERNS FOR TIMING OF FINANCIAL POLICY

Variations in the cost of money and its availability are likely to be of great significance for decisions by financial managers. The importance of the sound timing of financial policy is further underscored by the mistakes observed in practice.[10]

Financial managers have tended to shift from short-term funds to long-term funds too late during the business upswing. Characteristically, firms have relied on short-term financing during the early stages of a business upswing. The reason for this can clearly be seen from Figure 30–5. The cost of short-term money remains below the cost of long-term money until well into the boom. Furthermore, as recovery takes place the major need for funds is for working-capital purposes. Although these needs are permanent, as has been demonstrated previously, many financial managers in the past have tended to regard the financing of working-capital needs as a need for temporary funds only.

As a consequence, the acquisition of long-term funds has been delayed until relatively late in the business upswing. Specifically, long-term funds have been acquired at point B in Figure 30–6, rather than at point A. At point B there is an apparent logic in obtaining long-term funds rather than short-term funds. Compared with acquiring long-term funds at point A, the timing of the acquisition of long-term funds is unsound. It leads to obtaining long-term funds at a $4\frac{1}{4}$ percent rate, when they could have been obtained at something like a $3\frac{3}{4}$ percent rate during the upswing. Another advantage of obtaining the funds at point A is that credit conditions are relatively much easier at this stage, and the terms under which funds may be acquired are likely to be much less onerous than they will be near the peak of the boom.

It is likely, therefore, that by making proper financial requirement

---

10 For illustrations, see J. Fred Weston, "Financial Implications of Growth," *Controller*, March 1958, pp. 118–120.

projections, as described earlier, and by keeping historical perspective on the growth of the economy and the pattern of interest rate behavior, financial managers can improve the timing of their acquisition of debt funds. They can lower the cost and improve the terms of financing by obtaining long-term funds early in the upswing. As the upturn in business conditions improves, the firm will have the benefit of trading on the equity with the use of long-term debt money.

Before the peak of the business upswing, the firm may properly sell equity securities, replacing some of its debt. By selling equities near the highs of common stock prices, the firm shall have been enabled to increase its equity base to the degree necessary to facilitate the sale of additional long-term debt money at the low point of the next business cycle.

Although all the strategies of the timing of financial policy are not encompassed by this brief overview, it does serve to focus attention on the need for awareness of changes in the cost of different forms of money during different stages of fluctuations in the level of business activity.

SUMMARY

In general, the financial manager should seek to time the acquisition of funds for his business enterprise in relation to trends and cycles in general business and in interest rates. At the beginning of a business upswing it is likely to be advantageous to raise funds through long-term debt sources. Although short-term rates are lower than long-term rates at this stage of the cycle, the magnitude of swings in short-term rates is large. In the later stages of a business upswing, short-term rates exceed long-term rates, and both are much higher. Qualitative aspects of financing reflected in credit terms will also be considerably more favorable if long-term borrowing is arranged during the beginning of the upswing. The firm will also obtain larger benefits from trading on the equity.

Later in the upswing, the equity markets are likely to be strong. Equity financing should be used for expansion and for replacing long-term debt financing arranged early in the upswing. At this time interest rates will be relatively high, and equity yields relatively low. This situation allows refunding of debt issues and builds the equity base for protection during the downswing and for trading on the equity during the next upswing.

SELECTED REFERENCES

"Business Financing in Early 1957," *Federal Reserve Bulletin*, 43 (June 1957), pp. 615–621.

"Financing of Business Expansion," *Federal Reserve Bulletin*, 42 (June 1956), pp. 553–558.

"Financing of Large Corporations, 1951–55," *Federal Reserve Bulletin*, 42 (June 1956), pp. 580–588.

Frazer, W. J., Jr., "Some Factors Affecting Business Financing," *Southern Economic Journal*, 25 (July 1958), pp. 33–47.

Freund, William C., "The Dynamic Financial Markets," *Financial Executive*, 33 (May 1965), pp. 11–26, 57–58.

Guthmann, H. G., "The Movement of Debt to Institutions and Its Implications for the Interest Rate," *Journal of Finance*, 5 (March 1950), pp. 70–87.

Johnson, N. O., "Financing Industrial Growth," *Journal of Finance*, 12 (May 1957), pp. 264–271.

Liebling, H. I., "Financing the Expansion of Business," *Survey of Current Business*, 37 (September 1959), pp. 6–14.

Luckett, Dudley G., "Professor Lutz and the Structure of Interest Rates," *Quarterly Journal of Economics*, 73 (February 1959), pp. 131–144.

Lutz, Friedrich A., "The Structure of Interest Rates," *Quarterly Journal of Economics*, 55 (1940–1941), pp. 36–63.

Malkiel, Burton G., "Expectations, Bond Prices, and the Term Structure of Interest Rates," *Quarterly Journal of Economics*, 76 (May 1962), pp. 197–218.

McFerrin, J. B., "The Structure of the American Capital Market," *Southern Economic Journal*, 21 (January 1955), pp. 247–260.

McKinley, Gordon W., "Forces Affecting Interest Rates," *Financial Executive* (January 1964), pp. 18–22.

McHugh, L. F., and J. N. Ciaccio, "External Financing of Small- and Medium-size Business," *Survey of Current Business*, 35 (October 1955), pp. 15–22.

Meltzer, Allan H., "Mercantile Credit, Monetary Policy, and Size of Firms," *Review of Economics and Statistics*, 42 (November 1960), pp. 429–437.

Payne, Wilson F., *Industrial Demands upon the Money Market, 1919–57: A Study in Fund-Flow Analysis* (New York: National Bureau of Economic Research, Inc., 1961).

"Recent Capital Market Developments in the United States," *Federal Reserve Bank of New York Monthly Review*, 45 (October 1963), pp. 152–159.

Segall, Joel, "The Effect of Maturity on Price Fluctuations," *Journal of Business of the University of Chicago*, 29 (July 1956), pp. 202–206.

Wood, John H., "Expectations, Errors and the Term Structure of Interest Rates," *Journal of Political Economy*, 71 (April 1963), pp. 160–168.

QUESTIONS

30-1 "It makes good sense for a firm to fund its floating debt, because this relieves the possibility that it will be called upon to pay off debt at an awkward time. However, from the standpoint of cost, it is always cheaper to use short-term debt than long-term debt." Discuss the statement.

30-2 Historical data indicate that more than twice as much capital is raised yearly by selling bonds than by selling common stocks. Does this indicate that corporate capital structures are becoming overburdened with debt?

30-3 Distinguish between the money market and the capital market. How are they related?

30-4 Is the Federal Reserve's tight-money policy restraining the country's economic growth? Discuss the pros and cons from the corporation's viewpoint.

30-5 Why do interest rates on different types of securities vary widely?

30-6 What does GNP represent? Why are its level and growth significant to the financial manager?

30-7 Figure 30-3 indicates that short-term interest rates are higher than long-term interest rates for most of the period 1900–1930. Is there any reason to believe that this relation may again prevail during the next decade?

30-8 Are short-term rates of any value in forecasting the rates for the long-term market?

PROBLEMS

30–1 In mid-1958 the Central Company made a reappraisal of its sales forecasts for the next one, two, and five years. It was clear that the product development program which had been under way for the previous five years was now coming to fruition. The officers of Central were confident that a sales growth of 12 to 15 percent per year (on a compound growth basis) for the next five years was strongly indicated unless general business declined.

The Central Company has total assets of $10 million. It has a debt-to-net-worth ratio of 40 percent. Since it has been spending heavily on research and development during the past five years, its profits have been depressed and the stock has not been favorably regarded by investors.

The Central Company learned that it could borrow on a short-term basis at 2.5 percent (the rate for prime commercial paper at mid-1958 was 1.6 percent) and sell some common stock or float some nonconvertible long-term bonds at 4 percent. Central financed by selling $2 million of common stock (the maximum to avoid control problems) and by short-term loans at the lower rates until early 1960, when it found that its growing financial requirements could not be met by short-term borrowing. Its need for financing was so great that Central sold $10 million convertible debentures at 5.5 percent (the rate on prime commercial paper at this time was almost 5 percent) and with terms requiring a strong current ratio and limitations on fixed-assets purchases. The price of its common stock had quadrupled by mid-1959 but had dropped by 10 percent in early 1960.

Evaluate the timing of the selection of forms of financing by the Central Company.

30–2 In July 1958, as the economy in general was emerging from the 1957–1958 downturn and the Flexible Container Corporation's business was resuming its strong growth in sales, Fred Bolden, the treasurer, had concluded that the firm would require more working-capital financing during the year ending June 30, 1959. Below are the historical and *pro forma* income statements and balance sheets of the Flexible Container Corporation.

How should the financing needs be met? Why?

FLEXIBLE CONTAINER CORPORATION
BALANCE SHEETS
1958 and 1959 Pro Forma
(dollar figures in thousands)

Assets	1958	1959
Cash	200	600
Receivables	800	1,200
Inventories	1,000	1,600
Total current assets	2,000	3,400
Fixed assets, net	1,000	2,000
Total assets	3,000	5,400

Liabilities and Capital		
Accounts payable	300	500
Accruals	100	200
Reserves for taxes	600	800
Total current liabilities	1,000	1,500

Additional financing	0	800
Common stock, $10 par	1,000	1,000
Surplus	1,000	2,100
Total liabilities and capital	3,000	5,400

FLEXIBLE CONTAINER CORPORATION
INCOME STATEMENTS
For Years Ended June 30, 1958 and 1959

	1958	*1959*
Sales, net	10,000	14,000
Cost of sales	8,000	10,000
Gross profit	2,000	4,000
Operating expenses	1,000	1,500
Operating profit	1,000	2,500
Other income, net	200	100
Profits before taxes	1,200	2,600
Taxes	600	1,300
Net profit after taxes	600	1,300
Dividends	100	200
Retained earnings	500	1,100

30–3 On August 18, 1965, the Southern California Edison Company issued $74 million 3⅛ convertible debentures, due August 15, 1980. The debentures are convertible into common stock at $44.50 per share. The proceeds would be used in part to retire $15 million short-term bank loans and to retire $38 million bonds due September 1, 1965. The remainder would be available for future construction programs.

1. What was the effective yield on the bonds issued?
2. Why were the debentures convertible?
3. Would the conversion price have been higher or lower if the bonds had been issued in April 1965?
4. Would the effective yield have been lower or higher if the bonds had been issued in October or November of 1965?
5. Comment on the timing of the issue in relation to the terms of the issue.

Chapter 31

The Financial Life Cycle
of the Firm

The financial manager should formulate policies in relation to the underlying changes in the economic and financial environment. In addition, financing patterns should change with the evolution in the characteristics of the firm itself. Analogies are always dangerous, but the analogy to the life cycle of the individual may be useful if it is not taken too literally and is not carried too far. The individual finds, as the old saying has it, that certain things are appropriate to the behavior of a child, to the behavior of a young man, to the behavior of the head of a mature and established family, and to an aged person in the years of his elder statesmanship and wisdom.

Just as the outside world changes, so the individual, regardless of his age or stage in life, must make adjustments. But further, even if the external environment does not change, the individual must adjust as the aging process goes on. In a similar fashion, the financial policies of a firm must be related to the stages of its development.

STAGES OF GROWTH AND FINANCING

The inspiration to view the financing of a firm over its life cycle comes from comments dealing with historical series on sources and uses of funds made by Professor George Evans at a National Bureau of Economic Research conference.[1]

---

[1] George Herberton Evans, Jr., "Discussion: The Development of Historical Series on

Evans's Hypothesis

Professor Evans's hypothesis is stated succinctly: "Asset financing during the early, rapid stages of growth is carried on largely through stock and bond issues; thereafter, retained earnings are likely to become very important and, finally, annual depreciation charges bulk large as a source of funds for gross additions to plant."[2] The hypothesis suggests that there are three stages of growth in a business firm, which might be referred to as (1) the early stage, (2) the maturity stage, and (3) the leveling-off stage. In stage one, the firm is said to rely on stock and bond issues; in stage two, on retained earnings; and in stage three, on depreciation charges.

A preliminary empirical basis for the generalizations is provided by Figure 31–1, which reproduces findings for the relative importance of different forms of financing over time for six steel companies and five chemical companies. The data are clearly consistent with the hypothesis set out.

A further corroboration of the Evans approach is suggested in the book by the Oxford financial economists analyzing the business financing of the firm. Their conclusion likewise was that for an understanding of the financial policies of business enterprise in the United Kingdom, it was much more important to group the firms by size and growth rate rather than by industry.

It is also highly significant that the contributors of the general studies (Chapters 2–8) usually found it more illuminating to compare and contrast the companies in different size and growth groups than those in different industrial groups. This is not to say that any of the size groups or growth groups were homogenous—far from it—but at least such groups were often found to be significantly different (and frequently in some systematic and explicable fashion) than were the twenty-one industrial groups.[3]

Rate of Growth

The influence of the rate of growth, referred to in the Oxford study, can be shown by the example in Table 31–1, which compares two firms. One grows from $800,000 sales to $1.2 million in one year; the other grows by the same amount, but over a four-year period.[4]

Sources and Uses of Corporate Funds," *Conference on Research in Business Finance* (New York: National Bureau of Economic Research, Inc., 1952), pp. 28–34.
[2] *Ibid.*, p. 23.
[3] Brian Tew and R. F. Henderson (eds.), *Studies in Company Finance* (Cambridge, England: Cambridge University Press, 1959), p. 255.
[4] Parenthetically, it may be observed that a 50 percent growth rate is not at all unusual for a new firm starting out in the electronics industry, plastics industry, or almost any small firm in other than retail or wholesale trade. Even in the latter industries, in the early stages of the life cycle of the firm, if a firm is going to succeed it must have a very rapid growth rate.

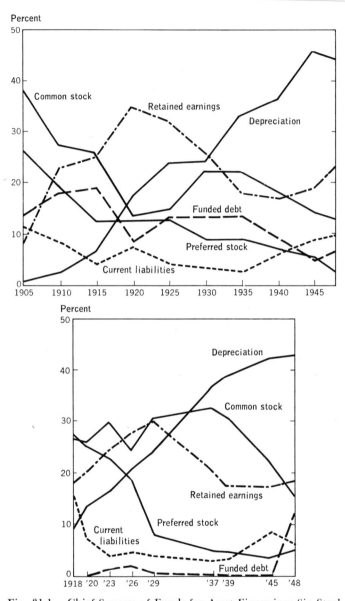

Fig. 31-1.   Chief Sources of Funds for Asset Financing: Six Steel
Companies and Five Chemical Companies. (upper) Six Steel
Companies, (lower) Five Chemical Companies
*Medians of percentage of total are computed for
each company on data cumulated to indicated dates.*
Source: Loc. cit., p. 33. Reprinted by permission
of the National Bureau of Economic Research.

It will be observed that, when the firm achieves a 50 percent growth in one year the current ratio, which was weak to start with, deteriorates further. The debt-equity ratio, which was 100 percent initially, moves beyond generally accepted prudent levels. The financial community always likes to feel that the owner has as much money in the business as the creditors have, but in situation two, the creditors have $1.16 to every $1 in the business by the owners. The profit rate has improved, because the firm is using debt more heavily; that is, it is receiving the benefit of trading on the equity.

The consequences may be contrasted when the firm uses four periods

TABLE 31-1

FINANCIAL EFFECTS OF DIFFERENT RATES OF GROWTH
(in thousands of dollars)

	Firm 1		Firm 2				
	1	*2*	*1*	*2*	*3*	*4*	*5*
Sales	$800	$1,200	$800	$900	$1,000	$1,100	$1,200
Current assets (30%)	240	360	240	270	300	330	360
Fixed assets (20%) . .	160	240	160	180	200	220	240
Total assets . . .	$400	$ 600	$400	$450	$ 500	$ 550	$ 600
Accounts payable (10%)	80	120	80	90	100	110	120
Notes payable	96	172	96	79	56	27	(8)
Other accruals (3%) . .	24	36	24	27	30	33	36
Current liabilities	$200	$ 328	$200	$196	$ 186	$ 170	$ 148
Common stock . . .	100	100	100	100	100	100	100
Retained earnings*	100	172	100	154	214	280	352
Net worth . . .	$200	$ 272	$200	$254	$ 314	$ 380	$ 452
Total claims . . .	$400	$ 600	$400	$450	$ 500	$ 550	$ 600
Key ratios							
Current ratio (times)	1.2	1.1	1.2	1.4	1.6	1.9	2.4
Debt to equity (percentage)	100	111	100	77	59	45	33
Sales to total assets (times)	2	2	2	2	2	2	2
Profit to net worth (percentage)	24	26.5	24.0	21.3	19.1	17.3	15.9

* Profit is 6% of sales, retained earnings are equal to profit plus retained earnings from the previous year.

to achieve the same amount of growth. The financial ratios give a profile of what has happened. The current ratio has improved; it has risen above the bankers' rule of thumb to 2.4 to 1. The debt-to-equity ratio has dropped to 33 percent, very low compared with the average of 45 percent for all manufacturing. However, the profit-to-net-worth ratio has returned to the 14-to-16 percent level, which is normal for all manufacturing.

A paradox is encountered. Rapid growth means high profitability but a precariousness in the firm's financial position unless external financing is obtained in relatively large amounts. On the other hand, slow growth can be encompassed by the plowback from retained earnings and depreciation charges. The example suggests that a firm growing by only 10 percent per year should not have serious financial problems if it obtains normal profits and retains a high percentage in the business. But owners of rapidly growing firms will ask why, when their sales are growing, their financial difficulties are growing even faster. Or alternatively, a firm that is holding funds in the business cannot understand why its profit rate on net worth is declining. Both paradoxes are readily unraveled if one looks at the simple dynamics of this growth situation.

FINANCING IN RELATION TO A CROSS SECTION OF STAGES

The situation described in Table 31–1 purports to be a general statement of a particular kind of phenomenon comparing rapid growth with less rapid growth, and high retention of earnings with other alternatives. We may generalize further by considering a conspectus of firms and their financial characteristics from a cross-section standpoint, in terms of their different sizes and ages.

The relation between the growth of a firm and its requirements is exhibited by Figure 31–2, which presents the sales and the total assets of the Bethlehem Steel Corporation during the last half century. With the exception of the perturbations brought about by World War I and World War II and their aftermaths, the growth of sales of the Bethlehem Steel Corporation has roughly followed the S-shaped growth curve.

Financing requirements of the firm have paralleled the growth pattern in sales. After 1940 the firm has been able to achieve a sales-total-asset ratio exceeding 1 during most years. Yet the sales-total-asset ratio is substantially below the characteristic 2-to-1 ratio observed for all manufacturing firms.

A relation exists between the growth of a firm and the nature of its financing requirements. A general framework for obtaining perspective on the financial life cycle of the firm can be developed. Table 31–2 sets forth a conspectus of leading financial characteristics of manufacturing firms, classified by the stage at which one finds them: small, medium, large; and, among the small and medium, new and old. This panorama is based on a review of studies of the growth of individual firms and on the Financial Research Program of the National Bureau of Economic Research on capital formation and its financing in a number of industries.

TABLE 31-2

GENERAL CONSPECTUS OF FINANCIAL PATTERNS IN RELATION TO SIZE AND AGE OF FIRM*

	Growth Rate (in percentages)	Profit to Sales	Financial Position		Main Forms	Main Sources	Dividend Payout (in percentages)	Mergers
Small								
Rapid growth	20–30	8	Current ratio . . . . Asset turnover . . . Debt to net worth . .	1 3 200%	Current liabilities	Trade credit	0–10	Need for full range of management capabilities
Moderate growth	5–8	5	Current ratio . . . . Asset turnover . . . Debt to net worth . .	2 2 50–100%	Long-term debt Common stock Retained earnings	Bonds, publicly issued	20–25	Cost reduction incentives
Medium								
Rapid growth	16–20	6–7	Current ratio . . . . Asset turnover . . . Debt to net worth . .	1.4 2.5 100%	Long-term debt Current liabilities Common stock	Bonds, publicly issued	5–15	Cost reduction, rounding out of sales lines
Moderate growth	4–7	5	Current ratio . . . . Asset turnover . . . Debt to net worth . .	2 2 50%	Long-term debt Common-stock Retained earnings	Bonds, equity capital market	40–50	Diversification into new product lines
Large								
Moderate growth	4–6	5	Current ratio . . . . Asset turnover . . . Debt to net worth . .	2 2 50%	Retained earnings, Depreciation	Retained earnings	50–60	Diversification into new product lines

* Based on the institutional framework of the United States.

Millions of dollars

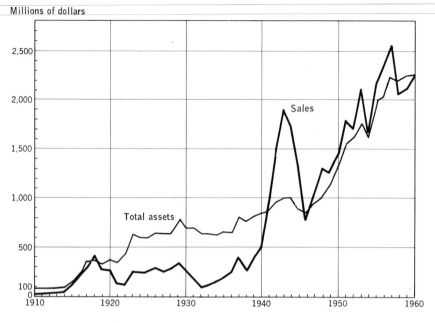

Fig. 31-2. Bethlehem Steel Corporation, 1910-1960

The conspectus is idealized in that many exceptions can be found in actuality. It is not an ideal picture in the sense that each set of characteristics represents the optimal situation. It indicates how the age and the growth rate of a firm, and the nature of its financial environment, are reflected in its financial patterns over time. The table is discussed horizontally rather than vertically, to convey the idea of how a firm is likely to move from one stage to another.

Small, Rapidly Growing Firm

The small, successful firm will typically have a very good growth rate—20 to 30 percent a year. Its profit rate on sales will be somewhat higher than the average for large manufacturing companies. Compared with traditional and customary standards, its financial position is relatively weak. The current ratio is probably under 1 to 1. The sales-to-total-assets ratio will be high. The debt-to-net-worth ratio is 200 percent.

Because the table provides the profit on sales, the asset turnover, and the debt-to-worth ratio, the return on net worth can be calculated. In the present instance the return on total assets would be 24 percent, more than double the norm of about 10 to 12 percent for all manufacturing. The return on net worth would be 72 percent (after taxes). Because of its precarious financial position, the underfinanced small firms show a high return on net worth. With a relatively normal profit on sales, the high turnover of total assets results in a favorable profit rate on total assets. The relatively high debt-to-net-worth ratio further magnifies the return on net worth. The result is a profit rate on net worth of 72 percent after taxes, or 144 percent before taxes. Starting from a moderate return on sales, the small firm earns enough profit before taxes to equal almost 150 percent of its investment.

Studies of the financing of new, small firms indicate that 80 to 90 percent of the initial financing comes from the funds of the owners of the business and their relatives and friends. As the sales grow, the major initial source of external financing is likely to be trade credit. Suppliers provide credit of both an informal and a formal kind. This practice may be fortunate, because trade credit thereby performs the very useful social function of providing small firms with financing otherwise unavailable.

With regard to dividend policy (the term is here used to include withdrawals), the small firm should pay out very little, if anything, in dividends. Here is a case where the pattern is idealized in the sense that many small firms may fail to observe this rule or guide to action.

Small firms will sometimes sell out to large firms as they grow to a certain point. A small firm is created and receives its initial propulsion because of a specific ability of the owner-manager-entrepreneur. He may be a good salesman, a good engineer, or a good production man. He strikes out on his own because of his one strong competence. While the firm is small, a specific ability may be sufficient for the firm's success.

But very soon a firm reaches "that awkward age" in which more than the dynamic force of one or two individuals is needed to enable it to continue to prosper. At this stage the owner-managers of the firm realize that it takes a full range of managerial abilities to succeed. It is not enough to have only sales, technical, or financial skills. A firm begins to find that it is making numerous mistakes because it does not have a full range of balanced managerial skills. As a consequence, it may join with other firms with which it can complement strengths and weaknesses. Or, more typically, a large firm sees that it can use the particular managerial talents that the small firm has and can supply everything else the small firm needs. For these reasons, many small firms are likely to sell out to larger firms.

Small, Long-Established Firm

If a firm is small and old, it is probably not in a growing industry. Since manufacturing firms are being discussed, the long-established firm is probably producing a particular product splinter to which large firms do not give much attention. Its growth rate in sales is probably no better than the over-all average of the industry. The profit rate is not likely to be more than normal.

Its financial position is likely to meet conventional standards. It meets the traditional standard for the current ratio, the bankers' rule of thumb of 2 to 1. Its sales-to-total-assets ratio approximates the 1.9 for all manufacturing. The debt-to-net-worth ratio probably is from 50 to 100 percent, reflecting the fact that because it is small it may have difficulty raising equity funds.

Because the firm has been in existence for a time, its past performance record may have enabled it to obtain moderate amounts of long-term debt. Also, it probably has had time to build up fairly large retained earnings. As it meets the bankers' traditional financial standards, it qualifies for bank financing to the extent required.

Dividend payouts are probably still on the low side, because the small firm by nature has only limited access to the external financial markets. Hence it relies on internal financing to a great degree.

The firm is likely to engage in mergers. It may be acquired by a large firm for its special product contribution. Large firms seek vertical integration as they reach the stage of maturity. In older firms, in the later stages of the life cycle of an industry, profit margins may decline. For this reason, such firms may engage in mergers to encompass an additional product stage or product splinter to broaden its product line. If larger volume per dollar of investment can thereby be generated, improved profit margins may be achieved.

Medium-Sized, Rapidly Growing Firms

The remainder of the firms in this panorama have some relation to the two categories already discussed. For the medium-sized firms, growth rates and net profit rates will not be so high as those for the new, small firms. They will have a somewhat better financial position. Because it is medium-sized, although new, it probably has been in operation long enough to have established a performance record which gives it access to bank financing and to the external capital markets at least to a limited degree.

Such a firm's dividend payout is still relatively on the low side because of its high profit rate and the need to finance further growth. It is likely to seek mergers to round out production or sales lines. Thus it can spread the relatively fixed costs of the sales organization or production organization over a larger number of product lines and compete more effectively with the larger firms in its line of business.

Medium-Sized, Moderately Growing Firm

The firm of medium size with a moderate growth rate will have characteristics similar to those of small firms of moderate growth rates. The profit rate will be slightly lower, approximating the profit rate of industry generally. It will satisfy the financial standards generally regarded as sound. It will doubtless achieve a current ratio of at least 2 to 1. It will have a normal sales-to-total-assets ratio of about 2. It will have reduced its debt ratio to about 50 percent of net worth.

The medium-sized firm will have greater access to the capital markets than will the small firm of moderate growth rate. The fixed costs of capital flotations will bear less heavily on the larger firm than on the small firm. For this reason, the medium-sized firm of moderate growth and profitability will have a somewhat higher dividend payout than will the smaller firm.

The lower growth rate of the medium-sized firm may lead it to seek product diversification in an effort to enter new product-market areas with more favorable growth opportunities. It will seek to acquire smaller, rapidly growing firms which have products with favorable growth potentialities.

Large Firm with Moderate Growth Rate

The large firm with a moderate growth rate is likely to be an established firm in an industry that has reached its maturity. The firm will generally exhibit the characteristics of a medium-sized firm. However, its larger size implies a higher fixed-assets-to-total-assets ratio. Thus the fixed assets will provide a throw-off of funds from depreciation charges. The large firm will therefore draw on the capital markets for financing to a smaller degree. Instead, it will rely to a greater extent on internal financing.

Illustrative Patterns

The influence of industry, age, size, and rate of growth on financing of firms can also be indicated by Table 31–3. Firms in the textiles and shoe-manufacturing industries generally have a large peak seasonal investment in receivables. This seasonal investment does not justify a proportionate amount of permanent capital. Consequently, such firms are likely to make use of receivables to provide a secured basis for financing large temporary investment requirements during each year.

Similarly, a canning manufacturer is likely to experience a peak seasonal growth in inventories. Again, such large investments do not justify permanent capital sufficient to finance the seasonal peak inventories. Therefore field warehousing or other types of commodity loans are the strategic financing requirements.

The many new scientifically oriented firms with rapid growth have a different financing requirement. Their investment in equipment is likely to be heavy, and their large outlays on research may require a number of years before a profitable series of products results. The initial outlays for research must require venture capital—capital willing to assume substantial risks. Permanent investment requirements are reduced by the opportunities for leasing their heavy equipment needs.

The small, basic manufacturing company is likely to have its heaviest investment in equipment. Conditional sales contracts or leasing may take care of this strategic financing requirement. In addition, the initial period

TABLE 31–3

ILLUSTRATIVE FINANCING STRATEGIES

Characteristic of Firm	Critical Financing Need	Strategic Financing Requirement
Small		
Textiles and Shoes	Peak seasonal in receivables	Receivables financing
Scientific	Equipment and research outlays	Leasing, venture capital
Canning	Peak seasonal in inventories	Field warehousing, other commodity loans
Manufacturing	Equipment	Conditional sales contract, leasing, venture capital
Moderate Size		
Manufacturing	Plant and equipment	Long-term debt and equity financing
Rapid growth	Working capital and fixed assets	Convertible debt or debt with warrants
Large		
Moderate growth	Replacement	Internal funds

of operations is likely to require an investment of venture capital. On the other hand, a manufacturing firm that has been in business for a number of years and has achieved moderate size is likely to have heavy investment in both plant and equipment. With a record of sales, profitability, and some stability of management, a moderate-sized manufacturing firm is likely to have access to the open capital market. It will have access to long-term debt and equity financing from the financial markets.

The rapidly growing, moderate-sized firm will probably have a record of reasonably stable and rising sales and profits, and it will experience a need to finance both fixed assets and working capital. Such a firm is likely to use a certain amount of straight debt, supplemented by subordinated convertibles or debt with warrants that will, in time, provide additional equity capital.

The large firm in a mature industry is likely to be experiencing only moderate growth. With reasonably stable profits and a heavy investment in fixed assets (which contributes to cash flow due to depreciation charge-off), its main financing requirement is for replacement of fixed assets. Most of these needs will be met from internal sources.

The purpose of this review of some illustrative financing strategies has been to place characteristic financing needs in proper perspective and to relate them to financing forms and sources. It has not been possible to generalize on the financing patterns and requirements of every type of firm and every type of industry. However, these illustrations have served to indicate that some basic patterns emerge when firms are viewed analytically in terms of their industry characteristics, ages, size, and growth rate. With a foundation based on an understanding of the basic patterns and relationships, in addition to a sound analytical framework, practical experience will develop the maturity and good judgment essential to making good financial decisions.

INFLUENCE OF ECONOMIC CLIMATE

These broad patterns and the financing of the firm over its life cycle are likely to be substantially modified by variations in money market conditions over time. During a strong bull market in equities, such as occurred in the late 1920s, the advantages to equity financing become substantial. During depressed periods like that of the 1930s the characteristic life cycle pattern of growth and sales is likely to be seriously disturbed. The occurrence of wars will cause erratic disturbances in the growth cycle of the firm.

In addition, characteristics of the general economic environment are likely to influence the forms of financing employed. For example, during the post-World War II period, the fear of inflation, coupled with the danger of a postwar depression, made convertible securities popular. The convertible securities, of course, provided a hedge against deflation and at the same time offered some participation in the growth potentialities of firms and industries during a period characterized by attractive growth records among many firms.

FINANCIAL GUIDELINES

On the basis of the perspectives provided by a review of the financial life cycle of firms, some generalizations may be drawn. These generalizations present a form of summary of the many topics discussed, and provide a statement of guidelines for the financial manager.

1. Permanent needs should not be financed from short-term sources.
2. A substantial portion of current assets represents permanent investment and should not be financed from short-term financing.
3. Financing should be arranged before needs become immediately pressing. "The best time to get money is the time at which it is not needed."

4. It is better to obtain financing in larger chunks than in a series of small amounts, because each financing transaction carries a large element of fixed costs, which will mount in repeated financing.

5. Anticipate needs so that future needs will also be met.

6. Financing is a personal business. Personal and professional contacts with credit men, bank-loan officers, investment bankers, and financial executives of insurance companies and finance companies should be cultivated by the financial manager.

7. The financial manager should keep some element of flexibility in his financing programs so that the unexpected does not find him in a vulnerable position.

8. The financial manager should be prepared to bargain strenuously on the terms of financial agreements. He should not permit his firm to be tied up in loan terms which will hamper its freedom of action in the future.

9. Especially in a new firm, the commitment of funds should be held to a minimum. Buildings and equipment should be rented initially, or used equipment should be employed to the extent permitted by fund-raising capacity.

10. Irrational aversion to debt reduces profits. Judicious use of debt provides valuable leverage.

11. On the other hand, small and new firms, especially, must recognize that growth requires a large plowback of earnings if excessive debt is to be avoided or equity ownership is not to be shared. Growth of sales may lead to a feeling of prosperity and large withdrawals, which may hamper the healthy growth of a firm.

SUMMARY

The framework provided by the concept of the financial life cycle of the firm gives perspective on the financing alternatives available to the firm. Acquisition of funds at one stage of a firm's development should be made with a view to establishing the best foundation for the forms of financing most likely to be required at subsequent stages.

The overview of the financial life cycle of firms also highlights the interrelations between growth rates, financial position, forms and sources of financing, and dividend and merger policy. Understanding of these relations will prevent mutually inconsistent policies.

A widespread fault of small firms in their early stages is excessive withdrawals of funds by owner-managers. Failure to recognize the financing requirements of rapid growth and the necessity for obtaining the major portion of such financing from internal sources during the early stages of a firm's development will lead to financial difficulties. As a firm establishes a performance record, the opportunities for financing are broadened. The possibilities for obtaining external sources of funds on favorable terms improve during the later stages of a firm's development. At the same time, the reduced rate of growth makes it probable that a larger proportion of needs will be provided from internal sources.

Application of the life cycle framework can yield useful guidelines for financial decisions. The financial policies of the firm constitute an important area of managerial decisions required for successful operations.

SELECTED REFERENCES

Dauten, C. A., "The Necessary Ingredients of a Theory of Business Finance," *Journal of Finance,* 10 (May 1955), pp. 107–120.

Kuznets, Simon, *Capital in the American Economy—Its Formation and Financing* (Princeton, N.J.: Princeton University Press, 1961).

Marris, Robin, "A Model of the 'Managerial' Enterprise," *Quarterly Journal of Economics*, 77 (May 1963), pp. 185–209.

McLean, J. G., and R. W. Haigh, "How Business Corporations Grow," *Harvard Business Review*, 32 (November–December 1954), pp. 81–93.

O'Neal, F. Hodge, "Minority Owners Can Avoid Squeeze-Outs," *Harvard Business Review*, 41 (March–April 1963), pp. 150–160.

Schroeder, G. G., *The Growth of Major Steel Companies, 1900–1950* (Baltimore: Johns Hopkins Press, 1953).

Seltzer, L. H., *A Financial History of the American Automobile Industry* (Cambridge, Mass.: Houghton Mifflin, 1928).

Simon, H. A., and C. P. Bonini, "The Size Distribution of Business Firms," *American Economic Review*, 48 (September 1958), pp. 607–617.

Weston, J. Fred, "Toward Theories of Financial Policy," *Journal of Finance*, 10 (May 1955), pp. 130–143.

White, K. K., *Financing Company Expansion* (New York: American Management Association, 1964).

QUESTIONS

31-1 Explain how each of the following could be expected to influence the extent to which actual firms conform to the life cycle hypothesis:

1) Development of the corporate form of organization
2) Corporate diversification
3) Research and development expenditures
4) Trend toward larger firms

31-2 If the average cost of capital is actually minimized when the firm has a certain amount of debt in its capital structure, is it logical for older, slower growing firms to retire all their debt by retaining earnings? If such a tendency is observed, what is the implication for the economists' notion that firms seek to maximize profits?

31-3 A fast-growing firm usually has a higher profit rate than a firm growing more slowly. Yet the former will be less able to finance its growth from retained earnings. Explain.

31-4 A large, well-established firm typically retains a lower percentage of its earnings than does a smaller, faster growing firm. Yet the larger firm finances a higher percentage of its financing needs from retained earnings than does the smaller firm. Explain.

31-5 Two firms each earn 6 percent on sales and have an asset turnover of 2 times. Firm A has a debt-to-total-assets ratio of one third. Firm B has a ratio of two thirds. What is the respective profit rate on net worth for each firm?

31-6 A firm has a 5 percent return on sales. It has a debt-to-worth-ratio of 100 percent. What turnover of total assets is required for a 20 percent return on net worth?

31-7 Which firms are likely to have the higher asset turnover—new, small, rapidly growing firms or the largest firms in American industry?

31-8 What are the major sources of initial financing of new, small firms? Why?

31-9 Are large firms likely to have a higher or a lower ratio of trade-receivables-to-trade-payables than have smaller firms in the same line of business?

31-10   At what stage in its development is an industrial firm likely to make the greatest use of long-term debt? Explain.

31-11   Explain the characteristics of the economy and the stage of development of a firm and of its financial structure that will favor the use of convertible debt to raise funds equal to 20 percent of its present total assets.

PROBLEMS

31-1   Match each firm in list 1 with the most appropriate form of financing found in list 2. Present the key factors which determine your choice.

List 1

a) A medium-sized specialty steel company in Texas expects to double its sales in 12 years. Stock prices are expected to more than double over that period. Existing short-term debt is somewhat high; it has no long-term debt.

b) A laundromat plans expansion by the installation of ten additional washing machines and three new driers.

c) A plastics manufacturing company of $8 million sales volume, 70 percent owned by the founder and chief engineer, sells 60 percent of its output to a small number of large aircraft firms and finds itself continually short of working capital.

d) An electronics company doing $25 million of sales needs $5 million to finance its expansion. It has a debt-to-total-assets ratio of 60 percent, and its common stock, which is widely held, has tripled in price during the past year.

e) A manufacturing company with steadily growing sales (currently at $20 million) needs $2 million to finance new equipment which will substantially increase sales 10 to 14 months after the investment is made. Profits are expected to increase more than proportionally to the sales increase. Its debt-to-total-assets ratio runs about 30 percent.

f) A finance company with good prospective sales growth, relatively low debt ratio, stock prices temporarily depressed, and very good banking relations seeks to finance a prospective 10 percent increase in assets during the forthcoming year.

g) A medium-sized electrical utility ($100 million total assets) with a net-worth-to-total-assets ratio of 60 percent needs an additional $20 million to finance the growth taking place in the early stages of a business upswing.

h) A small chemical company producing many competitive lines has been growing on the average at about 10 percent per year—larger in good years and smaller in poor years. To finance growth the firm is attempting to decide between a convertible debenture issue or debt with warrants to buy common stock. Its existing total debt ratio is 10 percent of total assets.

List 2

1) Common stock
2) Convertible preferred stock
3) Subordinated debentures
4) Conditional sales contract
5) Accounts receivables financing or factoring
6) Mortgage bonds
7) Debt with warrants
8) Convertible debentures

31-2 United Engineers, Inc., has experienced the following sales, profit, and balance sheet patterns. Identify the financial problem that has developed, and recommend a solution for it.

UNITED ENGINEERS, INC.
FINANCIAL DATA
1965–1974
(in millions of dollars)

Income Statements	1965	'66	'67	'68	'69	'70	'71	'72	'73	'74
Sales	$50	$70	$90	$100	$120	$200	$180	$220	$240	$340
Profits after tax . . .	5	7	9	10	12	20	18	22	24	34
Dividends	4	5	6	6	7	10	10	14	18	24
Retained earnings . .	1	2	3	4	5	10	8	8	6	10
Cumulative retained earnings . . .	1	3	6	10	15	25	33	41	47	57
Balance sheets										
Current assets . . .	10	15	20	25	30	50	40	55	60	80
Net fixed assets . . .	15	20	25	25	30	50	50	55	60	90
Total assets . .	$25	$35	$45	$ 50	$ 60	$100	$ 90	$110	$120	$170
Trade credit	$ 4	6	8	9	10	18	15	20	40	60
Bank credit	4	6	10	10	13	29	14	20	—	20
Other	1	5	6	6	7	8	8	9	8	8
Total current liabilities . .	9	17	24	25	30	55	37	49	48	88
Long-term debt . . .	0	0	0	0	0	5	5	5	10	10
Total debt . . .	9	17	24	25	30	60	42	54	58	98
Common stock . . .	15	15	15	15	15	15	15	15	15	15
Retained earnings . .	1	3	6	10	15	25	33	41	47	57
Net worth	16	18	21	25	30	40	48	56	62	72
Total claims on assets	$25	$35	$45	$ 50	$ 60	$100	$ 90	$110	$120	$170

31-3(a) A firm judges that it is at the beginning of a three-year growth cycle. It is a manufacturing firm with a total-debt-to-equity ratio of 20 percent. It expects sales and net earnings to grow at a 10 percent rate per year.

Stock prices are expected to rise 30 percent per year over the three-year period. The firm will need $2 million at the beginning of the three-year period and another $1 million by the middle of the third year. It is at the beginning of a general business upswing, when money and capital costs are what they generally are after about a year of recession and at the beginning of an upswing. By the middle of the third year, money and capital costs will have their characteristic pattern near the peak of an upswing.

How should the firm raise the $2 million and the $1 million?

(b) An aerospace company with sales of $50 million per year, needs $10 million to finance expansion. It has a debt-to-total-assets ratio of 65 percent. Its common stock, which is widely held, is selling at a price-earnings ratio of 25 times. It is attempting to compare the sale of common stock and convertible debentures.

Which do you recommend? Why?

(c) A chemical company has been growing steadily. To finance a growth of sales from $80 million per year to $100 million over a two-year period, it needs $4 million in additional equipment. When additional working-capital needs are taken into account, the total additional financing required during the first year is $10 million. The profit increase will come in about 14 months, and the price of the stock is expected to reflect the profit increase in about ten months. Profits will rise by 50 percent after the first ten months. The stock is currently selling at 20 times earnings. It can borrow on straight debt at 5½ percent. It could borrow with a convertibility or warrant "sweetener" for ¾ percent less. The present debt to total asset ratio is 25 percent.

Which form of financing should it employ?

Compound Interest Tables

Compound Sum of $1

Year	1%	2%	3%	4%	5%	6%	7%	8%	9%	10%
1	1.010	1.020	1.030	1.040	1.050	1.060	1.070	1.080	1.090	1.10●
2	1.020	1.040	1.061	1.082	1.102	1.124	1.145	1.166	1.188	1.21●
3	1.030	1.061	1.093	1.125	1.158	1.191	1.225	1.260	1.295	1.33
4	1.041	1.082	1.126	1.170	1.216	1.262	1.311	1.360	1.412	1.46●
5	1.051	1.104	1.159	1.217	1.276	1.338	1.403	1.469	1.539	1.61●
6	1.062	1.126	1.194	1.265	1.340	1.419	1.501	1.587	1.677	1.77●
7	1.072	1.149	1.230	1.316	1.407	1.504	1.606	1.714	1.828	1.94●
8	1.083	1.172	1.267	1.369	1.477	1.594	1.718	1.851	1.993	2.14●
9	1.094	1.195	1.305	1.423	1.551	1.689	1.838	1.999	2.172	2.35●
10	1.105	1.219	1.344	1.480	1.629	1.791	1.967	2.159	2.367	2.59●
11	1.116	1.243	1.384	1.539	1.710	1.898	2.105	2.332	2.580	2.85●
12	1.127	1.268	1.426	1.601	1.796	2.012	2.252	2.518	2.813	3.13●
13	1.138	1.294	1.469	1.665	1.886	2.133	2.410	2.720	3.066	3.45●
14	1.149	1.319	1.513	1.732	1.980	2.261	2.579	2.937	3.342	3.79●
15	1.161	1.346	1.558	1.801	2.079	2.397	2.759	3.172	3.642	4.17●

Year	12%	14%	15%	16%	18%	20%	24%	28%	32%
1	1.120	1.140	1.150	1.160	1.180	1.200	1.240	1.280	1.320
2	1.254	1.300	1.322	1.346	1.392	1.440	1.538	1.638	1.742
3	1.405	1.482	1.521	1.561	1.643	1.728	1.907	2.067	2.300
4	1.574	1.689	1.749	1.811	1.939	2.074	2.364	2.684	3.036
5	1.762	1.925	2.011	2.100	2.288	2.488	2.932	3.436	4.007
6	1.974	2.195	2.313	2.436	2.700	2.986	3.635	4.398	5.290
7	2.211	2.502	2.660	2.826	3.185	3.583	4.508	5.629	6.983
8	2.476	2.853	3.059	3.278	3.759	4.300	5.590	7.206	9.217
9	2.773	3.252	3.518	3.803	4.435	5.160	6.931	9.223	12.166
10	3.106	3.707	4.046	4.411	5.234	6.192	8.594	11.806	16.060
11	3.479	4.226	4.652	5.117	6.176	7.430	10.657	15.112	21.199
12	3.896	4.818	5.350	5.936	7.288	8.916	13.215	19.343	27.983
13	4.363	5.492	6.153	6.886	8.599	10.699	16.386	24.759	36.937
14	4.887	6.261	7.076	7.988	10.147	12.839	20.319	31.691	48.757
15	5.474	7.138	8.137	9.266	11.974	15.407	25.196	40.565	64.359

Year	36%	40%	50%	60%	70%	80%	90%
1	1.360	1.400	1.500	1.600	1.700	1.800	1.900
2	1.850	1.960	2.250	2.560	2.890	3.240	3.610
3	2.515	2.744	3.375	4.096	4.913	5.832	6.859
4	3.421	3.842	5.062	6.544	8.352	10.498	13.032
5	4.653	5.378	7.594	10.486	14.199	18.896	24.761
6	6.328	7.530	11.391	16.777	24.138	34.012	47.046
7	8.605	10.541	17.086	26.844	41.034	61.222	89.387
8	11.703	14.758	25.629	42.950	69.758	110.200	169.836
9	15.917	20.661	38.443	68.720	118.588	198.359	322.688
10	21.647	28.925	57.665	109.951	201.599	357.047	613.107
11	29.439	40.496	86.498	175.922	342.719	642.684	1164.902
12	40.037	56.694	129.746	281.475	582.622	1156.831	2213.314
13	54.451	79.372	194.619	450.360	990.457	2082.295	4205.297
14	74.053	111.120	291.929	720.576	1683.777	3748.131	7990.065
15	100.712	155.568	437.894	1152.921	2862.421	6746.636	15181.122

Present Worth of $1

Year	1%	2%	3%	4%	5%	6%	7%	8%	9%	10%	12%	14%	15%
1	.990	.980	.971	.962	.952	.943	.935	.926	.917	.909	.893	.877	.870
2	.980	.961	.943	.925	.907	.890	.873	.857	.842	.826	.797	.769	.756
3	.971	.942	.915	.889	.864	.840	.816	.794	.772	.751	.712	.675	.658
4	.961	.924	.889	.855	.823	.792	.763	.735	.708	.683	.636	.592	.572
5	.951	.906	.863	.822	.784	.747	.713	.681	.650	.621	.567	.519	.497
6	.942	.888	.838	.790	.746	.705	.666	.630	.596	.564	.507	.456	.432
7	.933	.871	.813	.760	.711	.665	.623	.583	.547	.513	.452	.400	.376
8	.923	.853	.789	.731	.677	.627	.582	.540	.502	.467	.404	.351	.327
9	.914	.837	.766	.703	.645	.592	.544	.500	.460	.424	.361	.308	.284
10	.905	.820	.744	.676	.614	.558	.508	.463	.422	.386	.322	.270	.247
11	.896	.804	.722	.650	.585	.527	.475	.429	.388	.350	.287	.237	.215
12	.887	.788	.701	.625	.557	.497	.444	.397	.356	.319	.257	.208	.187
13	.879	.773	.681	.601	.530	.469	.415	.368	.326	.290	.229	.182	.163
14	.870	.758	.661	.577	.505	.442	.388	.340	.299	.263	.205	.160	.141
15	.861	.743	.642	.555	.481	.417	.362	.315	.275	.239	.183	.140	.123
16	.853	.728	.623	.534	.458	.394	.339	.292	.252	.218	.163	.123	.107
17	.844	.714	.605	.513	.436	.371	.317	.270	.231	.198	.146	.108	.093
18	.836	.700	.587	.494	.416	.350	.296	.250	.212	.180	.130	.095	.081
19	.828	.686	.570	.475	.396	.331	.276	.232	.194	.164	.116	.083	.070
20	.820	.673	.554	.456	.377	.319	.258	.215	.178	.149	.104	.073	.061
25	.780	.610	.478	.375	.295	.233	.184	.146	.116	.092	.059	.038	.030
30	.742	.552	.412	.308	.231	.174	.131	.099	.075	.057	.033	.020	.015

Year	16%	18%	20%	24%	28%	32%	36%	40%	50%	60%	70%	80%	90%
1	.862	.847	.833	.806	.781	.758	.735	.714	.667	.625	.588	.556	.526
2	.743	.718	.694	.650	.610	.574	.541	.510	.444	.391	.346	.309	.277
3	.641	.609	.579	.524	.477	.435	.398	.364	.296	.244	.204	.171	.146
4	.552	.516	.482	.423	.373	.329	.292	.260	.198	.153	.120	.095	.077
5	.476	.437	.402	.341	.291	.250	.215	.186	.132	.095	.070	.053	.040
6	.410	.370	.335	.275	.227	.189	.158	.133	.088	.060	.041	.029	.021
7	.354	.314	.279	.222	.178	.143	.116	.095	.059	.037	.024	.016	.011
8	.305	.266	.233	.179	.139	.108	.085	.068	.039	.023	.014	.009	.006
9	.263	.226	.194	.144	.108	.082	.063	.048	.026	.015	.008	.005	.003
10	.227	.191	.162	.116	.085	.062	.046	.035	.017	.009	.005	.003	.002
11	.195	.162	.135	.094	.066	.047	.034	.025	.012	.006	.003	.002	.001
12	.168	.137	.112	.076	.052	.036	.025	.018	.008	.004	.002	.001	.001
13	.145	.116	.093	.061	.040	.027	.018	.013	.005	.002	.001	.001	.000
14	.125	.099	.078	.049	.032	.021	.014	.009	.003	.001	.001	.000	.000
15	.108	.084	.065	.040	.025	.016	.010	.006	.002	.001	.000	.000	.000
16	.093	.071	.054	.032	.019	.012	.007	.005	.002	.001	.000	.000	
17	.080	.060	.045	.026	.015	.009	.005	.003	.001	.000	.000		
18	.069	.051	.038	.021	.012	.007	.004	.002	.001	.000	.000		
19	.060	.043	.031	.017	.009	.005	.003	.002	.000	.000			
20	.051	.037	.026	.014	.007	.004	.002	.001	.000	.000			
25	.024	.016	.010	.005	.002	.001	.000	.000					
30	.012	.007	.004	.002	.001	.000	.000						

Sum of an Annuity of $1 for n Years

Year	1%	2%	3%	4%	5%	6%	7%	8%
1	1.000	1.000	1.000	1.000	1.000	1.000	1.000	1.000
2	2.010	2.020	2.030	2.040	2.050	2.060	2.070	2.080
3	2 030	3.060	3.091	3.122	3.152	3.184	3.215	3.246
4	4.060	4.122	4.184	4.246	4.310	4.375	4.440	4.506
5	5.101	5.204	5.309	5.416	5.526	5.637	5.751	5.867
6	6.152	6.308	6.468	6.633	6.802	6.975	7.153	7.336
7	7.214	7.434	7.662	7.898	8.142	8.394	8.654	8.923
8	8.286	8.583	8.892	9.214	9.549	9.897	10.260	10.637
9	9.369	9.755	10.159	10.583	11.027	11.491	11.978	12.488
10	10.462	10.950	11.464	12.006	12.578	13.181	13.816	14.487
11	11.567	12.169	12.808	13.486	14.207	14.972	15.784	16.645
12	12.683	13.412	14.192	15.026	15.917	16.870	17.888	18.977
13	13.809	14.680	15.618	16.627	17.713	18.882	20.141	21.495
14	14.947	15.974	17.086	18.292	19.599	21.051	22.550	24.215
15	16.097	17.293	18.599	20.024	21.579	23.276	25.129	27.152
16	17.258	18.639	20.157	21.825	23.657	25.673	27.888	30.324
17	18.430	20.012	21.762	23.698	25.840	28.213	30.840	33.750
18	19.615	21.412	23.414	25.645	28.132	30.906	33.999	37.450
19	20.811	22.841	25.117	27.671	30.539	33.760	37.379	41.446
20	22.019	24.297	26.870	29.778	33.066	36.786	40.995	45.762
25	28.243	32.030	36.459	41.646	47.727	54.865	63.249	73.106
30	34.785	40.568	47.575	56.085	66.439	79.058	94.461	113.283

16%	18%	20%	24%	Year	9%	10%	12%	14%
1.000	1.000	1.000	1.000	1	1.000	1.000	1.000	1.000
2.090	2.100	2.120	2.140	2	2.160	2.180	2.200	2.240
3.278	3.310	3.374	3.440	3	3.506	3.572	3.640	3.778
4.573	4.641	4.779	4.921	4	5.066	5.215	5.368	5.684
5.985	6.105	6.353	6.610	5	6.877	7.154	7.442	8.048
7.523	7.716	8.115	8.536	6	8.977	9.442	9.930	10.980
9.200	9.487	10.089	10.730	7	11.414	12.142	12.916	14.615
11.028	11.436	12.300	13.233	8	14.240	15.327	16.499	19.123
13.021	13.579	14.776	16.085	9	17.518	19.086	20.799	24.712
15.193	15.937	17.549	19.337	10	21.321	23.521	25.959	31.643
17.560	18.531	20.655	23.044	11	25.733	28.755	32.150	40.238
20.141	21.384	24.133	27.271	12	30.850	34.931	39.580	50.985
22.953	24.523	28.029	32.089	13	36.786	42.219	48.497	64.110
26.019	27.975	32.393	37.581	14	43.672	50.818	59.196	80.496
29.361	31.772	37.280	43.842	15	51.659	60.965	72.035	100.815

Year	28%	32%	36%	40%	50%	60%	70%	80%
1	1.000	1.000	1.000	1.000	1.000	1.000	1.000	1.000
2	2.280	2.320	2.360	2.400	2.500	2.600	2.700	2.800
3	3.918	4.062	4.210	4.360	4.750	5.160	5.590	6.040
4	6.016	6.362	6.725	7.104	8.125	9.256	10.503	11.872
5	8.700	9.398	10.146	10.846	13.188	15.810	18.855	22.370
6	12.136	13.406	14.799	16.324	20.781	26.295	33.054	41.265
7	16.534	18.696	21.126	23.853	32.172	43.073	57.191	75.278
8	22.163	25.678	29.732	34.395	49.258	69.916	98.225	136.500
9	29.369	34.895	41.435	49.153	74.887	112.866	167.983	246.699
10	38.592	47.062	57.352	69.814	113.330	181.585	286.570	445.058
11	50.399	63.122	78.998	98.739	170.995	291.536	488.170	802.105
12	65.510	84.320	108.437	139.235	257.493	467.458	830.888	1444.788
13	84.853	112.303	148.475	195.929	387.239	748.933	1413.510	2601.619
14	109.612	149.240	202.926	275.300	581.859	1199.293	2403.968	4683.914
15	141.303	197.997	276.979	386.420	873.788	1919.869	4087.745	8432.045

PRESENT WORTH OF AN ANNUITY OF $1

Year	1%	2%	3%	4%	5%	6%	7%	8%	9%	10%
1	0.990	0.980	0.971	0.962	0.952	0.943	0.935	0.926	0.917	0.909
2	1.970	1.942	1.913	1.886	1.859	1.833	1.808	1.783	1.759	1.736
3	2.941	2.884	2.829	2.775	2.723	2.673	2.624	2.577	2.531	2.487
4	3.902	3.808	3.717	3.630	3.546	3.465	3.387	3.312	3.240	3.170
5	4.853	4.713	4.580	4.452	4.329	4.212	4.100	3.993	3.890	3.791
6	5.795	5.601	5.417	5.242	5.076	4.917	4.766	4.623	4.486	4.355
7	6.728	6.472	6.230	6.002	5.786	5.582	5.389	5.206	5.033	4.868
8	7.652	7.325	7.020	6.733	6.463	6.210	6.971	5.747	5.535	5.335
9	8.566	8.162	7.786	7.435	7.108	6.802	6.515	6.247	5.985	5.759
10	9.471	8.983	8.530	8.111	7.722	7.360	7.024	6.710	6.418	6.145
11	10.368	9.787	9.253	8.760	8.306	7.887	7.499	7.139	6.805	6.495
12	11.255	10.575	9.954	9.385	8.863	8.384	7.943	7.536	7.161	6.814
13	12.134	11.348	10.635	9.986	9.394	8.853	8.358	7.904	7.487	7.103
14	13.004	12.106	11.296	10.563	9.899	9.295	8.745	8.244	7.786	7.367
15	13.865	12.849	11.938	11.118	10.380	9.712	9.108	8.559	8.060	7.606
16	14.718	13.578	12.561	11.652	10.838	10.106	9.447	8.851	8.312	7.824
17	15.562	14.292	13.166	12.166	11.274	10.477	9.763	9.122	8.544	8.022
18	16.398	14.992	13.754	12.659	11.690	10.828	10.059	9.372	8.756	8.201
19	17.226	15.678	14.324	13.134	12.085	11.158	10.336	9.604	8.950	8.365
20	18.046	16.351	14.877	13.590	12.462	11.470	10.594	9.818	9.128	8.514
25	22.023	19.523	17.413	15.622	14.094	12.783	11.654	10.675	9.823	9.077
30	25.808	22.397	19.600	17.292	15.373	13.765	12.409	11.258	10.274	9.427

Year	12%	14%	16%	18%	20%	24%	28%	32%	36%
1	0.893	0.877	0.862	0.847	0.833	0.806	0.781	0.758	0.735
2	1.690	1.647	1.605	1.566	1.528	1.457	1.392	1.332	1.276
3	2.402	2.322	2.246	2.174	2.106	1.981	1.868	1.766	1.674
4	3.037	2.914	2.798	2.690	2.589	2.404	2.241	2.096	1.966
5	3.605	3.433	3.274	3.127	2.991	2.745	2.532	2.345	2.181
6	4.111	3.889	3.685	3.498	3.326	3.020	2.759	2.534	2.339
7	4.564	4.288	4.039	3.812	3.605	3.242	2.937	2.678	2.455
8	4.968	4.639	4.344	4.078	3.837	3.421	3.076	2.786	2.540
9	5.328	4.946	4.607	4.303	4.031	3.566	3.184	2.868	2.603
10	5.650	5.216	4.833	4.494	4.193	3.682	3.269	2.930	2.650
11	5.988	5.453	5.029	4.656	4.327	3.776	3.335	2.978	2.683
12	6.194	5.660	5.197	4.793	4.439	3.851	3.387	3.013	2.708
13	6.424	5.842	5.342	4.910	4.533	3.912	3.427	3.040	2.727
14	6.628	6.002	5.468	5.008	4.611	3.962	3.459	3.061	2.740
15	6.811	6.142	5.575	5.092	4.675	4.001	3.483	3.076	2.750
16	6.974	6.265	5.669	5.162	4.730	4.033	3.503	3.088	2.758
17	7.120	5.373	5.749	4.222	4.775	4.059	3.518	3.097	2.763
18	7.250	6.467	5.818	5.273	4.812	4.080	3.529	3.104	2.767
19	7.366	6.550	5.877	5.316	4.844	4.097	3.539	3.109	2.770
20	7.469	6.623	5.929	5.353	4.870	4.110	3.546	3.113	2.772
25	7.843	6.873	6.097	5.467	4.948	4.147	3.564	3.122	2.776
30	8.055	7.003	6.177	5.517	4.979	4.160	3.569	3.124	2.778

Industry Ratios

One useful guideline for arriving at a tentative formulation of the financial structure for a firm is the average ratios for the industry. If a firm conforms to the general practices of its industry, its financial statements are considered acceptable. For this reason, text and end-of-chapter problems have referred to average industry ratios. While a number of sources could be employed, this text has utilized judgment averages of the ratios provided by Dun & Bradstreet and the Robert Morris Associates. These ratios are to be used only as guides and not as inflexible determinants of what a firm's financial structure should be.

ILLUSTRATIVE INDUSTRY RATIOS, 1963–1964

Industry	Current Ratio (X)	Sales to Total Assets (X)	Sales to Inventory (X)	Aver. Collection Period (days)	Current Debt/Total Assets (%)	Long-Term Debt/Total Assets (%)	Pre-ferred/Total Assets (%)	Net Worth/Total Assets (%)	Profits to Sales* (%)	Profits to Total Assets* (%)	Profits to Net Worth* (%)
MANUFACTURING											
Agricultural Machinery	2.6	1.8	4.5	40	25	10–15	0–5	60–65	3.5	6.0	10.5
Bodies: Autos, Trucks, Buses	2.6	2.0	6.4	40	25	20–25	0–5	50–55	2.7	5.0	10.0
Canned & Dried Fruits and Vegetables	2.2	2.0	5.6	22	25–30	10–15	0–5	60–65	2.6	5.0	8.7
Drugs and Medicines	3.1	1.3	5.8	43	20–25	15	0–5	60–65	4.3	5.5	11.0
Electrical Appliances (Household)	2.6	1.7	5.0	50	25	15–20	40–45	60	3.5	6.0	10.5
Footwear	2.2	2.3	6.1	46	35	5–10	0–5	55–60	2.3	5.0	9.0
Machine Tools	2.5	1.6	4.6	46	25	10	0–5	60–65	4.0	6.3	9.7
Industrial Chemicals	2.6	1.3	6.1	46	20	20	0–5	55–60	4.3	5.7	9.7
Plastics and Synthetics	2.0	1.8	6.9	45	30	10	0–5	55–60	3.8	6.8	11.0
Precision Instruments	2.4	1.5	5.8	55	25	10–15	0–5	60–65	3.3	5.0	8.6
Steel Foundries	2.3	1.8	8.0	42	20–25	10	0–5	65–70	3.3	6.0	9.5

Industry	Current Ratio (X)	Sales to Total Assets (X)	Sales to Inventory (X)	Aver. Collection Period (days)	Current Debt/Total Assets (%)	Long-Term Debt/Total Assets (%)	Preferred/Total Assets (%)	Net Worth/Total Assets (%)	Profits to Sales* (%)	Profits to Total Assets* (%)	Profits to Net Worth* (%)
OTHERS											
Commercial Airlines	1.4	0.9	23.0	38	15–20	50–55	0–5	25–30	2.6	2.4	7.5
Department Stores	2.8	2.0	5.8	50	25	15–20	0–5	55–60	1.9	2.0	4.8
Public Utilities	2.6	0.3	—	28	5–10	45–50	10–15	30–35	—	5.9	10.1

* Profit ratios vary from year to year. In the judgment of the authors, more "normal" reference profit ratios should be about 5 percent on sales, 10 percent on total assets, and 15 percent on net worth.

Sources: Annual Statement Studies, 1965 edition (Philadelphia, Pa.: Robert Morris Associates); *Key Business Ratios,* 1963 (New York: Dun & Bradstreet, Inc.).

Indexes

Author Index

Subject Index